The Coveted Westside

The Urban West Series
Amy L. Scott, Bradley University, *Series Editor*

Urban West examines the development of primary and secondary cities in the Trans-Mississippi West including Texas and California. The series explores issues of class, race, ethnicity, gender, environment, suburbanization, municipal services, public works, community building, culture, and other relevant subjects within an urban context. All types of methodologies are welcome, but special attention will be given to those manuscripts offering important new insights, novel research approaches and sources, and comparative studies of multiple cities.

Sacramento and the Catholic Church: Shaping a Capital City
by Steven M. Avella

Class and Gender Politics in Progressive-Era Seattle
by John C. Putman

Urbanism and Empire in the Far West, 1840–1890
by Eugene P. Moehring

Cities, Sagebrush, and Solitude:
Urbanization and Cultural Conflict in the Great Basin
by Dennis R. Judd and Stephanie L. Witt

City Dreams, Country Schemes:
Community and Identity in the American West
by Kathleen A. Brosnan and Amy L. Scott

Cities and Nature in the American West
by Char Miller

Earning Power: Women, and Work in Los Angeles, 1880–1930
by Eileen V. Wallis

The Coveted Westside:
How the Black Homeowners' Rights Movement Shaped Modern Los Angeles
by Jennifer Mandel

The Coveted Westside

How the Black Homeowners' Rights Movement Shaped Modern Los Angeles

JENNIFER MANDEL

UNIVERSITY OF NEVADA PRESS | *Reno & Las Vegas*

University of Nevada Press | Reno, Nevada 89557 USA
www.unpress.nevada.edu
Copyright © 2022 by University of Nevada Press
All rights reserved
Cover design by David Ter-Avanesyan/Ter33Design

LIBRARY OF CONGRESS CATALOGING-IN-PUBLICATION DATA
Names: Mandel, Jennifer, 1975– author.
Title: The coveted westside : how the Black homeowners' rights movement shaped modern Los Angeles / Jennifer Mandel.
Other titles: Urban West.
Description: Reno ; Las Vegas : University of Nevada Press, [2022] |
Series: The Urban West series | Includes bibliographical references and index.
Summary: "The Coveted Westside explores the middle-class African American-led movement to challenge housing discrimination, gain equal access to twentieth-century Los Angeles, and ward off resegregation. Black professionals, from actors to entrepreneurs to doctors, made the city's distinguished neighborhoods of West Adams Heights in the 1940s and the Crenshaw area, View Park, View Heights, and Windsor Hills in the postwar era hubs in the fight for fair housing" —Provided by publisher.
Identifiers: LCCN 2021041576 | ISBN 9781647790349 (paperback) | ISBN 9781647790356 (ebook)
Subjects: LCSH: African Americans—Housing—California—Los Angeles—History—20th century. | Discrimination in housing—California—Los Angeles—History—20th century. | Housing policy—California—Los Angeles—History—20th century.
Classification: LCC HD7288.76.U52 M355 2022 | DDC 363.509794/94—dc23
LC record available at https://lccn.loc.gov/2021041576

The paper used in this book meets the requirements of American National Standard for Information Sciences—Permanence of Paper for Printed Library Materials, ANSI/NISO Z 39.48–1992 (R 2002).

FIRST PRINTING

Manufactured in the United States of America

*For my mother and grandparents
who instilled in me an appreciation for the past,
and my history professors who taught me to interrogate it.*

Contents

Abbreviations ix

Introduction 3

PART I. THE PIONEERS OF HOUSING INTEGRATION IN LOS ANGELES

Chapter 1. Demarcating the Westside from the Eastside 27

Chapter 2. Black Settlement in West Jefferson and West Adams Heights 58

Chapter 3. The Legal Demise of Racial Restrictive Covenants 89

PART II. POST-*SHELLEY* WESTWARD MIGRATION AND THE CASE FOR CRENSHAW

Chapter 4. The Affluent Black Westside Takes Shape 125

Chapter 5. A Campaign to Build "A Balanced Community" 161

Chapter 6. Brockman Gallery and the Art of Social Change 204

Chapter 7. Black Beverly Hills Redux 240

Acknowledgments 249

Notes 253

Bibliography 311

Index 333

About the Author 351

Illustrations follow page 122

Abbreviations

ACLU	American Civil Liberties Union
ACLU/SC	American Civil Liberties Union of Southern California Records, ca. 1935–64
APP	Ann Post Papers
AWA	Art West Associated, Incorporated
BAA	Black Artists Association
BAC	Black Arts Council
BGP	Brockman Gallery Productions
BOE	Board of Education
BPSN	Black Peace Stone Nation
CAP 14	Californians Against Proposition 14
CDC	California Democratic Council
CETA	Comprehensive Employment and Training Act
CHP	Committee for Home Protection
CN	Crenshaw Neighbors, Incorporated
COIN	Council of Integrated Neighborhoods
COPH	The Lawrence de Graaf Center for Oral and Public History, California State University, Fullerton
CORE	Congress of Racial Equality
CREA	California Real Estate Association
DMC	Democratic Minority Conference
FBP	Fritz Burns Papers
FHA	Federal Housing Administration
HACLA	Housing Authority of the City of Los Angeles
HL	The Huntington Library
HOLC	Home Owners' Loan Corporation
HUD	Department of Housing and Urban Development
HVS	Helene V. Smookler Collection of Material about the Desegregation of the Los Angeles Unified School District
IUSD	Inglewood Unified School District
JACL	Japanese American Citizens League
JAF	John Anson Ford Papers
JSP	James K. Strong Papers
KHC	Kenneth Hahn Collection
LACCHR	Los Angeles County Commission on Human Relations

LACMA	Los Angeles County Museum of Art
LALL	LA Law Library
LAP	Los Angeles Pacific Railway Company
LARB	Los Angeles Realty Board
LARy	Los Angeles Railway Company
LASC	Los Angeles Superior Court Archives
LASMC	Los Angeles School Monitoring Committee Records
LAUL	Los Angeles Urban League Records, 1933-1945
LAUSD	Los Angeles Unified School District
LMP	Loren Miller Papers
LMU	Loyola Marymount University, William H. Hannon Library, Department of Archives and Special Collections
LWV	League of Women Voters
LWVLA	League of Women Voters of Los Angeles
NAACP	National Association for the Advancement of Colored People
NAACP	NAACP Papers, pt. 5, The Campaign Against Residential Segregation, 1914–1955 (on microfilm)
NAACP/LA	Los Angeles NAACP Branch Files, 1913-1939
NEA	National Endowment for the Arts
NF/GSM	Nickerson Family, Golden State Mutual Life Insurance Company Papers, 1923-2000
PE	Pacific Electric Railway Project
APEX	Area Program for Enrichment Exchange
RRCC	Los Angeles County Registrar-Recorder/County Clerk
SCL	Southern California Library
SCLC	Southern Christian Leadership Conference
SNCC	Student Nonviolent Coordinating Committee
UCLA	University of California, Los Angeles
UCLA/MC	University of California, Los Angeles, Charles E. Young Research Library, Microform Collections
UCLA/OL	University of California, Los Angeles, Center for Oral History Research, Library Special Collections, Charles E. Young Research Library, online holdings
UCLA/SC	University of California, Los Angeles, Charles E. Young Research Library, Special Collections
UCRC	United Civil Rights Council
UN	United Neighbors
USC	University of Southern California
WAHIA	West Adams Heights Improvement Association
WAHPA	West Adams Heights Protective Association
WRA	War Relocation Authority
YB	Yellow Brotherhood

The Coveted Westside

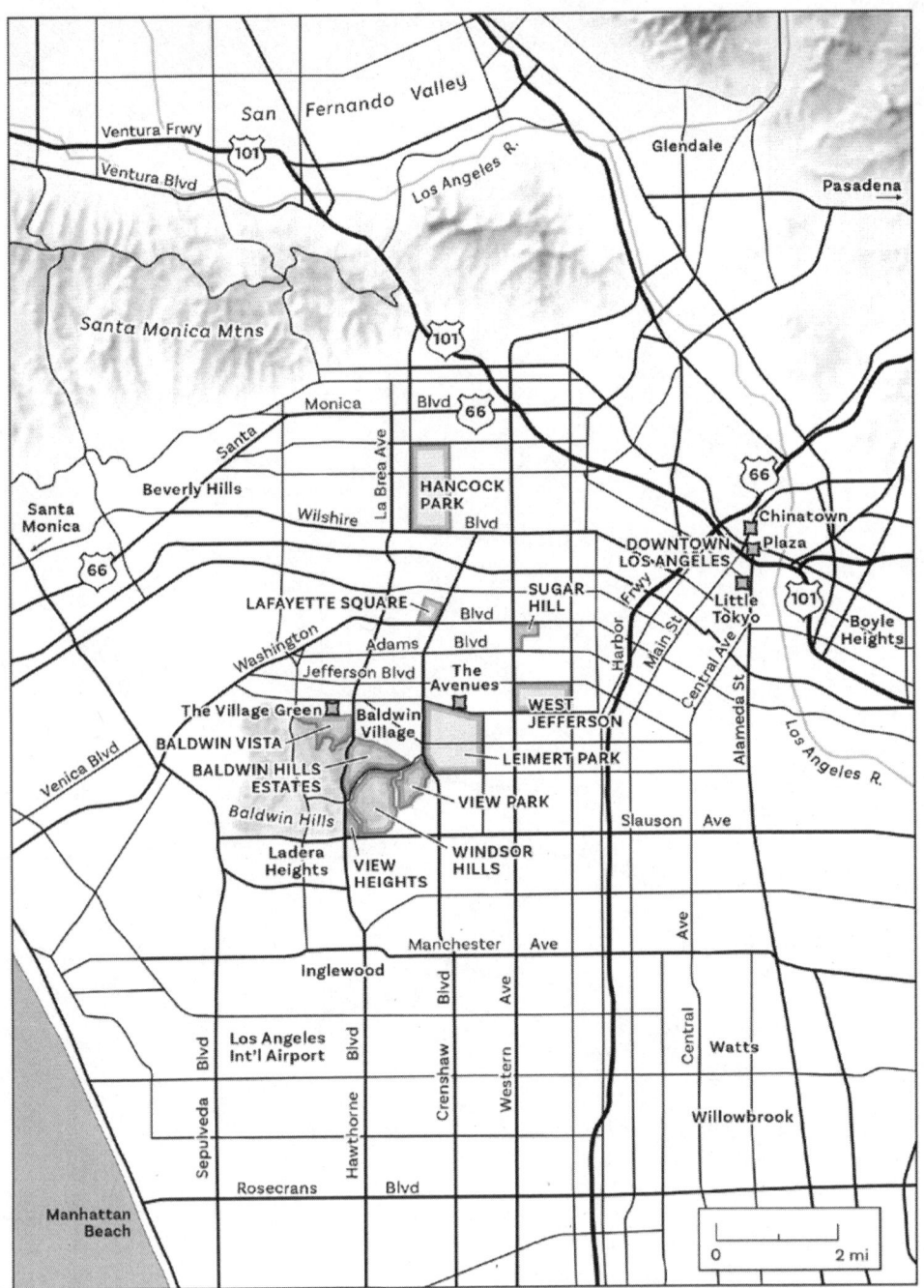

Los Angeles, ca. early 1950s. Amid the construction of the Harbor Freeway (Interstate 110), which would expand southward through the 1960s, Los Angeles's Eastside and Westside grew more divided and its affluent Black neighborhoods (highlighted here) took further shape. Map by Erin Greb Cartography.

Introduction

A FEW MONTHS SHY of his ninety-first birthday—in a 1982 interview with the University of California, Los Angeles (UCLA), Oral History Program—business executive and community activist George A. Beavers, Jr., recollected the long-standing pattern of residential settlement in Los Angeles. "There was a time when there were no Negroes west of Central Avenue," he explained. "They moved the line over to San Pedro [Street], then to Figueroa [Street], then to Vermont [Avenue].... Then they got to Crenshaw [Boulevard]." Beavers was referring to a multifaceted history of Black resistance to White suppression that spanned the twentieth century. White policymakers, developers, real estate interests, and homeowners in the 1910s and 1920s began escalating efforts to dominate the western city by restricting land west of Main Street to the mostly White middle and upper classes. As the primarily targeted group, Blacks responded by spearheading a decades-long migration westward to challenge housing discrimination and the resultant residential segregation and to secure full access to the expanding city and its services. In the years following the landmark 1948 *Shelley v. Kraemer* decision, when the US Supreme Court finally declared racial restrictive covenants legally unenforceable, Blacks and other marginalized Angelenos persevered across Arlington and Crenshaw Boulevards. Yet as they crossed the city's racial borders, Whites responded by fanning out into other, homogeneous communities, many of which were located farther west. "They can't live in the ocean," Beavers quipped, about the extreme measures Whites took to live away from people of color, but they got as close to the shore as possible.[1]

While Beavers left out the specific years when Blacks crossed the city's racial borders, he had a good understanding of the trajectory of Black westward migration in his hometown. He had lived it. Born in Atlanta, Georgia, in 1891, eleven-year-old Beavers moved with his family to Los Angeles in 1903, "in quest of full citizenship rights and better living conditions," and played an important role through the twentieth century in the growth of the city. He and his business partners, William Nickerson, Jr., and Norman O. Houston, established Golden State Mutual Life Insurance Company in 1925 in a one-room rental at the intersection of Newton Street and Central Avenue, near what was then the hub of Black cultural and commercial activity, and helped turn the business into an anchor of the Black community. In 1949, twenty-four years after its launch and one year after *Shelley*, Golden State advanced the Black westward movement by opening its newly constructed, spacious home office, abundant with amenities, on the corner of Western and Adams Boulevards, in Sugar Hill, the historically White, elite, and racially restricted neighborhood where affluent Blacks had begun to settle in the late 1930s. Beavers's business partner, Houston, and Houston's second wife, Edythe Pryce Houston, became the first African Americans to challenge the community's racial barrier by purchasing a home there in 1938, and in the face of White hostility, inspired other Blacks to follow.[2]

Fast forward to 1982 when Beavers was recollecting his past, and he and his wife, Lola Lillian Cunningham Beavers, were living in the Crenshaw area's Baldwin Hills Estates, which was then the center of affluent Black life. By the mid-1970s, newspapers had begun comparing the majority Black, affluent communities of the Crenshaw area to the mostly White, well-heeled, celebrity haven, Beverly Hills. In his 1975 editorial, *Los Angeles Times* writer and editor, J. K. Obatala, challenged the criticism, "especially by whites, and, unfortunately, younger generations of blacks," of middle- and upper-class Blacks as materialistic, arrogant, out of touch, and unconcerned with civil rights. Rather, Obatala extolled, Baldwin Hills "is to blacks what Beverly Hills is to whites." Crenshaw's affluent Black residents serve as "models of success" who worked hard to realize their goals, attain a comfortable standard of living, as southern Black ministers, teachers, and business owners had done in the sharecropper South, and help improve conditions for people of color. "Some of them are even interested in making life better for *every* Afro-American." Underlying the resentments of the Black middle class, "buried somewhere in the minds of most Afro-Americans...are the ruins of a secret utopia, a fossilized dreamland that, if unearthed, would probably look very much like Baldwin Hills."[3]

Starting in the 1980s, in local and national publications and reporting on a range of stories, journalists began to refer to the affluent Crenshaw area neighborhoods as well as nearby Ladera Heights by their nickname, the Black Beverly Hills. Surveying Black neighborhoods in Los Angeles in 1983, a *Christian Science Monitor* reporter mentioned the residents living near Baldwin Hills, or "the 'black Beverly Hills,'" as a possible political bloc supporting Jesse Jackson's presidential campaign. When a fire destroyed some fifty homes and resulted in several casualties in Baldwin Hills Estates in 1985, the *Los Angeles Times* used the moniker in its reports on the story. African American actor, choreographer, director, and producer Debbie Allen described her Baldwin Hills neighborhood, where she lived with her husband, professional basketball player Norm Nixon, according to a 1985 *Los*

Angeles Times article, "proudly as 'the black Beverly Hills.'" *Ebony* magazine published an article in 1995 on celebrities' places of residence across Los Angeles, including Baldwin Hills or the "black Beverly Hills," and in 2005 *L.A. Weekly* published a story on local rapper Kam, who was interviewed in Ladera Heights, "the black Beverly Hills." This modern pocket of Black affluence, which intensified working-class Blacks' feelings of resentment, had once been a zone of racial exclusion.[4]

African Americans endured decades of strife to keep up with twentieth-century Los Angeles's shifting social, cultural, geographic, political, legal, and economic patterns. They fought on all fronts, from the cultural sphere to the political arena and from the workplace to housing, to access, engage in, and shape the city. *The Coveted Westside* seeks to uncover the twentieth-century-long effort led by elite Black Angelenos to challenge housing discrimination and integrate restricted areas. With each racially restricted neighborhood block they breached, they opened up another part of the city, which gradually helped make available the adjacent neighborhoods to more Angelenos of color. Whites continually responded by using a multitude of discriminatory measures to maintain homogeneous communities that over time became embedded into the American political, legal, and economic structures. But when they found none of their tactics working any longer, they moved away. By 1960 historically White elite Sugar Hill was made up of a majority Black population. By 1970 most of the affluent Crenshaw area neighborhoods, including Leimert Park, View Park, View Heights, Windsor Hills, and Baldwin Hills Estates, had a majority Black population.[5] In their migration to the Westside, affluent Blacks faced the unfortunate byproducts of "White flight," as it was tersely phrased, and, as Obatala pointed out, a widening gap between them and their working-class counterparts who felt neglected and resentful for remaining confined to the Eastside.

FROM COLONIAL OUTPOST TO SEGREGATED CITY

Resistance against oppression has transpired throughout history in various forms, shapes, and sizes. It has surfaced in nonviolent and violent methods, from subversion and civil disobedience to armed rebellion and mutiny; it has manifested in various modes, from methodical and restrained to forthright and unreserved; and it has arisen in planned and spontaneous expressions with the help of individual leadership and group dedication. While efforts of resistance have developed in most eras and regions since the emergence of settled societies, taking shape in response to the existing conditions, the goals have varied from reforming a system to overthrowing a regime. In early twentieth-century Los Angeles, local elite African American men and women initiated a tactful and measured form of resistance by challenging housing discrimination to reform the urban environment and legal system. As American citizens, with a long history of contributing to the growth of the nation, they felt warranted to a stake at the wealth-building opportunities. Among other marginalized groups, including Chinese, Japanese, Mexican, and Jewish Angelenos, who faced the same restrictions, the Black elite headed the fight against housing discrimination in the decades between the world wars and bore the brunt of adversarial responses through the twentieth century. Using their social networks and financial resources, they purchased houses in racially restricted neighborhoods and defended themselves in the communities and the courts for their constitutional right to property. They came up against centuries-old racist social, political, legal, and economic practices that took root in the original thirteen colonies and spread into the western territory.

Since the time that the federal government took the West and Southwest in its 1848 victory in the Mexican American War and gave its newly acquired territories statehood in the subsequent years, including California in 1850, Anglo Americans set out to dominate the historically ethnically and racially mixed region. Fueled by the discovery of gold in Northern California, federal incentives, and the belief in Manifest Destiny, easterners and midwesterners, most of whom were Protestant Whites, traveled by boat or on the overland trails to settle the western land. As Los Angeles was transitioning from a Mexican town to an American city in the 1860s, Anglo Americans put down roots around the long-established Plaza, the indigenous territory that the Spanish and their subjects determined as their own in the 1780s. Los Angeles became another conquest in the colonial race as White settlers adopted policies that divided the public spaces between themselves and everyone else and appropriated or obliterated the city's ethnic and racial past.[6] *The Coveted Westside* begins by exploring the origins of White colonialism in the western city, and then centers on tracing the ways in which colonialism grew into a discriminatory legal system that local Whites shaped at the grassroots level and impelled the federal government to sanction.

Upon the late nineteenth-century advent of rail systems, Los Angeles saw a population influx and expanded outward from its downtown core toward all of the cardinal points. The completion of the transcontinental railroad, the reduction in ticket prices, and the work of boosters creating an image of Los Angeles bountiful in resources and a healthy climate drew peoples of European (including Russian), Latino, African, and Asian descent and led to the 1880s real estate boom. The construction of the interurban public transit system gave residents the impetus to traverse the growing city and establish streetcar suburbs. In 1900 African Americans made up 2.1 percent of the Los Angeles population, which was slightly more than Chinese residents. Many held out hope of escaping racism and violence that wreaked havoc on their daily lives and benefitting from the opportunities that they could not enjoy elsewhere.[7] What Beavers elided, in his explanation of Black migration, was that, until the early 1900s, African Americans had some freedom to reside in developed and undeveloped areas across early Los Angeles. They disembarked in the downtown train stations, settled around the central section, and migrated east of the Los Angeles River and as far west as the Pacific Ocean. But as the White population took control, Blacks and other ethnic and religious minorities faced discriminatory housing practices that pushed most of them south and east of downtown into what would later become the older and unrestricted Eastside.

While Los Angeles expanded outward from the central core, its White inhabitants used discriminatory measures to segregate the population and, among the city's many inner and outlying sections, essentially create the larger areas of the Eastside and the Westside. In the early twentieth century, the land west of Main Street and the downtown core, or what became known as the Westside, saw the growth of suburban, White, middle- and upper-class restricted neighborhoods. East of Main Street, or what became known as the Eastside, took shape as the primary place where people of color could find residence. Like most American cities, Los Angeles also linked neighborhood terms to the racial and ethnic demographics of its communities. Since its first decades as an American city, White Angelenos relegated people of color onto the Eastside and into ethnic neighborhoods, such as Chinatown, Sonoratown, Little Tokyo, Boyle Heights, and the East Los Angeles barrio, many of which held racially and ethnically particular names that identified their most prominent population.

Yet Los Angeles's ethnic enclaves comprised racially and ethnically diverse populations. Central Avenue and its adjacent streets included a mixed population of working-class Whites, Blacks, Mexicans, and Asians in the interwar years, and at the same time served as the city's center of Black life. Like the Japanese in Little Tokyo and the Jews in Boyle Heights, in the face of discrimination that sought to hinder their advancement, African Americans established businesses and religious institutions, headed local newspapers and political groups, and nurtured artistic and cultural pursuits along Central Avenue. But as the city expanded into a metropolis, Blacks and other ethnic minorities became cut off from the economic and cultural opportunities that were emerging on the Westside.[8]

Cultural, demographic, political, and economic shifts led to revisions in the Eastside's and Westside's borders and meanings. As Blacks migrated westward, the racial border that divided the Eastside and the Westside shifted. The boundary moved from Main Street to Western Avenue in the interwar interregnum, and Arlington Avenue and then Crenshaw Boulevard in the postwar era. That said, the terms "Eastside" and "Westside" have had historically different meanings to Los Angeles's varied racial and ethnic groups, have held politically and ideologically loaded connotations, and have served as symbols to understanding the imagined geography of the city. Some Angelenos, for instance, include as part of the Eastside, which has been predominantly known as a racially and ethnically diverse and distressed area, the Echo Park, Los Feliz, and Silver Lake neighborhoods, which, since late 1990s gentrification, have been viewed as White and affluent. Also, while White Angelenos initially used the Los Angeles River as their racial buffer zone and relegated Latinos and Mexicans to live east of it, and have referred to the area as East Los Angeles, scholars Victor M. Valle and Rodolfo D. Torres recognize mostly Mexican and Latino communities west of the river as part of what they call "the Greater Eastside."[9]

The Eastside has also undergone revisions to its name. While Central Avenue comprised a multiracial and multiethnic population in the interwar years, and at the same time served as the city's center of Black life, the area and its south-adjacent communities of Watts, Willowbrook, and Compton in the postwar years turned into, in common parlance, the city's "Black belt." The severe wartime housing shortage and systemic housing discrimination relegated the tens of thousands of African Americans, many of whom migrated to the city between the world wars, to the Eastside. By the 1960s Angelenos were referring to the Eastside as South Central, an area that extended from the historical Central Avenue corridor westward, around Western Avenue, southward to Compton, and eastward into the formerly White, working-class communities of the Alameda corridor. The name itself, South Central, carried negative connotations of a distressed and dangerous area. In a unanimous vote in 2003, the Los Angeles City Council changed the name to South Los Angeles to rebrand the area. Considering the goals of this study, which seeks to account for the twentieth-century's Black migration from Central Avenue westward as a means to challenge housing discrimination and gain equal access to the city, *The Coveted Westside* recognizes the historically contingent, shifting terminologies but, for the sake of consistency, has chosen to use the historical and comparatively less racially loaded labels Eastside and Westside throughout.[10]

Whites brought many well-established customs and comportments of the Jim Crow South and the acquiescent North into Los Angeles. Like other northern cities, the absence of "Whites Only" and "Coloreds Only" signs in Los Angeles might have made racial discrimination less noticeable, but racial and ethnic neighborhood segregation showed clear indication of an inequitable city. Whites at the grassroots level, who sought to protect their property and privileges in the urban system, exercised lawless and lawful practices to create neighborhood segregation and a racialized geography. They used overt methods of intimidation and aggression, from uttering racial epithets and making verbal threats to vandalizing property and burning crosses on lawns, to suppress the advancement of people of color. In the western city, Whites also effectively impelled the establishment of a discriminatory legal system by implementing exclusionary zoning laws and racial restrictive covenants, and then persuading the courts and federal government to support the practices, and thus kept racial and ethnic minorities from moving to certain neighborhoods for years.[11]

From the early 1900s onward, policymakers, developers, real estate brokers and agents, and homeowners in urban centers across the country began adopting discriminatory housing measures that created long-lasting, damaging effects. Los Angeles city officials instituted the nation's first use-based zoning laws that designated most of the Eastside as industrial, mixed-use districts and most of the Westside as residential, single-family communities. The laws helped populate the Eastside with the city's ethnically and racially diverse working class who could not afford single-family housing, and the Westside with the White middle class and upper class who could. Around the same time, local developers, real estate interests, and homeowners began to endorse and attach racial occupancy clauses, articles, and appendices to their housing contracts. While these covenants restricted White homeowners from renting, leasing, selling, and transferring their property to whom they commonly called non-Whites and oftentimes non-Christians, such as Blacks, Chinese, Japanese, Mexicans, and Jews for decades, apart from allowing service staff to live in the home, those covenants consistently targeted and afflicted African Americans. White homeowners pressured their neighbors to add these racial restrictive covenants to their properties, and in many communities, neighbors entered into these contracts together, allocating entire blocks and subdivisions exclusively to White settlement.[12]

In the 1920s and 1930s the federal government's judicial and executive branches cemented the discriminatory tools. After lower courts disapproved these practices for years, the US Supreme Court in 1926 made detrimental decisions on America's residential patterns when it sanctioned use-based zoning laws in *Euclid v. Ambler* and racial restrictive covenants in *Corrigan v. Buckley*. Then, in the depths of the Great Depression, and in the name of economic relief to reduce and avoid foreclosures, President Franklin D. Roosevelt and his administration joined the chorus. While Roosevelt's New Deal established the roots of racial liberalism, whose adherents denounced overt racism and embraced inclusion in the 1940s, and championed civil rights in the 1950s and 1960s, it institutionalized housing discriminatory measures at the national level under the Home Owners' Loan Corporation (HOLC) and the Federal Housing Administration (FHA) in the Great Depression. Postwar discriminatory practices took shape in other forms, such as speculative contract selling using installment land contracts that historian Beryl Satter discusses in Chicago.[13] The nation's White power structure came to accept the discriminatory measures as natural, while the practices left African Americans and ethnic minorities with little option but to live in what would become neglected communities or, to use the more loaded word, ghettos. As the consistently and systematically marginalized group, Black Angelenos became confined to the Eastside.

As racism, discrimination, and segregation intensified through the twentieth century, the Eastside turned into the city's Black belt. Meanwhile, newer and higher-quality residences, businesses, and services cropped up on the coveted and covenanted Westside. Local Black leaders and professionals who had the financial resources to do so responded by leading the migration westward. Norman O. Houston was one of many who led the charge. Black business owners and real estate agents; actors, comedians, singers, and musicians; doctors and dentists; teachers, police officers, and military officials; and community activists set out to attain equal access to the city. Moreover, Black men *and* women headed the charge to access the traditionally female sphere of housing and domesticity. Many Black men lent their names to property contracts and conveyances, while Black women and children, who often spent the most time in the neighborhood, also had to endure White resistance. Black women in particular faced the intersectional burdens of racial and gender discrimination in their quest for quality housing. Individuals, couples, and families chose properties that had expiring or expired restrictive covenants, collaborated with White or light-skinned Black intermediaries to make the purchase, and contended with White resistance and intimidation in the neighborhood and in the courtroom.

Their challenges to the discriminatory measures took significant toil, dogged resistance, and strategic organizing that manifested in Los Angeles's Black homeowners' rights movement. As early as the 1910s, when White Angelenos began to increasingly implement lawless and lawful measures to establish all-White neighborhoods across the Westside, local Blacks and their attorneys launched a decades-long movement to end housing discrimination and gain equal access to the city. Their efforts preceded the interracial "urban guerilla warfare" over territory and housing in 1940s Chicago that historian Arnold Hirsch describes and the "defensive localism" Whites used to maintain homogenous communities in 1940s Detroit that historian Thomas Sugrue identifies. *The Coveted Westside* seeks to push back the historiography of urban Black civil rights activism over homeownership to the 1910s and 1920s, the same time Whites began implementing those discriminatory measures. For some Black Angelenos, as historian Jeffrey Gonda argues, "Breaching covenants...rarely began as a political act." But this research reveals that, in Los Angeles, many of the first anti-covenanters deliberately and strategically fought these insidious measures.[14]

Migration became one of the more common forms of resistance twentieth-century Blacks used to escape poverty, discrimination, and violence. Between 1910 and 1980, in what became known as the Great Migration, more than 6.5 million African Americans left the South for the burgeoning northern and western cities. During the first wave of the mass movement, between 1910 and 1940, more than 1.5 million southern African Americans moved to New York, Chicago, Detroit, and other northern cities. During the 1940s, the first decade of the second wave, some 1.5 million Blacks, more migrants than during any other decade of the Great Migration, joined the exodus. Los Angeles experienced a substantial Black influx. The expansion of wartime manufacturing and the federal government's promise of equal employment in the defense industry drove Blacks to relocate.[15] The percentage of Blacks in the city steadily rose from 3.1 in 1930, to 4.2 in 1940, to 8.7 in 1950, to 13.5 in 1960.[16] Yet as they faced a defiant White population who sought to control the city and covet its financial prospects, their efforts to migrate for opportunity did not end at the downtown train stations. Black migration onto the Westside became an extension of the Great Migration and the drive for equity.

Blacks' move into restricted neighborhoods as a form of resistance served as one step in challenging housing discrimination. They also had to fight in the courts to delegitimize racial restrictive covenants and live in their new neighborhoods. Scholarship on the racial restrictive covenant cases has centered on the midwestern and eastern lawsuits that became part of and culminated in the 1948 *Shelley v. Kraemer* decision. Whites in cities across the country, in addition to Los Angeles, had begun implementing covenants since the early twentieth century, and the number of lawsuits over their legality grew in the 1930s and 1940s.[17] Los Angeles, however, was what legal scholar Kenneth Mack calls "ground zero" in the fight to overturn the discriminatory measures. Despite the emphatic disapproval of the National Association for the Advancement of Colored People (NAACP), St. Louis, Missouri, civil rights attorney George Vaughn persisted in getting the US Supreme Court to review his lawsuit and make it the namesake of the case. Yet Los Angeles attorney Loren Miller achieved the first greatest victory over covenants in the postwar era. The 1945 *Anderson v. Auseth* case, "a particular darling of the NAACP's legal staff," according to Gonda, and that included

Norman O. Houston and other Black leaders and professionals who moved into the historically White, elite Sugar Hill, became the nation's first lawsuit that declared racial restrictive covenants an infringement on citizens' constitutional rights.[18] *Anderson*, and the Black elite's organizing that led to the case, set the precedent for the 1948 *Shelley v. Kraemer* decision, and then the Los Angeles–originated 1953 *Barrows v. Jackson* ruling, which denied property owners the right to collect damage claims when restrictive covenants were breached.

Among many factors, including the resolve of the defendants and the NAACP attorneys, the political milieu also contributed to the *Shelley* and *Barrows* victories. Amid the city's Black homeowners' rights movement, California and Los Angeles underwent a political shift to a Democratic majority in the 1930s and 1940s, electing racially liberal leaders who decried political corruption, expressed concern over racial inequality, and sought to reform municipal services and improve conditions for all citizens.[19] The African American "Double V" campaign to defeat totalitarianism abroad and racial discrimination at home in World War II, and the atrocities committed by the Third Reich, additionally shined a light on the United States' own bigotries. Loren Miller's defense in the Sugar Hill case gained more strength from the support of state attorney general Robert Walker Kenny (California) as amicus curiae, and Miller found an unexpected ally in Judge Thurmond Clarke (Los Angeles Superior Court) who handed down the landmark decision. Also evincing the rise of racial liberalism, the national NAACP, in *Shelley*, relied heavily on amici briefs from activist organizations across the country, as well as US attorney general Tom Clark, and it finally received approval for judicial review from the high court that, since the mid-1920s, had refused to hear any covenant cases.

But despite hard-fought lawsuits against housing discrimination that culminated in the *Shelley* and *Barrows* victories, Angelenos of color found most of the city's White population clinging to and perpetuating racial segregation. When Blacks moved into majority White areas, they faced another set of problems that were cut from the same cloth. Some Whites made verbal threats, damaged Black-owned property, and pressured Blacks to leave. Most heeded the postwar, Cold War–inspired conservative anti-Communism, antistatism, and anti-integration call. By arguing Black in-migration would destroy property values and public schools, profit-seeking, blockbusting real estate agents exacerbated White fear. White flight and resegregation ensued. In the decades following World War II, as Blacks settled in Los Angeles proper, most Whites (including both Christians and Jews) migrated outward and took their assets with them. Asian Angelenos also migrated alongside Blacks, but after the 1965 Watts rebellion, many left, too. Some moved north, into areas such as Pasadena, the San Fernando Valley, and Ventura County. Others relocated east into San Bernardino and Riverside Counties, or south into Orange County. Still others migrated farther west to the beautiful, sandy beaches of the Pacific Ocean.[20] Angelenos who decided to stay engaged in counterforce efforts to stop resegregation, tout the benefits of racial integration, and further the appreciable potential of their home and community.

AFRICAN AMERICANS IN THE SUBURBAN METROPOLIS

As Beavers explained the city's westward migration pattern in his 1982 interview, he made sense of the reasons behind the Black-led migration onto Los Angeles's Westside. "We really have segregation, but it's not imposed by the law. It's imposed by the pattern of living." Since the early twentieth century, White Angelenos were, in part, exercising de facto segregation, he believed, acting in practice of custom and personal selection of their neighborhood. "They don't like to live in a situation where they are the minority, so they move out." Then, he added, the city's residential patterns took shape because of state-endorsed, de jure, discriminatory housing measures. "Long before" the *Shelley* decision, occupancy clauses "made it impossible for Negroes to get clear title" and move to restricted areas. His insurance company, Golden State, lent money to Blacks to purchase homes in White areas, a provision the California Supreme Court decided in the 1928 *Wayt v. Patee* case, in hope "some time that [the restrictions] would have to be lifted." But occupancy clauses kept people of color from living there, and the more comprehensive racial restrictive covenants prohibited them from purchasing property altogether.[21] Before and since Beavers's interview, scholars have sought to understand this history.

In fact, around the same time Beavers spoke to the UCLA Oral History Program, scholarship on suburban development was emerging as a major topic of discussion. While urban expansion marked the late nineteenth and early twentieth centuries, suburban growth fundamentally transformed the landscape through the mid-twentieth century. The installation of rail systems in the late nineteenth century helped urban centers, including Los Angeles, develop streetcar suburbs that became the forerunners of the suburban residential form in the twentieth century. But rather than a city centered on a downtown and encircled by suburbs, Los Angeles decentralized decades before the establishment of New York's Levittown, into self-contained, low-density, racially and economically homogeneous suburban neighborhoods comprising detached, single-family, and mostly ethnically, racially, and religiously restricted homes. Like in the 1880s, Los Angeles in the 1920s underwent a far-reaching real estate boom that led to the development of subdivisions north of downtown through greater Hollywood and the San Fernando Valley and west of downtown through the Wilshire district, Beverly Hills, and the Crenshaw area. The "suburban metropolis" scholar Robert Fishman dubbed it, in *Bourgeois Utopias* (1987), was coming into fruition, which the locally filmed television series, *Leave It to Beaver*, would fictionalize in the mid-twentieth century. People of color had access to only a portion of that world.[22]

Two distinct racialized narratives emerged in the mid-twentieth century—affluent, White, suburban growth, and poor, Black, urban decline—that scholars sought to unpack. Historian Kenneth Jackson, in *Crabgrass Frontier* (1985), spearheaded the discourse over the reasons suburban growth took place. Federal policies and programs, especially accelerated under the New Deal, he argues, led Whites to migrate to the suburbs. The implementation of transportation policies; tax incentives; self-amortizing, low-interest mortgages; and so-called security maps that redlined communities, among other practices, benefited Whites and contributed to residential segregation. If Whites wanted robust, ever-increasing property values to build a strong nest egg for their family and their retirement and to live in neighborhoods with quality public schools to help their children succeed, they were told to live in a nice, meaning White, and at minimum, middle-class, neighborhood populated by, in Cold War parlance, nuclear families. Jackson brought attention to the structural issues at play that scholars of cities have also explored.[23]

Especially since the mid-1960s urban uprisings, beginning with the Watts rebellion, social scientists sought to understand the reasons that caused urban poverty and decline, the commonly called "urban crisis." When Daniel Patrick Moynihan placed the onus on Black pathology and the Black family structure, and perpetuated Oscar Lewis's "culture of poverty" thesis, sociologists responded by scrutinizing the structural developments that created a Black "underclass." William Julius Wilson, in *The Truly Disadvantaged* (1987), argues that the withdrawal of industries from the inner cities caused a decline in the number of low-skilled industrial jobs and joblessness among Black men, while Douglas Massey and Nancy Denton, in *American Apartheid* (1993), find residential racial segregation as the primary driver.[24] Thomas Sugrue, in *The Origins of the Urban Crisis* (1996), pushed the debate further by scrutinizing the past's institutional frameworks to understand the roots of Detroit's urban crisis. He makes clear that "no one social program or policy, no single force" led to urban decline. Rather, between the 1940s and 1960s, in the so-called age of affluence, a "complex and interwoven" web of structural developments, from deindustrialization and economic restructuring to antiradical politics and racial discrimination, contributed to the crisis.[25]

The Coveted Westside builds on the works of scholars who brought attention to the handmade historical and structural developments that segregated America's cities. Practices and policies implemented at the neighborhood, city, county, state, and federal levels gave rise to Los Angeles's mostly White Westside and the decline of its mostly Black Eastside. White real estate interests and institutions, including banks, developers, appraisers, brokers, agents, school boards, family members, friends, and neighbors, encouraged each other to invest in what would probably become their largest asset, their house, in the Westside suburbs. But long before the federal government sanctioned discriminatory housing practices in the 1920s and 1930s, it took control of the western city and encouraged White easterners and midwesterners to settle there. White city dwellers then created tools to segregate the city that the federal government later endorsed. This study, therefore, pushes the narrative back, arguing Anglo American domination of the West gave local Whites the license to secure the city's opportunities and marginalize people of color.

The Jim Crow South created a binary landscape by segregating Whites and Blacks, and, in part, many northern and western cities like Los Angeles repeated the pattern. Yet, from its indigenous roots through the Spanish, Mexican, and American eras, Los Angeles gained a multiethnic and multiracial population that helped the city take shape as a multicultural center. This study is one contribution to the intersecting narratives that took shape in the city. African Americans rarely lived or fought for equal access in isolation from other urbanites. They resided among an ethnically and racially dynamic population that shaped their perspectives, their actions, and their relationship with the city. From the outset of the American city, Anglo nativist practices pushed Mexican Angelenos northeast of the Plaza, into Sonoratown, and then east of the Los Angeles River, into Boyle Heights and the East Los Angeles barrio. The Chinese, who began moving to the West Coast during the 1850s gold rush and 1860s transcontinental railroad construction, and who established the city's first Chinatown in the 1860s, experienced White hostility through the 1882 exclusion act, got pushed to an undeveloped section east of the Plaza, and then relocated in the early 1930s, when Union Station was built, to the new Chinatown. In the late 1800s, Japan's Meiji leaders lifted legal barriers that allowed for Japanese citizens to travel, many of whom went to Hawaii Territory and the North American west coasts of, for example, Canada, Washington state, and California. By 1910 Los Angeles had become home to the largest share of Japanese in the United States, many of whom in the 1920s made Little Tokyo the city's center of Japanese economic and cultural life. Blacks established alliances and coalitions with other racial, ethnic, and religious groups that experienced the same discriminatory forces.[26]

Black and Japanese Americans, the two largest groups of color that migrated onto the Westside around the same time, have become the center of recent scholarship. Historian Daniel Widener argues that Black and Japanese Angelenos often shared experiences living in the same and adjacent areas, drew inspiration from one another, and established coalitions to combat racism. "Where one group was found, the other was likely as well," Widener explains. Historian Scott Kurashige also challenges the White/Black racial binary by exploring the intersections of the city's Black and Japanese populations. To maintain hegemony in the interwar years, Kurashige shows, Whites grouped together Black and Japanese Americans in the same category. But within the multiethnic and multiracial milieu, Kurashige argues and this study seeks to further establish, local Black leaders and professionals spearheaded the legal effort against discriminatory housing measures that paved a path for other marginalized groups to access the Westside.[27]

In the postwar era, Whites pitted Black and Japanese Angelenos against one another, Kurashige argues, using relationship triangulation devices and exploiting their diverging racial and ethnic constructs. While the United States sought Japan as an anti-Communist Cold War ally, reframed internment as "a benevolent endeavor consistent with modernist notions of progress and racial integration," and dubbed Japanese Americans "model minorities," it pitched African Americans "as a problem minority that had to be contained." Around the same time the White power structure cast Jews and some Mexicans and Latinos as White, and accepted Asian Americans as paradigms of success, it continued to make African Americans the unwarranted scapegoats to society's issues.[28] Thus, Blacks led the westward migration in the interwar years and bore the brunt of antagonism through the twentieth century. Of the ways Angelenos resisted Black in-migration in the postwar era, relocation topped the list. But in multiethnic and multiracial Los Angeles, White flight also involved Asian and Jewish out-migration. Many of the marginalized ethnic and religious groups that formed coalitions with Blacks in the interwar interregnum broke those alliances in the postwar era.

Scholars of twentieth-century Black Los Angeles have uncovered a city abounding with opportunities and shortcomings. In the first study of African Americans in Los Angeles, a 1936 PhD dissertation, sociologist J. Max Bond found that, alongside the rise of the city's population in the early twentieth century, racial intolerance intensified and the urban landscape became segregated. Since then, historians Lawrence de Graaf, Douglas Flamming, and Josh Sides have shown that Black Angelenos acted to achieve equality. Flamming, in *Bound for Freedom* (2005), argues that the Black quest for freedom in Los Angeles emerged not as a distinct movement defined by a series of events but rather as "a way of life" that African Americans committed to and pursued. He centers his study on the "strivers and joiners," the city's early Black middle class who possessed bourgeois values of family, industry, and thrift, and who broke down racial barriers for later generations, including those in this study. Sides begins *L.A. City Limits* (2003) in the 1930s, where Flamming's work concludes, to examine the transformation of the city landscape through Black influx from the Great Migration. His broad scope of Black settlement in many of Los Angeles's neighborhoods, including those in this study, provides a basis for this work to explore the middle-class Black-led migration onto the Westside.[29]

As scholarship on the Black underclass and the urban crisis generated widespread interest in the 1980s and 1990s, a parallel discussion arose on the Black middle class that sought to underscore diversity within African America and yet received less attention. Leading the scholarship, sociologists essentially explored the roots of the Black middle class, the social, political, and economic forces that affected its growth, its defining status symbols, its driving philosophies, and its relationship with its working-class counterparts and the nation as a whole. The discussion culminated in a 1987 book by sociologist Bart Landry who, using empirical data on a national scope, sequenced the history of the Black middle class into three periods: the "old mulatto elite" who prospered between Emancipation and 1915; the "old black middle class" who thrived between 1915 and 1960; and, as his title states, the focus of his work, *The New Black Middle Class*, who have flourished since the 1964 Civil Rights Act and its ban on discrimination in education, employment, and public accommodations. Lacking a consensus on an official definition of middle-class status, scholars have instead used a range of markers.[30]

The Black elite of the Jim Crow era differed in many ways from those in the post–World War II years. With roots in the postbellum Black elite, the "old black middle class" of the interwar years expanded in part due to African Americans' attainment of undergraduate and graduate degrees, especially from the newly established Black colleges and universities, and their entrance into skilled, professional, and entrepreneurial fields, including business (such as hotels, retail shops, and funeral homes), finance (such as banks, building and loan associations, and insurance companies), medicine (medical and dental), ministry, law, education, real estate, and entertainment. In the era of racial uplift and self-help, primarily from the 1880s to World War I, Henry Lyman Morehouse and then W. E. B. Du Bois identified what they called the Talented Tenth, meaning the top 10 percent of African American men, as exemplars of the race. They earned a college education as opposed to getting industrial training, succeeded in their professions, and served as thought leaders. Despite the legal protections passed in the years following the Civil War, and opportunities from joining the Great Migration and settling in northern and western cities, the Black middle class earned its income serving a geographically bound and racially restricted clientele who had been shut out of White-run institutions. While they faced some censure from the Black working class who saw them as encountering the same racist practices, the Black middle class set high expectations of uplifting the race, maintaining a respectable character, and upholding the traditional patriarchal family as so-called Race Men and Race Women.[31]

Because African Americans faced a myriad of racist practices that hindered their education, employment, and thus economic position, historians have defined the Black middle class by additional markers. Flamming uses the values of family, education, industry, thrift, and civil rights as indicators of Los Angeles's early Black middle class. Homeownership has also served as a symbol of middle-class status, and the high rate of Black homeownership in Los Angeles illustrates middle-class Blacks' notable proportion in the city and the value they put on private property. In 1910, around the time Whites began using racial restrictive covenants to segregate the urban landscape, Los Angeles had the highest rate of Black homeownership in the nation at 36.1 percent. Black homeownership in Oakland, California, averaged 29.9 percent and in Seattle, Washington, it averaged 27 percent. New York City had a mere 2.4 percent rate. In 1930 and 1940 some cities surpassed Los Angeles in Black homeownership, including Portland, Oregon, and San Antonio, Texas, yet the rate stayed around 30 percent. The growth of the Black middle class nationwide, and the high rate of Black homeownership in Los Angeles, buttressed the effort against housing discrimination.[32]

African Americans were not the only ones who valued homeownership. In Los Angeles, homeownership served as a central mechanism that drove migrants from across the country to the city and to take measures to defend their property against the forces they believed would devalue it. To attract newcomers to the area, boosters promoted Southern California as a place where its warm climate restored medical ills, its jobs offered economic security, and its single-family houses provided stability. "It is no coincidence that migrants to California in the early twentieth century were labeled 'homeseekers,'" historian Becky Nicolaides explains. In the 1920s Whites escalated their use of discriminatory housing measures, including in the blue-collar suburbs of the Alameda corridor when they feared African Americans living in the west-adjacent Central Avenue district would migrate into their community. White working-class homeowners saw their property as a symbol of their hard work, class identity, autonomy, and financial security. Many built their homes themselves, in the after-work hours and on the weekends, lobbied to maintain low taxes and the area's affordability on a working-class wage by keeping municipal services to a minimum, and fervently guarded against the in-migration of African Americans. While Alameda Street served as the so-called cotton curtain that segregated its blue-collar White suburbs from Central Avenue, African Americans saw it only fair for them to own a house as well.[33]

Without standard criteria, sociologists use various datasets to measure the size of the Black middle class and its growth in the postwar years. Bart Landry considers all white-collar employees and small business owners, including those in entrepreneurial, professional, and managerial roles, and many clerical and sales positions, as part of the middle class. He finds that the Black middle class in the United States increased from 3 percent in 1910 (compared to a 23.8 percent White middle class) to 13.4 percent in 1960 (compared to a 44.1 percent White middle class) to 37.8 percent in 1981 (compared to a 54.3 percent White middle class).[34]

Among the factors, increased educational attainment and employment opportunities, passage of civil rights legislation, and nationwide prosperity in the postwar years helped expand the Black middle class. Sociologists Thomas Durant, Jr., and Joyce Louden find in census data a progressive rise in the median years African Americans completed school from 6.8 in 1950, to 8.2 in 1960, to 9.8 in 1970, to 11.9 in 1979. Durant, Louden, Sharon Collins, and Landry argue that, in addition to the fields the first Black middle class worked in, postwar Blacks found employment in more white-collar and public-sector jobs; when protected by civil rights legislation and buoyed by an economic boom, many moved into higher income brackets. Durant and Louden find the percentage of Blacks in white-collar positions, including in professional, technical, managerial, clerical, and sales roles, increased from 9.8 in 1950 to 15.2 in 1960 to 23.9 in 1970. Collins notes that more Blacks entered skilled government positions, especially in personnel, labor relations, social science, and social welfare, and Black business owners received more federal financial support. Collins and Landry contend that federal initiatives since the 1964 Civil Rights Act helped Blacks enter more fields, and Landry adds that nationwide prosperity aided job growth.[35]

In addition to education, employment, values, and homeownership, scholars have used the Black working class as a marker in which to identify and distinguish the Black middle class. Among the indicators he uses, historian Martin Summers defines the Black middle class in the twentieth-century's first three decades less by "the material benefits of the larger American middle class" and "more by its self-conscious positioning against the black working class."[36] As the postwar Black middle class expanded, its values and its relationship with its working-class counterparts changed. The

Black middle class continued to generally differ in values to its working-class counterparts, but more of them came directly from the working class and shared familial ties, physical proximity (especially with the help of new technologies), and work settings. Thus, the postwar Black middle class reflected Marxist features (or material conditions characterized by income, assets, and expenditures) and Weberian sensibilities (or status attributed to, for instance, education, elite club membership, or property holdings). Considering the different ways of distinguishing class and status in the United States, African Americans self-identified according to varied and sometimes dissimilar criteria. While some middle-class Blacks sought to set themselves apart from their working-class counterparts, others, such as those who lived or worked on the Eastside in the 1960s and 1970s, continued to identify with the area. That said, on the whole, and as the Black middle class increased, intra-racial class tensions intensified.

Censure of the Black middle class heightened in the 1940s and 1950s when some critics thought it was distancing itself from the Black working class. Novelist Chester Himes, in *If He Hollers Let Him Go* (1945), rebuked Los Angeles's Black middle class for perpetuating racial inequality by abandoning the Black working class and moving to the Westside. Sociologist E. Franklin Frazier emerged as the foremost detractor when he contended, in *Black Bourgeoisie* (1957), that the Black middle class improved its class and social status by adopting and accommodating to White middle-class values and snubbing its racial heritage. Frazier denounced the Black middle class as shallow and insular, and consumed with its social affairs and sororities and fraternities, while the Black working class suffered from racial restrictions and poor conditions. He saw the male-led, Black working-class household as the answer to achieving interracial cooperation and economic and civil rights. While serving as a visiting professor at the University of Southern California (USC) in the summer of 1948, Frazier met some of Los Angeles's Black middle class. He and his spouse, Marie Brown Frazier, who had put her husband and his career ahead of her literary work, attended a party at actor Hattie McDaniel's Sugar Hill home.[37]

Himes and Frazier raised valid points, particularly when considering that Black middle-class Angelenos moved away from Central Avenue to access better opportunities in White neighborhoods. Members of the Black middle class also set themselves and their children apart by participating in elite organizations, such as The Boulé, The Links, and Jack and Jill of America, and embraced many of those heteronormative standards.[38] But unpacking the past shows that many Black leaders and professionals saw their decisions differently, in that they faced racism and discrimination at every step of their lives. They combated a system that, over the twentieth century, manipulated housing markets to privilege Whites and endorsed discriminatory housing measures at every level of society. Like their forbearers following the Civil War, the twentieth-century's Black middle class secured financial resources and used social networks to challenge racial discrimination, improve their quality of life, and claim their right to the promises made under the Declaration of Independence and the US Constitution.[39] They were advocating for a consumer-based, free market ideology as the basis of citizenship. Considering the varied markers of middle-class status, and the high value placed on Los Angeles's single-family, middle-class neighborhoods, this study centers on the first African Americans who broke racial barriers and moved into the city's restricted affluent enclaves.

The Coveted Westside is divided into two parts. The first three chapters that make up part I, "The Pioneers of Housing Integration in Los Angeles," explore Los Angeles's rise of residential segregation and its racialized geography, and the middle-class Black-led effort to migrate into the earliest Westside neighborhoods and successfully argue the unconstitutionality of racial restrictive covenants in the courts. Chapter 1 discusses the federal government–led crusade to take control of the city, the White effort to restrict the Westside from the city's multiethnic and multiracial population, and the lawsuits that resulted in the high court sanctioning discriminatory housing practices. Chapter 2 centers on West Jefferson and Sugar Hill, two historically White, elite Westside communities that Black leaders and professionals accessed between the world wars. After migrating into West Jefferson, Norman O. Houston and other Black professionals turned to Sugar Hill. Whites mobilized into a so-called improvement association and brought lawsuits against the newcomers, the subject of chapter 3. Sugar Hill's prominent Black defendants, and their talented attorney Loren Miller, stepped into the forefront of the battle against restrictive covenants and became part of the legal precedent that led to the *Shelley* and *Barrows* decisions.

African Americans and people of color across the city found encouragement in the legal victories to push farther onto the Westside, but they had to enforce the high court's decisions through their own labor. The three chapters that make up part II, "Post-*Shelley* Westward Migration and the Case for Crenshaw," explore the desegregation of Los Angeles proper, and local efforts in the Crenshaw area to foster integration and inclusion. Postwar Los Angeles underwent profound systemic changes that, among many ways, surfaced in the battle between the power structure for the city's business center. As scholar Mike Davis puts it, postwar Los Angeles comprised "a city with two heads." Beginning in the interwar interregnum and accelerating in the postwar era, as Los Angeles underwent suburban expansion, assisted by the housing construction boom and the rise of the automobile and the freeway system, the old-moneyed, White, Protestant, conservative guard sought to revitalize downtown while the new-moneyed savings-and-loan and show business executives, many of whom were Jewish and Democrats, invested in the Westside. Amid the contestation over power, and the growth of the Westside, post-*Shelley* and *Barrows*, Angelenos of all backgrounds set their sights on Westside real estate. White homeowner activists then pivoted from creating racially homogeneous bourgeois utopias to defending their neighborhoods against, Davis explains, "unwanted development," such as apartments, freeways, and businesses, and "unwanted persons."[40]

While Blacks led the legal battle in interwar Los Angeles, they migrated onto the Westside alongside Jews, Asians, and Latinos throughout the twentieth century. Yet at the same time, they made up the largest numbers and bore the brunt of adversarial responses, including their neighbors' flight. Most Whites, including some Jewish Angelenos, whose predecessors had fought against the same discriminatory measures, perpetuated segregation, and abandoned the area. Chapter 4 focuses on the migration, following *Shelley* and *Barrows*, to settle north of Washington Boulevard in the prosperous neighborhoods of Lafayette Square and Hancock Park, and west of Arlington Boulevard in the affluent Crenshaw area, and the White resistance that the new Black middle class endured.

The Crenshaw area served as a prime locale in the westward migration pattern that middle-class Blacks led in the early 1900s. African American entrepreneurs, entertainers, politicians, professionals, and community activists, who desegregated the middle-class Crenshaw area in the post-*Shelley* years, were the successors of those who had moved into West Jefferson and Sugar Hill and beneficiaries of postwar middle-class expansion through increased educational attainment and white-collar and public-sector jobs. They initially faced White intimidation and harassment; when those tactics failed, they saw Whites yield to conservative claims and real estate blockbusting, and move away. Responding to the population shift, and concerns the neighborhood would become all Black, Crenshaw residents forged efforts across the color line to cultivate integration and inclusion and sustain the value of their communities.

Chapter 5 centers on an interracial group of White (Christian and Jewish), Black, and Asian homeowners in Crenshaw who, beginning in the early 1960s, established Crenshaw Neighbors, Incorporated (CN), hired their own real estate agent, organized events, published literature, and collaborated with local officials and groups. Chapter 6 explores the expansion of Black art and activism into Crenshaw's Leimert Park, which emerged under the leadership of brothers Alonzo and Dale Davis when they opened Brockman Gallery in 1967. Both artists and public-school teachers turned art entrepreneurs and local activists, the Davis brothers exemplify the benefits African Americans received from 1960s federal civil rights legislation and the expansion of public-sector jobs. The gallery became a central meeting place where artists of color not only sold their work, but also planned outreach programs and social events in the community and around the city to promote multiculturalism and inclusion.

Black migration onto the Westside made available more neighborhoods to more Angelenos of color. Over the second half of the twentieth century, Angelenos of color fanned out across greater Los Angeles into upper-, middle-, and working-class communities. Many moved into some of the most sought-after neighborhoods of the city, such as affluent Crenshaw, and gained access to better-quality goods and services. But Whites (Christian and Jewish) and then Asians (mostly Japanese) also used migration as a form of resistance. Adhering to the decades-long messages that Black influx would result in property deterioration and ghetto expansion, Whites and Asians in Crenshaw increasingly sold their homes and left Los Angeles proper. Some forward-thinking Whites, Blacks, and Asians joined forces to uphold the quality of their neighborhoods and the adjoining public services. In the Crenshaw area, they saw success in maintaining property values well above the city average and sustaining the esteemed reputation of their community. By the 1970s, however, the population of many Westside communities, including those in affluent Crenshaw, became majority Black, and the effort toward racial integration waned. Black migration and settlement could not put an end to the methodically defined and then consistently redefined racist practices and policies that influenced non-Black Angelenos from wanting to live near Black Angelenos.

PART ONE

The Pioneers of Housing Integration
in Los Angeles

Chapter One

Demarcating the Westside from the Eastside

IN 1924, DURING A DECADE when Whites in northern cities harnessed the power of racial restrictions to impede on Black migration and harden residential segregation, a working-class African American couple, William H. and Eunice Long, took a risk and put a down payment on a small bungalow at 771 East Forty-First Street in Los Angeles's Entwistle tract, a few blocks west of Central Avenue. Even though the deed included a long-established occupancy clause, the Longs made the purchase, knowing that Blacks had been living in the community for years without facing any legal challenges. In 1905 Lulu Nevada Entwistle Hinton (later Letteau) subdivided the land south of Fortieth Street, between Avalon Boulevard, and Vernon and McKinley Avenues. Born to James and Ellen Entwistle, the city's early wealthy White landowners, and a new widow of real estate broker John W. Hinton, Lulu Hinton continued her family's business of land development, and as other developers had begun to do, attached racial restrictive clauses to most of the tract's deeds that mandated the properties "never at any time be sold[,] rented to[,] or occupied by any person of Negro descent." A few years later, despite the occupancy clauses, African Americans began moving into the tract, and by the mid-1920s, they accounted for roughly half of the population. It was not until years after Lulu Hinton (then Letteau) died, when the Longs moved into the community, that her heirs, led by her second spouse, real estate broker George H. Letteau, tried to enforce the restriction.[1]

Initially inhabited by indigenous populations, the state of California and the city of Los Angeles were founded amid European and American competition for land and power. The Spanish arrived in the late 1700s, traveling northwestward from Mexico along the Pacific Coast and setting up missions (religious outposts), presidios (fortified settlements), and pueblos (agricultural villages), including El Pueblo de Nuestra Señora La Reina de Los Ángeles de Porciúncula, in 1781. Mexico became a sovereign nation and took control of the land, after winning the Mexican War of Independence in 1821, and then the United States obtained it in the Mexican American War in 1848. Each nation sought to claim the land, extract its natural resources, exploit or expel the indigenous populations, and attain access to the trade networks in the Pacific Ocean. After annexing much of the West and Southwest in the Treaty of Guadalupe Hidalgo, and mandating all Spanish and Mexican citizens living in the territory to either become US citizens or leave within one year of the treaty's ratification, the US government encouraged eastern and midwestern Americans with the prospect of gold, Manifest Destiny, and the Homestead Acts to travel westward, following the overland trails, through inclement weather and harsh conditions. The American effort to colonize California and Los Angeles continued through the 1900s as United States–supported citizens settled more of the city, expunged its multiethnic past, relegated people of color to certain areas, and asserted control over its social, political, legal, and economic structures.[2]

Land-locked and centered at the Plaza in the downtown core, Los Angeles in the late 1800s and early 1900s expanded its margins in all of the cardinal points, setting itself up to become a leading world city in the modern era. Entrepreneurs installed individual horse-drawn streetcar lines and then cable- and electric-powered systems that initially connected downtown to the adjoining neighborhoods and eventually radiated northward into Pasadena, southward to Long Beach, eastward across the Los Angeles River, and westward to the Pacific Ocean. Los Angeles increased its size with the 1906 shoestring annexation that connected the city to San Pedro through a corridor between downtown and the harbor. The city expanded again with its annexation of greater Hollywood in 1910 and the San Fernando Valley (including Burbank) in 1915. Amid expansion, developers and landowners paved roads, constructed residences and businesses, installed sewerage systems and street lighting, and incorporated towns. The city's total population multiplied nine times from 11,183 in 1880 to 102,479 in 1900, and then more than five times to 576,673 in 1920.[3]

Between the late 1800s and early 1900s, in what scholars call the golden era of Black Los Angeles, African Americans had some freedom to settle in many developing parts of the city, engage in local affairs, and seek economic advancement. The small Black population which, at the time, Whites believed posed only a minor threat, established businesses and churches, headed political groups and local newspapers, and participated in an emerging cultural life. African Americans settled on their own, in family units, and in small clusters in the developed and undeveloped areas of the city and lived among mostly Whites and some Asians, Mexicans, and Jews, who also had some freedom of movement. Some African Americans lived around the Plaza and railroad depots or moved into the adjoining neighborhoods or across the Los Angeles River to Brooklyn Heights or Boyle Heights. Others traveled westward to the Temple Street section or across Hoover Street and into West Jefferson and West Adams, what would become the early Westside neighborhoods, or they migrated even farther westward to the developing outskirts of Beverly Hills and Santa Monica. The majority migrated from the business district southward along the main roadway of Central Avenue and its adjacent ascending blocks from First Street to Ninth Street and beyond. By 1910 they were residing largely north of Washington Boulevard, and by 1920 they had made their way to Thirty-Fifth Street. Like Blacks in the Entwistle tract before the Longs moved in, many lived in properties covered by racial restrictions that Whites had let lapse, ignored, or forgotten about.[4]

But in the early 1900s, as the city developed and offered more opportunities for advancement, Whites imposed greater restrictions on land use. It is unclear if the Letteau heirs felt compelled to enforce the property restrictions because of racism, financial need, or financial reward, but they joined a nationwide movement of White property owners who sought to block or remove Blacks from their neighborhoods.[5] They attempted to hinder Black migration southward on Central Avenue around the same time other Whites implemented measures to divide the city between the Eastside and the Westside. While the racial border shifted over time, in the early 1900s Main Street (named Calle Principal in the Spanish and Mexican eras and situated several blocks west of Central Avenue) initially served as the unofficial White buffer zone to separate what would become the multiethnic and multiracial Eastside from the mostly White Westside. Whites used overt methods of intimidation and violence to curb the advancement of people of color and worked artfully within the legal system to persuade the initially unsupportive courts to back discriminatory housing policies. Los Angeles city officials established the nation's first use-based zoning ordinances in 1908 that formally delineated the Eastside as mostly industrial, for manufacturers and more-affordable multi-unit dwellings, and the Westside as mainly residential, for low-density, single-family housing.[6] For added defense, White homeowners also signed clauses or covenants to their property records that prohibited, often for decades, what they called non-Whites and oftentimes non-Christians, except for service staff, from renting, purchasing, or residing in the neighborhood.[7]

In the first decades of the legal battle over racial restrictive covenants, African Americans endured the constant stress of losing their home and financial investment, and while they fought forcefully in the courts, they lost the early challenge and bore witness to judicial sanctioning of residential segregation. NAACP attorney Edward Burton Ceruti took the lead on William and Eunice Long's case. A graduate of St. Lawrence University in New York in 1910, Ceruti moved to California, passed the state bar exam in 1912, opened a law office, and, in 1914, helped found and serve as attorney for the Los Angeles NAACP. One decade before the Longs made their purchase, the Los Angeles NAACP set out to combat early White efforts to restrict Black movement and advancement in the city. Ceruti and several other local Black leaders took their inspiration to establish the branch from W. E. B. Du Bois, a founding member of the national organization, and at the time, director of publicity and research, who traveled to the city in 1913 to promote the nascent group. Shortly after his visit, Du Bois lauded the opportunities Los Angeles offered African Americans in the July 1913 issue of *The Crisis*: "Nowhere in the United States is the Negro so well and beautifully housed." While Los Angeles had the highest rate of Black homeownership in the nation at 36.1 percent in 1910, Black Angelenos could not escape racial discrimination.[8] The motivations underlying westward migration and Jim Crow segregation came slithering into the western city.

Before the Los Angeles NAACP tried the Long's case in the Los Angeles Superior Court, it waited for the US Supreme Court to hand down its decision in the Washington, DC, lawsuits, docketed as *Corrigan v. Buckley*. "A favorable decision there will effect [sic] such cases here," the local branch wrote in the January 1926 *California Eagle*, "and an unfavorable decision would leave us helpless." Events took a turn for the worse and in fact the decision was unfavorable. The high court sanctioned racial restrictive covenants, seeing them as private contracts. Pledged and registered Republicans, the party of Abraham Lincoln, the Longs attempted to carry on with their lives, with William working as a cook and Eunice as a homemaker. But while they awaited their trial, under the weight of losing their home, their health suffered, and first William and then Eunice checked into a hospital. At the end of the year, the lower court ruled in favor of the Letteau heirs and endorsed occupancy clauses. William never recovered and passed away, and Eunice suffered a mental breakdown. The high court's decision emboldened the Letteau heirs to bring more lawsuits against other Black homeowners and White proprietors who rented to Blacks in the Entwistle tract. Ceruti promised Eunice Long he would appeal her case, but the following year, after Ceruti unexpectedly died of heart failure, as historian Douglas Flamming chronicles, the local NAACP neglected her paperwork, and Eunice was evicted from her home.[9] As Whites intended, African Americans saw their options decline. Whites blanketed the Westside with occupancy clauses and covenants and gave the city's multiethnic and multiracial population little option but to live on the Eastside.

WESTWARD AGGRESSION, WESTWARD EXPANSION

The history of the western United States and the origins of Los Angeles have been blurred in popular memory by ethnocentric tales of Indian warfare and cowboy heroism, rugged overland trails and pioneer resilience, the gold rush and economic opportunity, taking place on the uncharted and wild frontier. Mid-nineteenth century America believed in Manifest Destiny, and expanded its territory, its Christian tenets, and its power to the western corners of North America. Land acquisitions west of the Mississippi River, and the compromises that resulted in free and slave states, authorized easterners to settle the region. The Mexican American War, sparked by United States' annexation of Texas in 1845, typified American aggression and takeover. While abolitionists argued that proslavery states were using the war to extend slavery into the West, transcendentalist Henry David Thoreau refused to pay his poll tax to support the war, and then-Representative Abraham Lincoln proclaimed the federal government had carried out an unprovoked attack against Mexico, President James Polk pursued his longstanding dream to expand the United States from shore to shore. Polk triumphed in a Mexican retreat and annexed more than five hundred thousand square miles of western land. California came under United States rule in 1848 and received statehood in 1850, under the premise of aggression and expansion.[10]

Long before California became part of the United States, the region underwent the settlement and occupation of peoples from around the world. At least fifteen thousand years ago, hunter-gatherers migrated into California; over time they established hundreds of small, semi-autonomous, agrarian societies and, without the livestock that later came with European colonization, remarkably established and sustained trade as well as political and religious systems. Upon European settlement, California served as home to one of the largest indigenous populations in North America with 20 percent of North America's total languages.[11] In the late eighteenth century the Spanish Empire forged an effort to claim the territory along the Pacific Coast by sponsoring its subjects to travel northwestward from Mexico and set up Franciscan missions to convert the indigenous population to Roman Catholicism; presidios to defend their land claims; and pueblos to cultivate crops, rear animals, and stabilize colonial and indigenous relationships. Among the pueblos, Spanish governor Felipe de Neve, in 1781, founded El Pueblo de Nuestra Señora La Reina de Los Ángeles de Porciúncula on the edge of the Río Porciúncula (later Los Angeles River) and next to the Tongva village of Yaanga. Following de Neve's instructions, the *pobladores* (settlers) took possession of the land and laid out the settlement.[12]

De Neve expressed his vision for the pueblo. He mandated the *pobladores* to construct a plaza at the center of town that would draw together the village's political, economic, and cultural activities. From there, de Neve directed four main streets extend outward following the four compass points. The pueblo's earliest map, created by Sergeant José Arguello in the 1780s, who traveled to the village to confirm land titles, shows the *pobladores* encircling the Plaza with a guard house, a granary, two royal buildings, and several homes of the founding families. The right-hand side of the map indicates that the *pobladores* grouped their lands between the *zanja* (irrigation canal) and the Río Porciúncula, a reflection of de Neve's orders to centralize the location of work and supervise the settlers. Severe floods in the 1810s and 1820s blocked the Los Angeles River channel with trees, rocks, and debris, and rerouted the water flow from Santa Monica Bay to San Pedro Bay. By the time the *pobladores* had rebuilt the village northwest of the first site on higher ground, Mexico had won its War of Independence and taken control of the region.[13]

While the policies of Mexican Los Angeles restructured the dynamics of the pueblo, the newly built Plaza continued to serve as the center of social, economic, and political life. The Mexican government implemented a secularization program in the 1830s and 1840s that emancipated Native Americans residing in the missions and converted properties to self-governing ranchos. A landowning class of Spanish-speaking Californios, many of whom received land grants from Spain and Mexico in exchange for settling the land and amassed their fortune from cattle ranching on rancho land, took control, and a large labor class of Native Americans had to yield to the new hierarchy. As at the Spanish Los Angeles location, the wealthiest settlers clustered their homes around the Plaza, but, in the Mexican era, Californios extended their landholdings beyond the ranchos and purchased the most highly prized property in town. In 1822 José Antonio Carillo, the alcalde (mayor) of Mexican Los Angeles, built his home directly across from the Plaza. During the subsequent decades, around a dozen wealthier Californios settled near Carillo's home, including Pío Pico and Agustín Olvera. The location of their homes around the Plaza served as a symbol of their high status.[14]

The early Spanish-led *pobladores* had ancestral backgrounds from societies around the world and established a richly diverse population in the Spanish pueblo and later the Mexican republic. When they made their way to the Americas in the late 1400s, Spaniards themselves came from mixed race or mestizo families of European, African, and Middle Eastern descent who had commingled with Jews and Muslims alike. The Spanish Empire had gained much of its diverse population by acquiring subjects and enslaved people from those same regions, intermarrying and integrating them into the empire, and giving many the opportunity to help settle distant territories. More than half of Los Angeles's first *pobladores* in the 1780s claimed either African or part-African ancestry, while the others came from Spanish, American Indian, Chinese, or mixed-race families. In the regions of the Spanish frontier, including parts of what became the western

United States, Spanish subjects suffered injustices but had some opportunities to serve in leadership roles. The early African pioneers in California, all of whom had their freedom, most likely served the empire as soldiers or settlers.[15] Then, in the decades following statehood, and as the gold rush and Manifest Destiny inspired American westward migration, Anglo Americans not only became the majority population, but also took the most advantageous areas of the city and developed public facilities and amenities in those areas to benefit only themselves.

LOS ANGELES'S EARLY SEGREGATION PATTERNS

In the 1860s, as Los Angeles was transitioning from a Mexican town to an American city, three residential and commercial areas emerged that highlighted its early residential segregation patterns and racialized geography. By then, the culture of violence, including mob rule and lynch law, had become commonplace. Guns were widespread and often used as a first resort to settle disputes, seek justice, or assert dominance.[16] Los Angeles had only a three-mile radius, conducive for traveling to work, conducting business, and visiting friends and family, yet the settlers and their adjoining neighborhoods were becoming geographically divided. The Plaza continued to serve as the ruling elite's domain, yet, during this liminal phase, it deteriorated into a contentious and rundown area. Buildings and homes were unfinished or in disrepair, and the unpaved roads brushed up dust in the warm weather and turned into mud in the rain. The three primary areas extending from the Plaza illuminate the emerging city's racial and class divides.[17]

Calle de los Negros, the designation for the short contiguous street that extended immediately east and south of the Plaza, would become a central road of the emerging Chinatown. Initially named after the dark-skinned or Black Californios in the Mexican era, which likely reflected the Spanish colonial *casta* system that ranked Negro in the middle of the racial and socioeconomic order, the marker became used in the pejorative in the American era to racialize Angelenos. Chinese immigrants who began arriving on the West Coast during the 1850s gold rush and 1860s transcontinental railroad construction, and moved to Los Angeles to find work and escape anti-Chinese violence settled there. The Calle had fallen into disrepair years before Chinese immigrants arrived, yet before the 1882 Chinese Exclusion Act virtually ceased Chinese immigration and restricted Chinese Angelenos' movements for some sixty years, the Calle's positioning as a "place of least resistance," scholar César López argues, and its low-rent rooms attracted them to the block, since they could save money to take back with them to China. Despite becoming a mostly Chinese-residential block, settlers from all racial, ethnic, and religious backgrounds frequented the Calle for its social and business life. Like other early settlers, Chinese immigrants initiated, took part in, and defended themselves on the streets and in court. But in the late 1860s, as the Chinese population increased, and Anglo Californians felt threatened by their presence, Chinese immigrants found themselves barred from certain jobs, relegated to the Calle, and faced with more attacks. Those attacks culminated in the 1871 Chinatown massacre when a conflict between rival *huiguan* (societies) drew in a mob of vigilantes and resulted in the brutal murder of at least eighteen Chinese Angelenos.[18]

A second neighborhood took shape north of the Plaza and east of Calle Principal (Main Street) that became derogatively known as Sonoratown. *Vecinos*, those who had previously settled in Los Angeles, and immigrants from the northern Mexican state of Sonora, many of whom became known for their mining techniques in the gold rush, erected adobe storefronts and homes in the area. By 1870 more than half of Angelenos with Spanish-surnames were living in the ten-block-square community. Anglo Americans viewed Sonoratown residents as indulgent with tobacco, alcohol, and gambling (activities that many Anglos also engaged in), and, despite their familial ties to the region that predated the Treaty of Guadalupe Hidalgo, as outsiders and as inferior. The 1872 election of Mayor James Toberman and the Common Council tipped the power structure of the city to Anglo Americans who oversaw the installation of much-needed infrastructure, including a public sewerage system and paved roads. However, when the city installed the sewerage system and paved the roads, historian David Torres-Rouff explains, it neglected Sonoratown and Chinatown. "Two sewers grazed Sonoratown's southern boundary, and one ran along Chinatown's southern edge." Taking their cue from US imperialism, the newly elected city officials seized control of the city, attempted to stem any prospects of Mexican and Chinese Angelenos, and kept municipal services from Sonoratown and Chinatown, despite the residents' tax contributions. By the 1870s Anglos had established what would become a long-lasting pattern of pushing Latinos, Asians, and other people of color east of the Plaza and the Los Angeles River, and then isolating and neglecting those communities.[19]

Anglo Americans and Californios developed the third noteworthy community southwest of the Plaza in the mid-nineteenth century. In 1857, two decades after Massachusetts-born Abel Stearns with his wife, Arcadia Bandini de Stearns (later Baker), had built a stately house known to locals as "El Palacio," on Calle Principal, they constructed a two-story brick business center, Arcadia Block, on Arcadia and Los Angeles Streets. Jewish settlers held the city's first religious services there. One year later, Massachusetts-born Jonathan Temple, who had converted to Catholicism and changed his name to Juan, helped further shift the pueblo's commercial district southwest of the Plaza when he built Temple Block, a grand three-story business center on Main, Spring, and Temple Streets. In contrast to Sonoratown's adobe structures, Anglo Americans built wood and brick buildings that reflected the American tradition. After Abel Stearns died, Doña Arcadia remarried, and she and her second spouse, Rhode Island–born entrepreneur and landowner Robert Symington Baker, tore down El Palacio and built the towering, three-story retail and residential building Baker Block. Pío Pico, the last Mexican governor of California, opened his new hotel, the Pico House, on Calle Principal, and Mercedes Abbott, daughter of successful *vecinos*, opened the Merced Theater next door. Anglo Americans dominated the commercial activity on the southwestern side of the Plaza and reaped the benefits from English- and Spanish-speakers' patronage. As Torres-Rouff points out, the area also enjoyed the public sewerage system and paved roads.[20]

Between the mid- to late-nineteenth century, the federal census claimed that Anglo Americans ascended to Los Angeles's leading population group. In 1850 Los Angeles County, the census enumerated Native Americans as making up 50 percent of the population and Anglos as making up 49 percent. Blacks consisted of 0.4 percent, a proportion at that time too insignificant to alarm the dominant base. The 1880 census then recorded, in the county, Whites remarkably surpassing all other ethnic and racial groups by making up 95 percent of the population, followed by Chinese and Japanese residents at 3.5 percent, Native Americans at 0.9 percent, and African Americans at 0.6 percent. In Los Angeles's brief history, the 1880 census touted, "Americans now predominate, and to their energy and perseverance the prosperity of the place is due." The striking jump in the data within thirty years, however, tells a story not only of the transition to White dominance, but also of the census's consolidation of the nation's many ethnic and racial groups into a few categories. Since the census began in 1790, the racial and ethnic categories have expanded and contracted, depending on government officials' control of political power and budgetary resources, immigrant patterns in the United States, and changing ideological beliefs on race and ethnicity. The 1880 census's "White" category, its oldest population taxonomy, included those born in the United States to families from the western and eastern hemispheres. Through the subsequent decades' major wave of European immigration, the census further consolidated its racial and ethnic taxonomies to create the five-part demographic structure of African, Asian, European, Indigenous, and Latino Americans that prevented a more precise collection of population data.[21]

Moreover, Los Angeles's multiethnic foundation, in the words of historian William Deverell, became "whitewashed" or covered up by White ethnocentrism. From Spanish occupation of California, interracial mixing among the indigenous, Spanish, Mexican, African, and Anglo settlers obscured the rich diversity of the population. Disease and warfare also reduced the numbers of indigenous, Spanish, and Mexican peoples. In the decades following California statehood, Anglo Angelenos "worked diligently to invent" Los Angeles by "appropriating, absorbing, and occasionally obliterating the region's connections to" peoples not of Anglo descent. Seeking its own identity, the young American city appropriated its Spanish and Mexican past for its community events and celebrations, city landmarks and public spaces, and architecture and literature. Thus, the city rewrote its history into a narrative rooted in ethnocentrism, nostalgia, and White privilege. As the Anglo population grew and claimed Los Angeles, the city saw fewer Latino representatives, a greater use of English in public documents, and clearer demarcations of public spaces between Whites and everyone else.[22]

Meanwhile, increasing opportunities for work and leisure and declining prices of the transcontinental railroad in the 1880s drew more people to the city. For several decades thereafter, Harrison Gray Otis, Charles Lummis, Joseph Widney, and other boosters conjured up and spread stories of Los Angeles's unclaimed territory, abundant resources, and healthy climate to populate and bring money to the city. The completion of the Santa Fe transcontinental railroad link to Los Angeles in the mid-1880s became the catalyst that brought thousands of migrants to the western city. Competition and a fare war between the Santa Fe and Southern Pacific railroads also made traveling more affordable when the companies lowered their prices.[23] Between 1880 and 1890, in an economic and real estate boom, the county's population more than tripled from 33,381 to 101,454, and the White proportion grew from 31,707 (95 percent) to 95,033 (93.7 percent). The number of Native Americans dwindled from 316 (0.9 percent) to 144 (0.1 percent), while the proportion of Chinese and Japanese residents, the largest minority group at the time, rose from 1,170 (3.5 percent) to 4,460 (4.4 percent). Around the time of the 1882 Chinese Exclusion Act, Japan's Meiji leaders lifted legal barriers that permitted Japanese citizens to travel, and many went to the Hawaii Territory and the North American western coasts of, for example, Canada, Washington state, and California. By 1910 Los Angeles became home to the largest proportion of Japanese (known as Issei, or first-generation immigrants) in the United States. The Jewish population also steadily increased from 136 in 1881 to 2,500 in 1900. Meanwhile, African Americans in the county multiplied their population almost ten times from 188 (0.6 percent of the population) in 1880 to 1,817 (1.8 percent) in 1890. The 1890s economic depression temporarily slowed the growth in the Black proportion, but in the subsequent decades the number steadily increased. Anglo Americans worked hard to erase Los Angeles's multiethnic and multiracial roots, yet Asian, Latino, Jewish, and African Americans were heeding the advertisements' call in hopes of reaping the benefits of the burgeoning city.[24]

BEYOND DOWNTOWN AND INTO LOS ANGELES'S FIRST WESTSIDE

Before the 1880s, the small Los Angeles population, which mainly resided around the Plaza, had little demand for transportation outside of the business district. But the transcontinental railroad link, population growth, and economic boom sparked an interest in creating communities beyond downtown. Real estate developers outside of the Plaza set out lobbying the city for long-term contracts to provide transportation to their land holdings and secure monopolies over the transit routes, asking landowners for subsidies, and requesting railway companies to subdivide the land. They started by building individual horse-drawn lines to areas adjacent to the Plaza, and then, with the advent of electricity, constructed electric-powered streetcar lines radiating from downtown toward all of the cardinal points across what became the city. Public transit lines expanded the scope of and helped decentralize Los Angeles, transformed the Mexican and early American ranchos and undeveloped land outside of the business district into subdivisions, and gave Angelenos access to areas that were previously out of their reach. West of Main Street was becoming the Westside.

Not surprisingly, the emerging White, upper-class community of Bunker Hill obtained the first public transit line that connected the streetcar suburb to the Plaza. Located on an elevated section west of the business district, roughly between Fourth, Hill, First, and Figueroa Streets, Bunker Hill in the pre–Civil War years was barren and difficult to reach. Following the Union victory, future city mayor Prudent Beaudry and government official Stephen H. Mott, among others, subdivided the land and advertised lots as affordable for middle-class families to build on. Beaudry also initiated the construction of a water-pumping system and graded streets. California district judge and Bunker Hill resident, Robert M. Widney, noticed the need in his neighborhood for transportation. Widney petitioned the city for a long-term contract in 1873; one year later he oversaw the construction of a two-and-a-half-mile-long, single-track, horse-powered line that connected Bunker Hill at Sixth Street to the Plaza by running along Spring and Main Streets. By the 1890s, Widney's Spring and Sixth Street Railroad Company helped Bunker Hill become Los Angeles's highly desirable, White residential refuge. Many affluent doctors, bankers, and attorneys seeking some distance from the Plaza constructed elaborate mansions adjacent to luxury hotels in

Queen Anne, Eastlake, and American Renaissance architectural styles. Widney's brother, Joseph P. Widney, founder of the USC medical school and that university's second president, who, in his two-volume work, *Race Life of the Aryan Peoples* (1907), saw the United States as the culmination of the Aryan Empire, also lived there. Meanwhile, more affordable cottages, duplexes, and boarding houses cropped up in the community. Not long after, in 1901, Bunker Hill residents and visitors enjoyed further ease of travel with the installation of the Third Street Tunnel and the Angels Flight Railway, a funicular cable system from Hill and Third Streets that traversed a steep incline to Olive Street.[25]

In the mid-1880s, the decade following the introduction of the first cable cars in San Francisco, Los Angeles saw the consolidation of many horse-drawn streetcar lines and the installation of cable- and electric-powered cars. In 1887 James Crank purchased, combined, and extended several horse-drawn lines under the auspices of the Los Angeles Cable Railway Company. But it was Frank J. Sprague's electric interurban system that caught national attention. An assistant to Thomas Edison, Sprague broke from the famous inventor, established the Sprague Electric Railway and Motor Company, and installed his electric streetcar in Richmond, Virginia, before other cities adopted his invention. Inspired by Sprague's streetcar, developer Charles H. Howland in 1887 installed the Los Angeles Electric Railway in a rural area west of Vermont Street and north of Pico Street. But as the small traction companies struggled to make ends meet, brothers-in-law Moses H. Sherman and Eli Clark took the opportunity to purchase the disparate lines and unify them into the Los Angeles Consolidated Electric Railway Company.[26]

Sherman and Clark's streetcar system expanded Los Angeles's reach by consolidating and adding lines to more outlying areas and providing the impetus to develop those areas. Like Bunker Hill, elite White Angelenos in Pasadena benefited from Sherman and Clark's efforts. Located roughly ten miles northeast of Los Angeles, established by Indiana transplants in 1873, and incorporated as a city in 1886, Pasadena grew into a destination with the help of Sherman and Clark reconstructing its horsecar lines into a trolley system and establishing a line between Pasadena and Los Angeles in the 1890s. Many wealthy eastern and midwestern tourists who traveled to the area to find respite in the grand hotels, thriving commercial district, and warm climate opted to stay.[27] In 1895, after opening the Pasadena line, Sherman and Clark began construction on the Santa Monica system, which made more available the city's Westside by commencing the route at Echo Park Avenue, traversing Sunset Boulevard through Hollywood, and then following what became Santa Monica Boulevard to the Pacific Ocean.[28]

In the early 1900s the brothers-in-law purchased, merged, and further developed several lines that gave them a monopoly on the western side of Southern California with the 180-mile-long Los Angeles Pacific Railway Company (LAP). The LAP included multiple lines and cross lines that essentially connected three different eastern parts of Los Angeles, the Cahuenga Valley, the downtown business district, and Inglewood, to the Pacific Ocean, creating easier access to and therefore the development of towns along the routes. More sections and towns took shape that were annexed to the city. The Mexican and early American ranchos gave way to the communities of, for example, Beverly Hills, Sawtelle, the Palms, and Culver City. The LAP traveled next to the shore, making stops at and further developing the ocean side towns of, among others, Santa Monica, Ocean Park, Venice, Playa del Rey, Manhattan Beach, Hermosa Beach, and Redondo Beach.[29]

THE GOLDEN ERA OF BLACK LOS ANGELES

Before discriminatory housing practices became widespread and legally valid in the 1920s and hemmed Los Angeles's multiethnic and multiracial population into the Eastside, African Americans, similar to most other minority ethnic and religious Angelenos, had some freedom to reside across the city. For the most part, African Americans could live in communities that appealed to them, offered employment and recreational opportunities, and had not yet developed a reputation of racial hostility. Unlike most major cities before the 1920s that had established highly segregated, spatially isolated Black neighborhoods, Los Angeles had a small Black population that Whites had not yet sought to systematically remove. For those and other reasons, African Americans generally dispersed throughout the city. Upon their arrival, many Black newcomers initially lived in the residential sections adjacent to the railroad depots and the downtown district and then moved farther away from the city center. During what historians call the golden era of Black Los Angeles, African Americans had considerable freedom of movement.[30]

The 1880 census shows that the 102 African Americans, of the city's 11,183 total population, lived in a variety of arrangements. Black Angelenos resided on their own or with their family units on city blocks inhabited by all or mostly Whites. Many lived scattered, alongside White residents on the same road, such as on San Fernando Street (particularly north of the Plaza and east of the Los Angeles River) and Los Angeles Street (particularly south of the Plaza and west of the river). The census reported Charity Street (later renamed Grand Avenue) with the highest number of Black and mixed-race residents, around sixteen altogether, most of whom resided with family, often including spouses, children, and sometimes in-laws, nieces, nephews, or grandchildren. While most Blacks appear to be living with their families, others show in the census living alone, as boarders, laborers, or servants. The census shows no signs of African Americans concentrated in one section of the city. Chinese Angelenos, on the other hand, mostly lived in Chinatown.[31]

The first Blacks to settle in the American city established "a small but sturdy foundation for community building," explains historian Douglas Flamming, and business enterprise. Flamming highlights Robert and Minnie Owens, Bridget "Biddy" Mason, and Hannah, all of whom fought for their freedom and went on to lead lives that overlapped as their family and friends married and had children. The Owens family had purchased their freedom, moved from Texas to Los Angeles in 1853, and accumulated capital from real estate holdings in the young city. Born in 1818 Georgia, Mason endured the precariousness of bondage. She had been sold by one enslaver to another, was separated from her family, and moved to Mississippi at a young age; she was subsequently forced, with her three children, to join the Mormon migration to Utah, and then, in 1851, settle a Mormon community sixty miles outside of Los Angeles, in San Bernardino. She and Hannah, another enslaved woman whose existing records exclude any surname, carried out midwifery work there. Despite California's status as a newly admitted free state, Robert and Rebecca Smith, who were Mason's and Hannah's enslavers, kept them and twelve others, including Mason's and Hannah's children, in bondage. But when the Smiths planned to return to Texas, local authorities intervened. The battle to determine Mason's and Hannah's status, and that of the other twelve individuals, played out in a lawsuit that resulted in the Smiths' flight from California and the 1856 emancipation of all fourteen people.[32]

Mason, who adopted the surname after her manumission, subsequently achieved significant success and, among many other individuals, helped establish the cultural and commercial foundation of modern Black Los Angeles. In the 1860s she earned income as a midwife and a nurse, and purchased land on Spring Street between Third and Fourth Streets, nearly one mile south of the Plaza, in an area that would merge with downtown and make her property highly valuable. She cofounded the city's First African Methodist Episcopal Church in 1872 in her home. The small but significant congregations of Mason's church and the Second Baptist Church contributed to the community's development. By the 1890s, around the time of Mason's death, African Americans had opened businesses a few blocks north of her residence, between First and Second Streets, on San Pedro Street. Brick Block became the city's first established Black area. Along with Mason, Robert and Minnie Owens, Hannah, and their families also helped create the foundation of the city's Black community. For instance, Mason's daughter, Ellen, and the Owens's son, Charles, married. Also, while Hannah and her husband, Toby Embers, lived in San Bernardino, Hannah frequently visited Los Angeles to see her children and grandchildren.[33]

At the turn of the twentieth century, Blacks further dispersed across the city. As in the 1880 census, the 1900 census shows the 2,131 Blacks, out of the 102,479 total population, scattered across Los Angeles on blocks occupied by some or mostly Whites, living on their own, as boarders, laborers, or servants, with their immediate and sometimes extended family members, and occasionally next to other Black families. A small number of Blacks lived in the neighborhoods east of the Los Angeles River. In East Los Angeles, located in the upper-east corner of the city, fewer than one hundred Blacks dispersed, but many lived close to the river and took up residence on Avenue Nineteen. In Brooklyn Heights and Boyle Heights, situated south of East Los Angeles, fewer than one hundred Blacks lived among mostly Whites, some Chinese, and a growing number of Jews and Mexicans. Directly west of the Los Angeles River, surrounding the Plaza, which included former Sonoratown and the railroad depots, also saw a diffusion of African Americans, but, as found in the 1880 census, the area had a concentration of Chinese Angelenos in Chinatown.[34]

Some communities, however, became more concentrated with Blacks than others. Flamming finds that "blacks with middle-class sensibilities" who sought to establish a business center separate from Brick Block, moved southward, out of downtown, along San Pedro Street and then to Central Avenue. In the early 1900s, the Central Avenue corridor saw significant numbers of Blacks sharing the area with Whites, Mexicans, and Asians. In the northernmost section, from First to Third Streets, Hewitt Street and Stephenson Avenue, the census recorded some 5 percent of the city's Black population living near White, Chinese, and Japanese Angelenos. Between Alameda Street, and Fifth, Ninth, and Central Avenue, the census recorded more than 9 percent of the city's Black population living near Whites. Between Alameda Street and Ninth, Twentieth, and Central Avenues, the census recorded about 7 percent of the city's Black population living near some Asians and Mexicans and mostly Whites.[35]

African Americans also settled in some early Westside communities, before those areas became highly restricted in the 1920s. The Temple Street section, named after Jonathan Temple, who helped shift the pueblo's commercial activity southwest of the Plaza in the 1850s, expanded westward along Temple Street and its adjacent blocks with the installation of the streetcar in the 1870s and became one of the earliest and more noticeable areas of Black settlement in the early 1900s. The 1900 census indicates that a high number of Blacks lived among mostly Whites (Protestants and Jews) in the area. African Americans indeed spread farther westward across Hoover Street, in what was becoming the White elite areas of West Jefferson and West Adams, and lived on their own or with their families, among mostly Whites (also Protestants and Jews). But in 1900 Whites overall saw the small Black population as nonthreatening.[36]

At the turn of the twentieth century, African Americans also moved to the western limit of the state and enjoyed ocean property in Santa Monica and its adjacent resort towns. Linked to Los Angeles by the railroad in 1875, incorporated in 1886, and then connected further to the city by electric railway in the 1890s, Santa Monica saw the migration of local city and business leaders, entertainers, wealthy eastern tourists, and health-seekers who visited the seaside village and its adjacent towns for the hotels, bathhouses, and attractions. In the late 1800s, as the seaside communities were taking shape, small numbers of Blacks, Chinese, Japanese, old Californios, Jews, and Mexican immigrants also moved to the area, seeking the same opportunities as other city dwellers. Before the 1920s, the small Black population in Santa Monica and its adjacent towns faced racism and discrimination, yet they enjoyed some freedom. They settled in small clusters, established their own churches, bought property, opened businesses, worked in the service sector, and sunbathed at the lesser populated beaches, including North Beach (located north of the Santa Monica Pier), Ocean Park (between Pico and Ocean Park Boulevards), and Playa del Rey (south of Venice Beach).[37]

In addition to the small beach spaces in and near Santa Monica, before the 1920s African Americans could swim and sunbathe at a second shoreline farther south in Manhattan Beach known as Bruce's Lodge (later Bruce's Beach). When Manhattan Beach was incorporated in 1912, developer George H. Peck, Jr., subdivided oceanfront property; that same year, amid a barely established area where residents drew water from the two wells and mostly lived in wooden sheds, White real estate agent Henry Willard sold two adjoining, undeveloped, and unrestricted lots between Twenty-Sixth and Twenty-Seventh Streets to African American Willa Bruce. Historian Alison Rose Jefferson notes that Willa and her husband, Charles, a dining car chef, secured their upwardly middle-class income through property ownership and their own labor. Seeking to create a resort space where African Americans could bask on the beach, the Bruces built a small cottage and bathhouse with private changing tents and sold food and rented bathing suits. Around eight years later, Willa Bruce extended the length of her property by purchasing an adjacent parcel where she built overnight guest accommodations. In a time when Whites increasingly segregated the city and its surroundings, the Bruces heeded the call of Peck's advertisement, "Los Angeles grows towards the beach. Be there when it arrives!"[38]

Continued construction of the interurban transportation system not only expanded the scope of the city, but also helped the White elite take control of more land. While Sherman and Clark ran into financial difficulties, Henry E. Huntington emerged as the most successful of the traction entrepreneurs when he purchased the existing lines, under the auspices of the Pacific Electric Railway (PE), and built a wide-ranging interurban system that linked Southern California. Born in Oneonta, New York, in 1850, Huntington received his start in business with the help of his railroad magnate uncle, Collis P. Huntington. In 1898, three years before he arrived in Los Angeles, Henry Huntington set out to connect Los Angeles to its outlying communities by purchasing the Los Angeles Railway Company (LARy), which transported people on streetcars; and, two years later, incorporating the PE, which transported passengers and freight. Together with the LARy and the PE, Huntington dominated transportation in Los Angeles. He extended and modernized the Yellow Cars of the LARy and the Red Cars of the PE from the downtown business district eastward to San Bernardino; southward to Watts, Compton, San Pedro, and Newport Beach; northward to Pasadena and San Fernando; and westward to Santa Monica, El Segundo, and Redondo Beach. The interurban system enabled the development of suburbs across the city, many of which had their own commercial centers.[39]

But over time, the transit system struggled to keep up with the expanding city. The configuration of Huntington's railway, radiating from the central business district, required Angelenos to travel through downtown to reach other neighborhoods. By the 1920s city dwellers were complaining that the railways ran late, drivers drove drunk and ignored passengers' safety, the wealthy owners failed to maintain the trains' conditions, and the system had few connections into less-populated communities. Angelenos saw the private automobile as their answer to travel more freely across the city. As scholar Mike Davis puts it, "The centrifugal influence of Southern California's precious automobilization...subverted Downtown's central-place monopoly," which improved mobility and further broadened real estate opportunities beyond the central core.[40] Yet Los Angeles was also becoming visibly and intensely defined by race, ethnicity, class, and, in some areas, religion. The automobile and increased mobility gave White Angelenos better access to land that they could restrict from Angelenos of color.

Through the 1910s and 1920s, African Americans saw increasing restrictions over access within and beyond the city limits. Whites in Ocean Park, Santa Monica, for instance, confined Blacks to a short stretch of the shoreline between Bay and Bicknell Streets, in what became known as Bay Street Beach, or, derogatively, the "Inkwell." Soon after the Bruces opened Bruce's Beach in Manhattan Beach, George Peck posted "No trespassing" signs around his property that forced Black guests to walk half-a-mile to get to the shoreline. Black beachgoers also faced harassment, had sand thrown at them, and got their cars vandalized. Some Black-owned properties were set on fire. The Ku Klux Klan, which reemerged across the country and in Los Angeles, ignited a mattress underneath the Bruces' property. The city also joined segregation efforts, and in 1924 used eminent domain to procure the Bruces' property at an undervalued price in the pretext of building a public park. The Bruces relocated to the Eastside, returned to blue-collar jobs, and died soon thereafter.

Jackie Robinson moved from Georgia to Pasadena in 1920 at the age of one year with his mother and siblings. He would later integrate major league baseball, eleven years after his older brother, Matthew ("Mack"), won a silver medal in the 200-meter race behind Jesse Owens at the 1936 Olympics. Robinson described Pasadena's rampant racism and discrimination: "Pasadena regarded us as intruders," he explained. "My brothers and I were in many a fight that started with a racial slur.... We saw movies from segregated balconies, swam in the municipal pool only on Tuesdays, and were permitted in the YMCA on only one night a week." He went on, "In certain respects Pasadenans were less understanding than Southerners and even more openly hostile." Through the 1920s, as automobiles were replacing streetcars, Whites were also implementing exclusionary zoning laws and racial restrictive covenants to set apart the Westside from the Eastside. As in areas across and adjoining the city, though, Blacks continued to fight back.[41]

STATE-SANCTIONED HOUSING DISCRIMINATION CULMINATING IN *EUCLID* AND *CORRIGAN*

Residential segregation in the United States occurred by no accident. White southerners constructed a system backed by the US Supreme Court in *Plessy v. Ferguson* (1896) that segregated Blacks and Whites in nearly every aspect of life, from water fountains and department store dressing rooms to public transportation and public education. The court-ordered authorization to create "equal but separate" (referred to, in common parlance, as separate but equal) facilities and institutions never developed into a fair system, and Blacks in the South lived in a profoundly disproportionate society that continually hindered them from advancing beyond their means.[42] While southerners principally carried out the *Plessy* decision, White northerners and westerners also sought to separate themselves from those of a different race, ethnicity, religion, and class. As the North and West developed through the nineteenth and twentieth centuries, Whites continued to use the legal system to keep the multiethnic and multiracial population at a distance, and housing served as a key component to ensure that separation. Policymakers, developers, real estate interests, and homeowners used established techniques and formulated new methods to control the racial, ethnic, and class composition of neighborhoods that they had to convince the courts to endorse. By the 1920s they had succeeded: discriminatory housing practices had been codified in the legal system, and in Los Angeles people of color became relegated to the Eastside.

The earliest reported California lawsuits on racial land restrictions centered on the exclusion of Chinese Americans, illustrations of the extended effort that the exclusion act codified to ultimately drive out Chinese presence, and yet initially resulted in some protective measures for the multiethnic and multiracial population. Two of the major cases—one on districting (later known as zoning) and the other on deed restrictions—demonstrated the various legal tools Whites used to segregate. In 1890, amid a nativist movement, policymakers in San Francisco passed the Bingham Ordinance to remove all Chinese inhabitants from Chinatown, which was in the center of the city, to an isolated district "set aside for slaughterhouses, tallow factories, [and] hog factories." Any Chinese resident living or conducting work outside of the designated area, the 1890 ordinance stated, would face up to six months in prison. Before receiving approval from the courts, city officials began to implement the ordinance and arrest Chinese residents. But the federal circuit court intervened, and in the case *In re Lee Sing* (1890), that court denied San Francisco the right to carry out the ordinance on the grounds that it violated the Fourteenth Amendment.[43]

Another lawsuit arose in a Ventura County community when a White homeowner violated a deed restriction by leasing property to Chinese tenants. The restriction, which had been placed on the property by the previous owner, forbade the sale or rental of land to anyone of Chinese descent. But in *Gandolfo v. Hartman* (1892) a federal circuit court judge ruled that the deed restriction violated the Fourteenth Amendment. In the opinion, the judge argued that "a very narrow construction of the constitutional amendment" might sanction deed restrictions but "certainly not in a court of equity of the United States."[44] Yet as the courts defended the constitutional rights of state residents, Whites found other ways to manipulate the legal system and prevent people of color from moving to their neighborhoods.

Use-based zoning laws became popular legal tools to demarcate the urban landscape for residential and business purposes, and Los Angeles emerged at the forefront of the movement. Amid industrialization, construction advancements, the influx of immigrants, and increasing city density, planners and realtors took inspiration from the City Beautiful movement, which sought to bring what they saw as order and beauty to chaotic and immoral urban environments by lobbying for projects to develop the city and for laws that defined land and building use. From its establishment in 1903, the Los Angeles Realty Board (LARB) emerged as the driving force to market Los Angeles as attractive, to draw homebuyers, and, ultimately, to make sales by implementing policies that racially, ethnically, and economically segregated the city. LARB led efforts to, for example, clean up vacant lots, limit building height, carry out city projects such as parks and boulevards, and implement use-based laws that designated or zoned sections of the city for specific purposes and to specific classes, ethnicities, and races.[45]

Impelled by LARB's campaigning, policymakers passed two of the nation's first citywide exclusionary zoning ordinances in 1908 that essentially assigned the Eastside as mixed-use and industrial and the Westside as residential. The aptly named Industrial District Ordinance established six mixed-use districts that included manufacturing centers, artisans' workshops, stores, restaurants, and single-family and multi-use dwellings. Each of the three mixed-use districts situated around San Pedro Street and west of Main Street, in what was becoming the Westside, covered only a few blocks. The other three mixed-use districts contained large sections of land alongside both western and eastern sides of the Los Angeles River and the railroad depots. One of those zones stretched from San Fernando Street on the north (or just south of Elysian Park) to what was then the southern boundary of the city. The Residence District Ordinance established three residential areas that prohibited "works or factory where power other than animal power is used." Two of the three residential districts were situated on the Eastside, one at the intersection of Central Avenue and Washington Boulevard near the end of the existing racial border of Black settlement, and the other in part of Boyle Heights. The largest residential district was carved out on the Westside between roughly Figueroa Street on the east and Western Avenue on the west.[46]

While planners, realtors, and policymakers implemented zoning laws to secure land for specific purposes, they had underlying, racially prejudiced motives to segregate the urban landscape. W. L. Pollard, an attorney for LARB and its counterpart, the California Real Estate Association (CREA), made clear that "racial hatred played no small part" in the decision to implement zoning laws. Founded in 1905, two years after LARB, as the California State Realty Federation, CREA formed an alliance with the city's realty board that would persist for decades to establish and maintain segregationist policies to privilege its clients, White property buyers. From the early 1900s, LARB and CREA lobbied for use-based restrictions to encourage class and racial segregation by demarcating single-family communities for affluent White homebuyers, and low-income dwellings near the industrial workplace for the ethnically diverse working class. In other words, the Westside residential district and the Eastside industrial districts carved out in the 1908 ordinances made clear the city's intentions to delineate the western side of the city for White middle- and upper-class, single-family housing and the eastern side of the city for everyone else. Through the 1910s and 1920s, the California courts endorsed use-based zoning, and policymakers continued their efforts by expanding the laws and establishing the Los Angeles County Regional Planning Commission to regulate land use and ensure suburban growth.[47]

But the effort to demarcate the urban environment did not take place without a challenge. The NAACP sought to outlaw zoning laws; while the NAACP succeeded in banning race-based zoning laws, the US Supreme Court sanctioned use-based restrictions. In one of the NAACP's first major legal victories, the high court in the Louisville, Kentucky, case, *Buchanan v. Warley* (1917), found race-based zoning laws unconstitutional. Robert Buchanan, a White property owner, filed a claim against William Warley, president of the local NAACP and a Black buyer, for refusing to fulfill their sales agreement and make payment on a lot covered by a Louisville zoning ordinance that prohibited Blacks from residing in the White area. The high court struck down the law, because it infringed on Buchanan's property rights under the due process clause of the Fourteenth Amendment. Yet the judgment failed to stop the spread of use-based zoning laws across the country.[48]

Nearly two decades after Los Angeles passed the first comprehensive land-use ordinance, the high court in *Euclid v. Ambler* (1926) put to rest the debate over the constitutionality of use-based zoning and sanctioned the practice. The conflict arose when Euclid, Ohio, passed a land-use ordinance that restricted the Ambler Realty Company from completing its industrial development. In 1924 the federal district court invoked *Buchanan* and declared the ordinance unconstitutional. But two years later, in an appeal, the high court reversed the judgment, finding that use-based zoning laws represented a valid use of municipal police power that "had no substantial relation to the public health, safety, morals, or general welfare." Within ten years after the decision, 85 percent of the nation's cities had demarcated their urban landscapes with exclusionary zoning ordinances.[49]

Whites used racial restrictive covenants, in addition to use-based zoning laws, to prohibit people of color from occupying their properties, oftentimes for decades, and ultimately to segregate the urban landscape. But in the early twentieth century covenanters also had to seek approval from a judicial system that barred racial restrictions. In one of the earliest cases heard in Los Angeles, the court prohibited the use of restrictive covenants. When Homer L. Garrott, an African American police officer, and his spouse Pearl Garrott, bought a home west of Main Street, on 420 West Fifty-Ninth Place, in a subdivision covered by racial restrictions, housing developer Title Guarantee and Trust Company filed a grievance with the Los Angeles

Superior Court accusing Garrott of violating its covenant, which prohibited the right to "lease or sell the property to any person of African, Chinese or Japanese descent." Without hearing the case before the bench, the Los Angeles Superior Court in *Title Guarantee & Trust Company v. Garrott* (1915) granted Garrott's objection of the claim and declared the restrictive covenant invalid. The court found that the covenant infringed on land conveyance rights protected under the California civil code and sanctioned the Garrotts, with their three children, to live there.[50]

While restrictive covenants affected most Angelenos of color, a handful of African American attorneys in early twentieth century Los Angeles led the effort to impede the use of restrictive covenants; one of these attorneys was Willis O. Tyler, who represented Garrott. Since 1878 when the California State Assembly had lifted the race and gender ban from the bar, and, after several years of resisting the legislation, the legal profession had admitted its first Black lawyer in 1887, civil rights attorneys had demonstrated steadfast determination in their work against racial discrimination. Tyler was born in 1880 in Bloomington, Indiana, graduated from Harvard Law School in 1908, worked as an attorney in Illinois until 1911, then moved to Los Angeles and opened a law firm with fellow Harvard Law graduate Hugh Ellsworth Macbeth in 1912. Tyler and Macbeth, along with Edward Burton Ceruti and other Black attorneys, paved an unmarked path in the local courts fighting for equality. Tyler defended Garrott in the plaintiffs' appeal in 1919 against the lower court decision that invalidated the restrictive covenant and enjoyed a victory when the California Supreme Court concurred with the initial judgment.[51] But the fight against covenants had only just begun. White housing developers and homeowners in California learned from the verdict and set out to reword restrictive covenants to make the documents legally permissible.

Through the 1910s, White housing developers and homeowners mastered the language needed to attain judicial sanction of restrictive covenants. Five months after the 1919 *Title Guarantee* proceedings, the California Supreme Court heard another appeals case on racial restrictions that began when Alfred Gary, an African American janitor, purchased a property in 1916, not long after the Garrotts' move. Like the Garrotts' case, the real estate developer and covenanter filed a complaint. This time, it was the Los Angeles Investment Company who claimed that Gary violated the covenant. Gary had managed to push the racial boundary farther westward than the Garrotts by buying a house at 1728 West Fifty-First Street, immediately west of Western Avenue. Three weeks after he moved in, "several hundred home owners," reported the *Los Angeles Times*, "assembled in a mass meeting" at Forty-Eighth Street and Western Avenue, near Gary's new home, in protest. The southwest property owners' association rallied, raised money, and called on the California Supreme Court to reverse the lower court's decision in *Garrott*, evict Gary, and uphold restrictive covenants in Los Angeles and across the country.⁵²

The Los Angeles Superior Court granted Gary's objection to the claim by citing the California civil code's protection against alienation in land conveyance, but in the appeal the California Supreme Court reversed the judgment. The court supported the original ruling on the covenant's first condition, which stated, "The property shall not be sold, leased, or rented to any persons other than of the Caucasian race." Yet in the second condition, which specified, "No person or persons other than of the Caucasian race shall be permitted to *occupy* the property," the California Supreme Court found no grounds that restricted the real estate developers from deciding on land use. Put another way, the court asserted that while the Fourteenth Amendment provided citizens equal protection of the law in state actions, it included no stipulations against private actions. Therefore, in the appeals verdict of *Los Angeles Investment Company v. Gary* (1919), the appellate court granted Gary permission to own his house, but he had no right to live there. He had to rent, lease, or sell his property to Whites and find residence in an unrestricted neighborhood. Segregationists had succeeded in creating a legal loophole. Immediately following the decision, with encouragement from realty boards, White homeowners added occupancy clauses to their restrictive covenants.⁵³

One year before the US Supreme Court ruled on restrictive covenants, the California Supreme Court heard another related lawsuit. The Janss Investment Company claimed that, in 1922, James J. Henry Walden, a White man, breached the subdivision's racial restrictive covenant when he sold his property to Betty Walling, an African American. Like the Los Angeles Investment Company, Janss learned to adopt a covenant with an occupancy clause. "No part of said real property shall ever be leased, rented, sold or conveyed to any person who is not of the white or Caucasian race," the covenant stated, "nor be used or occupied by any person who is not of the white or the Caucasian race whether grantee hereunder or any other person." When the lower court ruled in favor of Janss, Walden appealed the case. The California Supreme Court, in *Janss Investment Co. v. Walden* (1925), referred to the *Gary* ruling to affirm the lower court's decision.⁵⁴

Then in 1926, as William and Eunice Long suffered from health problems, weighed down by the stress and financial hardship while awaiting their trial in the Los Angeles Superior Court to challenge the occupancy clause attached to their home in the Entwistle tract, the legal battle over racial restrictive covenants headed to the US Supreme Court. In the early 1920s, after Irene Corrigan and twenty-nine other White residents of a Washington, DC, suburb agreed to cover their properties with a restrictive covenant that prohibited Blacks from the neighborhood for twenty-one years, Corrigan entered a contract to transfer her property to Helen Curtis, an African American woman, and her physician spouse. Angered by the breach of contract, John Buckley, a White resident and covenanter in the neighborhood, requested an injunction from the trial court to stop the sale of the property, which the court had authorized. With the help of their attorney James A. Cobb, a graduate of Howard Law School and head of the NAACP legal committee (and who had also served on the *Buchanan* case), Corrigan and Curtis petitioned the District of Columbia Circuit Court of Appeals to reconsider the ruling of the trial court on the grounds of the equal protection clause of the Fourteenth Amendment. But again, in *Corrigan v. Buckley*, the court struck down their argument and ruled in favor of the plaintiff.[55]

Unwilling to give up after the appellate court's judgment, Cobb turned to the national NAACP attorneys for help. The national NAACP had been fighting against residential discrimination since its formation in 1909, achieved its first major legal victory against race-based zoning in the 1917 *Buchanan* case, and continued to battle in the courts through the 1920s. But *Corrigan* became the NAACP's first major attempt to end restrictive covenants in the US Supreme Court. The NAACP's legal counsel, headed by Louis Marshall and Moorfield Storey, drafted an argument that stated the use of restrictive covenants violated public policy under the Fifth (right to due process), Thirteenth (abolishment of slavery), and Fourteenth (equal protection of law) Amendments of the US Constitution. But in 1926, the same year that the US Supreme Court in *Euclid* sanctioned use-based zoning laws, the high court found that the NAACP lacked sufficient evidence to further defend its case. The court perceived restrictive covenants as private contracts entered by private citizens, rather than state measures that violated public policy. "None of these Amendments," the court claimed, "prohibit private individuals from entering into contracts...of their property."[56] In a climate of the first Red Scare, the 1921 Tulsa massacre, heightened nativism, the reemergence of the Ku Klux Klan, the rise of eugenics, and the passage of anti-immigration laws, racial restrictive covenants prevailed. The decision was a blow to the NAACP and the fight against housing discrimination around the country. In two major cases the same year, the highest court in the country endorsed Whites' efforts to continue to segregate through use-based zoning laws and racial restrictive covenants.

THE EASTSIDE

After California entered the Union as a free state in 1850, it passed a few laws that curbed racial discrimination and advanced gender equality. While the 1882 exclusion act heightened intolerance against Chinese Americans, relegated them to Chinatown, and fueled White animosity, the end of Black testimony restrictions in 1863, of legal segregation of African Americans in education by 1890, and of discrimination in public transportation in 1893 indicated a movement toward racial parity.[57] In 1911 California became the sixth state in the Union to enfranchise women, nine years before the ratification of the Nineteenth Amendment. Partly due to the availability of affordable housing and mostly due to increasing housing discrimination, as more Whites moved onto the Westside, most people of color and working-class Whites through the early 1900s remained on the Eastside and made its adjoining neighborhoods ethnically, racially, and religiously diverse. Despite rising citywide racial discrimination, marginalized Angelenos shaped their communities and the city. While Black Angelenos lived throughout the Eastside among a diverse population, they mainly resided, established businesses, and supported cultural and artistic activities along the Central Avenue corridor, making it the city's center of Black culture and commerce. Over time, they had little choice but to live on the Eastside.

While many Eastside enclaves, such as Chinatown, Little Tokyo, Boyle Heights, the East Los Angeles barrio, and Central Avenue, made up the city's multiethnic and multiracial population, they became known for having one leading ethnic or religious group. Despite their significant contributions to the development of the West, as exemplified in their backbreaking work constructing the transcontinental railroad, the Chinese faced obstacles to achieving economic stability. As early targets of nativism that culminated in the 1882 exclusion act, the Chinese population dwindled. Los Angeles County saw a decrease from 4.4 percent in 1890 to 1.9 percent in 1900, 0.5 percent in 1910, and 0.3 percent in 1920. Following the 1871 Chinatown massacre on Calle de los Negros and amid city officials' repeated efforts to marginalize and displace the Chinese population, Chinatown's location shifted to a more remote and undeveloped area east of the Plaza and Alameda Street, along Apablasa and Marchessault Streets. On roads the city continued to neglect, Chinese Angelenos persisted, occupying residences and running churches, schools, shops, and restaurants. Then, in 1931, after decades-long litigation over land rights, the California Supreme Court approved the construction of Union Station on the site and, henceforth, the removal of the Chinatown residents.[58]

In the late 1930s two neighborhoods replaced old Chinatown. Christine Sterling led the development of China City. Sterling had recently completed Olvera Street, a fabrication of a nineteenth-century neighborhood of the historic Plaza that mythologized the early wealthy settlers as heroes who founded the American city; omitted its history as a contested space among indigenous, Spanish, Anglo, and Asian settlers; and contrived a Mexican marketplace replete with blissful Mexican vendors selling archetypal Mexican goods and cuisine in traditional attire. Sterling also envisioned China

City as a tourist attraction and appropriated it as a walled Chinese village using the set, props, and costumes of Cecil B. DeMille's 1937 film, *The Good Earth*, and including curio shops, a theater, Cantonese restaurants, and rickshaws. On the other hand, city engineer Peter SooHoo, Sr., and an exclusively Chinese American group purposefully planned, purchased land, designed, and developed the new Chinatown. Guided by the hard-fought legacy of their Chinese predecessors who had no choice but to live on neglected city blocks, and the desire for self-determinism and inclusion, SooHoo and others designed the new Chinatown in their own vision to represent the uniquely Chinese American experience that, for instance, had restaurants with cuisines that represented a blend of cultures. In 1938, about three weeks after China City was completed, the new Chinatown opened a few blocks north of China City and old Chinatown for Chinese Angelenos and all other city dwellers to enjoy alike. The sign, at the west gate's entrance, broadcast the founders' goal: "Cooperate to achieve."[59]

Chinese and Japanese trajectories diverged through the late 1800s and early 1900s, but both groups immigrated to a country that sought to hinder their advancement. As the exclusion act halted Chinese immigration, Meiji Japan modernized its nation to match Western, imperial powers, and permitted Japanese citizens to immigrate to the United States. Los Angeles County's Japanese population accordingly rose from 0.04 percent in 1890 to 0.1 percent in 1900 to 1.7 percent in 1910 to 2.1 percent in 1920. By then, Japanese Angelenos made up the largest proportion of Japanese in the United States.[60] But despite their small population size, the Japanese found that the United States continually sought to complicate their entry with alien land laws, such as the California laws in 1913 and 1920 that targeted the Japanese and essentially forbade them and other noncitizens from owning agricultural land. In 1924, the same year William and Eunice Long made a down payment on their house in the Entwistle tract and two years before the *Euclid* and *Corrigan* decisions, the United States government passed the Immigration Act that set national quotas on European immigrants and virtually ended Asians' entry. While the act reduced Japanese immigration to a "trickle," it "did not thwart the Issei's entrepreneurial spirit," historian Lon Kurashige explains. "Exclusion failed to severely damage their ethnic economy."[61]

Like Blacks in Los Angeles's golden era, before racial restrictive covenants prevailed, Japanese Angelenos dispersed across the city. From the late 1800s and early 1900s, they moved near or beyond the city's borders, including to Pacoima and Sun Valley, in the San Fernando Valley, to work in agriculture and floriculture; and to Terminal Island, near San Pedro, where they established the state's tuna fishing industry. They settled northwest of downtown, in Hollywood, and around Virgil and Madison Avenues, or what became known as the J-Flats for its sizeable Japanese population. They resided in Westside communities, including West Jefferson, Uptown (situated north of West Adams, around Vermont Avenue and Pico Boulevard), Sawtelle (around Sawtelle and Olympic Boulevards), and Venice (along Ballona Creek). They also stayed in Eastside neighborhoods, including around Alameda and Temple Streets (south of the Plaza), Boyle Heights, and along the Central Avenue corridor. While they continually lived among racially, ethnically, and religiously diverse populations, by the 1920s they made Little Tokyo along East First Street, around the intersection of San Pedro Street, the center of Japanese economic and cultural life. The principal hub, next to Terminal Island and then the smaller Japanese communities, Little Tokyo comprised residences, retail shops, grocery stores, restaurants, cultural and religious institutions, and medical services that supported Japanese Angelenos living in the neighborhood; because of its central location, it also supported those working in, among other industries, the outlying farming, fishing, and service sectors.[62]

The city's racial, ethnic, and religious markers further appeared in East Los Angeles. The history of the land east of the Los Angeles River dates back as a Tongva village and Spanish and then Mexican settlements. In 1858 Irish immigrant Andrew Boyle purchased land along El Paredón Blanco or the White Bluffs (later Boyle Avenue), and affluent Angelenos and local leaders soon moved. Over the following decades, Boyle Heights stretched outward along Brooklyn Avenue (later Avenida César Chávez), toward the Evergreen Cemetery, and underwent shifts in the racial, ethnic, and religious makeup of its residents. By the early 1900s the area drew in Angelenos of varied descents, including Mexican, Japanese, African, Italian, Russian Orthodox, and Jewish, for its affordable, single-family, unrestricted housing that, unlike the increasingly congested downtown neighborhoods, offered yard space and a suburban-like environment. Since Jewish Angelenos faced exclusionary measures from the city's major social clubs and economic engines, they built their own institutions. In 1891 they established the Concordia Club, an elite social institution; in 1894 it opened in the Burbank Building on Main Street, and by 1902 it boasted a clubhouse at Sixteenth and Figueroa Streets. In the 1920s and 1930s, while the Temple Street section saw a growing Jewish population, Boyle Heights and its Brooklyn Avenue served as the center of Jewish cultural and economic life. While Jewish and Mexican experiences overlapped on the same blocks, Mexican Angelenos would become the community's dominant population in the postwar years.[63]

The city's Mexican population remained stable through the late nineteenth century and mostly resided around the Plaza, but as major push and pull factors prompted immigration, many newcomers arrived in a hostile city that consigned them to East Los Angeles. The Mexican Revolution, United States industrialization and wartime labor needs, and the availability of rail transportation, among other forces, contributed to the rise of Los Angeles's Mexican population from an estimated five thousand in 1910 to thirty thousand in 1920 to ninety thousand in 1930, by that time the largest of any American city. Before the 1920s the hub of the Mexican community remained around the Plaza. But Mexican Angelenos dispersed across the city. Many with the financial means to do so moved to the largely White Westside communities, such as West Adams, Hancock Park, and Hollywood. Most others migrated northward, around Chavez Ravine, and southward along the Central Avenue corridor, into Watts; with the introduction of interurban transportation and the rise in housing discrimination, they migrated east of the Los Angeles River to Boyle Heights, Brooklyn Heights, Lincoln Heights, Belvedere, Maravilla, and City Terrace. Alongside the eastward migration, many Mexican-run and -supported businesses relocated from the Plaza to East Los Angeles. By 1930, although Belvedere had the city's largest concentration of Mexican population, the contiguous enclaves together made up the unincorporated East Los Angeles barrio.[64]

Meanwhile, through the early 1900s most African Americans resided along Central Avenue and its adjacent blocks. They migrated over time southward along the thoroughfare, settling on and around the ascending blocks, from First Street to Seventh Street to Ninth Street. By 1910 Blacks resided largely north of Washington Boulevard, and then by 1920, they made their way to Jefferson Boulevard and Thirty-Fifth Street. Whites tried to contain Blacks at nearly every intersection, but Blacks insisted on their right to live in the area. By 1920 the area between Eighth and Twentieth Streets, and especially the intersection of Twelfth Street, emerged as the city's center of Black cultural and commercial activity. Many Black-owned landmarks, including the *California Eagle* newspaper headquarters, the Booker T. Washington building (which housed shops, offices, and apartments), and the Angelus Theater helped create a vibrant space. Like other communities dispersed around the city, the Central Avenue corridor reflected Los Angeles's multiethnic and multiracial character. By 1920, Blacks made up less than 20 percent of the Seventy-Fourth Assembly District. But while Blacks negotiated space with Protestant Whites, Asians, Latinos, European immigrants, and Jews, they boasted significant influence, exemplified in the district's 1918 election of California's first Black legislator, Frederick Madison Roberts, the great grandson of Thomas Jefferson and Sally Hemings, to the state assembly, where he served for sixteen years.[65]

In the 1920s, as Blacks migrated southward along Central Avenue, the center of Black life along what was affectionately called "the Avenue" shifted southward. While the intersection of Twelfth Avenue remained a hub of Black enterprise, key Black institutions, including the Colored YMCA and the Elks Hall, followed the trend of Black migration and relocated farther south. Black-owned apartments, real estate agencies, dry goods stores, dressmaking shops, beauty parlors, and furniture retailers lined the Avenue. Then, in 1928, when Black dentist, entrepreneur, and Los Angeles NAACP cofounder, J. A. Somerville, opened the Somerville Hotel in time to host the national NAACP convention, the center of Black culture and commerce shifted to the intersection of Central Avenue and Forty-First Street. The four-story hotel (later purchased by Lucius Lomax, Sr., who renamed it the Dunbar Hotel after the Harlem Renaissance poet Paul Laurence Dunbar) included one hundred rooms as well as beauty parlor, barbershop, drug store, flower shop, real estate office, tailor, and coffee shop. Soon thereafter, a host of Black-owned establishments relocated to the area. The hotels and nightclubs helped give Central Avenue its nickname, the "Harlem of the West." The Apex (later Club Alabam), the Downbeat Club, and Club Memo, among other nightclubs, featured artists such as Duke Ellington, Louis Armstrong, and Nat King Cole. While Whites in New York City headed to Harlem in the evenings to escape the social restrictions in their lives and check out the new sounds, Whites in Los Angeles did the same on Central Avenue.[66]

As the Black community along the Central Avenue corridor strengthened, Whites further demarcated the city's racial boundaries through discriminatory measures. Several blocks east of Central Avenue, historian Becky Nicolaides explains, working-class Whites clung to their communities with all of their might. In the blue-collar suburbs of the Alameda corridor, which included Bell, South Gate, Lynwood, and Maywood, situated south and east of Central Avenue, White working-class homeowners saw their property as a symbol of their hard work, class identity, autonomy, and financial security. As the Great Depression led to the rise of unemployment, bank failures, and property taxes, White homeowners guarded their local schools and neighborhoods fervently "by juxtaposing them against the ever-sensitive issue of race" and thwarting the in-migration of African Americans who were migrating into the west-adjacent communities. "Alameda Street soon became a racial dividing line...known as 'the wall' and the 'cotton curtain'...separating the suburbs of working-class blacks and whites." Through the interwar years, Whites in the area south of Slauson Avenue, between the Central Avenue corridor and the blue-collar community of Watts, also fought against racial integration. Housing contractors marketed their properties to local White workers and then encouraged White homeowners to maintain segregation by covering properties with racial restrictions. Consequently, African Americans skipped over the section and continued their migration southward into Watts, which, by the 1920s, comprised a population of Blacks, Whites, Asians, and Mexicans.[67]

For African Americans, living on the Eastside had both advantages and disadvantages. On one hand, the Eastside served as a space for Black newcomers to get their bearings in the bustling metropolis, network, and try their hand at the available opportunities. Alongside the steady influx of Blacks into the city, Black entrepreneurs acquired more clients, built their companies, and enjoyed some financial success. Central Avenue also provided a supportive space for Black artists to experiment with their craft, engage with other artists, and acquire a broader audience. But racial discrimination became a constant hindrance to Black advancement. Because most Whites refused to provide any support, African Americans felt they had no other option than to establish their own businesses and organizations. As the city expanded and racial discrimination intensified, African Americans also grew concentrated along the Central Avenue corridor, or what became Los Angeles's Black belt. Blacks persistently sought to improve their quality of life and challenge the racial limits, but they were faced with a system that would legally sanction them into neglected communities or what became damagingly labeled ghettos.

SUCCESSES AND SETBACKS OF THE BLACK HOMEOWNERS' RIGHTS MOVEMENT

The decades-long effort to legally validate use-based zoning ordinances and racial restrictive covenants in the court system that culminated in the mid-1920s pointed toward a pattern of hardening racial segregation in the city. Hundreds of lawsuits over zoning ordinances and restrictive covenants emerged in California and across the country throughout the first half of the twentieth century. Legal rulings varied by district and state, but, in the earliest cases around the turn of the twentieth century, the courts prohibited use-based zoning and racial restrictions on the grounds of the Fourteenth Amendment, which required all states to provide their citizens with the equal protection of law. Whites learned from their losses, reworked the language, and made arguments that convinced courts to endorse their ordinances and contracts for decades thereafter. Their effort culminated in the 1926 US Supreme Court cases *Euclid v. Ambler*, which sanctioned use-based zoning laws, and *Corrigan v. Buckley*, which sanctioned racial restrictive covenants. Through the 1920s, Los Angeles essentially became divided between the middle- and upper-class White Westside and the working-class, multiethnic, and multiracial Eastside.

While the NAACP suffered its loss in the *Long* case and the *Corrigan* decision, it had outstanding lawsuits to challenge. Riding on their win, the Letteau heirs pursued lawsuits against more Entwistle tract residents, including Black homeowners and White proprietors who were renting to people of color. While the Los Angeles NAACP could not afford to finance all of the cases and most of the defendants could not pay for representation, the local branch proposed the Entwistle homeowners follow the *Gary* ruling, move out of the property but "retain every other right," selling, renting, or leasing it "to any person except a Negro, and all of their equities in the property would be preserved," while the attorneys pursue a test case in the court. In 1928, the local branch celebrated a small victory in its defense of Pauline Ellis, another African American Entwistle tract property owner who the Letteau heirs took to court. Los Angeles Superior Court Judge Carl A. Stutsman ruled in favor of Ellis and the other defendants, finding the Entwistle tract's "changed conditions...made it oppressive and inequitable to enforce the restrictions and the original purpose for the restriction was no longer served." The lawsuit made its way to the California appellate court which, in 1932, validated Stutsman's decision.[68] In the face of defeat, Whites clamped down harder, spreading onto the Westside, writing airtight racial restrictive covenants to ensure their neighborhoods underwent no change in their racial makeup, and in effect, confining Blacks to the Eastside.

African Americans sought to make the most of the opportunities in the city. Along Central Avenue they purchased property and established businesses, religious institutions, and social clubs and made the area the city's center of Black art and culture. But as racial discrimination intensified, African Americans found themselves with little other option but to live on the Eastside. In response, African Americans with financial resources and social connections, including business owners and real estate agents, doctors and dentists, teachers and public servants, community activists and entertainers, challenged the racial restrictions by migrating westward into some of the city's historically desirable areas on the Westside. In the 1910s and 1920s they set their sights on West Jefferson, a highly restricted neighborhood several miles southwest of Jonathan Temple's original Temple Street section, challenging White recalcitrance and lawsuits along the way. Then, in the 1930s, they moved into the historically White elite West Adams Heights, a community that originated the nation's first successful lawsuit against restrictive covenants after the *Corrigan* decision that ultimately led to the demise of racial restrictions in the US Supreme Court.

Chapter Two

Black Settlement in West Jefferson and West Adams Heights

FROM THE MOMENT her son learned to walk and talk, Norman O. Houston's mother encouraged him to pursue a career in business. Living near burgeoning San Francisco in the late 1890s, Lillian Jackson Houston was struck by the city's vibrant and lucrative commercial activity and urged her son to make use of the opportunities. After high school, young Norman enrolled at the University of California, Berkeley, and majored in business administration. World War I cut short his completion of a degree. The US armed forces commissioned him to serve in the 92nd Infantry Division, or Buffalo Soldiers, an all-Black unit of the segregated military, and he worked his way up to lieutenant. But Houston never gave up on his professional goals. When he returned to Northern California after the war, he found a position as an office assistant in a San Francisco insurance firm. Then, on his trek home from work one day, he encountered a friend who offered him a job at a Los Angeles White-owned insurance agency selling policies to Pullman cooks and waiters at the railroad commissary. Houston needed little convincing, packed his belongings, and traveled south to the city.[1]

In Los Angeles, Houston discovered a recipe for success when he went into business with William Nickerson, Jr., and George A. Beavers, Jr. Understanding that African Americans had little opportunity to obtain reasonably priced, full coverage life insurance, the entrepreneurs set out to fill the void by establishing their own insurance company. The hundreds of thousands of African Americans who flocked to the city through the world wars wanted to protect themselves and their families in the unpredictable urban climate with an insurance company they could trust. In a matter of years, their business, Golden State Mutual Life Insurance Company, far surpassed its original goals. Nickerson, Houston, and Beavers multiplied their assets, opened offices across California, and extended their services into home and business loans. Amid widespread job and housing discrimination, they created hundreds of white-collar jobs for African Americans, invested hundreds of thousands of dollars in loans to help Blacks get credit and improve their conditions, and championed the NAACP's and Urban League's local branches and other civil rights groups.[2] Success allowed Houston and his colleagues not only to improve their quality of life, but also to advance the conditions of Black Angelenos.

By the time Houston arrived in Los Angeles, however, the relative freedom that Blacks had enjoyed at the turn of the century had begun to erode. Throughout the Roaring 1920s the city had experienced a population surge, doubling its size within the decade, including a residential and commercial construction boom that decentralized the city and resulted in 3,200 new subdivisions and 250,000 new houses.[3] Alongside these changes, White developers, real estate interests, and homeowners implemented exclusionary zoning laws and racial restrictive covenants to what they believed would protect the quality and value of their dwellings. White homeowners also established homeowners' improvement associations and urged their neighbors to cover their properties with racial restrictive covenants and prohibit people of color from moving to the area. Through the interwar years, the Westside became blanketed with restrictive covenants, and people of color had little option but to live on what was becoming the overcrowded and rundown Eastside. The city's Black leadership refused to stand by and accept these measures. In the 1910s and 1920s a small group of elite Blacks began to mobilize on the grassroots level to challenge racial restrictive covenants and the 1926 *Corrigan v. Buckley* decision.[4]

By the time Houston reached his mid-forties in the late 1930s, he and Edythe Pryce Houston could see an opportunity to move into West Adams Heights, a historically White, elite neighborhood situated on an elevated portion of the eastern edge of Westside Los Angeles. Although they moved to the neighborhood after Asians and Mexicans had done so, the Houstons were the first African Americans to purchase property in the area and contend with neighbors who fought to keep them out. Before the Houstons bought their house, White residents rushed out to instate a community-wide restrictive covenant and stop Blacks, Asians, and Latinos from living in the neighborhood (other than as service staff). While the Houstons' seller abstained from signing the contract, White neighbors mobilized in their homeowners' improvement association and pressured the Houstons to sell their recently purchased home. But the Houstons remained resolute, and their feat encouraged other Black professionals and entertainers with the financial means to move to the area; they faced legal complaints, and defended their actions against the racial restriction in court. They wanted to live in a high-quality neighborhood, with beautifully designed and spacious homes, but like the Houstons, those newcomers also aimed to dismantle the deeply rooted system of racial inequality. Their move turned the center of the nationwide battle over racial restrictive covenants to the elite neighborhood.

WEST JEFFERSON: A GATEWAY TO THE WESTSIDE

As Los Angeles developed from downtown outward, establishing public transit lines, and then paving roads for automobiles that allowed for greater access to the city, the Westside became highly sought after and highly restricted. Middle-class Blacks chose the Westside community of West Jefferson as a logical location to challenge restrictive covenants. Centered primarily between Vermont and Western Avenues, and Jefferson and Exposition Boulevards, but affecting blocks beyond its borders as far west as Arlington Avenue, in one of the first developed Westside suburbs, West Jefferson housed a majority White population who covered at least part of the area in restrictive covenants before World War I. In the interwar years, as the district became populated and some White homeowners converted their houses to rental units, the high reputation of West Jefferson began to decline. Middle-class Blacks, however, saw the area and its moderate-size, single-family homes as a gateway to the Westside. Like other Los Angeles neighborhoods, by 1940 West Jefferson comprised a diverse population of Whites, Blacks, Asians, and Latinos. But the local Black elite, who had the income and resources to contend with segregationists, led the legal battle to break the restrictive covenants.[5]

From the 1920s onward, and some two decades before White Chicagoans' "urban guerilla warfare" and White Detroiters' "defensive localism" against aspiring Black homeowners, White Angelenos mobilized in communities across the city that were experiencing Black in-migration, including West Jefferson. In 1926 Charlotta Bass and the *California Eagle*, one of the city's leading voices for racial equality, reported eighty-one White homeowners' protective associations in Los Angeles alone. In 1922 Whites near USC formed the Anti-African Housing Association (renamed the University District Property Owners Association) to halt Black in-migration. Around 1925 some fifteen families in West Jefferson, around West Thirtieth Street and Western Avenue, formed the paradoxically named Equal Rights Protective Association. Among their tactics for hindering Black in-migration, the *California Eagle* reported, West Jefferson covenanters: distributed literature, such as the weekly bulletin, the *West Jefferson Street News*, "devoted to the interests of the white people in the vicinity of West Jefferson Street," and the *West Jefferson Press*, "a white anti-Negro publication"; renewed restrictive covenants; and filed lawsuits against the sellers and buyers.[6]

White homeowners in West Jefferson initially reacted with shock when Blacks managed to get around the restrictive covenants. In the first study of African Americans and housing in Los Angeles, sociologist J. Max Bond found that White homeowners in West Jefferson not only overlooked the expiration date of the covenants on their properties, but also underestimated Blacks' capabilities to purchase property in the high-priced area. One White resident revealed to Bond how Whites had become less vigilant in guarding the homogeneity of their neighborhoods. "We white people had forgotten that the forty year deed restriction prohibiting Negroes from buying property in our community had expired." The resident continued, "In truth, we thought that no Negro would be ambitious enough to move into our community, especially at the price we were asking for property. But one did move in, and he paid $10,000 cash for his place." Blacks initially operated under the radar of White residents and selected houses with care. But as Whites organized, Blacks struck back in their neighborhoods and in the courts.[7]

In the mid-1920s, the *California Eagle* kept two West Jefferson lawsuits in the news that attorney Willis O. Tyler defended. In the Hopper and Sons tract, around West Thirtieth Street and Western Avenue, the all-White Equal Rights Protective Association president, Edward W. Walker, and his neighbors entered into a lawsuit "based upon a ten-year old restriction" against the newcomers. Meanwhile, the Crestmore tract saw a related, albeit more decisive court battle, due to its location around West Thirtieth Street and the Arlington Avenue racial border that ultimately went to the California Supreme Court. In 1925 the all-White Crestmore Improvement Association signed a twenty-five-year renewal on their expiring racial restrictions. But a few months later, two White signers, Fred R. Stewart and Nellie Stewart, sold their property at 2245 West Thirtieth Street to a working-class, African American couple: Adolphus D. Kinchlow, who at the time was earning a living as a porter, and Mattie Kinchlow. By then, the Los Angeles transplants had lived in the Midwest and been married for some eighteen years. The transaction incited a group of White homeowners to sue fifteen Black families for violating the covenant.

While Tyler headed the defense in both cases, he received support from the community. The Blackstone Club, a group of the city's leading Black attorneys, including its president, Hugh Ellsworth Macbeth, offered free services for the cases, and the Black-run Progressive Federation of Improvement Associations of California, called for, according to the *California Eagle*, "a day of fasting and prayer for our people in this district and...a day's earnings to aid them in their fight." The Crestmore tract case, *Wayt v. Patee*, persisted in the courts for the next several years. The Los Angeles Superior Court ruled in favor of the defendants, including the Stewarts and the Kinchlows, but the plaintiffs sought an appeal. The case went to the California Supreme Court in 1928, which upheld the 1926 *Corrigan v. Buckley* decision, permitting Blacks to own property in the tract, yet forbidding them from occupying their homes. The court found that the covenant "did not invalidate the conveyance to the purchasers nor their legal title," but "it did prevent them from occupying or residing upon the property," essentially evicting the defendants from their homes. By then, following the *Corrigan* decision, the Kinchlows had relocated to the Central Avenue area temporarily before moving into a house in Pasadena, where they remained for the next several decades. *Wayt* stalled Black migration onto the Westside, but African Americans continued to press forward.[8]

Through the 1930s several Black professionals, including Norman O. Houston, moved into the blocks east of Cimarron Street, the racial border identified in the *Wayt* case. Houston understood that moving to West Jefferson would provide his family with more opportunities, and the success of Golden State Mutual Life Insurance Company allowed him the means to challenge the covenants. He and his business partners, Nickerson and Beavers, saw an opportunity in the 1920s to support and profit from the city's growing Black population when they established Golden State. Across the country, White-owned insurance companies refused to cover Blacks altogether, or overcharged them for policies that included minimal coverage, which was yet another tool to oppress aspiring Black homeowners. Some companies, such as Houston's first employer in Los Angeles, hired Blacks to sell overpriced and limited policies to people of color. Some Black entrepreneurs offered alternative opportunities by setting up fraternal insurance organizations, but those often provided only short-term policies. By the 1920s full-line Black-owned insurance companies in other parts of the country had gained national reputations for their success. Atlanta Life Insurance Company and North Carolina Mutual Insurance Company, for example, grew into highly lucrative enterprises that supported multiple branches and employees.[9]

While Golden State became the leading, Black-owned insurance agency in Los Angeles, it was founded around the same time that other Black-owned financial institutions sought to support the city's Black population when White-owned institutions refused aid. In 1924, one year before Golden State opened, physician Wilbur C. Gordon, entrepreneurs Louis Matthew (L. M.) Blodgett and Norman O. Houston, and other Black professionals founded Liberty Savings and Loan Association to provide Blacks with savings and loans services and encourage homeownership. They raised $16,000 for a charter and opened at 2510 South Central Avenue, near East Twenty-Fifth Street. In its first two years, the company more than tripled its assets from $38,895 to $141,277 and increased the number of its members and investors from 392 to 559. Also, within two years, Georgia-born Blodgett, who had fled the South in fear of his life after he hit a streetcar conductor while fighting over seating, took over Gordon's role as president and steered the bank through the Great Depression, successfully petitioned the federal government to insure its assets, and acquired multimillion dollars in holdings. As a developer, he also led home and neighborhood tract construction that created jobs and housing for Blacks and helped him amass a multimillion-dollar fortune. Before Houston turned his attention to Golden State, he worked as Liberty's insurance sales manager. In the mid-1920s the Black-owned bank Unity Finance Company also set out to provide loans to African Americans, but after around ten years in operation, the company closed as a result of its leaders' lack of business acumen.[10]

From 1925, its opening year, Golden State steadily developed into a fixture of Black Los Angeles. The founders rented a room in a small building at the intersection of Newton Street and Central Avenue, near the city's first center of Black cultural and commercial activity, and turned it into their office. They next found a space at the intersection of Jefferson Boulevard and Central Avenue to better run their business. Then when J. A. Somerville began building his hotel at Forty-First Street and Central Avenue, and Golden State's founders had enough resources, they purchased a lot across the street and hired Blodgett to construct a larger office. In 1928, the opening year of the Somerville Hotel, Golden State relocated to the spacious two-story building. The company leased the first floor to various businesses, including a barber and beauty shop, and occupied the second floor, where it stayed for the next two decades.[11] "The Growing Giant of the West," according to *Who's Who in Colored Los Angeles*, saw significant success. Between 1927 and 1938 Golden State multiplied its staff from 54 to 214. By 1928 its services extended to the California cities of Bakersfield, El Centro, Fresno, Pasadena, Sacramento, and San Diego; in 1938 the firm opened an office in Chicago. The company's overall income rose from $34,000 in 1925 to $392,000 in 1938, while its total assets increased from $19,000 in 1925 to $341,000 in 1938. As business grew, the founders used their resources to help improve the conditions of Blacks in the city.[12]

Before he moved to West Jefferson, Houston lived with his first spouse, Los Angeles–born Doris Talbot Young Houston, and their three children, in the Central Avenue district. In 1925, Golden State's opening year, they lived on East Fifty-Fourth Street, a block adjacent to Central Avenue, in the Furlong Tract. Located east of Central Avenue, between Long Beach Avenue and Alameda, Fiftieth, and Fifty-Fifth Streets, the tract in the early 1900s offered reasonably priced homes where working- and middle-class Whites, Blacks, and Mexicans settled. In the late 1920s, when Golden State relocated to Central Avenue's new Black hub, the Houstons purchased their first house at East Forty-First Street, closer to the office's headquarters.[13]

Then in the mid-1930s, Norman and Doris divorced; Doris stayed in a home near Central Avenue and Norman bought a house near USC at 1225 West Thirty-Sixth Street in West Jefferson. While their children lived with their mother, the youngsters commuted daily to their father's neighborhood to attend John H. Francis Polytechnic High School. Norman Houston, his son Ivan explained, "thought it best that we go to Poly High instead of Jefferson High [School]" in the Central Avenue district. "I guess it was the feeling that you got a better education at Poly than you might at Jeff." Even though some of the most prominent African Americans graduated from Jefferson High, including Ralph Bunche and Augustus Hawkins, West Jefferson and the Westside developed a reputation not only for its high-quality residences, but also for its public services.[14]

In a clear act of defiance against the *Wayt* decision, some Black entertainers purchased properties abutting the Cimarron Street border. Actor Eddie Anderson, best known for his role as Rochester, Jack Benny's raspy-voiced, quick-witted valet and butler on *The Jack Benny Program*, and Mamie Nelson Wiggins Anderson built a twenty-two-room mansion for roughly $50,000 in the 1930s between West Thirty-Sixth and West Thirty-Seventh Place, on what has been aptly named Rochester Circle. While Benny bought an estate in Beverly Hills, the fashionable, White, rich community, racial restrictions prohibited Anderson from moving near his Hollywood peers. In response, the actor purchased three lots "as far [west] as he could go," his second spouse, Eva Simon Anderson, explained, and constructed a mansion nearly identical to Benny's Beverly Hills estate that "takes the whole dead-end" of the road. "The house was just glamorous," Eva gushed about the first time she saw the massive white colonial. "This was like a fairy-tale to me." Eddie and Eva raised their three children in the neighborhood. The local children played together on the street and swam in the Andersons' Olympic-size pool. The family entertained illustrious guests, such as Duke Ellington, Nat King Cole, Mantan Moreland, and Benny.[15]

Through the 1930s and 1940s the area west of USC's University Park campus also became home to Black entertainers and athletes. Tap dancer Bill Robinson (known professionally as Bojangles) and Fannie Clay Robinson, a trained pharmacist who managed his career, moved into a spacious home designed by African American architect Paul R. Williams that boasted formal dining and living rooms, a billiards room and bar in tiki decor, a balcony off the largest bedroom, his-and-hers closets, and a meticulously landscaped outdoor living space, at 1194 West Thirty-Sixth Place. Actor Horace Winfred Stewart, often billed as Nick or Nicodemus Stewart who later became known for playing the janitor Lightnin' on the *Amos 'n' Andy* television show, along with his spouse, Edna Stewart, founded Los Angeles's

Ebony Showcase Theater and settled into 3409 Walton Avenue. Down the block, actors and spouses Laura Bowman and Le Roi Antoine lived at 3430 Walton Avenue. Actor and comedian Mantan Moreland and Hazel Moreland lived north of Jefferson Boulevard at 2940 South Kenwood Avenue. Kenny Washington, star UCLA football player who broke a long-time ban against Blacks in the National Football League, lived across Western Avenue, at 1807 West Thirty-Fifth Street. Meanwhile, accomplished African Americans continued to settle directly east of Cimarron Street, the racial border that the *Wayt* decision established. Actor and comedian turned casting agent Ben Carter and his wife, Betty J. Carter, lived at 3753 Ruthelen Street. Composers, musicians, and spouses William Grant Still and Verna Arvey resided at 3670 Cimarron Street, around the corner from the Andersons. Actor Hattie McDaniel, just before she landed the role as Mammy in *Gone with the Wind* (1939), lived at 2177 West Thirty-First Street, and actor Louise Beavers, cousin of George Beavers, Jr., Golden State cofounder, best known for her character Delilah Johnson in *Imitation of Life* (1934), lived at 2130 West Twenty-Ninth Street.[16]

Through the 1940s, as more of the area's racial restrictive covenants came undone, African Americans moved west of Cimarron Street and pushed up against Arlington Avenue, yet another racial border. Newlyweds Harold Nicholas, of the Nicholas Brothers tap dance duo, and actor Dorothy Dandridge moved into a modest two-bedroom home at 2272 West Twenty-Seventh Street. They spent their free time redecorating and entertaining guests, such as William James Basie (known professionally as Count Basie), Louis Armstrong, and Herb Jeffries as well as their neighbors, the Andersons. Fayard Nicholas, the other half of the Nicholas Brothers, and Geraldine (Geri) Pate Nicholas (later Branton), bought a home at 3706 South Van Ness Avenue. Hattie McDaniel's older brother, actor Sam McDaniel, and Lulu McDaniel resided at 3735 South Van Ness Avenue. Actor James Baskett, best known for his role of Uncle Remus and his rendition of the song "Zip-a-Dee-Doo-Dah" in Walt Disney's *Song of the South* (1946), and Margaret Elizabeth Bonvill Baskett resided at 3442 South Arlington Avenue.[17]

Anti-covenanters developed deliberate and calculated strategies to access the Westside. University of California, Berkeley, professor Lloyd H. Fisher, in a mid-1940s report, explained African Americans carefully chose property with restrictive covenants that they could challenge. They might have waited for the covenant to expire or incurred the fine for purchasing property under a racial contract. Because creating a valid restrictive covenant required planning and diligence, anti-covenanters could find gaps or ambiguities in the contract to overturn it. A covenant should have no "technical flaws," Fisher explained, such as no errors in the property's description, or mismatched signatures on the covenant and property deed. In addition, the neighborhood should show no change in demographics, he wrote, or "non-Caucasian infiltration," to make the contract legally enforceable. Anti-covenanters might seek a tract that had a series of covenants and buy a house "covered by one of the minor covenants with only a few signatories." The likelihood remained minimal that the contract's cosigners would file a lawsuit, especially if "they are few and scattered." Also, neighborhood associations with short membership rosters and limited resources were less likely to pursue litigation. After anti-covenanters breached the minor covenants, they set out to challenge the full contract. Then, once they had broken a covenant and moved in, Whites came out in "a new flurry of covenant signing" to restrict other blocks.[18]

Around the time of Fisher's report, some two decades after Angelenos of color had begun moving into West Jefferson, "a number of Negro organizations" were still seeking to break all the covenants in the middle-class community. The 1940 census, Fisher explained, shows West Jefferson in a transitional state with only one out of the seven tracts comprising a majority Black population and three of those seven tracts comprising between 23 and 33 percent Black residents. Of all the tracts combined, Whites made up 70.6 percent, Blacks comprised 19.3 percent, and Asians and other people of color accounted for 10.1 percent. The fight to live in West Jefferson was protracted, and while most members of the anticovenant organizations paid dues, Fisher wrote, they declined to appear in court for their lawsuits, and thus the "actual work of covenant breaking falls on a few," the Black elite. "The Negro anti-covenant associations of West Jefferson represent Negro organization at its most rational. The ends are clear, specific and agreed upon; the methods and techniques employed are appropriate. Members and agents of these associations are the Negro elite, the group from which the leadership of the Negro community today must come." Fisher found Black elites to be the most suited to break covenants because of their connections and resources. They had to take risks and make themselves more visible and vulnerable to public scrutiny if they were to challenge the mostly anonymous covenanters.[19]

Amid Black westward migration, intra-racial tensions intensified as elite Westside Blacks faced criticism for abandoning working-class critics for better conditions and better opportunities, and, the critics argued, adopting White norms. Seven years before sociologist E. Franklin Frazier published *Black Bourgeoisie* (1957), writer and social critic Chester Himes, in his first published novel, *If He Hollers Let Him Go* (1945), criticized not only racial inequality in Los Angeles, but also the Black elite who resided in West Jefferson for perpetuating that inequality. The semi-autobiographical account set in World War II centered on African American defense industry laborer Bob Jones as he attempted to navigate the city's discriminatory practices. The expansion of aircraft and shipbuilding manufacturing, and the federal government's promise of equal employment in the defense industry in the early 1940s, impelled tens of thousands of African Americans, mostly from the South, to take part in the Second Great Migration and relocate to Los Angeles. Himes joined the wave of migrants seeking to leave behind racial segregation, take advantage of the employment boom, and achieve a better quality of life for themselves and their families. However, in his brief three years in Los Angeles, while working in a succession of low-wage jobs, he discovered the hypocrisy of a city known for its abundance of opportunities.[20]

On one level, throughout *If He Hollers* the protagonist confronted the city's racial inequalities by challenging Whites who attacked him. When a White female coworker refused to work under Jones at the shipyard, Jones boldly retorted with an acerbic slur and an intimidating glare. After the department superintendent ordered Jones to contain his temper and cultivate a courteous relationship with his White colleagues, the protagonist adamantly defended his actions.[21]

The Black middle class also served as a major barrier blocking the attainment of racial equality. Throughout the novel, the relationship between Jones and his love interest, Alice Harrison, remained burdened with distress. Raised by affluent parents, Harrison learned at a young age that success came to those who received a formal education, worked hard, and resisted the temptation to protest openly against racial discrimination. The formula resembled the conservative teachings of Booker T. Washington. Dubbed by his critics as the great accommodator in the post–Reconstruction South, Washington urged Blacks to acquire vocational skills, respect the law, and defer to segregation instead of fighting for civil rights and against discriminatory policies, until southern Whites adjust to and meet the promises of emancipation. But like W. E. B. Du Bois, Ida B. Wells, and William Monroe Trotter, Himes knew White segregationists never intended to see Blacks as equals. While Jones sought to "get even" with Whites who curbed Black advancement, Alice's mother, Mrs. Harrison, advised the protagonist to show Whites respect. "You must accept whatever they do for you and try to prove yourself worthy to be entrusted with more." Alice echoed her mother's sentiment, and although she encouraged Jones to set goals, she also recognized the limitations of her race. "You need some definite aim, a goal that you can attain within the segregated pattern in which we live," Alice stressed. "We *are* Negroes and we can't change that. But *as* Negroes, we can accomplish many things."[22]

While the Harrisons saw themselves as exemplars of the Black race, living proof that more people of color possessed the ability to advance beyond their means, Jones found their actions rather arrogant and hypocritical. The Black middle class, Jones believed, used their Westside address to differentiate themselves from their working-class counterparts. "When you asked a Negro where he lived, and he said on the West Side," Himes wrote, "that was supposed to mean he was better than the Negroes who lived on the South Side; it was like the white folks giving a Beverly Hills address."[23] Their two-story house, Himes went on, situated in the "clean, quiet, well bred" West Jefferson neighborhood, as well as the well-manicured lawn and the plant and flower beds surrounding the property, served as lavish symbols of their success. The Harrisons furnished their home in high-priced décor and modern amenities, and they relied on hired help to take care of their routine needs. "Their house reminded me of a country club," Jones chided. "You knew they had dough, you saw it, it was there." Himes used the Harrisons to condemn affluent Blacks for making as their priority the attainment of wealth and prestige in White society, rather than racial equality. He argued that affluent Blacks conformed to White standards and lacked sympathy for working-class Blacks who struggled to make ends meet.[24]

Others believed that middle-class Black westward migration hindered working-class Blacks' prospects for getting support and moving out of the Eastside. In a 1940 study of Black communities in Los Angeles, for instance, Karl Holton, Chair of the Deteriorating Zone Committee of the Los Angeles Urban League, noted Westside Blacks felt responsibility to serve as role models and help advance the city's larger Black community. But while Holton claimed West Jefferson as "the best district" of all the areas inhabited by a sizeable Black population, he understood that "social programs in the large district [of Central Avenue] will have little chance for permanent success unless the aid of this element [of Black professionals] can be enlisted." By moving westward, middle-class Blacks risked creating a deeper divide between poor communities and what many commonly believed as, in Holton's words, "the best" neighborhoods, and diverting public and private investments away from the Eastside.[25]

Black elites saw their decisions differently. In an era when Hollywood typecast African Americans in one-dimensional roles as menial laborers, Black entertainers saw that by moving to the Westside they could challenge housing discrimination and attain better access to opportunities in the city. Historian Donald Bogle, paraphrasing Geri Branton, explained that Black entertainers in Los Angeles felt a "communal cohesiveness" as they bonded over their shared experiences, celebrated their successes, and commiserated over their defeats. Their radio, film, and television characters of often agreeable or dim-witted maids, cooks, chauffeurs, and butlers differed starkly from their off-screen lives. In their homes and communities, they served as role models and leaders. They navigated into restricted areas of the city that Whites fervently defended with legal contracts and neighborhood associations. Once Black professionals settled in, they sought not only to share their successes with others, but also to continue to work toward racial acceptance. They hosted parties, offered their spare bedrooms to out-of-town guests, and held meetings of local organizations in their living rooms. Most importantly, the migration of Black leaders into West Jefferson opened the door for more Blacks to move to the Westside. White-collar Blacks, from mail carriers to police officers to teachers to civil servants, settled in the area. Between 1940 and 1950, West Jefferson's Black proportion had increased from 19.3 percent to 48.6 percent. They shared the area with Whites, Asians, and Latinos, and ultimately challenged the nation's deeply racist policies and practices.[26]

Affluent Blacks saw West Jefferson as one step in the campaign to attain full access to housing on the Westside. Shortly after moving into West Jefferson, Black professionals turned their attention northward to the historically affluent community of West Adams Heights. West Jefferson offered good schools and public services as well as starter and mid-range homes with ample garden space, but the modest-size dwellings and repetitive gridiron street pattern on the flatlands of the city did little to honor the achievements of African American professionals. West Adams Heights, on the other hand, had a history of illustrious White residents who appeared regularly in the society pages of the late nineteenth-century newspapers. The city's most successful and envied White pioneers and socialites founded the area on the elevated section of the city, leaving behind elaborately constructed estates with panoramic views overlooking the city. While elite Blacks continued to combat housing segregation, they also wanted their homes and living spaces to reflect their hard work and achievements, and West Adams Heights offered that space. But the process to move into the area took several years as the federal government added more layers onto residential discrimination policies and programs and extended the struggle for equal access to housing further into the twentieth century.

STATE-SANCTIONED HOUSING DISCRIMINATION
AFTER *EUCLID* AND *CORRIGAN*

In the 1920s *Los Angeles Times* publisher Harry Chandler envisioned creating the city as a "white spot," a place free of crime, corruption, unionism, Communism, and, he implied, free of people of color; his newspaper peddled this vision through the mid-twentieth century. Urban expansion between the world wars put additional pressures on the city, which inflamed White animosity toward people of color. The Ku Klux Klan exemplified and escalated racial, ethnic, and religious xenophobia when it reemerged in the South and established klaverns across the country, including in Los Angeles.[27] Amid heightened tensions, Black Angelenos continued to challenge housing discrimination. In 1927, one year after the NAACP lost *Euclid v. Ambler*, which validated use-based zoning laws, and *Corrigan v. Buckley*, which sanctioned racial restrictive covenants, Willis O. Tyler insisted, "The fight against residential segregation has in fact just begun." But for more than a decade thereafter, the country's lower courts deferred to *Euclid* and *Corrigan*, and the US Supreme Court refused altogether to hear any restrictive covenant case.[28] During the Great Depression the federal government institutionalized the discriminatory contract and financial tools at the national level that northern and western Whites had been using at the grassroots, neighborhood, and municipal levels since the early twentieth century. The New Deal's housing programs and policies exacerbated residential discrimination when they validated the measures that White homeowners, real estate interests, housing developers, and private sector lenders had been using, supposedly to protect the value of their properties.[29]

As the restricted Westside took shape, and people of color settled into West Jefferson, the Black elite looked to alternative approaches to counter housing discrimination and gain access to the Westside. In the mid-1920s, physician, Liberty Savings' first president, and real estate investor Wilbur C. Gordon set out to construct a Westside subdivision for affluent Blacks on 213 acres of undeveloped land north of Torrance and outside of the Los Angeles city limits. For his subdivision, which he dubbed Gordon Manor, Gordon envisioned a community that stayed on pace with the development of the White Westside but challenged the city's demographic pattern that was heading toward segregation. With a group of Black realtors and White financiers, Gordon raised the funds and began installing the infrastructure, drafting the housing plans, and selling lots on the barley fields. Unsurprisingly, however, Whites in the adjacent communities led a year-long campaign to stop construction under the guise that the public wanted to put a park on the land. Among "the greatest and wealthiest aggregation of monied interests ever assembled in a legal battle against Negro realty acquisition," a reporter for the Black-owned *Pittsburgh Courier* explained, attorney Henry O'Melveny stood at the forefront as the public face of the group to pressure the Los Angeles Board of Supervisors to stop the development. Landscape architect Frederick Law Olmsted, Jr., also joined the White opposition, which resembled his late father's 1857 effort to evict through eminent domain free Blacks and Irish and German immigrants, including those who owned property in Seneca Village, from the land on which he designed New York's Central Park. O'Melveny's group successfully persuaded county officials to stop construction and give Gordon a $700,000 settlement that covered his expenses, but not his time and effort. Despite White urgency in stopping Gordon Manor, the area, many years later, became the site of Alondra Park, El Camino College, and a golf course.[30]

Elite Blacks had also sought areas outside of Los Angeles for their respite and recreation, and their health and wellness. In the late 1880s and early 1900s, many of the city's leading Blacks purchased vacation homes in Lake Elsinore Valley. Located south of Los Angeles, in Riverside County, Lake Elsinore Valley became a popular retreat for its hotels, sanatoriums, hot springs, and leisure activities. Prominent Black Angelenos, including Gordon, Charlotta Bass, Paul R. Williams, and H. Claude Hudson, owned homes there. In the mid-1920s, as Bay Street Beach and Bruce's Beach became less safe for Blacks, Texas-born and Los Angeles–transplant real estate developer and broker, insurance agent, filmmaker, and actor Sidney P. Dones established Eureka Villa (later known as Val Verde), another place where Blacks could find respite from racial prejudice and the urban environment. Located near Santa Clarita Valley, around fifty miles northwest of Los Angeles, Val Verde was previously owned by Laura C. Janes, a wealthy White woman from Pasadena, who opened her Chiquito Canyon family ranch to African Americans for weekend picnics to reportedly counter racism and segregation in the city, although she might have also been motivated by financial gain. The ranch grew into a Black resort after Dones obtained the land in 1924 and appointed an advisory committee, which included the *California Eagle*'s editor, Joseph Blackburn Bass, who married the newspaper's owner Charlotta Bass, to help develop and promote it.[31]

Dones believed that hard work, thrift, and family responsibility would lead African Americans to financial stability and social mobility. In his 1914 *Eagle* column, Dones advised Black men, whom he viewed as the family breadwinners, to live in a low-rent apartment, cut back on household expenses, save money, and purchase a house. His line of work as a real estate broker and developer—and his recommendations in the article—highlight his belief in Black male-led homeownership as a means toward upward mobility in the United States: "Get a nice little house large enough to comfortably house [your] wife and the little ones, do not worry about living far out, and don't worry about being on the car line—a few blocks walk will do you good."[32]

Engaging in Progressive-era respectability politics, Dones spelled out the steps his readers should take to improve their quality of life, one of which was purchasing property. He advocated for participating in a consumer-based, free market system as the basis of asserting citizenship, by way of racial uplift that Himes (and later Frazier) scorned and that inflamed intra-racial tensions. Himes's fictional characters, the Harrisons, claimed they worked hard to move into West Jefferson and to seek White respect. But, Himes believed, they abandoned the Black working class and drove a wedge in Los Angeles's Black population when they moved westward. The court-endorsed discriminatory housing policies and practices provide a more complex picture of the challenges Blacks faced to improve their conditions. Housing and employment discrimination, among multiple other systemic factors, limited Blacks' movement and opportunities in the city and impeded on Blacks' citizenship rights. While elite Blacks focused on ending the practice of restrictive covenants, those without the financial means to save money or acquire a home loan remained restricted to substandard rentals.[33]

Similar to Blacks' intentions for Lake Elsinore Valley, Dones sought to provide a break from racism and discrimination, and a space for respite and recreation, by developing Val Verde. But he also sought to establish a permanent, residential community that lived there year-round. He sold lots, rented cabins, and offered recreational activities. Then in 1928, as Dones's Eureka Villa became a township, residents changed its name back to its earlier designation, Val Verde, and the resort town continued to thrive through the subsequent decades. Thanks to local leaders, investors, developers, and residents, Val Verde secured additional private and public amenities, including an African Methodist Episcopal Church and a public park, clubhouse, bathhouse, and Olympic-size pool, and made improvements to, for example, the landscaping and the water system. Crowds gathered at the clubhouse for holidays and celebrations. Black entertainers, including Hattie McDaniel and Louise Beavers, and local leaders, such as Norman O. Houston and George Beavers, regularly visited the area. By the 1940s, some referred to Val Verde as the Black Palm Springs. But despite these recreational opportunities, Los Angeles's multiethnic and multiracial population saw more impediments put on them to owning a home altogether or one that would likely appreciate over time. Visiting Lake Elsinore, Val Verde, and other recreation spots provided temporary relief from persistent racism and discrimination.[34]

Amid economic turmoil and a foreclosure crisis, Depression-era New Deal programs sanctioned and exacerbated racial discrimination and residential segregation in cities nationwide. Passed in 1933, the HOLC became the first federal agency in the Great Depression aimed to rescue the plummeting housing market by refinancing home mortgages that were headed toward default and offer low-interest loans to those who had lost their homes to foreclosure. In the process, the agency institutionalized at the federal level redlining, a discriminatory ratings system that ranked lenders' risk of granting loans in each urban neighborhood. The HOLC's inaptly named security maps of the nation's cities graded areas (from first to fourth) using a color-coding system (from green to blue to yellow to red) at the block-level, indicating most to least appreciable and desirable. First grade (green) marked the most desirable communities where banks could safely provide loans, while fourth grade (red) indicated "hazardous" locales where banks, the HOLC warned, took significant risk in lending to homebuyers. The HOLC also often ranked communities at the fourth-grade if they were older and included even the smallest racial or ethnic population. Evidence suggests that, before the HOLC, many private sector lenders had already created their own discriminatory identifiers, been avoiding what they believed were at-risk areas, and did not come into possession of the HOLC maps whatsoever. But the HOLC advised some developers and lenders to contain or even raze fourth-grade redlined neighborhoods as a method of protecting what it believed were the best parts of the city, and, most significantly, it sanctioned these discriminatory tools at the federal level, adding another tier of residential discrimination to the nationwide system.[35]

The 1939 Los Angeles HOLC redlining map resembled the industrial and residential districts established by the 1908 zoning ordinances. The HOLC gave many of the Eastside communities situated east of the Los Angeles River, including Boyle Heights, and west of the Los Angeles River, including Chinatown and the Central Avenue corridor, running from Washington Boulevard southward into Watts, on Los Angeles's 1939 HOLC map, third (yellow) or fourth (red) grades. The HOLC assigned the White, blue-collar communities of the Alameda corridor, including Bell, Huntington Park, and South Gate, however, either second (blue) or third (yellow) grades. Even the area descriptions used alarming language that reflected Whites' racial anxieties. The area description of a Central Avenue section, south of Washington Boulevard, which the HOLC assigned a fourth, or "low red," grade, explained that the "population is uniformly of poor quality." The HOLC gave many of the communities located west of Main Street, in what was considered the desirable Westside one decade before, a solid third, or yellow, grade. It marked West Jefferson with a third, "low yellow," grade; and West Adams Heights with a third, "high yellow" grade. Even the smallest population of color influenced the HOLC to downgrade its neighborhood ranking. Not surprisingly, the HOLC gave Hancock Park a first, "medial green," grade, and Beverly Hills a first, "high green," grade.[36]

In 1934 President Roosevelt also established the FHA to stimulate residential construction by insuring private sector loans for home building and sales. The FHA took no part in construction, but the agency set guidelines

HOLC's Los Angeles Security Map, September 30, 1939. Recreated in grayscale, the HOLC's discriminatory security map ranked Los Angeles's neighborhoods from most appreciable (first grade) to least desirable (fourth grade). The white areas represented undeveloped, sparsely developed, or commercial spaces. (Later developed roads included for orientation.) Map by Erin Greb Cartography.

on its insurance policies that privileged the building of single-family homes (rather than multiple-use dwellings), favored new properties (instead of modernizing rentals), and offered better insurance policies to homes in financially secure areas. It also created block-level maps that graded neighborhoods' risk level. Moreover, the FHA's widely distributed *Underwriting Manual* advised contractors and lenders to maintain home values by covering properties with racial restrictive covenants.[37]

The 1944 Servicemen's Readjustment Act, more popularly known as the G.I. Bill, accelerated racial inequality and residential segregation in the postwar years. The federal government set up the G.I. Bill to provide World War II veterans with precollege and college education grants (including tuition and a living stipend), on-the-job training, job placement services, and subsidized business and mortgage loans, and then decentralized administration of the funds by giving states, localities, local Veterans Administration offices, and private and public institutions (e.g., banks and colleges) authority to distribute them. Many of these institutions followed the FHA federal regulations and adhered to Jim Crow laws and customs while making those decisions. The G.I. Bill excluded any language that prohibited racial discrimination in the distribution of its benefits. Black veterans expected to receive these supports, and while thousands did, significantly more faced obstacles in, for example, getting accepted into college, finding a job that was comparable to the skills they developed in the war, and securing a home loan. The legislation helped build the postwar suburban White middle class while leaving most Blacks behind. Black-owned insurance companies and real estate agencies attempted to offset the discriminatory practices and policies by providing African Americans with home loans and insurance policies; but they lacked the scope to finance a vast proportion of the nation's housing market, and lacked the power to prohibit the discriminatory tools that grassroots efforts had implemented by the early twentieth century, that the courts had sanctioned in the mid-1920s and the federal government had endorsed from the early 1930s.[38]

For more than two decades after *Euclid* and *Corrigan*, cities across the United States grew segregated, and most urban Blacks found themselves relegated to what became known, disparagingly, as ghettos. African Americans continued to dispute the constitutionality of use-based zoning laws and racial restrictive covenants by moving into restricted areas and pursuing lawsuits against covenanters; Black-owned newspapers, from the *California Eagle* to the *Chicago Defender* to the Baltimore *Afro-American*, kept those lawsuits in the public eye. As Los Angeles continued to expand and Whites implemented discriminatory measures to segregate the urban landscape, the city's multiethnic and multiracial population became isolated in overcrowded and rundown neighborhoods. The flourishing Central Avenue corridor of the 1910s and 1920s suffered an acute housing shortage that affected the entire city in the 1940s. Black Angelenos with the financial means found no other option but to challenge restrictive covenants and move westward into White neighborhoods. Some faced little resistance, but many risked their lives and livelihoods. Yet they pursued the fight in hopes that one day they would reap the rewards, enjoy their full right to property, and make available to everyone the same opportunities. After moving into West Jefferson, they set their sights on historic West Adams Heights.[39]

HISTORICALLY WHITE WEST ADAMS

In the late 1800s and early 1900s, few residential areas in Los Angeles compared to the wealthy settlements of the West Adams district. The main section, stretching from Figueroa Street to Arlington Avenue on the east and west, and Washington and Adams Boulevards on the north and south, became the center of White upper-crust society. West Adams was not the first affluent area in Los Angeles. In the late 1800s, Bunker Hill became highly desirable as many successful, White entrepreneurs and professionals seeking distance from the Plaza constructed elaborate mansions and luxury hotels in the hilltop community. But with the streetcar installation, West Adams became an early White, elite community outside of the downtown center, before Beverly Hills emerged to eminence in the 1920s as home to the White Hollywood elite, and the escapades of Douglas Fairbanks and Mary Pickford at Pickfair alerted the press to the homes of entertainers.[40] Elite Whites looking for distance from the city center migrated westward, along the streetcar line, in the late 1800s, and settled in the West Adams district. Recently arrived easterners and midwesterners who pioneered industries, as well as doctors, attorneys, and socialites, commissioned noted architects to design grand estates in Victorian, Italian Renaissance, colonial, and Tudor styles that topped each other and astonished passersby.[41]

The early White, upper-crust West Adams residents settled on the eastern side of the district around West Adams Boulevard and Figueroa Street. Self-made lumber millionaire Thomas Stimson, former Arkansas Republican Senator Stephen Wallace Dorsey, and entertainer Roscoe Conkling Arbuckle (known as Fatty Arbuckle professionally) helped give the area its distinction. The affluent residents on West Twenty-Eighth Street, or what became known as Bankers' Row, brought prestige to the district. Chester Place, immediately west of Figueroa Street, became the jewel of the district's eastern end. Real estate developer and federal court judge Charles Silent bought a two-story farmhouse and the surrounding grounds, and in the 1880s and 1890s turned his property into a residential compound comprising twenty acres, which he sheltered with gates, trees, and shrubbery. Silent named the center square St. James Park, after his first son, James, and the surrounding area Chester Place, after his youngest boy, Chester.[42]

Chester Place especially attained prominence when Edward L. Doheny and his family moved in. Born into a poor Irish family in Wisconsin, Doheny was swept up in the excitement of the gold rush, and as a teenager he prospected across the western territories. After years of hard work without reaping any reward, Doheny traveled to Los Angeles in hopes of striking it rich. After a difficult year, Doheny hit black gold (oil) hundreds of feet below the city. He amassed a fortune from his first oil well, and several others thereafter, and used his wealth to buy property in Chester Place. In the early 1900s, he paid for in cash a 10,500-square-foot, three-story, Gothic revival mansion for $125,000 at 8 Chester Place. According to Doheny's biographer, the Doheny family added to the more than twenty-room estate a "private bowling alley, music room, and wildlife menagerie."[43]

The western side of West Adams (and the western limit of the city) also included impressive residences in subdistricts, such as Berkeley Square, Gramercy Park, Adams Place, and Kinney Heights. Berkeley Square stood out, the *Los Angeles Times* in 1909 explained, as "one of the show streets of the west...[and] marvels of the recent growth of Los Angeles."[44] Situated between Twenty-First and Twenty-Second Streets, Gramercy Place and Western Avenue, Berkeley Square offered homes in a variety of prices and styles. Through the 1910s and 1920s, property values ranged upward from $10,000. William G. McAdoo, railroad executive and former secretary of the US Department of the Treasury under President Woodrow Wilson, bought a fifteen-room estate surrounded by about one acre of land at 5 Berkeley Square for $60,000. Lee Allen Phillips, vice president of Pacific Mutual Life Insurance Company, bought a mansion at 4 Berkeley Square for $80,000 and hired an architectural firm to renovate and enlarge the property. A. L. Cheney, president of Stimson Oil Company, and his spouse built a Tudor-style home that included a reception hall, terrace, sunroom, library, dressing room, sewing room, and servants' quarters.[45] Like Chester Place, attorney and journalist Carey McWilliams chided, Berkeley Square "was designed as an inner fortress to hold the line against the invading forces of mediocrity." Stone entryways and gates kept the community separate from the city and its varied residents.[46]

West Adams Heights was situated between Chester Place and Berkeley Square. In the 1860s and 1870s, Charles Victor Hall, a college student working as a land surveyor, recorded a section of territory just south of what would become West Adams Heights, which he aptly named after himself, while Mary E. Hall, his sister and a schoolteacher, patented the adjacent territory on the north. Mary and her spouse, William Moore, a surveyor and engineer, were among the first occupants in the tract. George Ira Cochran, attorney and insurance company executive, saw the tract's potential and bought the title from the Moores. In 1902 he subdivided the elevated portion, specifically to sell to wealthy Whites, and named the area West Adams Heights. Western Avenue, Washington Boulevard, Normandie Avenue, Twenty-Second Street, La Salle Avenue, and Adams Boulevard bounded the Heights.

Elevation became a key element throughout much of modern Los Angeles history that affluent urbanites used to distinguish and distance themselves from the rest of the population. As the city expanded and migrants arrived, historian Robert Fishman writes, "The wealthy seized upon the hills as a sign of wealth and status." This trend became apparent with Bunker Hill in the late 1800s and Beverly Hills in the early 1900s, which Fishman calls the "archetypal hill suburb."[47] Affluent Whites in the late nineteenth century who sought homes in West Adams Heights had the same objectives. The sloping streets, private cul-de-sacs, and panoramic views overlooking the city gave West Adams Heights residents privacy from city congestion, as well as attention from envious onlookers. Cochran and his business associate, Frederick Hastings Rindge, built the first mansions in the area.[48]

Rindge and his family owned one of the most noted homes in the Heights. At around the age of thirty, Rindge had inherited $3 million from his father, who had made his fortune as a woolen manufacturer in the Northeast. In the 1880s Rindge married Rhoda May Knight and moved to Southern California. The couple is most remembered as the founders of Malibu, and for the war Rhoda May waged against squatters and the court to preserve her beachfront property after her spouse's death. They also owned land in Santa Monica. Their two-acre home at 2263 South Harvard Boulevard, dubbed Castle Rindge, became the centerpiece of the Heights. Castle Rindge included several parlors and thirteen fireplaces, all of which were made from imported Italian marble, as well as domed ceilings, a study, a chandelier suspended in the large dining room, an elaborate oak staircase, and a carriage house. The Rindge mansion and other estates in the Heights became symbols of the possibilities of Los Angeles. At the turn of the twentieth century, those opportunities stood at a far distance for Angelenos of color.[49]

But in the 1920s and 1930s, as many illustrious Whites passed away and the Great Depression drained the riches of some remaining residents, African Americans sensed a weakness in the armor of West Adams's contract-based racial apartheid and seized the opportunity to move in. As the older generation of Whites died, their children sold their homes and moved to newer Westside communities, such as Brentwood, Bel Air, and Beverly Hills. The stock market crash of 1929 and ensuing depression further affected the community. While some residents managed to hold on to their wealth, others faced difficulty maintaining their properties. Some long-time residents converted their homes into apartments, others filed for bankruptcy, and a few took their own lives. African Americans with the financial resources found an opening and began moving in.[50]

THE HOUSTONS MOVE IN

After years of chipping away at housing discrimination, moving from Central Avenue to West Jefferson, Norman and Edythe Houston broke ground in 1938 by becoming the first African Americans to purchase a home in West Adams Heights. They were not the first people of color to move to the area. In the late 1800s and early 1900s golden era, before Whites implemented housing restrictions, and ethnic, racial, and religious minority groups had more freedom of movement, some prosperous city dwellers of color settled there. Then, "for at least a decade before Mr. Houston purchased a home in the Heights," Cary McWilliams reported, "a Korean merchant, a Chinese character actor, two Italian-American families, a Hungarian-American, and several Armenian-American families" had moved to the community. Elite Jews and Mexicans also moved to the district. When the Houstons purchased their home, however, Whites openly panicked and tried to evict them, and to deter all other people of color from moving into the neighborhood.[51]

Whites had a history of responding with hostility to the settlement of people of color in their neighborhoods, and they often prohibited in their restrictive covenants the sale of their property to all non-Whites, yet no existing reports have indicated that the White West Adams Heights residents panicked before the Houstons moved in. While Whites refused to welcome Blacks into the neighborhood, they "tolerated but never really accepted," according to McWilliams, a handful of ethnic minorities of the same class, contradicting the conservative argument that multiculturalism creates societal disintegration. Typifying their movement westward, elite Jewish Angelenos, with Rabbi Edgar Fogel Magnin's leadership, for instance, relocated one of the city's first synagogues, which served Congregation B'nai B'rith since 1896, from Ninth and Hope Streets, immediately north of West Adams, to 3663 Wilshire Boulevard, in 1928. Temple B'nai B'rith became Wilshire Boulevard Temple. Excluded from the city's social clubs, Rabbi Magnin and some elite B'nai B'rith congregants also led the establishment of Hillcrest Country Club in 1920 on 142 vacant acres directly south of Beverly Hills. Hillcrest became a highly exclusive place to play golf and tennis, dine, conduct business, and fundraise. Over the decades, Hollywood's Jewish elite, from actors Milton Berle to the Marx Brothers, and executives, from Louis B. Mayer to Adolph Zukor, many of whom had established their studios on what was then the largely undeveloped Westside, had memberships there. Many other racial, ethnic, and religious minorities followed.[52]

More than ten years before the Houstons purchased their West Adams Heights' house, Mexican American actor Ramon Novarro settled in the area. In 1899 he was born José Ramón Gil Samaniego in Durango, Mexico, into an affluent and influential family. According to his family's accounts and the Hollywood studio's marketing, Novarro's father's family had roots in Greece, moved to Spain, and then seized Mexico with conquistador Hernán Cortés; his mother's family had both Spanish and Aztec origins that had connections with the last sovereign Aztec emperor, Motecuhzoma II Xocoyotzin. Novarro's paternal grandfather worked as a physician and political leader. His maternal grandfather was a landowner. His dentist father wanted him to join the practice, but Novarro developed a passion for music and theater. He moved to Los Angeles in 1915, rented a room with his brother, Mariano, in the downtown business district, and then rented a house about five miles west of West Adams Heights. He worked in low-paying positions, including a grocery store clerk and an usher. He played small acting roles in the theater and then landed larger roles with the Metro-Goldwyn-Mayer studio, who changed his last name to Novarro.[53]

Before shooting the silent film *The Midshipman* (1925), the same year he also starred in *Ben-Hur*, Novarro purchased a new Lincoln Coupe and a seventeen-room house at 2265 West Twenty-Second Street in West Adams Heights. To his house, his biographer explains, he "added his own private wing with a suite of dressing rooms, servants' quarters, and something that had been a dream for him—his own theater" that sat sixty people and boasted a bright neon sign that read "Novarro's Teatro Intimo." Perhaps the property's location, on the tract's western edge, helped his White neighbors feel less threatened about his move. Perhaps Novarro's light skin and good looks made the White homeowners less reactionary. They might have seen him the same way as the federal census, which, about the same time, listed him in the Heights as "White." Novarro's family roots in Greece, Spain, and indigenous Mexico seemed to have helped him transcend, to some degree, America's rigid color lines. He played characters of all different nationalities, including American, English, French, and Polynesian, and could easily pass for non-Hispanic. Moreover, historian Scott Kurashige explains, "While in some cases restrictive covenants explicitly excluded occupancy by 'Mexicans,' in other cases Mexicans were judged fit to occupy housing restricted to 'Caucasians.'" Perhaps it was Novarro's affluence that provided him more mobility and acceptance into the White neighborhood. While working-class Mexicans had little option but to reside in the East Los Angeles barrio, Novarro and other well-off Mexicans purchased property on the Westside. Yet, McWilliams clarifies, the newcomers "socially...never became part of the Heights." White residents might not have protested their arrival, but they refused to accept the new residents as part of their social circle. When African Americans moved in, however, Whites believed they had lost control of their community.[54]

In 1938, when hearing the news of the Houstons' purchase, the West Adams Heights Improvement Association (WAHIA) called a meeting to come up with a plan to block the couple from moving in. In Los Angeles, along with cities across the country, as people of color moved into White communities, Whites responded by mobilizing themselves into so-called homeowners' improvement associations. To maintain the White makeup of the community, these associations took various measures, such as intimidating Black newcomers, threatening real estate agents who might sell to people of color, administering restrictive covenants, raising funds to purchase property from recent Black buyers, buying vacant lots, refusing to patronize stores that sold to Black shoppers, lobbying city officials to pass and enforce exclusionary zoning laws that, for example, prohibited multi-unit rentals, or pursuing legal action.[55]

In 1937, around a year before the Houstons bought property in the area, White residents set out mobilizing their White neighbors to instate a community-wide restriction. Over the next few years, with the WAHIA's help, some one hundred property owners in and around the area signed their name before a witness to the contract, which they then notarized and filed in the county recorder's office. In the covenant they agreed "that no portion of any of said lots, pieces, or parcels of land shall ever be occupied, as a residence or for residential purposes, by any person other than of the Caucasian, or White Race," and, evidential of the antebellum-originated, one-drop rule's enduring existence, and yet an unviable argument in mid-twentieth century courts, "that no person whose blood is not entirely that of the White Race shall live upon any of said real property during said term...save and except in the capacity of a domestic servant." The signers promised to adhere to the contract until December 31, 2035, almost a century from when it was recorded, a willful and "fantastically remote" duration of time, McWilliams derided, considering the migration and mobility patterns that characterized urban history. While her neighbors signed the covenant, Naomi Freeney, a divorced White mother of two children, avoided it. She had been running her property as a guesthouse to earn an income, but in the face of her neighbors' relentless objections for defying land-use laws, she "decided to settle scores," McWilliams wrote, and sell to the Houstons.[56]

The spacious residence located at 2211 South Hobart Boulevard, near the corner of Twenty-Second Street, seemed perfect for the Houstons' combined families. Norman had three children with his first spouse, and Edythe had one child from her previous relationship. The property needed some repairs to reverse Freeney's guesthouse operations. It also had been used as a private club for professional football players and a meeting place for community groups. But, McWilliams wrote, "as the first Negro to purchase a home in the Heights, Mr. Houston was a little hesitant about moving in." For a few years the Houstons continued to live in West Jefferson while they rented their Hobart house to various White tenants, similarly following Freeney's practice that had angered the White neighbors. The WAHIA offered to purchase the Houstons' home, and, under pressure, the couple gave the association a time frame in which to come up with the money. But the WAHIA failed to agree on an amount each homeowner should contribute to pay for the Houstons' house and sought another resolution to their crisis. Then, in late 1940, as the Houstons moved in, the WAHIA agreed in an emergency meeting "to take legal action to protect the exclusive character of the

Heights." While the Houstons avoided a lawsuit by buying an unrestricted property, other Blacks, Asians, and Latinos who moved in afterward faced a legal battle.[57]

By moving in, the Houstons inspired local leaders and professionals of color in Los Angeles to do the same. After decades of exclusion from the covenanted area, they seized the opportunity. While properties remained expensive for the average city dweller, their values in the Great Depression had declined. Economic loss forced White property owners to skimp on home repairs and improvements and sell at reduced prices. But houses in West Adams Heights continued to hold historical value and distinction from a bygone era of Los Angeles's White wealthy class. In 1944, reporter Malcolm Thurburn noticed, "There is an air of grandeur, even though some of the buildings are falling into disrepair."[58] Once the Houstons moved in, they motivated others to buy property in the area.

HISTORICALLY BLACK WEST ADAMS HEIGHTS

As word spread of the Houstons' purchase, elite African Americans began to purchase homes in the area, many of which were covered by the community-wide covenant. Whites who believed their property values would fall and feared living near Blacks rushed to sell their homes.[59] But a group of Whites who aimed to maintain an all-White neighborhood hired attorneys and filed lawsuits against many Black and a few Asian and Latino newcomers. Rather than suing White homeowners for violating the covenant and selling their properties to people of color, this group focused on prosecuting the newcomers. The defendants had knowingly breached the legal contract, the plaintiffs claimed, and their residence in the community "is causing and will continue to cause these plaintiffs great and irreparable injury."[60] White fears did not reflect the reality. On the contrary, the newcomers brought public attention to the historical community, improved the quality of their homes, and ultimately helped broaden the possibilities for a better quality of life in the city to everyone.

Among the many Black entertainers who settled in West Adams Heights, or what became popularly known as Sugar Hill, actor Hattie McDaniel received much attention. About one year after the Houstons moved into their home, newlyweds McDaniel and James Lloyd Crawford, a real estate agent, bought a two-story, seventeen-room, white stucco mansion at 2203 South Harvard Boulevard for $7,000, well above the city's $3,958 median property value.[61] By the early 1940s, McDaniel had achieved significant professional and personal success, celebrating her triumph in 1940 as the first African American to win an Academy Award for her performance as Mammy in *Gone with the Wind*, and enjoying her recent marriage to Crawford. After the wedding, McDaniel moved out of her West Jefferson home and into a grand estate with her spouse. Newspapers around the country reported the wedding and their move into Sugar Hill, and McDaniel embraced the accolades that came with her accomplishments.[62]

McDaniel grew up in meager conditions, but her natural talent and hard work helped her succeed. She was born the youngest of seven children in Wichita, Kansas, in 1893; her parents struggled most of their lives to feed and clothe their offspring, who often went without the necessities. To escape menial labor and poverty, McDaniel's brother urged his siblings to become entertainers. They worked in minstrel shows, carnivals, and plays, and McDaniel traveled the country singing the blues in front of an orchestra.[63] Then, in the 1930s, she joined her sister, Etta Goff, in Los Angeles to seek opportunities in show business. Goff had moved to Los Angeles in the 1920s, lived on the Eastside, and worked as a housekeeper for a wealthy, White family north of USC in the West Adams district. When McDaniel arrived, she rented an apartment near Central Avenue, and, as she landed small roles in films, she earned enough money to buy a modest dwelling in West Jefferson. But she had higher goals, and in less than a decade from her arrival to the city, McDaniel had bought a home in the same district where her sister had once labored.[64]

McDaniel embraced her success as a professional actor. During the filming of *Gone with the Wind*, while she was earning a steady salary, she bought a green Packard automobile and cruised around the city with her head held high. En route to the studio, she stopped by the Dunbar Hotel on Central Avenue to show off her prized possession. "I just couldn't help driving by the Dunbar that day," she told a reporter. "I felt mighty happy driving that Packard." In her previous visit to the studio, she explained, "I remember to myself the last time I was there I only had bus fare one way," she continued, "So I just had to show them all standing around there dressed up so big. I had to show 'em I done it."[65] Her purchase of a Sugar Hill mansion lifted her status to a higher level. Her home stood at the center of the neighborhood, on one of the best spots in the area overlooking the city. Trees, shrubbery, and flowers adorned the house's façade, which featured a wrap-around porch and towering front doors. Each room boasted its own unique design. She furnished the drawing room in French period style; the lounge had rattan furniture; the dining room featured an ivory table and chairs; and the upstairs bedrooms matched each of their bathrooms. Around the home, McDaniel displayed her prized possessions, including her Academy Award, a white grand piano, and autograph portraits of famous entertainers.[66] The hard-working, well-paid actor devoted her free time to giving back to her race and her country.

McDaniel's commitment to the community made her, according to scholar Donald Bogle, the "grand matriarch of Sugar Hill." At her South Harvard Boulevard address, elite Blacks gathered together to share ideas, honor their achievements, and escape from the confines of White-dominated society. Historian and biographer Jill Watts explains that McDaniel's home "was private and intimate, but it was also independent and unfettered, free of white interference." Prominent African American musician Cab Calloway, actor Louise Beavers, and scholar E. Franklin Frazier spent time at her estate. Frazier might have gathered more support for his argument in *Black Bourgeoisie*, his 1957 provocative critique of the Black elite, while visiting her home. At her parties, guests Duke Ellington, Ethel Waters, and Butterfly McQueen entertained the room. In the era of segregation, McDaniel also welcomed into her home Hollywood's White elite: Greg Belcher, Janet Blair, Joan Davis, Clark Gable, Agnes Moorehead, and Esther Williams.[67]

Faced with deeply rooted layers of oppression that intersected at her race, gender, and class, McDaniel refused to let her critics limit her goals. While the motion picture industry offered McDaniel only the roles within the established character archetypes of mammy, sassy and/or tragic mulatta, and jezebel, and marginalized her at work, the NAACP argued that McDaniel yielded to Hollywood's superficial preconceptions of African Americans and perpetuated negative racial stereotypes. NAACP executive secretary Walter White singled out McDaniel as an example of how Blacks were degraded in film, and the Black press called for boycotts across the country, including in her hometown, of *Gone with the Wind*. By refusing to denounce the film industry and sacrifice her career, McDaniel had a hand in maintaining racism in show business, but, as Watts concluded, "In a harsh, unforgiving, and racist industry…the only options were to comply or get out." Responding to her critics, McDaniel famously chided, "I can be a maid for $7 a week, or I can play a maid for $700 a week." She sought to improve Blacks' conditions from within a deeply racist business, as Bogle explained, by creating "rich, dazzling characterizations" of her on-screen maids, and emerging "as the one servant of the era to speak her mind fully." In the face of multiple burdens of oppression, she became a pioneer for Black access to show business and housing. Likewise, she challenged traditional gender norms by earning her own money, heading her household as the primary breadwinner, and remarrying four times. Her acceptance speech at the Academy Awards revealed the duality of her goals. "I sincerely hope I shall always be a credit to my race and to the motion-picture industry," she said.[68]

Accomplished and high-profile Blacks who moved to Sugar Hill continued to revive the area as respectable and fashionable. Several months before McDaniel and Crawford finalized their purchase, Lieutenant Leslie U. King, retired officer of the US Army, and his wife, Mamie King, moved from West Jefferson to a home at 2215 South Harvard Boulevard, one block north from the McDaniel and Crawford residence.[69] Horace and Vera Clark, owners of the Clark Hotel, one of the finest Black-owned establishments on Central Avenue since the 1910s, which lodged guests and provided a stage for Black musicians, became neighbors of the Houstons when they moved from Central Avenue to 2205 South Hobart Boulevard.[70]

In late 1941, singer and actor Ethel Waters also heightened the reputation of the area when she bought a three-story, ten-room mansion at 2127 South Hobart Boulevard. Waters faced a difficult upbringing and learned to rely on herself early in her life. In her 1951 autobiography, *His Eye Is on the Sparrow*, she began, "I never was a child. I never was coddled, or liked, or understood by my family. I never felt I belonged." In her early years, she shifted between relatives, lived on the streets, mixed with prostitutes, stole food, got married and divorced, and worked as a maid. Her career as a recording artist took off in the 1920s, and she began to work in film in the 1930s. She recollected the day she moved into her Sugar Hill home: "I shook with happiness that first evening when I walked into my house. During the day the moving men had brought my things, and when I saw that they had placed each chair and table exactly where I wanted it, I burst into tears. 'My house,' I told myself. 'The only place I've ever owned all by myself.'"[71] Waters felt overcome with relief to own a house and settle down near her peers. Her long-time yearning for an established and secure residence throughout her turbulent childhood and her demanding tour schedule as an adult materialized in Sugar Hill. She could decorate her house in her own style, unwind in the privacy of her own home, and keep company with trusted friends. For Waters, homeownership signified security and self-sufficiency, and, like McDaniel, she also challenged racism and sexism, and earned the means to purchase, by herself, that refuge.

African Americans who relocated to the neighborhood in 1942 helped solidify Sugar Hill's new reputation as home to the city's Black elite. McDaniel's close friend and colleague Louise Beavers moved from West Jefferson to 2219 South Hobart Boulevard, located next to the Houstons (the Clarks resided on the opposite side of the road). She bought the home for $6,500 from Isabel Cryer, spouse of former Los Angeles mayor George E. Cryer, who only a few years earlier had signed the racial restriction on the property.[72] Ben Carter moved into 2133 South Harvard Boulevard, which, actor and local activist Frances Williams explained, "was so grand that it became a showplace, and when anyone came to town, if they could they wanted to see Ben Carter's house."[73] Juan Tizol, Puerto Rico–born trombonist and composer for the Duke Ellington and Harry James bands, who was often viewed as White but who experienced the persistent forces of racism working with Black musicians, and his spouse, Washington, DC–born, African American, Rosebud (Rose) Browne Tizol, bought a home for $7,575 at 2150 South Hobart Boulevard. While Juan Tizol toured most of the first years they owned the Sugar Hill home, Rose Tizol lived there, managed the couple's business affairs, and secured their lifelong financial well-being. Dr. William E. Bailey and Edith B. Bailey moved to 2115 South Hobart Boulevard, and Dr. W. Clyde Allen and Aulette D. Allen bought a home on 2069 South Oxford Avenue.[74]

Moving into Sugar Hill remained one part of the larger goal of overcoming racial inequality. Like many Black professionals, Drs. J. A. and Vada Somerville sought more than housing equality. Born and raised by two educators in Jamaica, J. A. wrote in his autobiography, he grew up experiencing no racial prejudice in his hometown. His first encounter with discrimination occurred at age nineteen, during his first days in California, when he was denied restaurant service, lodging, and employment. But Somerville persevered. As the first African American student enrolled at the USC School of Dentistry, he withstood threats from his White classmates who initially demanded his dismissal. In 1906 Somerville finished at the top of his class and earned distinction as the first Black graduate of the university. Pomona, California–born Vada Jetmore Watson Somerville became the second Black graduate, the first Black female graduate, and the first Black woman to attain certification to practice dentistry in California.[75] J. A. helped establish the Los Angeles NAACP branch in 1913, and Vada served as director of the branch's junior division; both became prominent leaders in the community. In the 1920s they built a twenty-six-unit residential high-rise for low-income Blacks, called La Vada Apartments, and constructed Hotel Somerville (later renamed the Dunbar Hotel) on Central Avenue to host the national NAACP convention and provide first-rate accommodations for Blacks. In 1943 the Somervilles moved from their home on Jefferson Boulevard and bought an estate (sitting on two lots) at 2104 South Harvard Boulevard in Sugar Hill for $12,000, directly across the street from the Kings.[76] But their battle against racial inequality had just begun.

Through the mid-1940s, more Black leaders and professionals moved into Sugar Hill. Physician and surgeon J. Phyromn Taylor and community activist Pearl S. Taylor relocated from Shreveport, Louisiana, and purchased the house at 2210 South Hobart Boulevard. Real estate agent and future city council official Courtland G. Mitchell and community activist Rosa Lee Mitchell moved to 2048 South Oxford Avenue. US Army personnel Alfred Green and schoolteacher Senola Maxwell Green purchased the house at 2215 South Harvard Boulevard. Bandleader Noble Sissle and Ethel Sissle lived at 2126 South Harvard Boulevard.[77] Asian and Latino Angelenos also settled in the area and faced the same obstacles and confrontations. At the time the Houstons moved into their home, in 1940, the census accounted for five units occupied by people of color, or 0.8 percent of all occupied units in Sugar Hill. At the beginning of the next decade, through the central years of the legal battle against the newcomers, the number of units inhabited by people of color had grown to 175, or 22.9 percent of the community's total population.[78]

While White homeowners worried that Black in-migration would hurt the reputation of the neighborhood and refused to change their perspective over its value, property values rose after people of color moved in. The fame and renowned reputations of the newcomers revived Sugar Hill, and their renovations increased property values. When African American oil producer Mitchell B. Miles and homemaker Mabel C. Miles bought their house at 2119 La Salle Avenue, according to reporter Malcolm Thurburn, "The place had been allowed to run down completely through neglect." But the couple "immediately had it brought up to date both to interior decoration and landscape gardening" by spending $12,000 on restoration.[79] Properties previously used as private clubs, or sectioned off into guesthouses and rental units, were transformed into charming single-family homes. In 1950, when the city's average property value stood at $11,925, and the tract averaged $12,614, homes on McDaniel's block averaged $20,333, almost three times the amount she paid in 1941. The properties on the block where the Houstons, the Clarks, and Louise Beavers lived reached an average of $21,000.[80] Sugar Hill's Black residents had revived the status and value of the area.

The Houstons' 1938 purchase of a West Adams Heights house added fuel to the long-standing White effort to control the racial and ethnic makeup of neighborhoods. Through the Great Migration, as the city's Black population increased from 2.7 percent in 1920 to 3.1 percent in 1930 to 4.2 percent in 1940, Whites tightened their grip through, among many practices, discriminatory housing measures.[81] But before African Americans could live freely and unconditionally in their Sugar Hill homes, they had to challenge restrictive covenants in a court system that had defended them for decades. Throughout the 1940s their purchases remained insecure, and at any moment the newcomers faced eviction from their own property. White homeowners pulled their resources together and prepared to force out any resident who failed to fit into their criteria. Many Whites living in the area continued to believe that the courts would confirm the restrictive covenant and return the neighborhood to its supposed rightful status as a center of the White elite. But Sugar Hill's new residents refused to relent. They mobilized into their own group, held meetings out of their homes, hired the city's leading civil rights attorneys, and presented a united front with the goals of holding on to their most hard-earned possession and putting an end to residential discrimination. Their lawsuit resulted in a precedential decision that declared restrictive covenants an infringement on citizens' constitutional rights and thus legally unenforceable, nearly three years before the US Supreme Court made the same ruling on other covenants cases.

Chapter Three

The Legal Demise of Racial Restrictive Covenants

ON APRIL 15, 1943, eight White Sugar Hill homeowners filed a complaint with the Los Angeles Superior Court requesting both judicial support of their racial restrictive covenant and a judicial order to evict Sydnetta Dones Smith, Sidney P. Dones, and nine other tenants residing at 2045 South Hobart Boulevard. Dones Smith had recently bought and moved into the property a few years after the seller, Jennie V. Robinson, had signed the covenant. Dones Smith and her father, Sidney P. Dones, a successful insurance agent and real estate developer who was also charged in the complaint, might not have set out to willfully break the restriction, especially as World War II gripped the country, but Dones had a history of challenging housing discrimination by purchasing and developing land, including his Val Verde resort, and believed African Americans had equal right to property. The White plaintiffs alleged, "The use and occupancy...by the said Negro defendants...makes the plaintiffs' property undesirable to them, and others of the Caucasian race...[language reminiscent of the HOLC's gradations of supposed desirable neighborhoods] and greatly injures the rental and sale value of the premises," a common argument among Whites. A little more than a month later, defense attorneys Loren Miller and Clarence A. Jones responded that the covenant violated the Fourteenth Amendment of the US Constitution, and Article I, Section I, of the California State Constitution. The complaint launched a series of lawsuits in Sugar Hill that affirmed Los Angeles as "ground zero" in the struggle for equal access to housing and foreshadowed the legal demise of racial restrictive covenants nationwide.[1]

Two years after the eight White homeowners filed the claim, more Whites in Sugar Hill filed seven other separate legal complaints, with similar charges. Whites filed five of those complaints on a single day in March 1945. Among the plaintiffs, Francis L. Smith stood out. He was living at 2082 South Harvard Boulevard with his spouse, Mildred Taylor Smith; he worked as an accountant and led the WAHIA as president. In the eight Sugar Hill cases, a total of nineteen White plaintiffs sued more than one hundred African Americans and some Asian and Latino Americans. Whites summoned to court included local civil rights leaders and professionals such as Vada Somerville, Horace and Vera Clark, William and Edith Bailey, and Leslie and Mamie King, and celebrated Black entertainers, including Hattie McDaniel, Louise Beavers, and Ethel Waters. While the plaintiffs demanded the legal sanction of restrictive covenants and the expulsion of people of color from the neighborhood, the defendants argued that racial restrictions violated their basic constitutional rights. The Los Angeles Superior Court consolidated the eight lawsuits under Dones Smith's case and named it *Anderson v. Auseth* after the litigants' alphabetized surnames; the public commonly knew it as the Sugar Hill case. Thus, on December 5, 1945, when the Sugar Hill case went to trial, the campaign against restrictive covenants found its spokespeople.[2]

Interwar civil rights efforts, including Los Angeles's Black homeowners' rights movement, fostered the emergence of racial liberalism, the successor of 1930s New Deal liberalism and precursor to the 1950s and 1960s modern civil rights movement that saw race as a construct, believed in inclusion, and sought government intervention and legislation to achieve equality. In the 1930s and 1940s, as the country wrestled with an economic collapse and a world war, California voted more liberal-minded leaders to office who promised to root out political corruption and racial discrimination, and the state shifted to a Democratic majority.[3]

But racial liberalism had its flaws that manifested in uneven approaches and outcomes. Although racial liberals sought inclusion and integration, they often overlooked dismantling institutional discriminatory practices. Moreover, amid a multiethnic and multiracial population of competing interests, historian Mark Brilliant argues, "Civil rights reformers...[were] divided over the specific antidiscrimination measures they prioritized in their litigation and legislation agendas." He goes on, "Different axes of discrimination demanded different avenues of redress." Reform groups centered their efforts on challenging a range of issues, including the state's alien land laws that targeted Japanese Americans and local public schools that segregated Mexican Angelenos for their supposed deficiency in the English language. These issues required a strategy of their own. Moreover, scholar Daniel Martinez HoSang explains, reformers cherry-picked the issues they sought to address and, limited by their own blind spots, neglected or perpetuated racial and ethnic discrimination in other areas. Amid significant political and legal achievements, for instance, the city sustained Japanese wartime incarceration, the 1942 Sleepy Lagoon murder, and the 1943 zoot suit attacks. In a city known for its postwar progressivism, "the logics that naturalized racial distinctions and hierarchies lingered."[4]

Meanwhile, African Americans persisted in seeking greater opportunities. The national campaign against Nazism and Fascism overseas and the mass mobilization on the home front gave African Americans the impetus to demand equality. The Double V campaign, spearheaded by the widely circulated Black-owned newspaper *The Pittsburgh Courier*, inspired African Americans to fight for victory over the Axis powers abroad and over racial discrimination at home. As the US government expanded the defense industry, awarded local employers with more than $10 billion in contracts, and catapulted Los Angeles into one of the leading manufacturing centers in the country, tens of thousands of African Americans sought the growing employment opportunities by relocating to the city. Between 1940 and 1950, through the second Great Migration, the percentage of Blacks in the city's population more than doubled from 4.2 percent to 8.7 percent. But, in this rising metropolis, Blacks faced challenges.[5]

Preeminent African American sociologist Horace R. Cayton took note of the racial advances in a 1947 *Negro Digest* article, when he named Los Angeles one of the top ten best livable cities for African Americans. Measuring cities by their public services, cultural activities, job openings, and overall treatment of African Americans, Cayton found Los Angeles teeming with opportunities for African Americans to acquire an education, find employment, and own property. But as the Black population swelled, racial discrimination intensified and most African Americans found themselves relegated to the Eastside. Cayton recognized parts of Black Los Angeles as "overcrowded, tense, and tawdry."[6] Through the 1940s Angelenos faced a severe housing shortage. The influx of migrants combined with residential discrimination in Los Angeles and other cities nationwide gave way to a scarcity of housing. The federal government sought to alleviate the crisis by passing public housing measures, and, after several years of intense debate, anti–public housing activists succeeded in dismantling the program. The local Black elite found further reason to migrate westward.

While courts across the country saw a growing number of lawsuits over restrictive covenants through the 1940s, the Sugar Hill case not only raised public awareness of the fight, but also took a major step toward a national legal victory in the long campaign against racial contracts. Reporters from leading newspapers and journals across the country took notice of the case, and prominent Black entertainers, professionals, and community leaders stepped into the forefront of the legal campaign. The *New York Times, New York Herald, Chicago Defender, Time* magazine, and the NAACP's *The Crisis*, as well as local Black- and White-owned newspapers, kept readers informed of the Los Angeles story.[7] But, more importantly, the judge's surprising verdict in the case helped set the precedent for subsequent proceedings that resulted in the legal demise of restrictive covenants. While courts across the country refused to acknowledge that restrictive covenants violated the

Fourteenth Amendment, Judge Thurmond Clarke in the Los Angeles Superior Court saw, in the Sugar Hill case, the contracts as unequivocal infringements on citizens' constitutional rights. Three years before the US Supreme Court in *Shelley v. Kraemer* (1948) declared restrictive covenants legally unenforceable, Clarke took a stand against housing discrimination.

LOS ANGELES'S SHIFTING POLITICAL CLIMATE AND DEMOGRAPHICS

Los Angeles's political shift to a Democratic majority through the 1930s and 1940s provided civil rights activists with an added layer of support. Liberal-minded public officials worked toward undoing political corruption, reforming public services, and ending racial discrimination. Before 1932 California and Los Angeles primarily voted Republican candidates into office. The party of President Abraham Lincoln claimed a legacy of combating Confederate Democrats and passing the Thirteenth, Fourteenth, and Fifteenth Amendments. But from the 1920s, as the Republican Party increasingly supported big business, limited regulation, and lowered taxes for the rich, its constituents began to question their party affiliation. Then in 1932, because of the landslide election of President Franklin D. Roosevelt, Los Angeles's political climate underwent a "dramatic change," as explained by California attorney general Robert Walker Kenny. Californians elected more Democrats to office. African Americans still had to proceed on the grassroots level in fighting against racial discrimination, but the Democratic majority helped bolster their efforts.[8]

Through the 1930s Democratic candidates in California won political positions. They obtained seats in the state senate, and in 1936 they achieved a majority in the state assembly and chose the speaker. Los Angeles also voted more Democrats into office. In 1934 African American Democrat Augustus Hawkins defeated sixteen-year-long incumbent Republican Frederick Roberts in the state assembly race, thus becoming representative of the Sixty-Second district that included Central Avenue. Midwest-born, reform-minded, White Democrat John Anson Ford also gained a seat as Los Angeles County supervisor. His efforts to clean up local government, improve education, advance the arts, end racial discrimination, and promote positive race relations, particularly through his Commission on Interracial Progress, which he established in 1944, made Ford a leading liberal figure throughout the subsequent decades.[9]

The 1938 mayoral election of Democrat Fletcher Bowron also reflected the shifting political climate to racial liberalism. Bowron came to office in a recall election against Frank Shaw, a centrist Republican who began his second term in office under a cloud of scandals and facing a well-organized reform movement determined to expose his transgressions. Bowron served as mayor during a transformative period of Los Angeles's history. Under his leadership from 1938 to 1953, historian Tom Sitton explains, Los Angeles evolved "from a regional center to a national powerhouse." Bowron facilitated this change by rooting out corruption from the Shaw administration and implementing reforms to improve the police department, public works, health department, and other civil service agencies. Before World War II Bowron showed little concern for the racial issues plaguing the city. The growth in defense industry jobs, the influx of migrants into the city, and residential discrimination led to a severe housing shortage. In 1943, following the Sleepy Lagoon murder and the zoot suit attacks, as well as race riots across the country, the mayor finally turned his attention to the issue.[10]

Through the 1940s tens of thousands of African Americans migrated to the city to find employment and improve their quality of life. The federal administration's expansion of the defense industry helped Los Angeles become one of the foremost industrial manufacturing hubs in the nation. California became a leading center in aircraft and shipbuilding, and Los Angeles alone received more than $11 billion worth of contracts for war production. African Americans benefited from the wartime exigencies, but only after they had mobilized for equal protection. Pressured by A. Philip Randolph, head of the Brotherhood of Sleeping Car Porters, President Roosevelt passed Executive Order 8802 in 1941, which prohibited discrimination in national defense work. While Blacks continued to face discrimination, to be hired last, and to get shut out of unions, by 1944 the defense industries in Los Angeles employed more than thirty thousand African Americans. No longer having to settle for domestic or janitorial work, Blacks found skilled positions as riveters, welders, and machine-operators. But, as the city expanded, new challenges arose for them: compounded by the rise in population and state sanction of housing discrimination, and the pause in housing construction through the war, Los Angeles, like many cities across the country, suffered an acute housing shortage that left thousands living in squalid conditions.[11]

Despite the progress made toward equal treatment in the defense industry, the few residential areas available to Black Angelenos became overcrowded. The population of Central Avenue, the city's foremost Black area since the early twentieth century, grew from 45,000 in 1940 to more than 70,000 in 1946. As more Blacks moved into the corridor, they challenged its racial boundaries and found housing in the adjacent communities. Upon the 1942 federal order that enforced the removal of some 120,000 Japanese Americans on the West Coast, which included around 37,000 in Los Angeles County alone, to concentration camps in the interior West,

African Americans moved into Japanese American residences, including those in Little Tokyo, West Jefferson, Uptown, Hollywood/J-Flats, and Boyle Heights. While thousands of Japanese Americans relinquished their jobs, sold their property, and lost their savings, wartime incarceration opened space for African Americans to find homes, particularly in Little Tokyo, and establish businesses and religious and cultural institutions in the commercial center. But the population jumped from thirty thousand before forced removal to roughly eighty thousand in mid-1944, turning Little Tokyo into what was called Bronzeville, an overcrowded community that existed for about three years.[12]

African Americans also challenged the Eastside's southern and eastern racial borders. During the 1940s more Blacks migrated to the multiethnic, multiracial, blue-collar community of Watts. Long before it incorporated into Los Angeles in 1926, the sleepy enclave offered affordable, unrestricted housing near the public transit system to a diverse population comprising Blacks, Whites, Asians, and Latinos. Alongside Black influx, the population of Watts grew from 16,955 in 1940 to 25,799 in 1950. Willowbrook, the area directly south of Watts, also underwent an increase in the Black population. But when Blacks attempted to migrate eastward into Lynwood and southward into Compton, they faced White resistance. The 1950 census reported only sixteen African Americans residing in Lynwood. White blue-collar workers also guarded Compton against Black settlement. Through the 1940s a small number of African Americans successfully cracked Rosecrans Avenue. But as Blacks migrated closer to Rosecrans, Whites defended each neighborhood block with fervor, proclaiming, "Keep the Negroes North of 130th Street," and then "Keep the Negroes North of 134th Street."[13]

Consequently, the unrestricted Eastside neighborhoods fell into disrepair. Rather than maintaining or improving their properties, many White landowners exploited the critical need for housing. They partitioned their Eastside apartments into smaller living spaces and inflated rental fees. Renters had to share rooms with extended family members, friends, and strangers. The small living spaces provided little space, and some roommates had to rotate turns sleeping in limited beds. As landowners neglected their properties, apartments became dilapidated, unhygienic, and disease-ridden. Renters lived without adequate space, proper ventilation, or a functioning sanitation system, remindful of the substandard conditions in tenements in industrial cities at the turn of the twentieth century and camps of impoverished itinerant workers in the Great Depression. "In place after place children lived in windowless rooms, amid peeling plaster, rats, and the flies that gathered thick around food," Dorothy Baruch of the *Nation* reported on Bronzeville in 1945. Typhus, tuberculosis, meningitis, and other diseases thrived in these environments. African Americans who lacked the financial resources or good fortune to find housing had to make homes out of abandoned businesses, automobiles, garages, and chicken coops. Others slept in train stations or on the streets. Out of sheer racism and disregard for the basic needs of Black city dwellers, local officials initially overlooked the problems. "By such means we create hopelessness in our midst," Baruch warned, in hindsight of the race riots in Los Angeles, Detroit, Harlem, and elsewhere, "We create protest, and hatred that strikes out blindly. We cause the desire for retaliation to mount until it finds release."[14]

For his first five years in office, Bowron provided limited support despite the housing shortage, while the city's housing authority took action. In 1938, one year after the Roosevelt administration signed the Wagner-Steagall Housing Act into law, a New Deal initiative that financed state agencies with loans for low-cost housing, and the same year Bowron first won the mayoral race, California established the Housing Authority of the City of Los Angeles (HACLA) to provide housing support to low-income and working-class residents. While Bowron initially had doubts about public housing, progressive Angelenos rallied behind the welfare state's initiative, viewing it as a means to aid the neediest city dwellers, provide them with a space to foster their well-being and financial conditions, and cultivate community development. After months of delay from city council members and the mayor, who pressed supporters to prove the value of public housing, the first developments received approval.[15]

From 1939 to 1942, with the backing of the 1937 Housing Act, the HACLA forged ahead with the construction of ten permanent housing projects that, in total, provided 3,468 units for low-income Angelenos. These housing projects—all but one of which had an Eastside address—were designed by some of the city's preeminent architects, including Richard Neutra, Robert Alexander, and Paul R. Williams, all of whom considered in their plans residents' range of daily activities, from work to housework, and from recreation to social interactions. During the war HACLA also oversaw five permanent, federally financed public housing war projects, located around the harbor's wartime plants that, in sum, provided 1,538 units, and were expected to be transferred or sold at war's end. Additionally, HACLA managed twenty-two temporary public housing war projects mainly on the Eastside, aimed at quickly and inexpensively furnishing defense workers with housing, which, in total, amounted to 7,293 units. And it constructed five temporary projects for veterans mostly in the city's central and harbor areas that totaled 3,670 units.[16]

Bowron finally took steps to ease the housing crisis in 1943, out of concern that the city would undergo further racial unrest following the Sleepy

Lagoon murder, the zoot suit attacks, and riots across the country, and under mounting pressure from local activists. That August he scheduled a meeting and appointed Norman O. Houston, Los Angeles Urban League director Floyd Covington, and Judge Edwin L. Jefferson as his advisors; he expanded the board in January 1944. Some of the appointees represented the Los Angeles Negro Victory Committee, a coalition of local Black leaders who set forth an ambitious agenda to fight against discrimination in housing, employment, and the armed forces; increase Black political representation; end racial violence; and attain better educational opportunities for African Americans. Part of the broader Double V campaign, the local victory committee used its support of the war as leverage to pressure authorities to meet its demands. Among his housing initiatives, Bowron raised the quota that apportioned only 7 percent of Blacks to live in public housing. In early 1944 he implemented measures that entailed condemning buildings and removing residents from Bronzeville, while health officials tested them for syphilis and gonorrhea. In March 1945, seeking to address the one hundred thousand outstanding housing applications, Bowron appealed for federal aid to construct eighty thousand temporary units, which would add to the twenty-four thousand units that private industry was expected to build. When Covington stepped down from the HACLA commission board, Bowron appointed long-time activist and entrepreneur George Beavers to the position. Beavers served as the sole Black member between 1946 and 1962, rising to acting vice-chair and then chair.[17]

Despite these efforts, the housing shortage persisted, and as Japanese Americans returned from incarceration, accommodations remained limited. Soon after December 1944, when the US Department of War rescinded President Roosevelt's Executive Order 9066 and the War Relocation Authority (WRA) began the resettlement process, Japanese Americans had to face the decisions of where to return and how to rebuild after losing their jobs, property, and savings. In 1945 alone, more than fifteen thousand Japanese Americans relocated to Los Angeles County. The WRA set up intentionally meager, temporary housing to hasten the thousands of homeless Japanese to find permanent residence. With few options, some capitulated to makeshift homes, cramped living spaces, or boardinghouses. Many returned to the communities they had evacuated before their deportation and faced hostile residents who had settled there in their absence. In Bronzeville rumors of Blacks planning to riot upon the return of Japanese residents fueled tension but never came to fruition. Still, others attempted to move into restricted areas. When Takeshi Saito and his family moved into a house in West Jefferson at 2947 Dalton Avenue, White residents filed a lawsuit claiming the Saito family violated a restrictive covenant. In 1946 Judge Henry M. Willis of the

Los Angeles Superior Court sided with the plaintiffs and forbade the Saitos from occupying the house; that same year the Sugar Hill case headed to the California Supreme Court, which upheld Willis's decision. As the displaced Japanese reestablished their lives, they had to compete for housing with other marginalized Angelenos.[18] On the southern end of Central Avenue, Watts faced its own set of challenges. By the end of the 1940s, the previously diverse community had become solidly Black and neglected. While Watts's Black population rose from around 31 percent in 1940 to 70 percent in 1950, defense industries closed, joblessness increased, Whites moved away from the area, and Blacks had no political representation.[19]

Bowron also failed to ease the housing crisis, and in many ways he intensified the racial and ethnic tensions in the city. Alongside his California colleagues, state attorney general Earl Warren and Governor Culbert Olson, Bowron supported the forced removal of Japanese Americans from the West Coast. He then exacerbated Japanese postwar struggles when he refused to aid their transition home and helped spread fabricated rumors of an imminent riot in Bronzeville upon their return. He showed the same disregard for Mexican Americans. Despite his response to ameliorate the housing crisis after the zoot suit attacks (when bands of soldiers and sailors raided Mexican American neighborhoods, and assaulted pachucos, Mexican American youths with a flashy sartorial style, in the summer of 1943), Bowron defended the actions of the police and sympathized with the rioters. Like many racial liberals, Bowron simultaneously furthered racial equity and racial discrimination.[20] Amid these conflicts over living conditions in Los Angeles and other growing western and midwestern cities, affluent Blacks pulled together their resources and drew on the Democrat-led establishment and the work of reform-minded thinkers to challenge restrictive covenants.

THE WAHPA TAKES ACTION

Beginning in 1943, while many Sugar Hill newcomers lived in precarious conditions, anticipating their White neighbors would file a legal complaint against them, the newcomers began meeting to formulate their defense. In March seventeen homeowners gathered at William and Edith Bailey's South Hobart Boulevard house; after discussing the community's restrictive covenant and two legal opinions that stated reasons for the covenant's possible invalidity, they moved to form an organization to defend their right to live in the neighborhood. They unanimously agreed on their name, the West Adams Heights Protective Association (WAHPA), in contrast to their White neighbors' WAHIA, and elected Norman O. Houston president, Louise Beavers vice president, Edith Bailey secretary, Leslie King treasurer, and Ben Carter chair of public relations. They also appointed a committee to establish a constitution and bylaws, and decided to notify the press about their formation.[21]

At its second meeting, in April 1943, the WAHPA approved its structure, procedures, and leadership roles. It adopted a constitution and bylaws. Under Article I, the association sought to "maintain and improve the standard of the homes"; share news and information on neighborhood codes and assessments; protect the legal rights "of any member regardless of race, color or creed, to peacefully occupy any properties"; and educate residents on "maintaining the tract as the outstanding residential district in the City." The WAHPA purported in its constitution to elect officers; run committees, including a committee on legal rights; collect membership fees (a $1 initial fee and a 50¢ monthly fee); and hold monthly meetings. Through the subsequent years, the WAHPA met regularly, sometimes more than once a month, rotating the meetings' locations at each of the members' homes, and concluding each meeting with a prayer or what they called a "mizpah," a reference to a covenant or agreement Jacob and Laban made in the Hebrew biblical story to commemorate their pact. Leslie King, WAHPA's treasurer and chair of the legal committee, further formalized the association by gifting it with printed stationary, notecards, and a records book.[22]

Four days following the second meeting, Sydnetta Dones Smith, Sidney Dones, and their nine renters faced a lawsuit over their right to live in their home. While Dones Smith and her father had not yet attended a WAHPA meeting, and none of its existing members had yet been served, the group mobilized, knowing anyone could be next, and met consistently throughout May. Maintaining traditional, mid-twentieth-century male responsibilities, Sidney Dones worked directly with the WAHPA and managed the case against his daughter's property. At the May 2 meeting, Secretary Edith Bailey recorded, Dones granted the legal committee "power of attorney to take all legal actions necessary." At the May 4 meeting, he joined the group and paid membership fees. Hattie McDaniel also attended and paid membership fees, and attorney Loren Miller came to provide counsel. On May 6, 1943, the WAHPA met again, and agreed to secure Miller as chief counsel for the Dones Smith case. The next day, May 7, with Miller present, according to Edith Bailey WAHPA members readily agreed to pitch in, support their neighbors, and pay Miller $500 ($250 up front for the retainer) for his legal fees. By the meeting's end, members had contributed their $20 share for the retainer, and the group needed only $30 more, which it collected and more within a week. Challenging housing discrimination came with a high cost. The effort not only drained Sugar Hill residents' time and energy as they juggled working full-time jobs, raising children, and fighting a legal battle but it also required their financial resources. The WAHPA hired Miller to serve as lead attorney; like a few other Sugar Hill residents who soon thereafter faced a similar legal complaint, Dones also hired his own attorney, Clarence A. Jones.[23]

Loren Miller, however, ultimately headed the case. Miller began his legal career in Los Angeles a little more than a decade before the Sugar Hill case. Born in 1903 to an interracial couple in Pender, Nebraska, and in the face of unceasing poverty, Miller pursued his education at the University of Kansas, spent some time at Howard University, and in 1928 earned a law degree from Washburn College (later Washburn University) in Topeka, Kansas, where he passed the Kansas bar exam. For about a year, Miller practiced in the Midwest. Then in 1929, he joined his family in Los Angeles to attend his sister's funeral. His mother had moved to the city several years earlier, and because the California economy was faring better than the Midwest at the onset of the Great Depression, Miller decided to stay. He also needed a reason to leave his profession. "I...wasn't enamored [with] the law to put it mildly," he explained. Miller worked on Black-owned newspapers, including the *California News* and the *California Eagle*. In the 1930s he also became active in far-left-wing politics. He criticized the NAACP and the established Black leadership as conservative, cautious, and self-interested. He grew more emboldened on a trip he took to the Soviet Union in 1932 with poet Langston Hughes and other Black activists. They sought to make a film on race relations in the American South; the film never came to fruition, much to the delight of the Western press. But, echoing muckraker Lincoln Steffens, Miller stated, "I've seen the future and I believe that it worked." Upon his return he continued writing for left-wing publications and Black-owned newspapers, and then in 1933 founded the *Los Angeles Sentinel*, with his cousin, Leon Washington, Jr.[24]

Miller's far left political stance came from his drive to eradicate poverty and achieve racial equality, and he ultimately returned to the legal profession to achieve his goals. In 1934, after passing the California state bar exam, he launched his law practice in Los Angeles. Miller later revealed that he returned to law "more in self defense than anything else." Journalism paid little, and the more friends questioned Miller on his law school background, the more he needed to prove to them his capabilities. But Miller had deeper motives for returning to the profession. He saw the law as an avenue to fight against racial injustice. Since the early twentieth century, his attorney colleagues had demonstrated steadfast determination in their work against racial discrimination. Until 1878 the state of California prohibited African Americans from being admitted to the bar. In the subsequent decades, particularly through the early twentieth century, African American litigators in Los Angeles, such as Charles S. Darden, Burton Ceruti, Hugh E. Macbeth, and Willis O. Tyler, paved an unmarked path, and their efforts set an example for future Black attorneys. In the 1930s Miller emerged as one of the next generation of attorneys to carry the torch. He earned admiration for his bold journalism and passionate speeches, but his legal work catapulted him into the national arena as an ardent civil rights crusader.[25]

In his first few years as a Los Angeles litigator, Miller handled routine disputes, such as probate and divorce matters, while he secured new clients and developed his reputation, but he also undertook lawsuits in the 1930s and 1940s that championed racist policies and practices. For instance, he sued the Rollerdome Ice Skating Rink for denying African American youngsters' admission and the Gunther Drug Store in Beverly Hills for refusing to serve two African American women. With the Southern California branch of the American Civil Liberties Union (ACLU), he challenged Japanese American evacuation and incarceration. He fought city officials at the regional planning commission against a zoning ordinance that prohibited an African American family from using part of their home for their electric business. He submitted an amicus brief on behalf of Black workers confronting inequitable auxiliary union fees from the shipyard.[26] Beyond his law practice, he managed Augustus Hawkins's 1934 state assembly campaign that defeated Roberts and helped shift California to ruling by the Democratic Party; he became further involved in numerous local and national groups, including the NAACP, National Urban League, ACLU, National Negro Conference, and US Commission on Civil Rights; and he continued to write for left-wing and Black-owned publications. In 1935, with the emotional and financial backing of his spouse, USC-graduate Juanita Ellsworth Miller, who had for years supported his endeavors with her steady income as a social worker, he went to New York to work for a brief stint at the *New Masses*. But it was his fight against restrictive covenants, starting in the late 1930s, that earned him much of his esteemed reputation.[27]

His work against racial restrictions accelerated in the early 1940s, especially after he teamed up with Willis O. Tyler. Before Miller became involved in the legal campaign, starting in the 1910s Tyler had enjoyed some victories fighting against restrictive covenants in the California courts. He helped secure the appeal against Homer Garrott in the California Supreme Court in 1919, and he defended the residents in West Jefferson's Crestmore tract in the late 1920s, but because of the US Supreme Court case *Corrigan v. Buckley* (1926) and judicial impediments, he achieved little success against racial contracts until the 1940s.[28] The first major victory for Miller and Tyler came in a lawsuit that had been filed against a Black couple who had purchased a home in a restricted section of Pasadena. Hazel Fairchild and several other White homeowners tried to prohibit Ross and Helen Raines from residing in the home they had bought. The trial court and California Court of Appeals affirmed the plaintiffs' claim, but the California Supreme Court reversed the decision. In the final opinion in *Fairchild v. Raines* (1944), the judge found that, counter to the trial court's records, since the adjacent, unrestricted blocks underwent a "change in the character" when Blacks moved to the area, "it would be oppressive and inequitable to give the restriction effect" in the Raines's community. Put another way, Black migration to the nearby blocks negated the objective of the restrictive covenant. *Fairchild* showed that a "change in the character" of the community brought Blacks closer to defeating covenants.[29] The decision represented a breakthrough for Miller and Tyler, but they had further steps to take. The verdict made no reference to the Fourteenth Amendment, which the attorneys needed to proclaim covenants unconstitutional.

While men, including Norman O. Houston and then J. A. Somerville, headed the WAHPA, and male attorneys such as Miller, Tyler, and Jones argued the case, women had central roles in fighting the Sugar Hill case. The WAHPA secretaries Edith Bailey (1943–44), Aulette Allen (1944–45), and Pearl S. Taylor (1945 to at least 1947), meticulously kept track of the members and dues owed and paid; managed the meeting schedule and locations; penned meeting minutes; sent communications to WAHPA members, Sugar Hill homeowners, and community leaders; took part in neighborhood maintenance and improvement projects; and fought against the restrictive covenant. Louise Beavers served as WAHPA's first vice president, and with McDaniel and teacher Senola Green, also led the WAHPA's committee on social interest. Meeting minutes likewise demonstrate that the female WAHPA members consistently shared their ideas and views, and volunteered their time to win the case. Through the mid-1940s, as more Blacks moved to Sugar Hill and Whites' antagonism increased, WAHPA membership rose. In 1943, its first year, forty-two residents, representing twenty-three households, joined the association. By the late 1940s, according to the WAHPA's master list, membership had more than doubled. Some ninety people, representing fifty households, affiliated themselves with the association.[30]

After many planning and organizing meetings, and then a summer hiatus, the WAHPA reconvened on September 24, 1944, to an intensified environment. The Los Angeles Superior Court had scheduled the Dones Smith case for October 18, and, according to Secretary Allen, WAHPA member Yolanda Billingsley reported that the WAHIA urged its members "to fight." Mr. Williams (first name unknown) added, the WAHIA "had secured 27 volunteers to canvass the neighborhood to determine the extent of colored invasion." Miller joined the meeting to update the group on the *Fairchild* decision; although it was different from the Dones Smith case, its "spirit...is advantageous." Miller urged the WAHPA to bring "a large audience" to the trial, and asked Leslie King to serve as a witness and Norman O. Houston and Angelus Funeral Home secretary-treasurer Lorenzo Bowdoin to testify. Miller also explained that, as the title company verifies the covenant's signatures, "he believes about 70% of the properties are restricted." Feeling uneasy that they could lose, WAHPA members mobilized. Leslie King agreed to gather an inventory of the neighborhood's homeowners, including their names, addresses, home purchase dates, and any home renovations. The WAHPA legal committee aimed to ask White sellers Deborah O'Reilly and George and Isabel Cryer to testify. Aulette Allen agreed to write letters to the WAHPA members and homeowners with information on the "trial date, legal fees," and more. When the WAHPA met on October 12, six days before the scheduled trial, its female members had used a call tree to disseminate the trial date and location, and to encourage residents to attend.[31]

In highly tense conditions pending the upcoming trial, the WAHPA received frustrating news. The plaintiffs' attorneys "asked for postponement"; while Miller refused to accept their appeal, according to Allen's October 29 minutes "the case was thrown off the docket." The WAHPA would have to wait longer for the court to schedule another date. "Apparently the opposing group did not put up sufficient funds to fight the case," J. A. Somerville explained. At the next meeting, on November 26, 1944, according to Allen, Leslie King assured attendees, "We are in a good condition, but...we must be on our guard." Anticipating future events, Houston then warned, "Since the Dones case is off the docket the opposing force may sue anyone else." Meanwhile, the WAHPA continued to monitor the case's press coverage, correct any misinformation, track local covenant cases, and prepare for trial.[32]

Almost half a year later, or two years after Dones Smith was served with the legal complaint, conditions again intensified. According to then-secretary Pearl Taylor's March 25, 1945, minutes, White homeowners had filed five additional legal complaints against other Sugar Hill newcomers. More White neighbors brought more Black neighbors into a lawsuit. Miller, who again joined the meeting, advised the group, "It is better to have all defendants sued together...[because] the more cases the less expensive" legal fees the WAHPA and the defendants would incur. He believed he could make a persuasive argument since "some of the properties are not restricted" and thus, if the judge upholds the covenant, some people of color could remain in the area. Since "the defendants have improved the property," he can also challenge the plaintiffs' arguments that the newcomers contributed to neighborhood deterioration. Both Norman Houston and William Bailey recommended that WAHPA members hire Miller as their attorney, if they had not already, and, Bailey added and Taylor recorded, "as soon as [they get] served to notify" the WAHPA secretary or president. Most meeting attendees agreed to hire Miller, and at the WAHPA's next meeting, on May 27, Miller collected $75 toward his fee from his clients, including Sidney Dones and J. A. and Vada Somerville. WAHPA members also continued to pay the association's dues. While the court had not yet scheduled a trial date, Miller explained, and he had not yet identified other attorneys to work with him, Taylor recorded, "all would be tried at the same time." Houston reiterated, Taylor wrote, it "would be a 'team case.'"[33]

Throughout the 1940s Miller's workload increased. Months before the litigants of the Sugar Hill case met in the courtroom, Miller alone was involved in nearly twenty covenant cases. While "Los Angeles was ground zero for the process," writes legal scholar Kenneth Mack, lawsuits against racial contracts cropped up across the country. As Miller was battling restrictive covenants in Los Angeles, he was corresponding with attorneys and organizations across the country over the issue. Black homeowners facing lawsuits hired attorneys if they could afford to, such as many of those in Sugar Hill, or turned to local civil rights organizations, including NAACP branches, for aid. Many of those legal activists, some of whom volunteered or worked for little pay, built a national communication network that exchanged ideas, strategies, and struggles. While the national NAACP had been fighting housing discrimination since its establishment in 1909, Thurgood Marshall, who founded its Legal Defense and Educational Fund in 1940, saw an opportunity with the rise of covenant cases to pull together a group in July 1945. At the two-day Chicago conference, he and legal activists and attorneys, including Miller, discussed a strategy to challenge restrictive covenants and which legal claims to try in the US Supreme Court. Marshall then announced at the meeting's end that the NAACP would devote its work to the fight against covenants.[34]

By the time of WAHPA's September 23, 1945, meeting, the Los Angeles Superior Court had scheduled a trial date for December 5, which, Taylor recorded, Houston "stressed the necessity of" attending. The WAHPA continued to prepare for trial by hiring a photographer to create a portfolio with pictures of their homes and streets as proof of the community's high quality. While the NAACP was organizing against covenants, WAHPA members agreed that they did not need the national association's financial support, but might consider asking it to "sit in on the case." The following month, when the WAHPA met again, Miller again updated the group on the case. By that time, Miller explained and Taylor recorded, the plaintiffs had employed five White attorneys to argue for the covenant's validity, and Miler had hired Willis O. Tyler to assist him. Miller also urged, as he had done before, for "a large number of persons" to come to the trial.[35]

"A DECISION OF GREAT MOMENT"

On December 5, 1945, after several years of organizing and preparing for trial, the Sugar Hill case convened in the Los Angeles Superior Court to settle arguments on the constitutionality of racial restrictive covenants. Local and national Black- and White-run newspapers reported the events as they unfolded. On the first day of the trial roughly 250 litigants and spectators filed into the "packed courtroom," according to one account, to observe the hearing and causes célèbres.[36] For two hours the lawyers presented their opening arguments to the court. Leading the defense, Miller argued that introduction of evidence or testimony in court remained futile, because restrictive covenants not only defined racial identity on illogical and unscientific terms, but also and ultimately violated the equal protection clause of the Fourteenth Amendment. After hearing opening arguments, in a rare turn of events, Judge Thurmond Clarke adjourned the proceedings and went with the attorneys to investigate and "determine the present status" of the Sugar Hill population.[37] What happened in the next twenty-four hours foreshadowed the legal demise of racial restrictive covenants.

Despite one reporter's prediction that "the trial seems destined to last more than a month," Clarke handed down his ruling one day after the opening proceedings.[38] The native Californian, who had earned his law degree at USC in 1927 and climbed the ranks in the legal profession rather quickly from district attorney to city attorney, and then Los Angeles municipal court judge to superior court judge in the mid-1930s, made a groundbreaking decision.[39] Based on the litigators' opening arguments and Clarke's subsequent investigation into the so-called character of the neighborhood, the judge granted Miller's objections against the introduction of evidence or testimony. Miller took a risk, deciding against including any briefs or testimonies; rather than challenging covenanters' individual rights to engage in private contracts, he relied exclusively on using the state action strategy. Backed by the work of legal scholars, he argued state enforcement of restrictive covenants violates the equal protection clause of the Fourteenth Amendment. Some attorneys before Miller had tested the argument to no avail, but Clarke found it persuasive, departed from precedent in *Corrigan*, and ruled that the plaintiffs' complaints presented insufficient cause of action under the equal protection clause for his court to continue the proceedings. "It is time members of the Negro race are accorded without reservations and evasion the full rights guaranteed them under the 14th Amendment," he made clear. Clarke's reading of constitutional law set him apart from his colleagues, and, in line with the state action argument, he called on the judiciary to correct the problem. "Judges have been avoiding the real issue for too long," he scorned.[40]

While Miller decided against introducing evidence, he "furnished" Clarke with two 1945 scholarly articles from Harold Kahen and Dudley Odell McGovney, both of whom had made a case for the state action strategy. "Those two reviews seem to me to exhaust the law on the matter," Miller explained.[41] In "Validity of Anti-Negro Restrictive Covenants: A Reconsideration of the Problem," which was published in *The University of Chicago Law Review*, Illinois attorney Kahen advised attorneys to include sociological, census, and demographic data, which Miller decided against, and argue before the court that, "For constitutional purposes, judicial enforcement of restrictive covenants is state action which should not be permitted where legislation to the same effect would be invalid." McGovney helped lead the shift in legal views in California, and create a new intellectual environment, by coming out against restrictive covenants. After earning a law degree at Columbia University in 1907, McGovney built an extensive academic résumé in teaching, administration, and scholarship. As a law professor at the University of California, Berkeley, McGovney published an article in the *California Law Review* arguing that by sanctioning restrictive covenants, the state violated the US Constitution. McGovney stated in his title, "Racial Residential Segregation *by State Court Enforcement of* Restrictive Agreements, Covenants or Conditions in Deeds Is Unconstitutional." His article would support the defense not only in the California court, but also in the US Supreme Court.[42]

In addition to Miller's state action argument, the war and its exigencies influenced Clarke to depart from legal precedent. The horrific goals of Adolf Hitler to exterminate Jews, Romani, Poles, homosexuals, and other "non-Aryans" awakened the United States to its own racism. Black involvement in World War II also shaped Clarke's decision. "Certainly there was no discrimination against the Negro race when it came to calling upon its members to die on the battlefields in defense of this country in the war," he asserted. He was evoking the more than 1 million African Americans who served the US armed forces in segregated units, and others who became riveters and welders in the defense industry, rationed food and gasoline, and waited for their loved ones to return home. The WAHPA members and Sugar Hill case defendants became some of the leaders of the Double V campaign. On the Hollywood Negro Victory Committee, Hattie McDaniel toured military camps, visited wounded soldiers, and led war bond rallies. Ethel Waters entertained Black troops and sponsored servicewomen. Henry Taylor and Jessie Elmore welcomed service members into their seventeen-room 2156 South Hobart Boulevard home, providing "full course dinners, long distance telephone calls and comfortable beds," the *Los Angeles Sentinel* reported.[43]

The defense's dedication, financial resources, and fame helped bring about a legal victory. Miller had a reputation as dynamic and gifted, and formed alliances in the community and across the country for years before the case. The Sugar Hill's Black residents, including those who ultimately did not get served, also contributed their own money, time, and energy to the campaign. Most began fighting against racial discrimination decades before the Sugar Hill case went to trial. Houston, the Somervilles, and the Clarks established businesses to improve the conditions of Blacks in the city. McDaniel and Waters challenged racial stereotypes as best they could in their on-screen roles. Shortly after J. A. Somerville helped found the NAACP Los Angeles branch in 1913, many of the defendants joined the group, and they remained long-time members. They also joined forces with the Los Angeles Urban League and the ACLU of Southern California. In the Double V campaign, they led the fight for victory abroad and at home. Then in 1943, before Dones Smith faced the formal legal complaint, they formed the WAHPA. As successful professionals, they had financial resources and personal connections to challenge restrictive covenants. Dones, and McDaniel and Crawford, for instance, hired their own attorneys to represent them. While Miller collaborated with several attorneys, including Tyler, Macbeth, and Jones, he served as lead defense attorney in the trial.[44]

As the defendants prepared for court, Hattie McDaniel, Ethel Waters, Louise Beavers, Juan Tizol, and other entertainers received most of the press's attention. Criticized for conforming to Black stereotypes in her roles in the entertainment industry, McDaniel refused to give into racial discrimination in her personal life. She censored herself at the studio but put her name on the line to defend her and her neighbors' properties by joining the WAHPA, hiring her own attorneys, and appearing in court. McDaniel and the other entertainers had that star quality that would help attract the news. Not surprisingly, references to the entertainers appeared in many of the newspaper reports on the case. More than a year before the case went to trial, the *Chicago Defender* reported the case using the title, "Film Stars Face Eviction from West Coast Homes." One day after the trial began, the *Los Angeles Times* reported that "film Academy Award winner" McDaniel and "blues songbird" Waters led the Black property owners into the courtroom. Following the victory, *Time* magazine reported, "many [of the defendants] were movie folk—Actresses Louise Beavers, Hattie McDaniel, Ethel Waters, etc." Entertainers raised public awareness and pressured the courts, and the defendants and litigators worked hard to win the case.[45]

In fact, the press's emphasis on the entertainers made some WAHPA members, who believed they had put more work into the case, resentful. Pearl Taylor recorded that, at the June 30, 1946, meeting, WAHPA member Elizabeth Edwards and others maintained "that more publicity was given [to] movie stars living in the tract than those of us who had really engaged a lawyer to defend us." Houston suggested "that emphasis be placed upon the line of importance of the neighborhood and not the movie column."[46] The WAHPA saw their fight within the larger context of racial equality. For instance, as they prepared for the Sugar Hill case they discussed building connections with new residents and the community at large, Edith Bailey recorded, "to bring about better conditions among Negroes." Yet they also believed that to maintain the high quality of the neighborhood, they had to push out "undesirable roomers" from rental properties, which validated working-class Blacks' criticism that middle-class Blacks abandoned them for the Westside.[47]

Civil rights activists celebrated the Sugar Hill victory. On its front page, in bold and capital letters, the *Los Angeles Sentinel* acclaimed, "Sugar Hill Victory Sets U.S. Precedent." McDaniel extolled, reported *Time* magazine, "Words cannot express my appreciation." Miller received congratulations letters from across the country. Noah Griffin, Regional Director of the West Coast NAACP, based in San Francisco, wrote that "reverberation [of the case] will be felt throughout [the] nation." Theodore Spaulding, a Philadelphia attorney, anticipated the decision as the "first step towards the ultimate elimination of restrictive covenants in America." William Hastie, Howard University Dean, celebrated, "We in the East are almost as enthusiastic as you are about the decision." Rufus Clement, president of Georgia's Atlanta University, described the decision as an "epochal victory." Miller also wrote to others in celebration, including Norman O. Houston, the first African American to purchase a home in Sugar Hill, with a rhetorical question: "Won't you consider yourself thanked?"[48]

After he handed down his decision, Judge Clarke received an outpouring of letters that reflected the mixed reaction in the city. Parents, ministers, and other supporters praised his decision as brave and bold. Mothers of sons who fought beside African Americans in the war believed Clarke made the right decision. Yet Clarke also received mail from detractors, some of whom warned him that he would lose his position as judge in the coming election and be forced to scrape by on meager earnings representing Blacks on Central Avenue. Newspapers reported one letter writer railing that, because of his decision, Clarke, a race traitor, will have to get by "practicing law on Central avenue among his Negro friends." The writer implied Blacks should be relegated to the lowest-paying jobs and the city's de facto segregated neighborhoods. Clarke, however, remained undeterred by the criticism and stood by his decision. When Clarke faced a 1948 reelection as Los Angeles Superior Court judge, the WAHPA extended its support. Clarke maintained his position on the court until 1955 when President Dwight Eisenhower nominated him to the US District Court, Southern District of California. He rose to chief judge there until the mid-1960s, and then transferred to the

US District Court, Central District of California, where he served until his death in 1971.[49]

Upon its victory, the defense team braced for another fight ahead. Tyler hailed Clarke's ruling as "a decision of great moment" but indicated a degree of uncertainty, explaining, "It is hoped that it will be the turning point in the efforts of the Negro people of this city" to freely exercise their right to property. The defense team, he asserted, stood prepared to take the case to the California Supreme Court and the US Supreme Court. Miller also regularly updated Thurgood Marshall on the progress of the Sugar Hill case. On the day of the decision, Miller wrote to Marshall with the good news that "the Court sustained our motion," yet warned, "We are certain that there will be an appeal" and asked for "any suggestions" as well as amicus briefs to strengthen the defense. Miller continued, "We hope that in the event of an adverse decision in the [state] Supreme Court, the United States Supreme Court will grant a review." Less than one week later, noting the significance of the ruling and yet acknowledging the fight ahead, Marshall replied, "Congratulations on the victory so far" and promised to provide Miller with support to take the case to the high court. "Maybe this is it," Marshall hoped. "At any rate, you may be assured of our fullest cooperation."[50]

COVENANTS IN THE CALIFORNIA SUPREME COURT

Immediately after the Sugar Hill victory, Miller began asking his colleagues for assistance to prepare the case for the California Supreme Court. In response to Miller's letter on the day of the decision, Marshall assured him the case would have amicus briefs from the NAACP, National Bar Association, ACLU, and Lawyers' Guild and promised to send either NAACP attorney William Hastie or himself to help represent the defense. Miller also sought out colleagues to build positive public opinion, an area he understood as valuable in shifting public thought when he worked on newspapers. "What we need is a chance in those decisive sectors of public opinion which exert the greatest influence on such topics as this one," Miller wrote to Lester Granger, executive secretary of the National Urban League. He asked Granger to oversee printing "at least one article" in magazines, such as *Survey Graphic*, the *Nation*, and *New Republic*. On New Year's Day 1946 Miller also wrote to Robert Weaver, Rufus Clement, Maurice Weeks, and Hastie for articles. "It seems to me that the judges have difficulty in brushing these things aside when the public eye is fixed on them," Miller wrote to Hastie. As anticipated, the prosecution appealed the case to the California Supreme Court.[51]

While both legal teams prepared for the appeal, the judgment in the Sugar Hill case emboldened Blacks to action. In the mid-1940s Miller served on one of the most publicized cases over restrictive covenants in the city.

Henry and Anna Laws, an African American couple, bought a home in 1937 near Central Avenue covered by a restrictive covenant and decided to defy the restriction in 1940 by moving in. A group of Whites filed a lawsuit, and in 1944 both the trial and appellate courts found the racial restriction valid and ordered the Laws to vacate the property. Yet the Laws refused to leave. In mid-December 1945, weeks after Clarke handed down his decision in the Sugar Hill case, Los Angeles Superior Court judge Allen W. Ashburn held the Laws in contempt of court and sentenced them to five days in jail. The story made headlines in the city's major Black newspapers. On the front page, the *Los Angeles Sentinel* proclaimed, "Laws Put in Jail for Living in Own House." The *California Eagle* reported that at an NAACP-led rally demonstrators cried, "We are going to smash restrictive covenants!" and "paid tribute to the courageous stand taken by the Laws family." Charlotta Bass, editor of the *Eagle* and president of the Home Protective Association, which met weekly at the *Eagle*'s office, aiming to put an end to restrictive covenants, raised $2,000 for the Laws. The California Supreme Court released the Laws from jail, but the courts would not yet resolve the use of restrictive covenants.[52]

In early 1946 Miller also defended seven lawsuits consolidated for trial in the Charles Victor Hall tract, a neighborhood located directly south of Sugar Hill, which White homeowners claimed had been covered under a racial restriction since the mid-1920s. As usual, the Los Angeles Superior Court handed down its judgment in favor of the plaintiffs and endorsed the restrictive covenant. But that failed to deter Miller from further action.[53]

In the summer of 1946 the appellants' attorneys for the Sugar Hill case filed an opening brief maintaining *Corrigan* and its definition of restrictive covenants as private contracts that private citizens engaged in. "Until the decision in this [Sugar Hill] case it had been uniformly held that the...Fourteenth Amendment was imposed solely upon the states and...did not apply to agreements between citizens." By prohibiting citizens to exercise their "right to choose their own associations, the right by private contract," the attorneys contended, the court exercised "intolerance." In the respondents' brief, filed two months later, Miller contended, "State action *is* involved in every step of the process of giving effect to a race restrictive covenant." He found the appellants' arguments "absurd" but "ingenious," and he compared restrictive covenants to use- and race-based zoning ordinances, because "they determine where certain American citizens may live." Furthermore, he blamed restrictive covenants and other practices of residential discrimination for creating an urban ghetto and maintained that the ensuing consequences "redound...to the ultimate disadvantage of all Americans."[54]

The Sugar Hill case received a significant boost when California attorney general Robert Walker Kenny joined the lawsuit as amicus curiae. Born in Los Angeles in 1901, Kenny graduated from Stanford University in 1920, worked as a newspaper reporter, took courses at USC and Loyola College law schools, and passed the bar exam in 1926. He served as deputy counsel for Los Angeles County, became a municipal judge, and joined the Los Angeles Superior Court. Meanwhile, Kenny became involved in liberal politics. A registered independent until 1937, he registered as a Democrat in his run for the state senate and won the seat. While serving his term, he maintained his law practice and defended the head of the state's Communist Party. Between 1943 and 1947, as California attorney general, Kenny continued to take up liberal causes, leading a lawsuit that revoked the corporate charter of the Los Angeles Ku Klux Klan, and defending the Hollywood Ten in the House Un-American Activities Committee (HUAC) hearings. But, he made clear, "The one single act of which I was most proud during my four years of service as Attorney General" was his Sugar Hill case brief. Written by law professor McGovney and signed by Kenny, the brief stuck to Miller's strategy, maintaining that the state violates the Fourteenth Amendment's equal protection clause when it sanctions restrictive covenants. "The suit is *nothing but* a petition for *action by the State* to make effective an agreement, otherwise ineffective, by a decree ousting the respondents from their homes." The brief went on, "These agreements are motivated by race prejudice and operate without regard to the culture or refinement of the individuals affected." Kenny's involvement in the case reflected Los Angeles's changing political and judicial landscape, as liberal-minded Californians rose to high-ranking positions and stood against racial discrimination.[55]

The defense team added another piece of evidence to its case. In addition to insisting on their constitutional rights, the defendants used the newly established charter of the United Nations to make their case. Signed in 1945 at the end of World War II, the international treaty for global security and human rights signaled the continuing national shift in the political and judicial climate toward racial equality that the Double V campaign set out to achieve. In addition to the development of a liberal coalition among elite Blacks, their attorneys, and the elected Democrats in Los Angeles, the United Nations charter represented the rise of a cross-class coalition that bridged together diverse socioeconomic groups across the country and the globe. The defense claimed that the charter protected African Americans' right against racial discrimination. "The U.N. charter is a treaty which has the effect of law," Miller argued. One month before Miller stood before the California Supreme Court, he wrote an article for the NAACP's *The Crisis* forecasting the months ahead. "There has to be a showdown, and soon," he demanded. The lawsuits against restrictive covenants accumulated around the country, and more and more courts had to confront the issue. Miller stood at the forefront of the fight and sensed a sea change ahead when he predicted, "There are signs of an awakening."[56] In June 1946 he argued twelve covenant cases in front of the California Supreme Court. The *Los Angeles Sentinel* reported, "250 people, colored and white, who filled every available seat and overflowed into the corridor, listened intently to the legal arguments presented." The following October Miller argued eight covenant cases in front of the court, which included the Sugar Hill case.[57]

Awaiting the state court's decision, Miller strengthened his collaboration with fellow attorneys and pursued cases against racial restrictions. For instance, Miller and civil rights attorney A. L. Wirin worked with the Japanese American Citizens League (JACL) in a campaign against restrictive covenants in Los Angeles, and they collaborated on a lawsuit against racial restrictions in South Pasadena. Through the mid-1940s Miller's cases piled up. In 1948, when the US Supreme Court ultimately ruled restrictive covenants legally unenforceable in *Shelley v. Kraemer*, Miller "had more than a hundred cases pending" over racial restrictions, he later explained. Meanwhile, advocates across the country continued to mobilize. Because the National Association of Real Estate Boards, which held the trademark for the term "realtor," prohibited Blacks from joining the group, Black realtors founded the National Association of Real Estate Brokers, or "realtists," in Tampa, Florida, in 1947, to support Black real estate professionals.[58] Miller and the NAACP believed Sugar Hill was one of the more promising lawsuits to bring to the US Supreme Court. He later explained that Clarke in the Sugar Hill case had "anticipated" the high court's ruling against racial restrictions. But before the California Supreme Court handed down its decision on the Sugar Hill case, which would have allowed Miller to submit his case for review to the high court, the US Supreme Court agreed to preside over four midwestern and eastern covenant cases.[59]

COVENANTS IN THE US SUPREME COURT

For more than a decade after the *Corrigan* decision, despite petitions to reconsider the constitutionality of racial contracts, the US Supreme Court refused to hear any cases on the matter. The 1940 proceedings in *Hansberry v. Lee* marked a shift in the high court's willingness to reassess the agreements. After Carl Hansberry, African American real estate agent, civil rights activist, and father of future playwright Lorraine Hansberry, purchased a house on a White neighborhood block in Chicago, several property owners filed a lawsuit, claiming Hansberry was violating a covenant. The defense team based its argument on a previous case that found a restrictive covenant valid when 95 percent of homeowners signed the contract. Only 55 percent of property owners in Hansberry's area endorsed the agreement. While the Illinois Supreme Court upheld the plaintiffs' argument, the US Supreme

Court reversed the decision. The high court found that the ruling in the previous case could not be applied to the *Hansberry* defendants, yet it refused to address the validity of racial contracts. After his victory, Miller believed the Sugar Hill case served as the ideal model to take to the US Supreme Court, but another attorney first convinced the high court to review his lawsuit from Missouri.[60]

In January 1947, two years after the first meeting, Thurgood Marshall gathered together attorneys for a second conference to discuss legal strategy and choose lawsuits to submit for review in the US Supreme Court. Rather than attending the meeting, African American attorney George Vaughn set out to petition the high court to review his St. Louis, Missouri, case. In the proceedings, White couple Louis and Fern Kraemer sued Black couple J. D. and Ethel Lee Shelley for violating a covenant and purchasing a house in the area. While the trial court ruled in favor of the defendants, finding the covenant valid only when all of the homeowners in the community signed it, the Missouri Supreme Court reversed the decision. Unlike the Sugar Hill case, which had to wait for the California Supreme Court's decision, the Missouri lawsuit was ready to pursue in the high court. Despite Marshall's insistence to slow down and work together, Vaughn applied for certiorari, and, under pressure, compelled Marshall to ask the court to hear the Michigan and Washington, DC, cases. Before the court went to summer recess in 1947, the justices granted the petitions to review the Missouri and Michigan cases. When the court reconvened the following October, it also approved two Washington, DC, cases. "I regret very much that their decisions came down before ours," Miller wrote to Marshall, but offered "to assist in whatever way I can." Meanwhile, Marshall organized a third conference in the NAACP's New York headquarters for September 1947 to coordinate the effort. In 1948 the four cases, all of which had originated in cities with no de jure segregation laws, were consolidated under the St. Louis lawsuit *Shelley v. Kraemer*, and went to trial.[61]

While the NAACP legal team collaborated, the defense attorneys allocated the work and relied heavily on social science data to make their central argument that judicial sanction of restrictive covenants violated the equal protection clause. Since attorney and future US Supreme Court justice Louis Brandeis and his sister-in-law, labor reformer Josephine Clara Goldmark, pioneered the inclusion of social science data in legal arguments in 1908, the "Brandeis brief" has been implemented as a legal strategy, including by the NAACP in the late 1930s. The *Shelley* litigators strengthened their argument to the high court by using the Brandeis tactic. Miller, Marshall, and other NAACP attorneys crafted the brief for the Detroit case, a ninety-two-page statement that described the sociological and economic implications of racial agreements. Drawing on eighty-three official and published sources, many of which included social science works, government and census publications, and journal and magazine articles, they argued that restrictive covenants forced rental prices up and housing standards down, and created overcrowded, disease-ridden ghettos in Detroit and other cities nationwide. Black settlement in White neighborhoods, the brief continued, showed no harmful effects on property values. In the United States' early Cold War free market economy, which was at odds with Communist governments, the argument held extra weight.[62]

Charles Hamilton Houston and the attorneys for the two Washington, DC, lawsuits also took the Brandeis approach in their 149-page brief that presented an innovative and multifaceted analysis of the cases. First, they cited more than 150 studies in sociology and economics, and appended more than fourteen pages of maps and tables, to show the detrimental costs of restrictive covenants on the Washington, DC, communities. They also used examples of earlier court opinions and relied on law review articles, including one written by Dudley Odell McGovney. While attorneys in previous cases had argued that restrictive covenants violated the US Constitution, the counsel in the Washington, DC, cases backed its arguments with considerable evidence and legal analysis that showed judicial sanction of covenants had obstructed civil rights. For the St. Louis case, the attorneys drew on sociological data but centered their position on the unconstitutionality of restrictive covenants. The NAACP would use the Brandeis approach as a legal framework in subsequent cases, including *Brown v. Board of Education*, to attack racial apartheid. *Shelley* provided further impetus for the efficacy of this approach.[63]

The amici curiae for the defense team served as another significant source of support that helped lead to a legal victory. A host of racial, ethnic, religious, labor, and human rights organizations, including the ACLU, JACL, and Congress of Industrial Organizations, submitted a total of eighteen briefs to the US Supreme Court endorsing the defendants' case. In an important turn of events that also provided a major boost to the defense, the federal government announced its support for racial equality. Responding to the reports of racial discrimination and violence against Black veterans after World War II, in late 1946 President Harry Truman appointed the fifteen-member Committee on Civil Rights to prepare a report with reforms aimed to end discrimination and advance equality. Issued in October 1947 the committee's report, *To Secure These Rights*, proposed thirty-four recommendations that, among others, urged the government to take the lead in civil rights reforms and get involved in pending lawsuits concerning racial equality. The day after the report's release Attorney General Tom C. Clark announced his decision to file an amicus brief for the *Shelley* defendants. Echoing the appeal of the report, Clark argued, "The Federal Government has a special responsibility for the protection of the fundamental civil rights guaranteed to the people by the Constitution." While *Corrigan* viewed racial agreements as private contracts that in no way infringed on state laws, Clark found the court failed to "deal with…the constitutional validity of judicial enforcement" of racial agreements. The "enforcement of racial restrictive covenants," Clark concluded, "is contrary to the public policy of the United States."[64]

On May 3, 1948, the US Supreme Court handed down a decision in *Shelley v. Kraemer* that marked a noteworthy step in the civil rights struggle. The six participating justices reversed the judgment of the lower courts and unanimously ruled racial restrictive covenants were unenforceable by a court of law. While honoring legal precedents, Chief Justice Fred M. Vinson clarified that the defense team presented a new angle to the argument that had never been heard before in the court. The decision came down to the interpretation of state action under the Fourteenth Amendment. The court found that restrictive covenants "standing alone cannot be regarded as violative of any rights guaranteed to petitioners by the Fourteenth Amendment." However, when the court in *Corrigan* gave its judicial sanction of the agreements, Vinson argued, it infringed on the rights protected under the Fourteenth Amendment. "The purposes of the agreements were secured only by judicial enforcement by state courts," Vinson found. Therefore, "We hold that in granting judicial enforcement of the restrictive agreements… the States have denied petitioners the equal protection of the laws." In his closing remarks, Vinson harkened back to "the historical context in which the Fourteenth Amendment became a part of the Constitution," and underscored the framers' fundamental objective of establishing "equality in the enjoyment of basic civil and political rights" as the goal of the court.[65]

Upon the ruling, newspapers celebrated the win and some changes began to take place. Beside a photo of Hattie McDaniel's home, the front page of the *Los Angeles Sentinel* featured the headline, "California Negroes Can Now Live Anywhere!" The *New York Times* reported that racial, religious, and labor groups "hailed" the decision. Days after the verdict, *U.S. News & World Report* warned, "A mild revolution…is in sight." Miller received congratulations letters from friends and colleagues across the country. George Beavers remarked, "Not only our race, but all Americans who believe in the high ideals and lofty principles enunciated in the Bill of Rights and our Constitution owe a great debt of gratitude to you and the [NAACP] for this remarkable victory." Courts around the country dismissed the pending lawsuits on restrictive covenants. Based on the *Shelley v. Kraemer* decision, the

California Supreme Court affirmed Judge Clarke's ruling in the Sugar Hill case. Thus, the Sugar Hill defendants won the right to stay in their homes.[66]

But limitations of the decision arose quickly and clearly. Despite the NAACP's effort both to illustrate the consequences that racial restrictive covenants had had on the American landscape, and to appeal to wholly prohibit the use of covenants, Chief Justice Vinson argued that the contracts did not infringe on the Fourteenth Amendment's equal protection clause. While the court would not enforce the contracts, it continued to allow private citizens to use racial agreements.[67] By early 1950 the FHA and the Veterans Administration changed their guidelines and refused to aid or insure lenders or borrowers on properties with racial restrictive covenants. The FHA announced that it would not use a neighborhood's racial composition as a factor in determining loan eligibility, and it removed its support for restrictive covenants from the *Underwriting Manual*. But the FHA made no meaningful effort to prohibit private lenders or homebuyers from upholding redlining, and would enable real estate blockbusting and speculation, discriminatory measures that Whites increasingly turned to after *Shelley*, by allowing buyers to rapidly acquire federally insured mortgages thus accelerating White flight. When the Lyndon Johnson administration established the Department of Housing and Urban Development (HUD) in 1965 and folded the FHA into the new agency, it spurred what historian Keeanga-Yamahtta Taylor calls "predatory inclusion" practices that kept low-income African Americans tied to the inner city and perpetuated racial segregation. The high court, in 1948, ultimately took a narrow view by examining only the restrictive covenants and lost the opportunity to scrutinize the baked-in beliefs and institutional practices that enabled more discriminatory housing measures.[68]

Meanwhile, *Shelley*'s detractors responded with defiance and forged a concerted effort to circumvent the ruling. In Los Angeles, after the US Supreme Court handed down its decision, LARB, with CREA's backing, launched a citywide campaign to pass an amendment to the US Constitution that would give courts the power to enforce private agreements at their own discretion. Formed in 1903 and 1905, respectively, the two groups, LARB and CREA, succeeded in their efforts to protect and elevate property values of White homeowners, in the name of making sales for themselves, by persuading policymakers to pass the first citywide exclusionary zoning ordinance and, through the subsequent decades, strengthening zoning laws, defending restrictive covenants, and promising to maintain the all-White make-up of neighborhoods. In the face of *Shelley*, LARB insisted that restrictive covenants ensured social and economic stability for middle- and moderate-income White homeowners. LARB upheld that covenants sustained property values and staved off racial conflict by segregating Whites from everyone else. Milton Senn, director of the regional Anti-Defamation League, reported that realty boards in neighboring areas, such as the San Gabriel Valley and Culver City, backed the amendment. The campaign to pass an amendment thawed until the 1963 passage of the Rumford Act impelled realtors to resume their crusade. Whites turned to other judicial and extrajudicial discriminatory housing methods to keep people of color out of their neighborhoods.[69]

In the early 1950s, the legal battle over restrictive covenants returned to the US Supreme Court in a case that had begun in Los Angeles. While *Shelley* ruled covenants legally unenforceable, the US Supreme Court left unaddressed homeowners' right to file damage claims against covenanters that breached their contracts. Olive Barrows and a group of White residents in Los Angeles tested this theory when they sued their former neighbor, Leola Jackson, for selling her property to an African American family. Although the property conveyance occurred after *Shelley*, the plaintiffs claimed that, since Jackson violated a covenant, they deserved compensation for their losses. The trial and appeals court granted the defendants' objection, and the California Supreme Court refused to hear arguments altogether, but the US Supreme Court decided to review the case. Thanks to Miller and Marshall, who stepped back into the courtroom to head the defense team, *Barrows v. Jackson* (1953) reaffirmed the campaign against restrictive covenants. The US Supreme Court held that covenants "standing alone cannot be regarded as violative of any rights," but judicial approval of the damage suit indirectly supported the agreements, which infringed on citizens' Fourteenth Amendment rights. The fight against restrictive covenants in the courtroom resulted in another win. But the campaign against residential discrimination persisted long after *Shelley* and *Barrows*.[70]

THE FIGHT CONTINUES

One of the most significant and visible signs of Black migration onto Los Angeles's Westside after *Shelley* materialized on August 23, 1949, the grand opening of Golden State Mutual Life Insurance Company home office in Sugar Hill. After years of planning, Golden State had left its office on Central Avenue, where it had been a staple of the Black community for more than twenty years, and moved to the center of what became elite Black Los Angeles. Located on the corner of Western and Adams Boulevards, at 1999 West Adams Boulevard, which was the southwest entrance to Sugar Hill, the new office stood as a showpiece of Black achievement in Los Angeles. The move to Sugar Hill was bold for the Black-owned insurance agency. Central Avenue continued to serve as the hub of Black culture, and relocation to the Westside risked hurting the company's well-regarded reputation, losing its faithful clientele, and fueling intra-racial tensions. But Golden State set its goals high. Founders Nickerson, Houston, and Beavers established the insurance agency to improve the conditions of African Americans in the city. Also, by moving to Sugar Hill they were anticipating further Black migration onto the Westside.

About a week before the grand opening, cofounder and chair of the board George Beavers circulated a letter around the office informing his employees of the event. The last momentous occasion for Golden State, he recollected, occurred in 1925 when the company was founded. He took pride in the achievements to date. The company had more clients and brought in more revenue than ever before. Total income rose from roughly $392,000 in 1938 to more than $3.8 million in 1950. Total assets increased from more than $341,000 in 1938 to more than $4.8 million in 1950. Moving into the West Adams district allowed Golden State to honor its achievements, provide more services and opportunities, grow its clientele, increase its staff, and continue to give back to the city's Black population. Nickerson had died unexpectedly four years before the grand opening, but his vision lived on in the cofounders and employees. Beavers articulated the purpose of the company's relocation in his letter to the staff: "Your new building has been acclaimed as truly a prideful achievement in the business development of your race and the nation." The founders created Golden State not only to provide insurance to Black Angelenos, but also to advance their social and economic conditions. The grand building, centered in the heart of the West Adams district, served as a symbol of Black triumph over racial restrictive covenants, and Black migration into the sought-after Westside.[71]

The new home office boasted the latest technological advances as well as more facilities to better serve the staff. Renowned African American architect Paul R. Williams designed the triangular-shaped marvel. A promotional pamphlet written for employees and clients around the time of the grand opening explained that the new office included an "auditorium, cafeteria, research and information library, lounge, and elevator service." The building had a modern intercom system that could play music throughout the workday, make office-wide announcements, and address the entire staff. Employees had access to health care in the building's medical facility, which was run by a medical director, assisted by a nurse, and equipped with "examination and recuperating rooms." Overall, the new building represented, the pamphlet read, "a promise of greater future achievement."[72]

While the modern improvements represented the company's success, the building's artwork commemorated California's Black past. During the month of the grand opening, the company unveiled in the lobby a two-panel mural that honored the struggles and contributions of African Americans throughout the history of California and Los Angeles. Charles Alston and Hale Woodruff, well-known Harlem Renaissance painters, illustrated in the mural African American pioneers of California, including laborers rigging an oil drill and building the Golden Gate Bridge, and protesters picketing for equal educational and housing opportunities. On his panel, Woodruff depicted a man holding a picket sign asserting, "Let Us Own Homes." For the next several decades, but especially after the appointment of William Pajaud as art director in 1957, the company commissioned, collected, and displayed its substantial collection of works by local and national Black artists. Beavers explained that the artwork imparted "the spirit of our company's tradition; the elements of vigor, social protest, and group consciousness."[73] Golden State had come a long way from the modest office on Central Avenue. The new building symbolized past Black achievements as well as the possibilities for the future of African Americans in Los Angeles.

But Golden State's relocation into Sugar Hill made it a target of attack. After moving into Sugar Hill, Golden State faced White intimidation. In the first few years of operation in the West Adams district, Ivan Houston, Norman O. Houston's son, explained, "We had a few bomb threats." The company also fueled intra-racial tensions by, many argued, abandoning the Eastside's Black population. Although an increasing number of Blacks were moving to the Westside in the late 1940s, most of the area west of Western Avenue remained unavailable to people of color. Financial constraints and racial discrimination continued to limit working-class Blacks to low-income housing on the Eastside. "I remember when...we built the Golden State Mutual home office at Western and Adams, some of the people complaining about the Golden State moving away from the Negroes," Beavers explained. "People sort of thought we were leaving the community when we moved here," Ivan Houston recalled. The Black elite's victory against restrictive covenants, many believed, primarily aided Angelenos of color who had the financial means to secure a loan on a single-family house. Writing in retrospect on the compounded causes of the 1965 Watts rebellion, historian Gerald Horne finds, "Civil rights organizations," including the NAACP, "focused more on restrictive covenants—a particular concern of the middle class—than on public housing, a particular concern of the strapped sector of the working class."[74]

While Golden State relocated in the early years of what became a decades-long migration onto the Westside, the insurance company joined a movement that involved many others. In addition to the individual Black families who moved to West Jefferson, Sugar Hill, and the adjacent neighborhoods, Black entrepreneurs began establishing businesses in those areas. Four years before Golden State completed construction on its home office,

Chicago transplant William B. Watkins opened Hotel Watkins at 2022 West Adams Boulevard, near the corner of Adams and Western Boulevards, two blocks west and across the street from where Golden State's home office would sit. According to jazz trumpeter Clora Bryant, who had been performing on Central Avenue and developing a distinguished career playing for jazz greats, including Louis Armstrong, Count Basie, and Duke Ellington, Watkins opened the Westside's first Black-owned hotel that, over time, included seventy rooms and suites and live entertainment in the Rubaiyat Room. "That's where all the bands stayed," Bryant explained, and where many performed. Bryant lived a few blocks west of the hotel. Soon thereafter, other enterprises opened along Western Avenue, making the thoroughfare a hub of Black culture and commerce on the Westside.[75]

Yet amid that westward expansion, Eastside Blacks' feelings of resentment and abandonment were further intensified by the breakdown of public housing. Public housing was intended to alleviate the housing shortage; from the late 1930s through the late 1940s, the planned communities provided hope for low-income city dwellers to improve their well-being, achieve economic stability, and flourish in a supportive community. The 1937 Housing Act and the 1938 establishment of HACLA created the foundation to build public housing. But since the passage of the Housing Act, and especially in the booming postwar housing market, private real estate groups saw the law as infringing on their interests and had a hand in curbing the program. California's Community Redevelopment Act of 1945, for instance, intended to empower local redevelopment agencies to secure support, raise the funding, and take the lead on urban renewal projects. Although progressive housing activists initially backed the legislation, the power struggle among opposing forces over redevelopment resulted in so-called "slum clearance"—the displacement of residents, many of whom were low-income and not White, and the replacement of low-income housing with commercial property.[76]

Moreover, amid early Cold War hysteria and McCarthyism, support for public housing ultimately gave way to red-baiting and anti-Communism. In 1948 advocates backed by the NAACP, Urban League, JACL, and others collected enough signatures to add Proposition 14 on the November ballot that would secure the establishment of a state housing agency and allocation of $100 million in loans to local agencies to construct low-income housing and $25 million annually for operation costs. The conservative Committee for Home Protection (CHP), which was funded by affluent real estate developers, including Fritz B. Burns, who had built racially restricted communities before *Shelley*, led an aggressive campaign that persuaded most voters to oppose the initiative. CHP branded the initiative a Communist plot that would enable dictatorial rule and force all Californians to fund. Federal support for public housing received a boost under President Truman's Fair Deal with the Taft-Ellender-Wagner Housing Act of 1949, which, among the provisions, financed slum clearance programs and expanded federal funding for public housing, covering an additional 810,000 units nationwide over six years. But the law intensified the debate over public housing nationwide, including in Los Angeles.[77]

The Right's campaign, and successful use of Red Scare indictments, led to public housing's downfall. To counteract the 1949 Housing Act, CHP lobbied for more initiatives, including Proposition 10 of 1950, for which, again, Burns and other developers fundraised. Using the same accusations that public housing had Communist intentions, CHP persuaded the electorate to pass the measure, adding as Article 34 to the state constitution voters' right to decide by election on any housing project. At the end of 1951, as the city was using eminent domain to uproot residents from areas such as Chavez Ravine, the Los Angeles Chamber of Commerce and the City Council voted to cancel the 1949 federal program altogether. By late 1952 the anti–public housing campaign had won more than forty measures, including Proposition B that ended the program through election. Citizens Against Socialist Housing, CHP's successor, which comprised much of the same leadership, including Burns as fundraiser, used the same aggressive, red-baiting tactics to win. Meanwhile, the anti-Communist crusade persuaded federal agencies to question Americans' loyalty, including public housing residents, and required them to sign loyalty oaths or face eviction. Bowron also became a target of red-baiting and the anti–public housing campaign, and in the 1953 election he lost his tenure as a four-term mayor to Republican Norris Poulson. Under Poulson, in 1953 the city cut 57 percent of the units from the 1949 contract and two of the eleven approved housing projects, which had not yet been built, and abandoned any future projects within the vision of the 1937 and 1949 measures. Without the support of public housing, low-income Angelenos saw yet another barrier to improving their conditions and leaving the Eastside.[78]

Meanwhile, Black Angelenos with the financial means continued to create alternative ways to finance homebuying by opening banking institutions. When dentist, financier, and long-time Los Angeles NAACP president H. Claude Hudson helped found Broadway Federal Savings and Loan Association in 1947, he knew that "it was almost impossible to secure a loan. A Negro was given a smaller loan, for a shorter period of time, and a higher rate of interest." Hudson and several Black professionals, including architect Paul R. Williams, real estate broker H. J. Howard, business owners M. Earl Grant and Norman O. Houston, and city judge Thomas Griffith, Jr., raised funds, obtained a federal charter, and opened Broadway Federal at 4325 South Broadway Street, a few miles south of USC. Hudson's leadership at the bank, where he served as president from 1949 to 1973, scholar Abigail Rosas writes, was "an extension of his mission for social, political, and economic African American equality." He trained and employed Blacks when other financial institutions hired only Whites, and he celebrated Black culture and history through the bank's interior design and print advertisements. In 1947 World War II–veteran James M. Woods founded Safety Savings and Loan Association and, by the mid-1950s, had moved into an office at 2638 South Western Avenue in West Jefferson. Then, by 1948 several of the same entrepreneurs who founded Broadway Federal had also established Watts Savings and Loan Association, which was later renamed Family Savings and Loan Association, and moved from Watts to 3683 Crenshaw Boulevard in the Crenshaw area. Under Earl Grant's leadership, Family Savings aimed to support the community by awarding scholarships and offering rent-free space to local groups.[79]

After 1948 White homeowners had no judicial support to enforce discriminatory private contracts, and after 1953 they had no legal support to sue their neighbors for damage claims for breaching racial agreements. The 1948 US Supreme Court ruling, *Oyama v. California*, which forbade enforcement of the 1913 and 1920 California alien land laws, and the 1948 California Supreme Court decision in *Perez v. Sharp*, which struck down the ban on interracial marriage, revealed the shift to end discriminatory practices. But Whites used other methods to control the racial composition of neighborhoods: "Restrictive covenants," Thomas Sugrue writes, "were the weakest link in the armor of racial segregation." Among the many obstructers, real estate interests persisted as a major force in upholding racial apartheid. The all-White National Association of Real Estate Boards maintained its policy that it implemented in the 1930s that members should never sell property to anyone who could change the "character" of the neighborhood. Following those guidelines, local realty boards ousted realtors who had violated the established racial boundaries. Until the early 1960s, among its two thousand members, LARB, which gave only its realtors access to the multiple listing service, had not one Black realtor. In 1966 LARB's Southwest Branch finally gave Black realtors access to its listings. Grounded in its history of promoting exclusionary zoning laws to segregate the city, LARB launched a campaign after *Shelley* to add an amendment to the US Constitution sanctioning the enforcement of property restrictions that would come to fruition in the state's 1964 passage of Proposition 14. White homeowners also continued to mobilize in neighborhood improvement or protective associations to intimidate their Black neighbors.[80]

Moreover, when no other judicial or extrajudicial methods worked, Whites exercised their most common act of resistance: selling their properties and moving away. Amid the celebration of *Shelley*, Miller recognized the battle against housing discrimination needed to continue: "Laws and court decisions do not solve social problems; they merely set limits within which those problems may be tackled and ultimately solved. It is up to us to give effect to the decision." As more Blacks gained access to Los Angeles's Westside, they faced the burden yet again of challenging institutional racism and persuading their neighbors of the value of their presence and the value of racial integration. At the same time that intra-racial tensions intensified, education and white-collar and public-sector jobs for Blacks expanded, civil rights legislation was passed, and a flourishing economy in the postwar years gave rise to the "new" Black middle class that, thanks to its larger size, could make a greater impact of the city's landscape. The next generation resumed their predecessors' work in what became known as the "open" or fair housing movement.[81]

Postcards of Eddie Anderson's and Jack Benny's estates, ca. 1930s–40s. In the 1930s actor Eddie Anderson, who played the role of Rochester on *The Jack Benny Program*, built this twenty-two-room mansion abutting the Cimarron Street racial border on what became Rochester Circle. He modeled his house after Benny's estate in racially restricted Beverly Hills. Postcards from Western Publishing & Novelty Co., Los Angeles, California.

Bill and Fannie Clay Robinson's house. In the 1930s tap dancer Bill Robinson (known professionally as Bojangles) and Fannie Clay Robinson, a trained pharmacist who managed his career, moved into a Paul R. Williams–designed house (photo, ca. 1943) at 1194 West Thirty-Sixth Place in West Jefferson that included formal dining and living rooms, a billiards room and bar in tiki decor, and a meticulously landscaped outdoor living space (July 1939). *Top photo*: Miriam Matthews Photograph collection (Collection 1889), Library Special Collections, Charles E. Young Research Library, University of California, Los Angeles. *Bottom photo*: Maynard L. Parker, photographer. The Huntington Library, San Marino, California.

Golden State Mutual Life Insurance Company founders, George A. Beavers, Jr., William Nickerson, Jr., and Norman O. Houston (*left to right*), 1945. When White-owned institutions refused to serve African Americans or overcharged them for services, George A. Beavers, Jr., William Nickerson, Jr., and Norman O. Houston established Golden State Mutual Life Insurance Company in 1925. Over time, Golden State became the leading Black-owned insurance agency in Los Angeles, opened offices across and beyond California, extended its services into home and business loans, and championed civil rights groups and causes. Golden State Mutual Life Insurance Company records (Collection 1434), Library Special Collections, Charles E. Young Research Library, University of California, Los Angeles.

Norman O. Houston and family, ca. 1930s. In 1938, Norman O. Houston (*center*) and Edythe Pryce Houston (*right*) became the first African Americans to purchase a house in Sugar Hill. Their residence at 2211 South Hobart Boulevard fit their combined families, including Norman's sons Norman Benjamin (left of his father) and Ivan James (right of his father). Lillian Jackson Harris (*left*), Norman O. Houston's mother, joined them in this photo. Golden State Mutual Life Insurance Company records (Collection 1434), Library Special Collections, Charles E. Young Research Library, University of California, Los Angeles.

Hattie McDaniel with group in front of her house, ca. early 1940s. Actor Hattie McDaniel (*center*) became one of several high-profile defendants in the Sugar Hill case. In 1941 she moved from West Jefferson to Sugar Hill with her husband, James Lloyd Crawford. Their estate at 2203 South Harvard Boulevard (*background*), served as a space for social and political gatherings. As chair of the Negro Division of the Hollywood Victory Committee, McDaniel led entertainers to Minter Field air base, in Shafter, California, to perform for World War II service members. Courtesy of National Archives (photo no. 208-NS-4264–5).

J. A. and Vada Somerville, 1930s, and their Sugar Hill house, ca. mid-1940s. When dentists, entrepreneurs, and civil rights activists J. A. (*left*) and Vada (*right*) Somerville, purchased an estate at 2104 South Harvard Boulevard in Sugar Hill (*below*) in 1943, they added fuel to White residents' resistance to the Black newcomers that led them to court two years later in the Sugar Hill case. Miriam Matthews Photograph collection (Collection 1889), Library Special Collections, Charles E. Young Research Library, University of California, Los Angeles.

Loren Miller, ca. 1950. With Loren Miller as lead attorney, the Sugar Hill defendants triumphed in an unprecedented victory that declared racial restrictive covenants violated the Fourteenth Amendment. The dynamic and gifted attorney, shown here a few years following the case, went on to help the national NAACP succeed in *Shelley v. Kraemer* and *Barrows v. Jackson*, and merit a Los Angeles County Municipal Court judgeship. Papers of Loren Miller, The Huntington Library, San Marino, California.

Golden State Mutual Life Insurance Company's home office, ca. 1950s. Golden State Mutual's home office grand opening in Sugar Hill in 1949, the year following *Shelley*, served as a symbol of the hard-fought Black migration onto Los Angeles's Westside and a showpiece of Black excellence. The Paul Williams–designed, triangular-shaped structure on the corner of Western and Adams Boulevards included advanced technologies and enhanced facilities to best serve the staff and clientele. Golden State Mutual Life Insurance Company records (Collection 1434), Library Special Collections, Charles E. Young Research Library, University of California, Los Angeles.

Tina Turner in her View Park Home, 1970. In 1962, two years after their single "A Fool in Love" had made the *Billboard* rhythm and blues and pop charts, Ike and Tina Turner and their four children joined the first African Americans who moved into View Park. *Look* magazine photographer recorded the couple in their 4263 Olympiad Drive house and Tina Turner cooking in the kitchen. Douglas Jones, photographer, *Look* Magazine Photograph Collection, Library of Congress, Prints & Photographs Division [Negative number LC-L9–70–5465-UU, #13].

Integration of Baldwin Hills Elementary School, Los Angeles, 1962. In 1962 Baldwin Hills Elementary School became a center in the fight over school segregation in Los Angeles. Ever since African Americans began moving west of Crenshaw Boulevard after *Shelley*, they faced White resistance in the neighborhoods and the schools. After Principal Metz (*center*) initially refused to register a group of African Americans, the Los Angeles NAACP pressured school authorities to desegregate and the Los Angeles BOE intervened. Todd (*left*) and Randall (*right*) Garr became the first Black youngsters to transfer to the school. Harry Adams Photograph Collection, Tom & Ethel Bradley Center, University Library, California State University, Northridge.

Degnan Boulevard Commercial Center, ca. 1938. In the mid-1920s, the Walter H. Leimert Company carved a 230-acre lot into racially restricted Leimert Park for residential and commercial uses. Located along the southern end of Degnan Boulevard, between West Forty-Third Street and West Forty-Third Place, Leimert Park Village emerged as the community's business center. Nearly two decades after *Shelley*, as Leimert Park transitioned into a majority Black population, Alonzo and Dale Davis opened Brockman Gallery that helped make the Village into a hub of Black art and activism. Herman J. Schultheis photographer, Herman J. Schultheis Collection/Los Angeles Public Library.

Brockman Gallery, Opening Night, 1967. Brockman Gallery Archive, Los Angeles Public Library, Special Collections.

Alonzo Davis (*right*) with Sidney Poitier (*left*) and Joanna Shimkus (*center*) at Brockman Gallery, ca. 1970s. Brockman Gallery Archive, Los Angeles Public Library, Special Collections.

Dale Brockman Davis in his studio, ca. 1970s–80s. Brockman Gallery Archive, Los Angeles Public Library, Special Collections.

PART TWO

Post-*Shelley* Westward Migration and the Case for Crenshaw

Chapter Four

The Affluent Black Westside Takes Shape

> *We discussed all this when we began house-hunting in this neighborhood. You wanted to live here because it's near the office, close to shopping centers, and an excellent school.... The house was priced right and it fit our dream. We knew we were to be the first Negroes in the area, and both of us expected enmities even to the point of cross-burnings on the front lawn. We're thankful it hasn't come to that! Put on your hard outer shell, honey, because we're here to stay.*
> — Jim Burton, calming the fears of his wife Rose,
> in Evelyn Allen Johnson's *My Neighbor's Island* (1965).[1]

TWO WEEKS OF HOSTILITY from her new neighbors left Rose Burton troubled about her move into a mostly White, affluent neighborhood. Rose, a nurse, and her obstetrician spouse, Jim, the fictional characters of Evelyn Allen Johnson's prize-winning novel, *My Neighbor's Island*, represented upwardly mobile Blacks who settled in desirable, White communities after the *Shelley* and *Barrows* decisions. Although the US Supreme Court had declared racial restrictive covenants legally unenforceable, African Americans had to enforce the orders through their own labor in their daily actions. The fictional Burtons took pride in their home, honored their heritage by decorating the interior with African artwork, and invited their friends over for gatherings. But the protagonists had to fight a war waged by George and Sybil Armstrong, their White neighbors, who doggedly protested Black in-migration. Sybil antagonized the Burtons by standing at her front window and glaring at them, by ignoring Rose when they were both outdoors, by not allowing her daughter to talk to theirs, and by calling the police to break up a party at the Burtons' home. Yet the Burtons persevered, under Jim's advice, with a "hard outer shell." They saw their efforts within a larger struggle, wrote the author, "in obtaining those rights essential to the pursuit of happiness."[2]

Johnson based *My Neighbor's Island* on her experiences as one of the first African Americans to move into Baldwin Hills Estates, an affluent community on Los Angeles's Westside, north of where Stocker Street and La Brea Avenue meet, in the sought-after Crenshaw area. She and her spouse,

Raymond, purchased a four-bedroom, three-bathroom, single-family house there in 1962, only a few years after Black neighbors began moving in. The couple represent part of what sociologist Bart Landry dubbed the new Black middle class, which took shape thanks to the expansion of educational opportunities and white-collar and public-sector jobs for Blacks, the passage of the 1964 Civil Rights Act, and a flourishing economy in the postwar years. Like Rose Burton, Johnson was a registered nurse. Born in Pittsburgh, Pennsylvania, in 1929, she defied her teacher's advice to become a maid, and instead pursued academic degrees at Howard University and California State University, Los Angeles. She met Raymond, a former Tuskegee airman, at Howard University, where he was pursuing a law degree. After relocating to Los Angeles, the couple purchased a house that met the needs of their growing family and honored their achievements. Yet the family faced a rocky transition into the community. Johnson later recollected several incidents when her White neighbors prohibited their offspring from playing with the Johnson children. She also believed that school officials questioned her children's academic abilities because of their skin color. But the Johnsons refused to yield to White intimidation. Raymond practiced law and joined the local Democratic Party and the Los Angeles NAACP. The couple hosted political fundraisers and social gatherings in their home to guests as illustrious as Mayor Tom Bradley. Evelyn worked as a full-time nurse; was active in organizations such as Jack and Jill, the Wives of the Bench and Bar, and the Los Angeles NAACP; and wrote several books that grappled with class identity, interracial and intra-racial relations, and racial discrimination.[3]

Among its many significant systemic changes in the war and postwar years, Los Angeles saw a battle between the downtown and Westside power structures for the city's cultural, economic, and political center that reflected the competing interests within the sprawling, decentralized pattern. As the city expanded westward in the interwar and postwar years, the old moneyed, White, Protestant, conservative guard and business executives in downtown Los Angeles, Pasadena, and San Marino, some of whom descended from boosters, sought to revitalize downtown, while the new moneyed savings-and-loan and show business executives, many of whom were Jewish and Democrats, invested in the Westside. Dorothy Buffum Chandler, who married Norman Chandler, the eldest son of *Los Angeles Times*'s Harry Chandler, bridged the downtown and Westside divide when she persuaded representatives from both camps to donate to what became The Music Center. Opened in 1967, the downtown multimillion dollar, three-theatre complex comprised the Dorothy Chandler Pavilion, named in honor of Chandler, as well as the Ahmanson Theater and the Mark Taper Forum, named after Westside savings-and-loan executives Howard Ahmanson and Mark Taper, both of whom made a fortune financing the postwar housing construction boom and donated more than $1 million to the center. While the downtown elite tried to retain their command, the Westside positioned itself as a center for wealth and power.[4]

Meanwhile, African Americans continued to extend Los Angeles's existing racial borders. They moved into more Eastside communities along Central Avenue, including Watts, Willowbrook, and Compton. And the Westside underwent a significant demographic shift. Tracts lined directly north along Washington Boulevard saw an increase in the city's minority populations. Hancock Park and Lafayette Square serve as notable examples. Both shared a reputation for their affluent White residents who clung to their communities' restricted order, but while Hancock Park Whites maintained their majority and stayed put, Lafayette Square Whites fled the area. African Americans also moved west of Figueroa Street, and what was becoming the Harbor Freeway, into Exposition Park and Vermont Square. Settling in the Crenshaw area, which is the focus of this chapter and the next two, became a key step toward full access to the city.[5] While African Americans headed the movement in the pre-*Shelley* years, they migrated alongside Jews, Asians (most of them Japanese), Latinos, and other people of color in the post-*Shelley* years. Japanese Angelenos made a significant mark on Crenshaw. They had progressed with Blacks in the pre-*Shelley* westward pattern, mainly from Little Tokyo; after their return from incarceration they likewise purchased homes, opened businesses, and influenced the Crenshaw culture. By 1950 Angelenos of color had settled west of the Arlington Avenue racial border, and by 1960 they had moved across Crenshaw Boulevard.[6]

Shaped by the rolling Baldwin Hills, which received their name from nineteenth-century land investor Elias Jackson "Lucky" Baldwin, the Crenshaw area largely bordered Arlington and Slauson Avenues, and Exposition and La Cienega Boulevards. The spacious houses, panoramic views of the city, and high-quality public facilities were major selling points. Starting in the 1920s when they began carving out the area, developers insisted that property owners cover their homes in restrictive covenants. When the high court handed down *Shelley* and *Barrows*, however, Whites lost judicial support to use their primary mechanism to restrict people of color from the area. They then pivoted from creating what historian Robert Fishman calls racially homogeneous bourgeois utopias to defending their neighborhoods against, as scholar Mike Davis puts it, "unwanted development" and "unwanted persons." In the 1940s the middle-class suburb of Leimert Park, located on the eastern flatlands immediately west of Arlington Avenue, became the main entry point for Black and Asian migration into Crenshaw's affluent sections. Through the 1950s and 1960s they migrated farther westward into View Park, View Heights, and Windsor Hills, situated on the southerly slope, and Baldwin Hills Estates and Baldwin Hills Vista (later Baldwin Vista), on the hilly northern section.[7] In the decentralized, sprawling, suburban metropolis, living on the hills served as a long-time marker of distinction. "A family that moves up literally in height above sea-level," one Crenshaw resident wrote, "also moves up in cost of living and in status and prestige."[8] *Shelley* and *Barrows* were essential in invalidating Whites' major segregation tool, but after the verdicts countless individuals at the grassroots level had to endure daily encounters of White intimidation to enforce their right to housing.

One of Los Angeles's most damaging byproducts of White neighborhood defense against people of color transpired in the 1940s, several blocks east of Central Avenue, in the working-class Huntington Park, Bell, and South Gate neighborhoods. The decade after the first Chicano and Japanese gangs assembled, resentful White teenagers formed street clubs, led by the notorious Spook Hunters, to single-handedly thwart *Shelley*. Named after the racial epithet "spook" and identified by their jackets that had a graphic on the back of a Black person's face with a noose around the neck, the Spook Hunters violently attacked African Americans they spotted in White schools and communities across the city. While White clubs claimed the Alameda corridor, Blacks responded in self-defense by forming their own street clubs, first in the Central-Vernon area near Jefferson High School, and then southward along the Central Avenue corridor and westward across the Harbor Freeway, onto the Westside. "When you can't live where you want to live, when you can't go where you want to go, without someone saying something to you, there's a problem," former Black club member "Bird" explained. In response, "I began fighting the little White kids every day." Slausons's founder, Chinaman, considered he and his cohorts were "the pioneers that open[ed] up Los Angeles."[9]

In the 1950s Black and Japanese gangs began forming on the Westside, and in the Crenshaw area they emerged in the working-class neighborhoods. While the racial border dividing the Eastside and the Westside shifted westward over time, Black Eastside and Westside gangs maintained historic Main Street as their dividing geographic marker and a reason for rivalry. Yet clashes occurred both inside and outside their professed territories. Their initial motives of defying White bigotry and domination turned into a lethal, mostly intra-racial and intra-ethnic contest over control of territory and, over time, of the market for illicit drugs. The affluent Crenshaw communities, including View Park, Windsor Hills, and Baldwin Hills Estates, dodged gang control of their immediate surroundings, but they had to watch their northern and eastern neighbors become gripped by drug trafficking and violence, share public services (including public schools) with gang members, either traverse or circumnavigate the perilous and gang-controlled communities, and take measures to prevent crime from spreading to their blocks.[10]

While street gangs used violence to claim and defend their territories, middle-class homeowners of color mandated full access to the city within the culture of their higher income bracket. Even as they became recast from the "yellow peril" to the "model minority" in the postwar era, a change that was part of the United States agenda to make East Asia an ally in the fight against Communism, Japanese Americans encountered White hostility in Crenshaw. Yet Blacks became the main targets and bore the brunt of White resistance. Some White homeowners packaged their efforts in neighborhood improvement or then-dubbed protective associations that privately pressured individual Black families to sell their homes and raised money to file lawsuits and purchase Black-owned property. Others refused altogether to acknowledge their Black neighbors, or resorted to scornful stares, verbal insults, or property damage. But White intimidation failed to deter Blacks from exercising their rights. While the middle-class, cookie-cutter, postwar suburbs represented White consumerism, conformism, and escapism from the supposed lurking Cold War dangers, Los Angeles's Westside neighborhoods emerged as sites in the civil rights struggle where middle-class Blacks, alongside Japanese Americans and other targeted groups, used their financial resources and resolve to assert their right to the entire city landscape. After *Shelley* and *Barrows*, Asian Angelenos first outnumbered Blacks by a small margin in some of the affluent Crenshaw neighborhoods. But White and Asian residents fled out of concern the area would deteriorate into a so-called ghetto, making the new Black middle class the majority within two decades.[11]

HANCOCK PARK AND LAFAYETTE SQUARE— A TALE OF DIFFERING OUTCOMES

Following the wartime housing shortage, and prompted by the *Shelley* and *Barrows* victories, African Americans expanded the city's racial borders by moving beyond Central Avenue in all cardinal directions. Among the postwar migration patterns, middle- and upper-class African Americans moved northward into the historically restricted tracts lined directly above Washington Boulevard and made their way into two highly distinguished neighborhoods: Hancock Park and Lafayette Square. White politicians, business magnates, show business executives, doctors, and wealthy heirs established the communities' high reputation in the early twentieth century by building mansions designed in varied architectural styles. Despite *Shelley*, Black newcomers had to prove their right to live in these enclaves. Hancock Park and Lafayette Square serve as case studies that represent Whites' differing responses to Black in-migration that affected long-term demographic patterns. After trying to intimidate Blacks into leaving, Hancock Park Whites remained in the exclusive enclave, while Lafayette Square Whites fled.

The lofty ideals of Los Angeles's first White elite have resonated in the culture of Hancock Park. Major Henry Hancock, attorney and land investor, acquired the territory in the second half of the nineteenth century. His family extracted oil from the land, and then gradually sectioned off and sold or donated it. Over time the city dedicated the area, bordered by Wilshire Boulevard and Melrose, Rossmore, and Highland Avenues, as Hancock Park. Wealthy Angelenos built massive and elaborate homes with the finest materials. The Wilshire Country Club, a private golf course and social establishment constructed in 1919 in the center of the neighborhood, set the area's tone. Many Hancock Park residents intermingled and conducted business on the green. They attempted to set themselves apart from the flamboyance and hedonism of Beverly Hills by affiliating with philanthropic causes and taking pride in their forebearers who contributed to Los Angeles's early Anglo settlement. But like other affluent neighborhoods, Hancock Park and its country club were available to only Protestant Whites.[12]

Virtuoso jazz pianist and singer Nat King Cole, and singer Maria Ellington Cole, purchased a house in 1948 that changed the neighborhood dynamic. Born in segregated Montgomery, Alabama, in 1919, young Nathaniel developed a lifelong love of music when playing it in his home and listening to it on the radio. The Coles relocated to Chicago in the 1920s, during the Great Migration, and Nat grew up in the South Side jazz clubs. He learned from talented musicians, including Benny Goodman, Louis Armstrong, and Art Tatum, and honed his craft on stage. He also met his first spouse, dancer Nadine Robinson, who entertained audiences on the road with him. They arrived in Los Angeles in 1937, and Cole eked out a living on unrestricted Central Avenue, playing in the clubs, touring, and recording for the jazz race market with the King Cole Trio. Forced to use the back door to enter clubs, stay in segregated motels and boarding houses while touring, and observe the color line, Cole persevered. During World War II the Trio achieved widespread success when their song, "Straighten Up and Fly Right," struck a chord in the wartime climate and crossed over to the Billboard White pop chart. At twenty-five years old, Cole began to prosper, earning a sizeable income from his recordings, royalties, live performances, radio appearances, and movies that included his music. He and Nadine purchased a house at 1977 West Twenty-First Street in Sugar Hill, but their marriage fell apart, and Cole fell in love with Ellington. Then in

1948, the same year as *Shelley*, Cole and Ellington married, and bought a home in Hancock Park.¹³

Nat and Maria immediately fell in love with the house. The red-bricked, English Tudor–style, 401 Muirfield Road mansion, with twelve rooms and twelve-foot ceilings, symbolized Nat's success. Since Nat and Maria had decided to buy the house only a few months after *Shelley*, they proceeded with caution; despite Nat's widespread popularity, they used a light-skinned African American colleague to make the transaction. Their approach of a straw-party sale, historian Jeffrey Gonda explains, using a third-party White buyer or, in the Coles' case, a light-skinned African American buyer, became a common indirect method of Black homebuyers to secure better financing and a lower interest rate, purchase restricted property, break a covenant, and integrate the neighborhood. Even after *Shelley*, African Americans, as the Coles' experience evinces, were using the method. Nat and Maria agreed to purchase the house for $85,000, more than seven times the city's 1950 average property value of $11,925. In July they made the $6,000 down payment in cash, and in August they finalized the property conveyance.¹⁴

But before Nat, Maria, and their children could move in, their new neighbors fought back. While White audiences across the country swooned to Nat's music, White residents in Hancock Park, the *Los Angeles Times* reported, created a "quandary" out of the Coles' purchase. Nat's celebrity status made no difference to them. The seller, Colonel Harry Gantz, and his real estate agent, Ann Winters, received anonymous phone calls threatening their jobs and their lives. White residents hurriedly formed the Hancock Park Property Owners Association, and attorney and resident Andrew J. Copp served as president. Copp sought out Cole at a Sunset Strip nightclub to persuade him to back out of the decision by offering to buy the house for the sale price plus a small profit. But Nat and Maria refused to submit to the pressure. They spoke to the press, requested support from First Lady Eleanor Roosevelt, and eventually moved in.¹⁵

White hostility persisted after the Coles settled in the neighborhood. The association threatened the couple with legal action. Vandals desecrated the Coles' front lawn with an abhorrent racial slur and a burning cross, threw spoiled meat over the wall that killed the family dog, placed fireworks in their rose bushes, and, while the family was away from home on a trip, fired a bullet through a window. But the Coles carried on. At a homeowners' meeting, Maria later recalled, when residents voiced their opposition to allow "any undesirable" people to move into the community, Nat responded that if "anybody undesirable [came] in here, I'll be the first to complain." As he did in his professional career, he challenged the color line by acting in kindness and humility, hoping his charisma would overcome White racism and break down racial stereotypes. But underlying his exterior, Nat insisted to a reporter, "I am an American citizen and I feel that I am entitled to the same rights as any other citizen." Maria hired a Beverly Hills interior decorator to design the house in the latest California modern style. *Ebony* magazine featured photos of the living room, the couple's large bedroom and bathroom, patio, dining room, front hallway, three-car garage, and recreation room. The Coles raised their five children and entertained illustrious guests such as Louis Armstrong, Dorothy Dandridge, Ella Fitzgerald, Peggy Lee, and Danny Thomas. Nat went on to achieve greater success and singularity in the American music art form as a solo artist, a host of his own variety show, and an actor.[16]

Unlike other affluent neighborhoods that experienced Black in-migration, however, Hancock Park remained largely White. Through the second half of the twentieth century, Whites stayed put. The federal census recorded the proportion of Whites at 97.1 percent in 1950, 98.1 percent in 1960, and 97.1 percent in 1970. The proportion of Blacks notably fell from 2.3 percent in 1950, to 1.2 percent in 1960, to 0.7 percent in 1970. The Coles opened Hancock Park to other African Americans, as the census figures indicate, and after Nat's death in 1965, Maria and the children stayed there until the early 1970s. Professional boxer and civil rights icon Muhammad Ali purchased a 14,500-square foot Italian Renaissance-style mansion there in 1979.[17] But unlike other neighborhoods that underwent Black in-migration, Hancock Park experienced no significant demographic shift. Homes remained too expensive for most Americans, and residents clung to the culture of the first inhabitants that set the community apart from other areas of the city.

Lafayette Square took shape a few years before Hancock Park. In the early 1910s, George L. Crenshaw and his realty company began developing the area between Venice, Crenshaw, Washington, and West Boulevards. Aiming to sell properties to wealthy and worldly buyers, Crenshaw made Lafayette Square into a residential park with an international flair. The company described the gateways "Parisian," called the streets "pasears," and cited the inspiration for the layout and landscape of St. Charles Place, the "central Pasear," the surroundings of the Theatro Municipal in Rio de Janeiro, Brazil. Even the other street names, such as Victoria Avenue, Wellington Road, and Buckingham Road, evoked an air of English distinction. Attorneys, architects, company presidents and vice presidents, and other professionals built and bought multiple-room mansions there. Despite the area's global theme, the new residents were ensured before their purchase, a 1914 *Los Angeles Times* advertisement stated, that Lafayette Square would remain "Restricted for 50 years."[18]

Architect Paul R. Williams and his family became one of the first African Americans to move there. As a student in the city's public schools, the native Angeleno aspired to become an architect. He made the decision to pursue his dream after his high school teacher doubted he had the ability to succeed in the profession and discouraged him from trying. Williams enrolled in architectural classes, worked at several firms, and, when he was in his twenties, won awards for his plans. The opportunity to open his own business came in the early 1920s when a wealthy classmate hired Williams to build him a home. From then on, Williams designed houses for the rich and famous in California cities such as Bel Air, Beverly Hills, Brentwood, Hancock Park, Hollywood, Malibu, and Pasadena, and in other states and countries. He also designed airports, churches, department stores, movie sets, office buildings, public housing projects, and schools.[19]

Throughout his career Williams walked the color line. He worked for some of the wealthiest White Angelenos, became the first Black member of the American Institute of Architects, and served on local, state, and federal commissions. Yet racial prejudice shaped many aspects of his life. He avoided parties attended by White women and learned to write upside-down to give his clients distance. For decades, racism also kept him from building his own house. In a 1937 essay Williams began, "Today I sketched the preliminary plans for a country house which will be erected in one of the most beautiful residential areas in the world." He continued, "Sometimes I have dreamed of living there. I could afford such a home. But this evening, leaving my office, I returned to my small, inexpensive home in an unrestricted, comparatively undesirable section of Los Angeles. Dreams cannot alter facts; I know that, for the preservation of my own happiness, I must always live in that locality, or in another like it, because…I am a Negro." Since he was a child, he endured a rollercoaster of emotions that moved from "bewilderment, inarticulate protest, resentment, and, finally, reconciliation to the status of my race." He came to accept Booker T. Washington's teachings of hard work, accommodation, and self-reliance. "I found in my condition an incentive to personal accomplishment." He called on Black America to "solve its own problems, raise its own standards, [and] *earn* its right to self-respect." Although conservative in his stance, Williams exhibited a fierce determination to succeed and inspire other Blacks to do the same. He warned Whites, "A race is beginning to stir beneath your feet and to demand a place in the sun."[20]

In the early 1950s, Williams fulfilled a lifelong dream when he designed his family home in Lafayette Square. He had developed a reputation in his profession for his ability to work in a range of period revival styles from

English Tudor to Spanish Colonial to Mediterranean, and to link the indoors to the outdoors. He built his two-story Lafayette Square house in the California modern form. The open floor plan and large glass doors connected the indoors to the garden where family and friends gathered for barbecues. Architectural historian David Gebhard noted that the house showed a mixture of contemporary elements, represented in the curved and horizontal lines, and traditional components, featured in the formal entrance. Paul and his spouse and, grassroots organizer Della Mae Givens Williams, hired Hollywood designers to decorate the interior and a weaver to create the fabrics.[21]

African Americans continued to move to the area. The 1950 census reported no people of color living within the borders of Lafayette Square. A little more than a decade after *Shelley*, the racial composition had shifted: In 1960 people of color resided in 10.3 percent of the total occupied housing units. In 1970 Blacks made up 75.2 percent of the population.[22] Judges, attorneys, ministers, doctors, educators, entertainers, and other professionals enjoyed the large houses, landscape, and air of distinction. Harry Belafonte bought a home for his mother on Victoria Avenue, and civil rights attorney Leo Branton, Jr., who later defended political activist Angela Davis, with Geraldine Pate Nicholas Branton, who had first married Fayard Nicholas of the Nicholas Brothers tap dance duo, moved to the area in the 1960s.[23]

While the city's racial borders expanded, transitional blocks a few streets west of Lafayette Square became targets of White intimidation and violence. In two consecutive years, 1951 and 1952, between Adams and Washington Boulevards on Dunsmuir Avenue, bombs detonated in four different homes. In July 1951 explosions occurred in two residences steps from each other. One of the bombs destroyed the corner of a house recently acquired by a Japanese American physician; the other bomb damaged the home of a real estate agent. In March 1952, one block north on the same street, bombs exploded on two different properties, one in the home of an African American science teacher and the other in the home of two White men reportedly planning to rent to African Americans. Police also received news of threatening phone calls and letters, and sidewalk markings several blocks away with "KKK."[24] Vandalism sightings continued into 1955 when the *Los Angeles Tribune* reported a "For Rent" sign and a sidewalk defaced with an egregious racial slur, and another block marked, in all capital letters, with the threat, "DOWN WITH NAACP." Neighborhood protective associations also formed around the city in reaction to Black in-migration.[25]

By the mid-1950s Black migration out of the Eastside had become more noticeable. Reporter Paul Weeks, in a 1956 *Mirror-News* article, identified the trend "as dramatic as" Black arrival into Los Angeles in the Great

Migration. Weeks opened his article by noting Black families moving into the "stately" mansions on Buckingham Road, St. Charles Place, and Victoria Avenue in Lafayette Square. "In the old days, this was one of the finest residential districts in the city. And it still is," Weeks confirmed. He reported that Central Avenue, "a section of tired and worn old buildings," as well as downtown Los Angeles, Watts, and other Eastside areas witnessed a decline in Black inhabitants. Meanwhile "the Negro community is expanding mainly by taking over the urban homes of whites."[26] Another significant trend was taking shape. The once multiracial and multiethnic Central Avenue, Watts, and West Adams communities were becoming predominantly Black. Most of the tracts from Jefferson Boulevard to Artesia Boulevard, along Central Avenue, by 1960 comprised a 75 percent or higher Black population. Black gangs did not form north of Washington Boulevard in the postwar era, but they did consume the Eastside and develop in and around the West Adams district. Meanwhile, the first people of color to move into the affluent Westside enclaves surely demonstrated bravery. But after withstanding White intimidation, they saw their neighbors turn to the most effective method for dealing with *Shelley* and *Barrows*: flight.[27]

LEIMERT PARK—POINT OF ENTRY INTO CRENSHAW

After *Shelley*, Crenshaw emerged as the major Westside area where Angelenos of color sought to tackle housing discrimination, and among all of its enclaves, Leimert Park served as the entry point. Located on the area's easternmost side, roughly bordered by Van Ness and Vernon Avenues, and Exposition and Crenshaw Boulevards, Leimert Park used its location, in what was becoming central Los Angeles, to initially draw in buyers in the 1920s and 1930s. The community was situated "only 15 minutes," a brochure boasted, from downtown Los Angeles, Santa Monica, Hollywood, and Beverly Hills, and on the Los Angeles Railway's trolley car lines. Likewise, Leimert Park was one of Crenshaw's most varied, planned communities, offering accommodations in a range of prices for the middle and upwardly middle class. The charming single-family houses, lower-priced apartment dwellings, high-quality public schools, and quaint business district (later known as Leimert Park Village) made Leimert Park desirable. *Life* magazine and *Architectural Forum*, working in collaboration during the 1940s, deemed a Leimert Park house to be one of eight noteworthy residences in the United States. The article showcased a two-bedroom dwelling built in California colonial style with a family-friendly floor plan and an outdoor living space. "Leimert Park," the article touted, "was created in the belief that beautiful surroundings should not be the luxury of the wealthy few." Until *Shelley*, however, Leimert Park remained covered by racial restrictive covenants.[28]

The developer Walter H. Leimert Company aimed to set Leimert Park apart from other Los Angeles areas with its unique design, range of accommodations, and assortment of amenities. Walter Leimert began working as a land subdivider in the San Francisco area, moved to Los Angeles in the 1920s, and continued his career there. He bought a 230-acre lot that included bean fields from Lucky Baldwin's daughter and heir, Clara Baldwin Stocker, in the mid-1920s, subdivided it for residential and commercial use, and commissioned the highly regarded architectural landscape firm, the Olmsted Brothers, which was owned by the sons of Frederick Law Olmsted, Sr., who had planned New York's Central Park, to help with the design. Leimert Boulevard, the main artery running diagonally below Santa Barbara Avenue (later Martin Luther King Jr. Boulevard, or simply King Boulevard), allowed for more-efficient traffic flow. The community's three public schools were planned in the layout and built in the first years of development. Forty-Second Street Elementary School and Audubon Junior High School sat on each side of Leimert Boulevard, and Thirty-Eighth Street School was built on the northeastern section. Running north on Degnan Boulevard, and past Santa Barbara Avenue (King Boulevard), roads fanned out to the main residential portion. Multifamily units lined the main boulevards, while single-family homes were situated in the interior roads. To create a family-friendly environment the developers ended several roads with cul-de-sacs and added walkways behind lots.[29]

Leimert also set aside parcels of land around the southern end of Degnan Boulevard for public and commercial use and then advertised the business section as second in importance to downtown Los Angeles. In late 1928 the Mesa Vernon Market opened. Situated at the intersection of Crenshaw and Leimert Boulevards and Vernon Avenue, the Mesa Vernon Market provided residents with easy access to goods and services. Over time, the market and its immediate surroundings included a butcher and produce shop, delicatessen, fountain café, bakery, beauty salon, jeweler, pharmacy, and medical offices with dentists and doctors. Citizens National Bank set up a branch in 1930. Directly north of Mesa Vernon Market sat a public park and square, known as Leimert Park Plaza, that included what would become its iconic pedestal fountain. Then, north of the park along Degnan Boulevard, from West Forty-Third Place north to West Forty-Third Street, another business section took shape. Famed aviator and film producer Howard Hughes built the Leimert Theater near the corner of West Forty-Third Place and Degnan Boulevard in 1932 that established the center of the business section or what would become known as Leimert Park Village. Its art deco tower served as a landmark to Leimert Park. The grand auditorium, encircled by a promenade that was decorated with a hand-painted mural, played the latest motion pictures. Over time, as more businesses opened along Degnan Boulevard—from restaurants and delicatessens, to paint stores and photography studios, to optician and chiropractor offices, to plumbing services and television repair shops—Leimert Park Village became the heart of the community.[30]

For roughly two decades after its initial development, however, Leimert Park was covered in racial restrictive covenants. The Leimert Company set out to make homeownership more accessible by selling affordable homes but only sold them to Whites, while ensuring them that their communities would be safe, and their property values would appreciate. To do so, Leimert followed federal standards and covered the area in restrictive covenants. In one of its earliest advertisements in the *Los Angeles Times* the company publicized in commonly used code words that the area upheld, in all capital letters, "PERMANENT protective restrictions."[31] But people of color gradually managed to move in. The 1950 census recorded Leimert Park had a 99.5 percent White population. Mexican-born Angelenos numbered 146 (1.1 percent), Asian-born urbanites reached 128 (1 percent), and African Americans trailed behind at 51 (0.4 percent).[32]

The Avenues section, located directly north of Leimert Park between Exposition and Crenshaw Boulevards and Arlington Avenue, saw noteworthy Japanese inhabitation. Resettling after their incarceration in the mid-1940s, Japanese Americans and their blockbusting realtors began breaching the Arlington Avenue racial border and establishing their homes and community institutions that reflected their culture and history. Like the city's past ethnic neighborhoods, the Avenues included an ethnically and racially diverse population. The 1950 census recorded a population of 70.9 percent Whites, 18.8 percent Blacks, 0.7 percent Mexican-born Angelenos, and 0.6 percent Asian-born city dwellers. Yet the area became a center of Japanese cultural and economic activity. Japanese Angelenos designed their houses and yards in and outside of the Crenshaw area in the Japanese architectural and landscape forms, including incorporating elements of the Zen garden around the exterior. At the same time, Japanese business owners opened restaurants, grocery and dry goods stores, barbershops, photography studies, credit unions, banks, and real estate offices along Jefferson Boulevard that catered to the growing Japanese market. Within a decade, what became known as the Seinan (southwest) Japanese district would rival the cultural spirit and economic offerings of Little Tokyo.[33]

But while Japanese Angelenos moved into the area, Black presence in Leimert Park especially rankled Whites. By early 1950 Leimert Park residents formed Neighborly Endeavors, Incorporated, to stave off Black in-migration. In the meeting minutes from a group in an adjacent area, a representative of Neighborly Endeavors by the name of Mr. Lund urged homeowners to sell their properties only to White buyers. Recognizing the *Shelley* ruling, Lund stated, "Negroes and the other non-Caucasians...have a right to live wherever they want to." Yet he encouraged White homeowners to circumvent court orders and continue to prohibit people of color from the area. "The only way to protect yourselves," he argued, "is to make certain that none of your neighbors sells to a non-Caucasian." Lund accused White homeowners of behaving in a "selfish" manner by allowing people of color to purchase property in the area, and he advised residents to resist the inclination to "hurt" the community. "This experience has drawn us much closer together in Leimert Park," he touted. "We had to buy up one piece of property and we're going to sue the person who sold it to a Negro." He urged the group to follow the same steps and purchase any properties that had been recently sold to African Americans. Since they lost the high court's authority to enforce restrictive covenants, Lund argued to the group, make a "moral agreement with your neighbors," and sell only to Whites. "The law doesn't protect you so we will have to rely on each other."[34]

As Lund advised, White Leimert Park homeowners pursued legal action against those who sold to Blacks. On June 6, 1950, three years before the *Barrows* decision in which the US Supreme Court struck down the right to collect damages when restrictive covenants were breached, some forty White residents filed a lawsuit against White sports writer and radio broadcaster Oscar Reichow and his spouse, Mabel, for damages for violating a deed restriction and selling their 3913 Sixth Avenue home to an African American couple. Citizens United, Incorporated, the homeowners' group that raised money against the Reichows, alleged, "Such violations depreciates [sic] the value of other property, creates social unrest and exposes the District to conditions damaging to personal welfare and safety." While the Reichows' White neighbors requested roughly $185,000 in damages, Reichow lost his job over the conflict, and died unexpectedly the next month, *Barrows* would ultimately dismiss such claims.[35]

Segregationists also used extralegal methods to supposedly "protect" the neighborhood from Black in-migration. On June 21, 1950, two weeks after White homeowners filed a claim against the Reichows, vandals targeted a home on the same road at 3817 Sixth Avenue that had been recently placed in escrow to Mr. and Mrs. A. J. Hunter, an African American couple. Reports showed that vandals emptied the flowerpots outside the premises and wedged a water hose inside an opening to the house made for milk bottles, which flooded the kitchen and basement and damaged the heating system. Neighbors also filed a lawsuit against the White sellers for $45,000 in damages, an argument that had no grounds under *Barrows*.[36]

As the local Democratic Party gained more power, and civil rights activism grew, Blacks found support. In response to the lawsuit against the

Reichows and the vandalism at the Hunter residence, a small group of religious leaders, doctors, attorneys, and homemakers known as the Sixty-Third Assembly District Community Council organized to stop the violence. The group was initially established to elect political candidates to office; as racial hostility heightened in Leimert Park, however, members redirected their goals and stood behind the Black newcomers. In July 1950 the Council organized a mass meeting to present, one newspaper explained, "a clear picture of the facts and the situation, as well as the legal, ethical, and spiritual issues involved." Some two hundred community members gathered at the local junior high school to air their grievances. "The meeting," another newspaper reported, "was free from physical violence but was verbally stormy." The Council insisted on more protection from the police department and requested assistance from the Los Angeles County Committee on Human Relations, the agency established by Democratic County Supervisor John Anson Ford in 1944 to end racial discrimination and improve race relations in the city.[37] The ACLU's Southern California branch also offered support and a monetary reward for information that would lead to an arrest of the vandals who had flooded the Hunters' home. The executive director encouraged the Hunters to stay in the neighborhood and endure "such lawlessness on the part of Caucasians," in the name of attaining "a genuine democracy."[38]

Los Angeles police officer and future mayor Tom Bradley understood the importance of moving into Leimert Park. Bradley was born and raised in Texas for the first five years of his life, where his parents found themselves falling ever deeper into sharecropper debt. "The amount of money advanced to them [for their work] always seemed to amount to more than their income at the end of the year," Bradley recalled. In hopes of escaping poverty, six-year-old Tom and his family migrated to Arizona where they shared a residence with relatives. The backbreaking work in the Arizona cotton fields left them worn out and with little money. Consequently, in the mid-1920s they moved to Los Angeles. Once more Bradley's parents found few opportunities for financial relief. The family barely made ends meet as they worked in various jobs and moved frequently from one place to the next.[39]

In high school Bradley started to carve out a bright future for himself. Among an overwhelmingly White student body, he transcended the school's assumptions about minority students. He broke records in track, became a football star, formed and served in student clubs, and made the honor society. In his senior year he began to date another displaced Texan, Ethel Mae Arnold. He received an athletic scholarship for college and attended UCLA, while Arnold opened and ran beauty salons around the city. Bradley left UCLA after his third year to join the Los Angeles Police Academy, an offer he received after earning top marks on the entrance exam. The chance to "earn enough money to marry and support a family" appealed to him. He confronted racial discrimination in the department at every step, spoke out against the striking inequalities, and, despite the objections of his colleagues, climbed the ranks from the juvenile to detective division.[40]

Then in the early 1950s, a few years after his promotion to detective, Bradley and his family moved to Leimert Park. The couple had spent several years saving their earnings to purchase a home in the neighborhood. From the time they married in 1941, they had lived next to Ethel's parents in a mostly Black community on East Fifty-Seventh Street, but they longed to raise their two daughters, Phyllis and Lorraine, in a neighborhood with good schools and public services. Obtaining property in Leimert Park, however, required skill and ingenuity. Disguised in overalls, Bradley pretended to be a worker employed in the neighborhood and selected a house on Welland Avenue. White friends purchased the property in December 1950 and turned it over to the Bradleys.[41]

The Bradleys' fight to live there had only begun. Their neighbors possessed no judicial support to remove the Bradleys from their home, but they attempted to scare the family into leaving. During the Bradleys' first days in the neighborhood, local children taunted and scorned the family. The Bradley children often felt the brunt of the abuse. Far from Norman Rockwell's 1967 painting of the two Black young newcomers and their three White young neighbors inquisitively meeting for the first time, in *New Kids in the Neighborhood*, the Bradleys' seven-year-old daughter Lorraine got into a fistfight with a local boy who shouted racial epithets at her and demanded she move. She ran home to her father with a bloody nose who said she had "two choices" to deal with the situation: either return outside and play or "stay here in the house all the time, afraid to ever leave, which in essence means that this hatred has beaten you." In an interview with a *Los Angeles Times* reporter, Bradley explained, "You win people over by demonstrating to them that you can be a good neighbor," a common tactic that Nat King Cole used.[42]

For months after the Bradleys moved in, incidents of racial violence continued to occur against other Black newcomers. In March 1951 the Los Angeles County Committee on Human Relations reported that the day after Charles and Bertha Williams unloaded some of their belongings into their 3775 Olmsted Avenue home, they discovered "an oily substance which appeared to be crank case oil...spread over the walls, draperies and floors of every room of the house except the kitchen." The Williams contacted Bradley for help, who immediately spoke to the local police. The police, however, failed to unearth any leads. "No clues, other than a few smudgy finger prints [sic], were found," read the statement.[43] Several months later, hatemongers terrorized John Caldwell and his family in their recently purchased 543 Sixth Avenue home by burning a four-foot-tall cross on their front lawn in the middle of the night.[44]

Despite White intimidation, the Bradleys made friends. Tom Bradley aimed "to create a spirit of good neighborliness" by helping neighbors with projects around their homes. He took pride in assisting the two elderly women that lived next door with home repairs, and he spent his time off from work making improvements on his own property. The Bradley children also made friends, attended the local schools, played on sports teams, and joined local social groups. For Ethel Bradley, planting and pruning the flowers and plants in her garden provided her a diversion from the pressures and demands of her spouse's political career.[45]

From the late 1940s onward, and only a few years before he moved to Leimert Park, Bradley was active in the local Democratic Party. Following Black political strategy of the 1940s, he initially sought to develop his personal connections by working on the election campaigns of candidates Edmund "Pat" Brown and Edward Roybal. While Los Angeles voters helped build a liberal coalition to elect more Democrats to the state legislature, until the late 1940s Augustus Hawkins was the only Black representative on the state assembly. Hawkins succeeded Frederick Roberts in 1934 to represent Central Avenue as the second African American elected to the legislature. For the next fifteen years, Hawkins spent most of his time thwarting the passage of racist legislation and seeing his civil rights laws obstructed. Concerned about the possibility of remaining underrepresented and attending to more powerful White liberals, Black activists from the mid-1940s sought public office for themselves. While Charlotta Bass lost the Los Angeles City Council election in 1945, William Byron Rumford won an assembly seat in Northern California in 1948. Starting in 1949 Hawkins and Rumford took turns introducing civil rights bills to the assembly. "One year, I'd sponsor them; the next year, Rumford would sponsor them," explained Hawkins, only to see them defeated, that is until 1959.[46]

In the early 1950s Bradley stepped up his political activism. He became a founding member of the Democratic Minority Conference (DMC), an organization begun by Black activists that pushed for affirmative action, increased voter registration, district reapportionment, and more Black representation. Bradley and his DMC cohorts also joined the California Democratic Council (CDC), a largely White, liberal reformist group founded in the early 1950s to mobilize local Democrats. He continued to build a biracial coalition in 1953 by getting involved in the Crenshaw Democratic Club, a CDC affiliate, and helping organize and lead its spin-off group, the Leimert Park Democratic Club. "Black and white members of the Leimert Park and other CDC clubs," scholar Raphael Sonenshein wrote, "became Bradley's most enduring loyalists and comprised the inner circle of his campaign organization." Meanwhile, the state assembly election of White liberals Jesse Unruh in 1954 and Phillip Burton in 1956, and then Pat Brown's gubernatorial win against Republican senator William Knowland in the 1958 general election, helped make Democrats the leading party in California. Their victories set the stage for the passage of three civil rights bills in the 1959 landmark session of the state legislature. California's legislation included the Fair Employment Practices Act (1959) that prohibited discrimination in employment (and evolved into the 1963 California Fair Housing Act or Rumford Act), the Unruh Civil Rights Act (1959) that outlawed discrimination in business and housing transactions, and the Hawkins Fair Housing Act (1959) that outlawed discrimination in public housing and urban renewal projects. As Democrats achieved groundbreaking victories, and racial discrimination thwarted his goals in the police force, Bradley began to look to politics as a career.[47]

In 1963, when the Tenth District city council position became available, Bradley ran for office. Located directly north and east of the Crenshaw area, Sonenshein wrote, the Tenth District emerged as the "seedbed of the biracial alliance" in the 1960s. West Jefferson and West Adams Heights made up a portion of the district, which the Black elite had broken in half decades before, while the overwhelmingly White majority included a large Jewish population and the core of CDC liberals. Bradley campaigned for the improvement of public services and facilities and promised to serve as a more visible representative in a district that he believed had been "largely... abandoned by the elected leadership." His rags-to-riches story from a poor Texan boy to Los Angeles police lieutenant, involvement in the CDC, and his ability to build a biracial alliance garnered him votes. He won the election as well as an additional two terms in office. In the early 1960s Blacks gained seats to three of the fifteen Los Angeles City Council districts. Gilbert Lindsay became the first Black member of the city council upon his appointment to the Ninth District in 1962, and Billy G. Mills won a seat to the Eighth District in 1963. As council member, Bradley furthered the biracial coalition, collaborated with civil rights organizations, and fought for better opportunities for Blacks. Then in 1973, one decade after his election, he became Los Angeles's first African American mayor, where he served for five terms.[48]

The arrival of African American entertainers to Leimert Park in the latter half of the 1950s heightened the neighborhood's prestige. Jazz singer Ella Fitzgerald purchased a two-story house at 3971 Hepburn Avenue in 1957. Born in Virginia in 1917 and raised in New York in a struggling working-class home, Fitzgerald showed ambition at an early age to become an entertainer.

She began singing and recording in the 1930s; over her career she sold millions of records, received numerous awards, and toured overseas. Because she spent most of her time recording albums and performing her songs on the West Coast, she made the decision to relocate from New York City to Los Angeles. Fitzgerald took pride in decorating her Leimert Park house, but she lived there for only part of the year while her career kept her on the road.[49]

One year after Fitzgerald purchased her house, musician Ray Charles and his family moved into the neighborhood. Born in segregated Albany, Georgia, in 1930, and raised by his single mother in rural and impoverished Greenville more than one hundred miles north of Albany, Ray Charles Robinson learned to navigate the world as he faced his brother's terrifying death and lost his sight. He started learning the piano at age eight, and after getting expelled from school at age fifteen, he focused on music. Three years before he and his family moved to Leimert Park, Charles crossed over from the rhythm and blues chart to the pop market with his song, "I Got a Woman," and positioned himself among the architects of rock 'n' roll. In 1958 he married Della Beatrice Howard Robinson (she took his surname) and they decided to relocate from Dallas, Texas, for year-round warm weather and a larger home for their expanding family. Della especially wanted to move out of their rented house in Dallas and into a more permanent residence to raise the children. The Robinsons bought a two-story stucco residence at 3910 Hepburn Avenue, located a couple houses up the street from Fitzgerald, paying more than $30,000 in cash, which was well above the 1960 tract median of $20,400 and the 1960 city median of $17,300. The entrance of their home opened into the kitchen and housekeeper's quarters in one section, and the dining room and living room in another, where Charles put his baby-grand piano. They converted the cellar into a recreation room, and Charles used the upstairs bedroom as his office. His touring schedule kept him away most of the time, and biographers later revealed that infidelity and drug abuse clouded his relationships. Della and the children lived in Leimert Park year-round.[50]

While Leimert Park Village served as the community's business center, the area's new residents created a market that led to commercial expansion along Crenshaw Boulevard. In the mid-1950s, Japanese-owned businesses opened along Crenshaw Boulevard that further denoted Crenshaw as an emerging multiethnic and multiracial area. In 1958, the same year Harry Oshiro and three other Nisei (second-generation Japanese) entrepreneurs opened Holiday Bowl, geographer Midori Nishi wrote, "[The] Westside community is now the best Japanese residential area, and its expansion is further evidence of an improved socio-economic status." The instantly popular, thirty-six-lane bowling alley, Holiday Bowl, included a

Japanese-themed lounge, a pool hall, bar, and coffee shop that attracted a cross-section of Angelenos. Holiday Bowl became known to promote "intra-ethnic solidarity, and cross-cultural interaction," historian Scott Kurashige explains, reflected in its menu that offered Japanese and Chinese food, as well as Black soul food. But it also "provided a place where a sense of cultural autonomy might reign on a small scale" as exemplified in the entirely Japanese American and exclusively African American bowling leagues. In 1959, about one block south of Holiday Bowl, Nisei developers constructed the $7 million Crenshaw Square shopping center on Crenshaw Boulevard, between Coliseum and West Thirty-Ninth Streets, in an Asian aesthetic that included offices and retail shops not only to meet the needs of the area's Asian population, but also to promote Japanese culture and heritage. Local merchants and a Nisei veterans' organization sponsored a Japanese summer festival called Bon Odori "that rivaled Little Tokyo's long-established Nisei Week," featuring Japanese foods, martial arts such as judo and kendo, and folk dancing.[51]

The 1960 census recorded a reasonably integrated community. Leimert Park comprised 51.7 percent Whites, 30 percent Blacks, and 18.2 percent Asians. (In comparison, Los Angeles city comprised 83.2 percent Whites, 13.5 percent Blacks, and 3.3 percent Asians.) But as Blacks moved to Leimert Park, they faced another challenge: Although the high court, in *Shelley* and *Barrows*, had declared racial restrictive covenants legally unenforceable, housing discrimination endured, and Blacks had to not only assert their right to live where they pleased, but also endure their neighbors' flight. Whites and then Asians adhered to the historical, government-backed trend of segregating themselves from Blacks, this time by moving, to safeguard their capital. Within a decade, census data showed a shift toward a Black majority and a community moving toward segregation. The Leimert Park population in 1970 comprised 12.9 percent Whites and 69.2 percent Blacks. Moreover, like their White neighbors, many Asian residents grew concerned over interracial dating, juvenile delinquency, and gang violence, concerns made worse by the 1965 Watts rebellion, and moved away. The Asian population fell from 18 percent in 1970 to 10.3 percent in 1980.[52] Before then, however, Angelenos of color had crossed over the Crenshaw Boulevard racial border and settled in the more affluent Crenshaw neighborhoods.

SETTLING ON CRENSHAW'S SOUTHERLY SLOPE—
VIEW PARK, VIEW HEIGHTS, AND WINDSOR HILLS

The exclusive single-family enclaves of View Park, View Heights, and Windsor Hills, located directly southwest of Leimert Park on the southerly slope, became the next major site in the westward trend into Crenshaw. View Park, View Heights, and Windsor Hills shared much in common, including a hilly landscape, views overlooking the city, high property values, and good public schools; residents tended to be in a higher income bracket than those in Leimert Park. The developers initially made clear in all three enclaves that only Whites had the right to purchase property in the area. But from the 1950s onward, on the cusp of the *Shelley* and *Barrows* rulings, Angelenos of color refused to let discrimination prohibit them from the area. They faced White resistance and their neighbors' exodus, but over a short period, property values increased, and View Park, View Heights, and Windsor Hills became some of the most sought-after Los Angeles neighborhoods.[53]

In the late 1920s the Los Angeles Investment Company began to carve out two areas on the opposite ends of the southerly slope as View Park and View Heights. Taking advantage of the rising demand for Westside property, the company subdivided a small section directly west of Leimert Park and across Crenshaw Boulevard, named the site View Park, and placed on the market several newly constructed houses. The developer dug gutters, installed underground utilities, paved sidewalks and streets, erected lampposts, planted trees, and designed parks to appeal to solidly middle-class buyers. In addition, an article in the *Los Angeles Times* assured readers, "The home owners [*sic*] are being protected by restrictions." On the opposite end of the slope, between Overhill Drive and La Brea Avenue, the company also began to develop a small residential enclave named View Heights. It had to briefly postpone construction when Los Angeles used the land for the athletes' living quarters of the 1932 Summer Olympics. But once the games concluded, the celebration of diversity came to an end and the company continued to subdivide the land into restricted enclaves.[54]

In the late 1930s, on the portion of land between View Park and View Heights, Marlow-Burns and Company carved out Windsor Hills. Before getting involved in real estate, Colorado-born Fred H. Marlow had attended West Point, served overseas after World War I, and studied engineering at Massachusetts Institute of Technology. When he arrived in Los Angeles in 1920, amid the nascent land boom, he and his real estate partner, Clifford F. Reid, made millions of dollars subdividing and selling tracts in the San Fernando Valley and then along the Pacific Coast, between Redondo Beach and the Palos Verdes Peninsula. Born to Irish and German immigrant parents in Minnesota, Fritz B. Burns got into real estate when he was a child and his uncle's land development firm, Dickinson and Gillespie, hired him to ride his bicycle to distribute handbills around Minneapolis that advertised lots for sale. In his teenage years, he purchased his first two lots in the Minneapolis suburbs from the same firm, sold his first piece of property, and worked in the office and in sales. After traveling both domestically and abroad, selling land in the western states, and briefly attending the University of Pennsylvania's Wharton School, he returned to Dickinson and Gillespie to expand their business nationwide. In 1921, with the company's financial backing, Burns opened an office with about a hundred agents in Los Angeles, and became a millionaire selling tracts around the San Gabriel Valley and then Palisades del Rey (later Playa del Rey). Like other land developers, Burns followed customary real estate practices and added racial restrictive covenants to the lots. He and Marlow prospered until the Great Depression; then, in 1937, amid financial turmoil, they joined forces and formed their own company.[55]

Buoyed by the New Deal programs, including the HOLC and FHA, both of which standardized housing discrimination, Marlow and Burns purchased their first piece of land together in 1937 from the Lucky Baldwin holdings and began carving out Windsor Hills. For the first time in their careers, thanks to the FHA's mortgage insurance, they not only sold vacant tracts, but also built houses on those parcels and succeeded in large part because of the postwar housing boom and racial restrictions. Marlow-Burns used several promotional techniques to attract White buyers to the area. The company took advantage of the press coverage after Prince Edward's abdication and named the community after the United Kingdom's House of Windsor to convey an air of White nobility and wealth. It also used print advertisements to set the tone of the area. A pamphlet depicted the ideal homeowners as a cheerful, White family. It featured a pale-skinned girl in a yellow dress reaching for the house's front door knocker while her doting mother and father looked on. Moreover, in the Windsor Hills building restrictions code, composed around 1938, "Caucasian race only" topped the list. Number nine made clear, "Racial restrictions are perpetual and binding forever." Burns continued after *Shelley* and *Barrows*, defending private housing interests and White homeowners by, for example, funding the aggressive campaigns of the CHP and Citizens Against Socialist Housing in the late 1940s and early 1950s to halt federally financed public housing projects.[56]

Despite White efforts to restrict the area, beginning in the 1950s people of color settled in. Compared to Leimert Park, integration in View Park, View Heights, and Windsor Hills came at a slower rate. The 1950 census recorded these communities as comprising a 99.7 White population. Asian-born Angelenos numbered 39 (0.4 percent of the population), Blacks numbered 25 (0.2 percent), and Mexican-born Angelenos accounted for 23 (0.2 percent). While the 1960 census recorded that the number of Blacks increased to 512 (4.2 percent of the population), more African Americans lived east of Valley Ridge Avenue, mainly in View Park, a clear illustration of the slow but steady westward migration trend.[57]

As in Leimert Park, westward migration into these communities initially proved to be a difficult task. When twin sisters and elementary school teachers Evangeline Woods Johnson and Elly Woods Redmond joined a handful of African Americans and moved into a house in View Park on 4025 Olympiad Drive in 1957, they endured continual racial slurs, threats, and vandalism. Whites, at least one of whom was identified as living in View Park, walked by the house yelling racial epithets, made death threats over the phone, sent hostile letters, and burned a seven-foot cross on the lawn; they also threw things: a rock at the door, a brick and a golf ball through the window, a lead pipe at the house, and a flare onto the lawn. "I want them to know we're not running.... This is a thing we're going to have to fight," Evangeline asserted, nearly ten years after *Shelley*. Johnson and Redmond notified the police who responded that the acts were merely "the pranks of teenagers," the *California Eagle* reported. She and her sister continued their fight throughout the years, including speaking on a panel at an NAACP meeting with Loren Miller, George Beavers, and Floyd Covington to advise more African Americans on ways to face White resistance. The *California Eagle* proposed and the panel sought to grapple with, "Who is going to win the battle of housing segregation in Southern California?" At that moment, the question remained up for speculation. In its early January 1958 report of the highlights from 1957, the newspaper put the View Park story on its front page with the Little Rock Nine and the Prayer Pilgrimage for Freedom. The *Eagle* understood the event within the spectrum of the civil rights movement.[58]

African American View Park resident David K. Carlisle recalled the struggles he and his family also faced when they moved to the neighborhood in his letter to the *Los Angeles Times* in 1989. When he and his spouse bought a house there in 1959, "Some of our immediate neighbors immediately put up 'For Sale' signs." He faced problems from parents when he attempted to register his oldest child in kindergarten at Windsor Hills Elementary School. "The well-intentioned but condescending attitude of some parents led me to enroll him instead at 54th Street Elementary School," a public school located on Windsor Hills's easternmost side. But the Carlisle family stayed as "most neighbors and parents soon made us realize how wonderful this close-in community would be." He continued, "Eventually, we began to experience the joy and enrichment of living in what became a truly integrated environment. Our children knew that black was beautiful, but they also learned that yellow, brown and white are just as beautiful." Unfortunately, integration in View Park in the mid-twentieth century was fleeting as most White residents left the area. Carlisle held out hope that, "By the time my grandson reaches kindergarten age in two years, View Park will again be an integrated community, in which children of all races...will have an opportunity to grow up together harmoniously."[59]

While Whites initially resisted Black in-migration in the postwar years, View Park's esteemed reputation continued to develop, particularly when entertainers Ike and Tina Turner moved in. Born in segregated Mississippi, Ike Turner had endured a turbulent childhood, including when, at around age five, he bore witness to his father's death. A White gang broke into the Turner home, forced his father into a truck, and, several hours later, returned him bruised and bloodied with "holes in his stomach." After the White hospital refused to help, the health department set up a tent in the yard for his father to heal. He died a few years later. While his mother made a living as a seamstress, young Ike worked between school hours, collecting scrap metal, selling chickens, and delivering goods. But Turner's passion for music led him to seek bigger dreams. After he completed the third grade, his mother bought her son a piano, and from then on Turner honed his musical skills.[60]

In the early 1950s, Turner began to receive recognition for his talent. Months after he and his band recorded "Rocket 88" at Sun Records in Memphis, Tennessee, the song topped the Billboard rhythm and blues chart. Success validated Turner's musicianship, but he continued to crave respect. Each band member received only $20 for the recording, and while Turner requested top billing for the song, singer Jackie Brenston received the honor. Turner continued to work in the music business as a talent scout for a Los Angeles–based record label. The work led him to Los Angeles in the early 1950s, where he first saw a house in View Park that he would later buy. "On the way to the airport" to catch his return flight, Turner's driver told him, "Ike, when you get some real money, this is the neighbourhood you'll stay in." Turner continued, "I saw this woman opening the garage. I'd never seen an electric garage-door-opener before. I said, 'Man, did you see that?' Man, that was exciting to me. When a record company gave me $20,000 for 'A Fool in Love,' I went back up in them hills and I bought the exact same house where I'd seen the woman open the garage door—4263 Olympiad Drive." But in the early 1950s, the house would have to wait. Turner and his band moved to East St. Louis, Missouri, where they played the nightclub circuit. There, he crossed paths with Anna Mae Bullock, who he would later marry and rename as Tina Turner.[61]

From an early age, Bullock yearned to shed her rural upbringing. Born in Tennessee, young Anna Mae felt overlooked by her parents and spent much of her childhood moving from one household to the next. She found little comfort in the religion of her church but flourished in the choir. "I knew I wanted to wear my hair differently—I hated those braids. And I had a feeling about the piano, too, and it had nothing to do with church songs. I wanted…glamour." In the mid-1950s, at age sixteen, she followed her mother and sister Alline to St. Louis, Missouri, where she absorbed the energy of the city. Alline introduced Anna Mae to the nightclub scene, and the two young women quickly became followers of the most popular band in town, Ike Turner and the Kings of Rhythm. During intermission one night, Bullock showed off her natural musical talent. When the drummer began to tease Alline to sing, gutsy Anna Mae grabbed the microphone from his hand and began to accompany Turner as he played the organ. Stunned and amazed, Turner "ran down off that stage and he picked me right up!" He invited her to return to sing at the nightclub and join the band on the road.[62]

In the early 1960s, Turner found a reason to relocate to Los Angeles. The recording of "A Fool in Love," with Bullock as lead vocalist, caught the attention of Sue Records head Henry "Juggy" Murray, who flew to St. Louis to convince Turner to sign a record deal with his label. Turner received a $25,000 advance, released the song under Ike and Tina Turner, and in August 1960 the single reached number two on the Billboard rhythm and blues chart. Then in October, the same month Ike and Tina performed on Dick Clark's show *American Bandstand*, the song crossed over to the White market and reached number twenty-seven on the pop chart. Turner had outgrown St. Louis. Between touring and recording, the couple returned to Los Angeles and purchased the one-story, three-bedroom ranch house at 4263 Olympiad Drive in View Park. After they had bought the property, the Turners moved their four children and caretaker in. Ike Turner decorated the interior extravagantly with custom-made couches, red carpet, and a guitar-shaped coffee table. *Look* magazine photos of the couple on the driveway in front of their sports cars and of Tina Turner cooking in the kitchen portrayed an idyllic picture of married, suburban life, yet this time, the couple was Black. For decades, the Turners and their close friends hid from public view Ike Turner's drug and spousal abuse.[63]

In 1963, roughly one year after the Turners had moved in, Ray Charles and Della Robinson bought three vacant lots only a few blocks away to build their family home. By then, Charles had achieved greater success, had moved from Atlantic Records to ABC-Paramount, and had recorded hit songs, including "Georgia on My Mind" and "Hit the Road Jack." Taking the advice of his manager, they invested $100,000 in Los Angeles property, and, after two years of construction, the family moved into their custom-built home at 4863 Southridge Avenue. The twelve-thousand-square foot structure, which symbolized Charles's wealth and success, stuck out among the adjacent moderately sized homes. "Our house at the top of the hill was a sanctuary and a refuge," wrote Ray Charles Robinson, Jr., the Robinsons' eldest son. "From our vantage point we could see the entire Los Angeles basin spread out beneath us." The white marble entryway, staircase, and fireplace as well as the white carpet and walls looked dignified, but Della thought that the design and color choice was unsuitable for raising children. She and the children spent most of their leisure time in the den. The boys enjoyed swimming in the pool, with its image of a piano shaped in tile on the shallow end's floor, and playing basketball with the net they had erected on the tennis court.[64]

The arrival of the first people of color into View Park, View Heights, and Windsor Hills gave others the opportunity to move to the area. Between 1960 and 1970, the census reported, while the White population fell from 94.6 percent to 33.5 percent, the Black proportion grew from 4.2 percent to 62.6 percent. Moreover, like Leimert Park, this area also saw a rise and fall in the Asian population from 1.2 percent in 1960 to 3.9 percent in 1970 to 2 percent in 1980. Asians, mostly of Japanese and then Chinese descent, gained access to the area around the same time as Blacks, and yet fled alongside Whites out of the same fears.[65] For decades, the government, courts, banks, real estate associations, and other White-dominated institutions spread the notion that integrated neighborhoods would depress property values and damage neighborhoods. But median owner-occupied property value and income stayed well above the city median. The median property value of the entire area rose from more than $27,000 in 1960 to more than $35,000 in 1970, while the city median increased from $17,300 in 1960 to $26,700 in 1970. The median income rose from more than $11,000 in 1960 to more than $14,000 in 1970, while the city median increased from $6,896 in 1960 to $10,535 in 1970.[66]

Through the 1960s, more esteemed African Americans moved to the area, including singer Nancy Wilson, musician Earl Grant, and musician Oliver Nelson, as well as doctors, judges, attorneys, teachers, and other professionals. "Most of the families who lived in View Park had arrived there through courage and hard work, not through birthright or privilege," Robinson Jr. explained. "We all lived by the same rules: dinner, homework, home by dark, good sportsmanship, and respect for others." Yet most Whites and Asians refused to remain in the area. Crenshaw's enclaves on the northern slope faced a similar trajectory.[67]

THE HIGHS AND LOWS OF BALDWIN HILLS

Westward migration persisted on to Crenshaw's northern slope that gave way to an area of contrasts. In the 1940s, land developers began subdividing the former Lucky Baldwin holdings between Stocker Street, Santa Barbara Avenue (King Boulevard), Rodeo Road (later President Barack Obama Boulevard, or simply Obama Boulevard), and La Cienega Boulevard for White city dwellers in a range of incomes, and branded the communities after their past proprietor. Both northern sections, Baldwin Village and the Village Green, offered multifamily rental units to the low- and middle-income urbanites, while both southern sections, Baldwin Hills Estates and Baldwin Vista comprised single-family houses, many with panoramic views of the city, for the solidly middle class. As Angelenos of color migrated into the area in the 1950s and 1960s, Whites fought back, first through intimidation and then, along with Asians, by abandoning the area altogether. While many new and older residents persevered, they grew concerned their communities would deteriorate and be labeled ghettos. Baldwin Hills Estates, Baldwin Vista, and the Village Green held on to their high reputations, but Baldwin Village fell victim to drug trafficking and gang violence. Residents faced an uphill battle to defend their long-desired and hard-earned communities from the historic forces of White disinvestment and neglect.

Baldwin Hills's northwest section situated between La Brea, Santa Barbara, and Marlton Avenues, and Santo Tomas Drive, and comprising single-family houses and multifamily rental units, has taken several names. Despite its location, the area has been described as the lower Baldwin Hills for its topography in the Baldwin Hills flats, and dubbed "the Jungle," which, according to legend, referred to its tropical palm trees, banana trees, and begonias. By the 1970s, however, locals used "the Jungle" as a metonym for its gang-ruled and drug-ridden environment. In the late 1980s, thanks to a local drive to repair and rebrand the area, it adopted Baldwin Village as its new name.[68]

Developers reserved the hilly, triangular-shaped interior south of Santo Tomas Drive, between Stocker Street and La Brea Avenue, which they named Baldwin Hills Estates, for the middle class. Baldwin Hills Estates featured unique characteristics that distinguished the enclave from its contiguous surroundings. The developers marked the entrance with stone columns; to avoid the cookie-cutter, postwar housing patterns, they designed custom-built, single-family residences in early American, French provincial, farmhouse, Cape Cod, and contemporary modern styles. They also attempted to set Baldwin Hills Estates apart by heading each street name with "Don," the Spanish title of respect for a nobleman. Appellations such as Don Quixote Drive, Don Luis Drive, and Don Milagro Drive romanticized the city's Spanish and Mexican eras and set a tone of distinction and privilege, and "the Dons" became the community's commonly used nickname.[69]

Through the 1950s, as people of color settled in the area, Whites tried to preserve the homogeneous racial composition with zeal. The 1950 census recorded Baldwin Village and Baldwin Hills Estates combined as having a 99.8 percent White population. Twelve Asian-born Angelenos, twelve Mexican-born urbanites, and one African American lived there. In 1960 the

Baldwin Village population comprised 4.4 percent Asians, 2 percent Hispanics, and 0.6 percent Blacks. Baldwin Hills Estates consisted of 1.6 percent Asians, 2.4 percent Hispanics, and 3 percent Blacks.[70] White hostility and intimidation drove some Blacks away. For instance, in 1955, the Los Angeles County Conference on Community Relations reported an African American family that recently purchased a house on Don Diablo Drive, "sold, under pressure, its contract of purchase." The incident, however, failed to dissuade others from moving in.[71]

Black migration west of La Brea Avenue, into the Village Green (originally Thousand Gardens and then Baldwin Hills Village) and Baldwin Vista (originally Baldwin Hills Vista) occurred at a slower rate. Like the area to its east, this area also offered multifamily rental units on its northwest section and single-family houses to the south. The Village Green became known for its unique design of rental units. Architectural magazines, including *Pencil Points*, published articles on the community, and *Architect and Engineer* granted it a distinguished honor award. Even Lewis Mumford took note in 1944 that the Village Green "stands out as a fundamental advance in both planning and architecture." Formulated in 1939 and built in 1941, between Sycamore Avenue, Coliseum Street, Hauser Boulevard, and Rodeo Road (Obama Boulevard), the interconnected Village Green was marketed as an idyllic complex intended to offset the bustling city for White urbanites seeking mid- to low-priced apartments. Associated architects Reginald Johnson, Robert Alexander, Lewis Wilson, and Edwin Merrill, and landscape architects Fred Barlow and Fred Edmondson, drew their inspiration for the project from consulting architect Clarence Stein and his previous housing projects. Since the 1920s Stein had been working to fulfill Ebenezer Howard's concept of garden cities: self-sufficient, bucolic residential enclaves situated amid the larger, teeming, industrial cities. Using the key components of Howard's garden city, the architects designed the Village Green within an eighty-acre superblock that included rental units facing spacious and meticulously landscaped central greens, playgrounds, service courts, and other communal spaces. The exclusion of roadways within the property provided residents more security and serenity from the urban environment. The community would serve as a model for Boyle Heights' Estrada Courts public housing that Robert Alexander later designed.[72]

Baldwin Vista also aimed to become an idyllic, exclusively White, postwar oasis that felt separate from the city; unlike the Village Green, though, it consisted of single-family housing for the solidly middle class. Situated between La Brea Avenue, La Cienega Boulevard, and Coliseum Street, Baldwin Vista, in 1954, offered sites with a view in a range of prices between roughly $9,000 and $16,000, at a time when the city averaged $11,925.

Residents could enjoy properties with "unobstructed" views of the city, the *Los Angeles Times* reported, and "gracefully contoured streets with all utilities underground." Beyond the southern boundary sat an open field, formerly used as a golf course, and portioned off for a water reservoir. The area also remained within the borders of Crenshaw's good public schools.[73]

But as in the main thoroughfares of Arlington Avenue and Crenshaw Boulevard, La Brea Avenue had become another roadblock for marginalized Angelenos seeking full access to the city. Consequently, Blacks joined other people of color across La Brea Avenue at a markedly slower rate than the other Crenshaw communities. The 1950 census recorded the Village Green as comprising a 99.7 percent White population. Thirteen Asian-born urbanites, ten Mexican-born Angelenos, and four Blacks lived there. From 1950 to 1960 the number of Blacks fell from four to one. The 1960 census recorded no Asians living there. Meanwhile, the 1950 census documented Baldwin Vista with a 99.8 percent White population. Ten Asian-born Angelenos, three Mexican-born city dwellers, and two Blacks lived there. From 1950 to 1960 the number of Blacks increased from merely two to six, and Asians from ten to twenty-eight.[74]

African Americans believed that these communities provided an opportunity to improve their quality of life. K. D. Patton understood the significance of moving into Baldwin Hills Estates. Born in Texas, Patton arrived in Los Angeles in 1946, following his discharge from the Army. With $4,500 in his pocket, he bought a restaurant on Central Avenue and moved into a nearby apartment. He ran the business for a year and a half, and then explored other options, attending business school and working at the post office. Meanwhile, he discovered his passion for real estate. "Every time we got a couple thousand dollars," he recalled years later, "I bought a property." He purchased properties in communities around Los Angeles, hired a crew to renovate, and then, with the help of realtors, sold them for profit. In Baldwin Hills Estates, he appreciated that no house "had the same floor plan" or "same exterior," and he enjoyed the various "short streets [and] long streets" in the landscape. Baldwin Hills Estates also marked his progress. He "wanted to do better," he explained, "live in better places," and "improve my living" conditions. In 1961 Patton and his family purchased a two-bedroom, two-bathroom split-level house for $32,500 on Don Luis Drive, impressively more expensive than the 1960 city median of $17,300. They resided among mostly Jewish and White neighbors for four years, and then relocated to a newly constructed, four-bedroom, four-bathroom house in View Park.[75]

Drs. Lawrence and Gertrude Paxton moved to Baldwin Hills Estates with similar intentions. Born in North Carolina, young Gertrude grew up with the expectation of completing college. Her mother, who taught economics at Shaw University, was "very determined" to have all of her children earn advanced degrees. As a student in the Teacher's College at Howard University, Paxton changed her career plans and pursued dentistry. Male students resented her for "taking up space that a man could have," but Paxton finished near the top of her class. While teaching at the dental school, she met Lawrence Paxton. The couple married, relocated to New York, and then moved to Los Angeles. In the early 1960s they settled in a two-bedroom apartment on Forty-Third Place in Leimert Park. "That was…*the* place to live then," Gertrude Paxton later recalled. A Leimert Park residence in the 1960s was a symbol of success. Within a few years, the Paxtons had grown into a family of five and were too large for their apartment. But also, Paxton explained, "We wanted to take the next step up." Around 1963 they purchased a three-bedroom, two-bathroom house on Don Mariano Drive for $40,000. Gertrude focused on raising their three children and participating in local church and social groups, while Lawrence ran his dental practice.[76]

Through the 1960s, as Blacks migrated into the single-family homes of Baldwin Hills Estates and Baldwin Vista, Whites and Asians moved away. Between 1960 and 1970, the White population fell from 95.4 percent to 18.9 percent in Baldwin Hills Estates, and 99.2 percent to 52.6 percent in Baldwin Vista. The Black population jumped from 3 percent to 74.8 percent in Baldwin Hills Estates, and from 0.1 percent to 34.2 percent in Baldwin Vista. Meanwhile, like the adjacent neighborhoods, the Asian population rose and fell. In Baldwin Hills Estates the Asian population swung from 1.6 percent in 1960 to 6.4 percent in 1970 to 2.3 percent in 1980. In Baldwin Vista it went from 0.6 percent in 1960 to 13.2 percent in 1970 to 8.5 percent in 1980.[77] Yet in the face of White exodus residents maintained the reputation and value of their communities. From 1960 to 1970, as the median owner-occupied property value rose from $17,300 to $26,700 in the city, it jumped from more than $25,000 to $44,300 in Baldwin Hills Estates, and more than $25,000 to $37,200 in Baldwin Vista. As the median income increased from $6,896 to $10,535 in the city, it rose from $11,873 to $14,907 in Baldwin Hills Estates, and $9,307 to $13,448 in Baldwin Vista.[78] But during the demographic shift toward a Black majority, residents grew deeply concerned that their thriving, middle-class communities would deteriorate and be called ghettos.

The Village Green, with its prize-winning architectural design that prevented automobile traffic from traversing the complex and its location west of La Brea Avenue, held on to its exclusive reputation. Between 1960 and 1970, its Black population slightly increased from 0.08 percent to 9.9 percent, while its White population held its majority at 99.9 percent and then 89.9 percent. Between 1970 and 1980 the Asian population also slightly increased from 0.2 percent to 5.9 percent. The community's median rent and median income remained above the city medians.[79]

But Baldwin Village concerned the affluent Crenshaw residents. Echoing trends in Baldwin Hills Estates, its southern neighbor, Baldwin Village's Black population substantially increased between 1960 and 1970 from 0.56 percent to 72.5 percent, while its White population fell from 95.1 percent to 18.1 percent. Also like its neighbor, Baldwin Village's Asian population rose and fell from 4.4 percent in 1960 to 9.3 percent in 1970 to 4.6 percent in 1980. The community's median rent remained above the city median, but its median income fell below the city median, an indication of the difficulty residents could have had in making ends meet. In 1970, for instance, while the city had a $10,535 median income, Baldwin Village's highest median income, of its four census tracts, was $9,395. Its lowest, of those four tracts, was $6,983. The decline of Central Avenue in the 1940s, the demolition of Sugar Hill in the mid-1950s, the upswing in gang activity in the 1950s and 1960s, and the formation of gangs in Baldwin Village in the early 1970s validated residents' concerns.[80]

COMMUNITIES TORN APART

Although middle-class Blacks succeeded in challenging Los Angeles's racial borders in the post-*Shelley* years, their struggles manifested in other ways. For one, in the mid-1950s the California Highway Commission announced its plans to construct the Olympic freeway (later the Santa Monica freeway, or I-10) on an east-west path running on the southern border of downtown Los Angeles to Santa Monica. While the freeway promised a more efficient route between downtown and the Pacific Coast Highway, some city dwellers protested after hearing that the road would cut through and destroy many predominantly Black communities, including Sugar Hill. Also, as Whites moved out of the central city, the Eastside Black belt took shape, police brutality against African Americans worsened, deindustrialization led to significant job loss, and gang membership and rivalry increased. While gangs claimed their right to the urban space, they turned against each other and ignited a deadly war over turf rights. African Americans put an end to racial restrictive covenants, but they could not stop racial prejudice, oppression, or violence.

Through the 1950s, after the announcement of the Olympic freeway construction, the struggle to protect the integrity and value of Sugar Hill waged on. Within a decade after *Shelley* and *Barrows*, as more Blacks settled in the area, most Whites sold their properties and moved. The proportion of people of color residing in Sugar Hill's total occupied dwellings increased from 22.9 percent in 1950 to 75.7 percent in 1960. But despite

White fears that property values would decline, the value of homes in Sugar Hill remained competitive. The 1950 census reported that the median owner-occupied property value of the entire tract had increased to $12,614, slightly above the city average of $11,925. But the freeway contributed to hurting the 1960 median property value of $16,900, which fell below the city median of $17,300.[81] While Black residents invested in their homes, a *California Eagle* reporter held out hope that, "Although the cards seemed heavily stacked against a reversal [of the decision to construct a freeway], there was an encouraging possibility that a victory might still be achieved." City officials put "the most prosperous, best kept and most beautiful Negro-owned property in the country" in harm's way. Yet Sugar Hill homeowners and advocates understood that they had to confront another powerful group of policymakers who showed little concern for the historic enclave.[82]

Sugar Hill residents and civil rights activists gathered together to agree on a plan of action. They established a citizens' committee and appointed three representatives to speak on behalf of the community. Los Angeles Urban League executive director Floyd Covington, attorney Bernard Jefferson, and real estate agent John Saito traveled to the state capital of Sacramento in February 1954 to make a case at a hearing of the California Highway Commission against the placement of the freeway. They attempted to persuade the commission to redirect the path of the freeway to a largely White area north of Washington Boulevard by arguing that racial discrimination prevented Black and Asian homeowners in Sugar Hill from moving to other comparably desirable neighborhoods. Despite *Shelley* and *Barrows*, Jefferson insisted, "We do not have equal opportunities to move elsewhere, a right which Caucasians enjoy." Saito explained that although finding a house "is a little easier" for Asians, "the problem is essentially the same." They convinced the commission to delay the construction for a few months. But in May, the *California Eagle* reported, the commission "unanimously approved" the plan. City council member Charles Navarro, one of the few policymakers who opposed the route, rebuked the commission, "All they care about is dollars and cents!"[83]

The reasons for positioning the freeway through Sugar Hill were rooted in economics and racism. The population boom and economic expansion through World War II accelerated the need for more-efficient transportation routes around the city. Under the Eisenhower administration, Congress helped boost interstate construction with the passage of the National Interstate and Defense Highways Act of 1956 that led to a national movement of highways. But the dubious placement of freeways in Los Angeles suggests motivations based in racial prejudice. Historian Eric Avila finds that urban planners used highway construction as an opportunity to clear out some of the city's predominately Black, rundown communities. While Sugar Hill had high property values, its high esteem endured mainly in the eyes of Angelenos of color. Most Whites saw little value in the community, and the largely Black population of Sugar Hill, and its adjacent lower-income, Black communities gave the highway commission a reason to forge ahead with the plan. Freeways served as "a symbol of such middle-class ideals as physical mobility, individual freedom, and civic progress," Avila maintains. Thus policymakers aimed "to coordinate highway construction with slum clearance." Replacing Sugar Hill and its adjacent Black communities with a freeway helped preserve those White, middle-class standards.[84]

The freeway razed the historic properties of some of the most celebrated Sugar Hill residents and literally tore the neighborhood in half. The houses formerly owned by Hattie McDaniel, Norman O. Houston, Horace and Vera Clark, and Louise Beavers, which were located directly below Twenty-Second Street, escaped the bulldozer. Yet a swath of highways and the resulting vehicular traffic obstructed their privacy and their expansive views of the city. The block of land that ran east and west between Twenty-Second and Twenty-First Streets fell victim to the construction. The properties that J. A. and Vada Somerville, Ethel Waters, and Juan and Rose Tizol worked so hard to attain were reduced to rubble. A community once known for its famous and affluent residents, who had determinedly set in motion the end of racial restrictive covenants, had become a passageway for commuters.

Despite the destruction caused by the freeway, many elite African Americans refused to give up on the area. Golden State Mutual's home office, built one year after *Shelley* on the corner of Western and Adams Boulevards, remained a staple of the community. The company continued to offer insurance policies, home mortgages, and employment opportunities. Founders Norman O. Houston and George A. Beavers continued to dedicate their time to civil rights causes. Houston served on the national board of the NAACP and the Urban League. Beavers worked with the Los Angeles Housing Authority Commission, the Los Angeles Urban League, Freedom Fund Campaign, Los Angeles NAACP, local YMCA, and United Negro College Fund, among other organizations. They also encouraged the Golden State Mutual staff to volunteer in the community. In a 1966 interview, Houston explained, "You'll find Golden State interwoven in practically every progressive movement that's going on in our city."[85]

Ray Charles also invested a portion of his wealth in the community. In 1963, the same year he purchased his View Park property, Charles bought two lots for $52,000 on the corner of Washington and Westmoreland Boulevards and built a state-of-the-art studio and office building for his company, Ray Charles Enterprises. Charles called the building RPM International, an acronym for the recording measurement, revolutions per minute. RPM employees carried out the recording, publishing, and management duties of Charles's three companies—Tangerine Records, Tangerine Music, and Racer Personal Management. His biographer explained that RPM International became Charles's "castle, his fortress, his faraway island; the place where he could work and play and live and love and be by himself whenever he pleased." He enjoyed the freedom of recording music on his own time without the pressure of a major studio and running the operations of his companies.[86]

Meanwhile, Black street clubs emerged out of an established history of youth mobilization. The city's first gangs developed in the 1930s largely Mexican American East Los Angeles barrio. The same systemic and systematic forces that pushed Blacks southward along the Central Avenue corridor had impelled Mexican Angelenos and immigrants since the mid-nineteenth century east of the Plaza, into Sonoratown, Boyle Heights, and then the East Los Angeles barrio. Following the pachucos who organized into gangs in 1920s El Paso, Texas, young Chicano Angelenos in the 1930s formed the city's first clique, El Hoyo Maravilla, which they named after their enclave, Maravilla. Others followed, including the Cuatro Flats and White Fence cliques in the 1940s. Organized for a range of reasons, including to resist discrimination, reject assimilation, and maintain ethnic traditions, pachucos soon gained public attention for wearing oversized zoot suits and becoming targets in the 1942 Sleepy Lagoon murder and the 1943 zoot suit attacks. By the late 1930s, Nisei youths had also formed their own cliques for a range of reasons, including rebelling against social pressures, resisting discrimination, and seeking self-protection. Some gangs were made up of members from different ethnic and racial groups. In the 1950s the mostly Japanese Westside gang, the Constituents, for instance, took inspiration from Black thinkers, such as Eldridge Cleaver, and from Black culture: they admitted Chinese, Filipino, and Black members, and bonded over White oppression and police abuse of power. Other gangs formed in opposition to other racial and ethnic sets.[87]

In the 1940s the decade after Chicano and Asian youths first established cliques, Black street clubs formed in self-defense against White clubs. Impelled by the rise of the Spook Hunters, Black clubs, such as the Devil Hunters, the Businessmen, and the Gladiators, arose. Through the 1950s and 1960s, as notorious Los Angeles Police Department chief William H. Parker set out to dismantle Black life and livelihood on Central Avenue, Black street clubs radicalized, increased in membership, and turned against one another. First allied to defend themselves against White oppressors, they adopted the oppressors' behavior and ignited a lethal war that wreaked havoc on themselves and the city. "Most clashes were actually rooted in socioeconomic differences," scholar Alex Alonso explains. The Eastside and Westside, which Black gangs partitioned at historic Main Street, the city's first racial border, served as one of many dividing lines. "Eastsiders resented the upwardly mobile Westsiders, who came from families that were able to break out of the Central Avenue ghetto.... Westside youth wanted to prove their toughness even though they lived in communities comprised of single-family stucco homes and manicured lawns." Interracial and interethnic hostility and class conflict existed long before the postwar era, but the rise of gang rivalry worsened infighting and violence.[88]

While gangs mostly steered clear of the affluent Crenshaw neighborhoods, such as View Park, Windsor Hills, and Baldwin Hills Estates, they wreaked havoc on the adjacent working-class enclaves. Sections to the north and east, adjacent to Leimert Park and Baldwin Hills Estates, saw the greatest gang formation and activity. In 1959 a group of Sansei (third-generation Japanese, largely those born to parents who had endured wartime incarceration) Dorsey High School students organized the Ministers, and over the subsequent years, recruited more than one hundred members, some of whom lived in the working-class Avenues section north of Exposition Boulevard, around the railroad tracks, and in Leimert Park. The Ministers asserted their power over anyone they believed was a threat, including their middle-class Leimert Park neighbors and any Angelenos living outside of the Crenshaw area. Among the Black Westside gangs, the Gladiators in the 1960s grew into the largest. Identified by a patch on their jackets of a gladiator wielding a sword and standing with his foot atop his victim's chest, the gang engaged in intra-racial fighting mostly using their fists, tire irons, pipes, or knives (and gradually guns) with rivals, including the Eastside's Businessmen and Slausons.[89]

Beginning in the early 1970s, after a hiatus from the Watts rebellion, Los Angeles underwent a third wave of gang formation, and as gang violence turned more lethal, Baldwin Village, the area north of Baldwin Hills Estates, fell victim to the devastating Bloods and Crips rivalry. Eugene "Bull" Hairston and Jeff Fort established the Black Peace Stone Nation (BPSN) amid rampant racial discrimination and segregation in early 1960s Chicago under a different name. Chapters formed in late 1960s and early 1970s Los Angeles, including the City Stones in the West Adams area and then the Jungle Stones in Baldwin Village, both of whom were affiliated with the Bloods, which was a rival gang of the Crips. Like most Chicago gangs, BPSN took its name to reference its Muslim identity and honor the sacred Islamic site, the Kaaba (a large black stone structure), in Mecca, Saudi Arabia. Like Chicano gangs, Black sets took their name from geographic locations, Alonso explains, to signify "turf ownership and group identity." The Jungle Stones named themselves after Baldwin Village's moniker, "the Jungle." Initially used to denote its tropical vegetation, the moniker over time connoted the community's "savage" and "uncivilized" gang-ruled and drug-ridden environment, racially loaded words fifteenth-century European colonists erroneously used to describe Africans and Native Americans. In the name of territorial rights over the community, the Jungle Stones graffitied property, engaged in drug trafficking, and used firearms to commit murder.[90]

African Americans who migrated to Hancock Park, Lafayette Square, the Crenshaw area, and other Westside enclaves aimed not only to improve their quality of life, but also to surmount housing inequality and gain equal access to the city. They faced White intimidation and racism at all levels, from their neighbors' daily threats to government-endorsed legal restrictions. They remained determined to enjoy the best opportunities that Los Angeles had to offer, yet through the 1960s, as the racial composition in these Westside enclaves like Lafayette Square and those in Crenshaw shifted toward a Black majority, middle-class Blacks faced another protracted struggle. Once they began purchasing property and moving to the area, a wave of White and then Asian Angelenos sold their homes and moved. Decades of housing discrimination created and carried out at the neighborhood, city, state, and federal levels caused damage to the American psyche that could not be undone merely by judicial decisions. "We saw the neighborhood change very drastically," Gertrude Paxton observed years later, from mostly White to mostly Black. After *Shelley* and *Barrows*, Crenshaw became one of countless areas in California, including those in San Francisco, Oakland, and Berkeley, where Whites fled. Hundreds of thousands in greater Los Angeles found new residence in outlying communities, such as Torrance and the San Fernando Valley, where they also forged efforts to restrict to Whites only.[91] But many Crenshaw homeowners refused to accept racism and mobilized in a campaign to sustain the integrity and diversity of their communities.

Chapter Five

A Campaign to Build "A Balanced Community"

BEGINNING IN THE SPRING OF 1961, in homes around the Crenshaw area, a small, multiracial group of women of various political leanings convened for monthly meetings to talk about the growing race-related conflicts in their community. They initially gathered in concern over "some serious racial problems" at Susan M. Dorsey High School, the local public high school, explained Windsor Hills homeowner and one of the White founders Jean Gregg. Rumors spread that classes, extracurricular activities, and social cliques had become separated by race; both White and Black students faced discrimination; fights among students broke out; and school officials took little disciplinary actions. The group's discussions led into a host of issues over property values, racial stereotypes, and interracial dating. "It was a very exciting time for me personally," explained Joan Suter, Baldwin Vista homeowner and one of the first Black members. As the women revealed their fears and assumptions, they discovered similarities with each other, developed meaningful friendships across racial and ethnic lines, and mobilized into an informal, loosely based group that they called United Neighbors (UN).[1]

As word spread in the area about the meetings, more residents joined. One year after the initial gathering, UN began scheduling evening meetings to give residents with daytime work hours an opportunity to get involved. Within two years attendance had grown from twenty to more than one hundred members. UN moved the meetings' locations from private homes to public places, invited local officials and school representatives to the discussion, addressed the Los Angeles Board of Education (BOE), and participated in panels. The meetings created what Gregg called "a large nucleus of people who had genuinely overcome the fears of each other." Neighbors worked together to resolve the racial tensions in their community and advocate for integration. "We see ourselves...as primarily a communications group which tries to involve more and more people and more and more groups and organizations; which tries to open up closed or clogged channels of communication, stimulate ideas, spark action by other groups, [and] improve understanding and knowledge." Several UN members also teamed up with other community groups to create programs aimed to give all Crenshaw residents equal respect and opportunity.[2]

Beyond the group's camaraderie, racial intolerance persisted, and UN knew it had a larger and more complex task at hand. In addition to the conflicts in the school district, White fear manifested in another form in the Crenshaw area and across the country: residents accused local real estate agents of using blockbusting, or panic selling, techniques that accelerated racial turnover. Used as far back as the early 1900s, with the term coined and the policy popularized in the 1950s, real estate agents across the country seeking to make a profit hastened resegregation by putting fear in White residents of what many viewed as what they called "a Black invasion." Generally, blockbusting real estate agents selected what they believed was an imminent transitional neighborhood, rented or sold properties to a few people of color, and then persuaded White residents that the area would decline in a matter of time. They capitalized on the transition by going door to door, circulating flyers, and making phone calls that impelled White homeowners to move.[3]

Blockbusting took shape differently across the country. In some cases, real estate agents would initiate racial turnover by purchasing White-owned properties at a low price and then, in what scholars call the dual housing market, renting or selling them at a high rate, which included what deridingly became known as the "Black tax," to Black families who sought access to the area. Once a few Black families had moved in, Whites yielded to their anxieties of racial mixing, a decline in the schools, services, and property values, along with an increase in crime, and sold their homes. In the single-family Crenshaw homes, affluent Blacks, such as Tom Bradley, Ray Charles, and Ike and Tina Turner, used White intermediaries, paid a high price in cash, or purchased property from Whites who were willing to sell to them. Their actions, as well as the help of cooperative real estate agents, allowed more people of color to move in. Scholars recognize that real estate blockbusting exploited both the buyers and the sellers. To complicate matters, realtors who sold in these transitional neighborhoods, such as those in Crenshaw, breached long-standing racial borders, making the restricted communities available to all city dwellers. Their aptitude for working in the market, their willingness to sell to buyers of color, and their substantial real estate earnings made them targets for White rebuke. White realtors and realtors of color alike faced blockbusting accusations. UN, for instance, struck back against blockbusting in an organized manner to realize their vision of an integrated community.[4]

Three years after the first meeting, the informal, ad hoc group established itself as a nonprofit organization. In July 1964, after collecting membership fees from one hundred Crenshaw residents, UN leaders obtained a charter and established Crenshaw Neighbors, Incorporated (CN). Shortly thereafter, CN rented an office, purchased a real estate license, hired its own real estate agent, and set out to counteract blockbusting, improve race relations, and sustain integration. While UN's agenda exhibited what historian Scott Kurashige calls a "moderate integrationist agenda focused on promoting tolerance," which emerged in Los Angeles after World War II when activists' attempts to create a multiracial coalition collapsed and consequently shifted "from militancy to assimilation," the breadth and depth of CN's work evinces an effort toward structural reform within the Crenshaw area, through members' own time, labor, and volition. Amid the height of the open or fair housing movement in the mid- to late 1960s, the group established a multiracial alliance of Whites, Blacks, and Asians mainly living in affluent Baldwin Hills Estates, Baldwin Vista, View Park, View Heights, and Windsor Hills, to thwart White flight. And within a few years, CN had gained public attention by organizing committees, community programs, block clubs, and watch groups; teaming up with other neighborhood associations; collaborating with the public schools and local officials; publishing a monthly newsletter and a quarterly journal; stopping the construction of a freeway through Crenshaw; and leading the development of a public park. CN forged an effort across the racial and ethnic divide that was, in the words of its slogan, "dedicated to building a balanced community." In the process, it developed a national example of racial integration that some of its leaders used to form and lead a national organization, National Neighbors. But, despite its efforts, CN's campaign was no match for Angelenos' fear of living near African Americans. Its approach lacked the scope and authority to dismantle institutional racism and stop the resegregation of its communities.[5]

THE PUBLIC SCHOOLS TAKE CENTER STAGE

As early as the 1940s, while absorbed in litigation against racial restrictive covenants, Loren Miller spelled out the ripple effect that residential segregation had on the entire community structure. Housing discrimination leads to racial segregation in public schools, parks, libraries, and swimming pools, as well as in neighborhood clubs, organizations, businesses, and religious institutions. Local facilities, Miller repeated in the 1960s, "take on the color, or lack of it, of the communities in which they function." The effort to gain access to housing on the Westside was part of a broader agenda to fully integrate the urban environment, and, as the Westside's racial composition changed, the public schools experienced racial conflict. The schools' high academic standards and solid reputation drew homebuyers to the area. But as the student population grew diverse, racial tensions increased that became a source of anxiety in the community. UN formed in response to the turmoil and initially made the schools its priority.[6]

The age-old institution of the neighborhood school became a contentious issue in mid-twentieth-century United States. The practice, which dated back to the eighteenth-century common school movement, based pupil assignment to a school on proximity to their residence. But Jim Crow laws in the South and racial prejudice across the nation also dictated student placement and forced African American youngsters to study in underfunded, substandard schools that were usually farther away from their homes. The 1954 US Supreme Court case, *Brown v. Board of Education*, which declared separate schools under Jim Crow laws unconstitutional, brought to the forefront the nationwide educational inequalities and helped spark the modern civil rights movement. Through the 1950s and 1960s, as White and Black civil rights activists demanded racial equality, some Whites relentlessly refused integration. Like other school boards, the Los Angeles BOE contributed to racial segregation by adjusting the neighborhood concept to meet its needs. Administrators had a reputation for racial gerrymandering of school zones and deciding on pupils' transfer requests based on their race. To enroll their children at their preferred schools, rather than the schools closest to their homes, White parents also evaded the neighborhood concept by lying about their home address.[7]

In the late 1940s and early 1950s, the local NAACP began pressuring the Los Angeles BOE to take steps toward school integration. But, as expected, school authorities denied that racial inequality in the system existed and paid no heed to the warnings of civil rights leaders. Despite Miller's frequent calls for change, he doubted administrators "either knew or cared about" racial segregation in the city's public-school population. Since the Los Angeles BOE collected no statistical data on the racial or ethnic background of its students in the Los Angeles Unified School District (LAUSD), civil rights groups had little documentation to support their case. The Pasadena BOE, however, had been collecting data on its students since 1946.[8]

As in Los Angeles, school administrators and parents in Pasadena—the mostly White community northeast of Los Angeles—perpetuated school segregation. The Pasadena BOE adopted a policy that promoted fair zoning practices and denounced racial segregation, yet the figures proved that, throughout the 1950s, as more people of color moved to the community, the public-school student population became segregated by race and ethnicity. Some school populations remained solidly White, while others had become heavily Black, Asian, and/or Latino. The local NAACP fired back in 1953 with a lawsuit after the Pasadena BOE approved a measure to build more classrooms at an all-White school when another local school consisting mostly of students of color had additional space. After *Brown*, the Pasadena BOE believed it had little basis to defend its actions. School administrators suspended their plans and promised to modify their policies toward racial inclusion. Nevertheless, school segregation worsened.[9]

In the early 1960s, the battle between the local NAACP and the Pasadena BOE landed in court. Seeking to attend a school closer to his home, Jay Jackson, a thirteen-year-old African American student, filed a request with the school district to transfer from his mostly Black junior high school to a White school. The school district denied his application, and although Jackson filed a complaint with the Los Angeles Superior Court, the judge upheld the decision. Backed by Loren Miller and the NAACP Jackson took his grievances to the California Supreme Court. The 1963 case, *Jackson v. Pasadena City School District*, revealed the school district's practices of racial gerrymandering. Evidence became clear that in 1961 the Pasadena BOE had responded to White parents' protestations and redrawn its school zones to allow White youngsters to attend the mostly White junior high school. Basing its ruling on *Brown*, the California Supreme Court called on school boards to "take steps, insofar as reasonably feasible, to alleviate racial imbalance" in the school district, mainly by allowing transfers to take place. While Jackson won his case, the court set neither a deadline for racial desegregation nor proposed any methods to achieve integration.[10]

The Los Angeles BOE continued to postpone school desegregation. At a meeting in June 1962, the year following UN's formation, representatives from the local ACLU, NAACP, and CORE joined forces to push for desegregation. They urged school administrators to set up a committee that aimed to create equal educational opportunities for all pupils in Los Angeles and begin desegregating the schools in the 1962–63 school year. While the Los Angeles BOE agreed to form a committee, school authorities spent the summer months organizing delegates, soliciting advisors, and planning the meetings schedule, rather than beginning to desegregate the school district. Meanwhile, racial violence continued in the city, including when African Americans Thomas Wells and Eleanor Wells had to contend with their White neighbors in July who "hurled beer bottles and fired a shotgun into the front window" of their newly purchased house, which they moved into with their two-year-old nephew, at 800 West 120th Street, some fifteen miles southeast of the Crenshaw area.[11]

In September 1962 members of the ad hoc committee on equal educational opportunities finally gathered for the first of a series of meetings that would be spread over the subsequent months. Civil rights groups had anxiously waited throughout the summer for board officials to begin taking steps toward school desegregation. At the first hearing, however, they learned that the committee planned six hearings, several weeks apart, over half of the school year, from September through January. The first meeting confirmed to civil rights groups that the Los Angeles BOE resisted any genuine change. School officials spent the meeting defending the neighborhood school concept and arguing against the recommendations for desegregation. The committee rejected the ACLU's suggestions to document the racial distribution of LAUSD schools and to make integration "a positive determinant" in pupil placement. The Los Angeles NAACP threatened a boycott unless officials adjusted enrollment before the school year. Since the Los Angeles BOE refused to act, the NAACP took matters into its own hands.[12]

Days before the start of the 1962 school year, the NAACP made Baldwin Hills Elementary School, which sat north of the Baldwin Hills on Rodeo Road (now Obama Boulevard), a center in the fight for school desegregation in Los Angeles. When sixteen African American and four Japanese American youngsters tried to register for class, Principal Elizabeth Metz turned them away. Metz argued that the twenty students and their parents resided in a different district and had to enroll at Marvin Avenue Elementary School, located north of Jefferson Boulevard. The students had come from the majority Black and, Loren Miller for the *California Eagle* reported, "seriously overcrowded," Cienega Elementary School, also located north of Jefferson Boulevard. While Cienega Elementary attempted to deal with its large enrollment by placing "at least half of the pupils on half-day sessions," the NAACP sought a better solution by enrolling their children in Baldwin Hills Elementary. Two of the children who attempted to register at the school, brothers six-year-old Todd and five-year-old Randall Garr, lived closest to Cienega Elementary School, but nearly the same distance from Marvin Avenue and Baldwin Hills Elementary Schools. While school authorities directed the students to Marvin Avenue Elementary, the NAACP wanted to provide the children with the best educational opportunities at the highly regarded school.[13]

The event brought public attention to the striking differences in the schools' racial composition. Baldwin Hills Elementary served residents in one of Crenshaw's least integrated communities. Until the 1960s Baldwin Hills Elementary had reflected the racial composition of Baldwin Vista with a solidly White student body. Cienega and Marvin Avenue Elementary Schools, on the other hand, mirrored the racial makeup of their surrounding communities and had a majority Black enrollment. In 1968 Asians were 1.9 percent and Blacks 95.7 percent of the student body at Cienega Elementary, while Asians were 3.6 percent and Blacks 95 percent at Marvin Avenue Elementary. Metz defended the district lines that the Los Angeles BOE demarcated in 1948 when, the *Los Angeles Times* reported, "all residents in the area were white." She also proudly noted that two Black teachers worked at Baldwin Hills Elementary, and that the previous year the school had graduated one Black student. At the time, the school reflected the small number of Blacks who had lived within the district borders. But as Angelenos of color moved into the area, school authorities had trouble covering up their racially driven intentions.[14]

The Los Angeles NAACP held its stance, defended the students, and pressured school authorities to desegregate. Theodore Wright, representative of the local chapter and father of a student that Principal Metz refused to enroll, pointed out that eight years after *Brown*, children in Los Angeles continued to study in segregated schools. "The situation is even more impermissible... since children who live six or seven blocks from Baldwin Hills [Elementary] must go twice that far—14 or 15 blocks to Marvin Avenue [Elementary]," the *California Eagle* reported on Wright's response. The behaviors of the Jim Crow South made their way into Los Angeles's public-school system. While civil rights activists demanded the desegregation of public facilities in the South, the Los Angeles NAACP planned to picket outside both Baldwin Hills Elementary and Marvin Avenue Elementary on the first day of school.[15]

But before the NAACP could carry out the protest, the Los Angeles BOE intervened. After "a lengthy meeting with Board of Education officials," Loren Miller reported, school authorities and the Los Angeles NAACP came to a resolution. Superintendent Jack Crowther mandated Baldwin Hills Elementary to grant transfer requests of fifty students from Cienega Elementary, and the NAACP agreed to withdraw its plans for the protest. The *California Eagle* and the *Los Angeles Sentinel* printed a photo on the front page of the Garr brothers on September 20, 1962, the first Black youngsters transferred to Baldwin Hills Elementary. They began their respective kindergarten and first grade classes at the beginning of the 1962–63 school year. The NAACP was "satisfied" with the results, Miller wrote, politely conceding that the "school system is attempting to arrive at solutions equitable to all." He understood school integration represented a pivotal point in the process toward full racial equality, yet he remained unimpressed by the sluggish pace of the school board's actions. The "issue... should have been looked into a decade ago."[16]

In the 1962–63 school year, the ad hoc committee on equal educational opportunities continued to attend to racial inequality in the school district. The hearings held between September and January addressed a host of race-related issues, including student placement, transfer policies, district zones, teacher assignments, curriculum standards, counseling needs, discipline guidelines, and dropout rates. Attendance by nearly all seven board members at every meeting, as well as the participation of citywide civil rights groups and community organizations, demonstrated a willingness to reform the system. UN emerged as an important voice in the debate. Among the meeting's many presenters, UN gave a statement that focused on a topic most troublesome to the Crenshaw residents by bringing attention to Dorsey High School and the rumors circulating in the community of hostile students and apathetic teachers. Because Dorsey High's school zones extended into the city's low-income and primarily Black areas, the school enrolled White, Black, and Asian students from a range of racial, economic, and educational backgrounds. UN urged the ad hoc committee to improve communications between school officials and parents, clarify misconceptions, and resolve the social and educational gaps in the student body.[17]

Despite the rumors of racial and ethnic conflict among students, and reports on the fight over integration between civil rights groups and school officials, some Crenshaw residents saw the advantage of sending their children to ethnically and racially diverse schools. A UN report around 1963 highlighted another side to the story. "People of all races express pride when watching the easy mixing of the children on the Windsor Hills elementary school playground." They believed, "these youngsters have a chance to grow up knowing that people are no more nor less than human beings." At Dorsey High, the source of concern that initially brought UN members together, the report explained, "The students...two years ago expressed in an evaluation study their overwhelming consensus that the interracial character of their school was an asset." A 1964 editorial in the *Los Angeles Sentinel* also addressed the rumors, explaining that, while some rumors were based on truth, others were simply false: "We must rejoice in the fact that we are a part of a cosmopolitan environment." UN members saw the value in integration, which included Crenshaw's primarily White, Black, and Japanese residents.[18]

Although UN characterized itself as a "study, or communications, group" aimed at facilitating the exchange of ideas and improving relations, its involvement in the community grew. In its first years, explained steering committee member and Los Angeles Urban League affiliate John Davies, UN remained a loosely based organization with "no formal memberships, no constitution or by-laws, no officers, not even a regular meeting schedule." Yet the group continued to expand in size and influence in Crenshaw and across the city. Rescheduling meetings to an evening hour and moving the locations from living rooms into public places brought in more than one hundred participants. UN established a steering committee that met "several times a month" to outline the agenda for the larger discussions and work on building a partnership with other local institutions. Representatives met privately with school administrators and pushed for resolutions to student hostility and educational inequalities in the public-school system. The group invited school officials and local leaders to speak at the larger discussions, and members participated in panel discussions sponsored by other local groups.[19]

Jean Gregg, Ann Post, and Othelia "Fifi" Boger initiated the idea for UN at their local League of Women Voters (LWV) meetings. Launched by suffragist Carrie Chapman Catt as a nonpartisan advocacy group for women's political participation in 1920 when the Nineteenth Amendment underwent ratification, the mostly White, middle-class LWV revived in the postwar era and second-wave feminist movement. Gregg, Post, and Boger met each other at LWV's Los Angeles chapter (LWVLA) meetings. All three women lived in the affluent, single-family Crenshaw area neighborhoods, had husbands and children, and were active in local affairs.[20]

Over time, Jean Gregg (later Jean Gregg Milgram) became UN's and later CN's earliest driving force. Born in Chicago, Gregg had earned a master's degree in psychology at Columbia University and moved to Los Angeles in the late 1940s to support her first spouse, Paul, who was completing a master's degree in business administration at UCLA. Through the mid- to late 1950s, as the Greggs expanded their family, they moved into a home at 4512 Whelan Place on the western end of Windsor Hills. At the time, Gregg was also working on a doctorate in psychology at UCLA; she passed her qualifying exams, but family matters interfered with her degree completion. While raising her children, working on her PhD, and working as a research assistant in the psychology department, she also served as a director and on the board of the LWVLA.[21]

Post was also an active member of the LWVLA. Born in St. Paul, Minnesota, Post married her first spouse, David, when she was twenty years old; they moved around to various cities until eventually settling in Los Angeles. In the late 1940s she and David purchased a house at 5163 Sanchez Drive in mostly White Baldwin Vista, and then moved less than a mile away to 3978 Cloverdale Avenue, also in Baldwin Vista. Their home was destroyed in the 1963 Baldwin Hills dam collapse, yet while some residents used it as a reason to leave the area, as Blacks began moving in and real estate agents used blockbusting tactics to accelerate the demographic shift, the Posts insisted on staying. Ann Post was politically active, serving in many positions, including vice president of the Los Angeles and state LWV, and on Mayor Sam Yorty's Citizens' Advisory Committee. Both she and her husband were highly involved in CN. Ann Post served as the group's founding president, and David Post initially chaired the real estate committee.[22]

Unlike Gregg and Post, Fifi Boger felt the double-bind of gender and racial inequality. Born in "a little rural stop" in North Carolina, Boger moved with her first spouse to Los Angeles in the early 1940s; after their divorce, she married Chicago-born dentist Tom Boger. In the mid-1950s the Bogers moved to a two-bedroom house that had peach, lemon, and grapefruit trees at 3518 West Forty-Eighth Street in View Park, and in the early 1970s they moved a little more than a mile away to a larger two-bedroom house with a swimming pool at 4116 Kenway Avenue that was also in View Park. While she worked at a telephone company, Boger grew active in local affairs. At an LWVLA meeting, she befriended Gregg and Post, who encouraged her to invite African Americans to the group. While some came, Gregg recalled, Boger and her friends "were much more interested in race problems...than in water policies," which LWVLA had on its agenda. But, as the three women grew concerned about increasing racial hostility among the students at Dorsey High School and about blockbusting real estate agents who were seeking to turn over the housing market, they proposed gathering together more Crenshaw-area residents. Boger hosted the first meeting in her West Forty-Eighth Street home.[23]

Part of the silent generation, the liberal-minded and socially conscious women challenged their peers' inclination for tradition and conformity and took their inspiration from racial liberalism and the civil rights and second-wave feminist movements. They understood that Black migration onto Los Angeles's Eastside neighborhoods had led to White flight there and tried to prevent the same demographic shift from happening in their community by embracing racial inclusion and integration. Spurred by second-wave feminism, they also sought to carve out their own path in a White, patriarchal society. At UN, Gregg, Post, and Boger used LWV beliefs in representative government and individual liberties, and techniques of engaging in discussions that nurture understanding among one another and lead to concerted decisions. They served as a counterforce to the city's conservative housewife activists who, according to historian Michelle Nickerson, amid Cold War anxiety, in their own study groups, speaking engagements, writings, and campaigning, framed their anti-Communist, antistatist, and anti-integrationist beliefs in the interest of preserving White, heteronormative family, domesticity, and community.[24]

UN members also assumed leadership roles in other local organizations that reflected their support for President Lyndon Johnson's Great Society antipoverty and racial justice programs. Beginning in 1963, the Crenshaw Coordinating Council (Coordinating Council), a group established by the Los Angeles County government to prevent juvenile delinquency in Crenshaw, carried out "the most concrete and specific achievement so far in the Crenshaw area," as UN explained. Under Joan Suter's leadership, the Coordinating Council's education committee created a six-week summer reading improvement course to raise the reading levels of low-achieving elementary school students. Suter worked within the broader effort to resolve the tensions in the school system and ensure educational equality for all students in the district. Born in New York City, she "came from a very integrated background," attended a "highly academic" all-girls high school, and enrolled at Hunter College. In the early 1960s, she suspended her studies and moved with her spouse, Lyle, to Los Angeles. The couple first lived in View Park with family who introduced Suter to UN, and then they bought a house in Baldwin Vista. While Lyle Suter taught art at Beverly Hills High School, Joan Suter became a local activist. The Los Angeles BOE approved the reading program, a UCLA professor of education advised the staff, and a team made up entirely of volunteer community members and teachers ran the course at the nearby synagogue, B'nai Israel Congregation. The success of the first summer course, which had an enrollment of sixty-six children, encouraged the Coordinating Council to continue running the program and create educational programs for secondary school students.[25]

To "preserve the interracial character of the Crenshaw community," UN explained in the early 1960s, community activists also formed the Greater Crenshaw Town Council (Town Council). In the summer of 1963, "The Town Council began with a meeting between a local Episcopalian priest and several members of the Board of the Crenshaw Chamber of Commerce." At the second meeting several other community leaders, including UN representatives, joined in. Within a few months, the group agreed on a set of bylaws, elected officers, and initially established five action committees, each of which focused on education, housing, crime and safety, publicity, or community activities. There were 150 community members, from school administrators and real estate agents to city officials and business owners, who attended the Town Council's first public forum. The group also distributed a brochure, printed a newsletter, presented "a film on property values and race," and urged real estate agents to practice fair mindedness and racial tolerance. UN, the Coordinating Council, and the Town Council exhibited a local politics that was rooted in racial liberalism and informed by the New Left. Unlike postwar White hostility that manifested in Chicago's "urban guerilla warfare," historian Arnold Hirsch explains, and Detroit's "defensive localism," historian Thomas Sugrue argues, Crenshaw's citizen efforts demonstrated a desire for inclusion in their approach to tackling the challenges of the multicultural city.[26]

But UN understood that it faced an uphill battle to maintain integration in Crenshaw. Conflict over the schools continued to grow, and, while the group teamed up with school officials and helped improve communication, the Los Angeles BOE remained largely resistant to change. Furthermore,

UN faced another growing problem in Crenshaw. Real estate agents were becoming a powerful force. Using what many residents saw as blockbusting techniques, including making telephone calls, going door to door, and circulating flyers to spread the word of Black in-migration, real estate agents tapped into White homeowners' fears of so-called Black encroachment and imminent neighborhood deterioration. As early as 1952 the Los Angeles County Commission on Human Relations (LACCHR) received reports of a realtor in Leimert Park distributing postcards to residents with the words, "Sell your homes now, Negroes are moving in."[27] At the same time that real estate blockbusters were opening these long-standing restricted neighborhoods to people of color, they were also inciting White flight. UN had to act.

BLOCKBUSTING CRENSHAW

By the first half of the 1960s, real estate agents had made the Crenshaw area their focus. "Brokers appeared to be everywhere, ringing doorbells, telephoning, sending letters and circulars urging home owners to sell," worried Post. While real estate agents targeted their claims at White homeowners, Black newcomers became caught in the movement. An African American homeowner later explained that he and his spouse received two or three phone calls a week from real estate agents warning them of Black in-migration. Real estate agents also mistook a light-skinned Black homeowner for a White resident and warned him, "Colored people are moving in!" Even though Whites still made up a large proportion of the population in the mid-1960s, Gregg protested that "the brokers really felt that this was a Negro community." Real estate agents tapped into White homeowners' fears, with some claiming that Crenshaw would become part of Los Angeles's expanding Black belt and lose its value. White homeowners, real estate agents contended, needed to take advantage of the high demand and sell their homes. Many Whites heeded the warnings.[28]

Real estate agents of color became part of the long-lasting effort to dismantle the city's racial borders. Nisei broker Kazuo K. Inouye saw the potential in Westside real estate following World War II. Born in 1922 in Los Angeles to Issei parents, Inouye grew up in the multiethnic milieu of Boyle Heights where he learned the traditions of his Jewish, Black, and Mexican friends that would help him navigate the housing market in his adulthood. He and his family suffered the demoralizing actions of the United States government during World War II when they had to sell their possessions, including the family's hard-earned car, furniture, and washing machine, and evacuate to concentration camps. Inouye was first incarcerated at the Manzanar War Relocation Center, received permission to then leave the Sierra Nevada location to work in Montana, and eventually was drafted into the

US Army and fought overseas. When he returned from the war he got married; in 1947 he began working at his brother-in-law's realty business.²⁹

In Inouye's first years in real estate, he later recalled, "No Japanese was [living] on [the west] side of Arlington [Boulevard]." But his work would significantly contribute to the demographic shift. His brother-in-law R. M. Mizukami, who lived on Seventh Avenue and Jefferson Boulevard in the Avenues section north of Leimert Park, became one of the first Japanese American brokers in the area. While most Japanese returned to Los Angeles's unrestricted communities after incarceration, Roy Takai ran Takai Realty; later, Ty Saito opened Saito Realty and Sam S. Miyashiro led Seinan Realty to access the restricted Westside. Inouye soon launched his own enterprise, Kashu Realty, and, like several of his counterparts, set up his office on Jefferson Boulevard. An astute business owner who saw an opportunity to breach the area, Inouye designed his business's name using Chinese brush lettering to signify to Asian buyers the properties available to them, and he deliberately left his signs up after a sale to advertise his name. He also used Yiddish words to disarm Jewish patrons. Through his work, Inouye faced racism and discrimination. Banks initially refused to open escrow accounts and lend to his buyers; insurance companies refused to sell them fire policies for fear vigilantes would burn down Japanese-purchased houses. One real estate agent shattered the windows of a house adjacent to the one Inouye had sold. Inouye drew from his military experience fighting Nazis overseas to challenge racial intimidation. He sold homes in West Adams and then expanded his business into the Crenshaw area and beyond to Culver City and Venice Beach. At one point in the 1960s he was selling fifty to sixty houses a month, or two to three a day, to mostly Japanese and Black buyers. He witnessed Japanese businesses, including barbershops, restaurants, and banks, open in Crenshaw. "You didn't have to go down to Japanese town," another name for Little Tokyo, like in the prewar years. "You could get anything you wanted over here." While his Crenshaw office remained open the longest, he also had offices in Los Feliz, Wilshire, Monterey Park, Montebello, and the San Fernando Valley.³⁰

African American broker Deloy Edwards also contributed to changing the area's racial makeup. With ambition, hard work, and foresight, he rose, in his words, "from a country boy to a multi-millionaire." Racism and inequality affected Edwards's experiences growing up in Phoenix, Arizona. He lived two blocks from a local school but had to travel several miles to attend Phoenix Union Colored High School (later renamed George Washington Carver High School). Before the United States entered World War II he moved to Los Angeles where, he recalled, "I always had three jobs." Among his many positions, he worked as a ship fitter at the Long Beach shipyard, supervisor at a lock company, and in the post office. He earned a bachelor's degree in business administration at UCLA and found his niche in real estate. He first worked in the property management division at the Veterans Administration, and then transferred in 1953 to W. A. Robinson Realty Company, a Los Angeles Black-owned agency, where he rose in the ranks to broker-manager. Three years later, with three sales agents, Edwards opened his own office at 4034 Buckingham Road, a few blocks north of Baldwin Hills Estates.[31]

Edwards's first years working in the area proved risky and difficult. As he made his rounds, White homeowners "slammed the door" in his face and ordered him to leave. Hatemongers burned crosses on the front lawns and filled a swimming pool with sand at properties he helped acquire. But the self-proclaimed "fighter" sensed a community on the verge of change that Blacks had long desired to live in, and he felt compelled to create that opportunity. To open the market and advertise his agency, for instance, he mailed postcards to View Park homeowners that included a photo of his African American staff, which trepidatious Whites could have interpreted as a message that Blacks were staking a claim to the community. He also banked on the capital of his Black clients and promised high returns to White homeowners. Oftentimes, in various cities, when Black demand and White exodus peaked, Whites sought to sell their properties below market value. In a 1986 *Los Angeles Times* interview Edwards reinforced that outcome, explaining Whites "more or less gave their property away," the newspaper added, "sometimes for half price." But years later he revised his statement, illuminating the varied individual experiences in the market at the time. "White brokers couldn't get what I did," he explained, and White homeowners knew that "I was the only one that could get more money for the house." His reputation for getting high returns enticed many Whites to hire him.[32]

As more Whites wanted to sell their properties, Edwards's business expanded and his relationship with the community became complex and multifaceted. He developed a reputation as an ambitious and well-connected broker. Unlike White real estate agents working in the area, he was able to reach Black homebuyers who could afford the property. Black physicians, attorneys, city officials, teachers, entertainers, athletes, and other professionals found in Edwards a skillful and charming mediator who possessed the ability to access the area. His early sales in Crenshaw came from Ike and Tina Turner for the house on Olympiad Drive, and Ray Charles Robinson and Della Robinson for the three lots on Southridge Avenue. He also sold to singer Dionne Warwick, politician Yvonne Brathwaite Burke, and politician Bernard C. Parks.[33]

For Black buyers without the financial means, Edwards found the funds to help his clients purchase property in the area, a common practice of real estate agents across the country. The discriminatory policies of federal agencies, private lenders, and real estate appraisers, brokers, and agents kept most Blacks hemmed in to what were soon labelled ghettos. Black-owned lending institutions, such as Liberty, Broadway Federal, and Family Savings and Loan, improved homeownership opportunities by providing loans to thousands of Black Angelenos. Edwards also used his personal connections and wealth to help Blacks move into the affluent communities. He nurtured his relationship with the vice president of White-owned California Federal Savings and Loan, who provided Edwards and his clients with home mortgages. Whenever he needed a loan, the vice president told Edwards, "Just come to the office and sign your name and the money is yours." When his clients needed help with a down payment, Edwards also loaned them his own money. While Whites perceived Edwards's real estate work as blockbusting, African Americans such as one of his long-time employees described Edwards as "the Thurgood Marshall of real estate."[34]

At the cusp of the *Shelley* and *Barrows* decisions, Edwards used his skills to help unlock Crenshaw to people of color, while simultaneously earning substantial wealth. He initially chose to work in real estate, he made clear, "because I knew I could make a lot of money." Through the 1960s, he later said, "I was buying and selling like crazy." He found homes for Blacks, purchased several properties for personal use, and rented and sold many of his holdings. As his real estate business succeeded, Edwards expanded the size of his staff, supporting more than fifty employees on his payroll at a time, and moved into a larger office in the Crenshaw Center business district. Real estate made him rich. "I made more than the president of the United States," he boasted years later. "There's nothing I said I wanted that I couldn't get." Edwards spent his earnings on luxury cars, a boat, land in and outside of Los Angeles, and private school tuition for his children. In the late 1960s he also donated property in View Park to the Methodist Church.[35]

While both Japanese and Black settlement set off alarm bells, Whites had a stronger reaction to Black newcomers. A 1962 *Los Angeles Times* article reported anecdotal evidence of not only the dual housing market (or, in this case, the threefold market), but also the higher social stigma attached to African Americans. In Leimert Park one White seller "asked $18,500 from whites, $19,500 from Orientals and $21,500 from Negroes," an example of the so-called Black tax that the federal Fair Housing Act of 1968 (instituted formally as Title VIII of the Civil Rights Act of 1968) would soon prohibit. The first African Americans to move to the area established a path for further Black in-migration. By the mid-1960s, Edwards had found that African Americans had become "the only people buying in the area." He explained, "Every house I got, I sold it to Blacks because Whites wouldn't buy it." Especially after the 1965 Watts rebellion, many Japanese Americans also left the area. Edwards wanted African Americans to enjoy good quality housing, yet, as a business owner, he also needed to earn money. UN, however, argued that blockbusting real estate agents, such as Inouye and Edwards, encouraged White out-migration. The group accused realtors of lacking the desire to prevent resegregation and what it feared as the expansion of the city's Black belt into Crenshaw. Frustrated by the real estate agents and fueled by its concern over resegregation, UN organized a more formal group and real estate agency aimed at maintaining integration.[36]

CRENSHAW NEIGHBORS' FIRST YEAR

"When Caucasians were thrashing out of Baldwin Hills like grunion from the ocean," *Los Angeles Times* reporter Art Seidenbaum reflected, with a vivid analogy of the silvery fish that spawn on the Southern California beaches, UN acted with urgency to establish a fully fledged organization aimed at maintaining a racially balanced population in the Crenshaw area. Shortly after UN began holding meetings, the group discovered that the conflicts at the high school represented one symptom of other racist practices in the area. Blockbusting became even more apparent after the 1963 Baldwin Hills dam collapse when real estate agents discouraged many residents who had lost their homes, including Ann Post, from staying in the area. Running a discussion-oriented group alone would not solve the problems. In response, UN's racially diverse and liberal-minded leaders formed CN, an incorporated, nonprofit organization and real estate agency that sought to maintain integration in the area.[37]

After two years of growing participation and influence in the area, UN faced a major turning point. "In the spring of 1963, Dorsey High School erupted in a way that no one could misinterpret," Gregg explained. "Serious fights involving real injury, even hospitalization, occurred with alarming frequency." While more White parents either requested the Los Angeles BOE to transfer their children to another school, or sold their homes and moved away, UN members sought a resolution. They relied on their relationship with school officials and "frantically appealed" to the Los Angeles BOE for help. School officials responded with concern, replaced the high school principal, and, as a UN report explained, added "additional staff, and additional counseling and library hours." But tensions between school officials and the community grew.[38]

In May, after an entire academic year of deliberations, the ad hoc committee on equal educational opportunities finally drew up a resolution toward educational equality. The Los Angeles BOE agreed in a policy statement to nurture a school system that provided "pupils an opportunity for interaction with persons of different cultures and ethnic backgrounds." BOE officials resolved to create a staff position that aimed to support equal educational opportunities, to offer programs that taught racial understanding, and to begin taking a racial survey of the student population in the school district. Yet the small steps frustrated integrationists.[39]

Resentment against the Los Angeles BOE culminated during the following months in a series of demonstrations for school desegregation. Soon after Martin Luther King, Jr., traveled to Los Angeles to spread the message of the Black freedom struggle, some seventy-six civil rights groups in the city, including the NAACP, ACLU, and CORE, formed the more forceful United Civil Rights Council (UCRC). UCRC took its cue from the Southern civil rights movement and waged a series of nonviolent protests toward school authorities. On June 24, 1963, the group organized a march with a thousand demonstrators from the First African Methodist Episcopal Church through downtown Los Angeles to the BOE headquarters. For more than ten days in September, several CORE members engaged in a hunger strike at the Los Angeles BOE headquarters. The following month, around 350 demonstrators held a study-in.[40]

As the protests swelled, UN sensed a turning point or "change in attitude" in Crenshaw. While the area comprised a mostly White population at the time, Gregg lamented that "there was a shift from a feeling that this was an inter-racial community to a feeling that it was going to be an all-Negro community." UN especially became upset after learning that by the early 1960s realtors had altogether discouraged Whites from purchasing property in the area. Interested White buyers came to UN meetings to share their experiences of realtors giving advice to look elsewhere and refusing to help Whites acquire property in the area. "It was this one discovery, more than any other, that precipitated the formation of Crenshaw Neighbors," Gregg stated.[41]

Out of its discussion-oriented group, Gregg explained, UN launched a formal and structured action-oriented group. The group mailed letters to homes across Crenshaw, asking residents to pay $10 to join a newly forming organization that aimed to stop blockbusting and maintain integration. Their proposal received considerable support, especially from residents in the affluent neighborhoods of Baldwin Hills Estates, Baldwin Vista, View Park, View Heights, and Windsor Hills. In July 1964, after receiving one hundred membership applications, the group secured its charter as Crenshaw Neighbors, Incorporated (CN). UN continued to pursue its goal as a communications group by gathering for discussions, while CN built a formal organization made up of bylaws, officers, a board of directors, and individual committees. Members of both groups overlapped.[42]

CN became part of nationwide housing campaigns that developed after *Shelley*. Rooted in decades of activism against discriminatory housing measures and propelled by the Southern civil rights movement, the open or fair housing movement assumed the charge in the 1960s to draw attention to inequality in the urban North. By 1965 more than one thousand fair housing groups had formed in cities across the country. In July 1966, six months after Martin Luther and Coretta Scott King had moved into a rundown tenement on Chicago's mostly Black North Lawndale neighborhood to plan the Chicago freedom movement, also known as the Chicago open housing movement, they kickstarted a massive rally with the Southern Christian Leadership Conference (SCLC), the American Friends Service Committee, and the Coordinating Council of Community Organizations at Soldier Field. Taking inspiration from King and entertainers Stevie Wonder, Mahalia Jackson, and the group Peter, Paul, and Mary, some thirty-five thousand demonstrators pressured Mayor Richard Daley to enforce an established fair housing law and remove slum housing, and pushed the nation to pass a federal fair housing law. More protests and marches persisted in Chicago and across the country thereafter.[43]

CN, however, saw itself as part of the neighborhood stabilization movement. Seeking to slow the rate of White exodus and Black influx into their neighborhoods and maintain integration, middle-class homeowners established the neighborhood stabilization movement, or what sociologist Juliet Saltman, in the title of her book, calls a fragile movement. The first known group, the Hyde Park–Kenwood Community Conference, which formed in Chicago's affluent community abutting Lake Michigan and the University of Chicago in 1949, provided an alternative to the prosegregation, neighborhood improvement, or protective associations. Through the following two decades, similar groups cropped up in places such as Denver, Colorado; Hartford, Connecticut; Nashville, Tennessee; and Oak Park, Chicago. According to *Crenshaw Notes*, "Groups in the stabilization movement like Crenshaw Neighbors view the concept, activities, and thrust of 'stabilization' to be the reverse [side of the] coin of 'fair housing.'" They shared the same goal of inclusivity and needed each other to achieve it. "Fair housing will be more successful if stabilization is successful, and of course stabilization will succeed only if fair housing succeeds." But despite the efforts, Saltman finds, integration became "easier to attain...than to maintain." These groups faced unrelenting, "massive institutional forces" working against their goals.[44]

Two months after it incorporated, CN gathered for a meeting to sort out the details of the organization. The group elected officers and a board of directors and adopted bylaws. While Whites and Blacks served as CN's core leaders, and its initial one hundred members comprised one-third Black and two-thirds White residents, CN aimed to represent the area's diverse population and involve Japanese Americans. When setting up the officers,

Gregg recalled, CN "conscientiously made sure it was half Black and half White." Gregg and Post, two of UN's original White members, took the lead as respective executive director and president, and public-school administrator Theopolis D. Kimbrough and real estate agent John Laing, both African Americans, served as first vice president and second vice president, respectively. CN also established secretary and treasurer positions and a board of directors, which consistently included Japanese American representation.[45] CN likewise formed committees, which over time included real estate, education, membership, coordinating, nominating, home tour, standards, and publications.

For its first order of business, CN set out to encourage Whites to stay in Crenshaw. It launched "an educational campaign" to "show Crenshaw in its *true* light: beautiful homes, convenient location, fine schools, various races, and dynamic residents."[46] CN also resolved to obtain a real estate license and establish an agency to carry out property conveyances on its own terms. This decision set CN apart from other stabilization groups, but it also put the organization in a controversial position. CN encouraged Whites to stay in the area, but if they decided to put their house on the market, the group asked sellers to choose CN as their real estate agency. Then, to counteract agents who CN believed sold homes only to people of color, the agency primarily sought White buyers. Using the money from membership fees, the organization purchased a corporate real estate license, hired John Laing as the real estate agent, rented an office, and in February 1965, opened for business. Within its first six months in operation, CN sold eight houses—six to White buyers, one to a Black couple, and one to an Asian and White couple.[47]

CN understood that focusing its sales on Whites appeared to undermine its fundamental goals of inclusion and integration. Especially since in the mid-1960s, CN's own racial census showed that Whites made up most of the population and Blacks and Asians had only recently gained access to the area. In the May 1965 edition of its monthly newsletter, *Crenshaw Notes*, CN attempted to clarify its aims. "CN's policy of encouraging white buyers for our area may seem discriminatory to some. The explanation is simple. Minorities know they can buy here, whereas whites have doubts that this area is for them. Therefore, CN will concentrate on the latter, while at the same time always making sure that every home is available to anyone who wishes to purchase it." While CN's vision of a balanced community remained loosely defined, the group understood the direction it wanted to avoid. The opening article in the October 1965 edition of *Crenshaw Notes*, explained, from the inception, "We didn't really have any precise concept of balance. Instead, we had a very definite picture of imbalance, and we knew we didn't want that. An unbalanced community, we felt, was one in which only one kind of people lived." While CN decided against setting racial quotas, the group understood that a majority Black population would end any chance of maintaining integration. If Crenshaw's population became "substantially more than 50 per cent non-white," Gregg believed, CN's campaign "would pretty much be a lost battle."[48]

CN worked hard, using forethought and creativity, to broaden the visibility of its real estate agency around greater Los Angeles. Believing that it had a better chance of attracting White, educated liberals, who more likely supported integration, the CN real estate committee deliberately chose publications in which to advertise the agency and its properties. University magazines, such as UCLA's *The Daily Bruin*; art and architecture journals, including a Beverly Hills's publication, *FM and Fine Arts Guide*; as well as local theater playbills, fair housing bulletins, and industry bulletins ran advertisements. Local Japanese American–run newspapers, including the bilingual daily *Shin Nichi-Bei: New Japanese American News* and the JACL's weekly *Pacific Citizen*, also printed stories that discussed the group, its goals, its events, and its Japanese American members, and encouraged membership. CN advertised its properties in and outside of Crenshaw, including the highly exclusive Beverly Hills, and in Black-owned newspapers, such as the *Los Angeles Sentinel*, to attract Black homebuyers to the agency and expand housing opportunities for Blacks to mostly White areas. CN likewise spread its message of integration on a billboard and real estate signs that touted its effort of "Building a Balanced Community."[49]

Within its first few months, CN had launched a monthly newsletter and carried out a major letter writing campaign to increase membership. The newsletter, *Crenshaw Notes*, published officers' speeches, featured news briefs of local events, reprinted relevant articles from local newspapers, included columns such as the one written by a Dorsey High School student, and publicized upcoming events. Residents from around the area also received letters from the group. CN encouraged thousands of apartment tenants to support the effort, stay in the area, and, when they were ready, to use CN's real estate agency to purchase property. The group urged nearly one hundred White homeowners who placed their property on the market to either suspend their decision or use the CN real estate agency to sell their home. CN mailed copies of *Crenshaw Notes* to more than four thousand homes around Los Angeles, accompanied with a letter that encouraged readers to join the group. The membership committee also planned an orientation meeting made up of a panel of CN board members to present CN's story, and to answer questions about the organization.[50]

CN also attempted to clarify the community's racial composition by conducting its own census. While the 1960 federal census found most Crenshaw neighborhoods made up of a majority White population, the in-migration of

Blacks concerned White residents. "We were told that we were too late, that the area was already unbalanced," an article in *Crenshaw Notes* explained. "We were told that Baldwin Hills Estates was so predominantly Negro that there was no hope for it. We were told that same thing about View Park." From late spring to early summer in 1965, CN member Joyce Jacobson headed the research committee to collect data and compile a report of residents living in the single-family houses of Baldwin Hills Estates, Baldwin Vista, View Park, and Windsor Hills, which were those communities "believed to have changed the most since the 1960 U.S. Census" and with "the most Crenshaw Neighbors members to whom we could turn for help." The census showed that Blacks and Asians remained a minority. Of 4,453 single-family houses covered in the survey, 2,823 had Whites, 1,257 had Blacks, 275 had Asians, and 37 had mixed-race families living in them.[51]

In June 1965 CN began one of its most inventive endeavors by hosting the first annual home tour. The home tour committee gave prospective buyers the opportunity to meet and walk through the homes of Crenshaw's diverse residents. For the first three hours, guests had an open invitation to visit a variety of houses, including "a Spanish stucco furnished with authentic Spanish pieces," "a western farm-house," and a "remodeled do-it-yourself," and then convene for cocktail hour. Within its first two years, Crenshaw's "Catholic, Jewish and Protestant citizens; Negro and Caucasian residents; persons of Japanese ancestry; and Mexican-Americans, all have participated in the program." CN hoped the tour would debunk the myths and misconceptions associated with its residents and attract homebuyers. At the second annual tour, which included eight homes and ended with a cocktail party, CN sold 494 tickets and made a profit of $800.[52]

Some of the earliest opposition against CN came from real estate agents. Realtors working in the area, John Laing explained, responded to the organization's agency with "mixed" reactions and "some hostility." Some brokers believed that the group's nonprofit status created unfair business competition; and Gregg described "at least two brokers [that] have categorically refused to cooperate with us on any sale." CN adjusted its approach by removing the term nonprofit from advertisements, but criticism continued. Laing became uncomfortable with CN's plan to deliberately seek out Whites to buy homes in the area. He initially made a deal with CN to sell properties on increasingly Black blocks to White buyers, if he could also sell in White areas to Black buyers. But, Gregg pointed out, "we had such a hard time convincing him that what we wanted to do was sell houses to White people. He wanted to sell them to Black people.... We had some early problems with him, and then finally they got worse." By October 1965, Laing resigned from his position.[53]

Within one year of receiving its charter, as the roster and budget increased, CN gained more influence in Crenshaw. With the help of membership dues, private contributions, real estate commissions, and event proceeds, CN raised the funds to run the operation. The growth in membership of White, Black, and Asian residents from 100 in July 1964 to some 650 in October 1965 illustrated the high interest in the group. Members practiced various religions, including Christianity, Judaism, and Quakerism, and engaged in various professions: they were teachers, doctors, reverends, store managers, engineers, bankers, public officials, and political leaders. Most of the revenue went toward staff salaries, rent, a telephone and answering service, office supplies, and print advertisements. CN hired one full-time employee, an executive director, and two part-time employees—a secretary and a real estate agent—and moved into a larger office on Crenshaw Boulevard. In its first fiscal year CN nearly broke even, after expenses and after Gregg decided against taking her salary. In its second fiscal year, the group reported earning $7,636 in real estate commissions, $4,511 more than its first fiscal year; after expenses it had grossed $708 in its real estate dealings. Again and throughout her role as CN's executive director, Gregg never took a salary. In its title to Post's 1964 letter to the editor, the *Los Angeles Times* put it simply: "They [CN] are proving it really works." Yet, after a full year in operation, CN faced additional strains on its goal as Los Angeles underwent an uprising.[54]

THE DISINTEGRATION OF FAIR HOUSING AMID THE PASSAGE OF PROPOSITION 14

In April 1964, seven months before California voters approved Proposition 14, which upended the state's fair housing movement and gave property owners, in a state constitutional amendment, the right "to decline to sell, lease or rent such property to such person or persons as he, in his absolute discretion, chooses," real estate agents of the Wesley N. Taylor Company, following their sellers' instructions and the pro–Proposition 14 hype, refused to show a house at 4862 West Sixty-Third Street, in affluent Ladera Heights, which adjoined the Crenshaw area, to interested buyers after discovering the husband, Riley Jacobs, was African American. Jacobs, an interior decorator, and his spouse, Edythe, a White public-school teacher, responded with a lawsuit against the realty company. The Los Angeles Superior Court heard the case in early 1964 and, recognizing the 1959 Unruh Act, which outlawed discrimination by state licensed businesses, awarded the interracial couple $250 in punitive damages. But if the realty company discriminated against the Jacobses after the November election, the *Los Angeles Times* reported, "the real estate salesmen could not have been held liable.

Proposition 14 permits a homeowner to sell to whom he chooses and he can so instruct his broker." California had adopted yet another impediment to housing integration.[55]

In the late 1950s and early 1960s, when African Americans won more seats to the state legislature and California Democrats passed landmark civil rights legislation, the liberal coalition reached its peak. Buoyed by civil rights groups, labor unions, and the CDC, more Democrats won offices that culminated in the 1958 gubernatorial election of Pat Brown against Richard Nixon and the 1959 passage of three state civil rights bills—the Fair Employment Practices Act, the Unruh Civil Rights Act, and the Hawkins Fair Housing Act—that furthered racial liberalism into the next decade. Black representation received a major boost in the early 1960s with the election of Mervyn M. Dymally, F. Douglas Ferrell, and Willie Brown, Jr., to the California State Assembly, and Gilbert Lindsay, Tom Bradley, and Billy Mills to the Los Angeles City Council. Campaigning on a platform that supported antidiscrimination housing legislation, Brown also won reelection as governor in November 1962. Capitalizing on their political victories, the liberal coalition passed the 1963 California Fair Housing Act through the assembly, and after stalling in the senate, getting pressure from civil rights groups demonstrating in and outside of the Sacramento chamber, and making slight changes, the bill received approval minutes before the deadline. Amid the civil rights and open housing movements, California joined an increasing number of cities and states, including Colorado, Massachusetts, New Jersey, and Washington, to adopt fair housing laws.[56]

Compared to the *Shelley* and *Barrows* decisions, the California Fair Housing Act, commonly known as the Rumford Act, which Augustus Hawkins attempted to pass two years earlier and William Byron Rumford reintroduced in 1963, protected Californians more broadly against discriminatory housing measures. The act prohibited racial discrimination in the sale or rental of two housing sectors: owner-occupied, single-family, government loan–financed homes; and public and private housing that included five or more units. Moreover, while previous laws required renters and buyers to file a claim either as a civil suit or a complaint in the district attorney's office to challenge discrimination, which cost time and money, the Rumford Act gave the state Fair Employment Practices Commission, which was established under the Fair Employment Practices Act in 1959, authority to enforce the law. But while the act covered one-third of the state's housing market, two-thirds remained unprotected. It excluded owner-occupied, single-family houses without government financing; renter-occupied, single-family homes; and apartments with four or fewer units, including duplexes, triplexes, and fourplexes. Scholar Daniel Martinez HoSang also points out that the law addressed only rentals and sales and elided providing aid to low-income Californians who wanted to move out of segregated areas. It essentially covered members of the Black middle class, evinced by the fact that they filed the most complaints in the law's first year. Despite its omissions of protecting all Californians, the Rumford Act unnerved a segment of the population who led a movement to nullify the bill altogether and unseat the liberal coalition.[57]

Following the passage of the Rumford Act, real estate agents resumed the campaign they had begun after the *Shelley* decision, this time to pass an amendment to the state constitution using the ballot initiative process. The 1958 general election showed that their other strategies for maintaining residential segregation, from promoting neighborhood protective associations to proscribing agents from selling property in White areas to people of color, failed to curry statewide favor. Supported by the long-standing, White-run National Association of Real Estate Boards, who believed persuading California to reverse its fair housing law could impel other states to do the same, CREA and the California Apartment Owners' Association drafted the measure. Established in 1911 with the referendum and recall processes to further direct democracy, the initiative process, which allows California voters to collect signatures to place proposed laws or constitutional amendments on the ballot, can require significant resources and cost millions of dollars to succeed. Most proposed initiatives fail to meet the criteria to get on the ballot; for those that succeed with that step, most are rejected by voters. CREA and its allies triumphed.[58]

Months ahead of the Rumford Act's adoption, as the law went through the assembly and senate, real estate interests plotted their counterattack. CREA and the California Apartment Owners' Association drafted a state constitutional amendment, some twenty real estate boards statewide used advertisements to broadcast their support for the measure, and, under the CHP, the same group that helped slash federally financed housing project efforts in the late 1940s, finalized and sponsored the amendment, and led an aggressive statewide campaign to pass it. While William Byron Rumford understood that Proposition 14 "says a person shall have the right to discriminate," CHP used Californians' color-blind language to convince voters that the Rumford Act, or what CREA called the Forced Housing Act, would infringe on their basic property rights. To get the 468,259 required signatures for the ballot measure within 150 days, CHP called on CREA's forty-five thousand members and 171 local realty boards and the Apartment Owners' Association members to organize a grassroots movement and assemble petitions. In total, they collected 633,206 valid signatures, far beyond the needed number and reportedly the largest quantity in history.[59]

Over the months leading up to the November 1964 election, the battle heated up on both sides of the debate and appeared in many forms—from leaflets, car bumper stickers, and television and radio advertisements, to politicians' platforms, political parties, and advocacy groups. For the most part, CHP and its allies omitted any mention of race, segregation, or property values in their campaign literature, public talking points, or fundraising efforts, which were key pain points the real estate industry had used in the past to maintain homogenous neighborhoods. Rather, HoSang explains, "Proposition 14 supporters steeped their arguments in the rhetoric of egalitarianism and even *antiracism*." They worked the New Left, civil rights language, and Cold War anxiety into their argument, insisting that the Rumford Act denied *all* citizens their individual right to property and claiming that the new law represented the socialist menace edging its way into the country and forcing property owners to obey state-made decisions. One CHP flyer, among many in an aggressive publicity campaign, claimed, "Owners! Tenants! Neighbors! Get Back Your Rights!" Using scare tactics that suggested the initiative would give political officials authority over Californians' property rights, and gendered language of the day, another advertisement read, "The Rumford Act makes a man's home subject to the whims of a politically appointed State Board."[60]

The pro–Proposition 14 rights-based argument resonated with the blue-collar suburbanites of the Alameda corridor. Since the interwar years, White working-class homeowners of Bell, South Gate, Lynwood, Maywood, and other communities situated south and east of Central Avenue had fought to stave off the in-migration of Blacks who were settling in the west-adjacent communities of Central Avenue. Concerned that African Americans would soon move next to their homes, which they saw as symbols of their success, identity, and status, blue-collar Whites defended their neighborhoods using all of their resources. In the postwar years, they coalesced around conservatism, fiscal austerity, anti-unionism, anti-Communism, and racial segregation in the city council, public schools, workplaces, civic groups, and on neighborhood blocks. Months before the 1963 Rumford Act went into effect, they shifted their focus from staving off desegregation of the public schools to condemning fair housing, and their attacks continued through the acrimonious Proposition 14 debate. While some White Alameda corridor residents came out in support of civil rights, the majority believed Proposition 14 would devastate the principal source of their status and value: their house. "In 1964, residents took their heritage of fighting politically to protect their homes, and applied it to the new racialized politics of the suburb," historian Becky Nicolaides explains. Pro-Proposition 14 advocates and area groups ran newspaper stories, held fundraising and voter registration drives, hosted speaking engagements, and attacked the opposition for infringing on White rights.[61]

While the pro–Proposition 14 campaign used its long-established organizational structure to sway voters, the anti–Proposition 14 operation underestimated the strength of its opposition and failed to marshal its most likely supporters. Californians Against Proposition 14 (CAP 14) formed in response to CHP's signature collection campaign and to prevent the passage of the initiative in the election. Governor Brown prioritized defeating Proposition 14 by appointing key officials in his administration to run CAP 14, mobilize the liberal coalition that elected him, and warn voters that Proposition 14 would reverse the state's progressive achievements. CAP 14 spread the message that Proposition 14 promoted hate, bigotry, and extremism, and infringed on the United States' promise of equality. "Don't Legalize Hate," CAP 14 broadcasted, in the war of words against CHP, on brochures and billboards across the state, imposed beside symbols of democracy, such as the American flag, Abraham Lincoln, and John F. Kennedy. Despite CAP 14's widespread support among the state's key civil rights, liberal, religious, and professional groups and high-profile celebrities, its shortcomings led to the victory of the pro–Proposition 14 campaign in the poll booth. CAP 14 focused on mobilizing the mostly White voters within Brown's liberal coalition instead of carrying out a direct voter campaign across the state, cultivating multiracial coalitions with Black, Mexican, and Japanese American groups, and organizing mass demonstrations.[62]

Rather than developing an interracial coalition, Black, Mexican, and Japanese Americans led separate campaigns to defeat Proposition 14, campaigns that also contributed to the initiative's passage. Historian Max Felker-Kantor finds that, among Black and Mexican Americans, Blacks "mobilized…to a greater degree." Major civil rights organizations, including the NAACP, Urban League, CORE, and the UCRC, which were also waging a war against school segregation, led boycotts, demonstrations, and voter registration drives, and distributed flyers to unite African Americans across class lines over supporting racial equality and defeating the initiative. Yet "the bulk of the opposition to Proposition 14 may have rested with middle-class blacks." Loren Miller and other NAACP attorneys, in fact, led the appeal to block the measure from getting on the ballot, which the state supreme court denied. While the majority of African Americans opposed the initiative, working-class Blacks felt it further benefited their middle-class counterparts, like those living in the Crenshaw area, who had the financial resources to secure single-family houses using government-financed loans. One African American leader went as far as to argue in support of the measure to prevent Blacks from abandoning Central Avenue.[63]

Mexican and Japanese Americans also experienced intra-ethnic divisions in the debate over the initiative that were rooted in their "class, residence, and their relationship to whiteness." Viewing Proposition 14 as an infringement on their rights and racial progress, and contributed to the nation's long history of housing discrimination, Mexican American groups, including the Los Angeles chapter of the Mexican American Political Association, the Council of Mexican American Affairs, and, allied with CAP 14, Mexican American Californians Against Proposition 14, led the anti–Proposition 14 effort. However, Mexican American supporters of the initiative, many of whom resided in the suburbs in or near East Los Angeles, subscribed to CHP's argument that Proposition 14 protected their property rights and, by going along with the status quo, could solidify their place in the White middle class. Japanese American groups, such as the JACL, Japanese American Christian and Buddhist churches, and the Japanese Chamber of Commerce advocated for a coalition to defeat the measure to protect civil rights and fair housing. Scott Kurashige points out one campaign poster that invoked World War II incarceration to warn voters that the nation could again deny Japanese Americans their rights. Yet, like many Whites who expressed disdain for living next to people of color, pro–Proposition 14 Japanese Americans conveyed the same sentiment.[64]

Ahead of the statewide election, CN pushed for fair housing albeit with reservations on the initiative that illustrates their moderate liberal stance. While Crenshaw residents initially came together in 1961 as UN over race-related conflicts at the public schools, they quickly saw racial issues interrelated in all of the functions of their community. In 1963 and 1964, amid UN's growth and CN's development, California was embroiled in the debate over fair housing; four months after CN obtained a charter, California voters passed Proposition 14 in the November 1964 election. Among its efforts toward fair housing, CN followed Riley and Edythe Jacobs's case, and reported on it in its monthly newsletter. Records also show that Gregg and Post spent time educating the community on fair housing. They presented at LWVLA workshops on the history and current status of fair housing in the state, and Post moderated a public forum that, according to its flyer, encouraged residents to "Hear Both Sides" and "Decide for Yourself." Despite their effort to remain neutral while informing the public, CHP's argument—or the fiery debate over fair housing itself—seemed to have persuaded them of the supposed shortfalls of Proposition 14. Following the measure's passage, Gregg conceded, using CHP's rights-based rhetoric, "I have come to think that the Rumford Act, while it may have been a good approach to insuring the *right* of any person to buy or rent any housing, was a bad approach to achieving integration." Post agreed, "Instead of concerning ourselves only with the people trying to get housing, let us consider laws that would prevent people in the business of housing from discriminating." Unfortunately, Proposition 14 nullified that law.[65]

In the election, of the 84.6 percent of California's registered voters, 65.4 percent approved the amendment and 34.6 rejected it. Of California's 58 counties, 57 voted in support of the measure. Only Modoc County, situated in the state's northeastern corner, voted against Proposition 14, by a mere nineteen votes. An astounding 67 percent of voters in Los Angeles County approved the measure, while 33 percent rejected it. At the same time, though, they voted for Democratic incumbent Lyndon Johnson against Republican Barry Goldwater in the presidential election. On December 7, 1964, the state added Proposition 14 as Article 1, Section 26 to the California constitution, its first postwar initiative aimed at legalizing housing discrimination and nullifying parts of the Unruh, Hawkins, and Rumford acts that covered housing. Proposition 14 undid fair housing advocates' work since the early twentieth century, and while attorneys filed lawsuits against the measure, the lower courts refused to address the matter until the California Supreme Court heard the case in October 1965. Two months before then, Los Angeles's Eastside residents had already pressed the issue using their last resort: uprising.[66]

THE WATTS REBELLION

What began as a drunk driving arrest of a twenty-one-year-old African American man on a hot summer evening in Watts sparked a six-day-long rebellion throughout the central city. On August 11, 1965, near the Watts border at 116th Street and Avalon Boulevard, Lee Minikus, a White California highway patrol officer on a motorcycle, pulled over Marquette Frye who was driving his mother's 1955 Buick. After Frye failed a sobriety test, the officer arrested him for driving under the influence. Frye's twenty-two-year-old stepbrother, Ronald Frye, then stepped out of the vehicle; Minikus radioed his partner, who arrived with a car to take Frye to jail, and Ronald went to get Frye's mother, Rena Price, who came from her home two blocks away. Meanwhile, a small group of onlookers outside in the summer heat had swelled to some 250 to 300 people. They had cause for their anger. Added to the countless, long-standing systemic racist policies and practices that kept Angelenos of color hemmed in in the Eastside, Chief William H. Parker's Los Angeles Police Department had gained notoriety for its relentless brutality targeted at African Americans, and, at that moment, the Frye brothers, their mother, and the crowd confronted it. As the crowd grew angry, which by then had grown to a thousand bystanders, the officers detained Marquette, Ronald, and Rena, and took them to the police station. Reports of police abuse of power at the scene subsequently spread throughout greater Los Angeles and sparked a nearly weeklong protest.[67]

Once a thriving, multiracial, blue-collar community, Watts had become mostly populated by Blacks. Incorporated first as a self-governing city in 1907 and then part of Los Angeles after 1926, Watts developed alongside the construction of two major rail lines. Mexican laborers mostly working on the railroad at the turn of the century initially settled around the tracks, followed by a small number of African Americans in a section of the city known as Mudtown. In the first quarter of the twentieth century, Watts grew into a working-class enclave with affordable housing, a reliable mass transit system, and a multiracial population made up of Blacks, Whites, Asians, and Latinos. World War II brought employment opportunities and an influx of African Americans to the city, but the subsequent years wreaked havoc on the quaint community. Watts became part of Los Angeles's neglected and isolated Black belt that had dilapidated housing, no rent control, exploitative landowners, and a high rate of homelessness. The passage of Proposition 14 represented and added to the decades of discrimination, neglect, and isolation that many African Americans had felt. A constant succession of social, economic, and political developments devastated the enclave. Deindustrialization, high Black unemployment, the decline of labor unions, the loss of public transportation, persistent housing discrimination, city officials' neglect of antipoverty programs and indifference to local grievances, the rise of gangs, unapologetic police brutality, anti-Communism and the suppression of liberalism, and the rise of Black nationalism set the stage for the 1965 uprising that started on the Eastside, or what became known as South Central, and, later, South Los Angeles.[68]

The city's decades-long intra-racial class conflict, which surfaced in the debate over Proposition 14, also contributed to the Watts rebellion. While economic and political developments most deeply caused the Eastside's decline, historians find that the divisions within the city's Black population likewise affected Watts's residents' feelings of neglect, isolation, and resentment. In his 1945 novel, *If He Hollers Let Him Go*, Chester Himes acknowledged the class divisions in the early years of Black migration onto the Westside when he censured the Black middle class in West Jefferson for assuming the Black working class failed to set goals, work hard, and earn a good living. Those class divisions widened in the postwar years as more southern Blacks migrated to the western city, according to historian Gerald Horne, and faced criticism for any number of groundless reasons—from their rural mannerisms to their working-class attire to their darker skin, to them taking jobs and housing from other White, Latino, and Asian working-class city dwellers.[69]

Meanwhile, working-class Blacks continued to argue that their middle-class counterparts had both abandoned the Eastside and also sought to conform to White norms. In the interwar interregnum, the NAACP, for example, used many of its resources to fight against restrictive covenants, which Whites primarily used to limit their single-family houses to Whites only, and middle-class Blacks had the financial means to obtain, if they could thwart the mechanism. The city's housing authority began constructing housing projects for low-income city dwellers in 1939, and after mounting pressure from the wartime housing crisis, local activists, and the 1943 race riots, Mayor Fletcher Bowron finally backed the program. Yet those public housing projects mostly had Eastside addresses, which contributed to over-concentrating the city's poor in an already overcrowded area. "Building public housing in South LA was a source of contention," Horne argues. "Public housing was sited in this area that already had more than its share of the poverty-stricken," he later continues. By focusing efforts on prohibiting discrimination in owner-occupied, single-family, government loan-financed housing, the Rumford Act bridged the earlier fight against restrictive covenants and consequently put fewer resources into aiding the Black working class in moving out of the Eastside.[70]

Horne likewise finds that intra-racial generational tensions had a hand in contributing to the uprising. As the Southern civil rights movement failed to address the needs of northern city dwellers, the reputation of Malcolm X grew after his February 1965 assassination, and Black Angelenos became hemmed in in the Eastside, Black nationalists and gang members filled a much-needed void and voiced the bottled-up anger and resentment many Eastside residents of color had felt. Long-time local leader Norman O. Houston, who had cofounded Golden State Mutual Life Insurance Company and led the desegregation of Sugar Hill, admitted that the city's NAACP chapter as well as middle-class Blacks needed to do more to support their working-class counterparts and invest in housing, jobs, and education on the Eastside. The rise of Black nationalist groups in California after the uprising, including the Black Panther Party and the organization known as Us, detailed in chapter 6, evinces this younger generation's desire for a more radical approach that countered the measured tactics of elder civil rights leaders, and that proudly embraced and celebrated African American history and culture. "A remarkable consensus had developed, crossing even class and racial divides: black leadership was too middle class and had lost touch with the masses," Horne concludes. Black nationalists and gang members might have prolonged the uprising, but long-standing, systemic, discriminatory policies and practices, perpetuated at the neighborhood, city, county, state, and federal levels, ignited it.[71]

Unlike the prewar race riots that were initiated by White vigilantes seeking to suppress Black advancement, the Watts rebellion and the successive uprisings saw African Americans releasing their pent-up anger. Yet the days following the confrontation on August 11 illustrated government officials' chronic negligence. For more than forty-eight hours, while the city was enduring looting, fires, and fatalities, local and state leaders, including Mayor Sam Yorty, Police Chief Parker, and Governor Brown, kept their previous engagements and deflected their responsibilities to quell the rebellion onto each other. Finally, two nights after the Frye and Price arrests, while Brown was in Greece, his lieutenant governor, Glenn Anderson, made the decision to deploy the California National Guard and, the following day, issue a curfew for eight o'clock in the evening in a 46.5-square-mile area of the central city. The curfew zone stretched west to Crenshaw Boulevard, cutting into the Crenshaw area and putting Leimert Park under surveillance. Nearly one week later, the city lifted the curfew, and the uprising ended with thirty-four dead, more than a thousand injured, and some four thousand arrested. Property damage within the curfew zone was estimated at $200 million. The California Supreme Court, in its May 1966 decision in *Mulkey v. Reitman*, overturned Proposition 14, ruling the decree violated the Fourteenth Amendment, because it involved the state in discriminatory practices, the same reasoning the US Supreme Court put forth in *Shelley* nearly two decades before. The US Supreme Court affirmed *Mulkey*, in a 5–4 decision, one year later. Although the decision reinstated the Rumford Act as the state's fair housing law, the damage had been done.[72]

The Watts rebellion had long-lasting effects that surfaced in its immediate aftermath. At first, in 1963 and 1964, CHP's campaign divided conservative groups and politicians, many of whom believed Proposition 14 threatened property values and rights, business activity, and public sentiment. While Goldwater, who was running against Johnson in the presidential election, and Ronald Reagan, who was serving as cochair of Goldwater's California campaign, endorsed the measure, they sidestepped mentioning it in their speeches or strategies. In 1966, however, in Reagan's successful gubernatorial campaign against incumbent Brown, he used CHP's tactics, argued in opposition to any legislation that he believed violated individual rights, and denied the existence of housing discrimination. Southern California's New Right established the foundation for Reagan's gubernatorial win that set the stage for his 1980 presidential victory. Meanwhile, New Left radicals continued to protest in and after the 1967 long, hot summer and in the 1968 week-long school blowouts when some twenty thousand East Los Angelenos, mostly Chicano high school students walked out of their classes to demand schools better support them, which, in turn, launched the Chicano movement. The 1969 Los Angeles mayoral election of Tom Bradley, against incumbent Yorty, also signified voters' desire for new leadership. Amid the polarized milieu, CN grew laser-focused on achieving racial integration, which, in the second half of the 1960s, became the moderate liberal stance.[73]

WATTS SHAKES UP CRENSHAW

As Crenshaw residents reacted to the Watts rebellion and put their homes on the market, CN stepped up its effort to maintain a racially balanced population by creating more programs and expanding its reach. Among its initiatives, CN teamed up with organizations outside of Crenshaw; generated good publicity on the organization; held seminars promoting racial integration for apartment owners and managers; organized social gatherings, lectures, block clubs, community watch groups, and clean-up programs; stopped the construction of a freeway through Crenshaw; led the development of a public park; created children's educational programs; continued to publish its newsletter; and published a nationally recognized journal. CN leaders also persistently lobbied for support for city and state officials to recognize their value. Amid the upsurge of activities and concentrated effort, in the second half of the 1960s CN reached its peak, and the affluent Crenshaw neighborhoods comprised CN's ideal diverse population of mainly Whites, Blacks, and Japanese Americans. Yet the out-migration of White and then Japanese residents persisted, and the demographics changed to a Black majority.

Several months before the Watts rebellion, CN allied with other neighborhood organizations in Southern California. In the early 1960s, nearby communities also struggling with real estate blockbusting and White exodus, such as Inglewood, Compton, Altadena, and Long Beach, formed their own neighborhood stabilization groups. Seeing an opportunity to strengthen its effort, in the spring of 1965 CN asked the County Commission on Human Relations to assemble these organizations together. After several informal meetings, delegates from eight groups in Southern California decided to form an umbrella organization. In September, they approved a steering committee and adopted the Council of Integrated Neighborhoods (COIN) as their name. Two more groups joined thereafter. Raymond Weil, president of Inglewood's Morningside Park Neighbors (later renamed Inglewood Neighbors), and Jean Gregg headed the formation of the group, and served as chair and vice chair, respectively.[74]

COIN quickly got to work pushing for racial integration. The group pressured the state legislature to ensure that community colleges offered educational programs that attracted students "from all ethnic groups" and every LAUSD high school. COIN pressured planning agencies in Los Angeles to promote and build integrated neighborhoods; wrote a proposal to fund documentary films on fair housing; and filed incident reports with the National Committee Against Discrimination in Housing. At its monthly meetings, COIN also hosted speakers from the school district, nonprofit organizations, and real estate associations who were committed to racial integration and equality.[75]

In October 1965, Gregg received an "unexpected call" to speak on CN's behalf before the California Governor's Commission on the Los Angeles Riots. Commonly known as the McCone Commission, after former Central Intelligence Agency director and commission chair John A. McCone, the hearings investigated the causes of the Watts rebellion and proposed recommendations to heal and improve the city. With a forty-eight-hour notice, Gregg hurriedly prepared a statement on Crenshaw's population trends, residents' concerns over the schools and real estate agents, and CN's origin, goals, and work. At the foot of "a huge T-shaped table," representing Crenshaw and CN, Gregg fielded questions from the panel "about housing and schools and attitudes in Crenshaw." She praised residents for defending their community in the face of the rebellion and stressed the importance of achieving residential integration.[76]

The Watts rebellion worsened the public image of Black neighborhoods in the city, but the media took notice of CN's work. While the group invested a large portion of its donations and revenue on flyers, advertisements, and newsletters, CN received what its October 1965 bulletin called "that most wonderful brand of publicity—the free kind." Newspapers, magazines, radio stations, and television news channels worldwide reported on the positive contributions of mid-city Angelenos. CN was delighted to "show a better side of this shocked and somewhat mangled city." Several CN members responded to the often shortsighted and erroneous depictions of the area and its residents by writing letters and submitting editorials to newspapers. They extolled the group's achievements while admitting that they "still have a long way to go." CN also continued to promote itself and prevent blockbusting by creating "small wooden plaques" with the CN symbol and the words "Member of Crenshaw Neighbors" for residents to display on their front door "and perhaps protect you from the spring surge of canvassing real estate salesmen."[77]

CN's work toward racial integration came with setbacks. At the end of 1965, soon after Laing resigned, the CN real estate office stopped listing properties and began "operating entirely as a home-finding service for prospective buyers." CN provided a few reasons for its decision: For one, its attention to property sales distracted its staff and resources from carrying out other initiatives. Another reason CN gave was that its approach of selling houses to a targeted race to create racial balance put pressure on and caused dissatisfaction in real estate agents and sellers. CN continued to pay agents either a salary or commission and earned a commission itself, but instead of selling properties, it focused on finding homes for buyers and referring renters to available units.[78]

The group also faced an uphill battle to show more residents the value of integration. Between November 1965 and February 1966, UCLA sociology faculty Richard T. Morris and Vincent Jeffries conducted some six hundred interviews of White residents in integrated Baldwin Hills and Leimert Park, as well as nearby communities, to identify their mood following the Watts rebellion. Of their sample of Whites, Morris and Jeffries found that 33 percent in Baldwin Hills and 36 percent in Leimert Park believed Blacks "have less native intelligence" compared to Whites, and 34 percent in Baldwin Hills and 42 percent in Leimert Park had a "negative feeling toward [the] civil rights movement." The sociologists picked up on White residents who wanted to move out of the area. "It is our feeling that the integrated neighborhood in Los Angeles is an ephemeral situation—it is a white neighborhood which has been invaded by Negroes and is on its way to becoming all-Negro," they concluded, using racialized language of marking the area as White and describing Black in-migration as an invasion.[79]

In the fall of 1966, CN encountered another challenge when Gregg resigned as executive director, writing that she badly needed rest. The necessary amount of time, emotional labor, and resolve needed, which fell mostly on Gregg and Crenshaw's women, to challenge the social and structural forces, took a toll. Post assumed Gregg's role, and Kenneth Olsen, public-school administrator and White View Park resident, who initially had moved to the area through the assistance of realtor John Laing's service, was elected president.[80]

CN's work continued without Gregg at the helm, and among its concerns, the group turned to the apartments. Members grew alarmed amid White exodus and Black influx when apartment owners and managers began neglecting their properties in Baldwin Village or, as it was insensitively dubbed, "the Jungle." One CN member noticed "paint peeling, grass uncut; litter and untidiness in the alleys," and more children and more cars on the road, "indicating larger families, overcrowding and...more noise," historically common signs of decline that pointed toward exploitation and reminded CN of what had become of the late nineteenth century New York City tenements. If the community disregarded the problems, as CN expected, "in a very short time there will be no way to stop it." The group offered a free six-week seminar to apartment owners and managers that met once a week. Sponsored by and hosted at the nearby Black-owned Family Savings and

Loan Association, the seminars included speakers and discussions on, for example, screening prospective tenants, refinancing, and the costs of property neglect on the entire community. The seminar led to the establishment of the Apartment Owners' Association, which, Post explained, "screens tenants, maintains standards, and provides a healthy integrated environment." CN might not have foreseen gang violence overrun Baldwin Village, but it intuitively understood that the rental area would become a problem.[81]

Through the late 1960s, CN organized multiple events to nurture residents' relationships across the color line and maintain Crenshaw's integrity and value. The group hosted dinners, cocktail parties, coffee fellowships, and public lectures. It helped organize block clubs, neighborhood watch programs, and clean-up campaigns. In its Shop Crenshaw drive, CN encouraged residents to support local establishments. Members volunteered at the Foundation for the Junior Blind in Windsor Hills, serving as drivers, teaching classes, offering their clerical services, and attending social gatherings. The CN standards committee, under the leadership of Barry Siegel, successfully fought a projected plan to extend the Slauson Freeway (Route 90) through the southern half of Crenshaw. CN vice president and one of the first female CBS television executives, Anne Nelson, led a nearly two-decade effort to convert an overgrown field into a park named for African American baseball great Jim Gilliam.[82]

CN also carried on its work organizing and sponsoring additional educational programs in and outside of Crenshaw. The Coordinating Council continued to offer the summer reading improvement project for four years, and in that time an increasing number of students registered for the course. In 1965 Joan Suter and Barbara Tenan founded the Baldwin Hills Cultural Enrichment Center, a summer program financed by parents and held at Baldwin Hills Elementary School for primary and middle school students. Youngsters had the opportunity to take courses in art, drama, cinematography, creative writing, ethnomusicology, dance, science, and logic, taught by volunteer grade school teachers and college professors, and to go on field trips to places such as the Griffith Park Observatory. Lyle Suter was director of the program. The cultural enrichment center became so successful that the organizers had to put the overflow of applicants on a waiting list. In 1968, as a reflection of the center's widespread appeal, it changed its name to the Los Angeles Cultural Arts Center for Youth.[83]

The Watts rebellion prompted Fifi Boger to organize the countywide youth outreach program, Teen Post. This War on Poverty initiative, which began as a three-week program in August 1965 that offered extracurricular activities, established more than one hundred safe places across the city for low-income teenagers to learn, make friends, and discover new pursuits.

Each Teen Post branch offered a variety of activities, such as cooking, crafts, nursing, and auto mechanics classes; table tennis, checkers, bowling, and swimming; and dances, movies, and day trips. "The main [goal] was to keep the kids off the street," Boger explained, and to offer them opportunities that they might not have received elsewhere. After some twelve thousand youngsters had participated in the program, Boger convinced financial backers to continue their support. Teen Post ran into many obstacles, including teenagers fighting and vandalizing property, police exhibiting apathy, and financial cutbacks and mismanagement, that led to criticism. But Boger defended the program: "We said we wanted to reach the hard-to-reach kids and we feel we have achieved that." Over her career, Boger remained politically active, supporting politicians such as Augustus Hawkins, Pat Brown, and John F. Kennedy; serving as community relations director for the cooperative housing project, Concord Park; and serving on the board of directors of the local NAACP and Urban League chapters.[84]

CN also headed one of its most innovative programs aimed at integrating high schools, and after two years of negotiations and groundwork, its initiative came to fruition. An advisory committee made up of CN representatives, community members, and school officials created an exchange program among five senior high schools and eight junior high schools in LAUSD that allowed students to take courses outside of their home institution. Under Project APEX (Area Program for Enrichment Exchange), participating schools served as special subject centers, offering courses in, among others, aeronautics, anthropology, business, ceramics, Chinese, computer math, constitutional law, data processing, Hebrew, Japanese, jazz, play production, Portuguese, and Russian. In 1967, three years before Los Angeles Superior Court judge Alfred Gitelson mandated LAUSD implement busing to desegregate schools, students who enrolled in APEX schools voluntarily took the bus to their selected APEX program, attended a course for two class periods, and then returned to their home institution. "You had Black kids taking Hebrew at Fairfax High School," Joan Suter, the program's founder and executive director, extolled. "It was a life-altering experience." In 1967, financed by the federal government under the Elementary and Secondary Education Act and the San Francisco–based nonprofit Rosenberg Foundation, the program began.[85]

Project APEX saw immediate success. In the 1967–68 academic year, the first year in operation, 1,500 students voluntarily enrolled in the program. Racially mixed Dorsey High School and Crenshaw High School (which had opened in 1968), mostly Black Manual Arts High School, and majority White Fairfax High School and Hamilton High School, became special subject centers for senior high school students. Dorsey High alone brought in more than two hundred pupils a year. Members and employees of local institutions also got involved. Academics at USC gave informational lectures, helped improve facilities, and encouraged students to join the program. Local museums, hospitals, and community councils donated their time. "The change of atmosphere, a variety of courses and being able to meet a wider range of people stimulated both student interest and achievement," raved Dorsey High principal Clifford L. Davis, Jr., and Project APEX English coordinator Karen Kaub. By creating a racially mixed student body, Project APEX "gives us the chance to clear up any misconceptions of backgrounds different from our own," Dorsey High student Diedra Wilson explained.[86]

The Project APEX student advisory committee also organized extracurricular activities designed to further advance racial tolerance. The weekend retreats to the mountains in Idyllwild and Camarillo, California, Joan Suter recalled, remained "one of the highlights of my life." Students joined sensitivity workshops, engaged in lively discussions, and forged relationships across racial and class lines that challenged their point of view. Beverly Hills High students, feeling isolated in their own community and inspired by the civil rights struggle, got the chance to join the events. With the help of Joan and Lyle Suter, several Beverly Hills High students sat on the student advisory committee, attended the weekend retreats, and participated in other extracurricular activities. Writing in the school newspaper after an inspiring retreat in Idyllwild, one Beverly Hills High pupil charged, "Wake up, Beverly students!" While Beverly Hills High was investing millions of dollars into parking spaces, a cafeteria, and a planetarium, "our ghetto brothers have no books; many can't even read." Another student found, "Going up to Idyllwild, the white kids stuck with white kids, and the blacks with blacks." But "we left Idyllwild, brothers and sisters, and members of the Human Race."[87]

While CN encouraged Japanese Americans' leadership, that group often struggled to increase its representation. From the mid-1960s and into the early 1970s, only one or two Japanese Americans served on CN's board of directors. In 1965 Yoshinao Nakada became the first Japanese American to serve on the CN board. Nakada was born in Los Angeles, graduated from the California Institute of Technology, and was working at Hughes Aircraft Company as an aerospace engineer and living with his spouse and two daughters in the Crenshaw area when he joined the board. In 1966 Joseph Ozawa, Jr., succeeded Nakada. Los Angeles–born Ozawa was twenty-one years old at the time, a Harvard University student, and a civil rights activist who had advocated for integration in Alabama and Massachusetts. He represented CN on the East Coast while he was at school. Then in 1968 Masamori Kojima won a seat to the board. Los Angeles–born Kojima graduated from Haverford College in Pennsylvania, and worked as a field deputy to councilor (and later mayor) Tom Bradley. The *Los Angeles Times* later eulogized Kojima as "Bradley's chief representative to Los Angeles's Asian communities." But not until 1970 did CN see two Japanese Americans serve on the board, which at the time consisted of seventeen directors, when Kojima and Donald Misumi, chair of the biology department at Los Angeles Trade Technical College and Crenshaw resident, won an election.[88]

CN also sought, albeit with difficulty, to boost Japanese American membership and participation. Interviewed for a March 1965 article in *Shin Nichi-Bei*, Nakada explained that CN had only six Nisei members, a number he greatly sought to increase. The housing committee, in the March 1969 *Crenshaw Notes* issue, called on "our Black, Brown, or Oriental members" to seek assistance from the group. "There is no need for your choice of location to be influenced by fear of discrimination." To draw more Japanese American interest in the group and increase understanding of the Japanese American experience, the June 1970 issue announced, "Join with your neighbors" at the city's newly founded Asian American theater, East West Players, to see *Tondemonai—Never Happen*, a drama that grappled with the trauma of wartime incarceration. "We have discussed many ideas to involve the oriental community in CN," the membership committee explained in the September 1970 issue. Among the initiatives, according to the newsletter, the committee sold fifty tickets to *Tondemonai*, had plans to interview Reverend Peter Chen, who would soon lead the Centenary Methodist Church, which had "more than half of its 1000 members [living] in our area," and recently spoke to the Japanese American newspaper, *Crossroads*, for an article on CN. But the decline in affluent Crenshaw's Asian population made CN's work toward racial inclusion more difficult.[89]

At the end of 1967, CN released the first issue of its quarterly journal, *The Integrator*. As the title suggests, *The Integrator* aimed to advance racial integration. Despite persistent White resistance against the civil rights struggle and the Black cultural and revolutionary nationalist movements, CN insisted integration remained the answer to society's race-related conflicts. The journal's introductory page explained, "Integration is looked upon here as the hope, and the only answer, for America's racial problem. Only by really living with people of a different race can we overcome the fear of previously taught differences." The journal's editor, Olive Walker, or who one CN member called the "reader, author, fretter, [and] mail-sack-dragger," ran the publication. Born in Selma, Alabama, Walker attended the University of Denver and St. Louis University, and became a social worker before moving to View Park and joining the LWVLA and UN as one of UN's first Black members. Walker, CN members, and writers nationwide contributed articles on civil rights, fair housing, public schools, interracial marriage, and parenting. The journal included a suggested reading list with books on race, fair housing, Black history, and urbanism. A regularly featured piece, "The National Integration Scene," summarized local-, state-, and federal-level efforts toward fair housing and integration. *The Integrator* reprinted scholarly articles, highlighted Black artists' works, and featured cartoons.[90]

Although the journal pushed for racial integration, it was unafraid to publish works that critiqued Whites. In "The '9 to 5' Liberal" cartoon, Lyle Suter highlighted White liberals' contradictory beliefs. Suter depicted an average White man, working in an administrator role as a department head, appropriately named Charlie White, who was embracing Blacks sitting around the conference table and touting his accomplishments for improving race relations in the workplace, and then, in a suburban neighborhood in the evening, attending an all-White function where an African American woman served drinks. In the "'De Facto' Charlie" cartoon, Suter pictured a White middle-class family in a suburban neighborhood posting on his front lawn a "For Sale" sign, amid a line of the same signs along the block, when a Black family moved in, and then relocating to "Safeland Valley" where, "We don't mind freeway bumper to bumper jams commuting, because we know, deep in our hearts, our daughters are safe!"[91]

While *The Integrator* mainly focused on Black and White race relations, at least one of its issues featured the Japanese American perspective. In the late 1960s and early 1970s, Japanese, Chinese, and Filipino Americans took inspiration from the civil rights, Black nationalist, and antiwar movements, and coalesced in the Asian American movement. They formed collectives and study groups, published materials, and promoted self-determinism and a Pan-Asian identity. Between 1969 and 1970, the Avenues section along Jefferson Boulevard, where Kazuo Inouye had opened his real estate business after wartime incarceration, emerged as a hub of Los Angeles's Sansei-led Asian American movement. John Saito's essay, "Yellow Power," which *The Integrator* published in its summer 1968 issue, foresaw the rise of the movement. Saito began with a rhetorical question, "'Black Power!!' 'Chicano Power!!' and far in the background if you listen attentively, a faint voice is saying 'Yellow Power?'" Writing two decades after incarceration, Saito acknowledged that, despite what seemed like less discrimination against Asian Americans and the rise in a "standard of living never before imagined" among Asian Americans, "the faint voice in the background will become stronger and we will hear more and more of 'Yellow Power.'"[92]

Through the late 1960s, CN continued to make progress toward its goals. In 1967 the Black-owned Family Savings and Loan Association gave CN free office space and access to conference rooms for a year. CN increased its membership from roughly 650 in October 1965 to 800 in 1967 and then 1,200 in 1969. Of those members, CN counted on its roster distinguished political leaders and Leimert Park residents Yvonne Brathwaite Burke and Tom Bradley. By September 1968 *The Integrator* had achieved 700 subscribers nationwide and fielded requests from publications to reprint its works. In 1969 Los Angeles County supervisor Kenneth Hahn named May 18–24 Crenshaw Neighbors Week.[93]

Amid pressure from the civil rights, Black nationalist, and open housing movements, the federal government responded. In 1965, the same year President Johnson established HUD and folded the FHA into the new agency, the FHA had begun to soften its redlining practices and encourage its partners to consider insuring home mortgages in older neighborhoods that exhibited growth potential, rather than dismiss them altogether. Then, one week after the assassination of Martin Luther King, Jr., Congress passed—and Johnson signed—the Civil Rights Act of 1968. The legislation paid tribute to King's shift to campaigning for the urban north and open housing in the mid-1960s, and became one of Johnson's last Great Society measures. Under Title VIII, commonly known as the Fair Housing Act, the legislation made liable anyone who discriminated against any person based on race, color, religion, or national origin in the sale, rental, or finance of private housing. Later the act was expanded to include gender, disability, and families with children. A section of the law also directly addressed blockbusting. In its most up-to-date language, the law makes it illegal "to induce or attempt to induce a person to sell or rent a dwelling by [mentioning] the entry or prospective entry into the neighborhood of a person or persons of a particular race, color, religion, sex, familial status, or national origin or with a handicap." While the act marked an achievement in the fair housing movement, it had limitations. As they had been doing for decades prior, private individuals and activist groups, rather than federal agencies, had to uphold and enforce the law by raising money, filing claims, and litigating their cases in court. Moreover, legislation passed four months later comprising the 1968 Housing and Urban Development Act enabled lenders and realtors to continue using predatory tactics that perpetuated residential segregation and kept low-income Blacks in the inner city.[94]

CN's own members also expressed mixed views on the group's success that foretold the breakdown of their efforts. With the help of another census, which USC sociology graduate student Burt R. Baldwin and his spouse, Dianne, led in 1967, Ann Post and others believed that the racial composition of the population in Crenshaw's single-family communities had either stabilized or was moving in that direction. Post wrote, "After four years of operation, our latest survey indicated that the racial change in 1967 was reduced to one percent." But Kenneth Olsen, Post's successor as CN president, argued in 1968 that not only was CN dealing with an "internal crisis," which led to restructuring the CN leadership, committees, finances, and procedures, but also CN's effort to establish racial integration had "failed." Moreover, CN faced its fair share of criticism. Some argued that CN primarily comprised White members who either represented the rare few who supported integration or who, albeit incorrectly, wanted to make Crenshaw all White. Others believed CN was not moving quickly enough to combat White out-migration. After all, real estate blockbusting continued well into the late 1960s. At the same time that Crenshaw was undergoing a demographic shift to a Black majority, some of CN's leaders were turning their attention to establish a national neighborhood stabilization agency.[95]

A NATIONAL AGENCY, A LOCAL LET DOWN

At the end of the 1960s, with the help of the CN leadership, neighborhood stabilization groups around the country joined forces to organize a national agency committed to thwarting residential discrimination and supporting integrated neighborhoods nationwide. When Jean Gregg and fair housing advocate Morris Milgram teamed up in 1968, they set out to fulfill an idea, rooted in the open housing movement, to set up a national agency. Born to working-class, Jewish immigrant parents, Morris Milgram had built a national reputation constructing and managing open-occupancy communities across the nation and founding nonprofit organizations to buttress racial integration. After they received funding for their proposal, Gregg and Milgram planned a conference to bring together integrated groups from around the country. To create a setting that reflected their objectives, they asked twelve groups to invite an active Black member and an active White member as representatives to an all-expenses-paid trip, underwritten by Milgram's group, Sponsors of Open Housing Investment, to Carleton College in Minnesota. At the conference, which convened in March 1969, participants voted unanimously to set up the agency. They adopted the name National Neighbors, outlined their mission, and elected African American attorney Joseph Hairston as president. Gregg became the first executive director of National Neighbors. She relocated from Los Angeles to Philadelphia at the end of 1969, married Milgram in 1970, took her new husband's last name, and turned her focus to the national effort.[96]

National Neighbors embarked on an ambitious plan. The goals that the participants agreed on at Carleton College illustrated their boldness and determination for progress toward residential integration. National Neighbors set out to improve communication between local groups, provide consulting services, create a national directory and data bank, support conferences, conduct research, publish literature, lead action programs against racial discrimination in the real estate industry, advocate for legislation, develop national public relations, and spread the message of racial integration. With Jean Gregg Milgram as "the hub around which the organization functioned," scholar Juliet Saltman wrote, the group quickly began to tackle its goals. Except for the data bank, National Neighbors launched all of its plans. One of its most noteworthy projects, Shoppers' Sunday, encouraged local groups around the country throughout the 1970s to audit and file claims against discriminatory real estate agents. National Neighbors provided legal aid from its US Justice Department team of attorneys at no cost to act against real estate agents.[97]

Meanwhile, CN left behind a mixed legacy of trials and errors, successes and failures. Thanks to its dedication and drive toward racial integration, particularly throughout the 1960s, CN achieved noteworthy growth in its membership roll, committee work, local programs, and national outreach. Gregg later explained that UN and CN members felt part of the modern civil rights movement, striving to achieve racial integration. While White liberals, such as Gregg and Post, initially took the lead, both Whites and Blacks carried out initiatives, worked with local officials, wrote articles and ruminations, and established a collaborative interracial group that they wished to see in the area. Maintaining racial balance, however, proved too difficult to achieve.[98] Around the same time as the long, hot summer, the integrated Crenshaw neighborhoods became predominantly Black. Federal census reports indicated that, by 1970, resegregation had overpowered CN's efforts. Black residents far exceeded White residents in Crenshaw's single-family neighborhoods. "It is clear," Barry Siegel, CN president in 1973, wrote, "that Crenshaw is less integrated than when Crenshaw Neighbors began."[99]

The Los Angeles BOE finally began to carry out a racial census of its schools in 1966, and the data similarly reflected the residential figures. Between 1966 and 1970, eight years after the NAACP threatened to picket Baldwin Hills Elementary, the proportion of Black students at the school rose from 16.1 percent to 56.7 percent. The White proportion fell from 60.7 percent to 20.9 percent, and the Asian proportion decreased slightly from 18 percent to 16.8 percent. At Windsor Hills Elementary, the Black proportion rose from 74.3 percent to 89.2 percent, while the White share fell from 18.3 percent to 7.9 percent, and the Asian share fell from 6.4 percent to 2.3 percent. Black students in the other schools also comprised the majority. In 1970, at Dorsey High, Blacks made up 76.2 percent of the student population, and at Crenshaw High, two years after it opened, Black youngsters comprised 96.2 percent.[100] The summer reading improvement course, the

Baldwin Hills Cultural Enrichment Center, and Project APEX lacked the resources to permanently desegregate LAUSD.

Regardless, Crenshaw's single-family communities remained highly respected and prosperous. Median property values and median annual income in Crenshaw's single-family communities remained above the city median. The media also took notice when the Windsor Hills Elementary School sixth-grade class scored the highest average out of the 435 LAUSD elementary schools, a reporter for the *Los Angeles Times* explained, "including all the high-achieving predominately white schools," on the 1968 intelligence quotient test. Through the early 1970s, *Newsweek* reported, Windsor Hills Elementary "ranks among the top 5 percent of the city's schools in standard reading tests."[101] The warnings of federal agencies, private mortgage lenders, real estate agents, and White homeowners that Black settlement in White communities caused neighborhood deterioration fell short from the truth. The affluent Crenshaw communities endured racial discrimination and hostility, school clashes, real estate blockbusting, and a significant shift in their racial composition while remaining desirable places to live.

Chapter Six

Brockman Gallery and the Art of Social Change

DRIVING IN A VOLKSWAGEN BUG on their cross-country road trip in the summer of 1966, brothers Alonzo and Dale Davis discussed opening an art gallery centered on African American works in their hometown of Los Angeles. Twenty-four-year-old Manual Arts High School art teacher Alonzo Joseph Davis, Jr., and twenty-year-old USC art student Dale Brockman Davis had embarked on a journey to explore their Southern roots and connect with other Black artists around the United States. Born to middle-class parents in Tuskegee, Alabama, and residents of Los Angeles since the mid-1950s, the Davis brothers were inspired by the social and political climate. They wore their hair long, protested against the Vietnam War, and picketed for civil rights. Sleeping mostly in Alonzo's car, they drove from Los Angeles through the South, into the eye of the civil rights movement. Less than one year after they returned home, they rented a storefront in the commercial center of their mother's home in Leimert Park, spruced up the interior, recruited artists, sent out mailings, decided on a name that honored their family, and opened Brockman Gallery.[1]

The population of Leimert Park in the 1960s underwent a significant shift not only in the community's residential portions, but also in the commercial center. Designed in the 1920s by the Leimert Company, the commercial center (later known as Leimert Park Village) became an important part of the community's activities. The Mesa Vernon Market stood at the intersection of Crenshaw and Leimert Boulevards and Vernon Avenue; in the 1930s the Leimert Theater opened along Degnan Boulevard, the road running parallel to and a few blocks east of Crenshaw Boulevard, through the center of Leimert Park. The food vendors, clothiers, drug and beauty stores, and theater helped create Leimert Park's milieu of a small town within a large city where residents could gather and buy goods. Black and Asian in-migration and real estate blockbusting altered the community's demographics, prompting many White and then Asian homeowners and merchants to move away, yet the new residents enhanced its character. In late 1966, after the Davis brothers had returned home from their road trip, they noticed the population shift taking place. "The small merchants were beginning to make a move, and eventually the big ones left too," Alonzo recalled. Seeing an opportunity in what was becoming an affluent Black area, they rented the vacant 4334 Degnan Boulevard storefront and pioneered a Black-run art gallery, dedicated to exhibiting and selling works of artists of color.[2]

Brockman Gallery emerged within the nationwide Black arts movement that took place from the mid-1960s through the mid-1970s. African American visual artists, musicians, writers, and filmmakers in urban centers around the United States insisted on their value and importance in the European-biased, White-run art market. Deeply affected by the civil rights and Black nationalist movements, Black artists rejected European influences, took a stand against colonialism, and used their art to pay homage to their African ancestry, promote Pan-African unity, explore the African American past, demand racial equality, and celebrate Black culture and self-determinism. The movement stood on a centuries-long tradition of Black art that, in early 1900s Los Angeles, centered along Central Avenue, and following World War II, also developed along Western Avenue. In the early 1950s, historian Daniel Widener explains, amid the decline of Central Avenue and the mostly Black, working-class Eastside (later known as South Central, and later still known as South Los Angeles), the area saw a resurgence of Black art collectives and initiatives. Grounded in the postwar arts infrastructure, Black artists and their supporters after the 1965 Watts rebellion established more art collectives and led art initiatives primarily in Watts and its adjacent neighborhoods. The Davis brothers expanded the Black arts movement's reach onto the Westside's Leimert Park and Crenshaw area.[3]

In addition to Leimert Park Village, Jefferson and Crenshaw Boulevards served as major thoroughfares for commercial activity around the Crenshaw area. With *Shelley* and blockbusting realtors as driving forces, Japanese American Angelenos in the mid- to late 1940s established residences and businesses along Jefferson Boulevard, between Crenshaw Boulevard and Arlington Avenue, in the working-class Avenues section. In the 1950s, a few years after the Crenshaw Center (later the Baldwin Hills Crenshaw Plaza) opened on Santa Barbara Avenue (King Boulevard) and Crenshaw Boulevard, Nisei opened Holiday Bowl and Crenshaw Square.[4] Then, in the late 1960s, while Little Tokyo remained important to Japanese economic and political life, Sansei made the Westside central to the Asian American movement when they founded left-wing activist enterprises on and beyond Jefferson Boulevard to promote Pan-Asian identity and politics.

Meanwhile, the Crenshaw area emerged as the Black art and culture hub outside of Central Avenue. South of the Crenshaw Center, Black film actor and music producer John Daniels opened Maverick's Flat in 1966, which served as a restaurant and performance space for The Temptations, Ike and

Tina Turner, and Marvin Gaye, among others. About one mile eastward, near the corner of Santa Barbara and Arlington Avenues, African American Lawrence Hearn owned and operated the landmark Memory Lane Supper Club, another restaurant and performance venue for Black artists, including Nat King Cole. Other Black-owned businesses also found success in the area, including the long-standing Angelus Funeral Home, housed in a building designed by architect Paul R. Williams.[5] After Brockman Gallery opened its doors, Leimert Park Village, which centered along Degnan Boulevard, between West Forty-Third Street and West Forty-Third Place, became the Black art and culture hub on the Westside.

Brockman Gallery succeeded for twenty-three years, from 1967 to 1990, for many reasons. The Davis brothers' timing, dedication, support, and creativity kept the gallery running. They stood on the metaphorical shoulders of Black Los Angeles's well-established art scene that had its roots on Central Avenue and saw a resurgence with the Black arts movement. They and their contemporaries, who shared an urgency for broadening the White-dominated art market, rallied around the gallery, dedicating themselves to the exhibit calendar, creating marketable work, and organizing and attending meetings and events. "Equally important…was the gallery's location," Widener points out. Alonzo, Dale, and their supporters used the Leimert Park commercial center's design and small town feel to build community around the gallery. But community development took some time. Unlike most Black artists in the postwar era, who came from the working class, the Davis brothers had a solidly middle-class upbringing that led them to settle on the Westside. As heirs to the decades-long affluent Black-led westward migration, they believed their neighbors who made up the new Black middle class would become their regular customers. To their surprise, Brockman Gallery initially attracted White buyers outside of the area who expressed an interest in civil rights and Black culture, held an appreciation for art, and had discretionary income.[6]

As art administrators, the Davis brothers tapped into the long-established middle- and upper-class desire to display their wealth, knowledge, and sophistication by supporting and collecting art. But they unintentionally first attracted Whites as their customers. Grounded in a long-established tradition, which economist and social critic Thorstein Veblen admonished in the late nineteenth century, elites gained access to the highest echelon not only by inheriting wealth or serving in highly regarded occupations but also, and especially, by adopting a certain set of values or behaviors, a practice he called "conspicuous leisure and consumption," such as employing staff, enjoying luxury goods, and indulging in the arts and entertainment. "In order to gain and to hold the esteem of men it is not sufficient merely to possess wealth or power," Veblen sneered. "The wealth or power must be put in evidence." American collectors, dealers, and critics extended the age-old European art market to the United States in the late nineteenth century and helped make art more significant and, yet at the same time, more accessible to a wider swath of Americans by founding museums in the 1930s and 1940s. While Whites purchased art to demonstrate their wealth and sophistication and to acquire social capital, Brockman's White buyers in the 1960s and 1970s went beyond White-centric attitudes by using their purchasing power to invest in artists who were on the margins of the art market. Brockman steadily developed a racially diverse middle- and upper-class clientele who also saw supporting the arts as a way of engaging with the educated and elite and demonstrating their sophistication, while at the same time fostering artists of color.[7]

Consistent with the Black cultural nationalist movement, Brockman Gallery sought to foster Black culture, identity, and self-expression. Following Malcolm X's assassination and the Watts rebellion in 1965, the Black Power movement generally branched into two camps: cultural nationalism and revolutionary nationalism. Unlike the Black revolutionary nationalists, such as the Black Panther Party, who saw political revolution as the primary means to alter the existing racially defined power structures, Black cultural nationalists, such as Amiri Baraka and the Committee for a United Newark on the East Coast, and Maulana Karenga and the Us Organization on the West Coast, aimed for a cultural revolution that would align Black consciousness, self-determinism, and group identity with African history and heritage. With an interest in Black art and music, Black cultural nationalists often aligned with the Black arts movement. But while the cultural and revolutionary nationalists shared a broad agenda to create a Black collective identity that would lead to self-determinism and political power, they built up a rivalry that harmed their staying power. Among their disagreements, revolutionary nationalists contended that cultural nationalists' middle-class ideas and elite, academic backgrounds weakened the revolution and their connection to the Black working-class struggle. Poet and playwright Baraka studied at Rutgers, Howard, and Columbia Universities as well as at the New School. Karenga ultimately earned two doctorates and became a widely published author and university professor. Alonzo and Dale's middle-class roots, college education, and gallery ownership likewise buttressed the revolutionary nationalists' argument.[8]

But cultural nationalists censured Alonzo and Dale for some of their business decisions. For one, cultural nationalists, several of whom maintained natural hairstyles, wore dashikis and kufi caps, and replaced their given names with African designations, criticized Alonzo and Dale for using their slaveholding great-great-grandfather's surname for the gallery. In their defense, the Davis brothers argued that the name honored their mixed-race great-grandfather, who had endured the horrors of slavery, and represented the deeply interrelated lives of Blacks and Whites in the American past, which aligned with the Davis brothers' belief in racial integration. The visual artists selling at the gallery also had a complicated relationship with the Davises. Unlike the Black cultural and revolutionary nationalist movements, both of which advocated for cooperative economies, such as those driven by socialism and communalism, Alonzo and Dale leveraged capitalism to advance their goals of racial and ethnic inclusion. The artists were grateful for the space Brockman provided to exhibit and sell their work but felt Alonzo and Dale took a disproportionately high percentage off the sale. The Davis brothers argued that they had to strike a balance between furthering their political agenda and selling enough product to keep their business open. To provide access to artists of color, in other words, they had to gross enough income. Despite some of their artist contemporaries' middle-class sensibilities, the Davis brothers' affluent background again provided reason for censure.[9]

Regardless of the criticism, Brockman Gallery became a central meeting place where Black artists not only displayed and sold their work, but also planned outreach programs and social events around the city. While Alonzo and Dale steadily tapped into affluent city dwellers, they also struggled to reach working-class and poor Blacks, whom they particularly wanted to inspire. When they had the opportunity, Alonzo, Dale, and their artist contemporaries extended their work outside of the gallery walls. From 1973 onward the Davis brothers increased their activism and outreach after securing federal and state grants, and establishing Brockman Gallery Productions (BGP), a nonprofit division of the gallery. With Alonzo at the helm, BGP organized and sponsored a myriad of activities and programs, from street fairs and music performances to film festivals and citywide mural projects. The Davis brothers focused on enriching city dwellers with African American culture and history, but imbued with the value of inclusiveness, they also provided a platform for underrepresented and underserved Caribbean, Latino, and Asian American artists. They brought attention to marginalized voices, supported art that explored America's complex interracial and interethnic past, and fought for full equality and inclusion.[10]

FROM TUSKEGEE TO LOS ANGELES AND BACK AGAIN

The obstacles and the advantages that Alonzo and Dale Davis encountered as youngsters inspired them to create a space for artists of color to exhibit their work and to bring art to all Angelenos. Growing up in segregated Tuskegee, Alabama, at the historic Tuskegee Institute, the Davis brothers thrived in the security and self-sufficiency of campus life. Raised by scholarly parents in the Black conservative tradition established by Booker T. Washington, and in an environment driven by highly ambitious and competitive academics, the young men developed a strong work ethic as well as the confidence in their ability to carve out their own future. When they moved to Los Angeles after their parents divorced in the mid-1950s, Alonzo and Dale discovered bigotry and inequality in the fabric of the multiracial and multiethnic city. Yet they flourished in their new environment. As high school and college students in the 1950s and 1960s, the brothers became active in the civil rights struggle.

Founded in 1881 as the Tuskegee Normal and Industrial Institute in post–Reconstructed Tuskegee, Alabama, the school built by its first president, Booker T. Washington, set out to provide Blacks the tools to develop self-reliance by teaching practical skills in the agricultural and manual trades. Washington vowed, in the Atlanta Compromise, a speech he delivered to a mostly White audience, that Blacks would continue to work for Whites and defer to segregation, as Whites fulfilled emancipation's promises. While Washington built alliances with northern industrialists who were seeking a labor force, W. E. B. Du Bois found Washington an apologist for racism. Du Bois sought to expand opportunities for Blacks in higher education and called on Blacks to denounce the rise of Jim Crow segregation, lynchings, and other methods of racial terrorism. While Washington's school changed its emphasis from vocational instruction to academic higher education in the 1920s, following his 1915 death, and adopted the name Tuskegee Institute in 1937, it helped establish a long-standing debate over the method to achieve racial equality. Alonzo Joseph Davis, Sr., Alonzo and Dale's father, saw the rewards of his hard work materialize at Tuskegee. Born in Washington, DC, the elder Davis became the first college graduate in his family, earning a bachelor's and then a master's degree at Howard University and a doctorate at the University of Minnesota. He arrived at the Tuskegee Institute to teach courses in psychology and education, joined a group of faculty who pushed for Black voter registration, and rose to dean of education. Agnes Moses Davis, Alonzo and Dale's mother, also understood the value of education. She came from a large family in Anniston, Alabama, attended an all-Black girls' private school, taught grade school, and then worked at Tuskegee as a librarian.[11]

Amid deep-seated racism, Alonzo Davis explained, the Tuskegee Institute campus felt like an unfettered, "little family town." The Davis parents worked hard to shield their sons from racial discrimination and segregation, and, thus, "everything centered around this college." The Black-owned and operated businesses around the campus, including the grocery stores, dry cleaners, and gas stations, brought a feeling of self-reliance and determination to the rural community. Alonzo and Dale enjoyed having access to the campus facilities and events. They swam in the pool, played on the tennis courts, and cheered on Tuskegee at the basketball tournaments. "We were somewhat privileged for people in the South at that time," Alonzo recognized. They understood the advantages they had over other African Americans.[12]

But raised by ambitious, intellectual parents in the competitive environment imbued with the legacy of racial uplift, the Davis brothers felt pressure to become upright, contributing citizens. Although they remained safeguarded from racial segregation on campus, "We knew the conditions that were surrounding us," Dale explained. "We were aware of the signs" separating Whites and Blacks on buses, water fountains, movie theaters, and other public facilities. Surrounded by accomplished African American doctors, attorneys, teachers, and business owners, however, the brothers developed a sense of self-worth and an awareness of their responsibility to shape the future. The Tuskegee Institute instilled in them the need to become not only self-sufficient, but also valued. "We grew up feeling like we have to make a difference," Alonzo explained. Yet he understood that, as all African Americans ascertained, to persist in White-dominated America, "We have to be twice as good to be equal."[13]

When their parents divorced in the mid-1950s, their mother, with Alonzo and Dale, started anew in Los Angeles. She refused to accept the contempt and disapproval of divorce in her middle-class community. While their father stayed in Tuskegee, their mother contacted friends living in Los Angeles who helped her make the transition and find housing in the city. She and her sons moved into a one-bedroom rental house in a primarily working-class and increasingly Black area near Second Avenue and Exposition Boulevard and settled into their work and school routines. Los Angeles presented its own set of challenges, but Alonzo and Dale had the knowledge and skills to navigate the city. "We were immediately...schooled that just because everything looks cute out here—don't be innocent, don't be fooled by it," Dale explained. Los Angeles had "the same issues, practiced a different way." Raised in an academic family, they also understood that, "no matter what...we had to go to school." As Alonzo settled into Foshay Junior High School and Dale attended Sixth Avenue Elementary School, their mother enrolled at USC to earn a master's degree in library science. A few years later, they moved into a three-bedroom rental house across the street with their mother's sister.[14]

In the second half of the 1950s, as Alonzo attended high school, the racial landscape of his surroundings noticeably shifted. The Davis residence, which was located on the outskirts of Leimert Park, fell within the same zone in LAUSD as the Crenshaw area, putting Alonzo in Dorsey High School. As affluent Blacks purchased property in Crenshaw and Whites moved out, Dorsey High School became mostly Black. Alonzo noticed that "there was a lot of tension among adults during that time," which led to UN's and CN's establishment, and those events affected his point of view.[15]

Meanwhile, Alonzo picked up a part-time job at the *Los Angeles Tribune* that politicized his thinking. Funded by a $100 loan from entrepreneur Lucius Lomax, Sr., independent-minded Almena Lomax purchased a religious newspaper in 1941, and for nearly two decades transformed the *Tribune* into one of the few well-circulated, Black-run Los Angeles–based newspapers. After studying journalism and English in school, Lomax began working for Charlotta Bass at the *California Eagle* but grew critical of Bass's Republican politics, the party of most prewar Blacks, and sought pay equity and control of her own work. Initially teaming up with her spouse, Lucius Lomax, Jr., she developed a dedicated readership by reporting on working-class issues, racial injustice, and the civil rights struggle. In the mid-1950s, with funds raised from her readers, she traveled to Montgomery, Alabama, to report on the bus boycott, one of the demonstrations that launched the modern civil rights movement. While she befriended Martin Luther King, Jr., Lomax criticized his nonviolence stance, believing Blacks should defend themselves in the face of violence. Before Lomax closed the *Tribune* in 1960, she hired Alonzo to make coffee and run errands. There he developed more of an urgency to fight racism. Lomax "broke me into sort of a radical, left way of thinking, questioning authority." He would carry her influence into the 1960s.[16]

While his political beliefs took shape, Alonzo became more passionate about art. As children in Tuskegee, the Davis brothers enjoyed experimenting in the visual arts. Alonzo took up drawing, and Dale showed an interest in constructing three-dimensional pieces. LAUSD offered art courses that furthered their artistic skills. Mostly to please his parents, who expressed concern over their eldest son's future, Alonzo took a more practical path by choosing science as his major. But his enthusiasm for the visual arts remained strong, and he continued to take elective and summer school art courses.[17] In the early 1960s, around the time Alonzo was attending college and Dale was completing his junior year at Dorsey High School, the Davis family moved to middle-class Leimert Park. Their mother and two aunts pooled their money together to make a down payment on a Spanish Mediterranean style, two-story house on Edgehill Drive, a few blocks north of Leimert Park Village.[18]

Through the early 1960s, while the Davis brothers continued their education, they joined the civil rights struggle. Alonzo began Los Angeles City

College and then transferred to Pepperdine College (later Pepperdine University). At the 1960 Democratic National Convention, he "picketed for a stronger civil rights platform." In the summer of 1963, he also joined hundreds of thousands of demonstrators at the pinnacle March on Washington. He continued to pursue art in college, while appeasing his parents with a more stable career path by taking education courses. After graduating from Pepperdine in 1964, Alonzo began a master's program in education at USC, but before he had completed his degree, he found a job teaching art at Manual Arts High School, a predominantly Black, LAUSD school, located south of USC.[19] Dale likewise tried to balance his interest in art with a practical career. After graduating from Dorsey High School in the early 1960s, he earned an associate's degree at Los Angeles City College, and then transferred to USC for its art program. To please his parents, however, Dale took English courses. The social and political milieu also shaped his decisions and inspired his growing activism. Like his older brother, Dale demonstrated for civil rights and protested the Vietnam War, a conviction he would convey in *Viet Nam War Games*, his 1969 sculpture that was made of a cluster of clay and metal objects of varied sizes that resembled ammunitions.[20]

Then in August 1965, as the Watts rebellion broke out, attention turned to the Eastside. Alonzo traveled to Europe earlier that summer feeling "really naïve to the energy that was happening in the Watts area and its problems." When he returned, Dale informed his older brother that the United States National Guard, bearing machine guns, was blocking off Leimert Park, preventing residents from going home, and enforcing a curfew on the community. Alonzo initially was stunned that the state government, under the direction of Lieutenant Governor Glenn Anderson, included affluent Leimert Park in the riot zone. But, Alonzo came to realize, the riot forced him and Crenshaw's middle-class Black community to pay attention and support low-income Blacks in Watts and on the Eastside. "The whole black community was shut down, which meant that middle-class people and affluent people couldn't get away from it, and they had to deal with it."[21]

Of the activists the Watts rebellion emboldened, Black cultural and revolutionary nationalists rose to the forefront. Derived from the Black conservative tradition, both Black nationalist factions advocated for the development of structural pluralism or separate, independent institutions based along racial lines. Cultural nationalists, led by Los Angeles–based Maulana Karenga, believed African Americans needed to rid themselves of White influence and solely embrace African culture to attain any political or social power. Born Ronald Everett, the UCLA graduate student changed his name after the uprising to Maulana ("master teacher" in Swahili) Karenga, and in 1965 formed the patriarchal and Afrocentric Us Organization. Karenga urged his followers to learn Swahili, study African history, adopt African names, wear traditional West African garments, and observe a host of rituals and holidays, including Kwanzaa ("first fruit" in Swahili). The African American Cultural Center, Us Organization's headquarters and its Kwanzaa Resource Center, opened in 1965, at 3018 West Forty-Eighth Street, directly south of Leimert Park Village, an illustration of the emergence of Black cultural nationalism in the Crenshaw area and its middle-class connection. Among his projects, Karenga teamed up with *Los Angeles Sentinel* columnist Booker Griffin, civil rights activist Tommy Jacquette, and attorney Stan Sanders to commemorate the thirty-four dead from the uprising and to promote African and African American culture in the Watts Summer Festival. The event convened annually from August 1966, one year following the revolt, through the 1980s. Revolutionary nationalists—including Us Organization's rival, the Black Panther Party—had different goals. Established in 1966 by college students Huey P. Newton and Bobby Seale in Oakland, California, the Black Panther Party for Self-Defense sought a Marxist agenda of, for example, arming African Americans in self-defense against police brutality; insisting on full educational, employment, and housing opportunities; and transforming society's existing racially based power structures to give African Americans control over their own lives and communities. Its Southern California chapter formed two years later.[22]

Meanwhile, in 1966 Alonzo and Dale remained on the fringe of the civil rights movement. "I was just trying to get it together...just finished college, trying to teach," Alonzo later explained. But that summer, when the Davis brothers set out on a cross-country road trip to reconnect with their southern heritage and connect with artists of color, they found their purpose. From Los Angeles, they drove southeast to Arizona, first to meet artist Eugene Grigsby in Phoenix, and then to meet artist Paolo Soleri in Scottsdale. They then drove southeastward to find John Thomas Biggers in Texas and connect with the art department at the historically Black Jackson State College (later Jackson State University) in Mississippi, where they found themselves at the center of the civil rights struggle.[23]

On June 5, 1966, civil rights activist James Meredith, known for integrating the University of Mississippi, embarked on a 225-mile, solo march from Memphis, Tennessee, to Jackson, Mississippi, to urge Blacks to vote. On his second day, Meredith was shot and wounded by a White supremacist. When SCLC leader Martin Luther King, Jr., CORE director Floyd McKissick, and Student Nonviolent Coordinating Committee (SNCC) head Stokely Carmichael visited Meredith in the hospital, they decided to continue his march. By that time, both CORE and SNCC were shifting their approach toward civil rights from nonviolence and integration to Black Power and Black nationalism. While McKissick and Carmichael compromised with King to lead an interracial, nonviolent march, the CORE and SNCC leaders asserted their new stance throughout the June demonstration. Their clear declaration of Black Power came in mid-June, after police arrested and imprisoned Carmichael for defying an order and erecting a tent on school property. At a rally that evening, Carmichael insisted, "This is the twenty-seventh time I have been arrested. I ain't going to jail no more!" Then, he began shouting "Black Power!" while the audience repeated his call. On June 26, two days after Meredith rejoined the march, thousands of protestors, including Alonzo and Dale, descended on the state capitol in Jackson for the final rally. The March Against Fear not only became a defining moment illustrating the splinter in the civil rights struggle and the rise of Black nationalism, but also inspired the Davis brothers to bring the civil rights struggle to their Los Angeles community.[24]

After visiting Jackson, Mississippi, Alonzo, and Dale carried on with their road trip, heading toward the East Coast. They stopped at Tougaloo College in Mississippi; reconnected with their childhood friends in Tuskegee, Alabama; visited their mother's family in Birmingham, Alabama; and saw their father in Durham, North Carolina. In New York City they formed valuable relationships with African American artists Romare Bearden, Charles H. Alston, Hale Woodruff, and Norman Lewis that would help them build the reputation of Brockman Gallery in the late 1960s.[25]

While the idea of establishing an art gallery initially seemed too difficult to accomplish, given their youth and their work and school schedules, Alonzo and Dale were determined to carry out their plan. In their discussion during the long car rides, the Davises knew they wanted to center their art gallery on the works of African American artists. They had grown up learning about Black accomplishments at the Tuskegee Institute and studying artists of color on their own, but they often encountered teachers in Los Angeles who knew nothing about the topic. Local museums and art galleries excluded African American artists' works from their collections, and art schools limited the number of Black students into their programs to a bare minimum. The Davises understood the dearth of opportunities for visual artists of color to showcase and sell their work and set out to fill that void and open an inclusive gallery. They represented a new generation of Black activists who connected the homeowner and entrepreneurial activism of previous generations to a politics of space-based community activism that was grounded in the civil rights and Black cultural nationalist movements. Yet they diverged from Black cultural nationalists by engaging in capitalist enterprise to advance their goals. Shortly after returning home to Los Angeles, Alonzo and Dale established their business.[26]

BLACK ART TAKES ROOT IN LOS ANGELES

The Davis brothers' approach to opening an art gallery was spontaneous and unsystematic. Before they had discussed a strategy or laid out a business plan, they signed a lease and invested their hard-earned savings in the space. Dale acknowledged in retrospect that he and his older brother were acting on youthful impulses that overrode any major concerns and compelled them to action. But the Davis brothers had the good fortune of opening an art gallery in a city where, especially since the early twentieth century on Central Avenue, Black artists and entrepreneurs had established a basis for support. As Central Avenue declined in the early 1950s, working-class artists and musicians rebuilt the culture in Watts, Willowbrook, and Compton that had allowed the Eastside to grow into a center of Black artistic expression and activism after the Watts rebellion. The Black arts movement in the mid- to late 1960s continued the charge in Los Angeles, and in other major cities across the United States, to support, explore, and bring attention to the Black experience. Brockman Gallery flourished with the help of the networks of artists and their supporters that formed in Los Angeles before and after the Watts rebellion.[27]

Before the 1920s, Black artists in Los Angeles had had few supporters who appreciated, promoted, and purchased their works. In 1929, the same year Abby Rockefeller, who was married to financier John D. Rockefeller, Jr., helped open the Museum of Modern Art in New York City, Black artists gained some exposure. The California Art Club hosted the city's first documented group show of Black artists, a traveling exhibit that originated in Chicago, at Los Angeles's Barnsdall Park. Despite the exhibit's success in attracting visitors, the city's foremost art critic, Arthur Millier, viewed the art through the lens of White superiority. While the show exhibited talented painters, such as John Wesley Hardwick, William Edouard Scott, and Hale Woodruff, Millier contended, the exhibit lacked a supposed authentic Black voice. After years of separation from their African traditions and White colonialism, Black artists have assumed the behaviors of the "so-called superior [White] race." Millier went on, "It would be much easier to assemble what looked like a negro art exhibit from among white artists than from the artists here represented." Representing the majority view of the Eurocentric art market, which artists of color had to contend with, Millier believed Black artists lacked any ability to distinguish themselves as unique or valuable.[28]

Los Angeles's first African American librarian, Miriam Matthews, set out to challenge White assumptions by supporting and documenting Black art. Born in Pensacola, Florida, in 1905, Matthews had relocated with her family to Los Angeles in 1907 to escape racism and segregation and to seek opportunities. Matthews pursued academic degrees, first at UCLA and University of California, Berkeley, where she studied Spanish and librarianship, and later at the University of Chicago, where she earned a master's degree in library science. As she worked her way up in the city, from substitute librarian to regional librarian who managed twelve libraries, she organized and curated programs on the Black experience in California that resembled the efforts of Arturo (Arthur) Schomburg in New York. Schomburg and Matthews provided a counter to Andrew Mellon, J. P. Morgan, Henry E. Huntington, and other late-nineteenth-century American industrialists who tapped into the long-established European art market, built their own private collections, and established a foundation for the nation's major art museums to open in the 1930s and 1940s, which then led New York City to replace Paris as the center of the art market. While Schomburg worked on the East Coast, Matthews amassed a collection of artifacts on Blacks in California. She helped establish Negro History Week (which later became Black History Month) and published *The Negro in California from 1780–1910: An Annotated Bibliography*.[29]

Matthews also fostered, exhibited, promoted, sold, and bought the works of Los Angeles's Black visual artists. Black artists and their supporters in the 1930s had slightly better exposure and support, but they still had to face White ignorance. Sculptor Beulah Woodard, in 1935, was the first African American to have a solo show, which took place at the Los Angeles County Museum of History, Science, and Art. However, historian Sarah Schrank points out, critics viewed her Afrocentric masks and sculptures as artifacts rather than as highly skilled work. In 1937, the same year Andrew Mellon founded the National Gallery of Art in Washington, DC, Woodard and Matthews formed the Los Angeles Negro Artist Association to support Black artists and organize exhibitions of their work. While the city developed an art scene in the postwar years, artists of color continued to fight for their value. In 1950 several artists, including Woodard, Curtis Tann, Alice Taylor Gafford, and Tyrus Wong, established the short-lived interracial art collective and gallery, Eleven Associated, that held shows at their downtown South Hill Street gallery.[30]

Meanwhile, in the mid-1950s, Los Angeles's White-led modern art scene emerged. Before Los Angeles had its own acclaimed art museum, Gallery Row took shape on La Cienega Boulevard, between Santa Monica Boulevard and Melrose Avenue, that put the city on a path toward global recognition. Among the many art galleries there, Ferus Gallery stood out. Despite his UCLA education in microbiology, Walter Hopps followed his love for the then-controversial abstract expressionist and assemblage works and joined Irving Blum in opening Ferus in 1957. Ferus provided a space for Ed

Kienholz, John Altoon, Ed Ruscha, and others to get their start; it found its way onto the art market's radar by hosting Andy Warhol's first solo exhibition of the Campbell's Soup Cans in 1962. Other galleries joined Ferus on Gallery Row, including Dwan, Huysman, and Nicholas Wilder. But few supported Black visual artists.[31]

Only a small number of African American artists in the White-run art spaces had opportunities to train, exhibit, and sell their work. Heritage and Ankrum galleries, both of which opened in the early 1960s on Gallery Row and were owned by Jewish entrepreneurs, sold works created by African American artists. Heritage Gallery represented Chicago-born and trained Charles White, who had developed an international reputation for his social realist paintings and prints before moving to Los Angeles in 1956 and accepting a teaching position at Otis Art Institute in 1965. Ankrum Gallery put on group shows of Black artists, including Betye Saar, John Riddle, Bernie Casey, Dan Concholar, and Samella Lewis. But most galleries, including the roughly thirty on and around Gallery Row, as well as art schools and museums, excluded Black artists. Nelbert Chouinard, Otis Art Institute teacher who founded Chouinard Art Institute in 1921, resisted admitting artists of color for decades. She first let in Asian Americans, including Tyrus Wong, and then, in 1952, allowed William Pajaud to study there. "I had the whole black race on my shoulders," Pajaud recounted, who paved a path for others to follow. But, through the 1960s, Black artists mostly used unconventional spaces to exhibit their work, including homes, libraries, churches, community centers, and Black-owned businesses.[32]

Ruth G. Waddy also took on the charge of supporting Black visual artists in a city that lacked the patronage. Born in Lincoln, Nebraska, in 1909, Waddy joined the Federal Writers' Project in Chicago during the Great Depression, and then moved to Los Angeles during World War II to work as a riveter in the aircraft industry before following her passion for the visual arts. Using her connections, she gathered together a group, including artist Charles White and Golden State Mutual Life Insurance Company's cofounder Norman O. Houston, to set up a juried art show at the Los Angeles County Museum to commemorate the 1963 centennial of the Emancipation Proclamation.[33]

In the 1950s the Los Angeles County Museum emerged as one half of the division of the Los Angeles County Museum of History, Science, and Art. The older county museum got its start from attorney, USC law professor, and Sunday school teacher William Miller Bowen; in the early 1900s Bowen had sought to bring culture and refinement to the city. Concerned by the racetrack, saloons, and brothels that had cropped up in the fairgrounds outside of the city's western limits of what was first called Agricultural Park, Bowen led a campaign that resulted in the annexation of the land and the opening of the Los Angeles County Museum of History, Science, and Art in 1913 in the renamed Exposition Park. Some forty years later, millionaire retail tycoon and University of California regent Edward Carter likewise set out to challenge popular notions of the city as uncultured by raising the funds to procure the County Museum's art collection and reposition it in a new facility. The Los Angeles County Museum of History and Science (later renamed Los Angeles County Museum of Natural History and then the Natural History Museum of Los Angeles County) stayed in Exposition Park; in 1965 the Los Angeles County Museum, renamed the Los Angeles County Museum of Art (LACMA), opened on the corner of Wilshire Boulevard and Fairfax Avenue, in well-heeled Hancock Park. LACMA joined the westward shift that reoriented the center of the city to the Westside. Seeking to advance its and the city's reputation, LACMA initially exhibited established artists over local practitioners of color.[34]

Although Waddy and her colleagues faced too many obstacles to carry out a juried art show at the new art museum, they continued their collaboration and in 1962 formed the seminal Art West Associated, Incorporated (AWA). The successor to Eleven Associated, AWA met weekly at a rotation of artists' homes, including Waddy's house on Western Avenue, where artist Samella Lewis later recalled, "We argued. We discussed our works. We had great sessions." AWA also staged exhibitions, ran Negro History Week at the Los Angeles City Hall, published literature, including *Prints by American Negro Artists*, and teamed up with Black artists across the country. Both AWA and Art-West Associated North, Incorporated, its Northern California counterpart, were pivotal in helping Black visual artists gain exposure for their work. More than one hundred artists, including Alonzo Davis, received support from and also supported these organizations.[35]

Shortly before the 1965 Watts rebellion, a group of artists and activists began setting up programs to enrich and empower low-income Watts residents. Accountant and art enthusiast James Woods gathered together friends and community leaders to brainstorm ideas for a multiracial art collective that would provide a space for community members to cultivate and advance their talents. Following the suggestion of civil rights activist and poet Jayne Cortez, and with the collaborative effort of local artists, in 1964 Woods opened Studio Watts Workshop in a former furniture outlet in the Watts commercial center at Grandee Avenue and 104th Street. Studio Watts held classes in art, drama, writing, and dance, and hosted public exhibitions, theater performances, poetry readings, and musical shows. With Woods as director and Cortez leading the writing and acting classes, the collective brought in hundreds of students and supporters from around the city.[36]

Los Angeles's own virtuoso avant-garde jazz musician Horace Tapscott also played an early role in forging community ties to Studio Watts. Born in Houston, Texas, in 1934, and a resident of Los Angeles from 1943, Tapscott honed his craft and learned to compose music from jazz greats on Central Avenue. His mother set aside money for her son to attend Julliard School in New York City, but Tapscott insisted he could get the best education at "SWU, 'sidewalk university,'" on the streets of Los Angeles. After high school, he took courses at Los Angeles City College, served in the United States Air Force, and then joined Lionel Hampton's orchestra on tour. After fewer than two years with the band, Tapscott became disillusioned by the commercially driven music business and its exploitation of Black artists; in early 1961 he walked away from the industry.[37]

Tapscott returned home, gathered together an eclectic group of musicians and artists, and set out to preserve and perform African American music in Los Angeles. His band, the Underground Musicians Association, soon became a mainstay on the Eastside, rehearsing daily at cofounder Linda Hill's home on Central Avenue, leading music classes at Studio Watts Workshop, performing at local schools and in South Park, and playing at SNCC and Black Panther Party meetings. By the early 1970s the band had changed its name to the Union of God's Musicians and Artists Ascension to reflect the expanding membership roll of musicians, poets, dancers, actors, students, and political activists. Performances included music, poetry readings, and dance pieces. The group became a nonprofit organization in the mid-1970s, turned its headquarters into a community center, appointed a board of directors, and received federal funding to support a staff and sponsor programs. Out of this umbrella organization, Tapscott also formed and conducted an avant-garde band, named the Pan Afrikan Peoples Arkestra, mainly to use for small ensembles and performances at political events.[38]

After the Watts rebellion, more artists and activists set out to rebuild the Eastside and support Black art. In October 1965 local activists turned an abandoned furniture store at 1802 East 103rd Street, or what became known as Charcoal Alley to reflect the devastation of the 1965 uprising, into the Watts Happening Coffee House. Funding from the US Department of Housing and Urban Development and the Southern California Council of Churches helped pay the rent. Activist Elaine Brown ran a field office for the Office of Economic Opportunity on the premises that administered antipoverty programs, and artists used the space for poetry readings, art classes, and musical and theatrical performances. Tapscott and his band rehearsed, led workshops, and entertained there. Novelist and Academy Award–winning screenwriter of film noir, Budd Schulberg, formed the

Watts Writers Workshop in 1965; within two years he had moved the meetings into Watts Happening. Schulberg and the Watts Writers yielded many accomplishments. Schulberg formed satellite groups around Southern California, television networks aired stories on the workshop, magazines published essays by its writers, and Schulberg compiled two anthologies of the writers' works. The workshop also brought together three poets: Father Amde (formerly Anthony Hamilton), Richard Dedeaux, and Otis O'Solomon, who began a long-term partnership as the Watts Prophets.[39]

Several other noteworthy grassroots organizations branched out of Studio Watts Workshop and the Watts Happening Coffee House: the Mafundi Institute, the Watts Repertory Theater Company, and the Inner City Cultural Center. Established in 1967 by Us founder Maulana Karenga, Watts Summer Festival planner Tommy Jacquette, and UCLA psychology professor J. Alfred Cannon, the Mafundi Institute initially opened its headquarters in the Watts Happening Coffee House. Unlike the multiracial Studio Watts Workshop, Mafundi (a word that means "artisans, creative people, or craftsmen" in Swahili) organized as an all-Black association allied with Black cultural nationalist groups, including the Sons of Watts and the Us Organization. It doubled as a community art space and job training center that offered a range of classes from art, dance, filmmaking, music, and theater to history, literature, political theory, and self-improvement. Due to internal disagreements, Jayne Cortez broke with Studio Watts Workshop and formed the Watts Repertory Theater Company. Cortez, along with musician and poet Stanley Crouch, led theater workshops and performances under the new name. Meanwhile, Cannon assisted UCLA colleague C. Bernard Jackson to establish the Inner City Cultural Center in the Boulevard Theatre on the corner of Vermont Avenue and Washington Boulevard, in the West Adams district. The center focused on supporting theater productions while hosting dance troupes, offering educational programs, publishing literature, and providing rehearsal space.[40]

When the survival of the Watts Towers was at risk, activists rallied behind its value and preservation. Between 1921 and 1954, at his East 107th Street home in Watts, Italian immigrant Sabato Rodia had constructed several one-hundred-feet-tall, triangular spires of steel pipes and rods, which he then adorned with pieces of tile, glass, shells, and other found objects. The towers, located about two miles south of the Watts Happening Coffee House and visible for miles, became a symbol of creativity, ingenuity, self-expression, and the artistic form of assemblage. After Rodia left the area in the mid-1950s and the site became vulnerable to demolition, a group of concerned citizens organized as the Committee to Save Simon Rodia's Towers in Watts to safeguard the piece. In 1964 the committee hired local African American artist Noah Purifoy to establish an art center adjacent to the Watts Towers. Committee members had been running rudimentary art classes and wanted Purifoy to launch a traditional program.[41]

During his two years as director, Purifoy established the Watts Towers and adjacent Watts Towers Arts Center into a vibrant community outlet of expression. Born to sharecroppers in Alabama in 1917, he went on to earn a bachelor's degree in education and a master's degree in social work. Upon his arrival in Los Angeles in the early 1950s, he worked at the Los Angeles County Hospital, and then enrolled at Chouinard Art Institute. His educational background in social service and art helped him get the job at the Watts Towers, but, Purifoy explained, the Watts rebellion "made me an artist." In the wake of the uprising, Purifoy, Judson Powell, John Riddle, and other fellow artists scavenged the wreckage to use as material for their art. Out of more than three tons of found objects, Purifoy and seven other artists collaborated on the art exhibition *66 Signs of Neon*, a collection of sixty-six assemblages that explored the causes, meanings, images, and views of the Eastside and the Watts rebellion. First exhibited at nearby Markham Junior High School in April 1966, and then four months later at the first annual Watts Summer Festival before traveling around the country, *66 Signs* catapulted Purifoy into the public's eye as a renowned artist. His work, which redefined the ruins of the Watts rebellion into meaningful pieces of art, illustrated that the capacity of those found objects in the Black community, if harnessed and cared for, could become whole, valued, and valuable entities.[42]

Purifoy used the Watts Towers Arts Center to raise the self-worth and confidence of the local African American youths. He believed that, by providing enjoyable experiences, the center could give students a better chance of making positive decisions in their own lives. But his unconventional approach to education, such as leading children on junk hunts around the Eastside to collect found objects for collages and assemblage pieces, generated criticism from the board. The committee wanted Purifoy to create a traditional art program that would attract and cultivate artists from beyond Watts. After two years as director of the center, he was pushed out of the position, yet Purifoy went on to have a successful career as an artist. When Black artist John Outterbridge took over as director of the Watts Towers Arts Center in the mid-1970s, he carried on Purifoy's vision by organizing activities around the needs of the community. Outterbridge's collaboration with Alonzo Davis, and the events that they organized in Watts, helped bridge the Eastside to Brockman Gallery and African Americans on the Westside.[43]

BROCKMAN GALLERY BRINGS BLACK ART TO LEIMERT PARK

Upon the Davis brothers' return from their 1966 road trip, Alonzo set out to find a place to open his business. He explored several areas around Los Angeles but quickly saw the potential of opening an art gallery in Leimert Park Village. As residents since the early 1960s, Alonzo and Dale had witnessed a steady influx of middle- and upper-class Blacks moving into the Crenshaw area and sensed that they would be the ideal customers for the gallery. "We felt like there was a market," Alonzo explained. "We moved into what was the wealthiest black neighborhood in the city of Los Angeles." Meanwhile, as the Davis brothers opened their gallery, more Black art initiatives and collectives in Los Angeles formed. African American artists and activists established their own galleries and organizations and carried out their own projects. They also joined forces, supporting each other's projects and aiding visual artists of color toward the common goal of creating an inclusive art world. The Davises joined the movement after the Watts rebellion and expanded the reach of Black art to the Westside.[44]

After looking at several vacant businesses in Leimert Park Village, Alonzo found the perfect place for the gallery. The quaint storefront situated at 4334 Degnan Boulevard, formerly used as a photography studio and frame shop, needed little renovation. The two large bay windows bookending the front door and facing Degnan Boulevard could look directly into the gallery. A small loft extending over part of the studio space would provide additional room for a private office and exhibitions, benefits, and meetings. After Alonzo made his decision, he returned to his mother's home on Edgehill Drive, told her about the discussion he and his brother had on their road trip, and announced his plan to open a gallery. He sought out the storefront's proprietor, Jack Sidney, whose family had owned several properties in the commercial center. Alonzo used his earnings from his teaching position, signed his name to the lease, and began renting the property in January 1967.[45]

Between January and March, Alonzo and Dale set up the space and sketched out a business plan. They installed lighting, put a fresh coat of paint on the walls, and laid down new carpet. While cultural and revolutionary nationalists were abandoning their given family names for African designations or, uncompromisingly, simply "X," Alonzo and Dale chose a name for the gallery that they felt paid tribute to their family, recognized their roots from both enslaved people and interracial unions, and gave power to the African American past and present. The gallery assumed the Davises' matrilineal surname, or what Alonzo explained as the family's "first slave name." The designation represented their varied influences, from their Tuskegee upbringing in the Black conservative tradition to their politicization in the civil rights and Black nationalist movements. On March 1, 1967, after they had recruited visual artists for their first show and mailed out invitations, the Davis brothers opened Brockman Gallery.[46]

Opening night drew an interracial crowd outfitted in suits and dresses and kicked off a year of exhibitions and events. From the end of March through the end of April, the gallery exhibited Alonzo's iron and stone paintings and sculptures and Dale's ceramic pottery, followed in the subsequent months by group shows of African American and Mexican American artists.[47] In July 1967 Brockman Gallery, with CN's sponsorship, organized the Festival of the Arts in Leimert Park Plaza, the public park with the iconic pedestal fountain, conveniently located about a block south of Brockman Gallery. The weekend-long festival included art exhibitions separated into crafts, graphics, paintings, drawings, posters, and sculptures, judged by artists Charles White and Carlton Ball; dance and musical performances; displays in Brockman Gallery and Raffles restaurant; and a sale of art supplies at the local paint store. CN member Olive Walker, who was serving at the time as editor of CN's newsletter, *Crenshaw Notes*, and who would soon launch its journal, *The Integrator*, helped raise funds for the festival by asking Crenshaw area businesses to purchase advertisements for the brochure. CN took the opportunity in the brochure to promote its goal, "to maintain a racially-mixed neighborhood."[48]

In her update on the Festival of the Arts in *Crenshaw Notes*, Walker provided an account of business owners' reactions to the demographic shift in Leimert Park Village. While recruiting event sponsors, Walker wrote, "I found panicky, nasty businessmen, with a thriving business, who seem to have a hostility toward the Negroes from whom they are earning the bulk of their living." Other business owners sold to "maybe one ethnic group," blamed African Americans for the population change, took no responsibility for Whites' actions in accelerating the shift, and then closed their businesses as soon as they could. Some business owners, however, welcomed the change. "The forward-looking businessmen...see customers as customers." She continued, "They are not fearful or threatened but look upon the area as an opportunity for growth." While most Whites left the area, open-minded Whites refused to resign themselves to fear-mongering policies and tactics.[49]

One year before Walker's piece, CN's *Crenshaw Notes* also published a story on two entrepreneurs' response to residents' complaints over "the quality and condition of our local retail operations." Milton Flicker, new general manager of May Company in the Crenshaw Center, formed a community advisory board that comprised members from local religious and civic organizations, including CN's Olive Walker and Suma Nakada; Nakada was married to CN board of director Yoshinao Nakada. At monthly meetings the advisory board discussed with Flicker and his executive team "the things that they are doing wrong and the things they are doing right" to improve community relations. Warren Ward bought Raffles restaurant, located at 4310 Degnan Boulevard, Brockman Gallery's neighbor, in the late 1950s, "when business instability and unrest—due to the transition in the area—was beginning to seriously hurt Leimert Park." As other businesses in the area moved away, went bankrupt, or closed, Raffles held steady. Ward attributed his success to his staff training program and his emphasis on customer service. His commitment to the community might have also been a factor. The restaurant was one of a few local businesses that sponsored and participated in Brockman Gallery's 1967 Festival of the Arts.[50]

Seeing an opportunity to bring awareness to their work, Brockman Gallery and CN occasionally worked together after the festival to further the integrationist model. Walker sought Alonzo Davis's advice and services when she was getting *The Integrator* off the ground. She published works and articles of Black artists, including Vertis Hayes and Charles White, in the journal. Brockman Gallery ran advertisements of its events, including the 1967 Festival of the Arts and a 1969 reception and exhibition of Herman Bailey's and Timothy Washington's art, and the gallery itself, in *Crenshaw Notes* and *The Integrator*. But their differing priorities, informed by their generational, household, and financial conditions, drove a wedge between them and their work. While CN members found common ground as homeowners, for instance, many of the baby boomers who became active in the community had yet to purchase a house. "This new breed" of Crenshaw residents, CN president Ken Olsen recognized in 1968, "feels we don't represent them." As CN struggled to achieve racial integration, Brockman Gallery pushed forward.[51]

Brockman Gallery thrived as more Black artists and supporters fought for representation. One year after Brockman Gallery opened, Cecil Fergerson and Claude Booker also set out to bring visibility to African American artists. Born in Oklahoma, Fergerson spent his formative years in Watts, graduated from Jordan High School, and then started in 1948 as a custodian at the Los Angeles County Museum of Natural History (later renamed the Natural History Museum of Los Angeles County). In 1953 he began working at LACMA; in more than three decades at LACMA he advanced from art preparator, to museum assistant, to LACMA's first Black curatorial assistant, after filing a lawsuit against the museum for racial discrimination. While painting galleries, installing exhibitions, and cataloguing the collections, Fergerson gained insight into the money-driven, European-biased politics of the museum. In the 1960s, as LACMA thrived on Wilshire Boulevard, the museum began hiring more Black personnel. Korean War veteran and former Los Angeles Police Department officer Claude Booker found work as a shipping clerk.[52]

As Black nationalist movements gained momentum, Fergerson saw the irony of his place of employment. While recuperating for nearly a year from acute injuries after a car accident, he received news of the uprisings in Watts and other urban centers. He read books on Malcolm X and decolonization, began attending meetings of the Black Muslims, and came to realize that, even after working at the museum for almost two decades, he knew no African American artists. "Up until that point, I just looked at art as a nightclub for the rich," Fergerson contended. "It was the white people's museum. A large number of black people worked there, black people's taxes paid for it, but they never had no sense of using it." Over lunch one day in 1968, Fergerson and Booker decided to form a group, the Black Arts Council (BAC), that pressured LACMA to become more inclusive.[53]

In their first weekly meetings that often included only the two of them, Fergerson and Booker began to plot out their ideas. Stan Sanders, attorney and Watts Summer Festival organizer, helped the BAC establish its bylaws and charter. Alonzo Davis, John Outterbridge, John Riddle, and other Black artists joined the group. The BAC implemented numerous successful projects. It pressured the museum's board of directors to establish an African American art department, hire a Black curator, and organize exhibitions of Black artists. The BAC also presented Black art to local public schools; brought students to Black art shows around California; organized exhibitions at the Watts Summer Festival; displayed the works of African American visual artists in banks, colleges, and other public spaces; held fundraisers; and pushed for the establishment of the state-supported California African American Museum.[54]

In late 1968, more than a year after Brockman Gallery opened, Suzanne Jackson set up Gallery 32, a nonprofit gallery at 672 South Lafayette Park Place, near MacArthur Park and the Otis and Chouinard Art Institutes, to showcase African American works. Born in St. Louis, Missouri, in 1944, and raised in Alaska, Jackson moved to California in the 1960s, earned a bachelor's degree at San Francisco State College (later San Francisco State University), and then studied under Charles White at Otis Art Institute. In its nearly two-year duration, Gallery 32 put on groundbreaking exhibitions, including David Hammons's first body prints and the first survey of female Black artists, called *Sapphire: You've Come a Long Way, Baby*. In an art market that venerated White male artists as geniuses and placed little value on female artists of color, *Sapphire* provided a space for Black female artists to process and challenge the oppression and discrimination they faced from the intersecting classifications of their race, gender, and sexuality. Named after the Sapphire caricature of an aggressive, domineering, and emasculating Black woman, or more commonly, the angry Black female, and the Virginia Slims cigarettes advertising campaign that doggedly targeted women, the show highlighted the multifaceted Black female experience through the works of Jackson, Saar, Senga Nengudi, and others. "What I paint attempts to express the conflicts within the mind...freeing oneself toward some continuous cycle of rediscovering who in fact I really might be," Jackson explained, in reference to her multidimensional identity. Although located on opposite sides of the city, Gallery 32 and Brockman Gallery became meeting places, exhibited many of the same artists, and participated in similar programs. Yet Gallery 32's Black female-centered leadership offset the shortfalls of the male-dominated civil rights movement and the White-centric second-wave feminist movement.[55]

African American artist and scholar Samella S. Lewis also emerged as a leading figure in the local Black arts scene who challenged the male-led and male-valued model. Before moving to Los Angeles in the 1960s, New Orleans–born Lewis excelled in school and in her career as an artist. She began her academic training studying under renowned artist Elizabeth Catlett at Dillard University, and then transferred to Hampton Institute (later Hampton University) to complete her bachelor's degree. Lewis continued her studies at Ohio State University, where she earned a doctorate in the early 1950s. She pursued a career in academe, teaching at Morgan State University, chairing the art department at Florida A&M University, and transferring to the State University of New York. In the 1960s she moved to Los Angeles and served as LACMA's education coordinator, but clashes with the administration led her to seek employment elsewhere, and she began a professorship at Scripps College.[56]

Lewis's contributions to the visual arts were vast and far-reaching. By the late 1960s art galleries across the country were adding her paintings to their permanent collections, and the Ankrum Gallery in Los Angeles represented her work. At a time when information on Black art remained scarce, Lewis took on the task of documenting the subject. Rooted in her formal education and professional experience, she made her first film in 1966 on the history of Black art, called *The Black Artists*, and then produced several pieces on individual Black practitioners. In 1969 and 1971, using her own press, Contemporary Crafts, she collaborated with Waddy and published a two-volume collection entitled *Black Artists on Art*. The success of her publications led Lewis to establish the journal, *Black Art: An International Quarterly* (later renamed *International Review of African-American Art*), in

1975. She wrote the textbook *Art: African American* (1978), on the history of African American art since slavery, which has been reissued several times and renamed *African American Art and Artists*. For a few years Lewis also opened and ran her own art galleries. With Bernie Casey she began Multi-Cul in the early 1970s at 1019 Redondo Boulevard, near LACMA, and then changed the name to The Gallery (later Gallery Tanner) and moved it a few blocks south to 5271 W. Pico Boulevard. In the mid-1970s, she transitioned into curatorship; in 1976, with the support of a National Endowment for the Arts grant, she founded the Museum of African American Art in the May Company department store building at 4005 Crenshaw Boulevard in the Crenshaw area.[57]

Brockman Gallery succeeded due to the loyalty and dedication of Black artists and supporters. "Artists, friends, and family were key to the success at Brockman," Dale later wrote. Black artists established the Black Artists Association (BAA) to present themselves as a distinct and noteworthy school of art. "In the beginning, we really did try to have it as a movement," Alonzo explained, like Cubism or Expressionism that came before them, adding that BAA artists used their craft to wrestle with similar questions of "civil rights and nationalism and African heritage and living in America." Alonzo and Dale Davis, David Hammons, Timothy Washington, Pajaud, Lewis, Concholar, Jackson, Outterbridge, and Riddle, among others, joined the group and met regularly at Brockman Gallery. The gallery functioned as "a work-think tank," Outterbridge explained, where artists posed questions, debated the answers, and experimented with ideas.[58]

BAA members overlapped with other groups and galleries. Those who associated with AWA, Art-West Associated North, Incorporated, and BAC also joined the BAA. Local Black visual artists exhibited their works at Brockman Gallery as well as at Ankrum Gallery, Heritage Gallery, Contemporary Crafts, and Gallery 32. BAA artists felt like they had a stake in the survival of Brockman Gallery. They committed themselves to the exhibit calendar and attempted to produce marketable work to sustain the gallery. Outterbridge understood: "You made sure that you did works that had the potential to sell along with works that you wanted no strings attached." For each sale, artists received around 70 percent of the proceeds and Brockman Gallery took 30 percent. In some cases, the percentage Brockman took was higher.[59]

Some artists resented the Davis brothers' business decisions. At the noteworthy 1971 LACMA exhibit, *Three Graphic Artists*, for instance, which featured the works of renowned artist Charles White and budding artists David Hammons and Timothy Washington, Alonzo, the artists' sponsor, negotiated the purchase of one painting from the show for $3,500. "Now, of course, Alonzo wanted that because Brockman Gallery would get 50 percent [off the sale of the works] of three artists," explained Cecil Fergerson, who had lobbied LACMA to put on the exhibit. "He'd make more money than anybody off the show. He'd get 50 percent of Timothy's [work], 50 percent of David's, and 50 percent of Charlie's." Compared to Suzanne Jackson's approach to running Gallery 32, Carmen Garrott Riddle, who was married to artist John Riddle, explained, "Alonzo was more administrative" and business-minded. Jackson, who went on after Gallery 32 closed to work for Alonzo, further described some artists' view of him: "A lot of people found Alonzo difficult for some strange reason. I think it was just that he was quiet and secretive sometimes. But basically his programs were always clean.... We tried to be as fair to the artists as we could." The Davis brothers argued that those commissions helped the gallery stay open. They set out to provide artists with the freedom to create original work, carry out their ideas, and, Outterbridge added, "made sure that some doors stayed open for us to go in and build whatever foundations we felt that we needed." Yet they steered the direction of the gallery, managing the business operations and advancing their primary goal of racial and ethnic inclusion in the White-centric art market.[60]

While the Davises juggled other responsibilities, their commitment and teamwork helped Brockman Gallery flourish. They generally opened the gallery doors from Wednesday to Saturday or Sunday, from the afternoon to the evening. Still a student at USC during Brockman's first years, Dale enrolled in morning classes, then opened the gallery around noon or one o'clock. Around four in the afternoon, after teaching at the high school all day, Alonzo took over the responsibilities. The same year that Brockman Gallery was established, Alonzo transferred from Manual Arts High School to Crenshaw High School, and remained committed to teaching in secondary education through the end of the decade. When Dale graduated from college in the late 1960s, he found a full-time position as an art teacher at his alma mater, Dorsey High School. Thereafter, he taught during the day, pursued a teaching credential, and worked part-time at the gallery. Both Alonzo and Dale also continued producing their own artwork. Meanwhile, family members, Dale explained, "provided money and advice as well as 'gallery sitting' time," and the property-owner, Jack Sidney, kept "the rent reasonable."[61]

The Westside also received a boost from Asian American leftist activism. As Brockman Gallery built a community around Leimert Park Village, many Sansei radicalized and made the Avenues section to the north a hub of the Asian American movement. Taking inspiration from the civil rights, Black nationalist, and antiwar movements, Japanese, Chinese, and Filipino Americans coalesced in their own political identity. Student activists' demands in Northern California's third world liberation front for Black and ethnic studies programs (including Chicano, Native American, and Asian American studies programs) made their way to Southern California. Among the universities who responded, UCLA in 1969 established the Asian American Studies Center. That same year, the center became headquarters for *Gidra*, a monthly student-turned community-oriented antiracist newspaper that five UCLA Sansei students founded. Soon thereafter, *Gidra* moved to Tenth Avenue and Jefferson Boulevard, where Nisei had opened businesses in the postwar years.[62]

The year 1969 also saw the formation of the Yellow Brotherhood (YB) on the Westside. When gangs disbanded in the early to mid-1960s, because of violence, imprisonment, military service, or a political awakening from the Watts rebellion, some ex-members turned to antiracist activism. Former member of the Renegade Slausons gang, Alprentice "Bunchy" Carter, became a founding member of the Black Panther Party's Southern California chapter; former members of the Businessmen gang joined Us Organization; and former members of the Ministers gang joined YB. The group formed over their concern for the rise in gang violence, drug abuse and poisoning, and the high school drop-out rate in the Asian American community. Faced with parental and societal pressures to live up to the label "model minority" and to catch up from losses incurred during wartime incarceration, some Sansei turned to self-destructive behaviors that their parents and local services failed to recognize. YB stepped in, mentoring young people through tutoring, counseling sessions, and social activities, and within half-a-year, had grown to 150 members. The group set up its headquarters on Ninth Avenue and Jefferson Boulevard and then opened a community center, the YB House, at 1227 Crenshaw Boulevard (near Pico Boulevard).[63]

Following the Nisei who established markets, restaurants, and real estate offices in the postwar years, Sansei opened enterprises on Jefferson Boulevard to foster Asian American identity. Before setting up the YB House on Crenshaw Boulevard, YB assembled on Ninth Avenue and Jefferson Boulevard. Visual Communications set out in 1970 on Twelfth Avenue and Jefferson Boulevard to portray Asian and Pacific Americans in the media as multifaceted and without racial stereotypes; to collect and produce photographs, films, and oral histories on their history and culture; and to organize exhibits and educational tools from the materials. The Storefront, a grassroots collective, opened in 1971 on Ninth Avenue and Jefferson Boulevard to promote multinationalism (or what they called third world unity) and self-determinism. Driven by a common bond of oppression, the mostly Japanese and a few Black, Chicano, and White Storefront members organized educational programs and forums and set up a library. Following in Marxist-Leninist tradition, leftist activists organized numerous collectives and study groups across the city, including on the Westside, to grapple with and find resolutions to society's major issues. *Gidra* associates also formed living study groups, including the Westside Collective in 1972, which had as its base a house near Twenty-Third Street and Arlington Avenue and ran six-week sessions that probed various issues.[64]

As Brockman Gallery gained attention, it attracted White buyers but struggled to draw in the Crenshaw area's affluent Black residents. While Alonzo believed that opening the gallery in Leimert Park would provide him with a built-in clientele, the business took a rather unexpected turn. "During the civil rights period, I noticed…somewhat of a pattern, that we had a lot of white clients" who expressed an interest in civil rights and Black culture. Carmen Riddle also noticed this trend taking place at the Watts Summer Festival. "All the white people came out there and they were buying art. They were the ones who were into art, for the most part." Grounded in a centuries-long European elitist tradition of art collection, White buyers in Los Angeles collected art to show off their wealth, knowledge, and sophistication. But unlike Eurocentric collectors, Brockman's patrons used their purchasing power to support artists of color. Meanwhile, the gallery had difficulty developing its relationship with Crenshaw's affluent Blacks. In part, like many Angelenos at the time, the Crenshaw residents viewed shopping outside of the area as being more attractive. "We would have probably been more successful" in drawing in Crenshaw's residents, Alonzo explained, "if we had moved to La Cienega [Boulevard]." More marketing could have helped. Over time, the gallery managed to attract a racially mixed clientele. White patrons, according to Alonzo, created a buzz that helped draw in Black customers. Brockman Gallery "grew into the kind-of social event that brought people to Leimert Park from all over the city of Los Angeles," Outterbridge described. It "catered to a diverse public," he explained in another interview. Luminaries such as actor Sidney Poitier were supporters, purchasing art from the gallery and attending its social functions.[65]

But the gallery struggled to draw in poor and working-class Blacks. In his controversial 1971 solo show at Brockman Gallery, which he entitled with an egregious racial slur and vulgar language, *Niggers Ain't Gonna Never Ever Be Nothin'—All They Want to Do Is Drink and Fuck*, Noah Purifoy intended to reach poor Blacks by illustrating the ways in which he saw them cope with poverty. In the gallery's small loft, Purifoy created a one-room apartment with a mattress on the floor, alcohol bottles on the nightstand, mannequins covered under blankets, and a putrid smell coming from the refrigerator. He intended to convey "the very essence of poverty and the way black people live" to encourage poor Blacks to "manifest some change in their general conditions and status" by, for instance, moving away from the

Eastside. But "I don't know to what extent the people whom it was meant for got to see it because they don't come to the Brockman Gallery." Purifoy elided the centuries-long, built-in systemic and systematic discriminatory policies and practices in his work that impeded many African Americans from financial stability, and instead, his art installation placed responsibility on the individual. His work also exemplified the long-standing criticism against affluent Blacks misunderstanding and disregarding low-income Blacks' challenges. The Davises and their colleagues indeed had a difficult mission, because art museums across the country also mostly drew in college-educated and well-off visitors and failed to appeal to the poor and working class.[66] Seeking to reach a broader swath of the public, the gallery and its affiliated artists turned to another approach.

TAKING ART TO THE STREETS

Throughout the 1970s, with the help of civil rights legislation that yielded state and federal grant programs, which sociologists attribute to the expansion of the new Black middle class, Brockman Gallery extended its work across the city.[67] Activists used Brockman Gallery as a springboard to carry out a host of artistic and philanthropic enterprises geared toward increasing the visibility of artists of color, empowering low-income Blacks, advancing Pan-Africanism, and seeking racial equality. In 1973, after the Davis brothers had secured a federal grant for the following fiscal year, they founded a nonprofit wing of the gallery named Brockman Gallery Productions (BGP) and set out to bring art to the streets of Los Angeles. In addition to hosting exhibitions, BGP sponsored a myriad of activities from street fairs and music performances to film festivals and citywide mural projects. When many Black-run art collectives, organizations, and galleries disbanded in the mid-1970s, Brockman Gallery expanded its influence beyond the borders of the Crenshaw area and into greater Los Angeles.

By 1970 the demands of the gallery and their full-time teaching positions left the Davis brothers with little time to rest. Alonzo became so busy juggling his work responsibilities and art projects that he found himself in the hospital on the verge of a physical breakdown. Consequently, he scaled back his schedule by resigning from his post at Crenshaw High School in 1970, and instead picked up a position as a college lecturer. Throughout the 1970s he taught courses at local community colleges and four-year universities, including Pasadena City College, Mount San Antonio College, UCLA, California State University, Northridge, and Otis Art Institute. Dale continued teaching at Dorsey High School while working at the gallery.[68]

Meanwhile, as its status and reputation grew, Brockman Gallery began to represent established African American artists. In its first years in operation, the gallery mainly held group shows featuring emerging Black artists, such as Gloria Rice, Dan Concholar, Timothy Washington, John Outterbridge, and John Riddle, many of whom went on to have successful careers. Once Brockman Gallery had established itself, Alonzo and Dale began hosting solo exhibitions of artists, such as Outterbridge and Riddle, and representing more well-known practitioners, including William Pajaud, Samella Lewis, Elizabeth Catlett, Jacob Lawrence, and Romare Bearden. African American art remained the central focus of the gallery, but from the outset, in the spirit of multiculturalism and inclusiveness, the Davises also showed the works of Latino, Asian American, and European-born artists. Near the end of 1967, for instance, the gallery held an exhibition solely of Mexican American artists, and in early 1969 it organized a show of Asian American artists. The gallery aimed to create a "multicultural setting," Alonzo explained, where artists from various backgrounds would have the opportunity to share their work and exchange ideas.[69]

From its inception, Brockman Gallery also got involved in community outreach that supported and increased the exposure of artists of color in the city. In 1968, in collaboration with Inglewood Neighbors, which was CN's counterpart to its south, Brockman Gallery and the BAA organized a month-long show at the Inglewood Public Library that included the works of ten Black artists and a panel discussion. As had happened in the Crenshaw area, as Blacks began migrating into the eastern half of the city of Inglewood, homeowners formed Morningside Park Neighbors (later renamed Inglewood Neighbors) shortly before the Watts rebellion to combat real estate blockbusting, integrate the public-school system, and improve race relations. Some locals worried about putting on the Black Artists Exhibit at the Inglewood Public Library, which was in the mostly White area of the city. A few White librarians who pushed back against Black in-migration and racial integration opposed the exhibit, and some Black artists believed Whites should go to Black communities to view the artwork. The exhibit, however, was a success. In her review, the branch librarian noted that the show "proved to be the most exciting and rewarding experience in a three-year history of library exhibits." More than three hundred attended the opening panel of artists, who addressed the topic, "What Art Means to the Black Community." Alonzo Davis, Dale Davis, Dan Concholar, David Hammons, and John Outterbridge, among others, exhibited their work at the show.[70]

Brockman Gallery's public outreach continued throughout the year. Also in 1969, the gallery, with the sponsorship of the Los Angeles Junior and Young Adult Clubs of the National Association of Negro Business and Professional Clubs, hosted an art exhibition and contest of high schoolers in the

Los Angeles area. The gallery worked with the BAA and the Church of the Good Shepherd to put on a film and slide show on contemporary African American artists in Los Angeles. That summer Brockman Gallery hosted the weekend-long Leimert Art Fair, with the sponsorship of the South District Recreation and Parks, in Leimert Park, that included art exhibitions, music, modern dance performance, and a fashion show.[71]

As Brockman Gallery found its niche, several of the early Black art groups and galleries in Los Angeles disbanded in the early and mid-1970s. In 1970, after two years in business, Suzanne Jackson closed Gallery 32. Internal disagreements and insufficient funds to finance their headquarters led to the breakup of Ruth Waddy's group, AWA. The full-time commitment that Cecil Fergerson and Claude Booker made to the BAC put strains on their marriages and families. They attempted to scale back their involvement and transfer their responsibilities onto other members, but the absence of their leadership hurt the group. In the mid-1970s, shortly before Booker passed away, the BAC was dissolved. Many of the pioneering art collectives in Watts also closed in the mid-1970s, including the Watts Writers Workshop, the Watts Happening Coffee House, and the Mafundi Institute. Key Asian American initiatives also folded, including the Storefront in 1973, *Gidra* in 1974, and YB in 1975. But Brockman Gallery had several elements that helped its staying power, including its supporters' dedication, its central location, and the Davis brothers' vision and leadership.[72]

The Davis brothers often faced "financial management problems," Alonzo explained, from pursuing their social agenda despite monetary limitations. But after following the advice of California State Assembly member (later representative to the US House of Representatives) Yvonne Brathwaite Burke, who urged them to apply for federal funding, Alonzo and Dale received a major boost toward their goals. The National Endowment for the Arts (NEA), under the Expansion Arts program, approved their grant application for fiscal year 1974 for $7,500. The Davises formed the nonprofit BGP and kicked off January 1974 with a free Winter Music Festival in Leimert Park. Every year from 1974 to 1985, and then again in 1988, Brockman Gallery and BGP secured NEA grants that, in total, ranged from $7,500 to as high as $33,250. In 1983, the year it received the most NEA grant funds, BGP received $20,000 under the Expansion Arts program to provide cultural programming in South Los Angeles, $3,250 under the Visual Artists Forums program to organize a two-day symposium on public art, and $10,000 under the Art in Public Places program to sponsor artist Kent Twitchell's downtown Los Angeles mural project. Brockman Gallery and BGP used the funds for many other initiatives, including outdoor music festivals, such as a Fourth of July Jazz and Rock Festival that included fireworks and a film presentation at UCLA in 1975, as well as workshops, exhibitions, concerts, and film series. BGP also expanded its work into Watts.[73]

When BGP affiliate John Outterbridge took over the Watts Towers Arts Center director position in 1975, he helped expand Brockman Gallery's efforts onto the Eastside. Born in North Carolina and educated at the North Carolina Agricultural and Technical State University and the American Academy of Art in Chicago, Outterbridge and his spouse moved to Los Angeles in 1963 to make a fresh start. Soon after settling in, he befriended Curtis Tann, who was then director of the Watts Towers Arts Center, joined the local Black art scene, and quickly became a leading figure in the movement. Despite his newcomer status, Outterbridge learned quickly about Los Angeles's racial geographic divide. In his assemblage piece, entitled *Eastside-Westside*, which he created around 1970 as part of his *Containment* series, Outterbridge soldered three metal circles onto wood, added rusted pins or nails to the center circle to represent downtown Los Angeles, and surrounded the circles with metal squares and rectangles of various shades of brown, grey, tan, and green that illustrate the neighborhood tracts that divided the city. The piece echoed Martin Luther King's insight, in *Where Do We Go from Here?* (King 1967), into the racial geography that defined metropolitan inequality. Two years into the Chicago open housing movement, King analogized, "The suburbs are white nooses around the black necks of the cities." In Los Angeles, Outterbridge worked to reduce that racial divide.[74]

As the Watts Towers Arts Center director, Outterbridge collaborated with Alonzo Davis and local musician Greg Bryant to bring an annual jazz festival to Watts. Inspired by the Watts Summer Festival and other outdoor concerts, the Simon Rodia Watts Towers Jazz Festival aimed to commemorate and celebrate African American musical heritage. The considerable turnout at the first concert, which took place on July 9, 1977, motivated the planners to continue holding the event. The second annual jazz festival met on the first day at the Watts Towers, and the next day in Leimert Park. Over the years, a wealth of talent, from Horace Tapscott to Don Cherry to Etta James, performed jazz, rhythm and blues, gospel, and other musical forms in the Black tradition. While the festivals centered on Black contributions, other musicians of color made their mark on the events. The Asian American band Hiroshima, known for its fusion of Japanese and world music and its association with the Asian American movement, received its start playing in Leimert Park. BGP sponsored the jazz festival for the first three years, and then turned over the responsibilities to the Watts Towers Arts Center staff.[75]

As BGP celebrated African American culture and heritage, the organization also exemplified its support for inclusiveness as it established its annual film festival. In June 1975, around two years after its formation, BGP used NEA funds to put together a Sunday evening film festival at the Scottish Rite Masonic Temple on Wilshire Boulevard of contemporary independent, student, documentary, children's, and feature films from Black filmmakers. Black mime Hayward Coleman hosted the event. The following year, the Brockman Gallery Film Festival, which moved to the California Museum of Science and Industry (later renamed the California Science Center) in Exposition Park, showed Black films over three days; offered workshops, seminars, discussions, and opportunities for participants to meet established actors, directors, and producers; and presented awards in the name of the late Paul Robeson to exemplary filmmakers. In 1977, using NEA and California Arts Council funding, BGP expanded its scope and created a truly international film festival over four days by featuring more than forty contemporary films from North America (Cuba, the United States), South America, Africa, and Asia. The film festival the following year spanned five days and played more than forty mostly African and Caribbean films, and included performances of Caribbean music and West African dance.[76]

In the 1970s Alonzo also began to use public spaces as a canvas for artistic and self-expression. He initially proposed the idea of painting murals as a teacher at Crenshaw High School, to engage his students and to provide graffiti artists with guidance and direction, but school officials and city administrators denied his many requests for a permit. At Brockman Gallery, he saw affluent art collectors and patrons frequent the exhibitions, but the working- and middle-class city dwellers that he primarily wanted to reach "weren't coming in the doors." Receiving no support from city officials, and following in the Mexican mural tradition and the community-based mural movement that took off in Chicago with the 1967 *Wall of Respect*, in the early 1970s Alonzo disregarded legal requisites and proceeded with his plan. He sketched a design, gathered together several artist friends and former students, and headed out during "church time" on an early Sunday morning to paint the concrete retaining wall along Crenshaw Boulevard and Fiftieth Street, directly east of View Park and Crenshaw High School, Alonzo's former employer. Despite police intervention, Alonzo and his cohorts not only completed their initial plan, but also reworked the mural every two years.[77]

Stretching along the main thoroughfare from Fiftieth to Fifty-Second Street and highlighting Black struggle and progress in the United States, the Crenshaw Wall, as it came to be known, obtained an iconic status. Over the years, countless artists have added scenes that pay tribute to civil rights leaders and Black dignitaries, honor Africa and African Americans, and convey messages of Black nationalism and pride. Like Alonzo, they took risks, including facing police harassment, criminal charges, and the expense of defending themselves against vandalism charges, to show onlookers the possibilities of sheer ingenuity and the value of the Black experience. Their method of taking art directly to the streets represents the articulation of a different vision of Black urbanism in the multicultural city. By painting on public-facing walls, the muralists claimed control of a city that historically sought to steer the direction of their lives, suppress their creativity and their livelihoods, and relegate them to the fringes.[78]

In 1976 BGP received another major boost when it received its first Comprehensive Employment and Training Act (CETA), Title VI, grant. The federal initiative, established in 1973 under the US Department of Labor to provide grants for jobs and job training programs, initially awarded BGP funds, which the city distributed, to establish its own Professional Artist Employment Program. In a similar vein as the New Deal's Works Progress Administration in the mid-1930s to mid-1940s, BGP's apprentice program commissioned ten unemployed artists between 1977 and 1978 to complete public artwork, especially murals, mainly in downtown Los Angeles. Artists contributed to the many components of producing a mural, including seeking potential public sites, appraising the costs, collaborating with colleagues, and then painting the pieces. "There was actually money to pay artists to work in L.A. And work they did—all over the city," Pat Johnson, a Brockman Gallery regular in the mid-1970s, reveled. Kent Twitchell completed murals at Otis Art Institute and the downtown YWCA; Joan de Bruin unveiled a mural at St. John of God Nursing Hospital and Residence, which was adjacent to historic West Adams Heights; Robert Delgado finished one on the Inner City Cultural Center; and Suzanne Jackson, who served as CETA's artist coordinator after closing Gallery 32, painted one on the Crenshaw Wall. The BGP program also held quarterly seminars aimed to give visual artists the tools to apply for grants, network with galleries and museums, and market and sell their work.[79]

BGP received its second CETA, Title VI, grant in 1977, and used it through the following year. For this grant, BGP carried out a Multimedia Public Arts Services Program, which focused on supporting the creation and promotion of multimedia works. Some artists from the first grant, including Jackson, Twitchell, and Concholar, continued their work on the second grant, and other artists, such as Wilhelmina Fortier, Linda Price, and Tatiana Long, joined the group. The artists used a variety of mediums, from painting, drawing, and sculpture, to photography, music, and video, to produce work under the grant. The CETA grants allowed Alonzo to quit his position as a college lecturer to lead BGP nearly full time.[80]

As a key contributor to the California mural movement, Alonzo continued through the 1970s and 1980s to bring art to the streets. He organized the muralists, including Twitchell, Kinshasha Holman Conwill, and Tony Riddle, in a group he dubbed the Los Angeles Street Graphics Committee, to paint public-facing walls on public streets and private buildings throughout the city, for commission and for free.[81] Among his many achievements, in 1980 Alonzo completed *Homage to John Outterbridge*, an abstract painting in honor of the community activist, artist, and long-time Watts Towers Arts Center director on the exterior walls of the facility. He also helped produce a series of abstract panels along the retainer walls of the freeways for the 1984 Olympic Games. He initially proposed extending the murals from downtown Los Angeles southward into Central Avenue, the city's historically Black cultural center, but after finding no financial backers, he and several other muralists painted the walls of the downtown freeways. Like their predecessors had done when they migrated westward to challenge housing discrimination, Alonzo and the Street Graphics Committee insisted on having a space in the urban landscape by adding illustrations of their values and views to its walls.[82]

By the mid-1970s, artists had set up their studios in the storefronts adjacent to Brockman Gallery and had transformed Leimert Park Village into a hub of Black expression. Because the property owner, Jack Sidney, kept rent reasonable, Brockman Gallery not only remained at its 4334 Degnan Boulevard location for twenty-three years, but, Dale explained, also subleased "as many as six of [Sidney's] other adjacent properties...to artists, writers, musicians, and other productive entrepreneurs" to use as art studios, apartments, and meeting and presentation spaces, helping create "an artist community" in the process. More planned and impromptu activities occurred, including artist-led seminars and workshops in the visual arts, mime and yoga classes in the park near the pedestal fountain, and jam sessions and performances in front of the gallery doors. Brockman Gallery marked milestones, including its tenth anniversary with an evening gala celebration, and its fifteenth anniversary with a day-long fish fry and street fair that included live music from Latin, Caribbean, Asian American, and African American bands; clowns for children; and art on display. While Alonzo and Dale steered the direction of the gallery and raised the funds to pursue their agenda of racial inclusion, the affiliated artists and activists helped the gallery thrive. "We all participated in being board members from time to time or formulating and influencing policy," explained Outterbridge. "It was a place where we got an opportunity to practice civic responsibility."[83]

While African American artists and activists went outside of the established, White-run realms of the art market to seek exposure and recognition, White establishments gradually bent to the pressure and the milieu, and, over time, organized exhibits of Black artists. The year 1966, one year following the Watts rebellion, marked a turning point in the museum world when *The Negro in American Art* opened at UCLA's Dickson Art Center and then traveled to other California galleries. Among the more than forty artists exhibited, the show included some nineteenth-century practitioners—Edward Bannister, Robert Scott Duncanson, and Henry Ossawa Tanner, among others—but mainly centered on contemporary national and California visual artists, including Los Angeles–based Noah Purifoy, Betye Saar, Ruth Waddy, and Charles White.[84]

Like other major art museums in the nation's major urban centers, LACMA also finally responded to the demand. In 1968 LACMA held the *Sculpture of Black Africa: The Paul Tishman Collection*, an exhibit of nearly two hundred pieces from African art collector Paul Tishman that explored what LACMA director Kenneth Donahue described as the "rich and proud heritage" of Africa and African America. In response to years of the BAC's lobbying efforts, LACMA also held several exhibits of African American artists. The noteworthy *Three Graphic Artists* 1971 show with more than forty works by renowned Charles White and emerging David Hammons and Timothy Washington did not escape criticism. The BAC felt Charles White deserved a solo exhibit. The following year, LACMA held the group show, *Los Angeles, 1972: A Panorama of Black Artists*, with more than fifty contemporary artists. Then, in 1976, LACMA's efforts culminated in the groundbreaking *Two Centuries of Black American Art*. Curated by David Driskell, Fisk University's art department chair, this comprehensive survey of Black art, which after its time at LACMA traveled around the country, challenged conventional notions that African Americans had not developed legitimate art. Consisting of more than two hundred works by sixty-three artists working from 1750 to 1950, *Two Centuries* showed that Black artists had made significant contributions to the collective American historical discourse.[85]

Brockman Gallery played a key role in carrying out what Outterbridge describes as "civic responsibility" that aimed to teach city dwellers of all racial and ethnic backgrounds to come together and celebrate their differences. While Brockman Gallery and BGP sought to empower Blacks in Los Angeles to take pride in their history, strive beyond their circumstances, and stand up for racial equality, through their art exhibits, street fairs, music performances, film festivals, mural projects, workshops, and seminars, they also worked within the integrationist model, intending to teach all city dwellers to practice racial tolerance and understanding. Buttressed by the history of Black art and entrepreneurship in the first half of the twentieth century, and the Black artists and activists who worked tirelessly toward attaining more exposure and recognition in the art market in the mid-twentieth century,

Brockman Gallery provided a conduit to interrogate racial inequality, heal wounds, and work toward a more just society in a city where racial discrimination took shape in the centuries before the gallery opened and continued in the years after the Watts rebellion. As secondary and postsecondary educators, Alonzo and Dale used their skills and background to bring the classroom to the streets of Los Angeles. "We're teachers," Dale simply put, "that's what we do."[86]

Chapter Seven

Black Beverly Hills Redux

KNOWN BY THE 1980s as the Black Beverly Hills, the affluent neighborhoods of the Crenshaw area and adjacent Ladera Heights have spurred the creation of many artistic and entrepreneurial projects. Scenes from motion pictures, including *What's Love Got to Do with It* (1993), *Love & Basketball* (2000), and *Ray* (2004), have been filmed in the area. Segments of television shows, including *Moesha* (1996–2001), *Insecure* (2016–21), and *Black-ish* (2014–22), also were filmed there. The reality television shows *Baldwin Hills* (2007–9) followed a group of African American teenagers growing up in the area, and *Sweet Life: Los Angeles* (2021) has portrayed the young adult experience there. Songs such as Frank Ocean's "Sweet Life" (2012) and Overdoz.'s "Black Beverly Hills" (2017), reference the nickname. Clothing company Black Beverly Hills sells apparel that include images and words related to the area. View Park received national attention in 2012 when President Barack Obama attended a fundraiser there for his reelection campaign. Four years later, thanks to residents' leadership, the National Park Service designated View Park's Doumakes House the first historic home in unincorporated Los Angeles County and added the house and the entire View Park neighborhood to the National Register of Historic Places. Then, in 2019, the city renamed Rodeo Road, which runs along the northern Crenshaw area border, Obama Boulevard, to honor the former president and expand "presidential row" to include Washington, Adams, and Jefferson Boulevards. The Black Beverly Hills and all of its byproducts have been a source of pride to the largely African American community who once could not live there.[1]

African Americans fought an uphill battle through the twentieth century to move onto the Westside and gain full access to the city. They defied racial restrictive covenants, endured relentless White intimidation, teamed up with civil rights attorneys, fought lawsuits, and joined a nationwide movement that ended some lawful discriminatory housing practices. After legal victories, including *Shelley* and *Barrows*, Black Angelenos had to continue to fight for full access to the city through their own labor. They surpassed Los Angeles's existing racial borders by expanding their reach across the Eastside, and settling north of Washington Boulevard and west of Arlington Avenue. Following age-old practices, rooted in American colonialism and made systemic and systematic throughout American history, Whites resumed their attempt to stave off Black migration. Most yielded to real estate agents who encouraged them to sell their homes upon Black inmigration; they believed property values would fall and their community would be turned into a so-called ghetto. Other White, Black, and Asian Crenshaw area residents responded to the demographic shift by encouraging racial integration. Inspired by the modern civil rights, Black nationalist, antiwar, second-wave feminist, and Asian American movements, they stood up against racism and discrimination by working across the color line, in grassroots organizations and outreach programs, to cultivate racial inclusion and understanding.

Crenshaw area efforts saw noteworthy achievements. CN's growth in membership through the 1960s illustrates residents' increasing interest in the group and its goals. Its real estate agency attracted some Whites and Asians to the area. Its regular meetings, social gatherings, community outreach programs, educational initiatives, and publications brought together neighbors who might otherwise have never met and opened the lines of communication across the color line. Partnerships with other neighborhood stabilization groups locally and nationally strengthened the movement and led to the establishment of National Neighbors. Brockman Gallery also connected Angelenos by creating a central meeting place where established and emerging artists of color not only exhibited and sold their works, but also planned outreach programs and social events across the city. From street fairs and music performances to film festivals and citywide mural projects, BGP's activities celebrated and honored African American identity, supported people of color across Los Angeles, and fostered a more inclusive city. By the late 1970s local artists had set up their own studios in the storefronts adjacent to Brockman Gallery and transformed Leimert Park Village into a hub of Black expression.

As CN and Brockman Gallery fought to maintain integration and the quality of their neighborhoods, nearby Ladera Heights residents waged a similar battle. Situated immediately south of the Baldwin Hills and west of Windsor Hills, Ladera Heights underwent a nearly parallel trajectory as its Crenshaw area counterparts. Several years before the start of World War II, Ladera Heights' developer, the Los Angeles Investment Company, who also built View Park and View Heights, set out to make Ladera Heights into another White oasis made up of valuable and highly sought-after houses by encouraging homeowners to cover their properties with restrictive covenants. In the years following *Shelley* and *Barrows*, Black migration into Ladera Heights came at a slower pace than into the Crenshaw area, partly because of Ladera Heights' location west of La Brea Avenue, which served as yet another racial border. By the 1960s, when Blacks began moving into the area, they faced White intimidation, real estate blockbusting, and White out-migration. But despite the rumors, Ladera Heights maintained its highly regarded reputation. The 1970 federal census recorded Ladera Heights with the highest median family income in all of Los Angeles County, including Beverly Hills. "The Cadillacs and Mercedes and other conspicuous signs of money runneth over," one reporter wrote. "Almost everyone has a gardener and there's hardly a kid without either a ten-speed bicycle or an ear-shattering trail bike."[2] Yet residents struggled to stave off segregation, particularly in Ladera Heights' public schools.

Like its Crenshaw area counterparts, Ladera Heights residents faced school officials who resisted racial integration. In the mid-1960s, in the Inglewood Unified School District (IUSD) that served Ladera Heights residents, schools situated east of Prairie Avenue grew heavily Black, while schools west of Prairie stayed majority White, reflecting the Black westward migration trend. Concerned that Black in-migration and White out-migration in the entire school district would create a mostly Black student body, residents reacted. While CN pressured the Los Angeles BOE to integrate its student body, Inglewood Neighbors and other proponents of integration urged the Inglewood BOE for years to correct its racial imbalance. When the BOE continued to delay taking actions, integrationists filed a lawsuit against IUSD for aiding educational inequality. In 1970, one year before *Swann v. Charlotte-Mecklenburg Board of Education*, in which the US Supreme Court approved busing as a method to desegregate schools, Judge Max F. Deutz in the California Superior Court case, *Janel Johnson v. Inglewood Unified School District*, ordered IUSD to carry out its own desegregation plan by the 1971–72 school year.[3]

But despite their hard-fought legal victories in LAUSD and IUSD to foster racial integration and inclusiveness, integrationists saw their goals fall short. As many working- and middle-class Westside communities adjacent to the affluent neighborhoods became majority Black, the public schools that they all shared underwent a similar shift in the racial composition of their student bodies. The proportion of Black students at Crenshaw's LAUSD Baldwin Hills Elementary School, for instance, rose from 16.1 percent in 1966 to 56.7 percent in 1970 to 65.9 percent in 1980. At Crenshaw's LAUSD Dorsey High School, the proportion of Blacks increased from 68.8 percent in 1966 to 76.2 percent in 1970 to 92.9 percent in 1980.[4] The IUSD desegregation plan also proved no match to the city's long-standing discriminatory practices. Within five years of the 1970 Johnson ruling, students of color comprised the majority of most IUSD schools on both the east and west sides of the district. Resentful that IUSD bused children to an equally segregated school located farther from their home, parents and school officials filed several appeals with the Los Angeles Superior Court to review the case. In 1975, five years after he handed down his decision, Judge Deutz overturned his order for desegregation and called for the return of the neighborhood school policy. The dramatic demographic change in the LAUSD and IUSD student bodies presaged the shift in the affluent Westside neighborhoods.[5]

By the 1980s the value of the affluent enclaves of the Crenshaw area and Ladera Heights matched the meaning of the "Beverly Hills" suffix of their "Black Beverly Hills" nickname. Despite White fears of property deterioration, median owner-occupied property values remained high in many Crenshaw area neighborhoods and Ladera Heights. For 1980, compare the national median of $47,200 and the Los Angeles city median of $96,100 to Baldwin Hills Estates, $135,200; Baldwin Vista, $115,900; View Park, View Heights, Windsor Hills, $111,500; and the two Ladera Heights census tracts, $85,000 and $188,100. For 2000, compare the national median of $119,600 and the Los Angeles city median of $221,600 to Baldwin Hills Estates, $317,000; Baldwin Vista, $242,700; View Park, View Heights, and Windsor Hills, $290,300; and Ladera Heights, $442,000.[6]

The communities' racial composition also reflected the "Black" prefix of their "Black Beverly Hills" nickname. Between 1960 and 2000, affluent Crenshaw and Ladera Heights underwent a population shift to an overwhelming Black majority. Leimert Park, View Park, View Heights, Windsor Hills, Baldwin Hills Estates, and Baldwin Vista, in aggregate, swung from 13.6 percent Black and 78.6 percent White in 1960, to 97.4 percent Black and 12.5 percent White in 1980, to 83.8 percent Black and 5.8 percent White in 2000. Albeit at a slower pace, Ladera Heights also underwent a shift to a Black majority. Its population changed from 0.2 percent Black and 99.4 percent White in 1960, to 39.6 percent Black and 54.3 percent White in 1980, to 57.1 percent Black and 31.4 percent White in 2000.[7]

One of the most notable achievements in the long campaign against housing discrimination was Black settlement across Greater Los Angeles. Once confined to the Eastside, increasing numbers of African Americans moved into the middle- and working-class communities of Los Angeles proper through the second half of the twentieth century. By 1970 nearly all of the census tracts situated between Alameda Street on the east and the Crenshaw area on the west, Washington Boulevard on the north and Artesia Boulevard on the south, comprised at least 75 percent Black populations. According to the 1980 census, African Americans began to take up residence beyond those borders and migrate farther west of the Crenshaw area into Culver City. Yet for those who fought against White flight and sought racial integration, the demographic shift remained a grave disappointment.[8]

In the late 1980s, while Black activism and engagement in Leimert Park Village waned, and Alonzo and Dale Davis closed their business, the spirit of Brockman Gallery endured. In the 1990s another generation of Black artists and activists took up the baton on Degnan Boulevard and its adjacent streets, opened art enterprises and Afrocentric shops, and led Leimert Park Village in a renaissance of African American artistic expression and social and political activism. The 1992 Los Angeles uprising, and the racially charged developments leading up to it, revived community engagement. When a jury found four Los Angeles police officers not guilty for beating African American motorist Rodney King, despite a filmed record of the episode that the television news media repeatedly played, thousands of city dwellers erupted in revolt across South Los Angeles. Almost thirty years after the Watts rebellion, the 1992 protestors sought to make clear that racial inequality and police brutality persisted in the city. Amid the turmoil, Black city dwellers found in Leimert Park Village a space to take control of the streets, come together on common ground, and engage in dialogue. One reporter, writing in 1997 for *Black Enterprise*, explained, "The success that the Brockman Gallery enjoyed during the '70s and early '80s planted the seeds for the bustling commercial district of today." That social and political engagement was stimulated by decades of needless racism and discrimination.[9]

Black-owned businesses helped elevate Leimert Park Village into a site of Black activism and expression. A few days before the 1992 uprising, a Vietnam veteran, recovering alcoholic, and formerly homeless man, Richard Fulton, opened 5th Street Dick's Coffee Company, which quickly became a local fixture after the revolt. Because of the uprising, Fulton explained, "We all became a community right then and there." More businesses that opened before the 1992 revolt received greater attention in the aftermath. Artist Ramsess, who first rented his studio at 4342 Degnan Boulevard from the Davis brothers in 1979, became a major presence in the community. Former Brockman Gallery intern, Ben Caldwell, founded the film media center Video 3333 and then KAOS Network in 1984, at 4343 Forty-Third Place, that offered classes, programs, and exhibits in the digital arts and a performance space for poetry readings and the hip-hop open mic night, Project Blowed. Brian Breye displayed his extensive collection of West African art pieces and American antebellum artifacts at Museum in Black. Jazz poet Kamau Daáood rented a Brockman Gallery space at 4344 Degnan Boulevard, and, with jazz drummer Billy Higgins, opened World Stage, where jazz and spoken word artists rehearsed, performed, and honed their craft. Following the footsteps of Brockman Gallery, Laura Hendrix's Gallery Plus displayed and sold works of local artists.[10]

Five-time Emmy-nominated actor Marla Gibbs invested heavily in the area, opening businesses that advanced the arts. Chicago-born Gibbs, who moved from Detroit to Los Angeles in 1969, began playing a role that aired on television six years later and would cement her reputation as a talented comedic performer. On the eleven-season-long sitcom, *The Jeffersons*, Gibbs played the feisty live-in maid, Florence Johnston, who worked for George and Louise Jefferson, a middle-class Black couple. The Jeffersons had relocated from New York's borough of Queens to Manhattan or, as the theme song celebrates, the "East Side," the equivalent in reputation to Los Angeles's Westside. Gibbs purchased the Memory Lane Supper Club at 2323 Martin Luther King Jr. Boulevard in the early 1980s and renamed it Marla's Memory Lane (and later Marla's Jazz Supper Club), where many musicians, including Horace Tapscott, performed. Soon thereafter, Gibbs opened the nonprofit Crossroads Arts Academy and Theater, at 8461 South Vermont Avenue in Leimert Park, which provided office and rehearsal space, put on concerts and theatrical shows, and offered drama, playwriting, voice, and music classes. In 1990 Gibbs purchased the landmark Leimert Theater complex near the corner of West Forty-Third Place and Degnan Boulevard in Leimert Park Village, opened it as the Vision Theater, and then added Crossroads Art Academy, which offered drama classes, staged theatrical performances, and hosted music concerts. Her subsequent major television series, *227*, was first performed at the academy.[11]

In the years following the 1992 uprising, countless more businesses opened and Leimert Park Village saw more patronage. Choreographers Pat Taylor and Lady Helena Walquer Vereen opened Dance Collective, which held workshops and performances in African American and West African dance. Laura Mae Gross moved her long-standing blues club, Babe's and Ricky's Inn, which she opened on Central Avenue in the early 1960s, to Leimert Park Village in 1997. Boutiques, eateries, bookstores, and art galleries, many of which specialized in Afrocentric goods, including Zambezi Bazaar and the Leimert Park Fine Art Gallery, lined Degnan Boulevard. Vocalist Dwight Trible recalled, "All of a sudden things started happening there. The next thing you know, I went around to Richard [Fulton]'s place one day and the whole street was just full." Through the mid-1990s, according to historian Steven Isoardi, "At night there were as many as four or five spaces within one and a half blocks offering live music. Peaceful, crowded sidewalks gave rise to continuous conversations with friends, acquaintances, and, just as often, strangers." Well-established performers, from drummer Max Roach to vocalist Nina Simone, worked with new artists. As it had been in the 1960s and 1970s, Leimert Park Village became a center for festivals and music performances, with Horace Tapscott and the Pan Afrikan

Peoples Arkestra regularly headlining shows. In Jeannette Lindsay's film, *Leimert Park: The Story of a Village*, which captured the vitality of the community in the 1990s, one man said simply, "It is a place that demands honesty from you."[12]

As Blacks moved westward and crossed the city's racial borders, they also found their neighborhoods' Eastside designation following them. Illustrating the city's continual imagined geography, comprising neighborhood borders shaped by cultural, demographic, economic, and political shifts, the White buffer zone that distinguished the Eastside became larger, covering a greater portion of Los Angeles proper, and the Westside label shifted northward, above the Santa Monica Freeway. As the Eastside's imagined borders spread westward, reports included the affluent communities of the Crenshaw area within the South Central designation. When news broke that biracial American actor Meghan Markle and Prince Harry of the British royal family planned to marry, the British tabloid, *Daily Mail*, brazenly and erroneously described the View Park home of Doria Ragland, Markle's mother, as being "plagued by crime and riddled with street gangs." For Crenshaw's affluent residents, who had worked tirelessly to maintain their community's esteemed reputation, the South Central designation hid the realities of their prosperous area. To defuse the negative connotations, in a unanimous vote in 2003 the Los Angeles City Council changed the name to "South Los Angeles." The initially sixteen-square-mile district excluded affluent Crenshaw. Although critics doubted that the modification would resolve the deep-seated problems of drug use and gang violence in the area, the measure illustrated Black Angelenos's continual struggle against racism and misinformation. Since the 2010s, the *Los Angeles Times'* "Mapping L.A." project has included the affluent Crenshaw neighborhoods within the South Los Angeles section.[13]

The movement against residential discrimination could not overcome age-old systemic and systematic racism and discrimination. The long history of government-supported, court-endorsed housing discrimination served as a key element in helping maintain residential segregation. But many other factors—from the failures of the public-school system to the perpetuation of Black stereotypes in American culture—inflamed the city's racial divisions. White exodus had far-reaching consequences on the urban landscape. While Blacks surmounted racial barriers and moved into Los Angeles's racially restricted enclaves, Whites packed their belongings and moved away. Residential areas as well as their surrounding public facilities resegregated. And, while the affluent communities of the Crenshaw area and Ladera Heights remained highly esteemed, many of the adjacent enclaves, such as Inglewood and Culver City, developed undeserved reputations as being rundown. Middle-class Blacks worked hard to gain equal opportunity by fighting residential discrimination, yet resegregation in the subsequent decades showed that racism and fear remained deeply embedded in the fabric of the city. As residents report Whites returning to their communities in the 2010s and 2020s, amid another housing and homelessness crisis, the next chapter of this Los Angeles history could take a turn.[14]

Acknowledgments

The idea for *The Coveted Westside* began with my initial inquiry into the origins of the "Black Beverly Hills" nickname, served as the basis for my PhD dissertation in the University of New Hampshire history department, and then evolved into this book on the varied ways in which White-dominated America created racially segregated Los Angeles and the African American urbanites who fought back. Working on this project over many years involved countless individuals, many archives and libraries, and a few academic institutions that helped me in small and large ways, all of which added significant value to sustain me and regularly remind me of the importance of this history and the need to document and examine it.

Many scholars have provided me with much-needed nudges to complete this work. As my PhD advisor, now University of New Hampshire professor emeritus, Harvard Sitkoff exercised a delicate balance of counsel and compassion that challenged and carried me throughout the program. The University of New Hampshire history department cultivated a supportive space to test ideas, make mistakes, and find my voice. Harvard Sitkoff, Lucy Salyer, Ellen Fitzpatrick, and Bill Harris, and Cliff Brown in the sociology department graciously served on my dissertation committee and offered some of the earliest feedback. Special thanks to Eliga Gould, who consistently provided support since my first semester there, and Molly Girard Dorsey and Kurk Dorsey, who opened up their home and family while I worked my way through the rigors of the program. My graduate student friends Keri Lewis, Alison Mann, and Glenn Grasso provided camaraderie. As I transitioned out of graduate school, the University of New England history faculty, especially Beth DeWolfe, Eric Zuelow, and Rob Alegre, offered me another space to continue studying, discussing, and interrogating the past. Special thanks to Rob Alegre who read early versions of the first two chapters.

The University of Nevada Press has maintained its interest in seeing this project to fruition. I am grateful to the press and all of the people there who have worked with me on the project. In 2012 Eugene Moehring, who was serving as coeditor of the press's Urban West series, and now University of Nevada, Las Vegas, professor emeritus, sowed in me the idea of turning my dissertation into a book by simply requesting a proposal. While Gene Moehring provided me with the impetus for shaping the project into book form, Amy Scott, since she began the Urban West series editor role, provided more much-needed nudges to complete the project. Her editorial suggestions, and those of the anonymous peer reviewers, brought to my attention the need to explore more of Los Angeles's developments that intersected with the Black homeowners' rights movement and to further refine my analysis. Their ideas, suggestions, and expressions are woven throughout this project. The phrase "Black homeowners' rights movement," in fact, comes from Scott herself. In the book's early and middle stages, Justin Race, Alrica Goldstein, and Clark Whitehorn generously responded to my questions and, in doing so, advanced my thinking. In the final stages, JoAnne Banducci, Margaret Dalrymple, and Jinni Fontana guided the manuscript to publication.

The bibliography and notes illustrate the indispensableness of libraries and archives that preserve the sources that made this project possible. Special mention goes to The Huntington Library; Southern California Library; UCLA Young Research Library, Special Collections and Center for Oral History Research; California State University, Fullerton, de Graaf Center for Oral and Public History; and the Los Angeles Public Library.

Many thanks are due to Louise Buckley at the University of New Hampshire Dimond Library for helping me locate census records. In the final years of the project, I relied heavily on the librarians at my own local library, Rice Public Library, in Kittery, Maine, and the library's association with MaineCat, the exceptional statewide catalog and interlibrary loan system. I am grateful to Rosemarie Knopka at the Los Angeles Public Library for sending me a draft of the container list and some photos and documents of the forthcoming Brockman Gallery Archive as she processes it for public view. In the coming years, the public will get access to more sources that could challenge this book's discussions and analyses. That essential disciplinary practice can lead us to better recognize and, I hope, confront and rectify the forces that have permitted racial discrimination and segregation.

Over the years, several institutions have generously supported my travel and research to the archives, and travel and fees to give conference presentations, with grants and fellowships. Many thanks to the University of New Hampshire history department; University of New Hampshire graduate school; The Huntington Library; Historical Society of Southern California; and Popular Culture Association/American Culture Association (now Popular Culture Association) for supporting my archival research and writing. The University of New Hampshire graduate school, Hesser College faculty development fund, and the University of New England history department also sponsored me to present portions of this work at conferences. I am also thankful to the audience members who listened to me work out some focus areas, asked probing questions, and offered suggestions to advance my thinking.

The bibliography also lists several individuals who shared their experiences with me on living in the neighborhoods that make up this study. I cannot express enough my gratitude to them for welcoming me into their homes, volunteering their time (oftentimes several hours of it), and opening up about their personal and family history for recorded history. The names listed in the bibliography, under the author-conducted oral histories subheading, not only provide a record of invaluable primary sources for this book, but also offer an expression of my deep appreciation for their contributions. More individuals sat with me for interviews than I list in the bibliography; their oral histories fit less into the work's final narrative so were not included, yet they too remain important to my understanding of this history. Some participants also shared with me some of the records that they had kept on their and their family's community work, which now appear throughout these chapters and in the notes. Special thanks to Deloy Edwards for providing me with some of his real estate records and photos; Ivan A. Houston and his family for lending me the astounding West Adams Heights Protective Association's notebook; Dale Davis for gifting me several documents, books, and photos on Brockman Gallery; Joan Suter for sending me records related to her work in the Crenshaw area; and Matthew Post for donating Ann Post's papers to the Southern California Library. Dale Davis, Joan Suter, and Matthew Post have also continued to remind me of the importance of publishing this history by staying in touch over the years. They have been wellsprings of information and inspiration.

My yearning to understand the city my family adopted in the mid-twentieth century and their experiences in it ultimately fueled me to pursue and complete this project. Growing up listening to stories about living in mid-twentieth century Los Angeles and experiencing the city for myself a few decades later sparked my interest to learn more. My grandparents moved to Los Angeles after World War II for many of the same reasons as everyone else then, including its proclaimed health benefits and employment opportunities. Their stories and my mother's and aunt's persisted in my mind as I sought to piece together Los Angeles's neighborhood development and change. A couple years before I began searching for a dissertation topic, Kerry Jones briefly mentioned in one of our many conversations the "Black Beverly Hills" nickname. A few years later, when I heard the reference again while watching the 1986 documentary *Ray Charles: The Genius of Soul*, which described the musician's move with his family into the Crenshaw area, I became hooked on the topic. What seemed like Kerry's casual mention of the area has led to this long-term project and the countless gifts that it has given me. Of those gifts, the best one has been him.

Notes

INTRODUCTION

1. George Beavers, Jr., interview by Ranford B. Hopkins (Los Angeles: UCLA Library, Center for Oral History Research, 1982), UCLA/OL (quotations). While they sit silent on pages, the varied ethnonyms used to refer to groups throughout United States history remain loaded with meanings that reflect their era's sentiments. This study uses the terms and letter cases that have become commonly used in recent years. Like W. E. B. Du Bois in the 1920s who campaigned to capitalize the word "Negro," activists and scholars in the early twenty-first century have pushed to capitalize the word "Black" to refer "to people of the African diaspora" who contributed significantly to the nation while having "to fight for the right to a proper name," argues journalism professor Lori L. Tharps. Moreover, in the spirit of using capitalization to signify a proper noun, a distinct race, and "how Whiteness functions in our social and political institutions and our communities," according to the Center for the Study of Social Policy, this study capitalizes Whites. That said, in an effort to highlight usages throughout history, this work has maintained the cited authors' letter cases in quotations, except for the oral histories that this author conducted. On another note, while recognizing the problems with the term "people of color" as a broad label to denote African, Asian, and Latino Americans, and other racial and ethnic groups other than Whites, this study relies on the phrase. See Tharps, "The Case for Black with a Capital B," *New York Times*, November 18, 2014 (first and second quotations in this note); Ann Thúy Nguyễn and Maya Pendleton, "Recognizing Race in Language: Why We Capitalize 'Black' and 'White,'" Center for the Study of Social Policy, March 23, 2020 (third quotation in this note).

2. Beavers, interview by Hopkins (quotation).

3. J. K. Obatala, "The Blacks of Baldwin Hills: Worthy Models for Youth?," *Los Angeles Times*, June 16, 1975, C7 (quotations, italics in original).

4. Marshall Ingwerson, "Jesse Jackson Tugs at Traditional Political Loyalty of L.A. Blacks," *Christian Science Monitor*, November 16, 1983, 3 (first quotation); Penelope McMillan, "Baldwin Hills on 'Day After': Grim Contrasts," *Los Angeles Times*, July 4, 1985; Robert Lindsey, "Weary Fire Fighters on Coast Battle Flames and Weather," *Los Angeles Times*, July 4, 1985, A1; Penelope McMillan, "Assistance Center Opens for Baldwin Hills Victims," *Los Angeles Times*, July 24, 1985; Nancy Mills, "Allen's Claim to 'Fame' is Making Right Moves," *Los Angeles Times*, August 5, 1985, F1, 5 (second quotation on 5); Aldore Collier, "Black Celebrities Have Become the Powerbrokers in the Boardroom and on the Glitzy Social Circuit," *Ebony* (September 1995): 52 (third quotation); Ben Quinones, "Brother Man," *L.A. Weekly*, June 24, 2005, 102 (fourth quotation).

5. For population data, see chapter 4.

6. For examples of works on Anglo settlement and efforts to appropriate or destroy Los Angeles's ethnic and racial past, see William Deverell, *Whitewashed Adobe: The Rise of Los Angeles and the Remaking of Its Mexican Past* (Berkeley: University of

California Press, 2004); and David Samuel Torres-Rouff, *Before L.A.: Race, Space, and Municipal Power in Los Angeles, 1781–1894* (New Haven, CT: Yale University Press, 2013).

7. *Twelfth Census of the United States*, Population, vol. 1, pt. 1 (Washington, DC: US Census Office, 1901), cxix.

8. Douglas Flamming, *Bound for Freedom: Black Los Angeles in Jim Crow America* (Berkeley: University of California Press, 2005), chap. 3. See also Clora Bryant et al., eds., *Central Avenue Sounds: Jazz in Los Angeles* (Berkeley: University of California Press, 1998); and Bette Yarbrough Cox, *Central Avenue—Its Rise and Fall (1890–c. 1955): Including the Musical Renaissance of Black Los Angeles* (Los Angeles: BEEM Publications, 1996).

9. Political scientist Benedict Anderson established the conceptual framework of socially constructed, in flux, imagined communities that has served as the basis of analysis for many subsequent studies. See Benedict Anderson, *Imagined Communities: Reflections on the Origins and Spread of Nationalism*, 3rd ed. (New York: Verso, 2006). For a report on the Eastside's meaning and Silver Lake's debate over removing the moniker as its location description, see Jessica P. Ogilvie, "Where Is LA's Eastside? A Brief History of Class, Gentrification and Maps," *LAist*, July 22, 2019. For discussion on the term "the Greater Eastside," see Victor M. Valle and Rodolfo D. Torres, *Latino Metropolis* (Minneapolis: University of Minnesota Press, 2000), 20–24 (quotation on 20). See also Victor Hugo Viesca, "The Battle of Los Angeles: The Cultural Politics of Chicana/o Music in the Greater Eastside," *American Quarterly* 56, no. 3 (September 2004): 720. The ethnonyms used to denote people of Spanish, Mexican, and South American descent have also varied throughout American history. In recent years, the gender-neutral Latinx has come into use among some scholars and media outlets. However, this study relies on the Spanish word "Latinos" to denote all Latin Americans, including those who identify as male, female, nonbinary, and nonconforming, with lineage in Spain and/or Latin America. But, when possible, this study uses terms that specify origin, such as Spain or Mexico.

10. For discussion on the South Central Los Angeles name, see Scott Kurashige, *The Shifting Grounds of Race: Black and Japanese Americans in the Making of Multiethnic Los Angeles* (Princeton, NJ: Princeton University Press, 2008), 234, 268. For a report on the South Los Angeles name change, see Matea Gold and Greg Braxton, "Considering South-Central by Another Name," *Los Angeles Times*, April 10, 2003.

11. For works that examine the tools Whites used to segregate their communities, see Douglas S. Massey and Nancy A. Denton, *American Apartheid: Segregation and the Making of the Underclass* (Cambridge: Harvard University Press, 1993); W. Edward Orser, *Blockbusting in Baltimore: The Edmondson Village Story* (Lexington: University Press of Kentucky, 1994); Amanda I. Seligman, *Block by Block: Neighborhoods and Public Policy on Chicago's West Side* (Chicago: University of Chicago Press, 2005); James W. Loewen, *Sundown Towns: A Hidden Dimension of American Racism* (New York: The New Press, 2005); and David M. P. Freund, *Colored Property: State Policy and White Racial Politics in Suburban America* (Chicago: University of Chicago Press, 2007).

12. Michael Jones-Correa, "The Origins and Diffusion of Racial Restrictive Covenants," *Political Science Quarterly* 115, no. 4 (Winter 2000–2001): 544. For recent works on restrictive covenants, see Richard R. W. Brooks and Carol M. Rose, *Saving the Neighborhood: Racially Restrictive Covenants, Law, and Social Norms* (Cambridge:

Harvard University Press, 2013); Jeffrey D. Gonda, *Unjust Deeds: The Restrictive Covenant Cases and the Making of the Civil Rights Movement* (Chapel Hill: University of North Carolina Press, 2015).

13. Jones-Correa, "Origins and Diffusion," 563–67; Beryl Satter, *Family Properties: How the Struggle over Race and Real Estate Transformed Chicago and Urban America* (New York: Henry Holt and Company, 2009).

14. Arnold R. Hirsch, *Making the Second Ghetto: Race and Housing in Chicago, 1940–1960* (Chicago: University of Chicago Press, 1998), 41 (first quotation); Thomas Sugrue, "Crabgrass-Roots Politics: Race, Rights, and the Reaction against Liberalism in the Urban North, 1940–1964," *Journal of American History* 82, no. 2 (September 1995): 557 (second quotation); Gonda, *Unjust Deeds*, 34 (third quotation). Sugrue borrows the phrase, "defensive localism," from Margaret Weir, and uses it as a building block to make his argument in *The Origins of the Urban Crisis: Race and Inequality in Postwar Detroit*, 3rd ed. (Princeton, NJ: Princeton University Press, 2014). See also Margaret Weir, "Urban Poverty and Defensive Localism," *Dissent* 41, no. 3 (Summer 1994): 337–42.

15. James N. Gregory, "The Second Great Migration: A Historical Overview," in *African American Urban History Since World War II*, edited by Kenneth L. Kusmer and Joe W. Trotter (Chicago: University of Chicago Press, 2009), 20–23; Lawrence de Graaf, "Significant Steps on an Arduous Path: The Impact of World War II on Discrimination against African Americans in the West," *Journal of the West* 35, no. 1 (January 1996): 27; Josh Sides, "Battle on the Home Front: African American Shipyard Workers in World War II," *California History* (Fall 1996): 252.

16. *Sixteenth Census of the United States: 1940*, Population, Characteristics of the Population, vol. 2, pt. 1 (Washington, DC: US Government Printing Office, 1943) (hereafter 1940 Census: Population), 630; *Census of Population: 1950*, Census Tract Statistics, Los Angeles, California, vol. 3, chap. 28 (Washington, DC: US Government Printing Office, 1952) (hereafter 1950 Census: Tracts), 9; *Census of Population and Housing: 1960*, Census Tracts, Final Report, Series PHC(1)-82, Los Angeles–Long Beach, Calif., pt. 5 (Washington, DC: US Government Printing Office, 1962) (hereafter 1960 Census: Tracts), 25.

17. For the earliest works on the cases, see Herman H. Long and Charles J. Johnson, *People vs. Property: Race Restrictive Covenants in Housing* (Nashville, TN: Fisk University Press 1947); and Clement E. Vose, *Caucasians Only: The Supreme Court, the NAACP, and the Restrictive Covenants Cases* (Berkeley: University of California Press, 1959). For more recent works, see Jones-Correa, "Origins and Diffusion"; Wendy Plotkin, "'Hemmed In': The Struggle against Racial Restrictive Covenants and Deed Restrictions in Post–WWII Chicago," *Journal of the Illinois State Historical Society* 94, no. 1 (Spring 2001): 39–69; R. Brooks and C. Rose, *Saving the Neighborhood;* and Gonda, *Unjust Deeds*.

18. Kenneth W. Mack, *Representing the Race: The Creation of the Civil Rights Lawyer* (Cambridge: Harvard University Press, 2012), 203 (first quotation); Gonda, *Unjust Deeds*, 120–22, 125–27 (second quotation on 121).

19. For more on racial liberalism in postwar California, see Mark Brilliant, *The Color of America Has Changed: How Racial Diversity Shaped Civil Rights Reform in California, 1941–1978* (New York: Oxford University Press, 2010).

20. For the conservative movement and its efforts to protect residential segregation in Southern California, see Michelle M. Nickerson, *Mothers of Conservatism: Women and the Postwar Right* (Princeton, NJ: Princeton University Press, 2012); and Lisa

McGirr, *Suburban Warriors: The Origins of the New American Right*, 2nd ed. (Princeton, NJ: Princeton University Press, 2015). See also maps of Black and White migration patterns between 1940 and 1980 in Josh Sides, *L.A. City Limits: African American Los Angeles from the Great Depression to the Present* (Berkeley: University of California Press, 2003), 210–14.

21. Beavers, interview by Hopkins (quotations); W. B. Wayt v. George Patee, 205 Cal. 46, 269 Pac. 660 (1928).

22. Robert Fishman, *Bourgeois Utopias: The Rise and Fall of Suburbia* (New York: Basic Books, 1987), chap. 6 (quotation in chapter title). As the city decentralized, the Westside took shape into what historian Scott Kurashige calls "a site for the preservation and renewal of whiteness." See S. Kurashige, *Shifting Grounds*, 2 (quotation).

23. Kenneth T. Jackson, *Crabgrass Frontier: The Suburbanization of the United States* (New York: Oxford University Press, 1985). Since Jackson's work, scholars have challenged the notion that suburban development was a solely White, middle-class phenomenon. See, for instance, Timothy P. Fong, *The First Suburban Chinatown: The Remaking of Monterey Park, California* (Philadelphia: Temple University Press, 1994); Andrew Wiese, *Places of Their Own: African American Suburbanization in the Twentieth Century* (Chicago: University of Chicago Press, 2004); and Charlotte Brooks, *Alien Neighbors, Foreign Friends: Asian Americans, Housing, and the Transformation of Urban California* (Chicago: University of Chicago Press, 2009).

24. Sugrue, in *Origins of Urban Crisis*, popularized the phrase "urban crisis" (first quotation in book title). E. Franklin Frazier, *The Negro Family in the United States* (Chicago: University of Chicago Press, 1939); Daniel Patrick Moynihan, *The Negro Family: The Case for National Action* (Washington, DC: US Government Printing Office, 1965); Oscar Lewis, "The Culture of Poverty," in *On Understanding Poverty: Perspectives from the Social Sciences*, edited by Daniel P. Moynihan (New York: Basic Books, 1969), chap. 7 (second quotation in chapter title); William Julius Wilson, *The Truly Disadvantaged: The Inner City, the Underclass, and Public Policy*, 2nd ed. (Chicago: University of Chicago Press, 2012) (third quotation in book subtitle); Massey and Denton, *American Apartheid*.

25. Sugrue, *Origins of Urban Crisis*, 5 (both quotations). Since Sugrue's work, other scholars have further discussed discriminatory housing measures and their effects on the American landscape. See, for instance, Satter, *Family Properties*; Gonda, *Unjust Deeds*; Richard Rothstein, *The Color of Law: A Forgotten History of How our Government Segregated America* (New York: Liveright Publishing, 2017); and Keeanga-Yamahtta Taylor, *Race for Profit: How Banks and the Real Estate Industry Undermined Black Homeownership* (Chapel Hill: University of North Carolina Press, 2019).

26. Daniel Widener, "'Perhaps the Japanese Are to Be Thanked?' Asia, Asian America, and the Construction of Black California," *Positions* 11, no. 1 (Spring 2003): 143–49; Midori Nishi and Young Il Kim, "Recent Japanese Settlement Changes in the Los Angeles Area," *Yearbook of the Association of Pacific Coast Geographers* 26 (1964): 23.

27. Widener, "Perhaps the Japanese," 148 (quotation); S. Kurashige, *Shifting Grounds*, 37, 49–50.

28. S. Kurashige, *Shifting Grounds*, 187 (first quotation), 205 (second quotation).

29. Flamming, *Bound for Freedom*, 3 (first quotation), 8 (second quotation); Sides, *L.A. City Limits*. See also J. Max Bond, "The Negro in Los Angeles" (PhD diss., University of Southern California, 1936); Lawrence B. de Graaf, "Negro Migration to Los Angeles, 1930 to 1950" (PhD diss., University of California, Los Angeles, 1962);

Lawrence B. de Graaf, Kevin Mulroy, and Quintard Taylor, eds., *Seeking El Dorado: African Americans in California* (Los Angeles: University of Washington Press, 2001).

30. Bart Landry, *The New Black Middle Class* (Berkeley: University of California Press, 1987), 5, 23 (both quotations on 23). In 2018 Landry published *The New Black Middle Class in the Twenty-First Century* (New Brunswick: Rutgers University Press), which examines the changes of the Black middle class since his 1987 book. For studies on the Black middle class leading up to Landry's 1987 study, see Sidney Kronus, *The Black Middle Class* (Columbus, OH: Charles E. Merrill Publishing Company, 1971); Richard B. Freeman, *Black Elite: The New Market for Highly Educated Black Americans* (New York: McGraw-Hill, 1976); David McBride and Monroe H. Little, "The Afro-American Elite, 1930–1940: A Historical and Statistical Profile," *Phylon* 42, no. 2 (2nd Qtr. 1981): 105–19; Sharon M. Collins, "The Making of the Black Middle Class," *Social Problems* 30, no. 4 (April 1983): 369–82; and Thomas J. Durant, Jr., and Joyce S. Louden, "The Black Middle Class in America: Historical and Contemporary Perspectives," *Phylon* 47, no. 4 (4th Qtr. 1986): 253–63.

31. For discussions on education and employment of the early Black middle class, see McBride and Little, "Afro-American Elite," 110–15; and Landry, *New Black Middle Class*, 1987, 38–57. For early references to "the Talented Tenth," see Henry Lyman Morehouse, "The Talented Tenth," *The American Missionary* 50, no. 6 (June 1896): 182–83; and W. E. B. Du Bois, "The Talented Tenth," in *The Negro Problem: A Series of Articles by Representative American Negroes To-day*, edited by Booker T. Washington (New York: James Pott & Company, 1903), 33–75. See also Kevin K. Gaines, *Uplifting the Race: Black Leadership, Politics, and Culture in the Twentieth Century* (Chapel Hill: University of North Carolina Press, 1996); and Martin Summers, *Manliness and Its Discontents: The Black Middle Class and the Transformation of Masculinity, 1900–1930* (Chapel Hill: University of North Carolina Press, 2004).

32. Flamming, *Bound for Freedom*, 8; Quintard Taylor, *In Search of the Racial Frontier: African Americans in the American West, 1528–1990* (New York: W. W. Norton & Company, 1998), 233.

33. See Becky M. Nicolaides, "The Quest for Independence: Workers in the Suburbs," in *Metropolis in the Making: Los Angeles in the 1920s*, edited by Tom Sitton and William Deverell (Berkeley: University of California Press, 2001), 80–91 (quotation on 89); and Becky M. Nicolaides, *My Blue Heaven: Life and Politics in the Working-Class Suburbs of Los Angeles, 1920–1965* (Chicago: University of Chicago Press, 2002), 156–58.

34. Landry, *New Black Middle Class*, 1987, 5–11, 21, 68, 219.

35. Durant and Louden, "Black Middle Class in America," 255–56; S. Collins, "Making of Black Middle Class," 369–74; Landry, *New Black Middle Class*, 1987, 67–78.

36. Summers, *Manliness and Its Discontents*, 6–7 (quotations on 6).

37. Chester Himes, *If He Hollers Let Him Go* (1945; repr., New York: Thunder's Mouth Press, 1986); E. Franklin Frazier, *Black Bourgeoisie*, 3rd ed. (1957; repr., New York: Free Press, 1966); Anastasia C. Curwood, *Stormy Weather: Middle-Class African-American Marriages between the Two World Wars* (Chapel Hill: University of North Carolina Press, 2010), 63–70, 121, 138. Other authors have also taken aim at the Black middle and upper classes, including Mary Pattillo-McCoy, *Black Picket Fences: Privilege and Peril Among the Black Middle Class* (Chicago: University of Chicago Press, 2000); and Lawrence Otis Graham, *Our Kind of People: Inside America's Black Upper Class* (New York: HarperCollins, 2000). For references to Frazier in Los Angeles, see Donald Bogle, *Bright Boulevards, Bold Dreams: The Story of Black Hollywood* (New

York: One World Books, 2005), 267; and Federal Bureau of Investigation, *E. Franklin Frazier: FBI File*, Internet Archive, added date March 4, 2016, https://archive.org/details/E.FranklinFrazierFBIFile.

38. See Graham, *Our Kind of People*, for discussions on Black elite organizations.

39. In the early 2000s, the World Health Organization (WHO) put forth a framework for understanding what has been phrased "quality of life" by describing the "social determinants of health." Besides individual behavioral and genetic risk factors, WHO argues "the conditions in which people are born, grow, live, work, and age" affect their health and well-being. Thus, "in their turn, poor and unequal living conditions are the consequence of poor social policies and programmes, unfair economic arrangements, and bad politics." While the twentieth-century's Black middle class did not have this language or the ensuing research to draw on, they sought to settle in higher quality neighborhoods to improve their and their children's personal and financial welfare. See Commission on Social Determinants of Health, "Closing the Gap in a Generation: Health Equity through Action on the Social Determinants of Health" (Geneva: World Health Organization, 2008), 1 (quotations in this note).

40. Mike Davis, *City of Quartz: Excavating the Future in Los Angeles* (New York: Vintage Books, 1992), 71–74, 102–5, 169–80 (quotations on 105, 170); Robert Gottlieb and Irene Wolt, *Thinking Big: The Story of the* Los Angeles Times*, Its Publishers, and Their Influence on Southern California* (New York: G. P. Putnam's Sons, 1977), 306–21; Max Vorspan and Lloyd P. Gartner, *History of the Jews of Los Angeles* (San Marino: The Huntington Library, 1970), 233–37. See also Eric John Abrahamson, *Building Home: Howard F. Ahmanson and the Politics of the American Dream* (Berkeley: University of California Press, 2013).

CHAPTER 1. DEMARCATING THE WESTSIDE FROM THE EASTSIDE

1. Flamming, *Bound for Freedom*, 221–25; S. Kurashige, *Shifting Grounds*, 50–51; *1900 United States Federal Census* (Provo, UT: Ancestry.com Operations Inc., 2004) (hereafter 1900 Census); "Rich Widow Bride of Young Partner," *Los Angeles Times*, July 13, 1906; "Residence Fight Won by Negroes," *Los Angeles Times*, July 4, 1928; George H. Letteau et al. v. Pauline Ellis, 122 Cal. App. 584 (1932) (quotation).

2. For histories of early California and Los Angeles, see, among others, Kent G. Lightfoot and Otis Parrish, *California Indians and Their Environment: An Introduction* (Berkeley: University of California Press, 2009); Torres-Rouff, *Before L.A.;* Leonard Pitt, *The Decline of the Californios: A Social History of the Spanish-Speaking Californians, 1846–1890* (Berkeley: University of California Press, 1966); and Robert M. Fogelson, *The Fragmented Metropolis: Los Angeles, 1850–1930* (Cambridge: Harvard University Press, 1967).

3. For discussion on the development of the Plaza, see Torres-Rouff, *Before L.A.*, 26–31. For works on the city's early public transit, see Spencer Crump, *Ride the Big Red Cars: How Trolleys Helped Build Southern California*, 4th ed. (Corona del Mar, CA: Trans-Anglo Books, 1970); William A. Myers and Ira L. Swett, *Trolleys to the Surf: The Story of the Los Angeles Pacific Railway* (Glendale, CA: Interurbans, 1976); and William B. Friedricks, *Henry E. Huntington and the Creation of Southern California* (Columbus: Ohio State University Press, 1992). Population data came from the *Sixteenth Census of the United States: 1940*, Population, Number of Inhabitants, vol. 1 (Washington, DC: US Government Printing Office, 1942) (hereafter 1940 Census: Inhabitants), 120.

4. For references to Black Los Angeles's golden era, see Cox, *Central Avenue*, 3; Lonnie G. Bunch, *Black Angelenos: The Afro-American in Los Angeles, 1850–1950* (Los

Angeles: California Afro-American Museum, 1988), 21; and Susan Anderson, "A City Called Heaven: Black Enchantment and Despair in Los Angeles," in *The City: Los Angeles and Urban Theory at the End of the Twentieth Century*, edited by Allen J. Scott and Edward W. Soja (Berkeley: University of California Press, 1996), 340. For a discussion on the city's racial landscape at the turn of the twentieth century, see Flamming, *Bound for Freedom*, chap. 3; and for Jewish settlement, see Vorspan and Gartner, *History of Jews of Los Angeles*, 117–18. Data on Black settlement in late 1800s and early 1900s Los Angeles came from *1880 United States Federal Census* (Provo, UT: Ancestry.com Operations Inc., 2010) (hereafter 1880 Census); 1900 Census.

5. Flamming, *Bound for Freedom*, 222.

6. For the 1908 zoning ordinances, see Los Angeles City Ordinance Number 17135 N.S. (New Series), Los Angeles City Archives; and Los Angeles City Ordinance Number 17136 N.S. (New Series), Los Angeles City Archives.

7. For discussions on the national battle over racial restrictive covenants, see Gonda, *Unjust Deeds*; Vose, *Caucasians Only*; and Massey and Denton, *American Apartheid*. For scholarship on restrictive covenants in Los Angeles, see Lawrence B. de Graaf, "The City of Black Angels: Emergence of the Los Angeles Ghetto, 1890–1930," *Pacific Historical Review* 39 (August 1970): 323–52; Flamming, *Bound for Freedom;* and Sides, *L.A. City Limits*.

8. For discussions on Ceruti, see J. Clay Smith, Jr., *Emancipation: The Making of the Black Lawyer, 1844–1944* (Philadelphia: University of Pennsylvania Press, 1993), 487–88; J. Alexander Somerville, *Man of Color: An Autobiography of Dr. J. Alexander Somerville* (Los Angeles: Lorrin L. Morrison Printing and Publishing, 1949), 81; Delilah L. Beasley, *The Negro Trail Blazers of California* (Los Angeles: Negro Universities Press, 1919), 192–94; and Flamming, *Bound for Freedom*, 143–44. For the quotation from Du Bois, see W. E. B. Du Bois, Editorial, "Southern California," *The Crisis* (July 1913): 131. Black homeownership data are published in Q. Taylor, *In Search Racial Frontier*, 233; S. Kurashige, *Shifting Grounds*, 18–19.

9. "NAACP Announcement for 1926," *California Eagle*, January 22, 1926, 1 (quotation); Flamming, *Bound for Freedom*, 221–25; S. Kurashige, *Shifting Grounds*, 50–51; *Index to Register of Voters, Los Angeles*, 1924, 1926; George H. Letteau et al. v. Pauline Ellis, 122 Cal. App. 584 (1932).

10. Amy S. Greenberg, *A Wicked War: Polk, Clay, Lincoln, and the 1846 U.S. Invasion of Mexico* (New York: Alfred A. Knopf, 2012), xvi, 34–37, 249.

11. Lightfoot and Parrish, *California Indians*, 4–7.

12. Fogelson, *Fragmented Metropolis*, 5–10; Torres-Rouff, *Before L.A.*, 23–26.

13. Fogelson, *Fragmented Metropolis*, 7; Torres-Rouff, *Before L.A.*, 26–29.

14. Torres-Rouff, *Before L.A.*, 29–31; Carlos Manuel Salomon, *Pío Pico: The Last Governor of Mexican California* (Norman: University of Oklahoma Press, 2010), 69–70; John Mack Faragher, *Eternity Street: Violence and Justice in Frontier Los Angeles* (New York: W. W. Norton, 2016), 42–59; Pitt, *The Decline*, 120–21.

15. Jack D. Forbes, "The Early African Heritage of California," in de Graaf, Mulroy, and Taylor, *Seeking El Dorado*, 74–80.

16. See Faragher, *Eternity Street*, entire.

17. Torres-Rouff, *Before L.A.*, 139, 145, 208; Scott Zesch, *The Chinatown War: Chinese Los Angeles and the Massacre of 1871* (New York: Oxford University Press, 2012), 9–12.

18. César López, "Lost in Translation: From Calle de los Negros to Nigger Alley to North Los Angeles Street to Place Erasure, Los Angeles 1855–1951," *Southern California*

Quarterly 94, no. 1 (Spring 2012): 28–38 (quotation on 37); Torres-Rouff, *Before L.A.*, 211–12; Zesch, *Chinatown War*, entire; Faragher, *Eternity Street*, chaps. 28–29.

19. Torres-Rouff, *Before L.A.*, 139–41, 219–27 (quotation on 223–24). See also Richard Griswold del Castillo, *The Los Angeles Barrio, 1850–1890: A Social History* (Berkeley: University of California Press, 1979), chap. 5.

20. Torres-Rouff, *Before L.A.*, 11, 141–45, 208–15; Jan Loomis, *Westside Chronicles: Historic Stories of West Los Angeles* (Charleston, SC: The History Press, 2012), 24–26; Vorspan and Gartner, *History of Jews of Los Angeles*, 55.

21. *Seventh Census of the United States: 1850* (Washington, DC: Robert Armstrong, Public Printer, 1853), 982; *Tenth Census of the United States:* Statistics of the Population (Washington, DC: US Government Printing Office, 1882) (hereafter 1880 Census: Statistics), 51, 382; *Tenth Census of the United States: 1880*, vol. 19, pt. II, Report on the Social Statistics of Cities (Washington, DC: US Government Printing Office, 1887), 779–80 (quotation on 780); Jennifer L. Hochschild and Brenna Marea Powell, "Racial Reorganization and the United States Census 1850–1930: Mulattoes, Half-Breeds, Mixed Parentage, Hindoos, and the Mexican Race," *Studies in American Political Development* 22 (Spring 2008): 59–66, 75–77. Historian David A. Hollinger dubbed America's five-part demographic structure as the "ethnoracial pentagon." See Hollinger, *Postethnic America: Beyond Multiculturalism* (New York: Basic Books, 1995) (quotation in this note on 8).

22. Deverell, *Whitewashed Adobe*, book title (first quotation), 5 (second quotation, italics removed), 7 (third quotation), 26, 29.

23. For discussions on boosterism, see Kevin Starr, *Inventing the Dream: California through the Progressive Era* (New York: Oxford University Press, 1985); William Deverell and Douglas Flamming, "Race, Rhetoric, and Regional Identity: Boosting Los Angeles, 1880–1930," in *Power and Place in the North American West*, edited by Richard White and John M. Findlay (Seattle: University of Washington Press, 1999), 117–43; and Mike Davis, *City of Quartz*. For reference to the transcontinental railroad, see Flamming, *Bound for Freedom*, 24–25.

24. 1880 Census: Statistics, 416; *Eleventh Census: 1890*, pt. 1, Report on Population of the United States (Washington, DC: US Government Printing Office, 1895) (hereafter 1890 Census, pt. 1), 404, 437, 442, 444; Nishi and Kim, "Recent Japanese Settlement Changes," 23. Because the census did not distinguish the Jewish population, Vorspan and Gartner used Jewish sources. See Vorspan and Gartner, *History of Jews of Los Angeles*, 287–88.

25. Pat Adler, *The Bunker Hill Story* (Glendale, CA: La Siesta Press, 1963), entire; Christina Rice and Emma Roberts, "Introduction," in *Bunker Hill in the Rearview Mirror: The Rise, Fall, and Rise Again of an Urban Neighborhood*, edited by Christina Rice and Emma Roberts (Los Angeles: Photo Friends of the Los Angeles Public Library, 2015), 9, 12–15; Merry Ovnick, "Early Suburb," in Rice and Roberts, *Bunker Hill in Rearview Mirror*, 19–37; Crump, *Ride Big Red Cars*, 19–20; Scott L. Bottles, *Los Angeles and the Automobile: The Making of the Modern City* (Berkeley: University of California Press, 1987), 28.

26. Crump, *Ride Big Red Cars*, 27–38; Fogelson, *Fragmented Metropolis*, 86–87; Myers and Swett, *Trolleys to Surf*, 11–13.

27. Myers and Swett, *Trolleys to Surf*, 13; Kevin Starr, *California: A History* (New York: Random House, 2007), 147–48.

28. Myers and Swett, *Trolleys to Surf*, 17–21; Friedricks, *Henry E. Huntington*, 9, 87.

29. Myers and Swett, *Trolleys to Surf*, 16, 21–28, 33–53; Friedricks, *Henry E. Huntington*, 9, 87.

30. Cox, *Central Avenue*, 3; Bunch, *Black Angelenos*, 21.

31. Lawrence B. de Graaf and Quintard Taylor, "Introduction: African Americans in California History, California in African American History," in de Graaf, Mulroy, and Taylor, *Seeking El Dorado*, 15; 1940 Census: Inhabitants, 120; 1880 Census.

32. Flamming, *Bound for Freedom*, 21–23 (quotation on 21).

33. Flamming, *Bound for Freedom*, 21–24, 118–19.

34. de Graaf and Taylor, "Introduction," 15; Vorspan and Gartner, *History of Jews of Los Angeles*, 117; 1940 Census: Inhabitants, 120; 1900 Census.

35. Flamming, *Bound for Freedom*, 25 (quotation); 1900 Census.

36. 1900 Census; Vorspan and Gartner, *History of Jews of Los Angeles*, 117–18.

37. Myers and Swett, *Trolleys to Surf*, 40–42; Alison Rose Jefferson, "African American Leisure Space in Santa Monica: The Beach Sometimes Known as the 'Inkwell,'" *Southern California Quarterly* 91, no. 2 (Summer 2009): 161–69; Alison Rose Jefferson, *Living the California Dream: African American Leisure Sites during the Jim Crow Era* (Lincoln: University of Nebraska Press, 2020), 75–85.

38. A. Jefferson, *Living California Dream*, 31–36; Jan Dennis, *Images of America: Manhattan Beach, California* (Chicago: Arcadia Publishing, 2001), 27–28, 44–45 (quotation on 44); "Colored People's Resort Meets with Opposition," *Los Angeles Times*, June 27, 1912; Flamming, *Bound for Freedom*, 271–75; Lawrence Culver, *The Frontier of Leisure: Southern California and the Shaping of Modern America* (New York: Oxford University Press, 2010), 71.

39. Friedricks, *Henry E. Huntington*, chaps. 2–4; Martin Wachs, "The Evolution of Transportation Policy in Los Angeles," in *The City: Los Angeles and Urban Theory at the End of the Twentieth Century*, edited by Allen J. Scott and Edward W. Soja (Berkeley: University of California Press, 1998), 108.

40. Myers and Swett, *Trolleys to Surf*, 52–53 (map); Bottles, *Los Angeles and Automobile*, 4, 40; Wachs, "Evolution of Transportation Policy," 118–19; Mike Davis, *City of Quartz*, 118 (quotation).

41. A. Jefferson, "African American Leisure Space," 169–71, 174–82; A. Jefferson, *Living California Dream*, 36–37, 39–42, 87–94; Culver, *Frontier of Leisure*, 71–72; Jackie Robinson, *Baseball Has Done It* (Philadelphia: J. B. Lippincott Company, 1964), 27–29 (quotations on 29). For information on the NAACP's battle over access to public swimming pools, see Flamming, *Bound for Freedom*, 216–18. For more on Robinson and his childhood in Pasadena, see Arnold Rampersad, *Jackie Robinson: A Biography* (New York: Alfred A. Knopf, 1997), chap. 2.

42. Plessy v. Ferguson, 163 U.S. 537 (1896) (quotation).

43. In re Lee Sing, 43 Fed. 359 C.C.N.D. Cal. (1890). See also Charles J. McClain, *In Search of Equality: The Chinese Struggle Against Discrimination in Nineteenth Century America* (Berkeley: University of California Press, 1994), 224 (quotation), chap. 9; C. Brooks, *Alien Neighbors, Foreign Friends*, 21–24; C. W. Y., "Enforcement of Race Restrictive Covenants and the Constitution," *Virginia Law Review* 34, no. 3 (April 1948): 307; and Loren Miller, *The Petitioners: The Story of the Supreme Court of the United States and the Negro* (New York: Pantheon Books, 1966), 246.

44. Gandolfo v. Hartman et al., 49 Fed. 181 C.C.S.D. Cal. (1892) (both quotations). See also Vose, *Caucasians Only*, 5–6; Charles Abrams, *Forbidden Neighbors: A Study of Prejudice in Housing* (New York: Harper & Brothers, 1955), 217; L. Miller, *The*

Petitioners, 251; C. W. Y., "Enforcement," 307–8; "Real Property, Restrictive Covenants, Prohibition against Use or Occupation by Racial Groups," *Virginia Law Review* 33, no. 5 (September 1947): 659; and D. O. McGovney, "Racial Residential Segregation by State Court Enforcement of Restrictive Agreements, Covenants or Conditions in Deeds is Unconstitutional," *California Law Review* 33, no. 1 (March 1945): 7.

45. For a discussion on the beginning of the City Beautiful movement, see Jon A. Peterson, *The Birth of City Planning in the United States, 1840–1917* (Baltimore: Johns Hopkins University Press, 2003), chap. 5. For reference to the LARB, see Marc A. Weiss, *The Rise of the Community Builders: The American Real Estate Industry and Urban Land Planning* (New York: Columbia University Press, 1987), 79–84.

46. Los Angeles City Ordinance Number 17135 N.S. (New Series), Los Angeles City Archives; Los Angeles City Ordinance Number 17136 N.S. (New Series), Los Angeles City Archives (quotation). See also Weiss, *Rise of Community Builders*, 83–84; and Peterson, *Birth of City Planning*, 309–10.

47. Weiss, *Rise of Community Builders*, 80, 83–84 (quotation on 83); M. Christine Boyer, *Dreaming the Rational City: The Myth of American City Planning* (Cambridge: MIT Press, 1983), 181. See also K. Jackson, *Crabgrass Frontier*, 241–42.

48. Buchanan v. Warley, 245 U.S. 60 (1917). See also Michael J. Klarman, *From Jim Crow to Civil Rights: The Supreme Court and the Struggle for Racial Equality* (New York: Oxford University Press, 2004), 79–83, 142–44; Massey and Denton, *American Apartheid*, 187–88; Vose, *Caucasians Only*, 3–4, 51–52; L. Miller, *The Petitioners*, 246–51; McGovney, "Racial Residential Segregation," 30–33; and Jones-Correa, "Origins and Diffusion," 548, 550–51. Jones-Correa identifies cities that continued to enact race-based zoning ordinances after *Buchanan* and discusses the reasons racial restrictive covenants did not simply replace those ordinances.

49. Village of Euclid, Ohio v. Ambler Realty Co., 272 U.S. 365 (1926) (quotation). See also Freund, *Colored Property*, 81–87. One year before the *Euclid* decision, a portion of Los Angeles's comprehensive zoning ordinance was tested when George and Francis Miller tried to build a four-family apartment building in an area zoned for single- and two-family dwellings. But in *Miller v. Board of Public Works of the City of Los Angeles*, the California Supreme Court upheld the ordinance. See Miller v. Board of Public Works of the City of Los Angeles, 195 Cal. 477, 234 P. 381 (1925).

50. Title Guarantee & Trust Co. v. Garrott, 42 Cal. App. 152 (1919) (quotation). The Los Angeles Superior Court cited Cal. Civil Code ß 711 in the verdict. See also Willis O. Tyler, "Defense Attorney Analyzes Historic 'Sugar Hill' Decision," *California Eagle*, December 13, 1945, 1, 24; and Flamming, *Bound for Freedom*, 153–55. While Tyler, in "Defense Attorney Analyzes," placed Garrott's address on West Fifty-Seventh Street, the *Los Angeles City Directory*, 1918, 1920, and *1920 United States Federal Census* (Provo, UT: Ancestry.com Operations, Inc., 2010), recorded the Garrotts on West Fifty-Ninth Place.

51. J. Smith, *Emancipation*, 485–87; Beasley, *Negro Trail Blazers*, 197; Joseph Clement Bates, ed., *History of the Bench and Bar of California* (San Francisco: Bench and Bar Publishing Company, 1912), 536–37; Title Guarantee & Trust Co. v. Garrott, 42 Cal. App. 152 (1919). See also Tyler, "Defense Attorney Analyzes," 1, 24; and Flamming, *Bound for Freedom*, 153–55.

52. "Race Restriction War to the Highest Court," *Los Angeles Times*, May 23, 1916 (both quotations); Los Angeles Investment Co. v. Gary, 181 Cal. 680 (1919). See also Flamming, *Bound for Freedom*, 155–56, 218–21; Tyler, "Defense Attorney Analyzes," 1,

24; L. Miller, *The Petitioners*, 252; and McGovney, "Racial Residential Segregation," 8–9. For Gary's address and occupation, see the *Los Angeles City Directory*, 1917, 1918.

53. "Race Restriction War"; Los Angeles Investment Co. v. Gary (both quotations, italics added). See also Flamming, *Bound for Freedom*, 155–56, 218–21; Tyler, "Defense Attorney Analyzes," 1, 24; L. Miller, *The Petitioners*, 252; and McGovney, "Racial Residential Segregation," 8–9.

54. Janss Investment Co. v. Walden, 196 Cal. 753, 239 Pac. 34 (1925) (quotation).

55. Corrigan et al. v. Buckley, 55 App. DC 30, 299 F. 899 (1924). See also Vose, *Caucasians Only*, 17–19; Mark Robert Schneider, *"We Return Fighting": The Civil Rights Movement in the Jazz Age* (Boston: Northeastern University Press, 2002), 286–87; L. Miller, *The Petitioners*, 252–53; and McGovney, "Racial Residential Segregation," 34–36.

56. Corrigan et al. v. Buckley, 271 U.S. 323 (1926) (quotation). See also Vose, *Caucasians Only*, 50–54; Schneider, *"We Return Fighting,"* 287–90; L. Miller, *The Petitioners*, 253–56; Klarman, *From Jim Crow to Civil Rights*, 144–46; William B. Hixson, Jr., *Moorfield Storey and the Abolitionist Tradition* (New York: Oxford University Press, 1972), 142–44; and Gregg D. Crane, *Race, Citizenship, and Law in American Literature* (New York: Cambridge University Press, 2002), chap. 5.

57. de Graaf, "City of Black Angels," 329; de Graaf and Taylor, "Introduction," 13–14. See also McClain, *In Search of Equality*.

58. For census data, see 1890 Census, pt. 1, 70, 442; *Fourteenth Census of the United States: 1920*, Composition and Characteristics of the Population by States, vol. 3 (Washington, DC: US Government Printing Office, 1922) (hereafter 1920 Census), 109, 114. For discussions on Los Angeles's Chinatowns, see Torres-Rouff, *Before L.A.*, 234–39; Roberta S. Greenwood, *Down by the Station: Los Angeles Chinatown, 1880–1933* (Los Angeles: UCLA Institute of Archaeology, 1996), 10–20; and Jenny Cho and the Chinese Historical Society of Southern California, *Images of America: Chinatown in Los Angeles* (Charleston, SC: Arcadia Publishing, 2009), 7–8.

59. William D. Estrada, "Los Angeles' Old Plaza and Olvera Street: Imagined and Contested Space," *Western Folklore* 58, no. 2 (Winter 1999): 107–22; R. Greenwood, *Down by the Station*, 35–40; Cho, *Images of America*, 7–8, 55 (quotation on 55); Jenny Cho and the Chinese Historical Society of Southern California, *Chinatown and China City in Los Angeles* (Charleston, SC: Arcadia Publishing, 2011), 37.

60. 1890 Census, pt. 1, 70, 442; 1920 Census, 109, 114; Nishi and Kim, "Recent Japanese Settlement Changes," 23.

61. Lon Kurashige, *Japanese American Celebration and Conflict: A History of Ethnic Identity and Festival, 1934–1990* (Berkeley: University of California Press, 2002), 16–24 (quotations on 17, 18).

62. S. Kurashige, *Shifting Grounds*, 40–42; L. Kurashige, *Japanese American Celebration*, 19–20. See also Naomi Hirahara and Geraldine Knatz, *Terminal Island: Lost Communities of Los Angeles Harbor* (Santa Monica: Angel City Press, 2015).

63. S. Kurashige, *Shifting Grounds*, 42; Mark Wild, *Street Meeting: Multiethnic Neighborhoods in Early Twentieth-Century Los Angeles* (Berkeley: University of California Press, 2005), 27–30; Vorspan and Gartner, *History of Jews of Los Angeles*, 94, 118–19, 153.

64. Wild, *Street Meeting*, 30–31; George J. Sánchez, *Becoming Mexican American: Ethnicity, Culture, and Identity in Chicano Los Angeles, 1900–1945* (New York: Oxford University Press, 1993), 13, 70–77; Ricardo Romo, *East Los Angeles: History of a Barrio*, 7th paperback ed. (Austin: University of Texas Press, 1998), 42–50, 61, 67–88.

65. Flamming, *Bound for Freedom*, chap. 3; Vorspan and Gartner, *History of Jews of Los Angeles*, 118.

66. Flamming, *Bound for Freedom*, 252–53, 261–62, 291–93; Bette Yarbrough Cox, "The Evolution of Black Music in Los Angeles, 1890–1955," in de Graaf, Mulroy, and Taylor, *Seeking El Dorado*, 256–60. For further discussion on the Somerville Hotel, see J. A. Somerville, *Man of Color*, 122–27. J. A. and Vada Somerville lost their hotel in 1929 after the stock market crash and the onset of the Great Depression.

67. Nicolaides, *My Blue Heaven*, 57–58, 156–58 (first quotation on 156; second quotation on 158); S. Kurashige, *Shifting Grounds*, 42–44; Wild, *Street Meeting*, 13.

68. "Legal Committee of L.A. Forum Makes its Report," *California Eagle*, October 21, 1927, 5 (first and second quotations); "Residence Fight Won"; George H. Letteau et al. v. Pauline Ellis, 122 Cal. App. 584 (1932) (third quotation); S. Kurashige, *Shifting Grounds*, 50–51.

CHAPTER 2. BLACK SETTLEMENT IN WEST JEFFERSON

1. Ivan J. Houston, interview by Ranford B. Hopkins (Los Angeles: UCLA Library, Center for Oral History Research, 1986–87), UCLA/OL; Norman O. Houston, interview by R. Donald Brown, October 27, 1966, The Lawrence de Graaf Center for Oral and Public History, California State University, Fullerton (COPH), 1–2; Beavers, interview by Hopkins; "Norman O. Houston," *Who's Who in Colored Los Angeles—California* (published by *California Eagle*, 1930–31), SCL, 83; Flamming, *Bound for Freedom*, 254.

2. N. Houston, interview by Brown, 2–7, 8–9; George A. Beavers, interview by R. Donald Brown, October 15, 1966, COPH, 1–3; Beavers, interview by Hopkins. For documentation on Golden State's value placed on providing white-collar jobs to Blacks, see William Nickerson, "Employment Opportunities," Before the Nineteenth Annual Session, National Negro Insurance Association, July 12, 1939, NF/GSM, Box 1, Folder 15, SCL. See also Flamming, *Bound for Freedom*, 258. The company's original name was Golden State Guarantee Fund Insurance Company of Los Angeles.

3. Scott Kurashige, "Between 'White Spot' and 'World City': Racial Integration and the Roots of Multiculturalism," in *A Companion to Los Angeles*, edited by William Deverell and Greg Hise (Malden, MA: Wiley-Blackwell, 2010), 57.

4. On zoning laws in Eastside and Westside Los Angeles, see Wild, *Street Meeting*, 53–56; and S. Kurashige, *Shifting Grounds*, 26. On racial restrictive covenants, see Vose, *Caucasians Only*, 7; and Massey and Denton, *American Apartheid*, 36. For scholarship on covenants in Los Angeles, see de Graaf, "City of Black Angels," 346; Sides, *L.A. City Limits*, 17; S. Kurashige, *Shifting Grounds*, 48–51; and Mike Davis, *City of Quartz*, 160–64.

5. Like most Los Angeles enclaves, the designation and boundaries defining West Jefferson vary by author. In "The Long Black Line," Mary Jane Hewitt describes the borders of what she calls the "West Side" as Normandie and Western Avenues, Jefferson Boulevard and Thirty-Fifth Place. See *California History* 60, no. 1 (Spring 1981): 12 (quotation in this note). Although Lawrence de Graaf calls it "the western area," and Donald Bogle calls it the "Westside," both historians center the area around Jefferson Boulevard and between Normandie and Western Avenues. See de Graaf, "City of Black Angels," 333 (quotation in this note); and Bogle, *Bright Boulevards, Bold Dreams*, 30–31 (quotation in this note on 30). In *Bound for Freedom*, Douglas Flamming defines a small section between Vermont and Western Avenues, Jefferson and Exposition Boulevards, as "the West Jefferson district" (quotation on 97). S. Kurashige, in *Shifting*

Grounds, locates West Jefferson within a larger section that includes the Crestmore tract (57–59). While this study recognizes Flamming's identified section as West Jefferson, as does Kurashige, it discusses the larger area's prominent Black residents and key developments related to the Black homeowners' rights movement.

6. Hirsch, *Making Second Ghetto*, 41 (first quotation); Sugrue, "Crabgrass-Roots Politics," 557 (second quotation); "Are You Sleeping?," *California Eagle*, February 12, 1926; S. Kurashige, *Shifting Grounds*, 59–60; "West Side Citizens Organize Defense," *California Eagle*, November 20, 1925, 1; "West Side Crackers," *California Eagle*, September 11, 1925, 6 (third quotation); "Improvement Ass'n. Notes: Article from 'West Jefferson Press' Brought to Attention of Board," *California Eagle*, April 30, 1926, 6 (fourth quotation).

7. Bond, "The Negro in Los Angeles," 45 (quotations).

8. For references to this paragraph and the one above, see "West Side Citizens Organize Defense," *California Eagle*, November 20, 1925, 1 (first quotation); "Ends West Side Restriction Fight," *California Eagle*, March 12, 1926, 8; "Improvement Ass'n Notes: Progressive Federation Pledges Support to Protect Negro West Side," *California Eagle*, June 4, 1926, 6; "Improvement Association Notes: West Side Association Meets Monday to Hear Full Details of Crestmore Situation," *California Eagle*, June 11, 1926, 10 (second quotation); "Improvement Association Notes," *California Eagle*, June 18, 1926, 6; W. B. Wayt et al. v. George Patee et al., 205 Cal. 46 (1928) (third and fourth quotations); "Right of Racial Ban Sustained: Property Restriction Upheld by State Supreme Court," *Los Angeles Times*, October 21, 1928, A6; S. Kurashige, *Shifting Grounds*, 60–61. For records on the Kinchlows, see *1910 United States Federal Census* (Lehi, UT: Ancestry.com Operations, Inc., 2006); *1930 United States Federal Census* (Provo, UT: Ancestry.com Operations Inc., 2002) (hereafter 1930 Census); *1940 United States Federal Census* (Provo, UT: Ancestry.com Operations Inc., 2012) (hereafter 1940 Census); *Los Angeles City Directory*, 1926, 1927; *Index to Register of Voters, Los Angeles*, 1960. Whites in Westside communities north of Washington Boulevard, particularly Pico Heights and Hollywood, also fought against Japanese in-migration. See John Modell, *The Economics and Politics of Racial Accommodation: The Japanese of Los Angeles, 1900–1942* (Urbana: University of Illinois Press, 1977), 56–66.

9. Flamming, *Bound for Freedom*, 66, 253–54; de Graaf, "City of Black Angels," 328–29; Bunch, *Black Angelenos*, 29; Lonnie G. Bunch III, "'The Greatest State for the Negro': Jefferson L. Edmonds, Black Propagandist of the California Dream," in de Graaf, Mulroy, and Taylor, *Seeking El Dorado*, 132–33. For studies on Black-owned insurance companies outside of Los Angeles, see Merah Steven Stuart, *An Economic Detour: A History of Insurance in the Lives of American Negroes* (College Park, MD: McGrath Publishing Co., 1969); and Alexa Benson Henderson, *Atlanta Life Insurance Company: Guardian of Black Economic Dignity* (Tuscaloosa: University of Alabama Press, 1990).

10. H. Claude Hudson, interview by R. Donald Brown, November 29, 1966, COPH, 4–5; Louie Robinson, "Richest Negro Family: Blodgetts of L.A. Have Savings-Loan Fortune," *Ebony* (December 1962): 151, 153–56, 158, 160–62; Flamming, *Bound for Freedom*, 239–42; Wendell P. Gladden, Jr., "'Home-Seekers' Form Loan Society in California," *Chicago Defender*, April 12, 1924; "A Sign of Real Progress: Coast Association Records A Remarkable Growth," *Pittsburgh Courier*, April 3, 1926; Charles Detrick, *Thirty-first Annual Report of the Building and Loan Commissioner of the State of California: 1924* (Sacramento: California State Printing Office, 1924), 68; A. E. Falch, *Thirty-third*

Annual Report of the Building and Loan Commissioner of the State of California: 1926 (Sacramento: California State Printing Office, 1926), 122.

11. "Golden State Insurance Company," *Who's Who in Colored Los Angeles—California* (published by *California Eagle*, 1930–31), SCL, 99; N. Houston, interview by Brown, 2–7, 8–9; Beavers, interview by Brown, 1–3; Beavers, interview by Hopkins; Flamming, *Bound for Freedom*, 261–62, 292–93.

12. "Golden State Insurance Company," *Who's Who*, 99 (quotation); Fourteenth Annual Statement of Golden State Mutual Life Insurance Company, December 31, 1938, NF/GSM, Box 2, Folder 4, SCL.

13. Flamming, *Bound for Freedom*, 64; S. Kurashige, *Shifting Grounds*, 43–46; Wild, *Street Meeting*, 98–99; I. Houston, interview by Hopkins; "Norman O. Houston," *Who's Who*, 83. For records of the Houstons' home situated west of Central Avenue, at 950 East Forty-First Street, see "Los Angeles, Calif. Crisis Report—Los Angeles Branch—Sept. 1929"; "Membership Report Blank," November 20, 1930; "Membership Report Blank," November 15, 1931; "Membership Report Blank," December 15, 1933, NAACP/LA, Reel 2, UCLA/MC.

14. I. Houston, interview by Hopkins (quotations). See also *Los Angeles City Directory*, 1938, 1939, and 1940.

15. Eva Anderson, interview by author, July 31, 2006, Los Angeles, California (quotations); Anthony F. Nicholas, interview by author, July 19, 2007, Los Angeles, California; Bogle, *Bright Boulevards, Bold Dreams*, 269–70, 273–74. Eddie and Eva Anderson married in 1955 (see Anderson, interview by author).

16. Bogle, *Bright Boulevards, Bold Dreams*, 152, 163–64, 264–65; *Los Angeles City Directory*, 1938, 1939, 1940, 1942; *Index to Register of Voters, Los Angeles*, 1940, 1944, 1946, 1948; 1940 Census; Beavers, interview by Hopkins; Meghan E. Cunningham, *Bill "Bojangles" Robinson: Dancer* (New York: Cavendish Square, 2017), 38–44; "The House that Blodgett Built," *California Eagle*, November 10, 1938 (article includes photo of the Robinsons' home). The Huntington Library has digital photos of the interior and exterior living spaces of the Robinsons' house. See Maynard L. Parker photographer, "Robinson, Bill [Bojangles], residence," Huntington Digital Library, HL.

17. *Los Angeles City Directory*, 1942; Bogle, *Bright Boulevards, Bold Dreams*, 202–4, 264–65; Donald Bogle, *Dorothy Dandridge: A Biography* (New York: Amistad Press, 1997), 202–4; Nicholas, interview by author.

18. Lloyd H. Fisher, "The Problem of Violence: Observations on Race Conflict in Los Angeles," n.d. (ca. 1945–46), John Randolph Haynes Papers, Box 230, Folder "American Council on Race Relations," UCLA/SC, 8–10 (quotations on 9-10).

19. Fisher, "The Problem," 6, 8–10, 16 (quotations on 9-10). For population data, see also tracts 204–5 and 211–15, which generally comprise the area between Vermont and Arlington Avenues, Adams and Exposition Boulevards, in *Sixteenth Census of the United States: 1940*, Population and Housing, Statistics for Census Tracts, Los Angeles–Long Beach, Calif. (Washington, DC: US Government Printing Office, 1942) (hereafter 1940 Census: Tracts), 5.

20. de Graaf, "Significant Steps," 27; Sides, "Battle on Home Front," 252. For biographical information on Himes and literary analysis of his works, see James Sallis, *Chester Himes: A Life* (New York: Walker & Company, 2001), 76–83; Gilbert H. Muller, *Chester Himes* (Boston: Twayne Publishers, 1989), chap. 2; and Stephen F. Milliken, *Chester Himes: A Critical Appraisal* (Columbia: University of Missouri Press, 1976), chap. 3.

21. Himes, *If He Hollers*, 27–30, 60–63.

22. Himes, *If He Hollers*, 48–52, 168 (first quotation on 51; second quotation on 51-52; third and fourth quotations on 168, italics in original). For the teachings and criticism of Booker T. Washington, see Booker T. Washington, *Up From Slavery: Authoritative Text, Contexts, and Composition History, Criticism*, edited by William L. Andrews (New York: Norton, 2006); and Michael Rudolph West, *The Education of Booker T. Washington: American Democracy and the Idea of Race Relations* (New York: Columbia University Press, 2006). For further criticism on the Black middle class, see Frazier, *Black Bourgeoisie*; Pattillo-McCoy, *Black Picket Fences*; and Graham, *Our Kind of People*.

23. Himes, *If He Hollers*, 48 (quotation).

24. Himes, *If He Hollers*, 49–51 (first and second quotations on 49; third quotation on 50). On West Jefferson, see S. Kurashige, *Shifting Grounds*, 58–59; and Flamming, *Bound for Freedom*, 97.

25. Karl Holton, "Notes on the Negro Districts in Los Angeles," Deteriorating Zone Committee, January 1940, LAUL, Box 1, Folder 14, UCLA/SC, 1–2 (all quotations).

26. Bogle, *Bright Boulevards, Bold Dreams*, xiv (quotation); S. Kurashige, *Shifting Grounds*, 58. For population data, see tracts 204–5 and 211–15, which generally comprise the area between Vermont and Arlington Avenues, Adams and Exposition Boulevards, in 1940 Census: Tracts, 5; 1950 Census: Tracts, 23–24. For a more nuanced analysis of the roles of Black entertainers, see Donald Bogle, *Toms, Coons, Mulattoes, Mammies, and Bucks: An Interpretive History of Blacks in American Films* (New York: Viking Press, 1973).

27. For discussions on Chandler's vision of Los Angeles as a so-called white spot, see Wild, *Street Meeting*, 38–39 (quotation); and Dennis McDougal, *Privileged Son: Otis Chandler and the Rise and Fall of the L.A. Times Dynasty* (New York: Perseus Books, 2001), 105–6 (quotation). For a discussion on the Ku Klux Klan in Los Angeles, see Flamming, *Bound for Freedom*, 196, 200–11.

28. Willis O. Tyler, "The N.A.A.C.P. and the Work for 1927," *California Eagle*, January 14, 1927, NAACP/LA, Reel 3, UCLA/MC (quotation). For examples of more cases in California that upheld restrictive covenants see Janss Investment Co. v. Walden, 196 Cal. 753, 239 Pac. 34 (1925); W. B. Wayt v. George Patee, 205 Cal. 46, 269 Pac. 660 (1928); and Shideler v. Roberts, 69 Cal. App 2nd 549, 160 P. 2nd 67 (1945). See C. W. Y., "Enforcement," 308–10, for more references to cases upholding restrictive covenants around the country.

29. Jones-Correa, "Origins and Diffusion," 563–67.

30. Flamming, *Bound for Freedom*, 239–42; George Perry, "New York Banking Interests Involved In Pacific Coast Race Restriction Litigation," in George P. Johnson, interview by Elizabeth Dixon (Los Angeles: UCLA Library, Center for Oral History Research, 1967–68), UCLA/OL; Paul J. Brindel, "Ask Courts to Protect their Homes: Fight Move to Condemn Land," *Chicago Defender*, May 15, 1926; George Perry, "California Superior Court Declares Million Dollar Bond Issue Valid in Negro Realty Condemnation Sale," *Pittsburgh Courier*, November 19, 1927 (quotation). For a discussion on Central Park, see Roy Rosenzweig and Elizabeth Blackmar, *The Park and the People: A History of Central Park* (Ithaca: Cornell University Press, 1992), chap. 3.

31. A. Jefferson, *Living California Dream*, 105–16, 184–94; Flamming, *Bound for Freedom*, 348–49.

32. Sidney P. Dones, "Avoid Hard Times: Mr. Dones Tells How: Timely Article on a Timely Subject," *California Eagle*, April 18, 1914 (quotation).

33. Sidney Dones, "Avoid Hard Times."

34. A. Jefferson, *Living California Dream*, 194–95, 201–11; Flamming, *Bound for Freedom*, 348–49.

35. K. Jackson, *Crabgrass Frontier*, 195–201 (quotation on 201); Massey and Denton, *American Apartheid*, 51–53; Amy E. Hillier, "Redlining and the Home Owners' Loan Corporation," *Journal of Urban History* 29, no. 4 (May 2003): 397–402; Dan Immergluck, *Credit to the Community: Community Reinvestment and Fair Lending Policy in the United States* (Armonk, NY: M.E. Sharpe, 2004), 92–94.

36. K. Jackson, *Crabgrass Frontier*, 197. The Los Angeles HOLC maps and their respective area descriptions are available online at LaDale C. Winling, *Mapping Inequality: Redlining in New Deal America*, Los Angeles, CA, accessed September 24, 2021, https://dsl.richmond.edu/panorama/redlining/#loc=12/33.9478/-118.4228&opacity=0.8&city=los-angeles-ca. For the noted area descriptions, see areas D52 for Central Avenue (first and second quotations), C122 for West Jefferson (third quotation), C121 for West Adams Heights (fourth quotation), A42 for Hancock Park (fifth quotation), and A37 for Beverly Hills (sixth quotation).

37. Federal Housing Administration, *Underwriting Manual: Underwriting and Valuation Procedure Under Title II of the National Housing Act* (Washington, DC: US Government Printing Office, 1936), part II, section 2, 228, 233; K. Jackson, *Crabgrass Frontier*, 203–5; Massey and Denton, *American Apartheid*, 53–55; Hillier, "Redlining and Loan Corporation," 402–7; Immergluck, *Credit to the Community*, 93–96.

38. Ira Katznelson, *When Affirmative Action Was White: An Untold History of Racial Inequality in Twentieth-Century America* (New York: W. W. Norton & Company, 2005), chap. 5; Josh Sides, "A Simple Quest for Dignity: African American Los Angeles since World War II," in *City of Promise: Race & Historical Change in Los Angeles*, edited by Martin Schiesl and Mark M. Dodge (Claremont, CA: Regina Books, 2006), 120–21; Beavers, interview by Brown, 11.

39. Attorney Loren Miller explained some of the devices Blacks used, especially in the 1930s to invalidate restrictive covenants in court and move into neighborhoods of their choice. See Loren Miller, interview by Lawrence B. de Graaf, April 29, 1967, COPH, 25. One of the more documented cases happened to Dr. Ossian Sweet and his family when they moved into an all-White, wealthy suburb of Detroit, Michigan, in the mid-1920s. Sweet and ten other African Americans were acquitted of murder after they defended themselves against a mob that attacked the Sweets' home. See Kevin Boyle, *Arc of Justice: A Saga of Race, Civil Rights, and Murder in the Jazz Age* (New York: Henry Holt and Company, 2004).

40. In *The History of the Normandie Program Area* (Prepared for the Community Redevelopment Agency of the City of Los Angeles, September 1, 1969), Patricia Adler finds the streetcar was an important factor in the development of West Adams, which connected downtown to the area in 1891 (p. 9). For Bunker Hill's history, see Adler, *Bunker Hill Story*. For references to Beverly Hills, see Walter Wagner, *Beverly Hills: Inside the Golden Ghetto* (New York: Grosset & Dunlap, 1976), 15; and David Weddle, *Among the Mansions of Eden: Tales of Love, Lust, and Land in Beverly Hills* (New York: William Morrow, 2003), 38–39.

41. Patricia Adler, *The History of the Normandie Program Area* (Los Angeles: Prepared for the Community Redevelopment Agency of the City of Los Angeles, 1969), 8–9; Carey McWilliams, "The Evolution of Sugar Hill," *Script* (March 1949): 24; Harry Anderson and Mary Wormley, *Historic West Adams: Now & Then: Remembering a Legacy* (Los Angeles: West Adams Heritage Association, 1987), 4.

42. McWilliams, "Evolution of Sugar Hill," 24; Michael Regan, *Mansions of Los Angeles* (Los Angeles: Regan Publishing Company, 1965), 21; Don Sloper, *Images of America: Los Angeles's Chester Place* (Charleston, SC: Arcadia Publishing, 2006), 9. Before moving to Los Angeles, Silent served as a federal judge in Arizona. He bought the property in West Adams from Nathan Vail, a New Jersey sea captain, and subdivided the surrounding area into Chester Place. After the land conveyance, Silent and Vail worked together investing in land development companies around Southern California, including in Inglewood and Redondo Beach (Sloper, *Images*, 9). For more on the West Adams district, see Suzanne Tarbell Cooper, Don Lynch, and John G. Kurtz, *Images of America: West Adams* (Charleston, SC: Arcadia Publishing, 2008).

43. Margaret Leslie Davis, *Dark Side of Fortune: Triumph and Scandal in the Life of Oil Tycoon Edward L. Doheny* (Berkeley: University of California Press, 1998), 8–9, 20–23, 26–27, 46–47 (quotation on 47). See also Regan, *Mansions of Los Angeles*, 27.

44. "Berkeley Square: Magnificent Mansions to Occupancy Sightly Lots in Fashionable Park Section," *Los Angeles Times*, December 26, 1909, V1 (quotation).

45. For homes prices, see "City Attracts Home Builders," *Los Angeles Times*, November 29, 1908, V1; "Merchant's Home Magnificent: In Berkeley Square Is One of City's Finest," *Los Angeles Times*, November 22, 1908, V1; "Home of Lee A. Phillips, Hunt & Burns, Architects: Will Be Show Place," *Los Angeles Times*, March 2, 1913, VI1. "McAdoo Buyer of Berkeley Square Home," *Los Angeles Times*, April 26, 1922; Regan, *Mansions of Los Angeles*, 49; "Oil Man Plans Fine Mansion: Berkeley Square Home to Be of Early Tudor Type," *Los Angeles Times*, January 29, 1911, V24.

46. McWilliams, "Evolution of Sugar Hill," 24 (quotation).

47. Fishman, *Bourgeois Utopias*, 167 (both quotations).

48. Adler, *History of Normandie Program Area*, 2; McWilliams, "Evolution of Sugar Hill," 24–25. See also the tract map of West Adams Heights in Book 2, 53–54, RRCC. Adams and Jefferson Boulevards, and Western and Normandie Avenues, bounded the Charles Victor Hall tract. In 1906 Conservative Life Insurance Company merged with Pacific Mutual Life Insurance Company, and Cochran became Pacific Mutual's first president (McWilliams, "Evolution of Sugar Hill," 24).

49. Anne S. Henshaw, "Frederick Hastings Rindge," *American National Biography Online*, February 2000, https://doi.org/10.1093/anb/9780198606697.article.2000865 (behind paywall); Cecilia Rasmussen, *L.A. Unconventional: The Men and Women Who Did L.A. Their Way* (Los Angeles: Los Angeles Times, 1998), 117–18; McWilliams, "Evolution of Sugar Hill," 25–26.

50. McWilliams, "Evolution of Sugar Hill," 28.

51. McWilliams, "Evolution of Sugar Hill," 28 (quotation); Wild, *Street Meeting*, 34; Romo, *East Los Angeles*, 85; Vorspan and Gartner, *History of Jews of Los Angeles*, 117–19; Grant Deed between Norman O. Houston, Edythe A. Houston, and Naomi Freeney, 1938, Book 16249, 36, RRCC. For reference on his marriage to Edythe, see I. Houston, interview by Hopkins. For documentation of the Houstons' address on South Hobart Boulevard, see *Los Angeles City Directory*, 1942. See also assembly district 231 in 1930 Census.

52. McWilliams, "Evolution of Sugar Hill," 28 (quotation); Vorspan and Gartner, *History of Jews of Los Angeles*, 90, 99, 153, 158–59; Neal Gabler, *An Empire of Their Own: How the Jews Invented Hollywood* (New York: Anchor Books, 1989), 273–76. For the quintessential conservative argument on the myth of multiculturalism, see David O. Sacks and Peter A. Thiel, *The Diversity Myth: Multiculturalism and Political Intolerance on Campus* (Oakland, CA: The Independent Institute, 1998).

53. Allan R. Ellenberger, *Ramon Novarro: A Biography of the Silent Film Idol, 1899–1968; With a Filmography* (Jefferson, NC: McFarland & Company, 1999), 5–14, 24. See also André Soares, *Beyond Paradise: The Life of Ramon Novarro* (Jackson: University of Mississippi Press, 2010).

54. Ellenberger, *Ramon Novarro*, 57–60 (first quotation on 57; second quotation on 59), 66, 70; S. Kurashige, *Shifting Grounds*, 42 (third quotation); Romo, *East Los Angeles*, 85; McWilliams, "Evolution of Sugar Hill," 28 (fourth quotation). Novarro shows up in assembly district 231 in 1930 Census.

55. McWilliams, "Evolution of Sugar Hill," 28. For more discussion on homeowners' improvement associations, see Massey and Denton, *American Apartheid*, 35–36.

56. "Real Property Restrictions Agreement," 1 (first and second quotations); McWilliams, "Evolution of Sugar Hill," 28–29 (third quotation on 29; fourth quotation on 28); Grant Deed between Norman O. Houston, Edythe A. Houston, and Naomi Freeney, 36. Freeney had a history of earning income by renting her properties to tenants. In 1930, eight years before her sale to the Houstons, according to the federal census, Freeney owned and lived at 2292 West Twenty-Second Street, on the West Adams Heights tract's western edge, with son, Phillip, daughter, Jane, and six White tenants. The years following her sale to the Houstons, she and Jane had moved between that house and her property at 2286 West Twenty-Second Street. See 1930 Census; *Los Angeles City Directory*, 1939, 1940, 1941.

57. McWilliams, "Evolution of Sugar Hill," 28–29 (first quotation on 28; second quotation on 29); I. Houston, interview by Hopkins. 1940 Census recorded the Houstons at their 1225 West Thirty-Sixth Street address. *Los Angeles City Directory*, 1939, and *Index to Register of Voters, Los Angeles*, 1940, listed the names and occupations of the White tenants, which included a few actors, who lived at the Houstons' Hobart property.

58. McWilliams, "Evolution of Sugar Hill," 25–26, 28; Malcolm Thurburn, "Restrictive Covenants: Homes Handsome Faultless," *Now*, Second half of December 1944, 4 (quotation), ACLU/SC, Box 30, Folder 3, UCLA/SC.

59. McWilliams, "Evolution of Sugar Hill," 29. Isabel Cryer, spouse of former Los Angeles mayor George E. Cryer, signed a restrictive covenant after the Houstons purchased property in the area, and then in 1942, sold her home to African American actor Louise Beavers. See "Real Property Restrictions Agreement," 1; Deed of Trust with Assignment of Rents between Louise Beavers and Isabel G. Cryer, 1942, Book 19161, 221, RRCC. Jennie V. Robinson, White homeowner of 2045 South Hobart Boulevard, also signed a restrictive covenant to her property a few years before selling it to African American Sydnetta Dones Smith. See "Real Property Restrictions Agreement," 2; Ane Marie Anderson et al. v. Earl F. Auseth et al., Complaint (for Declaratory Relief and Injunction), L.A. No. 484808, filed April 15, 1943, 2, LASC.

60. Anderson v. Auseth, Complaint, L.A. No. 484808, filed April 15, 1943, 9 (quotation), LASC.

61. Deed of Trust with Assignment of Rents between James Lloyd Crawford, Hattie McDaniel Crawford, and Marian Earle Stainback, 1941, Book 18984, 319–20, RRCC. For the city's median value of owner-occupied dwellings, see *Sixteenth Census of the United States: 1940*, Housing, vol. 3, pt. 2 (Washington, DC: US Government Printing Office, 1943), 85.

62. "Hattie McDaniel Becomes Bride, 'This Time Forever,'" *Los Angeles Times*, March 22, 1941; "Earl J. Morris in Grand Town: Day and Night," *California Eagle*, January 29, 1942; "The Trip," *Denver Star*, June 20, 1942. Descriptions of McDaniel and

Crawford's house vary. *The Denver Star*, for example, describes the Sugar Hill mansion with seventeen rooms, whereas Bogle, in *Bright Boulevards, Bold Dreams*, records thirteen rooms (p. 266).

63. Jill Watts, *Hattie McDaniel: Black Ambition, White Hollywood* (New York: Amistad, 2005), 17, 19, 28–29, 32–34, 56–57. See also Watts, *Hattie McDaniel*, 292, fn. 40, for a discussion on McDaniel's birth year.

64. Watts, *Hattie McDaniel*, 54, 77–80. For McDaniel's filmography see Watts, *Hattie McDaniel*, 283–86. For documentation of Etta Goff's residences on East Forty-Sixth Street and Portland Street, see 1930 Census. For records of McDaniel's residence at 2177 West Thirty-First Street, see *Los Angeles City Directory*, 1939, 1940. See also Carlton Jackson, *Hattie: The Life of Hattie McDaniel* (Lanham, MD: Madison Books, 1990).

65. Don Ryan, "A Personality Study," *Los Angeles Times*, February 11, 1940, I3, 8 (quotations), 10, 12, 20.

66. "The Trip"; Watts, *Hattie McDaniel*, 210–11; Bogle, *Bright Boulevards, Bold Dreams*, 266.

67. Bogle, *Bright Boulevards, Bold Dreams*, 265–67 (first quotation on 265); Watts, *Hattie McDaniel*, 212 (second quotation); Harry Levette, "City Mourns Death of Hattie McDaniel," *California Eagle*, October 30, 1952. For Frazier's critique, see Frazier, *Black Bourgeoisie*.

68. Watts, *Hattie McDaniel*, 139 (second quotation), 164 (first quotation), 174; Bogle, *Toms, Coons, Mulattoes*, 82 (third and fourth quotations); C. Jackson, *Life of Hattie McDaniel*, 99–101; "McDaniel, Hattie," Academy Awards Acceptance Speech Database, accessed November 14, 2021, aaspeechesdb.oscars.org (fifth quotation). Kimberlé Crenshaw coined the term "intersectionality" and created its framework to identify the multiple, overlapping axes such as race, class, and gender, that complicate, reinforce, and perpetuate oppression and discrimination. For her first major work on the topic, see Kimberlé Crenshaw, "Demarginalizing the Intersection of Race and Sex: A Black Feminist Critique of Antidiscrimination Doctrine, Feminist Theory and Antiracist Politics," *University of Chicago Legal Forum* 1989, 1, article 8 (1989): 139–67.

69. Grant Deed between Leslie U. King, Mamie King, and Douglas S. Mueller, 1941, Book 18414, 342, RRCC. For reference to the Kings' West Jefferson address, 2122 West Twenty-Ninth Street, see "Membership Report Blank," NAACP/LA, December 1938, Reel 3, UCLA/MC.

70. Deed of Trust with Assignment of Rents between Horace P. Clark, Vera Clark, and Robert Elliott, 1941, Book 18766, 381–82, RRCC; *Los Angeles City Directory*, 1938, 1939, 1942, 1943, 1945; Bogle, *Bright Boulevards, Bold Dreams*, 80; Cox, *Central Avenue*, 30.

71. Grant Deed between Ethel Burke Waters, Louis C. Venator, and Dorothy C. Venator, 1941, Book 18989, 115, RRCC; Ethel Waters with Charles Samuels, *His Eye Is on the Sparrow* (Garden City, NY: Doubleday & Company, 1951), 1 (first quotation), 8, 15, 24, 259 (second quotation).

72. Deed of Trust with Assignment of Rents between Louise Beavers and Isabel G. Cryer, 221; Bogle, *Toms, Coons, Mulattoes*, 63–67; Bogle, *Bright Boulevards, Bold Dreams*, 259, 262. See "Real Property Restrictions Agreement" for the covenant on Cryer's home.

73. Bogle, *Bright Boulevards, Bold Dreams*, 260; Frances Williams, interview by Karen Anne Mason and Richard Cándida Smith, 1992–93 (Los Angeles: UCLA Library, Center for Oral History Research, 1992–93), UCLA/OL (quotation).

74. Deed of Trust between Juan Tizol, Rose Tizol, and Inez L. Syminton, 1942, Book 19414, 321–22, RRCC; Deed of Trust between William E. Bailey and Edith B. Bailey, 1942, Book 19608, 299–300, RRCC; Deed of Trust (Purchase Money) with Assignment of Rents between William E. Bailey, Edith B. Bailey, and Winifred W. Coberly, 1942, Book 19652, 261–62, RRCC; Deed of Trust with Assignment of Rents between W. Clyde Allen, Aulette D. Allen, and Daisy Rose Montgomery, 1942, Book 19693, 303–4, RRCC. For more on the Tizols, see Basilio Serrano, *Juan Tizol: His Caravan through American Life and Culture* (San Bernardino, CA: Xlibris, 2012), chaps. 4 and 5.

75. J. A. Somerville, *Man of Color*, 21–34, 49–55, 63–67, 71, 97; Rasmussen, *L.A. Unconventional*, 124; J. Alexander and Vada Somerville, interview by Lawrence B. de Graaf, June 10, 1967, COPH, 23, 26.

76. J. A. Somerville, *Man of Color*, 81, 122–27; Rasmussen, *L.A. Unconventional*, 125; Bunch, *Black Angelenos*, 32; letter from Vada J. Somerville to Robert W. Bagnall, April 12, 1924, NAACP/LA, Reel 1, UCLA/MC; letter from Director of Branches to Vada J. Somerville, May 15, 1924, NAACP/LA, Reel 1, UCLA/MC. For the Somervilles' Jefferson Boulevard address, see *Los Angeles City Directory*, 1938, 1939, 1940, and 1942. For the deed on their West Adams Heights house, see Deed of Trust with Assignment of Rents between Vada J. Somerville and Anne B. Shine, 1943, Book 20128, 335–36, RRCC. The contract shows that the Somervilles paid $10,000 for their home in 1942. In 1967 J. A. Somerville told Lawrence de Graaf they paid $12,000 for the home (J. Alexander and Vada Somerville, interview by de Graaf, 32).

77. For references to the Taylors, see *Shreveport, Louisiana, City Directory*, 1931; *Index to Register of Voters, Los Angeles*, 1948. For the Mitchells, see Deed of Trust, Courtland G. Mitchell and Rosa Lee Mitchell, 1945, Book 21647, 167–68, RRCC; *Los Angeles City Directory*, 1943, 1945. For the Greens, see *Index to Register of Voters, Los Angeles*, 1944. For the Sissles, see *Index to Register of Voters, Los Angeles*, 1944, 1946. For photos of the Sissles' home, see Thurburn, "Restrictive Covenants," 5. Several sources, many of which reported on the Sugar Hill case, include more names of Black residents. Three good articles include "Celebrities in Spotlight as 'Sugar Hill' Trial Begins," *California Eagle*, December 6, 1945, 4; Tyler, "Defense Attorney Analyzes," 1, 24; and "Negro Property Owners Protest," *Los Angeles Times*, December 6, 1945. A2.

78. For the 1940 data, see census tract 208, blocks 1–14, 18–19, and 25 in *Sixteenth Census of the United States: 1940*, Housing Block Statistics, Los Angeles, California (Washington, DC: US Government Printing Office, 1942) (hereafter 1940 Census: Block Statistics), 141; *Census of Housing: 1950*, Block Statistics, Los Angeles, California, vol. 5, pt. 100 (Washington, DC: US Government Printing Office, 1952) (hereafter 1950 Census: Block Statistics), 161. The introduction of the 1940 census explains, "Nonwhite," or what I call people of color, "comprises Negro, Indian, Chinese, Japanese, Filipino, Hindu, Korean, or other nonwhite race, and persons of mixed white and nonwhite parentage." See 1940 Census: Block Statistics, 4. The 1950 census uses a similar definition. See 1950 Census: Block Statistics, 2. The five "nonwhites" listed in the 1940 census may include those noted by McWilliams.

79. Thurburn, "Restrictive Covenants," 4 (quotations); *Index to Register of Voters, Los Angeles*, 1944. (See photo of the Miles's home on 4.)

80. For the city's 1950 average property value, see 1950 Census: Block Statistics, 3. For Sugar Hill's 1950 property value, see census tract 208 in 1950 Census: Tracts, 158. Sugar Hill makes up roughly three-quarters of 1950 tract 208 and 1960 tract 2215, both of which border Washington and Adams Boulevards, and Western and Normandie

Avenues. For data at the block level, see 1950 Census: Block Statistics, 161. McDaniel lived on block 13 of tract 208, and the Houstons, the Clarks, and Beavers lived on block 12.

81. 1920 Census, 118; 1940 Census: Population, 629.

CHAPTER 3. THE LEGAL DEMISE OF RACIAL RESTRICTIVE COVENANTS

1. *Anderson v. Auseth, Complaint*, 2–4, 9 (first quotation), LASC; Ane Marie Anderson v. Earl F. Auseth, Answer, L.A. No. 484808, filed May 25, 1943, 4–5, LASC; Mack, *Representing the Race*, 203 (second quotation). See also "Real Property Restrictions Agreement," 2. For works on Sidney P. Dones, see Flamming, *Bound for Freedom*, 120–22; Frank Lincoln Mather, ed., *Who's Who of the Colored Race: A General Biographical Dictionary of Men and Women of African Descent*, vol. 1 (Chicago: Memento Edition, 1915), 93; and Beasley, *Negro Trail Blazers*, 205. For the HOLC's language of desirability, see K. Jackson, *Crabgrass Frontier*, 197–98, 363 (fn. 28). For Sugar Hill Whites' reasoning against Black in-migration, see also McWilliams, "Evolution of Sugar Hill," 29.

2. The complaints, answers, demurrers, cross-complaints, and judgment to the cases are located under Ane Marie Anderson v. Earl F. Auseth, L.A. No. 484808, filed June 19, 1948, LASC. The eight proceedings are (1) Anderson v. Auseth (L.A. No. 484808); (2) Francis L. Smith v. Omelia Craigen Crawford (L.A. No. 500054); (3) Victor J. Maricq v. James Sumner Pickett, Jr. (L.A. No. 500055); (4) Leila Daniels v. Hallie D. Johnson (L.A. No. 500056); (5) Josefa H. Tolhurst v. Nellie B. Venerable (L.A. No. 500057); (6) Edna I. White v. Russell T. Smith (L.A. No. 500058); (7) Elmer C. Weber v. Arthur Twyne, Sr. (L.A. No. 503450); and (8) Fred B. McComas v. Truman R. Lott (L.A. No. 503976). For information on Francis L. Smith, see *Index to Register of Voters, Los Angeles*, 1944; and WAHPA notebook, September 24, 1944, minutes, author's collection (from the Houston and Taylor families). Special thanks to the Houston and Taylor families, who have preserved the WAHPA notebook, which includes meeting minutes, membership lists, and documentation of the group's work from 1943 through 1947. The Los Angeles city directories include the Sugar Hill residents whose names headed the lawsuit. The 1939 directory listed plaintiff Ane Marie Anderson (spelled Andersen in the directory) as a stenographer residing at 2077 South Hobart Boulevard. The 1942 directory listed defendant Earl F. Auseth as a salesman living with his spouse, Helen Auseth, nearby at 2045 South Hobart Boulevard. See *Los Angeles City Directory*, 1939, 1942.

3. Brilliant, *Color of America Has Changed*, 7; Daniel Martinez HoSang, *Racial Propositions: Ballot Initiatives and the Making of Postwar California* (Berkeley: University of California Press, 2010), 14.

4. Brilliant, *Color of America Has Changed*, 9 (first two quotations); HoSang, *Racial Propositions*, 7 (third quotation).

5. de Graaf and Taylor, "Introduction," 27–30, 33 (for data); de Graaf, "Negro Migration to Los Angeles," 131. For a discussion on the effects of the Great Migration on Los Angeles, see Sides, *L.A. City Limits*, chap. 2.

6. Horace R. Cayton, "America's 10 Best Cities for Negroes," *Negro Digest* 5 (October 1947): 4–7, 9–10 (quotation on 9).

7. Several California newspapers reported on the case, including the *Los Angeles Times*, *California Eagle*, and *Los Angeles Sentinel*. For examples of articles in publications based outside the state, see "U.N. Cited by Negroes in Appeal for Homes," *New York Times*, October 3, 1946, 38; George Streators, "Negro Home Needs Rise as Coast

Issue," *New York Times*, April 27, 1947; Lawrence LaMarr, "Film Stars Face Eviction from West Coast Homes," *Chicago Defender*, October 7, 1944; "Victory on Sugar Hill," *Time*, December 17, 1945; Loren Miller, "Covenants in the Bear Flag State," *The Crisis* 53, no. 5 (May 1946), 138–40, 155; "Negroes Cite U.N. to End Segregation," *New York Herald*, ca. 1946, NAACP Papers, pt. 5; and Loren Miller, "Supreme Court Covenant Decision—An Analysis," *The Crisis* 55, no. 9 (September 1948): 265–66, 285.

8. Douglas Flamming, "Becoming Democrats: Liberal Politics and the African American Community in Los Angeles, 1930–1965," in de Graaf, Mulroy, and Taylor, *Seeking El Dorado*, 279–90; Robert W. Kenny, interview by Doyce B. Nunis, Jr. (Los Angeles: UCLA Library, Center for Oral History Research, 1960–61), UCLA/OL (quotation).

9. Flamming, "Becoming," 279–90. The Commission on Interracial Progress later adopted the name the Los Angeles County Committee on Human Relations, and then the Los Angeles County Commission on Human Relations. See also John Anson Ford, *Thirty Explosive Years in Los Angeles County* (San Marino, CA: Huntington Library, 1961).

10. Tom Sitton, *Los Angeles Transformed: Fletcher Bowron's Urban Reform Revival, 1938–1953* (Albuquerque: University of New Mexico Press, 2005), xv (quotation), chap. 1. For works on race riots in 1943, see Eduardo Obregón Pagán, *Murder at the Sleepy Lagoon: Zoot Suits, Race, & Riot in Wartime L.A.* (Chapel Hill: University of North Carolina Press, 2003); Mauricio Mazón, *The Zoot-Suit Riots: The Psychology of Symbolic Annihilation* (Austin: University of Texas, 1984); Edward J. Escobar, *Race, Police, and the Making of a Political Identity: Mexican Americans and the Los Angeles Police Department, 1900–1945* (Berkeley: University of California Press, 1999); Janet L. Abu-Lughod, *Race, Space, and Riots in Chicago, New York, and Los Angeles* (New York: Oxford University Press, 2007); Sugrue, *Origins of Urban Crisis;* Dominic J. Capeci, *The Harlem Riot of 1943* (Philadelphia: Temple University Press, 1977); and Nat Brandt, *Harlem at War: The Black Experience in World War II* (Syracuse, NY: Syracuse University Press, 1996).

11. For works on Los Angeles as a wartime manufacturing center, see Sides, "Battle on Home Front," 251; Sides, "A Simple Quest," 111; and de Graaf and Taylor, "Introduction," 27. For a discussion on Randolph and Executive Order 8802, see Paula F. Pfeffer, *A. Philip Randolph, Pioneer of the Civil Rights Movement* (Baton Rouge: Louisiana State University Press, 1990), 47–50, 89–91. Randolph's pressuring of President Roosevelt serves as one of many examples of the efforts against racial discrimination in the 1940s. African Americans won steps toward the desegregation of the armed forces. The Congress of Racial Equality (CORE), founded in 1942, used nonviolent direct action in protests. NAACP and Urban League membership also rose throughout the decade. See Harvard Sitkoff, *The Struggle for Black Equality, 1954–1992* (New York: Hill and Wang, 1993), 11–12. For works on the second Great Migration and its impact on Los Angeles, see de Graaf and Taylor, "Introduction," 27–30, 33 (for data); de Graaf, "Negro Migration to Los Angeles," 131; and Sides, *L.A. City Limits*, chap. 2. Historian Marilynn S. Johnson also examines the impact of World War II and the second Great Migration on Northern California. See Marilynn S. Johnson, *The Second Gold Rush: Oakland and the East Bay in World War II* (Berkeley: University of California Press, 1993).

12. de Graaf, "Significant Steps," 29–30; S. Kurashige, *Shifting Grounds*, 40–42, 158–61; Wild, *Street Meeting*, 24–25.

13. Abu-Lughod, *Race, Space, and Riots*, 199–203; Patricia Rae Adler, "Watts: From Suburb to Black Ghetto" (PhD diss., University of Southern California, 1977), chap. 10;

Wild, *Street Meeting*, 13; Josh Sides, "Straight into Compton: American Dreams, Urban Nightmares, and the Metamorphosis of a Black Suburb," *American Quarterly* 56, no. 3 (September 2004): 585 (first quotation), 603 (fn. 8; second quotation); 1950 Census: Tracts, 49–50 (Lynwood tracts 526-A, 526-B, 526-C, and 535-D). See also Sides, *L.A. City Limits*, 210–11 (census maps); and Nicolaides, *My Blue Heaven*.

14. Dorothy W. Baruch, "Sleep Comes Hard," *Nation*, January 27, 1945, 95–96 (first quotation on 95; second and third quotations on 96); Charles B. Spaulding, "Housing Problems of Minority Groups in Los Angeles County," *Annals of the American Academy of Political and Social Science* 248 (November 1946): 221–24; de Graaf, "Significant Steps," 30; de Graaf and Taylor, "Introduction," 29–30; and Sitton, *Los Angeles Transformed*, 69–70.

15. Don Parson, *Making a Better World: Public Housing, the Red Scare, and the Direction of Modern Los Angeles* (Minneapolis: University of Minneapolis Press, 2005), 1–9, 13–25; Don Parson, "'Houses for the Rich Were also for the Birds': Designing a Better World," in *Public Los Angeles: A Private City's Activist Futures*, edited by Roger Keil and Judy Branfman (Athens: University of Georgia Press, 2019), 56–58, 61–82.

16. Parson, *Making a Better World*, 32, 34–36; Parson, "Houses for the Rich," 61–82.

17. Parson, *Making a Better World*, 57, 69, 72, 76–77; Sitton, *Los Angeles Transformed*, 69–70, 112–14; S. Kurashige, *Shifting Grounds*, 135–44, 154, 163–64; Beavers, interview by Brown, ix, 17–32; Beavers, interview by Hopkins.

18. Midori Nishi, "Japanese Settlement in the Los Angeles Area," *Yearbook of the Association of Pacific Coast Geographers* 20 (1958): 41–42, 44–45; S. Kurashige, *Shifting Grounds*, 164–73; L. Kurashige, *Japanese American Celebration*, 110–16; "Negro Restriction Case Goes to Supreme Court," *Los Angeles Times*, June 7, 1946; "City Briefs: Curb on Japs Upheld," *Los Angeles Times*, June 21, 1946.

19. Adler, "Watts," 310 (for data), chap. 5 (transition during World War II). See also Keith E. Collins, *Black Los Angeles: The Maturing of the Ghetto, 1940–1950* (Saratoga, CA: Century Twenty One Publishing, 1980); and de Graaf, "City of Black Angels," 323–52. Located south of Watts, Compton became predominantly Black in the 1950s, but city dwellers did not view the area as a ghetto until the 1970s. Other factors—including White flight, deterioration of the business district, annexation politics, deindustrialization, loss of blue-collar jobs, and the emergence of street gangs—gave rise to blight. See Sides, "Straight into Compton."

20. Sitton, *Los Angeles Transformed*, 71–72; Kevin Allen Leonard, *The Battle for Los Angeles: Racial Ideology and World War II* (Albuquerque: University of New Mexico Press, 2006), 157, 159; S. Kurashige, *Shifting Grounds*, 164–69. For works on the Mexican American experience in Los Angeles and the zoot suit attacks, see Pagán, *Murder at the Sleepy Lagoon;* Mazón, *Zoot-Suit Riots;* and Escobar, *Race, Police, and the Making*.

21. WAHPA notebook, March 28, 1943, minutes, 5–6, author's collection (from the Houston and Taylor families).

22. WAHPA notebook, 1943 membership list, 1; April 11, 1943, minutes, 7–8; May 23, 1943, minutes, 17; constitution and bylaws, loose pages at front of notebook, author's collection (from the Houston and Taylor families) (all quotations). WAHPA first mentioned concluding its meeting with a prayer in March 28, 1943, minutes, 6, and a mizpah in May 2, 1943, minutes, 10.

23. WAHPA notebook, May 2, 1943, minutes, 9–10 (quotation on 9); May 4, 1943, minutes, 11; May 6, 1943, minutes, 12; May 7, 1943, minutes, 13–14; October 12, 1944, minutes, 36; "Legal Assessments Paid By," 250, author's collection (from the Houston and Taylor families).

24. Miller, interview by de Graaf, March 3, 1967, 1–5 (first quotation on 2), 8–10 (second quotation on 10); Flamming, *Bound for Freedom*, 302–3; Arnold Rampersad, *The Life of Langston Hughes*, vol. 1: 1902–1941, *I, Too, Sing America* (New York: Oxford University Press, 2002), 236–51; Mack, *Representing the Race*, 181–95. See also Kenneth W. Mack, "Dissent and Authenticity in the History of American Racial Politics," in *Dissenting Voices in American Society: The Role of Judges, Lawyers, and Citizens*, edited by Austin Sarat (New York: Cambridge University Press, 2012), 105–43; and Amina Hassan, *Loren Miller: Civil Rights Attorney and Journalist* (Norman: University of Oklahoma Press, 2015).

25. Miller, interview by de Graaf, March 3, 1967, 8–9 (quotation on 9); Miller, interview by de Graaf, April 29, 1967, 8; Mack, *Representing the Race*, 194–95. See also J. Smith, *Emancipation*, 485–89.

26. Mack, *Representing the Race*, 196–97, 200–202; Hassan, *Loren Miller*, 104–5, 126–28; Effie L. O'Rourke v. Roy Teeters, 63 Cal. App. 2d 349, 146 P. 2d 983 (1944); Joseph James v. Marinship Corporation, 25 Cal. 2d 721, 155 P. 2d 329 (1944). Miller also took on unpopular issues. For instance, as amicus curiae he defended the Communist Party's desire to participate in the primary elections against Los Angeles County administrators. See Communist Party of the United States of America v. Paul Peek, 20 Cal. 2d 536, 127 P. 2d 889 (1942).

27. Hassan, *Loren Miller*, 107–8, 111–23; Miller, interview by de Graaf, March 3, 1967, 8–9; Miller, interview by de Graaf, April 29, 1967, 8. See also Charlotta A. Bass, *Forty Years: Memoirs from the Pages of a Newspaper* (Los Angeles: Charlotta A. Bass, 1960), 102.

28. Title Guarantee & Trust Co. v. Garrott, 42 Cal. App. 152 (1919); W. B. Wayt v. George Patee, 205 Cal. 46, 269 Pac. 660 (1928). For more of Miller's covenant cases in the early 1940s, including one that involved Hattie McDaniel's brother, Sam McDaniel, on South Van Ness Avenue in West Jefferson, in 1941, see Hassan, *Loren Miller*, 132–34.

29. Hazel Fairchild v. Ross H. Raines, 24 Cal. 2d 818 (1944) (quotations). See also David Delaney, *Race, Place, and the Law, 1836–1948* (Austin: University of Texas Press, 1998), 164–67.

30. For Bailey's, Allen's, and Taylor's work, see the entire WAHPA notebook. For references to Beavers's, McDaniel's, and Green's roles, see WAHPA notebook, March 28, 1943, minutes, 5–6; May 23, 1943, minutes, 18, author's collection (from the Houston and Taylor families). For membership lists, see WAHPA notebook, 1, 252–55, author's collection (from the Houston and Taylor families).

31. WAHPA notebook, September 24, 1944, minutes, 32–34 (first and second quotations on 32; third, fourth, and fifth quotations on 33; sixth quotation on 34); October 12, 1944, minutes, 36–37, author's collection (from the Houston and Taylor families).

32. WAHPA notebook, October 29, 1944, minutes, 38–39 (first, second, and third quotations on 39); November 26, 1944, minutes, 41–42 (fourth and fifth quotations on 41); January 25, 1945, minutes, 47; February 25, 1945, minutes, 51, author's collection (from the Houston and Taylor families).

33. WAHPA notebook, March 25, 1945, minutes, 52–53 (first, second, third, and fourth quotations on 52); May 27, 1945, minutes, 55–56 (fifth and sixth quotations on 55), author's collection (from the Houston and Taylor families).

34. Vose, *Caucasians Only*, 50–64; Mack, *Representing the Race*, 203 (quotation); Hassan, *Loren Miller*, 142; Gonda, *Unjust Deeds*, 70–71, 103–14. For Miller's correspondence with attorneys and organizations across the country, see LMP, Boxes 6, 7, HL. For

more on the July 1945 NAACP meeting, see Mark V. Tushnet, *Making Civil Rights Law: Thurgood Marshall and the Supreme Court, 1936–1961* (New York: Oxford University Press, 1994), 88–89; and Rev. Bernard J. Sheil and Loren Miller, *Racial Restrictive Covenants* (Chicago: Chicago Council Against Racial and Religious Discrimination, 1946), ACLU/SC, Box 32, Folder 4, UCLA/SC.

35. WAHPA notebook, September 23, 1945, minutes, 57–58 (first quotation on 57; second quotation on 58); October 28, 1945, minutes, 59 (third quotation); November 25, 1945, minutes, 61, author's collection (from the Houston and Taylor families).

36. "Celebrities in Spotlight," 4 (quotation). See also "Negro Property," A2; and "Victory."

37. "Celebrities in Spotlight," 4 (quotation); "Negro Owners Win Contest on Occupancy," *Los Angeles Sentinel*, December 7, 1945; Tyler, "Defense Attorney Analyzes," 1, 24; "Victory." See also letter from Loren Miller to Thurgood Marshall, December 6, 1945, NAACP Papers, pt. 5; and Hassan, *Loren Miller*, 142.

38. "Celebrities in Spotlight," 4 (quotation).

39. "Clarke, Thurmond," *History of the Federal Judiciary*, Federal Judicial Center, accessed September 24, 2021, https://www.fjc.gov/history/judges/clarke-thurmond.

40. Ane Marie Anderson v. Earl F. Auseth, Judgment, L.A. No. 484808, filed December 18, 1945, 2–3, LASC; Gonda, *Unjust Deeds*, 84–86. For Clarke's remarks, see Anderson v. Auseth, Appellants' Opening Brief, L.A. No. 19759, filed July 1, 1946, 5 (both quotations), LALL; Letter from Loren Miller to Thurgood Marshall, December 12, 1945, NAACP Papers, pt. 5; and "The full text of his ruling," n.d., NAACP Papers, pt. 5 (also both quotations).

41. Letter from Loren Miller to Andrew D. Weinberger, January 1, 1946, LMP, Box 3, Folder 1, HL (both quotations). See also Letter from Loren Miller to Willis M. Graves, December 11, 1945, LMP, Box 5, Folder 2, HL.

42. Harold I. Kahen, "Validity of Anti-Negro Restrictive Covenants: A Reconsideration of the Problem," *University of Chicago Law Review* 12, no. 2 (February 1945): 198–213 (first quotation on 211); McGovney, "Racial Residential Segregation," 5–39 (second quotation from article title, italics added). See also Roger J. Traynor, "Dudley Odell McGovney," *California Law Review* 35, no. 3 (September 1947): 329; Vose, *Caucasians Only*, 68–71; and Gonda, *Unjust Deeds*, 84–85.

43. Anderson v. Auseth, Appellants' Opening Brief, 5 (first quotation); Christopher Paul Moore, *Fighting for America: Black Soldiers—The Unsung Heroes of World War II* (New York: One World, 2005), xiii; Watts, *Hattie McDaniel*, 208–10; Donald Bogle, *Heat Wave: The Life and Career of Ethel Waters* (New York: HarperCollins, 2011), 364, 371–72; "Sugar Hill Defendants' Generosity to GI's Told," *Los Angeles Sentinel*, December 10, 1945 (second quotation). For further discussion of the effects of World War II on the United States, see Bruce Zuckerman, Zev Garber, Jeremy Schoenberg, and Lisa Ansell, eds., *The Impact of the Holocaust in America: The Jewish Role in American Life, An Annual Review*, vol. 6 (West Lafayette, IN: Purdue University Press, 2008).

44. Several of the defendants appeared on the Los Angeles branch of the NAACP membership rosters. In the Los Angeles NAACP Branch Files, 1913–1939, at UCLA/MC, see "Membership Report Blank," November 20, 1930, Reel 2; "Membership Report Blank," November 15, 1931, Reel 2; "Membership Report Blank," December 15, 1933, Reel 2; "Membership Report Blank," April 8, 1934, Reel 2; "Membership Report Blank #35," December 13, 1937, Reel 3; and "Membership Report Blank," December 1938, Reel 3. The law office of Pacht, Pelton, Warne, Ross & Bernhard represented McDaniel. See

Josefa H. Tolhurst v. Nellie B. Venerable, Demurrer of Defendants James Lloyd Crawford and Hattie McDaniel Crawford to Complaint, L.A. No. 500057, filed May 16, 1945, LASC.

45. Watts, *Hattie McDaniel*, 238–39; Cecilia Rasmussen, "L.A. Then and Now: A Life that Defied Racial Stereotypes," *Los Angeles Times*, December 3, 2000; "Sugar Hill Victory Sets U.S. Precedent: Covenants Called Unconstitutional," *Los Angeles Sentinel*, December 10, 1945; "Celebrities in Spotlight," 4; LaMarr, "Film Stars," 1 (first quotation from article title); "Negro Property," A2 (second and third quotations); "Victory" (fourth quotation).

46. WAHPA notebook, June 30, 1946, minutes, 69–70 (first quotation on 69-70; second quotation on 70), author's collection (from the Houston and Taylor families).

47. WAHPA notebook, June 27, 1943, minutes, 19 (first quotation); February 25, 1945, minutes, 51 (second quotation), author's collection (from the Houston and Taylor families).

48. "Sugar Hill Victory" (first quotation from article title); "Victory" (second quotation). In LMP, Box 5, Folder 2, HL, see Telegram from N. W. Griffin to Loren Miller, December 7, 1945 (third quotation); Letter from Theodore Spaulding to Loren Miller, December 19, 1945 (fourth quotation); Letter from William H. Hastie to Loren Miller, December 20, 1945 (fifth quotation); Letter from Rufus Clement to Loren Miller, December 26, 1945 (sixth quotation); and Letter from Loren Miller to Norman O. Houston, December 12, 1945 (seventh quotation).

49. "'Sugar Hill' Judge Gets Threat Letters from White Bigots," *Tri-County Bulletin*, December 27, 1945, ACLU/SC, Box 30, Folder 3, UCLA/SC (quotation). The same article was published as "Bouquets, Brickbats Swamp 'Sugar Hill' Judge in Los Angeles," *Chicago Defender*, December 29, 1945. For WAHPA's expressed support for Clarke's 1948 reelection, see WAHPA notebook, February 24, 1947, minutes, 81, author's collection (from the Houston and Taylor families). For Clarke's résumé, see "Clarke, Thurmond."

50. Tyler, "Defense Attorney Analyzes," 1 (first and second quotations); Letter from Loren Miller to Thurgood Marshall, December 6, 1945, NAACP Papers, pt. 5 (third, fourth, fifth, and sixth quotations); Letter from Thurgood Marshall to Loren Miller, December 11, 1945, NAACP Papers, pt. 5 (seventh, eight, and ninth quotations). For more on the correspondence between Miller and Marshall, and other congratulatory letters that Miller received and responded to, see Hassan, *Loren Miller*, 143–45.

51. Letter from Thurgood Marshall to Loren Miller, December 11, 1945, NAACP Papers, pt. 5. In LMP, Box 3, Folder 1, HL, see Letter from Loren Miller to Lester B. Granger, December 18, 1945 (first and second quotations); Letter from Loren Miller to Robert C. Weaver, January 1, 1946; Letter from Loren Miller to Rufus E. Clement, January 1, 1946; Letter from Loren Miller to Maurice Weeks, January 1, 1946; and Letter from Loren Miller to William Hastie, January 1, 1946 (third quotation).

52. Dole M. Burkman v. Henry Laws, 63 Cal. App. 2d 230 (1944); In re Laws, 31 Cal. 2d 846 (1948). See also "Laws Put in Jail for Living in Own House," *Los Angeles Sentinel*, December 20, 1945 (first quotation from article title), ACLU/SC, Box 30, Folder 3, UCLA/SC, front page; "Citizens Push Battle Against Race Covenants," *California Eagle*, December 27, 1945, 1 (second and third quotations); Jessie Mae Brown, "A True Leader—Charlotta A. Bass" (draft of biography of Bass), Charlotta A. Bass Papers, Box 1, Folder 14, SCL, 2; and Bunch, *Black Angelenos*, 40–41. For discussion on the Home Protective Association, see Andrea Gibbons, *City of Segregation: One Hundred Years of Struggle for Housing in Los Angeles* (New York: Verso, 2018), 55–62.

53. Miller appealed the Charles Victor tract lawsuits in the California Supreme Court. For the briefs, see Appellants' Opening Brief by Loren Miller, M. A. Hester and Blair Hill v. Carlos J. Barbe, L.A. Nos. 19589–19594, filed February 8, 1946, 2, 8–13, LALL. Before handing down the verdict, the California Supreme Court waited until the US Supreme Court had made its decision on *Shelley v. Kraemer* (1948). For the decision made by the California Supreme Court, see Earl C. Cummings v. Frank Hokr, 31 Cal. 2d 844 (1948). See also "Court Reviews Right of Negroes to Live in Their Own Homes," *Los Angeles Sentinel*, June 6, 1946; and "Move to Evict Japanese from Harvard Home Fought," *Los Angeles Tribune*, October 26, 1946, ACLU/SC, Box 30, Folder 1, UCLA/SC.

54. Anderson v. Auseth, Appellants' Opening Brief, 6 (first quotation), 9 (second and third quotations); Anderson v. Auseth, Respondents' Brief, L.A. No. 19759, filed August 30, 1946, 16 (fourth, fifth, and sixth quotations; italics in original), 20 (seventh quotation), 47, 51 (eighth quotation), LALL.

55. Kenny, interview by Nunis (first quotation); Brief of the attorney general of the state of California, as Amicus Curiae, Ane Marie Anderson v. Earl F. Auseth, L.A. No. 19759, dated September 4, 1946, Foreword, ACLU/SC, Box 30, Folder 3, UCLA/SC, 5 (second quotation, italics in original), 9 (third quotation). See also Janet Stevenson, *The Undiminished Man: A Political Biography of Robert Walker Kenny* (Novato, CA: Chandler & Sharp Publishers, 1980).

56. "U.N. Cited by Negroes in Appeal," 38 (first quotation); "Negroes Cite U.N. to End Segregation"; L. Miller, "Covenants in the Bear Flag State," 155 (second and third quotations).

57. Letter from Loren Miller to Nelson C. Dreier, October 4, 1946, LMP, Box 6, Folder 2, HL; "Court Reviews Right," 1; "Citizens Pack Court at Covenant Hearing," *Los Angeles Sentinel*, June 20, 1946 (quotation); "'Sugar Hill' Cases Slated for Hearing on Oct. 2; No Date on Laws' Appeal," *California Eagle*, September 5, 1946; "Race Zoning Case in Supreme Court," *Los Angeles Times*, October 3, 1946, A3.

58. Greg Robinson and Tony Robinson, "*Korematsu* and Beyond: Japanese Americans and the Origins of Strict Scrutiny," *Law and Contemporary Problems* 68, no. 2 (Spring 2005): 40–42; Brian Niiya, ed., *Japanese American History: An A-to-Z Reference from 1868 to Present* (New York: Facts on File, 1993), 350–51; Miller, interview by de Graaf, April 29, 1967, 26 (quotation). For federal and state cases that both Miller and Wirin served on, see Communist Party of the United States v. Paul Peek; James v. Marinship Corporation; Mendez v. Westminster School District of Orange County, 64 F. Supp. 544 (1946). For information on the National Association of Real Estate Brokers (NAREB), see "NAREB History," accessed September 24, 2021, http://www.nareb.com/-our-history/

59. Miller, interview by de Graaf, April 29, 1967, 27 (quotation).

60. Hansberry v Lee, 311 U.S. 32 (1940). See also Tushnet, *Making Civil Rights Law*, 87; Vose, *Caucasians Only*, 55–56; and Stephen Grant Meyer, *As Long as They Don't Move Next Door: Segregation and Racial Conflict in American Neighborhoods* (Lanham, MD: Rowan & Littlefield, 2000), 56–57.

61. Tushnet, *Making Civil Rights Law*, 89–91; Gonda, *Unjust Deeds*, 120–30; Hassan, *Loren Miller*, 160–63; Letter from Loren Miller to Thurgood Marshall, January 29, 1947, NAACP Papers, pt. 5 (quotations). See also Letter from Thurgood Marshall to Loren Miller, February 5, 1947, NAACP Papers, pt. 5. *McGhee v. Sipes* began in Detroit, Michigan, while *Hurd v. Hodge* and *Urciolo v. Hodge* began in Washington, DC. For more on

the cases that the U.S. Supreme Court heard, see Vose, *Caucasians Only*, chaps. 4, 5, and 6.

62. Gonda, *Unjust Deeds*, 137–38, 146; Vose, *Caucasians Only*, 158–59, 184–86; Hassan, *Loren Miller*, 163–65.

63. Gonda, *Unjust Deeds*, 146, 215–17; Vose, *Caucasians Only*, 159–60, 186–90.

64. Vose, *Caucasians Only*, 163–74, 191–99; Tushnet, *Making Civil Rights Law*, 91–92; Gonda, *Unjust Deeds*, 150–55; President's Committee on Civil Rights, *To Secure These Rights: The Report of the President's Committee on Civil Rights* (Washington, DC: US Government Printing Office, 1947); Tom C. Clark and Philip B. Perlman, *Prejudice and Property: An Historic Brief Against Racial Covenants* (Washington, DC: Public Affairs Press, 1948), 22 (first quotation), 66–68 (second quotation on 66-67; third quotation on 68).

65. Shelley v. Kraemer, 334 U.S. 1 (1948) (all quotations). Vose, *Caucasians Only*, 205–10; L. Miller, *The Petitioners*, 324–26. At the hearing, Justices Robert Jackson, Stanley Reed, and Wiley Rutledge recused themselves from the case. Speculation ensued that they owned properties with restrictive covenants, but no records verify that information. See Gonda, *Unjust Deeds*, 174, 258 (fn. 45); and Hassan, *Loren Miller*, 169.

66. "California Negroes Can Now Live Anywhere!," *Los Angeles Sentinel*, May 6, 1948 (first quotation from article title); "Ruling is Acclaimed Here," *New York Times*, May 4, 1948, 2 (second quotation); "Real Estate: 'Exclusive…Restricted': Effect of Court Decision Upsetting Covenants," *U.S. News & World Report*, May 14, 1948, 22–23 (third quotation on 22); Letter from George A. Beavers, Jr., to Loren Miller, May 4, 1948, LMP, Box 8, Folder 3, HL (fourth quotation); Appellate Court Decision, part of Ane Marie Anderson v. Earl F. Auseth, L.A. No. 19759, filed May 18, 1948, LALL. For more congratulations letters, see LMP, Box 8, Folder 3, HL.

67. Gonda, *Unjust Deeds*, 185.

68. Immergluck, *Credit to the Community*, 96–97; Gonda, *Unjust Deeds*, 212; James Thomas Keane, *Fritz B. Burns and the Development of Los Angeles: The Biography of a Community Developer and Philanthropist* (Los Angeles: Historical Society of Southern California, 2001), 70–71; Loren Miller, "Residential Segregation and Civil Rights," Lawyers Guild Conference, Hollywood Athletic Club, California, May 12, 1956, ACLU/SC, Box 30, Folder 1, UCLA/SC, 5–6; K-Y Taylor, *Race for Profit*, 5 (quotation). For reference to the FHA's *Underwriting Manual*, see chap. 2, fn. 37.

69. Miller, interview by de Graaf, April 29, 1967, 30; L. Miller, *The Petitioners*, 326; Adler, "Watts," 300; Meyer, *As Long*, 95; Memo to Members of the County Conference on Community Relations, LMP, Box 3, Folder 5, HL; Milton A. Senn, "Report on Efforts in the Los Angeles Area to Circumvent the United States Supreme Court Decisions on Restrictive Covenants," December 31, 1948, LMP, Box 8, Folder 4, HL.

70. Barrows v. Jackson, 346 U.S. 249 (1953) (quotation). See also L. Miller, *The Petitioners*, 326–29; and Vose, *Caucasians Only*, 232–46.

71. George A. Beavers, Jr., Letter addressed to coworkers at Golden State Mutual, August 15, 1949, NF/GSM, Box 2, Folder 6, SCL (quotation); "Fourteenth Annual Statement of the Golden State Mutual Life Insurance Company," December 31, 1938, NF/GSM, Box 2, Folder 4, SCL; "35th Annual Report to Policymakers," December 31, 1959, NF/GSM, Box 2, Folder 4, SCL.

72. Pamphlet announcing the opening of Golden State's new office, ca. 1949, NF/GSM, Box 2, Folder 6, SCL, entire (first and second quotations on 9; third quotation on 14); Karen E. Hudson, *Paul R. Williams, Architect: A Legacy of Style* (New York: Rizzoli International Publications, 1993), 122–23.

73. James Prigoff and Robin J. Dunitz, *Walls of Heritage, Walls of Pride: African American Murals* (San Francisco: Pomegranate, 2000), 57 (first quotation); William Pajaud, interview by Karen Ann Mason (Los Angeles: UCLA Library, Center for Oral History Research, 1989), UCLA/OL; Beavers, interview by Brown, 10 (second quotation).

74. I. Houston, interview by Hopkins (quotations as indicated); Beavers, interview by Hopkins (quotations as indicated); Gerald Horne, *Fire This Time: The Watts Uprising and the 1960s* (Charlottesville: University Press of Virginia, 1995), 33–34 (last quotation in this paragraph).

75. Bogle, *Bright Boulevards, Bold Dreams*, 264; Clora Bryant, interview by Steven L. Isoardi (Los Angeles: UCLA Library, Center for Oral History Research, 1990), UCLA/OL (quotation); Hotel Watkins advertisement, *Ebony*, June 1962, 111.

76. Parson, *Making a Better World*, 139–47, 161–62.

77. Parson, *Making a Better World*, 90–91, 143; Parson, "Houses for the Rich," 82–90.

78. Parson, *Making a Better World*, 104, 110–17, 130–35; Parson, "Houses for the Rich," 91–92; Don Parson, "Breeding Grounds of Communism: The Gwinn Amendment in Los Angeles' Public Housing," in Keil and Branfman, *Public Los Angeles*, 122–31; Sitton, *Los Angeles Transformed*, 165–90. While Parson, in *Making a Better World*, uses the formal name Committee Against Socialist Housing, other scholars, especially on Chavez Ravine, such as Jerald Podair in *City of Dreams: Dodger Stadium and the Birth of Modern Los Angeles* (Princeton, NJ: Princeton University Press, 2017), and Eric Nusbaum, in *Stealing Home: Los Angeles, the Dodgers, and the Lives Caught in Between* (New York: PublicAffairs, 2020), refer to the group as Citizens Against Socialist Housing.

79. Hudson, interview by Brown, 6–10, 13 (quotation on 7); Abigail Rosas, "Banking on the Community: Mexican Immigrants' Experiences in a Historically African American Bank in South Central Los Angeles, 1970–2007, in *Black and Brown in Los Angeles: Beyond Conflict and Coalition*, edited by Josh Kun and Laura Pulido (Berkeley: University of California Press, 2014), 71–75 (quotation on 73); Richard L. Vanderveld, "Negro Business: Pride, Profit and Prejudice," *Los Angeles Times*, August 7, 1966; Display Ad for Safety Savings & Loan Association, *Los Angeles Times*, July 9, 1956; "The Story of Two Businessmen," *Crenshaw Notes* 24 (March 1967): 1–2, APP, Box 1, SCL.

80. Thomas J. Sugrue, "From Jim Crow to Fair Housing," in *The Fight for Fair Housing: Causes, Consequences, and Future Implications of the 1968 Federal Fair Housing Act*, edited by Gregory D. Squires (New York: Routledge, 2018), 18, 20 (quotation), 23; HoSang, *Racial Propositions*, 57; Lawrence B. de Graaf, "African American Suburbanization in California, 1960 through 1990," in de Graaf, Mulroy, and Taylor, *Seeking El Dorado*, 415.

81. Loren Miller, untitled article, May 26, 1948, LMP, Box 8, Folder 2, HL, 1 (quotation). For reference to the new Black middle class, see Landry, *New Black Middle Class*, 1987, 67–78.

CHAPTER 4. THE AFFLUENT BLACK WESTSIDE TAKES SHAPE

1. Evelyn Allen Johnson, *My Neighbor's Island* (New York: Exposition Press, 1965), 21.

2. E. Johnson, *My Neighbor's Island*, 21 (first quotation), 31 (second quotation). Johnson won the Vassie D. Wright Award for *My Neighbor's Island*.

3. Evelyn Allen Johnson, interview by author, September 30, October 23, and October 24, 2006, telephone. For more works by Evelyn Allen Johnson, see *Get the Show on the Road* (Los Angeles: Lynray Press, 1987); and Evelyn Allen Johnson, *Pillar of Salt* (Los Angeles: Lynray Press, 2006). See also Landry, *New Black Middle Class*, 1987, 67–78.

4. Mike Davis, *City of Quartz*, 71–74, 102–5, 120–25; Gottlieb and Wolt, *Thinking Big*, 241–45, 306–21; Vorspan and Gartner, *History of Jews of Los Angeles*, 233–37. See also Abrahamson, *Building*.

5. For census tract maps and the percentage of Black residents in them between 1940 and 1980, see Sides, *L.A. City Limits*, 210–14.

6. Scott Kurashige, "Crenshaw and the Rise of Multiethnic Los Angeles," *Afro-Hispanic Review* 27, no. 1 (Spring 2008): 47, 54; S. Kurashige, *Shifting Grounds*, 249–58.

7. Fishman, *Bourgeois Utopias*; Mike Davis, *City of Quartz*, 169–80 (quotations on 170); Paul Weeks, "Negroes in L.A. Moving Out from Center of City," *Mirror-News*, May 2, 1956, ACLU/SC, Box 28, Folder 3, UCLA/SC, 14-15; "Annual Report of the Committee on Human Relations," May 1955, ACLU/SC, Box 28, Folder 4, UCLA/SC. In the 1870s and 1880s Baldwin purchased more than 3,600 acres, spread across varied terrain, from 100 to 440 feet above sea level. See Sandra Lee Snider, *Elias Jackson "Lucky" Baldwin: California Visionary* (Los Angeles: Stairwell Group, 1987), 8–11.

8. United Neighbors (UN), "Problems and Challenges in the Crenshaw Area of Los Angeles, a Racially Mixed Community," ca. 1963, 2 (quotation), author's collection (from Joan Suter).

9. Alejandro Alonso, "Racialized Identities and the Formation of Black Gangs in Los Angeles," *Urban Geography* 25, no. 7 (2004): 659, 662–65; Alex Alonso, "Out of the Void: Street Gangs in Black Los Angeles," in *Black Los Angeles: American Dreams and Racial Realities*, edited by Darnell Hunt and Ana-Christina Ramón (New York: New York University Press, 2010), 140–43; Alex A. Alonso, "Territoriality Among African-American Street Gangs in Los Angeles" (master's thesis, University of Southern California, 1999), 71–78, 106–7; Cle Sloan, director, *Bastards of the Party* (2005; Los Angeles: Fuqua Films, 2009), 15:01 (first quotation), 15:15 (second quotation), 17:13 (third quotation). See also Stacy Peralta, director, *Crips and Bloods: Made in America* (2008; Los Angeles: Balance Vector Productions and Verso Entertainment, 2009). For discussions on the first Chicano and Japanese gangs, see James C. Howell, *The History of Street Gangs in the United States: Their Origins and Transformations* (Lanham, MD: Lexington Books, 2015), 26–31; and Lon Kurashige, "The Problem of Biculturalism: Japanese American Identity and Festival before World War II," *Journal of American History* 86, no. 4 (March 2000): 1646–49.

10. Alejandro Alonso, "Racialized Identities," 665, 670; Alex Alonso, "Out of the Void," 142–43; Alex Alonso, "Territoriality African-American Street Gangs," 71–78 (including fn. 12), 106–7; S. Kurashige, *Shifting Grounds*, 253–54, 283.

11. For a discussion on Japanese and Japanese Americans in Crenshaw, see S. Kurashige, "Crenshaw and the Rise"; and S. Kurashige, *Shifting Grounds*, 249–58.

12. Kevin Starr, *The Dream Endures: California Enters the 1940s* (New York: Oxford University Press, 1997), 185–86; Mildred Brooke Hoover, Hero Eugene Rensch, Ethel Grace Rensch, and William N. Abeloe, *Historic Spots in California*, revised by Douglas E. Kyle, 5th ed. (Stanford: Stanford University Press, 2002), 167–68; Tia Gindick, "Hancock Park: Half-Century Report," *Los Angeles Times*, November 23, 1975; Daniel Mark Epstein, *Nat King Cole* (New York: Farrar, Straus and Giroux, 1999), 178–79. As in other Los Angeles neighborhoods, Hancock Park's borders have changed over time. This study uses the community's early boundaries, while recognizing data from the census tracts go slightly beyond this study's stated Hancock Park borders.

13. Epstein, *Nat King Cole*, pt. 1, 65, 69, 85, 115–16, 128, 136–46; Jon Brewer, director, *Nat King Cole: Afraid of the Dark* (Cotswolds, UK: Cardinal Releasing, 2014), DVD.

14. Epstein, *Nat King Cole*, 178–79; Gonda, *Unjust Deeds*, 35–36; "Hancock Park Home Purchase Stirs Quandary," *Los Angeles Times*, August 3, 1948, B16. For the city's 1950 property value average, see 1950 Census: Block Statistics, 3. The *Los Angeles Times* documented the selling price as $65,000 ("Hancock Park Home," B16), while Cole's biographer, David Mark Epstein, cited the price as $85,000 (Epstein, *Nat King Cole*, 179).

15. "Hancock Park Home," B16 (quotation from article title); Epstein, *Nat King Cole*, 179–81.

16. Epstein, *Nat King Cole*, 181–83 (all quotations on 181); *Nat King Cole*; "King Cole Decorates His New $65,000 Home: Top-Drawer Beverly Hills Decorator Accents Bold Colors in furnishing Los Angeles House," *Ebony*, April 1949, 26–29; Natalie Cole, "An Unforgettable Dream House," *Wall Street Journal*, May 28, 2014.

17. Natalie Cole, "An Unforgettable Dream House." For census data, see tracts 80-B, 82, 93, and 98 in 1950 Census: Tracts, 15–16. See tracts 1923, 2116, 2141, and 2153 in 1960 Census: Tracts, 52, 59–61; *Census of Population and Housing: 1970*, Census Tracts, Final Report, Series PHC(1)-117, Los Angeles–Long Beach, Calif., pt. 1 (Washington, DC: US Government Printing Office, 1972) (hereafter 1970 Census: Tracts, pt. 1), P-56, P-62–64. The 1950, 1960, and 1970 tracts' borders go slightly beyond Hancock Park's borders. For reference to Muhammad Ali's home, see Jack Flemming, "Muhammad Ali's Former Hancock Park Home Seeks $17 Million," *Los Angeles Times*, January 17, 2019.

18. "La Fayette Square: An Unquestionable Investment Opportunity," *Los Angeles Times*, January 26, 1913, VI6 (quotations, "Parisian" and "pasears"); "The Pasear: La Fayette Square," *Los Angeles Times*, January 19, 1913, VI4 (quotation, "central Pasear," italics removed from Pasear); "La Fayette Square: Build Your Beautiful Home in La Fayette Square 'and Live Forever,'" *Los Angeles Times*, May 31, 1914, VI2 (quotation, "Restricted").

19. K. Hudson, *Paul R. Williams*, 11–15; David Gebhard, "Williams, Paul Revere," *American National Biography Online*, February 2000, https://doi.org/10.1093/anb/9780198606697.article.1701269; Paul Williams, "I Am a Negro," *American Magazine* (July 1937): 59, 161–62.

20. Williams, "I Am a Negro," 59 (first and second quotations, ellipses in original), 161–63 (third and fourth quotations on 161; fifth quotation on 162, "*earn*," italics in original; sixth quotation on 163); K. Hudson, *Paul R. Williams*, 16, 19–20, 27; Gebhard, "Williams, Paul Revere." For another good source, written for adolescent readers, see Karen E. Hudson, *The Will and the Way: Paul R. Williams, Architect* (New York: Rizzoli International Publications, 1994).

21. K. Hudson, *Paul R. Williams*, 16, 25–26; K. Hudson, *The Will and the Way*, 44. Photos of Williams's Lafayette Square home are printed in K. Hudson, *Paul R. Williams*, 157–61; and in K. Hudson, *The Will and the Way*, 45.

22. For 1950 data see tract 157, blocks 1–6 and 36–40, in 1950 Census: Block Statistics, 136–37. For 1960 data see tract 2182, blocks 1–7 and 24–27, in *Census of Housing: 1960*, City Blocks, Series HC(3), vol. 3, no. 46 (Washington, DC: US Government Printing Office, 1961) (hereafter 1960 Census: City Blocks), 154. According to the introduction of the 1950 census, "nonwhite," or what I call people of color, "consists of Negroes, Indians, Japanese, Chinese, and other nonwhite races." See 1950 Census: Block Statistics, 2 (quotation). The 1960 census uses a similar definition. See the introduction to 1960 Census: City Blocks. For 1970 data see tract 2182, blocks 101–4, 106–9, 202–3, 205–7, in *Census of Housing: 1970*, Block Statistics, Final Report, HC(3)-18, Los Angeles–Long Beach, Calif. Urbanized Area (Washington, DC: US Government Printing Office, 1972), 158–59.

23. Geraldine Branch, interview by author, July 27, 2007, Los Angeles, California; Nicholas, interview by author.

24. "Racial Trouble Blamed for Dunsmuir Ave. Blasts," *Los Angeles Times*, July 26, 1951, 16; "Bombs Rip Homes in W. Adams Area: Flying Glass From Blasts Perils Residents," *Los Angeles Times*, March 17, 1952, 1-2; "Protect Citizens in L.A., Veteran Group Demands: AVC Chairman Calls on Police and Brown to Prevent Recurrence of Home Bombings," *Los Angeles Times*, March 18, 1952, 2; "New Bombing Threat Sent to Teacher," *Los Angeles Times*, April 1, 1952, 2; "Home Blast Area Gets New Threats," *Los Angeles Times*, April 2, 1952, 2 (quotation).

25. "Rude 'Warning,' to Negroes Defaces Westside Sidewalks," *Los Angeles Tribune*, December 23, 1955, ACLU/SC, Box 28, Folder 3, UCLA/SC, 3 (quotations; all capital letters of second quotation in original). The ACLU of Southern California manuscript collection includes several documents from neighborhood protective associations. For associations in the Wilshire district, see Southwestern Wilshire Protective Association, "'Minutes' of meeting," September 17, 1947, ACLU/SC, Box 32, Folder 1, UCLA/SC; and Southwestern Wilshire Protective Association, "NOTICE To Property Owners Between Wilshire and Pico Crenshaw and Western," September 17, 1947, ACLU/SC, Box 32, Folder 1, UCLA/SC.

26. Weeks, "Negroes," 14 (all quotations).

27. See Sides, *L.A. City Limits*, 212, for percentages of the city's Black population in 1960 census tracts. For a map on Black gang formation in 1960, see Alejandro Alonso, "Racialized Identities," 665.

28. Cynthia E. Exum and Maty Guiza-Leimert, *Images of America: Leimert Park* (Charleston, SC: Arcadia Publishing, 2012), 36 (first quotation), 56–57; "*Life* Presents Your Home for Life in Leimert Park," ca. 1940s, California Ephemera Collection, Box 221, Folder: Leimert Park, Calif., UCLA/SC (second quotation).

29. Greg Hise, *Magnetic Los Angeles: Planning the Twentieth-Century Metropolis* (Baltimore: Johns Hopkins University Press, 1997), 15–17; "Your Homesite Permanently Improved in Leimert Park," *Los Angeles Times*, May 1, 1927, E7; "Homes Demand Indicated," *Los Angeles Times*, October 30, 1927, E6; "Community Development: Park Sees New Building Mark," *Los Angeles Times*, October 21, 1928, D4. See also Jeanette Lindsay, producer and director, *Leimert Park: The Story of a Village in South Central Los Angeles* (Los Angeles: Foster Johnson Studios, 2008), DVD. Thirty-Eighth Street School was renamed Thirty-Ninth Street School, then Dublin Avenue Elementary School, and is now named Tom Bradley Global Awareness Magnet Elementary School.

30. Exum and Guiza-Leimert, *Images of America*, 44; Hise, *Magnetic Los Angeles*, 17; "Plaza and Business Unit Dedicated," *Los Angeles Times*, November 18, 1928, E2. The Huntington Library, Digital Library, includes a panoramic photo of the Mesa Vernon Market taken by Charles C. Pierce, October 21, 1933, photCL 470 (084). The Los Angeles Public Library Photo and Digital Collections include many photographs of Leimert Park from the 1930s through the 1960s. See, for example, "Marquee, Leimert Theater," No. 00015010; "Lobby, Leimert Theater," No. 00015030; "Mural, Leimert Theater," No. 00015026; "Auditorium Interior, Leimert Theater," No. 00015028; and "Circular Promenade, Leimert Theater," No. 00015027. For a snapshot of active businesses along Degnan Boulevard in 1956 Leimert Park Village, see *Los Angeles Street Address Directory*, 1956, 210.

31. "Your Homesite Permanently," E7 (quotation, capitalization in original). See also Hise, *Magnetic Los Angeles*, 20, 26.

32. For 1950 data, see tracts 207-A and 207-B in 1950 Census: Tracts, 23. Mexicans faced White hostility in Crenshaw, yet their White legal status protected their property ownership and occupancy. See S. Kurashige, *Shifting Grounds*, 250; and Kazuo K. Inouye, interview by Leslie Ito, *REgenerations Oral History Project: Rebuilding Japanese American Families, Communities, and Civil Rights in the Resettlement Era*, vol. 2, edited by Japanese American National Museum, December 13, 1997, Calisphere, University of California Libraries, 194.

33. Exum and Guiza-Leimert, *Images of America*, 77; S. Kurashige, "Crenshaw and the Rise," 54; Inouye, interview by Ito, 196–97. For 1950 data, see tracts 197-A, 198–200, and 202, in 1950 Census: Tracts, 23. This study uses 1950 data from the census categories Mexico and Asia as birthplaces. The "other races" category, which includes groups other than White and Black, was 10.3 percent of the Avenues' population.

34. "Report on Meeting of Normandie Avenue Protective Association Held at Southwest Arena, 5301 S. Western Avenue," March 17, 1950, JAF, Box 76/ee, Folder 15, HL (all quotations in this paragraph). In this rare remaining document that recorded the aims and attitudes of Neighborly Endeavors, the minutes identified the speaker from Leimert Park only as Mr. Lund. The main purpose of the meeting was to raise money to purchase "a second trust deed on a piece of property which the Negro owner, Mrs. Wright, is willing to resell" in the Normandie Avenue neighborhood (quotation from source in this note).

35. Los Angeles County Committee on Human Relations, "Memorandum to Supervisor Raymond V. Darby," June 30, 1950, JAF, Box 5/a/cc, Folder 5, HL; Citizens United, Incorporated, "Property Owners Sued for Damages: Race Restrictions Violated!," (leaflet), ca. 1950, ACLU/SC, Box 32, Folder 4, UCLA/SC (quotation); "Owner who Sold Home to Negroes Faces Damage Suit," *Los Angeles Sentinel*, June 15, 1950; S. Kurashige, *Shifting Grounds*, 251.

36. Los Angeles County Committee on Human Relations, "Memorandum to Supervisor Raymond V. Darby"; Newspaper article, unknown source, ca. June 1950, ACLU/SC, Box 32, Folder 1, UCLA/SC.

37. Newspaper article, unknown source, ca. June 1950, ACLU/SC (first quotation); "Air Issues at Leimert Park Mass Parley," *Los Angeles Sentinel*, July 20, 1950, A2 (second quotation); County Committee on Human Relations, "Memorandum to Supervisor Raymond V. Darby." The County Committee on Human Relations was originally named the Commission for Interracial Progress. See also J. Ford, *Thirty Explosive Years*, on the committee's founder. Its name later changed again to the Los Angeles Commission on Human Relations.

38. Letter from A. A. Heist, Executive Director, ACLU, addressed to A. J. Hunter, July 11, 1950 (attached to a newspaper article, ca. June 1950), ACLU/SC, Box 32, Folder 1, UCLA/SC (both quotations). See also George L. Thomas, the executive director's report, "Los Angeles Conference on Community Relations: 7th Annual Report," ca. 1953, JAF, Box 68, Folder 2b, HL.

39. J. Gregory Payne and Scott C. Ratzan, *Tom Bradley: The Impossible Dream* (Santa Monica, CA: Roundtable Publishing Inc., 1986), 4–10; Thomas Bradley, interview by Bernard Galm (Los Angeles: UCLA Library, Center for Oral History Research, 1978–79), UCLA/OL (quotation).

40. Payne and Ratzan, *Tom Bradley*, 18–27, 30–42; Bradley, interview by Galm (quotation).

41. Payne and Ratzan, *Tom Bradley*, 49–50; Robert Scheer, "Notes 61st Birthday: Bradley Sees Today's Issues in His Past," *Los Angeles Times*, December 29, 1978, B1,

24, 26; Nancy Skelton, "'I'm a Prisoner Here...I'm Like a Bird in a Cage...' Mrs. Tom Bradley: Living the Life of a Political Wife," *Los Angeles Times*, December 4, 1983, A12, 14-17, 19. Payne and Ratzan, in *Tom Bradley*, record the White friends as Mr. and Mrs. John McTernan (p. 50), while the property deed on the Bradleys' purchase of the Welland Avenue home documented Stanley and Jeanne E. Friedman. See Deed of Trust between Stanley and Jeanne E. Friedman, and Alfred L. and Gertrude A. Buckman, 1951, Book 35318, 158, RRCC; Grant Deed between Stanley and Jeanne E. Friedman, and Thomas and Ethel Mae Bradley, 1951, Book 35318, 163, RRCC.

42. Payne and Ratzan, *Tom Bradley*, 51 (first and second quotations); Scheer, "Notes," 24 (third quotation). *Look* magazine used Norman Rockwell's *New Kids in the Neighborhood* painting for its May 16, 1967, cover.

43. Quotations in letter from Dale Gardner, Los Angeles County Committee on Human Relations, addressed to Police Relations Committee, "Vandalism in the residence of Charles L. Williams," March 29, 1951, JAF, Box 5/a/cc, Folder 7, HL.

44. Sides, *L.A. City Limits*, 102; Sides, "A Simple Quest," 120.

45. Scheer, "Notes," 24 (quotation); Skelton, "I'm a Prisoner Here"; Payne and Ratzan, *Tom Bradley*, 52.

46. Payne and Ratzan, *Tom Bradley*, 43–44; Bradley, interview by Galm; Sides, *L.A. City Limits*, 33–34, 154; Augustus F. Hawkins, "Oral History Interview with Augustus Hawkins," interview by Carlos Vásquez (California State Archives: State Government Oral History Program, 1988), 75 (quotation), Calisphere, University of California Libraries. See also Flamming, "Becoming," 279–308.

47. Payne and Ratzan, *Tom Bradley*, 44–46; Bradley, interview by Galm; Raphael J. Sonenshein, *Politics in Black and White: Race and Power in Los Angeles* (Princeton, NJ: Princeton University Press, 1993), 47, 60–61 (quotation on 61); Sides, *L.A. City Limits*, 154–56; Flamming, "Becoming," 297–98.

48. Sonenshein, *Politics*, 40–46, 55–58 (first quotation on 55); Payne and Ratzan, *Tom Bradley*, 57; Bradley, interview by Galm (second quotation); Sides, *L.A. City Limits*, 157. Sonenshein, in *Politics*, provides a detailed map of the council districts from 1965, including the Tenth District, Bradley's constituency (see p. 15). Bradley and his family lived in Leimert Park until the late 1970s. In 1978, after Bradley began his second term as Los Angeles mayor, he and his family moved from Welland Avenue to the mayoral mansion, known as the Getty House, in Windsor Square (located east of Hancock Park). Ethel deeply missed her friends and her garden in Leimert Park (Skelton, "I'm a Prisoner Here").

49. Stuart Nicholson, *Ella Fitzgerald: The Complete Biography* (New York: Routledge, 2004), 4–6, 25–39, 168–69. The *Colorato Magazine* of the *New York News* printed a photograph of Fitzgerald standing in front of her Leimert Park house. See May Okon, "She Still Gets Stage Fright: But Ella Fitzgerald Remains the First Lady of Song," *New York News, Coloroto Magazine*, September 8, 1957, 4.

50. Michael Lydon, *Ray Charles: Man and Music* (New York: Routledge, 2004), 5–6, 8–9, 18, 25, 146–48, 173; Ray Charles Robinson, Jr., *You Don't Know Me: Reflections of My Father, Ray Charles* (New York: Harmony Books, 2010), 43–51. For the median property value in tract 2341, where Ray Charles and his family lived, see 1960 Census: Tracts, 801. For the city's median property value, see *Census of Housing: 1960*, Metropolitan Housing, vol. 2, pt. 4, Kansas City-New Orleans Standard Metropolitan Statistical Areas (Washington, DC: US Government Printing Office, 1963) (hereafter 1960 Census: Housing), 104–58.

51. Nishi, "Japanese Settlement," 45 (quotation); S. Kurashige, *Shifting Grounds*, 255–57 (first and third quotations on 256; second quotation on 257).

52. For 1960, 1970, and 1980 data, see tracts 2341–44 in 1960 Census: Tracts, 67–68; 1970 Census: Tracts, pt. 1, P-71; *Census of Population and Housing: 1980*, Census Tracts, Los Angeles–Long Beach, Calif., section 1 (Washington, DC: US Government Printing Office, 1983) (hereafter 1980 Census: Tracts, sec. 1), P-472–73. For Los Angeles city data, see 1960 Census: Tracts, 25. The 1960 and 1970 censuses categorized Asians as "other races," while the 1980 census used "Asian and Pacific Islander." While the census recorded 2.2 percent Hispanics at the tract level in 1960, it provided no tract-level data in 1970 because the area included fewer than four hundred residents with Spanish surnames. See also S. Kurashige, *Shifting Grounds*, 253–54; and Scott Kurashige, "Growing Up Japanese American in Crenshaw and Leimert Park," KCET, January 30, 2014, https://www.kcet.org/shows/departures/growing-up-japanese-american-in-crenshaw-and-leimert-park

53. "New Unit of Tract to Be Put on Sale," *Los Angeles Times*, June 12, 1927, E4; "Spanish Type Home Favored: This Style Declared Most Popular Here," *Los Angeles Times*, July 7, 1929, D4; Keane, *Fritz B. Burns*, 69–71; Hise, *Magnetic Los Angeles*, 135–36.

54. "New Unit of Tract," E4; "Homes Demand," E6; "Spanish Type," D4 (quotation); "New Unit Will Open This Week," *Los Angeles Times*, March 10, 1929, E4; "A Village of All Nations For the Entertainment of Athletes," *Los Angeles Times*, December 4, 1931, D13; Gardner Bradford, "Feeding Athletes in Forty Languages," *Los Angeles Times*, July 24, 1932, I3. In early reports of the area, the *Los Angeles Times* used View Park and Viewpark interchangeably to identify the enclave. For Viewpark, for example, see "New Unit of Tract," E4; for View Park, see "Homes Demand," E6. Some recent maps have identified the area directly south of Slauson Avenue and Windsor Hills as View Heights. The Los Angeles Investment Company initially mapped View Heights directly west of Windsor Hills.

55. Keane, *Fritz B. Burns*, 29–52, 61–67.

56. Keane, *Fritz B. Burns*, 61–71; Hise, *Magnetic Los Angeles*, 41, 135–36; Windsor Hills brochure, ca. 1938, FBP, CSLA-2, Series 3, Box 20v, Portfolio 1953, LMU; "Windsor Hills. Summary of Building Restrictions," ca. 1938, FBP, CSLA-2, Series 3, Box 20v, Portfolio 1953, LMU (both quotations). The borders of Windsor Hills vary and change over time. For the early maps of the area, see "New 'Overhill Unit.' The 'Gold Plate Tract' of Windsor Hills Development," 1938, FBP, Series 3, Box 20v, Portfolio 1953, LMU; Windsor Hills brochure, ca. 1938.

57. For 1950 data, see tract 365-A in 1950 Census: Tracts, 36. For 1960 data, see tracts 7031 and 7032 in 1960 Census: Tracts, 132.

58. "Cross Burned on Teachers' Lawn," *California Eagle*, June 27, 1957, 1 (first and second quotations; ellipses in first quotation in original), 4; "Sisters to Tell how it Feels 'To Sit on a Keg of Dynamite,'" *California Eagle*, July 18, 1957, 1 (third quotation); "Highlights of 1957," *California Eagle*, January 2, 1958, 1.

59. David K. Carlisle, "Letter to the Editor," *Los Angeles Times*, September 22, 1989, 5.

60. Ike Turner with Nigel Cawthorne, *Takin' Back My Name: The Confessions of Ike Turner* (London: Virgin Books, 1999), 7–11 (quotation on 7), 24–39.

61. I. Turner, *Takin' Back My Name*, 46–55 (quotation on 55), 61–71.

62. Tina Turner with Kurt Loder, *I, Tina* (New York: Morrow and Company, 1986), 6–8, 18 (first quotation, ellipses in original), 37–39, 49–52 (second quotation on 50).

63. Joint Tenancy Grant Deed between Ike and Tina Turner, and Leavitt B. Glaze and Edith L. Glaze, 1962, Book D1675, 305, RRCC; T. Turner, *I, Tina*, 60–62, 67, 81, 125–29; Jennifer Seder, "Tina Turner," *Los Angeles Times*, June 2, 1978, J11; Buzzy Jackson, *A Bad Woman Feeling Good: Blues and the Women Who Sing Them* (New York: W. W. Norton & Company, 2005), 194, 233–34. For photos of Ike and Tina at their Olympiad house, see Ernest Dunbar, "Ike and Tina: They're Too Much," *Look* 34, no. 18 (September 8, 1970): 64; "Ike and Tina Turner," *Ebony*, May 1971, 89; and T. Turner, *I, Tina*, after 104 and 160.

64. Lydon, *Ray Charles*, 225–58, 432–33, 328; R. Robinson, *You Don't Know Me*, 124–30 (quotations on 125). While Lydon writes that the house was 6,500 square feet, Robinson Jr. explains it was twelve thousand (Lydon, *Ray Charles*, 243; R. Robinson, *You Don't Know Me*, 127). Ray and Della Robinson divorced in 1977; after splitting their assets in the settlement, Della stayed in the Southridge Avenue house.

65. See tracts 7031 and 7032 in 1960 Census: Tracts, 132; 1970 Census: Tracts, pt. 1, P-121; 1980 Census: Tracts, sec. 1, P-494.

66. See tracts 7031 and 7032 in all of the following sources. For their median income and property value, see 1960 Census: Tracts, 132, 833; 1970 Census: Tracts, pt. 1, H-121, P-526. For the city's median property value, see 1960 Census: Housing, 104–58; *Census of Housing: 1970*, Series HC(2)-120, Metropolitan Housing Characteristics, Los Angeles–Long Beach, Calif., pt. 7 (Washington, DC: US Government Printing Office, 1972), Table O-1. For the city's median income, see 1960 Census: Tracts, 25; 1970 Census: Tracts, pt. 1, P-408.

67. "New York Beat," *Jet*, July 1, 1965, 63; Phyl Garland, "The Many 'Bags' of Oliver Nelson," *Ebony*, November 1968, 109; R. Robinson, *You Don't Know Me*, 128 (quotations).

68. Darnell Hunt, "Introduction: Dreaming of Black Los Angeles," in Hunt and Ramón, *Black Los Angeles*, 6–7; William Overend, "A Neighborhood Watch Against Crime," *Los Angeles Times*, August 10, 1976; John L. Mitchell, "Community Wants More than a Name Change," *Los Angeles Times*, July 2, 1987; Edmund Newton, "Landlord Leads Anti-Pusher 'Jungle' Warfare," *Los Angeles Times*, April 1, 1988; "'The Jungle' is Renamed," *Los Angeles Times*, June 11, 1988. Like many communities in Los Angeles, sources conflict over the borders of Baldwin Village, some of which make Hillcrest Drive, rather than Marlton Avenue, the eastern limit.

69. "These Are Multimillion-Dollar Developments," *Los Angeles Times*, January 3, 1949, G10; "Baldwin Hills Plot Sold; Will Yield 1030 Sites," *Los Angeles Times*, June 11, 1950, E1; "Dwellings Rise in New Tract," *Los Angeles Times*, June 24, 1951, E2; "27 Dwellings With $675,000 Value Rising at Development," *Los Angeles Times*, May 11, 1952, F6; "Stone Columns to Stand at Entrance to Estate Tract," *Los Angeles Times*, June 29, 1952, E5; "19 Dwellings Are Rising in Newest Unit of Tract," *Los Angeles Times*, August 23, 1953, E9.

70. For the 1950 data, see tract 365-B in 1950 Census: Tracts, 29. The 1950 tract comprises Stocker Street, La Brea Avenue, Rodeo Road, and Coliseum Street, which includes Baldwin Village and Baldwin Hills Estates. For the 1960 data, see tracts 2361 and 2362 for Baldwin Village and tract 2364 for Baldwin Hills Estates in 1960 Census: Tracts, 68.

71. Los Angeles County Conference on Community Relations, Ninth Annual Report, September 30, 1955, ACLU/SC, Box 28, Folder 4, UCLA/SC (quotation).

72. "Distinguished Honor Awards...Baldwin Hills Village: Los Angeles, California," *Architect and Engineer* 168 (March 1947): 26; Lewis Mumford, "Baldwin Hills Village,"

Pencil Points 25 (September 1944): 45 (quotation); Catherine Bauer, "Description and Appraisal...Baldwin Hills Village," *Pencil Points* (September 1944): 46–60; Clarence S. Stein, *Toward New Towns for America* (New York: Reinhold Publishing Corporation, 1957), chap. 9, 188–216; Don Parson, "Houses for the Rich," 58–60, 63–65. The name changed from Thousand Gardens to Baldwin Hills Village to the Village Green. For a reference to the enclave as Thousand Gardens, see "Development of Extensive Home Community Scheduled," *Los Angeles Times*, October 8, 1939, E1.

73. "Formal Opening of Homes Set at New Tract," *Los Angeles Times*, June 20, 1954, E14 (both quotations); "Preview of View Sites Announced," *Los Angeles Times*, April 11, 1954, E8. For the city's 1950 average property value, see 1950 Census: Block Statistics, 3.

74. For 1950 data, see tract 197-B for the Village Green and tract 364-B for Baldwin Vista in 1950 Census: Tracts, 23, 29. For 1960 data, see tract 2202 for the Village Green and tract 2363 for Baldwin Vista in 1960 Census: Tracts, 63, 68. The 1950 tract borders include slightly more land than the borders of the Village Green and the 1950 and 1960 tract borders include slightly more land than the borders of Baldwin Vista.

75. K. D. Patton, interview by author, October 2 and 5, 2006, by telephone (quotations). For the city's 1960 median property value, see 1960 Census: Housing, 104–58.

76. Gertrude Paxton, interview by author, November 11, 2006, by telephone (quotations, italics in third quotation added for emphasis).

77. See tract 2364 for Baldwin Hills Estates and tract 2363 for Baldwin Vista in 1960 Census: Tracts, 68; 1970 Census: Tracts, pt. 1, P-72; 1980 Census: Tracts, sec. 1, P-473. The 1960 and 1970 tract borders include Baldwin Vista and a portion of land west of La Cienega Boulevard.

78. For the city's median property value, see 1960 Census: Tracts, 780; *Census of Population and Housing: 1970*, Census Tracts, Final Report, Series PHC(1)-117, Los Angeles–Long Beach, Calif., pt. 2 (Washington, DC: US Government Printing Office, 1972) (hereafter 1970 Census: Tracts, pt. 2), H-3. For the city's median income, see 1960 Census: Tracts, 25; 1970 Census: Tracts, pt. 1, P-408. For median property value of Baldwin Hills Estates (tract 2364) and Baldwin Vista (tract 2363), see 1960 Census: Tracts, 801; 1970 Census: Tracts, pt. 2, H-72. For median income of Baldwin Hills Estates (tract 2364) and Baldwin Vista (tract 2363), see 1960 Census: Tracts, 68; 1970 Census: Tracts, pt. 1, P-477. The 1960 census records the median owner-occupied property values in Baldwin Hills Estates and Baldwin Vista as $25,000+ or what it indicates as, "the terminal category [of] $25,000 or more" and "the highest median which could be shown." Thus this study describes the 1960 property values as more than $25,000. See 1960 Census: Tracts, 7 (both quotations in footnote).

79. For data on the Village Green, see tract 2202 in 1960 Census: Tracts, 25, 63, 780, 799; 1970 Census: Tracts, pt. 1, P-66, P-408, P-471; 1970 Census: Tracts, pt. 2, H-3, H-66; 1980 Census: Tracts, sec. 1, P-470.

80. Baldwin Village comprised tracts 2361 and 2362 in 1960 and tracts 2361, 2362.01, and 2362.02 in 1970. 1960 Census: Tracts, 25, 68, 780, 801; 1970 Census: Tracts, pt. 1, P-71–72, P-408, P-476–77; 1970 Census: Tracts, pt. 2, H-3, H-71–72; 1980 Census: Tracts, sec. 1, P-473.

81. For racial composition in Sugar Hill, see tract 208, blocks 1–14, 18–19, and 25, in 1950 Census: Block Statistics, 161; and tract 2215, blocks 1–13 and 18–21, in 1960 Census: City Blocks, 161. For the area's median property value, see tract 208 in 1950 Census: Tracts, 158; and tract 2215 in 1960 Census: Tracts, 799. Sugar Hill made up roughly three-quarters of 1950 tract 208 and 1960 tract 2215, both of which bordered

Washington and Adams Boulevards, and Western and Normandie Avenues. For the city's median property value, see 1950 Census: Block Statistics, 3; 1960 Census: Housing, 104–58.

82. "Sugar Hill's Fate to be Decided at Freeway Hearing," *California Eagle*, February 18, 1954, 1, 10 (quotations on 1).

83. "Freeway Hearing: Sugar Hill's Residents Plead to Cause," *California Eagle*, February 25, 1954, 1, 2 (first, second, and third quotations on 2); "Freeway Route Will Cut Swank Westside District: Owners Ask City Council to Save Homes," *California Eagle*, May 27, 1954, 1 (fourth quotation), 4; "Sugar Hill's Fate," 1, 10 (fifth quotation); Sides, *L.A. City Limits*, 124.

84. Eric Avila, *Popular Culture in the Age of White Flight: Fear and Fantasy in Suburban Los Angeles* (Berkeley: University of California Press, 2004), 185 (first quotation), 195–97, 206–7 (second quotation on 207).

85. N. Houston, interview by Brown, 18–19 (quotation on 19); Beavers, interview by Hopkins, biographical summary.

86. Lydon, *Ray Charles*, 233–34 (quotation on 234), 243, 250–51.

87. Howell, *History of Street Gangs*, 26–33; Joan W. Moore, *Going Down to the Barrio: Homeboys and Homegirls in Change* (Philadelphia: Temple University Press, 1991), 11–17; L. Kurashige, "The Problem," 1646–49; Roy Nakano, "Them Bad Cats: Past Images of Asian American Street Gangs," pt. I, *Gidra* (January 1973): 4–5.

88. Alex Alonso, "Out of the Void," 142–43 (first quotation on 142; second quotation on 142-43); Alex Alonso, "Territoriality African-American Street Gangs," 78. See also Peralta, *Crips and Bloods*. For discussions on Parker's war against Black Angelenos, see Mike Davis, *City of Quartz*, 293–300; and Daniel Widener, *Black Arts West: Culture and Struggle in Postwar Los Angeles* (Durham: Duke University Press, 2010), 58–60.

89. S. Kurashige, *Shifting Grounds*, 253–54; Nakano, "Them Bad," pt. I, 6; Jeff Furumura, Tom Okabe, and Roy Nakano, "Them Bad," pt. II, *Gidra* (June 1973): 1, 5–6; Jeff Furumura, "Them Bad Cats: A Follow Up," pt. III, *Gidra* (August 1973): 14; Alejandro Alonso, "Racialized Identities," 665; Alex Alonso, "Territoriality African-American Street Gangs," 77–78, 107; Robert Conot, *Rivers of Blood, Years of Darkness: The First Full Story of America's Long Hot Summer of Hate* (New York: Bantam Books, 1967), 124.

90. Alex Alonso, "Territoriality African-American Street Gangs," 42 (quotation), 119; Yusuf Jah and Sister Shah'Keyah, *Uprising: Crips and Bloods Tell the Story of America's Youth in the Crossfire* (New York: Scribner, 1995), 203–29; Hunt, "Introduction," 6–7. See also Peralta, *Crips and Bloods*. For more on the rise of the Black Peace Stone Nation in Chicago, see Natalie Y. Moore and Lance Williams, *The Almighty Black P Stone Nation: The Rise, Fall, and Resurgence of an American Gang* (Chicago: Lawrence Hill Books, 2011), introduction and chaps. 1 and 6.

91. Paxton, interview by author (quotation); HoSang, *Racial Propositions*, 58–60; C. Brooks, *Alien Neighbors, Foreign Friends*, 177.

CHAPTER 5. A CAMPAIGN TO BUILD "A BALANCED COMMUNITY"

1. UN, "Problems and Challenges in the Crenshaw Area of Los Angeles, a Racially Mixed Community," ca. 1963, 3–4, author's collection (from Joan Suter); Jean Gregg, "Statement to the Governor's Commission on the Los Angeles Riots," in *Transcripts, Depositions, Consultants' Reports, and Selected Documents of the Governor's Commission on the Los Angeles Riots*, vol. 7 (Los Angeles: Governor's Commission on the Los Angeles Riots, 1966), 4–6, 9 (first quotation on 9); "Testimony of Mrs. Jean Gregg," in *Transcripts, Depositions, Consultants' Reports, and Selected Documents of the Governor's*

Commission on the Los Angeles Riots, vol. 7 (Los Angeles: Governor's Commission on the Los Angeles Riots, 1966), 4–6; Jean Gregg Milgram, interview by author, November 11, 2006, by telephone; Joan A. Suter, interview by author, July 28, 2008, by telephone (second quotation); Juliet Saltman, *A Fragile Movement: The Struggle for Neighborhood Stabilization* (New York: Greenwood Press, 1990), 282; Ann Post, interview by author, September 24, 2006, by telephone; Ellen Shulte, "Good Neighbor Policy for a Troubled Neighborhood," *Los Angeles Times*, June 8, 1967.

2. Saltman, *A Fragile Movement*, 282; J. Gregg, "Statement to Governor's Commission," 4 (first quotation); UN, "Problems and Challenges," 4 (second quotation).

3. For descriptions of blockbusting and its history, see Seligman, *Block by Block*, chap. 6; and Massey and Denton, *American Apartheid*, 37–38. For discussion on the "Black invasion" reference in 1920s and 1930s Los Angeles, see Homer Fleetwood II, "You Can Hear Them a Mile Away: The Black Invasion of Los Angeles," *Negro History Bulletin* 64, nos. 1–4 (January–December 2001): 33–40 (quotation in article title).

4. Massey and Denton, *American Apartheid*, 37–38; Orser, *Blockbusting in Baltimore*, 84–58, 131; Seligman, *Block by Block*, 157, 160–62. For a discussion on the ways in which the Black tax manifested, see K-Y Taylor, *Race for Profit*, 48–54. For discussions on the experiences of Bradley, Charles, and the Turners moving into the Crenshaw area, see this volume, chapter 4.

5. J. Gregg, "Testimony of Jean Gregg," 6–8; J. Gregg, "Statement to Governor's Commission," 6–8; Shulte, "Good Neighbor Policy"; S. Kurashige, "Crenshaw and the Rise," 49–50 (first and second quotations on 50); "A Story of Balance," *Crenshaw Notes* 9 (October 1965): 1 (third quotation), JSP, Box 5, Folder 4, SCL.

6. Loren Miller, "Loren Miller Says...Long, Long Ago," *California Eagle*, September 27, 1962, 1; Gene Sherman, "The Negro's Role: Housing Is Key to Aspirations," *Los Angeles Times*, July 4, 1962, 2, 10; Loren Miller, "The Protest Against Housing Segregation," *The Annals of the Academy of Political and Social Science* 357 (January 1965): 76 (quotation).

7. "Prepared Statement by Dr. Burton Henry. Report of the Education Committee of the Community Relations Conference of Southern California," in *Hearings Held in Los Angeles and San Francisco, 25–28 January 1960* (Washington, DC: US Government Printing Office, 1960), 76–78; Sides, *L.A. City Limits*, 159–60. See also Meyer Weinberg, *Race and Place: A Legal History of the Neighborhood School* (Washington, DC: US Government Printing Office, 1967); and Richard Kluger, *Simple Justice: The History of Brown v. Board of Education and Black America's Struggle for Equality* (New York: Vintage Books, 1977).

8. "Prepared Statement by Dr. Burton Henry," 77–78; Miller, "Loren Miller Says," 1 (quotation); Sides, *L.A. City Limits*, 159–60.

9. "Prepared Statement by Dr. Burton Henry," 77–78.

10. Jay R. Jackson, Jr. v. Pasadena City School District et al., 59 Cal. 2d 876 (1963) (quotation); Sides, *L.A. City Limits*, 160. See also Charles M. Wollenberg, *All Deliberate Speed: Segregation and Exclusion in California Schools, 1855–1975* (Berkeley: University of California Press, 1976).

11. John Caughey and LaRee Caughey, *School Segregation on Our Doorstep: The Los Angeles Story* (Los Angeles: Quail Books, 1966), 5–7; John Caughey and LaRee Caughey, *To Kill a Child's Spirit: The Tragedy of School Segregation in Los Angeles* (Itasca, IL: F. E. Peacock Publishers, 1973), 15–18. For a report on racial violence at the Wells's residence, see "Home Owner Gets Gun, Routs Racists," *California Eagle*, July 12, 1962, 1 (quotation), 4.

12. Caughey and Caughey, *School Segregation on Our Doorstep*, 7, 10 (quotation); Dick Turpin, "Education Board Urged to Press Integration: Groups Ask that Race, Creed, Color Be Factors in Making School Boundaries," *Los Angeles Times*, September 6, 1962.

13. Johnny Otis, "Let's Talk," *Los Angeles Sentinel*, September 13, 1962; "Baldwin Hills School Rejects 20 Pupils; Picketing Planned," *California Eagle*, September 13, 1962, 1; "Negroes Try to Place 15 in School: Fail in Effort to Change District in Baldwin Hills," *Los Angeles Times*, September 12, 1962, A1, 2; Loren Miller, "NAACP Calls Off Boycott as Negroes Enter 'White' School," *California Eagle*, September 20, 1962, 1 (quotations), 4. Newspaper reports differ in the number of students who attempted to register at Baldwin Hills Elementary School; the *California Eagle* reported twenty students, while the *Los Angeles Times* reported fifteen.

14. "Baldwin Hills School Rejects," 1; "Negroes Try," A1 (quotation), 2; "NAACP Meets Rebuff on School Enrollment: Out-of-District Negro Students Turned Down at Two Predominately White Units," *Los Angeles Times*, September 14, 1962, 24; Los Angeles City Schools, "Racial and Ethnic Survey," Fall 1968, Research and Evaluation Branch, LASMC, Box 139, UCLA/SC.

15. "Baldwin Hills School Rejects," 1 (quotation); "Negroes Try," A1, 2. The Garrs lived at 2818 S. Mansfield Avenue. See Miller, "NAACP Calls," 1; "Integration at Baldwin School," *Los Angeles Sentinel*, September 20, 1962, A1.

16. Miller, "NAACP Calls," 1 (first, second, and third quotations); "Integration at Baldwin School," A1, A4; Miller, "Loren Miller Says," 1 (fourth quotation).

17. Caughey and Caughey, *School Segregation on Our Doorstep*, 7, 10–14; Caughey and Caughey, *To Kill a Child's Spirit*, 18; J. Gregg, "Statement to Governor's Commission," 9–10; UN, "Problems and Challenges," 2–3; John Davies, "One (Hopefully) Integrated Community," ca. 1964, 21–22, author's collection (from Joan Suter).

18. UN, "Problems and Challenges," 3 (first, second, and third quotations); Jacqueline Broxton, "An Editorial: Dorsey High—Myth or Fact," *Los Angeles Sentinel*, October 15, 1964, C10 (fourth quotation).

19. Davies, "One (Hopefully)," 21–22 (all quotations on 21); UN, "Problems and Challenges," 4; Saltman, *A Fragile Movement*, 282–83.

20. Barbara Burrell, *Women and Political Participation: A Reference Handbook* (Santa Barbara, CA: ABC CLIO, 2004), 7, 52–53. See also Louise M. Young, *In the Public Interest: The League of Women Voters, 1920–1970* (New York: Greenwood Press, 1989).

21. J. Milgram, interview by author, November 11, 2006 and August 18, 2008, by telephone. Gregg took the surname of her first spouse, Paul, from whom she was divorced. In 1970 she married fair housing advocate Morris Milgram.

22. Post, interview by author, September 14, 2006, and September 24, 2006, by telephone; "Meet Your Board," *Crenshaw Notes* 2 (February 1965): 2, APP, Box 1, SCL; "Ann Post Introduction," n.d., APP, Box 1, SCL.

23. Fifi Boger, interview by author, November 3, 2006, by telephone (first quotation); J. Milgram, interview by author, November 11, 2006 (second quotation); UN, "Problems and Challenges," 3; Ann Post, "Crenshaw Neighbors: A Lesson in Integration," *The California Voter* (November 1968), author's collection (from Joan Suter).

24. For LWV's principles and program, see *The National Voter: League of Women Voters of the United States*, ca. 1968, APP, Box 1, SCL. For a history on Los Angeles's conservative female activists, see M. Nickerson, *Mothers of Conservatism*.

25. UN, "Problems and Challenges," 5–6 (first quotation on 6); Suter, interview by author (second and third quotations); "Co-Council Sets Reading Instruction for Children," *Angeles Mesa News-Advertiser*, June 9, 1963, author's collection (from Joan Suter).

26. UN, "Problems and Challenges," 5–6 (first, second, and third quotations on 5); Davies, "One (Hopefully)," 21–22; Greater Crenshaw Town Council, "Where and What is the Crenshaw Area?," brochure, ca. early 1960s, author's collection (from Joan Suter); Hirsch, *Making Second Ghetto*, 41 (fourth quotation); Sugrue, "Crabgrass-Roots Politics," 557 (fifth quotation).

27. Dale Gardner, "Inter-Office Memo," L.A. County Commission on Human Relations, January 10, 1952, JAF, Box 5/a/cc, Folder 7, HL (quotation). According to the memo, a resident reported that an African American realtor was distributing the postcards. Jean Gregg attributed the blockbusting movement "largely to the real estate brokers, both Negro and Caucasian." See J. Gregg, "Testimony of Jean Gregg," 17 (quotation).

28. Ann Post, "Stabilizing an Integrated Neighborhood," *The Integrator* 1, no. 3 (Fall 1968): 9 (first quotation), SCL; Donald Cotterell with Perlita D. Clarke, interview by author, August 2, 2006, Los Angeles, CA; Phenella D. Perez and Gisele Perez, interview by author, October 19, 2006, by telephone (second quotation); J. Gregg, "Testimony of Jean Gregg," 17–18 (third quotation on 18).

29. Inouye, interview by Ito, 173–80, 185, 189. See also S. Kurashige, *Shifting Grounds*, 250–51.

30. Inouye, interview by Ito, 189–98 (first quotation on 189; second and third quotations on 197). See also S. Kurashige, *Shifting Grounds*, 250–51. For advertisements of Inouye's and his competitors' businesses, see *Shin Nichi-Bei: New Japanese American News*, September 3, 1955, 3; *Shin Nichi-Bei: New Japanese American News*, February 24, 1956, 2.

31. Deloy Edwards, interview by author, June 23, 2007, Los Angeles, CA (both quotations); "Deloy Edwards: 50 Years of Service," booklet from 50th Anniversary Gala Celebration, July 30, 2005, 3, 5, author's collection (from Deloy Edwards); Deloy Edwards's résumé, ca. 1980s, author's collection (from Deloy Edwards).

32. Edwards, interview by author (first, second, fifth, and sixth quotations); Bob Baker, "View Park," *Los Angeles Times*, August 25, 1986, 1-3 (third and fourth quotations on 3). For mention of Whites selling low and Blacks buying high, see Orser, *Blockbusting in Baltimore*, 131.

33. Edwards, interview by author.

34. Edwards, interview by author (first and second quotations); Massey and Denton, *American Apartheid*, 38, 51–55; K. Jackson, *Crabgrass Frontier*, 195–210; Hillier, "Redlining and Loan Corporation," 414–15.

35. Edwards, interview by author (all quotations); "Deloy Edwards," 3, 14–15; J. Gregg, "Statement to Governor's Commission," 6–7.

36. Sherman, "The Negro's Role," 10 (first quotation); Seligman, *Block by Block*, 157; Edwards, interview by author (second and third quotations); J. Gregg, "Statement to Governor's Commission," 1.

37. Art Seidenbaum, "Spectator, '67: Neighbors Stand for Integration," *Los Angeles Times*, November 2, 1967, D1 (quotation); J. Gregg, "Statement to Governor's Commission," 5–6; Shulte, "Good Neighbor Policy"; John Greenwood, Coro Foundation Intern in Public Affairs, "Racial Transition and Culver City," June 1968, 6, APP, Box 1, SCL; "Ann Post Introduction."

38. J. Gregg, "Statement to Governor's Commission," 10 (first, second, and third quotations); UN, "Problems and Challenges," 5 (fourth quotation). In "Problems and Challenges," UN explained that around 1963, the Audubon Junior High School principal also transferred to another position (5).

39. Caughey and Caughey, *School Segregation on Our Doorstep*, 12–16 (quotation on 15).

40. Caughey and Caughey, *School Segregation on Our Doorstep*, 16–23; Caughey and Caughey, *To Kill a Child's Spirit*, 20–23. The Los Angeles Public Library Photo and Digital Collections include several photos on the 1963 demonstrations against the Los Angeles BOE.

41. J. Gregg, "Testimony of Jean Gregg," 8–9, 17 (first and second quotations); J. Gregg, "Statement to Governor's Commission," 6–7 (third quotation on 6); J. Milgram, interview by author, November 11, 2006; LACCHR, "Neighborhood Stabilization, Los Angeles County: Report of an Informal Discussion," March 23, 1965, JSP, Box 4, Folder 3, SCL, 1.

42. J. Gregg, "Testimony of Jean Gregg," 4, 7–8; J. Milgram, interview by author, November 11, 2006; J. Gregg, "Statement to Governor's Commission," 4–5.

43. In Gregory D. Squires, ed., *The Fight for Fair Housing: Causes, Consequences, and Future Implications of the 1968 Federal Fair Housing Act* (New York: Routledge, 2018), see the following: Sugrue, "From Jim Crow to Fair Housing," 21; Wade Henderson, "Foreword: Legacy of a Movement," xviii–xix; Rigel C. Oliveri, "The Legislative Battle for the Fair Housing Act (1966–1968)," 30.

44. "The Story of Stabilization," *Crenshaw Notes* 21 (December 1966): 2, APP, Box 1, SCL (first and second quotations); Saltman, *A Fragile Movement*, xi (third quotation), 3 (fourth quotation), 10, 21, 22, 28 (fn. 13). For more on the Hyde Park-Kenwood Community Conference, see Morris Milgram, *Good Neighborhood: The Challenge of Open Housing* (New York: W. W. Norton & Company, 1977), 138.

45. J. Gregg, "Statement to Governor's Commission," 5; "The Crenshaw Neighbors Story," *Crenshaw Notes* 4 (May 1965): 1, author's collection (from Joan Suter); "Announcements," *Crenshaw Notes* 9 (October 1965): 7, JSP, Box 5, Folder 4, SCL; J. Milgram, interview by author, November 11, 2006 (quotation) and August 18, 2008; Post, interview by author, September 24, 2006. For mention of Kimbrough and Laing as first and second vice president, see "Board Candidate Biographies," *Crenshaw Notes* 8 (September 1965): 3, APP, Box 1, SCL. CN's newsletter, *Crenshaw Notes*, consistently listed CN's officers and board of directors.

46. "The Crenshaw Neighbors Story," 1 (quotations, emphasis in original).

47. J. Gregg, "Statement to Governor's Commission," 5–6; J. Gregg, "Testimony of Jean Gregg," 9, 19–20; J. Milgram, interview by author, November 11, 2006; "We Send Letters," *Crenshaw Notes* 4 (May 1965): 3, author's collection (from Joan Suter); LACCHR, "Neighborhood Stabilization," 1; "The Real Estate Story," *Crenshaw Notes* 8 (September 1965): 2, APP, Box 1, SCL. CN's first office was located at 4034 Buckingham Road, the same address where Deloy Edwards had opened his first office. See *Crenshaw Notes* 2 (February 1965): 4, APP, Box 1, SCL.

48. "The Crenshaw Neighbors Story," 1–2 (first quotation on 2); "A Story of Balance," 1 (second quotation); J. Gregg, "Testimony of Jean Gregg," 41–42 (third and fourth quotations on 42). For the results of CN's racial census, see "A Story of Balance," 2. For a discussion on the tipping point hypothesis, an assumption CN generally feared would come true in its communities, see Micheal W. Giles, Everett F. Cataldo, and Douglas S.

Gatlin, "White Flight and Percent Black: The Tipping Point Reexamined," *Social Science Quarterly* 56, no. 1 (1975): 85–92; and John R. Ottensmann, "Requiem for the Tipping-Point Hypothesis," *Journal of Planning Literature* 10, no. 2 (November 1995): 131–41.

49. Post, "Stabilizing an Integrated Neighborhood," 9; J. Gregg, "Testimony of Jean Gregg," 9; J. Milgram, interview by author, November 11, 2006. For mention of CN in local Japanese American-run newspapers, see "Crenshaw Group Organizes to Promote Racial Balance," *Shin Nichi-Bei: New Japanese American News*, March 12, 1965, 1; and "Crenshaw Neighbors," *Pacific Citizen*, May 27, 1966, 6. An update on CN's membership committee in *Crenshaw Notes* (issue September 1970, 6, APP, Box 1, SCL) also mentions an article on CN in the Japanese-run publication, *Crossroads*. For CN's advertisements of its Beverly Hills properties for sale, see "A Special House," *Los Angeles Sentinel*, April 1, 1965; "Look What You Can Buy All Over Town!" *Los Angeles Sentinel*, April 22, 1965. For references to the real estate signs, see "The Real Estate Story," 1; for the billboard, see "Have You Seen Our Billboard?," *Crenshaw Notes* 8 (September 1965), APP, Box 1, SCL, 5.

50. "We Send Letters"; "Come and See," *Crenshaw Notes* 4 (May 1965): 3, 7, author's collection (from Joan Suter).

51. J. Gregg, "Statement to Governor's Commission," 3–4; "Survey Starts," *Crenshaw Notes* 4 (May 1965): 6, author's collection (from Joan Suter); "A Story of Balance," 1–2 (all quotations on 1).

52. "Crenshaw Home Tour," *Crenshaw Notes* 4 (May 1965): 6 (first, second, and third quotations), author's collection (from Joan Suter); "Home Visits Set for Third Year," *Crenshaw Notes* 22 (January 1967): 3 (fourth quotation on 3), APP, Box 1, SCL; "Crenshaw Neighbors to Sponsor Home Tour," *Los Angeles Times*, May 26, 1966; "Home Tour Slated in Baldwin Hills," *Los Angeles Times*, June 3, 1966; "Home Tour Proves Major Success," *Crenshaw Notes* 17 (July–August 1966): 4, author's collection (from Joan Suter). See also Shulte, "Good Neighbor Policy"; Evelyn DeWolfe, "Home Tour Sunday: Neighbors Join Hands for Integration," *Los Angeles Times*, May 31, 1968.

53. LACCHR, "Neighborhood Stabilization," 1 (first and second quotations); J. Gregg, "Statement to Governor's Commission," 8 (third quotation); "Announcements," *Crenshaw Notes* 9 (October 1965): 7, JSP, Box 5, Folder 4, SCL; J. Milgram, interview by author, November 11, 2006 (fourth and fifth quotations).

54. J. Gregg, "Statement to Governor's Commission," 5; J. Milgram, interview by author, November 11, 2006; LACCHR, "Neighborhood Stabilization," 1; "Balance Sheet," *Crenshaw Notes* 8 (September 1965), APP, Box 1, SCL; "Balance Sheet," *Crenshaw Notes* 20 (November 1966), APP, Box 1, SCL; Ann Post, "They Are Proving It Really Works," *Los Angeles Times*, April 24, 1965, B4 (quotation). For CN members' biographies, see "Our Nominees," *Crenshaw Notes* 40 (September 1968): 1–2, APP, Box 1, SCL.

55. Thomas W. Casstevens, *Politics, Housing, and Race Relations: California's Rumford Act and Proposition 14* (Berkeley: University of California, Institute of Governmental Studies, 1967), 96 (first quotation); "Housing Case Won by Negro and White Wife," *Los Angeles Times*, January 4, 1966 (second quotation); "An Unusual Decision," *Crenshaw Notes* 12 (January 1966): 1, APP, Box 1, SCL; "Riley Jacobs Case," *Crenshaw Notes* 13 (February–March 1966): 5, APP, Box 1, SCL.

56. Flamming, "Becoming Democrats," 297–99; Sides, *L.A. City Limits*, 157–58; Casstevens, *Politics, Housing, and Race Relations*, 8–18, 22–40; HoSang, *Racial Propositions*, 61–62; Sugrue, "From Jim Crow to Fair Housing," 22.

57. HoSang, *Racial Propositions*, 61–63; Brilliant, *Color of America Has Changed*, 192; S. Kurashige, *Shifting Grounds*, 261. Casstevens, in *Politics, Housing, and Race Relations* (47), also mentions the Rumford Act primarily covering the Black middle class.

58. HoSang, *Racial Propositions*, 9–10, 63–64.

59. HoSang, *Racial Propositions*, 64–66; Max Felker-Kantor, "Fighting the Segregation Amendment: Black and Mexican American Responses to Proposition 14 in Los Angeles," in Kun and Pulido, *Black and Brown*, 148–49; Casstevens, *Politics, Housing, and Race Relations*, 41, 48–50; William Byron Rumford, "Legislator for Fair Employment, Fair Housing and Public Health," interview by Joyce A. Henderson, Amelia R. Fry, and Edward France (Berkeley: University of California, Berkeley, Bancroft Library, Regional Oral History Office, 1973), 44 (quotation).

60. HoSang, *Racial Propositions*, 65–70 (first quotation on 66, italics in original; second quotation on 69; third quotation on 65); Casstevens, *Politics, Housing, and Race Relations*, 48–49, 53, 57–67.

61. Nicolaides, *My Blue Heaven*, 272–315 (quotation on 312).

62. Casstevens, *Politics, Housing, and Race Relations*, 60–61; HoSang, *Racial Propositions*, 74–79 (quotation on 76); Felker-Kantor, "Fighting Segregation Amendment," 148–49.

63. Felker-Kantor, "Fighting Segregation Amendment," 144 (first quotation), 149–56 (second quotation on 154), 167 (fn. 6), 170 (fn. 30).

64. Felker-Kantor, "Fighting Segregation Amendment," 156–64 (quotation on 164); S. Kurashige, *Shifting Grounds*, 263–65; Raymond E. Wolfinger and Fred I. Greenstein, "The Repeal of Fair Housing in California: An Analysis of Referendum Voting," *American Political Science Review* 62, no. 3 (September 1968): 759.

65. "Unusual Decision"; "Riley Jacobs Case"; Jean Gregg, "Report on Current Fair Housing Legislation and Enforcement as it Applies to Los Angeles," August 27, 1963, APP, Box 2, SCL; Ann Post, "Report on Real Estate Organizations as it Applies to Los Angeles," August 27, 1963, APP, Box 1, SCL; Flyer, "Decide for Yourself," ca. February 1964, APP, Box 2, SCL (first and second quotations); J. Gregg, "Statement to Governor's Commission," 14 (third quotation, emphasis in original); Ann Post, "The Story of Open Housing Legislation," *Crenshaw Notes* 27 (June 1967): 2 (fourth quotation), APP, Box 1, SCL.

66. Casstevens, *Politics, Housing, and Race Relations*, 67–70, 81–83; HoSang, *Racial Propositions*, 65, 83–84.

67. Abu-Lughod, *Race, Space, and Riots*, 203–8. See also Jerry Cohen and William S. Murphy, *Burn, Baby, Burn! The Los Angeles Race Riot, August 1965* (New York: E. P. Dutton & Co., Inc., 1966); Conot, *Rivers of Blood*; Horne, *Fire This Time*; and Gerald Horne, "Black Fire: 'Riot' and 'Revolt' in Los Angeles, 1965 and 1992," in de Graaf, Mulroy, and Taylor, *Seeking El Dorado*, 377–404.

68. For reference to the history of Watts, see Abu-Lughod, *Race, Space, and Riots*, 199–203. For discussion on the causes of the Watts rebellion, see Horne, *Fire This Time*, 3–42, 217–18; Horne, "Black Fire," 379–88, 390–91; and Robert Bauman, *Race and the War on Poverty: From Watts to East L.A.* (Norman: University of Oklahoma Press, 2008), 31–37.

69. Felker-Kantor, "Fighting Segregation Amendment," 151–56; Horne, *Fire This Time*, 14–15, 33–36, 171–73; Horne, "Black Fire," 381–83.

70. Felker-Kantor, "Fighting Segregation Amendment," 151–56; Horne, *Fire This Time*, 14–15, 33–36 (first quotation on 35; second quotation on 36), 171–73; Horne, "Black Fire," 381–83.

71. Horne, *Fire This Time*, 14–15, 171–93 (quotation on 185); Bauman, *Race and the War on Poverty*, 38–42.

72. Abu-Lughod, *Race, Space, and Riots*, 208–14 (see map on 212 for the curfew zone and areas of significant violence within it); Horne, "Black Fire," 377; HoSang, *Racial Propositions*, 87.

73. Horne, "Black Fire," 389–90; HoSang, *Racial Propositions*, 72, 88–89; Felker-Kantor, "Fighting Segregation Amendment," 164. For works on the California origins of modern conservatism, see McGirr, *Suburban Warriors*; Kurt Schuparra, *Triumph of the Right: The Rise of the California Conservative Movement, 1945–1966* (Armonk, NY: M. E. Sharpe, 1998). For work on the Chicano blowouts, see Mario T. García and Sal Castro, *Blowout! Sal Castro & the Chicano Struggle for Educational Justice* (Chapel Hill: University of North Carolina Press, 2011).

74. J. Gregg, "Statement to Governor's Commission," 15; Jack Jones, "Fight to Stabilize Integrated Parts of City Showing Gain," *Los Angeles Times*, September 5, 1966; Los Angeles Commission on Human Relations, "Council of Integrated Neighborhoods, 'COIN,' Los Angeles County," n.d., JSP, Box 5, Folder 3, SCL, 1–3; Raymond Weil, "The Integrated Neighborhood—Unheralded Example and Bypassed Opportunity," address before the Housing and Urban Development Conference, October 26, 1966, JSP, Box 5, Folder 3, SCL, 1–4; "Los Angeles County Commission on Human Relations: A 25 Year History, 1944–1969 & Biennial Report 1967–1969," KHC, Box 1.25.1–1.25.4, Folder 1970 (#1), HL. *The Integrator* published a version of Weil's address for a wider audience. See Raymond Weil, "The Integrated Neighborhood Unheralded Example and Bypassed Opportunity," *The Integrator* 1, no. 1 (Winter 1967–68): 3–6.

75. Weil, "Integrated Neighborhood," address, 1–4; Los Angeles Commission on Human Relations, "Council of Integrated Neighborhoods," 3 (quotation).

76. "We Testify," *Crenshaw Notes* 10 (November 1965): 3 (all quotations in paragraph), JSP, Box 5, Folder 4, SCL; J. Gregg, "Statement to Governor's Commission," entire; J. Gregg, "Testimony of Jean Gregg," 16, 20–21.

77. *Crenshaw Notes* 9 (October 1965): 3 (first, second, and third quotations), 4, JSP, Box 5, Folder 4, SCL. For an example of an editorial in the *Los Angeles Times*, see Karen A. Freidson, "Integrated Housing Works in Crenshaw," *Los Angeles Times*, November 20, 1971. Freidson served as CN executive director in the early 1970s. For reference to CN's plaques, see "Membership Plaques Ready," *Crenshaw Notes* 11 (December 1965): 4 (fourth, fifth, and sixth quotations), APP, Box 1, SCL.

78. "New Real Estate Policy," *Crenshaw Notes* 11 (December 1965): 6 (quotation), APP, Box 1, SCL; "The Real Estate Story: Part II," *Crenshaw Notes* 20 (November 1966): 1–2, APP, Box 1, SCL. For real estate salaries and commissions CN earned and paid, see "Balance Sheet," (November 1966): 5–6; Crenshaw Neighbors, Inc., "Statement of Income and Expenses: For the Fiscal Year Begun July 1, 1966 and Ended June 30, 1967," ca. 1967, APP, Box 1, SCL.

79. Richard T. Morris and Vincent Jeffries, *The White Reaction Study* (Los Angeles: University of California, Los Angeles, Institute of Government and Public Affairs, 1967), 58–59 (quotations on 59).

80. Jean Gregg, "Our Executive Director Speaks," *Crenshaw Notes* 18 (September 1966): 4, APP, Box 1, SCL; "News Briefs," *Crenshaw Notes* 20 (November 1966): 7, APP, Box 1, SCL; Ken Olsen, "Editor's Notes," *Crenshaw Notes* 11 (December 1965): 3, APP, Box 1, SCL.

81. Hunt, "Introduction," 6–7; "Seminar for Apartment House Owners and Managers" and "Housing Seminar: Positive Action for Apartment Area," *Crenshaw Notes*

30 (September 1967): 3, 7 (first, second, and third quotations), APP, Box 1, SCL; Post, "Stabilizing an Integrated Neighborhood," 9, 15 (fourth quotation); "National Scene of Integrated Housing," *The Integrator* 1, no. 1 (Winter 1967–68): 7, SCL. For a 1970 update on the apartments, see "'The Jungle,' the Owners, and Crenshaw Neighbors," *Crenshaw Notes* 57 (May 1970): 1–2, APP, Box 1, SCL.

82. "RSVP An Invitation to Dinner," *Crenshaw Notes* 9 (October 1965): 8, JSP, Box 5, Folder 4, SCL; "Calendar of Events" and "Foundation for the Junior Blind," *Crenshaw Notes* 33 (December 1967): 3, JSP, Box 5, Folder 4, SCL; Saltman, *A Fragile Movement*, 284; Post, "Crenshaw Neighbors." For sources on the projected freeway, see "Shall CN Fight the Freeway(s)?," *Crenshaw Notes* 9 (October 1965): 5–6, JSP, Box 5, Folder 4, SCL; "Freeways Action," *Crenshaw Notes* 10 (November 1965): 5, JSP, Box 5, Folder 4, SCL; Barry Siegel, "'Rethinking in Order': Foes of Freeways Tell Stand," *Los Angeles Times*, May 7, 1966. For references to Anne Nelson and the park, see Ellen Shulte, "Area Turns to Greenery for Power," *Los Angeles Times*, November 7, 1968; Mollie Gregory, *Women Who Run the Show: How a Brilliant and Creative New Generation of Women Stormed Hollywood* (New York: St. Martin's Press, 2002): 99–101, 362; Claire Noland, "Anne Roberts Nelson Dies at 86; CBS Television Executive," *Los Angeles Times*, June 25, 2009.

83. "Summer Education Sessions Conclude," *Angeles Mesa News-Advertiser*, August 1, 1965, author's collection (from Joan Suter); "Center for Enrichment," *Angeles Mesa News-Advertiser*, May 5, 1966, author's collection (from Joan Suter); Ken Olsen, "Editor's Notes," *Crenshaw Notes* 17 (July–August 1966): 3, APP, Box 1, SCL; "3 Professors Lecture to Kids About Science," *University of Southern California Trojan*, July 29, 1966, author's collection (from Joan Suter); "The Third Session of the Baldwin Hills Cultural Enrichment Center," brochure, 1968, author's collection (from Joan Suter); "Mrs. Suter Tackles L.A. Education," *Angeles Mesa News-Advertiser*, February 23, 1969, author's collection (from Joan Suter).

84. Boger, interview by author (first quotation); "Teen Crash Program at Fremont High," *Los Angeles Sentinel*, August 26, 1965; Eric Malnic, "Youths Given Healthy Outlet for Energies," *Los Angeles Times*, August 29, 1965, G1, 3; George Garrigues and Lee Austin, "Busy Youths Free of Tensions," *Los Angeles Times*, September 5, 1965, B1, 5; Ernest Schonberger, "Extension of Poverty War Teen Posts OKd," *Los Angeles Times*, October 10, 1965, B; "Watts Teen Post Has Open House," *Los Angeles Sentinel*, June 30, 1966; Jack Jones, "Teen Post Sponsors Worried About Fiscal Cuts in Program," *Los Angeles Times*, June 13, 1966, 3, 32 (second quotation); Jack Jones, "Irate Mexican-American Units Demand Poverty War Equality," *Los Angeles Times*, September 25, 1966, B, 20; Peyton Canary and Bert Mann, "Sunset Strip Spectacle Sparks Study on Curfew," *Los Angeles Times*, December 18, 1966, B1, 6. For more on Boger's activism, see "Senator Kennedy at Elks Tuesday," *Los Angeles Sentinel*, October 27, 1960; "A Gift for the Governor," *Los Angeles Sentinel*, October 26, 1961; "Governor Brown to Lead Salute to 'Gus' Hawkins," *Los Angeles Sentinel*, September 6, 1962; "Concord Park Costs $30 Million," *Los Angeles Sentinel*, April 9, 1964.

85. Suter, interview by author (both quotations); Jean Gregg, "Apex Loves," *The Integrator* 1, no. 1 (Winter 1967–68): 8–12, SCL; Post, "Stabilizing an Integrated Neighborhood," 15; "APEX," brochure, April 1968, author's collection (from Joan Suter); "APEX Advisor Council: Mrs. Suter Elected to the Chair," *Angeles Mesa News-Advertiser*, December 25, 1969, author's collection (from Joan Suter); Saltman, *A Fragile Movement*, 284; Jack P. Crowther et al., "APEX Los Angeles City Schools. Division of Secondary Education—Area 'D.' A Special Informatory Report to the Board of Education," July 10,

1969, HVS, Box 1, Folder 2, UCLA/SC, 1–2; Office of Measurement and Evaluation, Los Angeles City Unified School District, "Mid-City Secondary Education Project. Area Program for Enrichment Exchange. APEX. Evaluation Reports," September 1969, HVS, Box 1, Folder 2, UCLA/SC, 21–22; Shulte, "Good Neighbor Policy"; "Community APEX Funded for a Third Time," *Angeles Mesa News-Advertiser*, October 2, 1969, author's collection (from Joan Suter). For Judge Gitelson's decision on busing in LAUSD, see Mary Ellen Crawford v. Board of Education of the City of Los Angeles, L.A. No. 822854, filed February 11, 1970.

86. Suter, interview by author; Crowther et al., "APEX Los Angeles City Schools," 7, 22, 25–26, 37 (first quotation), 40 (second quotation); Caughey and Caughey, *To Kill a Child's Spirit*, 33–34; Saltman, *A Fragile Movement*, 284.

87. Suter, interview by author (first quotation); "APEX Campers View Trip, tell Normans to 'Wake Up!'" *Highlights*, date unknown, author's collection (from Joan Suter; second and third quotations); "Beverly and APEX Students Make Excursion to Idyllwild Together as Brothers and Sisters in a Beautiful Adventure," *Highlights*, April 25, 1969, author's collection (from Joan Suter; fourth and fifth quotations, original emphasis).

88. "Candidates for Board of Directors: Yoshinao Nakada," *Crenshaw Notes* 8 (September 1965): 4, APP, Box 1, SCL; "Joe Ozawa Jr. Elected to Board of Directors," *Crenshaw Notes* 20 (November 1966): 4, APP, Box 1, SCL; "Our Nominees: Mr. Masamori Kojima," *Crenshaw Notes* 40 (September 1968): 2, APP, Box 1, SCL; George Ramos, "Rites Held for Bradley Aide Mas Kojima," *Los Angeles Times*, February 6, 1989 (quotation); "Board of Directors: Mr. Donald Misumi," *Crenshaw Notes* 60 (September 1970): 4, APP, Box 1, SCL; Board of Directors, *Crenshaw Notes* 61 (October 1970): 2, APP, Box 1, SCL.

89. "Crenshaw Group"; "Our Committees at Work," *Crenshaw Notes* 45 (March 1969): 5 (first and second quotations), APP, Box 1, SCL; "Join with Your Neighbors," *Crenshaw Notes* 58 (June 1970): 7 (third quotation), APP, Box 1, SCL; "Membership Committee," *Crenshaw Notes* 60 (September 1970): 6 (fourth and fifth quotations), APP, Box 1, SCL.

90. See introductory page on any edition, including *The Integrator* 1, no. 1 (Winter 1967–68), SCL (first quotation). For background on the making of *The Integrator*, see Seidenbaum, "Spectator, '67"; "New Horizons for CN," *Crenshaw Notes* 33 (December 1967): 5, JSP, Box 5, Folder 4, SCL. For Walker's biography, see "About *The Integrator*," *Crenshaw Notes* 54 (February 1970): 4 (second quotation), APP, Box 1, SCL; "Olive Walker," *Crenshaw Notes* 8 (September 1965): 4, APP, Box 1, SCL, and for mention of her on the LWVLA roster, see "League of Women Voters of Los Angeles: Know Your Housing Alphabet," 1968, APP, Box 1, SCL. For information on Olive Walker, including her involvement in UN as a steering committee member and her home address in the early 1960s, see UN, "Problems and Challenges," 4.

91. Lyle Suter, "The '9 to 5' Liberal," *The Integrator* 1, no. 2 (Summer 1968): 18, SCL; Lyle Suter, "'De Facto' Charlie," *The Integrator* 1, no. 3 (Fall 1968): 25–26, SCL.

92. John Saito, "Yellow Power," *The Integrator* 1, no. 2 (Summer 1968): 4–5 (first quotation on 4; second and third quotations on 5).

93. For mention of free office space, see Ken Olsen, "An Open Letter from Our President," *Crenshaw Notes* 22 (January 1967): 5, APP, Box 1, SCL. For membership numbers, see J. Gregg, "Statement to Governor's Commission," 5; "The Story of Membership," *Crenshaw Notes* 23 (February 1967): 1, APP, Box 1, SCL; "Crenshaw Group Endorses 3 School Proposals," *Los Angeles Sentinel*, February 6, 1969. For references to Burke and

Bradley, see, respectively, "Yvonne Brathwaite Elected to CN Board," *Crenshaw Notes* 22 (January 1967): 4, APP, Box 1, SCL; "Member of the Month," *Crenshaw Notes* 48 (June 1969): 3, APP, Box 1, SCL. For reference to *The Integrator*, see "Seven Hundred People across the Country," *Crenshaw Notes* 40 (September 1968): 7, APP, Box 1, SCL. For reference to CN Week, see "A Resolution," *Los Angeles Sentinel*, May 22, 1969.

94. K-Y Taylor, *Race for Profit*, 16, 74; Massey and Denton, *American Apartheid*, 195; Orser, *Blockbusting in Baltimore*, 168; Sugrue, "From Jim Crow to Fair Housing," 24. For the most up-to-date language on the Fair Housing Act's prohibition of blockbusting, see National Archives, "Code of Federal Regulations," 24 CFR § 100.85 Blockbusting, accessed September 24, 2021, https://www.ecfr.gov/current/title-24/subtitle-B/chapter-I/part-100.

95. For references to CN's 1967 census and Post's comments on stabilization, see "Story of Stabilization," *Crenshaw Notes* 31 (October 1967): 1–2, APP, Box 1, SCL; "Executive Director's Report to General Membership Meeting," September 28, 1967, 3, APP, Box 1, SCL; Post, "Stabilizing an Integrated Neighborhood," 9 (first quotation). For references to Olsen's comments, see Kenneth C. Olsen, "President's Report to the Board of Directors," April 16, 1968, APP, Box 1, 1–4 (second quotation on 1; third quotation on 2), SCL. For references to CN's critics, see Beverly Stearn, "Letters to the Editor," *Crenshaw Notes* 37 (May 1968): 6, APP, Box 1, SCL; "An Open Letter to the Black Community in Crenshaw," *Crenshaw Notes* 55 (March 1970): 2, APP, Box 1, SCL; "Crenshaw Neighbors and You," *Crenshaw Notes* 48 (June 1969): 1, APP, Box 1, SCL.

96. Lawrence Van Gelder, "Morris Milgram, 81; Built Interracial Housing," *New York Times*, June 26, 1997; Gwen Shaffer, "Philadelphia's First Integrated Housing Development Turns 50," *Philadelphia Weekly*, July 26, 2006; Saltman, *A Fragile Movement*, 313–14, 317; M. Milgram, *Good Neighborhood*, 11, 54–59, 62, 138–40; J. Milgram, interview by author, November 11, 2006; Jean Gregg Milgram, "National Neighbors: Fact Sheet," February 1970, APP, Box 2, SCL. Among his many projects, in the mid-1960s, Morris Milgram founded the National Committee on Tithing in Investment (NCTI), a nonprofit group of twenty-five thousand that sponsored housing integration, and Mutual Real Estate Investment Trust, a company that sought to purchase apartment buildings in all-White areas and maintain them with ethnically diverse tenants. NCTI eventually changed its name to Sponsors of Open Housing Investment. In 1975, Milgram and civil rights leader James Farmer also founded the Fund for an OPEN Society, a nonprofit organization that initially granted low-cost mortgages to integrate neighborhoods, and then worked to stabilize integrated communities. See Saltman, *A Fragile Movement*, 28–29 (fn. 15).

97. Saltman, *A Fragile Movement*, 322 (quotation), 336–39, 357–58; M. Milgram, *Good Neighborhood*, 139–40; J. Milgram, interview by author, November 11, 2006.

98. Jones, "Fight to Stabilize"; J. Milgram, interview by author, November 11, 2006.

99. LACCHR, "Neighborhood Stabilization," 1; Shulte, "Good Neighbor Policy"; Post, "Stabilizing an Integrated Neighborhood," 9; Barry Siegel, "Image and Reality," *Crenshaw Notes* 82 (December/January 1973): 1 (quotation), APP, Box 1, SCL. See chapter 4 for discussions on federal census data of the Crenshaw area.

100. Los Angeles City Schools, "Racial and Ethnic Survey," Fall 1966, Research and Evaluation Branch, LASMC, Box 138, UCLA/SC; Los Angeles City Schools, "Racial and Ethnic Survey," Fall 1970, Research and Evaluation Branch, LASMC, Box 139, UCLA/SC.

101. Jack McCurdy, "Black School Highest in IQ—Is Affluence the Reason?" *Los Angeles Times*, October 12, 1969, 1 (first quotation), 4–5; "Black Schools that Work," *Newsweek*, January 1, 1973, 57–58 (second quotation on 57).

CHAPTER 6. BROCKMAN GALLERY AND THE ART OF SOCIAL CHANGE

1. Alonzo Davis, interview by Karen Anne Mason (Los Angeles: UCLA Library, Center for Oral History Research, 1990–91), UCLA/OL; Dale Brockman Davis, interview by author, March 15, 2008, Los Angeles, California.

2. A. Davis, interview by Mason (quotation); D. Davis, interview by author; Hise, *Magnetic Los Angeles*, 14–17; Steven L. Isoardi, *The Dark Tree: Jazz and the Community Arts in Los Angeles* (Berkeley: University of California Press, 2006), 218–19.

3. Widener, *Black Arts West*, 81, 89, 126; Daniel L. Widener, "'Way Out West': Expressive Art, Music, and Culture in Black LA," *Emergences* 9, no. 2 (1999): 278. For monographs on the black arts movement, see James Edward Smethurst, *The Black Arts Movement: Literary Nationalism in the 1960s and 1970s* (Chapel Hill: University of North Carolina Press, 2005); Cheryl Clarke, *"After Mecca": Women Poets and the Black Arts Movement* (New Brunswick: Rutgers University Press, 2005); and Lisa Gail Collins and Margo Natalie Crawford, *New Thoughts on the Black Arts Movement* (New Brunswick, NJ: Rutgers University Press, 2006).

4. For reference to Japanese-owned businesses on Jefferson Boulevard, see Inouye, interview by Ito, 196–97. For reference to Crenshaw Square and Holiday Bowl, see S. Kurashige, *Shifting Grounds*, 255–57.

5. Exum and Guiza-Leimert, *Images of America*, 93–95, 101.

6. Widener, *Black Arts West*, 159 (quotation); A. Davis, interview by Mason.

7. Thorstein Veblen, *The Theory of the Leisure Class* (New York: Penguin Books, 1994), chap. 3, chap. 4 (first quotation on 85, second and third quotations on 36); Chin-tao Wu, *Privatising Culture: Corporate Art Intervention since the 1980s* (New York: Verso, 2002), 126–27; Paul Dimaggio and Michael Useem, "Social Class and Arts Consumption: The Origins and Consequences of Class Differences in Exposure to the Arts in America," *Theory and Society* 5, no. 2 (March 1978): 144. For a history of the art market, see Peter Watson, *From Manet to Manhattan: The Rise of the Modern Art Market* (New York: Random House, 1992).

8. Scot Brown, *Fighting for US: Maulana Karenga, the US Organization, and Black Cultural Nationalism* (New York: New York University Press, 2003), 107–13. For more on Black nationalist movements, see Peniel E. Joseph, *Waiting 'Til the Midnight Hour: A Narrative History of Black Power in America* (New York: Henry Holt and Co., 2006).

9. Lizzetta LeFalle-Collins, "The Brockman Gallery and the Village," *Journal of Contemporary African Art* 30 (Spring 2012): 11; A. Davis, interview by Mason; D. Davis, interview by author; Isoardi, *Dark Tree*, 218–19; Brown, *Fighting for US*, 50, 107, 110; John W. Outterbridge, interview by Richard Cándida Smith, 1989 (Los Angeles: UCLA Library, Center for Oral History Research, 1989–90), UCLA/OL.

10. Isoardi, *Dark Tree*, 218–19; Lindsay, *Leimert Park*.

11. A. Davis, interview by Mason; D. Davis, interview by author; Robert J. Norrell, *Reaping the Whirlwind: The Civil Rights Movement in Tuskegee* (Chapel Hill: University of North Carolina Press, 1998), 38–41. See also Washington, *Up from Slavery*; and West, *The Education*.

12. A. Davis, interview by Mason (all quotations); D. Davis, interview by author.

13. D. Davis, interview by author (first and second quotations); A. Davis, interview by Mason (third and fourth quotations); Kay Lindsey, "Brockman Gallery," *Art Papers* (July/August 1990): 23.

14. A. Davis, interview by Mason; D. Davis, interview by author (all quotations). In separate interviews, Alonzo and Dale gave two different locations of their first home

in Los Angeles. Alonzo cited the home near Fourth Avenue and Exposition Boulevard; Dale said the house was located near Second Avenue and Exposition Boulevard.

15. A. Davis, interview by Mason (quotation).

16. A. Davis, interview by Mason (quotation); Jennifer Mandel, "Setting the Record Straight: Almena Lomax, the *Los Angeles Tribune*, and a Lifelong Passion for Racial Justice and the Written Word," *Southern California Quarterly* 98, no. 1 (Spring 2016): 65–73, 78–81.

17. A. Davis, interview by Mason; D. Davis, interview by author.

18. D. Davis, interview by author.

19. A. Davis, interview by Mason (quotation).

20. D. Davis, interview by author. See also a biography of Dale Davis in Samella S. Lewis and Ruth G. Waddy, eds., *Black Artists on Art*, vol. 2 (Los Angeles: Contemporary Crafts, Inc., 1971), 125. For a photo of *Viet Nam War Games*, see Kellie Jones, ed., *Now Dig This! Art & Black Los Angeles, 1960–1980* (Los Angeles: Hammer Museum, 2011), 227.

21. A. Davis, interview by Mason (both quotations); Abu-Lughod, *Race, Space, and Riots*, 210–13.

22. Joseph, *Waiting 'til the Midnight Hour*, 217–18; Horne, *Fire This Time*, 202–4; Bruce M. Tyler, "The Rise and Decline of the Watts Summer Festival, 1965 to 1986," *American Studies* 31, no. 2 (Fall 1990): 62–66. See also Brown, *Fighting for US*. For information on the African American Cultural Center, see http://africanamericanculturalcenter-la.org

23. A. Davis, interview by Mason (quotation); D. Davis, interview by author.

24. A. Davis, interview by Mason; D. Davis, interview by author; Sitkoff, *The Struggle*, 194–200; Clayborne Carson, *In Struggle: SNCC and the Black Awakening of the 1960s* (Cambridge: Harvard University Press, 1995), 209–11 (quotation on 209).

25. A. Davis, interview by Mason; D. Davis, interview by author.

26. A. Davis, interview by Mason; D. Davis, interview by author.

27. A. Davis, interview by Mason; D. Davis, interview by author; Smethurst, *Black Arts Movement*, 14–16; Widener, *Black Arts West*, 81, 89; Widener, "Way Out West," 278.

28. Sarah Schrank, *Art and the City: Civic Imagination and Cultural Authority in Los Angeles* (Philadelphia: University of Pennsylvania Press, 2009), 60–62; Arthur Millier, "Negro Art Attracts," *Los Angeles Times*, December 8, 1929, 21 (first quotation), 30 (second quotation).

29. Miriam Matthews, interview by Robin D. G. Kelley (Los Angeles: UCLA Library, Center for Oral History Research, 1985–86), UCLA/OL; Kellie Jones, *South of Pico: African American Artists in Los Angeles in the 1960s and 1970s* (Durham: Duke University Press, 2017), 140–42; Robert Lee Johnson, *Notable Southern Californians in Black History* (Charleston: The History Press, 2017), 123–25. For the development of the art market in the United States, see Watson, *From Manet to Manhattan*.

30. Matthews, interview by Kelley; Judith Wilson, "How the Invisible Woman Got Herself on the Cultural Map: Black Women Artists in California," in *Art/Women/California: Parallels and Intersections, 1950–2000*, edited by Diana Burgess Fuller and Daniela Salvioni (Berkeley: University of California Press, 2002), 207–10. For references to the Museum of Modern Art and the National Gallery of Art, see Watson, *From Manet to Manhattan*, 230, 248.

31. Morgan Neville, producer and director, *The Cool School: The Story of the Ferus Art Gallery* (Los Angeles: Arthouse Films/Curiously Bright, 2008).

32. Jones, *South of Pico*, 160; Cecil Fergerson, interview by Karen Anne Mason (Los Angeles: UCLA Library, Center for Oral History Research, 1990-92, 1994), UCLA/OL; Outterbridge, interview by R. Smith; Peter Selz, *Art of Engagement: Visual Politics in California and Beyond* (Berkeley: University of California Press, 2005), 145-46; Robert Perine, *Chouinard: An Art Vision Betrayed: The Story of the Chouinard Art Institute, 1921-1972* (Encinitas: Artra Publishing, 1985), 40, 130-31; Pajaud, interview by Mason (quotation).

33. Ruth G. Waddy, interview by Karen Anne Mason (Los Angeles: UCLA Library, Center for Oral History Research, 1991), UCLA/OL.

34. Suzanne Muchnic, *LACMA So Far: Portrait of a Museum in the Making* (San Marino, CA: Huntington Library, 2015), chaps. 1-2, 8-10; Margaret Leslie Davis, *The Culture Broker: Franklin D. Murphy and the Transformation of Los Angeles* (Berkeley: University of California Press, 2007), 28-30; Widener, *Black Arts West*, 155.

35. Waddy, interview by Mason; Samella S. Lewis and Ruth G. Waddy, eds., *Black Artists on Art*, vol. 1 (Los Angeles: Contemporary Crafts Publishers, 1969), 86, 116-18, 128, 131; Samella S. Lewis, *African American Art and Artists* (Berkeley: University of California Press, 2003), 238, 252-53; Samella Lewis, interview by Eric Hanks, in *Distinctly Los Angeles: An African American Perspective*, edited by Eric Hanks (Santa Monica, CA: M. Hanks Gallery, 2009), 9 (quotation); Kellie Jones, "To/From Los Angeles with Betye Saar," in *Betye Saar: Extending the Frozen Moment*, edited by Karen Chassin Goldbaum (Ann Arbor: University of Michigan Museum of Art, 2005), 34. See also Art-West Associated North, Inc., *New Perspectives in Black Art* (Oakland, CA: Oakland Museum Art Division, October 5-26, 1968), 3, 24.

36. Smethurst, *Black Arts Movement*, 298-99; Isoardi, *Dark Tree*, 75-76; Widener, *Black Arts West*, 130; Nancy Adler, "Arts Center Born after Watts Riot," *New York Times*, March 19, 1967.

37. Horace Tapscott, interview by Steven L. Isoardi (Los Angeles: UCLA Library, Center for Oral History Research, 1993), UCLA/OL (quotation); Isoardi, *Dark Tree*, 1-2, 49. See also Horace Tapscott, *Songs of the Unsung: The Musical and Social Journey of Horace Tapscott*, edited by Steven Isoardi (Durham, NC: Duke University Press, 2001); Bryant et al., *Central Avenue Sounds*, 282-303 (discussion of Horace Tapscott).

38. Tapscott, interview by Isoardi; Smethurst, *Black Arts Movement*, 297-98; Isoardi, *Dark Tree*, 49-52, 62-64, 113, 181-87.

39. Widener, *Black Arts West*, 95-97, 134; Tapscott, interview by Isoardi; Smethurst, *Black Arts Movement*, 303-11; Daniel Widener, "Writing Watts: Budd Schulberg, Black Poetry, and the Cultural War on Poverty," *Journal of Urban History* 34, no. 4 (May 2008): 665-71; Tapscott, *Songs of the Unsung*, 105-8; Isoardi, *Dark Tree*, 75-87; Elaine Brown, *A Taste of Power: A Black Woman's Story* (New York: Pantheon Books, 1992), 149-51. See also Budd Schulberg, ed., *From the Ashes: Voices of Watts* (New York: New American Library, 1967).

40. Smethurst, *Black Arts Movement*, 299; Isoardi, *Dark Tree*, 75, 86-87; Widener, *Black Arts West*, 209; Victor Leo Walker, "The Politics of Art: A History of the Inner City Cultural Center, 1965-1986" (PhD diss., University of California, Santa Barbara, 1989), ix, 1-2, 7-8.

41. Noah Purifoy, interview by Karen Anne Mason (Los Angeles: UCLA Library, Center for Oral History Research, 1990), UCLA/OL; Isoardi, *Dark Tree*, 76-79; Richard Cándida Smith, "Reverencing the Mortal: Assemblage Art as Prophetic Protest in Post–World War II California," in *Betye Saar: Extending the Frozen Moment*, edited by Karen

Chassin Goldbaum (Ann Arbor: University of Michigan Museum of Art, 2005), 40; Sarah Schrank, "Picturing the Watts Towers: The Art and Politics of an Urban Landmark," in *Reading California: Art, Image, and Identity, 1900–2000*, edited by Stephanie Barron, Sheri Bernstein, and Ilene Susan Fort (Berkeley: University of California Press, 2000), 373–80.

42. Purifoy, interview by Mason (quotation); Lewis and Waddy, *Black Artists*, vol. 2, 138; Smethurst, *Black Arts Movement*, 305–6; Tyler, "The Rise," 64.

43. Purifoy, interview by Mason; Isoardi, *Dark Tree*, 77–78.

44. A. Davis, interview by Mason (quotations); D. Davis, interview by author.

45. A. Davis, interview by Mason; D. Davis, interview by author; Lindsey, "Brockman Gallery," 23.

46. A. Davis, interview by Mason (quotation); D. Davis, interview by author; Lindsey, "Brockman Gallery," 23.

47. Photos of opening night, April 1967, Brockman Gallery Archive, Los Angeles Public Library, Special Collections. For advertisements of the gallery's first shows, see "Brockman Art Gallery Open," *Los Angeles Sentinel*, April 27, 1967; "Prints on Display at Brockman Gallery," *Los Angeles Sentinel*, July 27, 1967; "Art: Opening," *Los Angeles Times*, August 6, 1967; "Brockman Showing Opens with Reception," *Los Angeles Sentinel*, October 5, 1967; "Community Calendar," *Los Angeles Sentinel*, November 9, 1967; "Brockman Gallery," *Los Angeles Times*, December 3, 1967.

48. Brochure, "Brockman Gallery Presents the Leimert Park Festival of the Arts," 1967, Brockman Gallery Archive, Los Angeles Public Library, Special Collections (quotation); Olive Walker, "Scribblings from the Editor," *Crenshaw Notes* 28 (July–August 1967): 3, APP, Box 1, SCL.

49. O. Walker, "Scribblings from the Editor," 3 (all quotations).

50. "The Story of Two Businessmen," *Crenshaw Notes* 13 (February–March 1966): 1–2 (first and second quotations on 1; third quotation on 2), APP, Box 1, SCL; Brochure, "Brockman Gallery Presents."

51. "New Horizons for CN," 5; "Brockman Gallery Presents the Leimert Park Festival of the Arts," *Crenshaw Notes* 28 (July–August 1967): 4, APP, Box 1, SCL; "Bits and Pieces," *Crenshaw Notes* 44 (February 1969): 6, APP, Box 1, SCL; Brockman Gallery advertisement, *The Integrator* 1, no. 1 (Winter 1967–68): last page, SCL; Kenneth C. Olsen, "President's Report to the Board of Directors," April 16, 1968, 3 (quotation), APP, Box 1, SCL. For examples of published articles and artwork of Black artists, see *The Integrator* 1, no. 2 (Summer 1968): 6, 8, SCL; "The Artistry of Charles White," *The Integrator* 1, no. 3 (Fall 1968): 4–5, SCL.

52. Fergerson, interview by Mason; Outterbridge, interview by R. Smith; Widener, *Black Arts West*, 159–60.

53. Fergerson, interview by Mason (quotations).

54. Fergerson, interview by Mason; Outterbridge, interview by R. Smith; Selz, *Art of Engagement*, 145.

55. Carolyn Peter and Damon Willick, "Gallery 32 and Los Angeles's African American Arts Community," *Nka: Journal of Contemporary African Art*, no. 30 (Spring 2012): 17–25; Samella S. Lewis, *Art: African American* (New York: Harcourt Brace Jovanovich, 1978), 161; Lewis and Waddy, *Black Artists*, vol. 2, 91–92, 137; Jane H. Carpenter with Betye Saar, *Betye Saar* (San Francisco: Pomegranate Communications, 2003), 26, 57; Fergerson, interview by Mason; Outterbridge, interview by R. Smith; Jones, "To/From Los Angeles," 34; Suzanne Jackson, interview by Karen Anne Mason (Los Angeles: UCLA Library, Center for Oral History Research, 1992), UCLA/OL (quotation). See

also Suzanne Jackson, *What I Love: Paintings, Poetry, and a Drawing* (Los Angeles: Contemporary Crafts, 1972); and Suzanne Jackson, *Animal* (Los Angeles: Continuity Transcript and Features, 1978).

56. Lewis and Waddy, *Black Artists*, vol. 1, 113–15, 127; Lisa E. Farrington, *Creating Their Own Image: The History of African-American Women Artists* (New York: Oxford University Press, 2005), 143–44; Floyd Coleman, *African American Art and Artists*, by Samella Lewis (Berkeley: University of California Press, 2003), "Foreword," xi–xii. See also Samella S. Lewis, interview by Karen Anne Mason (Los Angeles: UCLA Library, Center for Oral History Research, 1992), UCLA/OL.

57. Lewis and Waddy, *Black Artists*, vol. 1, 127; Farrington, *Creating Their Own Image*, 143–44; Jeanne Zeidler, "Lewis, Samella (Sanders)," in *St. James Guide to Black Artists*, edited by Thomas Riggs (Detroit: St. James Press, 1997), 326-28; Waddy, interview by Mason; Carpenter, *Betye Saar*, 26; Jones, *South of Pico*, 173–74. For a selection of works by Lewis, see Lewis and Waddy, *Black Artists*, vol. 1; Lewis and Waddy, *Black Artists*, vol. 2; Samella S. Lewis, *The Art of Elizabeth Catlett* (Claremont, CA: Hancraft Studios, 1984); and Lewis, *African American Art*.

58. Dale Brockman Davis, "Brockman Gallery as Community," in Hanks, *Distinctly Los Angeles*, 2–3 (first quotation on 2); A. Davis, interview by Mason (second and third quotations); Outterbridge, interview by R. Smith (fourth quotation); Waddy, interview by Mason. For a list of BAA members, see Jones, *Now Dig This!*, 284.

59. Outterbridge, interview by R. Smith (quotation).

60. Fergerson, interview by Mason (first and second quotations); John Riddle and Carmen Riddle, interview by Karen Anne Mason (Los Angeles: UCLA Library, Center for Oral History Research, 1992–93), UCLA/OL (third quotation); S. Jackson, interview by Mason (fourth quotation); Outterbridge, interview by R. Smith (fifth quotation).

61. A. Davis, interview by Mason; D. Davis, interview by author; D. Davis, "Brockman Gallery as Community," 2–3 (first quotation on 2; second quotation on 3).

62. Mike Murase, "Toward Barefoot Journalism," *Gidra* (April 1974): 1, 34-36. For more references on this paragraph and the next two, see S. Kurashige, *Shifting Grounds*, 283–84; S. Kurashige, "Growing Up Japanese American."

63. Widener, "Perhaps the Japanese," 171–72; Seigo Hayashi, "Yellow Brotherhood," *Gidra* (April 1970): 18; Scott Sheri Miyashiro, "Yellow Brotherhood," *Gidra* (1990): 122–23. For reference to YB's Jefferson Boulevard headquarters, see Jah and Shah'Keyah, *Uprising*, 203. For references to the YB House, see "Coming Attractions," *Gidra* (February 1973): 19; Nick Nagatani, "'Action Talks and Bullshit Walks': From the Founders of the Yellow Brotherhood to the Present," in *Asian Americans: The Movement and the Moment*, edited by Steve Louie and Glenn K. Omatsu (Los Angeles: UCLA Asian American Studies Press, 2001), 148–55.

64. Jah and Shah'Keyah, *Uprising*, 203; David E. James, *The Most Typical Avant-Garde: History and Geography of Major Cinemas in Los Angeles* (Berkeley: University of California Press, 2005), 338; "Storefront: Cooperation over Competition," *Gidra* (January 1972): 3; Laura Pulido, *Black, Brown, Yellow, and Left: Radical Activism in Los Angeles* (Berkeley: University of California Press, 2006), 108–13, 140–42; William Wei, *The Asian American Movement* (Philadelphia: Temple University Press, 1993), 111–12.

65. A. Davis, interview by Mason (first and third quotations); D. Davis, interview by author; Riddle and Riddle, interview by Mason (second quotation); Lindsay, *Leimert Park* (fourth quotation); Lindsey, "Brockman Gallery," 24; Outterbridge, interview by R. Smith (fifth quotation).

66. Purifoy, interview by Mason (all quotations). For discussions on museum audiences, see Wu, *Privatising Culture*, 131; and Dimaggio and Useem, "Social Class and Arts Consumption," 144–47.

67. S. Collins, "Making of Black Middle Class," 369–74; Landry, *New Black Middle Class*, 1987, 67–78.

68. A. Davis, interview by Mason; D. Davis, interview by author.

69. Brockman Gallery regularly advertised its exhibitions in local newspapers. See, for example, "Brockman Showing Opens with Reception," *Los Angeles Sentinel*, October 5, 1967; "Art: Continuing: Three Artists," *Los Angeles Times*, October 20, 1968; "Art: Opening: Three Artists," *Los Angeles Times*, November 3, 1968. For advertisements of solo exhibitions and established artists, see "Art: Opening: John Outterbridge," *Los Angeles Times*, October 19, 1969; "Art Opening: John Riddle," *Los Angeles Times*, November 9, 1969; "Your Social Chronicler," *Los Angeles Sentinel*, May 2, 1968; "Community Calendar," *Los Angeles Sentinel*, May 8, 1969; "Deltas Sponsor Art Show for History Week," *Los Angeles Sentinel*, February 4, 1971; "What's Doing in San Diego," *Los Angeles Times*, September 18, 1981; Josine Ianco-Starrels, "Art News: Auction to Benefit MOCA," *Los Angeles Times*, May 4, 1986. For advertisements on exhibitions of Mexican and Asian American artists, see "Community Calendar," *Los Angeles Sentinel*, November 9, 1967; "Art: Opening," *Los Angeles Times*, March 16, 1969. See also Jones, *South of Pico*, 148–50; Lindsey, "Brockman Gallery," 23; A. Davis, interview by Mason (quotation).

70. Adelaide Kerr, "A Record-Breaking Exhibit (Library) by a Group of Artists (Black)," *Wilson Library Bulletin* 43, no. 8 (April 1969): 756–59 (first quotation on 756; second quotation on 757). For more on Morningside Park Neighbors, see Weil, "Integrated Neighborhood," address, 1–4. For an advertisement of the exhibit, see Jones, *Now Dig This!*, 24.

71. "L.A. Junior and Young Adult Clubs Sponsor Art Exhibit for Local High Schools May 18," *Los Angeles Sentinel*, May 15, 1969; "A Film and Slide Show," *Los Angeles Sentinel*, June 12, 1969; "Area Art Exhibit in Leimert Park," *Los Angeles Sentinel*, June 19, 1969.

72. Peter and Willick, "Gallery 32," 24–25; Waddy, interview by Mason; Fergerson, interview by Mason; Widener, "Writing Watts," 681; Isoardi, *Dark Tree*, 87. For references to the end of key Asian American initiatives, see Bruce Iwasaki, "Dissolving the Storefront. It's a Long Story," *Gidra* (April 1973): 7, 18–19; Murase, "Toward Barefoot Journalism," 1; Miyashiro, "Yellow Brotherhood," 123.

73. A. Davis, interview by Mason (quotation); Outterbridge, interview by R. Smith; D. Davis, interview by author; Tapscott, *Songs of the Unsung*, 174; "Free Winter Music Festival," *Los Angeles Sentinel*, January 24, 1974; "4th of July Jazz & Rock Festival," *Los Angeles Times*, June 22, 1975. For mention of Brockman Gallery's and BGP's NEA grants, see NEA's *Annual Report*, 1974–85, 1988, at www.arts.gov/about/annual-reports. For NEA's first grant to Brockman Gallery, for instance, see National Endowment for the Arts, National Council on the Arts, *Annual Report 1974* (Washington, DC: US Government Printing Office, 1975), 38. For NEA's highest distribution of grants to BGP, see National Endowment for the Arts, *Annual Report 1983* (Washington, DC: US Government Printing Office, 1984), 56, 259, 263.

74. Outterbridge, interview by R. Smith; Martin Luther King, Jr., *Where Do We Go from Here: Chaos or Community?* (New York: Harper & Row, 1967), 201 (quotation). For photos and discussion of *Eastside-Westside*, see Jones, *Now Dig This!*, 84, 86–87, 167.

75. Outterbridge, interview by R. Smith; A. Davis, interview by Mason; Isoardi, *Dark Tree*, 187-88; Purifoy, interview by Mason; "Watts Towers Jazz Festival," *Los Angeles Times*, May 29, 1980; Lindsey, "Brockman Gallery," 24.

76. A. Davis, interview by Mason; D. Davis, interview by author; "Black Films Contemporary," *Los Angeles Sentinel*, June 26, 1975; "Brockman Gallery Film Festival," *Los Angeles Sentinel*, April 22, 1976; "Gallery Film Festival Set," *Los Angeles Sentinel*, April 21, 1977; "Festival of Black Films Set at Museum," *Los Angeles Sentinel*, April 20, 1978.

77. A. Davis, interview by Mason (first quotation); Alan W. Barnett, *Community Murals: The People's Art* (Philadelphia: The Art Alliance Press, 1984), 187-89, 279; Robin J. Dunitz and James Prigoff, *Painting the Towns: Murals of California* (Los Angeles: RJD Enterprises, 1997), 13; Lee Curtis Hampton, "Street Art," *Neworld* (Spring 1975): 24-29 (second quotation on 28). For a discussion on Chicago's *Wall of Respect* and the community-based mural movement, see Barnett, *Community Murals*, chap. 2.

78. A. Davis, interview by Mason; Dunitz and Prigoff, *Painting the Towns*, 13.

79. A. Davis, interview by Mason; Josine Ianco-Starrels, "Art News: Wachs Named to Arts Task Force," *Los Angeles Times*, August 21, 1977; Josine Ianco-Starrels, "Art News: Four N.Y. Artists Exhibit Tableaux," *Los Angeles Times*, November 6, 1977; "PAE Program Begins at Brockman Gallery," *Los Angeles Sentinel*, September 1, 1977; Pat Johnson, *Affirming a Visual Heritage: The Collection of Alonzo and Dale Davis*, California African-American Museum (Los Angeles: California African-American Museum, 1996), "Introduction" (quotation); Josine Ianco-Starrels, "Art News: 'Polar Crossing' Due at LAICA," *Los Angeles Times*, September 3, 1978; Edwards, "Essence Men," 42; S. Jackson, interview by Mason. See also Grace A. Franklin, CETA: *Politics and Policy, 1973-1982* (Knoxville: University of Tennessee Press, 1984). CETA awarded funds to BGP as well as to the Los Angeles Institute of Contemporary Art and Artists for Economic Action. See Suzanne Muchnic, "Art: Painting the Town for Fun, Profit and Jobs," *Los Angeles Times*, October 22, 1978.

80. "Brockman Gallery Productions," *Los Angeles Sentinel*, December 14, 1978; Suzanne Muchnic, "Art News: Social Criticism from the Artists," *Los Angeles Times*, July 29, 1979; A. Davis, interview by Mason.

81. Jones, *South of Pico*, 151; Jones, *Now Dig This!*, 302-3, 315; Barbaralee Diamonstein, *Inside the Art World: Conversations with Barbaralee Diamonstein* (New York: Rizzoli, 1994), 57.

82. Prigoff and Dunitz, *Walls of Heritage*, 35, 165, 167; Dunitz and Prigoff, *Painting the Towns*, 162; Robin J. Dunitz, *Street Gallery: Guide to 1000 Los Angeles Murals* (Los Angeles: RJD Enterprises, 1993), 41-42, 205, 208, 211, 230; Cheryl McKay Dixon, "Alonzo Davis," *International Review of African American Art* 6, no. 3 (1986): 17, 20, 28, 32.

83. D. B. Davis, "Brockman Gallery as Community," 3 (first and second quotations); D. Davis, interview by author; Invitation to the 10th Anniversary Celebration, November 18, 1977, Brockman Gallery Archive, Los Angeles Public Library, Special Collections; "Brockman Celebrates," *Los Angeles Sentinel*, November 10, 1977; "Live Music at Brockman Fair," *Los Angeles Sentinel*, September 9, 1982; Outterbridge, interview by R. Smith (third and fourth quotations).

84. Dickson Art Center, *The Negro in American Art* (Los Angeles: UCLA Art Galleries, Dickson Art Center, 1966); Jones, *South of Pico*, 162.

85. Kenneth Donahue, "Foreword," in *Sculpture of Black Africa: The Paul Tishman Collection*, edited by Roy Seiber and Arnold Rubin (Los Angeles: LACMA, 1969), 6

(quotation); Joseph E. Young, *Three Graphic Artists: Charles White, David Hammons, Timothy Washington* (Los Angeles: Los Angeles County Museum of Art, 1971); Jones, *South of Pico*, 162–66; Muchnic, *LACMA So Far*, 92. For a case study on the New York City museums, see Susan E. Cahan, *Mounting Frustration: The Art Museum in the Age of Black Power* (Durham: Duke University Press, 2016). For more discussion on Driskell's exhibit, *Two Centuries of Black American Art*, and its influence on the contemporary art world, see the Sam Pollard–directed film *Black Art: In the Absence of Light* (New York: HBO Documentary Films and Two Dollars and a Dream, 2021).

86. Outterbridge, interview by R. Smith (first quotation); D. Davis, interview by author (second and third quotations). In the early 1980s Brockman Gallery Productions shortened its name to Brockman Productions.

CHAPTER 7. BLACK BEVERLY HILLS REDUX

1. "Obama to Visit 'Black Beverly Hills,'" *Marketplace*, June 1, 2012; Pauline O'Connor, "View Park, the Neighborhood Nicknamed 'the Black Beverly Hills,' Now on the National Register of Historic Places," *Curbed Los Angeles*, July 23, 2016; Alexa Díaz, "Street Officially Renamed Obama Boulevard in Baldwin Hills/Crenshaw Ceremony," *Los Angeles Times*, May 4, 2019 (quotation). The Village Green received designation on the National Register of Historic Places in 2001.

2. Michael Creedman, "If This Be Our Camelot, How Come Nobody's Heard of It?," *Los Angeles Magazine* 19, no. 9 (September 1972): 41–42 (quotations on 42), KHC, Box 272 (8a), Folder 3.3.2.3.2, HL; 1970 Census: Tracts, pt. 1, P-526 (tract 7030). Tract 7030, which comprised Fairfax Avenue as its eastern border, excluded the easternmost portion of Ladera Heights. (The census included that section in the View Heights/Windsor Hills tract.)

3. For the classic account on the events in IUSD, see Edna Bonacich and Robert F. Goodman, *Deadlock in School Desegregation: A Case Study of Inglewood, California* (New York: Praeger Publishers, 1972). Documents on the lawsuit include Memorandum of Points and Authorities in Support of Petition for Peremptory Writ of Mandate, Janel E. Johnson et al. v. Inglewood Unified School District, L.A. No. 973669, filed March 19, 1970, LASC; Janel E. Johnson et al. v. Inglewood Unified School District, L.A. No. 948036, filed July 22, 1970, LASC; Judgment, Janel Johnson et al. v. Inglewood Unified School District, L.A. No. 948036, filed September 22, 1969, LASC. For the *Swann* case, see Bernard Schwartz, *Swann's Way: The School Busing Case and the Supreme Court* (New York: Oxford University Press, 1986).

4. Los Angeles City Schools, "Racial and Ethnic Survey," Research and Evaluation Branch, Fall 1970; Los Angeles Unified School District, "Racial and Ethnic Survey," Research and Evaluation Branch, Fall 1980, LASMC, Box 139, UCLA.

5. Creedman, "If This Be Our Camelot," 43; Noel Greenwood, "Inglewood to Ask Court OK to Abandon Busing: School Board Hopes to Return Soon to Neighborhood Plan," *Los Angeles Times*, November 20, 1972; Order Granting Respondent's Motion for Modification of Judgment, Janel E. Johnson et al. v. Inglewood Unified School District, L.A. No. 973669, filed June 3, 1975, LASC. For data on the IUSD student body, see Bonacich and Goodman, *Deadlock in School Desegregation*, 30; Informational Material, "Ethnic Survey by Individual Schools, School Year 1976–77," Janel E. Johnson et al. v. Inglewood Unified School District, L.A. No. 973669, filed March 2, 1977, LASC.

6. For 1980 data, see *Census of Population and Housing: 1980*, Census Tracts, Los Angeles–Long Beach, Calif., section 3 (Washington, DC: US Government Printing Office, 1983), H-5 (for Los Angeles city), H-8 (for View Park, View Heights, Windsor

Hills), H-94–95 (tracts 2341–44 for Leimert Park), H-96 (tract 2363 for Baldwin Vista and 2364 for Baldwin Hills Estates), H-176 (tracts 7030.01 and 7030.02 for Ladera Heights). For 2000 data, see tracts 2360 for Baldwin Vista and 2364 for Baldwin Hills Estates, and Ladera Heights CDP (or census-designated place) and View Park-Windsor Hills CDP, in US Census Bureau, accessed September 24, 2021, data.census.gov. For national rates, see US Census Bureau, "Historical Census of Housing Tables: Home Values," accessed September 24, 2021, https://www.census.gov/data/tables/time-series/dec/coh-values.html

7. For affluent Crenshaw data, see 1960 Census: Tracts, 67–68 (tracts 2341–44 for Leimert Park, 2363 for Baldwin Vista, and 2364 for Baldwin Hills Estates), and 132 (tract 7030 for Ladera Heights and 7031–32 for View Park, View Heights, and Windsor Hills); 1980 Census: Tracts, sec. 1, P-472–73 (tracts 2341–44 for Leimert Park, 2363 for Baldwin Vista, and 2364 for Baldwin Hills Estates), P-494 (tracts 7031–32 for View Park, View Heights, and Windsor Hills), and P-503 (tracts 7030.01 and 7030.02 for Ladera Heights). For 2000 data, see tracts 2340, 2342–43 (Leimert Park), 2360 (Baldwin Vista), 2364 (Baldwin Hills Estates), 7030.01 and 7030.02 (Ladera Heights), and 7031–32 (View Park, View Heights, and Windsor Hills) in US Census Bureau, data.census.gov

8. For maps of White and Black migration patterns between 1940 and 1980, see Sides, *L.A. City Limits*, 210–14.

9. Gil Robertson, "Inside Leimert Park," *Black Enterprise* 27, no. 11 (June 1997): 336 (quotation). For scholarship on the 1992 Los Angeles uprising, see Robert Gooding-Williams, ed., *Reading Rodney King, Reading Urban Uprising* (New York: Routledge, 1993); and Lou Cannon, *Official Negligence: How Rodney King and the Riots Changed Los Angeles and the LAPD* (Boulder, CO: Westview Press, 1999).

10. Lindsay, *Leimert Park*, 24:14 (quotation); Exum and Guiza-Leimert, *Images of America*, 83–90, 113. See also Edward J. Boyer, "A Heartbeat in Search of a Heart," *Los Angeles Times*, March 27, 1990; Don Snowden, "Cultural Spring in Crenshaw District: Arts Transform Degnan Boulevard," *Los Angeles Times*, October 3, 1992; P. J. Harris, "Leimert Park Village," *American Visions* 7, no. 3 (June/July 1992): 26; Michel Marriott, "Soul Central," *New York Times*, December 5, 1993; Robertson, "Inside Leimert Park," 336; Isoardi, *Dark Tree*, 218–21.

11. Gloria Calomee, "The Traveling Life," *The Crisis* 92, no. 6 (June/July 1985): 10; Exum and Guiza-Leimert, *Images of America*, 91, 93–94; Isoardi, *Dark Tree*, 184–87, 199, 211; Michelle Sorey, "'227' Her Third Series: Winning Numbers Are Coming Up For Gibbs," *Los Angeles Times*, September 17, 1985; "Marla Gibbs' Arts Group Buys Leimert Theater," *Los Angeles Times*, April 12, 1990; Don Shirley, "Ambitious Plans for Marla Gibbs' Crossroads Facility Theater," *Los Angeles Times*, June 21, 1990.

12. Isoardi, *Dark Tree*, 226–29 (first two quotations on 227); Exum and Guiza-Leimert, *Images of America*, 114; Lindsay, *Leimert Park*, 49:33 (third quotation).

13. For the analytical framework on imagined geographies, see B. Anderson, *Imagined Communities*. For reports that include affluent Crenshaw in South Central, see Ingwerson, "Jesse Jackson Tugs"; Ruth Styles, "Harry's Girl Is (Almost) Straight Outta Compton: Gang-Scarred Home of her Mother Revealed—So Will He Be Dropping by for Tea?," *Daily Mail*, November 2, 2016 (quotation). For reports on the name change, see Paul Feldman, "Neighborhoods in L.A. It's All in a Name," *Los Angeles Times*, June 18, 1989; Gold and Braxton, "Considering South-Central"; Lynell George, "What It Is (And What It Was)," *Los Angeles Times, West Magazine*, October 8, 2006, 14; "A Spin by Any Other Name," *Los Angeles Times*, April 14, 2003. For the *Los Angeles Times* "Mapping L.A." project, see http://maps.latimes.com/neighborhoods/

14. For recent reports of Whites moving into the affluent Crenshaw neighborhoods, see Angel Jennings, "'Black Beverly Hills' Debates Historic Status v. White Gentrification," *Los Angeles Times*, July 18, 2015; Angel Jennings, "Selfie of White Joggers in African American Neighborhood Sets off Debate, and Quest for Understanding," *Los Angeles Times*, March 10, 2017; Joseph Pimentel, "Residents Grapple with Change Coming to View Park, LA's 'Black Beverly Hills,'" *Bisnow*, February 22, 2018.

Bibliography

ARCHIVAL AND MANUSCRIPT COLLECTIONS

Los Angeles, California
Department of Archives and Special Collections, William H. Hannon Library, Loyola Marymount University
    Fritz Burns Papers

Library Special Collections, Charles E. Young Research Library, University of California, Los Angeles
    American Civil Liberties Union of Southern California Records
    California Ephemera Collection
    Helene V. Smookler Collection of Material about the Desegregation of the Los Angeles Unified School District
    John Randolph Haynes Papers
    Los Angeles School Monitoring Committee Records
    Los Angeles Urban League Records

Microform Collections, Charles E. Young Research Library, University of California, Los Angeles
    NAACP Branch Files, Los Angeles, California, 1913–39

Southern California Library
    Ann Post Papers (unprocessed)
    Charlotta A. Bass Papers
    James K. Strong Papers
    Nickerson Family, Golden State Mutual Life Insurance Company Papers

San Marino, California
Huntington Library
    John Anson Ford Papers
    Kenneth Hahn Collection
    Loren Miller Papers

ARCHIVED ORAL HISTORIES

Fullerton, California
Lawrence de Graaf Center for Oral and Public History, California State University, Fullerton
    Beavers, George A., Jr. Interview by R. Donald Brown, October 15, 1966.
    Houston, Norman O. Interview by R. Donald Brown, October 27, 1966.
    Hudson, H. Claude. Interview by R. Donald Brown, November 29, 1966.

Miller, Loren. Interview by Lawrence B. de Graaf, March 3, 1967, April 29, 1967.
Somerville, J. Alexander, and Vada Somerville. Interview by Lawrence B. de Graaf, June 10, 1967.

Online
   Center for Oral History Research, Library Special Collections,
      Charles E. Young Research Library, University of California, Los Angeles
   Beavers, George A., Jr. Interview by Ranford B. Hopkins, 1982.
   Bradley, Thomas. Interview by Bernard Galm, 1978–79.
   Davis, Alonzo. Interview by Karen Anne Mason, 1990–91.
   Fergerson, Cecil. Interview by Karen Anne Mason, 1990–92, 1994.
   Houston, Ivan J. Interview by Ranford B. Hopkins, 1986–87.
   Jackson, Suzanne. Interview by Karen Anne Mason, 1992.
   Johnson, George P. Interview by Elizabeth Dixon, 1967–68.
   Kenny, Robert W. Interview by Doyce B. Nunis, Jr., 1960–61.
   Lewis, Samella S. Interview by Karen Anne Mason, 1992.
   Matthews, Miriam. Interview by Robin D. G. Kelley, 1985–86.
   Outterbridge, John W. Interview by Richard Cándida Smith, 1989–90.
   Pajaud, William. Interview by Karen Ann Mason, 1989.
   Purifoy, Noah. Interview by Karen Anne Mason, 1990.
   Riddle, John, and Carmen Riddle. Interview by Karen Anne Mason, 1992–93.
   Tapscott, Horace. Interview by Steven L. Isoardi, 1993.
   Waddy, Ruth G. Interview by Karen Anne Mason, 1991.
   Williams, Frances. Interview by Karen Anne Mason and Richard Cándida Smith, 1992–93.

Calisphere, University of California Libraries
   Hawkins, Augustus F. Interview by Carlos Vásquez. California State Archives: State Government Oral History Program, 1988.
   Inouye, Kazuo K. "Interview by Leslie Ito." In *REgenerations Oral History Project: Rebuilding Japanese American Families, Communities, and Civil Rights in the Resettlement Era*, vol. 2, edited by Japanese American National Museum, December 13, 1997.
   Rumford, William Byron. "Legislator for Fair Employment, Fair Housing and Public Health." Interview by Joyce A. Henderson, Amelia R. Fry, and Edward France. Berkeley: University of California, Berkeley, Bancroft Library, Regional Oral History Office, 1973.

AUTHOR-CONDUCTED ORAL HISTORIES

Anderson, Eva. July 31, 2006, Los Angeles.
Boger, Othelia W. November 3, 2006, telephone.
Branch, Geraldine. July 27, 2007, Los Angeles.
Cotterell, Donald, with Perlita D. Clarke. August 2, 2006, Los Angeles.
Davis, Dale Brockman. March 15, 2008, Los Angeles.
Edwards, Deloy. June 23, 2007, Los Angeles.
Johnson, Evelyn Allen. September 30, October 23, and October 24, 2006, telephone.
Milgram, Jean Gregg. November 11, 2006 and August 18, 2008, telephone.
Nicholas, Anthony F. July 19, 2007, Los Angeles.
Patton, K. D. October 2 and 5, 2006, telephone.

Paxton, Gertrude. November 11, 2006, telephone.
Perez, Phenella D., and Gisele Perez. October 19, 2006, telephone.
Post, Ann. September 14 and 24, 2006, telephone.
Suter, Joan A. July 28, 2008, telephone.

LEGAL CASES (IN CHRONOLOGICAL ORDER)

In re Lee Sing, 43 Fed. 359 C.C.N.D. Cal. (1890)
Gandolfo v. Hartman, 49 Fed. 181 C.C.S.D. Cal (1892)
Plessy v. Ferguson, 163 U.S. 537 (1896)
Buchanan v. Warley, 245 U.S. 60 (1917)
Los Angeles Investment Company v. Gary, 181 Cal. 680 (1919)
Title Guarantee & Trust Co. v. Garrott, 42 Cal. App. 152 (1919)
Corrigan v. Buckley, 55 App. DC 30, 299 F. 899 (1924)
Miller v. Board of Public Works of the City of Los Angeles, 195 Cal. 477, 234 P. 381 (1925)
Janss Investment Co. v. Walden, 196 Cal. 753, 239 Pac. 34 (1925)
Village of Euclid, Ohio v. Ambler Realty Co., 272 U.S. 365 (1926)
Corrigan v. Buckley, 271 U.S. 323 (1926)
W. B. Wayt v. George Patee, 205 Cal. 46, 269 Pac. 660 (1928)
George H. Letteau v. Pauline Ellis, 122 Cal. App. 584 (1932)
Hansberry v Lee, 311 U.S. 32 (1940)
Communist Party of the United States of America v. Paul Peek, 20 Cal. 2d 536, 127 P. 2d 889 (1942)
Effie L. O'Rourke v. Roy Teeters, 63 Cal. App. 2d 349, 146 P. 2d 983 (1944)
Joseph James v. Marinship Corporation, 25 Cal. 2d 721, 155 P. 2d 329 (1944)
Hazel Fairchild v. Ross H. Raines, 24 Cal. 2d 818 (1944)
Dole M. Burkman v. Henry Laws, 63 Cal. App. 2d 230 (1944)
Shideler v. Roberts, 69 Cal. App 2nd 549, 160 P. 2nd 67 (1945)
Mendez v. Westminster School District of Orange County, 64 F. Supp. 544 (1946)
Anderson v. Auseth, L.A. No. 19759 (1948)
Earl C. Cummings v. Frank Hokr, 31 Cal. 2d 844 (1948)
In re Laws, 31 Cal. 2d 846 (1948)
Shelley v. Kraemer, 334 U.S. 1 (1948)
Barrows v. Jackson, 346 U.S. 249 (1953)
Brown v. Board of Education of Topeka, 347 U.S. 483 (1954)
Jay R. Jackson, Jr. v. Pasadena City School District, 59 Cal. 2d 876 (1963)
Janel E. Johnson v. Inglewood Unified School District, L.A. No. 948036 (1970)
Mary Ellen Crawford v. Board of Education of the City of Los Angeles, L.A. No. 822854 (1970)
Swann v Charlotte-Mecklenburg Board of Education, 402 U.S. 1 (1971)

SELECTED NEWSPAPERS, NEWSLETTERS, JOURNALS, INDICES, AND DIRECTORIES

California Eagle
Chicago Defender
Crenshaw Notes
Ebony
Gidra
Index to Register of Voters, Los Angeles
Integrator, The
Los Angeles City Directory

Los Angeles Sentinel
Los Angeles Telephone Directory
Los Angeles Times
Los Angeles Tribune
National Endowment for the Arts, *Annual Report*
New York Times
Pittsburgh Courier
Shin Nichi-Bei

REAL ESTATE RECORDS (IN CHRONOLOGICAL ORDER)
Norwalk, California
Los Angeles County Registrar-Recorder/County Clerk
   Tract map of West Adams Heights, 1902, Tract Maps, Book 2, 53–54.
   "Real Property Restrictions Agreement," Book 15896, 1–15.
   Grant Deed between Norman O. Houston, Edythe A. Houston, and Naomi Freeney, 1938, Book 16249, 36.
   Deed of Trust with Assignment of Rents between Louise Beavers and Isabel G. Cryer, 1942, Book 19161, 221.
   Deed of Trust with Assignment of Rents between James Lloyd Crawford, Hattie McDaniel Crawford, and Marian Earle Stainback, 1941, Book 18984, 319–20.
   Grant Deed between Leslie U. King, Mamie King, and Douglas S. Mueller, 1941, Book 18414, 342.
   Deed of Trust with Assignment of Rents [between Vance Young and Augusta Young, and Leslie U. King and Mamie King], 1941, Book 19016, 115–16.
   Deed of Trust with Assignment of Rents between Horace P. Clark, Vera Clark, and Robert Elliott, 1941, Book 18766, 381–82.
   Grant Deed between Ethel Burke Waters, Louis C. Venator, and Dorothy C. Venator, 1941, Book 18989, 115.
   Deed of Trust between Juan Tizol, Rose Tizol, and Inez L. Syminton, 1942, Book 19414, 321–22.
   Deed of Trust between Juan Tizol and Rose Tizol, and Inez L. Syminton, 1942, Book 19573, 161–62.
   Deed of Trust between William E. Bailey and Edith B. Bailey, 1942, Book 19608, 299–300.
   Deed of Trust (Purchase Money) with Assignment of Rents between William E. Bailey, Edith B. Bailey, and Winifred W. Coberly, 1942, Book 19652, 261–62.
   Deed of Trust with Assignment of Rents between W. Clyde Allen, Aulette D. Allen, and Daisy Rose Montgomery, 1942, Book 19693, 303–4
   Deed of Trust with Assignment of Rents between Vada J. Somerville and Anne B. Shine, 1943, Book 20128, 335–36.
   Deed of Trust, Courtland G. Mitchell and Rosa Lee Mitchell, 1945, Book 21647, 167–68.
   Deed of Trust between Stanley and Jeanne E. Friedman, and Alfred L. and Gertrude A. Buckman, 1951, Book 35318, 158.
   Grant Deed between Stanley and Jeanne E. Friedman, and Thomas and Ethel Mae Bradley, 1951, Book 35318, 163.
   Joint Tenancy Grant Deed between Ike and Tina Turner, and Leavitt B. Glaze and Edith L. Glaze, 1962, Book D1675, 305.

US CENSUS BUREAU RECORDS

1880 United States Federal Census. Provo, UT: Ancestry.com Operations Inc., 2010.
1900 United States Federal Census. Provo, UT: Ancestry.com Operations Inc., 2004.
1910 United States Federal Census. Lehi, UT: Ancestry.com Operations, Inc., 2006.
1920 United States Federal Census. Provo, UT: Ancestry.com Operations, Inc., 2010.
1930 United States Federal Census. Provo, UT: Ancestry.com Operations Inc., 2002.
1940 United States Federal Census. Provo, UT: Ancestry.com Operations Inc., 2012.
Census of Housing: 1950, Block Statistics, Los Angeles, California, vol. 5, pt. 100. Washington, DC: US Government Printing Office, 1952.
Census of Housing: 1960, City Blocks, Series HC(3), vol. 3, no. 46. Washington, DC: US Government Printing Office, 1961.
Census of Housing: 1960, Metropolitan Housing, vol. 2, pt. 4, Kansas City-New Orleans Standard Metropolitan Statistical Areas. Washington, DC: US Government Printing Office, 1963.
Census of Housing: 1970, Block Statistics, Final Report, HC(3)-18, Los Angeles–Long Beach, Calif. Urbanized Area. Washington, DC: US Government Printing Office, 1972.
Census of Housing: 1970, Series HC(2)-120, Metropolitan Housing Characteristics, Los Angeles–Long Beach, Calif., pt. 7. Washington, DC: US Government Printing Office, 1972.
Census of Population and Housing: 1960, Census Tracts, Final Report, Series PHC(1)-82, Los Angeles–Long Beach, Calif., pt. 5. Washington, DC: US Government Printing Office, 1962.
Census of Population and Housing: 1970, Census Tracts, Final Report, Series PHC(1)-117, Los Angeles–Long Beach, Calif., pt. 1. Washington, DC: US Government Printing Office, 1972.
Census of Population and Housing: 1970, Census Tracts, Final Report, Series PHC(1)-117, Los Angeles–Long Beach, Calif., pt. 2. Washington, DC: US Government Printing Office, 1972.
Census of Population and Housing: 1980, Census Tracts, Los Angeles–Long Beach, Calif., section 1. Washington, DC: US Government Printing Office, 1983.
Census of Population and Housing: 1980, Census Tracts, Los Angeles–Long Beach, Calif., section 2. Washington, DC: US Government Printing Office, 1983.
Census of Population and Housing: 1980, Census Tracts, Los Angeles–Long Beach, Calif., section 3. Washington, DC: US Government Printing Office, 1983.
Census of Population: 1950, Census Tract Statistics, Los Angeles, California, vol. 3, chap. 28. Washington, DC: US Government Printing Office, 1952.
Eleventh Census: 1890, pt. 1, Report on Population of the United States. Washington, DC: US Government Printing Office, 1895.
Fourteenth Census of the United States: 1920, Composition and Characteristics of the Population by States, vol. 3. Washington, DC: US Government Printing Office, 1922.
Seventh Census of the United States: 1850. Washington, DC: Robert Armstrong, Public Printer, 1853.
Sixteenth Census of the United States: 1940, Housing Block Statistics, Los Angeles, California. Washington, DC: US Government Printing Office, 1942.
Sixteenth Census of the United States: 1940, Housing. vol. 3, pt. 2. Washington, DC: US Government Printing Office, 1943.

Sixteenth Census of the United States: 1940, Population and Housing, Statistics for Census Tracts, Los Angeles–Long Beach, Calif. Washington, DC: US Government Printing Office, 1942.

Sixteenth Census of the United States: 1940, Population, Characteristics of the Population, vol. 2, pt. 1. Washington, DC: US Government Printing Office, 1943.

Sixteenth Census of the United States: 1940, Population, Number of Inhabitants, vol. 1. Washington, DC: US Government Printing Office, 1942.

Tenth Census of the United States: 1880, vol. 19, pt. II, Report on the Social Statistics of Cities. Washington, DC: US Government Printing Office, 1887.

Tenth Census of the United States: Statistics of the Population. Washington, DC: US Government Printing Office, 1882.

Twelfth Census of the United States, vol. 1, pt. 1, Population. Washington, DC: US Census Office, 1901.

US Census Bureau. "Historical Census of Housing Tables: Home Values," accessed September 24, 2021, https://www.census.gov/data/tables/time-series/dec/coh-values.html

FILMS

Brewer, Jon, dir. *Nat King Cole: Afraid of the Dark.* Cotswolds, UK: Cardinal Releasing, 2014. DVD.

Lindsay, Jeanette, prod. and dir. *Leimert Park: The Story of a Village in South Central Los Angeles.* Los Angeles, California: Foster Johnson Studios, 2008. DVD.

Neville, Morgan, prod. and dir. *The Cool School: The Story of the Ferus Art Gallery.* Los Angeles: Arthouse Films/Curiously Bright, 2008.

Peralta, Stacy, dir. *Crips and Bloods: Made in America.* 2008; Los Angeles: Balance Vector Productions and Verso Entertainment, 2009.

Pollard, Sam, dir. *Black Art: In the Absence of Light.* New York: HBO Documentary Films and Two Dollars and a Dream, 2021.

Sloan, Cle, dir. *Bastards of the Party.* 2005; Los Angeles: Fuqua Films, 2009.

Smith, Yvonne, dir. *Ray Charles: The Genius of Soul.* New York: Thirteen-WNET, 1986.

SELECTED PUBLISHED MATERIALS

Abrahamson, Eric John. *Building Home: Howard F. Ahmanson and the Politics of the American Dream.* Berkeley: Univ. of California Press, 2013.

Abrams, Charles. *Forbidden Neighbors: A Study of Prejudice in Housing.* New York: Harper & Brothers, 1955.

Abu-Lughod, Janet L. *Race, Space, and Riots in Chicago, New York, and Los Angeles.* New York: Oxford Univ. Press, 2007.

Adler, Patricia. *The Bunker Hill Story.* Glendale, CA: La Siesta, 1963.

———. *The History of the Normandie Program Area.* Los Angeles: Prepared for the Community Redevelopment Agency of the City of Los Angeles, 1969.

———. "Watts: From Suburb to Black Ghetto." PhD diss., Univ. of Southern California, 1977.

Almaguer, Tomás. *Racial Fault Lines: The Historical Origins of White Supremacy in California.* Berkeley: Univ. of California Press, 1994.

Alonso, Alex A. "Out of the Void: Street Gangs in Black Los Angeles." In Hunt and Ramón, *Black Los Angeles,* 140–67. New York: New York Univ. Press, 2010.

———. "Racialized Identities and the Formation of Black Gangs in Los Angeles." *Urban Geography* 25, no. 7 (2004): 658–74.

———. "Territoriality Among African-American Street Gants in Los Angeles." Master's thesis, Univ. of Southern California, 1999.

Anderson, Benedict. *Imagined Communities: Reflections on the Origins and Spread of Nationalism.* 3rd ed. New York: Verso, 2006.

Anderson, E. Frederick. *The Development of Leadership and Organization Building in the Black Community of Los Angeles from 1900 through World War II.* Saratoga, CA: Century Twenty-One Publishing, 1980.

Anderson, Harry, and Mary Wormley. *Historic West Adams: Now & Then: Remembering a Legacy.* Los Angeles: West Adams Heritage Association, 1987.

Avila, Eric. *Popular Culture in the Age of White Flight: Fear and Fantasy in Suburban Los Angeles.* Berkeley: Univ. of California Press, 2004.

Barnett, Alan W. *Community Murals: The People's Art.* Philadelphia: Art Alliance, 1984.

Barron, Stephanie, Sheri Bernstein, and Ilene Susan Fort, eds. *Reading California: Art, Image, and Identity, 1900–2000.* Berkeley: Univ. of California Press, 2000.

Bass, Charlotta A. *Forty Years: Memoirs from the Pages of a Newspaper.* Los Angeles: Charlotta A. Bass, 1960.

Bates, Joseph Clement, ed. *History of the Bench and Bar of California.* San Francisco: Bench and Bar Publishing, 1912.

Bauman, Robert. *Race and the War on Poverty: From Watts to East L.A.* Norman: Univ. of Oklahoma Press, 2008.

Beasley, Delilah L. *The Negro Trail Blazers of California.* Los Angeles: Negro Universities Press, 1919.

Bogle, Donald. *Bright Boulevards, Bold Dreams: The Story of Black Hollywood.* New York: One World Books, 2005.

———. *Dorothy Dandridge: A Biography.* New York: Amistad, 1997

———. *Heat Wave: The Life and Career of Ethel Waters.* New York: HarperCollins, 2011.

———. *Toms, Coons, Mulattoes, Mammies, and Bucks: An Interpretive History of Blacks in American Films.* New York: Viking, 1973.

Bonacich, Edna, and Robert F. Goodman. *Deadlock in School Desegregation: A Case Study of Inglewood, California.* New York: Praeger Publishers, 1972.

Bond, J. Max. "The Negro in Los Angeles." PhD diss., Univ. of Southern California, 1936.

Bottles, Scott L. *Los Angeles and the Automobile: The Making of the Modern City.* Berkeley: Univ. of California Press, 1987.

Boyer, M. Christine. *Dreaming the Rational City: The Myth of American City Planning.* Cambridge: MIT Press, 1983.

Boyle, Kevin. *Arc of Justice: A Saga of Race, Civil Rights, and Murder in the Jazz Age.* New York: Henry Holt, 2004.

Brandt, Nat. *Harlem at War: The Black Experience in World War II.* Syracuse, NY: Syracuse Univ. Press, 1996.

Brilliant, Mark. *The Color of America Has Changed: How Racial Diversity Shaped Civil Rights Reform in California, 1941–1978.* New York: Oxford Univ. Press, 2010.

Brooks, Charlotte. *Alien Neighbors, Foreign Friends: Asian Americans, Housing, and the Transformation of Urban California.* Chicago: Univ. of Chicago Press, 2009.

Brooks, Richard R. W., and Carol M. Rose. *Saving the Neighborhood: Racially Restrictive Covenants, Law, and Social Norms.* Cambridge: Harvard Univ. Press, 2013.

Brown, Elaine. *A Taste of Power: A Black Woman's Story.* New York: Pantheon Books, 1992.

Brown, Scot. *Fighting for US: Maulana Karenga, the US Organization, and Black Cultural Nationalism.* New York: New York Univ. Press, 2003.

Bryant, Clora, Buddy Collette, William Green, Steven Isoardi, Jack Kelson, Horace Tapscott, Gerald Wilson, and Marl Young, eds. *Central Avenue Sounds: Jazz in Los Angeles.* Berkeley: Univ. of California Press, 1998.

Bullough, Bonnie Louise. "Alienation among Middle Class Negroes: Social-Psychological Factors Influencing Housing Desegregation." PhD diss., Univ. of California, Los Angeles, 1968.

Bunch, Lonnie G. *Black Angelenos: The Afro-American in Los Angeles, 1850–1950.* Los Angeles: California Afro-American Museum, 1988.

Burrell, Barbara. *Women and Political Participation: A Reference Handbook.* Santa Barbara, CA: ABC CLIO, 2004.

C. W. Y. "Enforcement of Race Restrictive Covenants and the Constitution." *Virginia Law Review* 34, no. 3 (April 1948): 306–14.

Cahan, Susan E. *Mounting Frustration: The Art Museum in the Age of Black Power.* Durham, NC: Duke Univ. Press, 2016.

California African-American Museum. *Affirming a Visual Heritage: The Collection of Alonzo and Dale Davis.* Los Angeles: California African-American Museum, 1996.

Campbell, Marne L. *Making Black Los Angeles: Class, Gender, and Community, 1850–1917.* Chapel Hill: Univ. of North Carolina Press, 2016.

Cannon, Lou. *Official Negligence: How Rodney King and the Riots Changed Los Angeles and the LAPD.* Boulder, CO: Westview, 1999.

Capeci, Dominic J. *The Harlem Riot of 1943.* Philadelphia: Temple Univ. Press, 1977.

Carpenter, Jane H., with Betye Saar. *Betye Saar.* San Francisco: Pomegranate Communications, 2003.

Carson, Clayborne. *In Struggle: SNCC and the Black Awakening of the 1960s.* Cambridge: Harvard Univ. Press, 1995.

Case, Frederick E., and James H. Kirk. *The Housing Status of Minority Families, Los Angeles, 1956.* Los Angeles: UCLA Real Estate Research Program and Los Angeles Urban League, 1958.

Casstevens, Thomas W. *Politics, Housing and Race Relations: California's Rumford Act and Proposition 14.* Berkeley: Univ. of California, Institute of Governmental Studies, 1967.

Caughey, John, and LaRee Caughey. *School Segregation on Our Doorstep: The Los Angeles Story.* Los Angeles: Quail Books, 1966.

———. *To Kill a Child's Spirit: The Tragedy of School Segregation in Los Angeles.* Itasca, IL: F. E. Peacock Publishers, 1973.

Cho, Jenny, and the Chinese Historical Society of Southern California. *Chinatown and China City in Los Angeles.* Charleston, SC: Arcadia Publishing, 2011.

———. *Images of America: Chinatown in Los Angeles.* Charleston, SC: Arcadia Publishing, 2009.

Clark, Tom C., and Philip B. Perlman. *Prejudice and Property: An Historic Brief Against Racial Covenants.* Washington, DC: Public Affairs Press, 1948.

Clarke, Cheryl. *"After Mecca": Women Poets and the Black Arts Movement.* New Brunswick, NJ: Rutgers Univ. Press, 2005.

Cohen, Jerry, and William S. Murphy. *Burn, Baby, Burn! Los Angeles Race Riot, August, 1965.* New York: E. P. Dutton, 1966.

Collins, Keith E. *Black Los Angeles: The Maturing of the Ghetto, 1940–1950.* Saratoga, CA: Century Twenty-One Publishing, 1980.

Collins, Lisa Gail, and Margo Natalie Crawford. *New Thoughts on the Black Arts Movement.* New Brunswick, NJ: Rutgers Univ. Press, 2006.

Collins, Sharon M. "The Making of the Black Middle Class." *Social Problems* 30, no. 4 (April 1983): 369–82.

Conot, Robert E. *Rivers of Blood, Years of Darkness: The First Full Story of America's Long Hot Summer of Hate.* New York: Bantam Books, 1967.

Cooper, Suzanne Tarbell, Don Lynch, and John G. Kurtz. *Images of America: West Adams.* Charleston, SC: Arcadia Publishing, 2008.

Cox, Bette Yarbrough. *Central Avenue: Its Rise and Fall (1890–c. 1955): Including the Musical Renaissance of Black Los Angeles.* Los Angeles: BEEM Publications, 1996.

Crane, Gregg D. *Race, Citizenship, and Law in American Literature.* New York: Cambridge Univ. Press, 2002.

Crenshaw, Kimberlé. "Demarginalizing the Intersection of Race and Sex: A Black Feminist Critique of Antidiscrimination Doctrine, Feminist Theory and Antiracist Politics." *University of Chicago Legal Forum* 1989, 1, no. 8 (1989): 139–67.

Crump, Spencer. *Ride the Big Red Cars: How Trolleys Helped Build Southern California.* 4th ed. Corona del Mar, CA: Trans-Anglo Books, 1970.

Cuff, Dana. *The Provisional City: Los Angeles Stories of Architecture and Urbanism.* Cambridge: MIT Press, 2000.

Culver, Lawrence. *The Frontier of Leisure: Southern California and the Shaping of Modern America.* New York: Oxford Univ. Press, 2010).

Cunningham, Meghan E. *Bill "Bojangles" Robinson: Dancer.* New York: Cavendish Square, 2017.

Curwood, Anastasia C. *Stormy Weather: Middle-Class African-American Marriages between the Two World Wars.* Chapel Hill: Univ. of North Carolina Press, 2010.

Davis, Margaret Leslie. *The Culture Broker: Franklin D. Murphy and the Transformation of Los Angeles.* Berkeley: Univ. of California Press, 2007.

———. *Dark Side of Fortune: Triumph and Scandal in the Life of Oil Tycoon Edward L. Doheny.* Berkeley: Univ. of California Press, 1998.

Davis, Mike. *City of Quartz: Excavating the Future of Los Angeles.* New York: Vintage Books, 1992.

de Graaf, Lawrence B. "The City of Black Angels: Emergence of the Los Angeles Ghetto, 1890–1930." *Pacific Historical Review* 39 (August 1970): 323–52.

———. "Negro Migration to Los Angeles, 1930 to 1950." PhD diss., Univ. of California, Los Angeles, 1962.

———. "Significant Steps on an Arduous Path: The Impact of World War II on Discrimination against African Americans in the West." *Journal of the West* 35, no. 1 (January 1996): 24–33.

de Graaf, Lawrence B., Kevin Mulroy, and Quintard Taylor, eds. *Seeking El Dorado: African Americans in California.* Los Angeles: Univ. of Washington Press, 2001.

del Castillo, Richard Griswold. *The Los Angeles Barrio, 1850–1890: A Social History.* Berkeley: Univ. of California Press, 1979.

Delaney, David. *Race, Place, and the Law, 1836–1948.* Austin: Univ. of Texas Press, 1998.

Dennis, Jan. *Images of America: Manhattan Beach, California.* Chicago: Arcadia Publishing, 2001.

Deverell, William. *Whitewashed Adobe: The Rise of Los Angeles and the Remaking of its Mexican Past.* Berkeley: Univ. of California Press, 2004.

Deverell, William, and Greg Hise, eds. *A Companion to Los Angeles.* Malden, MA: Wiley-Blackwell, 2010.

Diamonstein, Barbaralee. *Inside the Art World: Conversations with Barbaralee Diamonstein.* New York: Rizzoli, 1994.

Dickson Art Center. *The Negro in American Art.* Los Angeles: UCLA Art Galleries, Dickson Art Center, 1966.

Dimaggio, Paul and Michael Useem. "Social Class and Arts Consumption: The Origins and Consequences of Class Differences in Exposure to the Arts in America." *Theory and Society* 5, no. 2 (March 1978): 141–61.

Dixon, Cheryl McKay. "Alonzo Davis." *International Review of African American Art* 6, no. 3 (1986): 16–32.

Drake, St. Clair, and Horace R. Cayton. *Black Metropolis: A Study of Negro Life in a Northern City.* Vols. 1 and 2. Torchbook ed. New York: Harper & Row, 1962.

Du Bois, W. E. B. "The Talented Tenth." In *The Negro Problem: A Series of Articles by Representative American Negroes To-day,* edited by Booker T. Washington, 33–75. New York: James Pott, 1903.

Dunitz, Robin J. *Street Gallery: Guide to 1000 Los Angeles Murals.* Los Angeles: RJD Enterprises, 1993.

Dunitz, Robin J., and James Prigoff. *Painting the Towns: Murals of California.* Los Angeles: RJD Enterprises, 1997.

Durant, Thomas J., Jr., and Joyce S. Louden. "The Black Middle Class in America: Historical and Contemporary Perspectives." *Phylon* 47, no. 4 (4th Qtr. 1986): 253–63.

Ellenberger, Allan R. *Ramon Novarro: A Biography of the Silent Film Idol, 1899–1968; with a Filmography.* Jefferson, NC: McFarland, 1999.

Epstein, Daniel Mark. *Nat King Cole.* New York: Farrar, Straus and Giroux, 1999.

Escobar, Edward J. *Race, Police, and the Making of a Political Identity: Mexican Americans and the Los Angeles Police Department, 1900–1945.* Berkeley: Univ. of California Press, 1999.

Estrada, William D. "Los Angeles' Old Plaza and Olvera Street: Imagined and Contested Space." *Western Folklore* 58, no. 2 (Winter 1999): 107–29.

Exum, Cynthia E., and Maty Guiza-Leimert. *Images of America: Leimert Park.* Charleston, SC: Arcadia Publishing, 2012.

Faragher, John Mack. *Eternity Street: Violence and Justice in Frontier Los Angeles.* New York: W. W. Norton, 2016.

Farrington, Lisa E. *Creating Their Own Image: The History of African-American Women Artists.* New York: Oxford Univ. Press, 2005.

Fishman, Robert. *Bourgeois Utopias: The Rise and Fall of Suburbia.* New York: Basic Books, 1987.

Flamming, Douglas. *Bound for Freedom: Black Los Angeles in Jim Crow America.* Berkeley: Univ. of California Press, 2005.

Fleetwood, Homer, II. "You Can Hear Them a Mile Away: The Black Invasion of Los Angeles." *Negro History Bulletin* 64, nos. 1–4 (January–December 2001): 33–40.

Fogelson, Robert M. *The Fragmented Metropolis: Los Angeles, 1850–1930.* Cambridge: Harvard Univ. Press, 1967.

Fong, Timothy P. *The First Suburban Chinatown: The Remaking of Monterey Park, California.* Philadelphia: Temple Univ. Press, 1994.

Ford, John Anson. *Thirty Explosive Years in Los Angeles County.* San Marino, CA: Huntington Library, 1961.

Franklin, Grace A. CETA: *Politics and Policy, 1973–1982.* Knoxville: Univ. of Tennessee Press, 1984.

Frazier, E. Franklin. *Black Bourgeoisie.* Glencoe, IL: Free Press, 1957. Reprint. 3rd ed. New York: Free Press, 1966.

———. *The Negro Family in the United States*. Chicago: Univ. of Chicago Press, 1939.
Freeman, Richard B. *Black Elite: The New Market for Highly Educated Black Americans*. New York: McGraw-Hill, 1976.
Freund, David M. P. *Colored Property: State Policy and White Racial Politics in Suburban America*. Chicago: Univ. of Chicago Press, 2007.
Friedricks, William B. *Henry E. Huntington and the Creation of Southern California*. Columbus: Ohio State Univ. Press, 1992.
Fuller, Diana Burgess, and Daniela Salvioni, eds. *Art/Women/California: Parallels and Intersections, 1950–2000*. Berkeley: Univ. of California Press, 2002.
Gabler, Neal. *An Empire of Their Own: How the Jews Invented Hollywood*. New York: Anchor Books, 1989.
Gaines, Kevin. *Uplifting the Race: Black Leadership, Politics, and Culture in the Twentieth Century*. Chapel Hill: Univ. of North Carolina Press, 1996.
García, Mario T., and Sal Castro. *Blowout! Sal Castro & the Chicano Struggle for Educational Justice*. Chapel Hill: Univ. of North Carolina Press, 2011.
George, Lynell. *No Crystal Stair: African-Americans in the City of Angels*. New York: Verso, 1992.
Gibbons, Andrea. *City of Segregation: One Hundred Years of Struggle for Housing in Los Angeles*. New York: Verso, 2018.
Giles, Micheal W., Everett F. Cataldo, and Douglas S. Gatlin. "White Flight and Percent Black: The Tipping Point Reexamined." *Social Science Quarterly* 56, no. 1 (1975): 85–92.
Goldbaum, Karen Chassin, ed. *Betye Saar: Extending the Frozen Moment*. Ann Arbor and Berkeley: Univ. of Michigan Museum of Art and Univ. of California Press, 2005.
Gonda, Jeffrey D. *Unjust Deeds: The Restrictive Covenant Cases and the Making of the Civil Rights Movement*. Chapel Hill: Univ. of North Carolina Press, 2015.
Gooding-Williams, Robert, ed. *Reading Rodney King, Reading Urban Uprising*. New York: Routledge, 1993.
Gottlieb, Robert, and Irene Wolt. *Thinking Big: The Story of the Los Angeles Times, Its Publishers, and their Influence on Southern California*. New York: G. P. Putnam's Sons, 1977.
Graham, Lawrence Otis. *Our Kind of People: Inside America's Black Upper Class*. New York: HarperCollins, 2000.
Greenberg, Amy S. *A Wicked War: Polk, Clay, Lincoln, and the 1846 U.S. Invasion of Mexico*. New York: Alfred A. Knopf, 2012.
Greenberg, Jack. *Crusaders in the Courts: How a Dedicated Band of Lawyers fought for the Civil Rights Revolution*. New York: BasicBooks, 1994.
Greenwood, Roberta S. *Down by the Station: Los Angeles Chinatown, 1880–1933*. Los Angeles: UCLA Institute of Archaeology, 1996.
Gregory, Mollie. *Women Who Run the Show: How a Brilliant and Creative New Generation of Women Stormed Hollywood*. New York: St. Martin's, 2002.
Hahn, Steven. *A Nation Under Our Feet: Black Political Struggles in the Rural South from Slavery to the Great Migration*. Cambridge: Harvard Univ. Press, 2003.
Hampton, Lee Curtis. "Street Art." *Neworld* (Spring 1975): 24–29.
Hanks, Eric, ed. *Distinctly Los Angeles: An African American Perspective*. Santa Monica, CA: M. Hanks Gallery, 2009.
Hassan, Amina. *Loren Miller: Civil Rights Attorney and Journalist*. Norman: Univ. of Oklahoma Press, 2015.

Henderson, Alexa Benson. *Atlanta Life Insurance Company: Guardian of Black Economic Dignity.* Tuscaloosa: Univ. of Alabama Press, 1990.

Hewitt, Mary Jane. "The Long Black Line." *California History* 60, no. 1 (Spring 1981): 12–13.

Hillier, Amy E. "Redlining and the Home Owners' Loan Corporation." *Journal of Urban History* 29, no. 4 (May 2003): 394–420.

Himes, Chester. *If He Hollers Let Him Go.* New York: Thunder Mouth's, 1945. Reprint, New York: Thunder's Mouth, 1986.

Hirahara, Naomi, and Geraldine Knatz. *Terminal Island: Lost Communities of Los Angeles Harbor.* Santa Monica, CA: Angel City, 2015.

Hirsch, Arnold R. *Making the Second Ghetto: Race and Housing in Chicago, 1940–1960.* Chicago: Univ. of Chicago Press, 1998.

Hise, Greg. *Magnetic Los Angeles: Planning the Twentieth-Century Metropolis.* Baltimore: Johns Hopkins Univ. Press, 1997.

Hixson, William B., Jr. *Moorfield Storey and the Abolitionist Tradition.* New York: Oxford Univ. Press, 1972.

Hoover, Mildred Brooke, Hero Eugene Rensch, Ethel Grace Rensch, and William N. Abeloe. *Historic Spots in California.* Revised by Douglas E. Kyle. 5th ed. Stanford, CA: Stanford Univ. Press, 2002.

Horne, Gerald. *Fire This Time: The Watts Uprising and the 1960s.* Charlottesville: Univ. Press of Virginia, 1995.

HoSang, Daniel Martinez. *Racial Propositions: Ballot Initiatives and the Making of Postwar California.* Berkeley: Univ. of California Press, 2010.

Howell, James C. *The History of Street Gangs in the United States: Their Origins and Transformations.* Lanham, MD: Lexington Books, 2015.

Hudson, Karen E. *Paul R. Williams, Architect: A Legacy of Style.* New York: Rizzoli International Publications, 1993.

Hudson, Karen E. *The Will and the Way: Paul R. Williams, Architect.* New York: Rizzoli International Publications, 1994.

Hunt, Darnell, and Ana-Christina Ramón, eds. *Black Los Angeles: American Dreams and Racial Realities.* New York: New York Univ. Press, 2010.

Immergluck, Dan. *Credit to the Community: Community Reinvestment and Fair Lending Policy in the United States.* Armonk, NY: M.E. Sharpe, 2004.

Isoardi, Steven L. *The Dark Tree: Jazz and the Community Arts in Los Angeles.* Berkeley: Univ. of California Press, 2006.

Jackson, Buzzy. *A Bad Woman Feeling Good: Blues and the Women Who Sing Them.* New York: W. W. Norton, 2005.

Jackson, Carleton. *Hattie: The Life of Hattie McDaniel.* Lanham, MD: Madison Books, 1990.

Jackson, Kenneth. *Crabgrass Frontier: The Suburbanization of the United States.* New York: Oxford Univ. Press, 1985.

Jackson, Suzanne. *Animal.* Los Angeles: Continuity Transcript and Features, 1978.

———. *What I Love: Paintings, Poetry, and a Drawing.* Los Angeles: Contemporary Crafts, 1972.

Jah, Yusuf, and Sister Shah'Keyah. *Uprising: Crips and Bloods Tell the Story of America's Youth in the Crossfire.* New York: Scribner, 1995.

James, David E. *The Most Typical Avant-Garde: History and Geography of Major Cinemas in Los Angeles.* Berkeley: Univ. of California Press, 2005.

Jefferson, Alison Rose. "African American Leisure Space in Santa Monica: The Beach Sometimes Known as the 'Inkwell.'" *Southern California Quarterly* 91, no. 2 (Summer 2009): 155–89.

———. *Living the California Dream: African American Leisure Sites during the Jim Crow Era*. Lincoln: Univ. of Nebraska Press, 2020.

Johnson, Evelyn Allen. *Get the Show on the Road*. Los Angeles: Lynray, 1987.

———. *My Neighbor's Island*. New York: Exposition, 1965.

———. *Pillar of Salt*. Beverly Hills: Lynray, 2006.

Johnson, Marilynn S. *The Second Gold Rush: Oakland and the East Bay in World War II*. Berkeley: Univ. of California Press, 1993.

Johnson, Robert Lee. *Notable Southern Californians in Black History*. Charleston, SC: History Press, 2017.

Jones, Kellie, ed. *Now Dig This! Art & Black Los Angeles, 1960–1980*. Los Angeles: Hammer Museum, 2011.

———. *South of Pico: African American Artists in Los Angeles in the 1960s and 1970s*. Durham, NC: Duke Univ. Press, 2017.

Jones-Correa, Michael. "The Origins and Diffusion of Racial Restrictive Covenants." *Political Science Quarterly* 115, no. 4 (Winter 2000–2001): 541–68.

Joseph, Peniel E. *Waiting 'Til the Midnight Hour: A Narrative History of Black Power in America*. New York: Henry Holt, 2006.

Kahen, Harold I. "Validity of Anti-Negro Restrictive Covenants: A Reconsideration of the Problem." *University of Chicago Law Review* 12, no. 2 (February 1945): 198–213.

Katznelson, Ira. *When Affirmative Action Was White: An Untold History of Racial Inequality in Twentieth-Century America*. New York: W. W. Norton, 2005.

Keane, James Thomas. *Fritz B. Burns and the Development of Los Angeles: The Biography of a Community Developer and Philanthropist*. Los Angeles: Historical Society of Southern California, 2001.

Keil, Roger, and Judy Branfman, eds. *Public Los Angeles: A Private City's Activist Futures*. Athens: Univ. of Georgia Press, 2019.

King, Martin Luther, Jr. *Where Do We Go from Here: Chaos or Community?* New York: Harper & Row, 1967.

Klarman, Michael J. *From Jim Crow to Civil Rights: The Supreme Court and the Struggle for Racial Equality*. New York: Oxford Univ. Press, 2004.

Kluger, Richard. *Simple Justice: The History of* Brown v. Board of Education *and Black America's Struggle for Equality*. New York: Vintage Books, 1977.

Kronus, Sidney. *The Black Middle Class*. Columbus, OH: Charles E. Merrill Publishing, 1971.

Kruse, Kevin M., and Thomas J. Sugrue, eds. *The New Suburban History*. Chicago: Univ. of Chicago Press, 2006.

Kun, Josh, and Laura Pulido, eds. *Black and Brown in Los Angeles: Beyond Conflict and Coalition*. Berkeley: Univ. of California Press, 2014.

Kurashige, Lon. *Japanese American Celebration and Conflict: A History of Ethnic Identity and Festival, 1934–1990*. Berkeley: Univ. of California Press, 2002.

———. "The Problem of Biculturalism: Japanese American Identity and Festival before World War II." *Journal of American History* 86, no. 4 (March 2000): 1632–54.

Kurashige, Scott. "Crenshaw and the Rise of Multiethnic Los Angeles." *Afro-Hispanic Review* 27, no. 1 (Spring 2008): 41–58.

———. *The Shifting Grounds of Race: Black and Japanese Americans in the Making of Multiethnic Los Angeles*. Princeton, NJ: Princeton Univ. Press, 2008.

Kusmer, Kenneth L., and Joe W. Trotter, eds. *African American Urban History since World War II*. Chicago: Univ. of Chicago Press, 2009.

Landry, Bart. *The New Black Middle Class*. Berkeley: Univ. of California Press, 1987.

———. *The New Black Middle Class in the Twenty-First Century*. New Brunswick, NJ: Rutgers Univ. Press, 2018.

LeFalle-Collins, Lizzetta. "The Brockman Gallery and the Village." *Journal of Contemporary African Art* 30 (Spring 2012): 4–15.

Leonard, Kevin Allen. *The Battle for Los Angeles: Racial Ideology and World War II*. Albuquerque: Univ. of New Mexico Press, 2006.

Lewis, Samella S. *African American Art and Artists*. Berkeley: Univ. of California Press, 2003.

———. *Art: African American*. New York: Harcourt Brace Jovanovich, 1978.

———. *The Art of Elizabeth Catlett*. Claremont, CA: Hancraft Studios, 1984.

Lewis, Samella S., and Ruth G. Waddy, eds. *Black Artists on Art*. Vol. 1. Los Angeles: Contemporary Crafts Publishers, 1969.

———. *Black Artists on Art*. Vol. 2. Los Angeles: Contemporary Crafts, Inc., 1971.

Lightfoot, Kent G., and Otis Parrish. *California Indians and their Environment: An Introduction*. Berkeley: Univ. of California Press, 2009.

Lindsey, Kay. "Brockman Gallery." *Art Papers* (July/August 1990): 23–24.

Loewen, James W. *Sundown Towns: A Hidden Dimension of American Racism*. New York: New Press, 2005.

Long, Herman H., and Charles J. Johnson. *People vs. Property: Race Restrictive Covenants in Housing*. Nashville, TN: Fisk Univ. Press 1947.

Loomis, Jan. *Westside Chronicles: Historic Stories of West Los Angeles*. Charleston, SC: History Press, 2012.

López, Ian Haney. *White by Law: The Legal Construction of Race*. New York: New York Univ. Press, 2006.

Louie, Steve, and Glenn K. Omatsu, eds. *Asian Americans: The Movement and the Moment*. Los Angeles: UCLA Asian American Studies, 2001.

Lydon, Michael. *Ray Charles: Man and Music*. New York: Routledge, 2004.

Mack, Kenneth W. "Dissent and Authenticity in the History of American Racial Politics." In *Dissenting Voices in American Society: The Role of Judges, Lawyers, and Citizens*, edited by Austin Sarat, 105–43. New York: Cambridge Univ. Press, 2012.

———. *Representing the Race: The Creation of the Civil Rights Lawyer*. Cambridge: Harvard Univ. Press, 2012.

Mandel, Jennifer. "Setting the Record Straight: Almena Lomax, the *Los Angeles Tribune*, and a Lifelong Passion for Racial Justice and the Written Word." *Southern California Quarterly* 98, no. 1 (Spring 2016): 59–105.

Massey, Douglas S., and Nancy A. Denton. *American Apartheid: Segregation and the Making of the Underclass*. Cambridge: Harvard Univ. Press, 1993.

Mather, Frank Lincoln, ed. *Who's Who of the Colored Race: A General Biographical Dictionary of Men and Women of African Descent*. Vol. 1. Chicago: Memento Edition, 1915.

Mazón, Mauricio. *The Zoot-Suit Riots: The Psychology of Symbolic Annihilation*. Austin: Univ. of Texas, 1984.

McBride, David, and Monroe H. Little. "The Afro-American Elite, 1930–1940: A Historical and Statistical Profile." *Phylon* 42, no. 2 (2nd Qtr. 1981): 105–19.

McClain, Charles J. *In Search of Equality: The Chinese Struggle Against Discrimination in Nineteenth Century America*. Berkeley: Univ. of California Press, 1994.
McDougal, Dennis. *Privileged Son: Otis Chandler and the Rise and Fall of the L.A. Times Dynasty*. New York: Perseus Books, 2001.
McEntire, Davis. *Residence and Race: Final and Comprehensive Report to the Commission on Race and Housing*. Berkeley: Univ. of California Press, 1960.
McGirr, Lisa. *Suburban Warriors: The Origins of the New American Right*. 2nd ed. Princeton, NJ: Princeton Univ. Press, 2015.
McGovney, D. O. "Racial Residential Segregation by State Court Enforcement of Restrictive Agreements, Covenants or Conditions in Deeds Is Unconstitutional." *California Law Review* 33, no. 1 (March 1945): 5–39.
McQuiston, John Mark. "Negro Residential Invasion in Los Angeles County." Master's thesis, Univ. of Southern California, 1969.
McWilliams, Carey. "The Evolution of Sugar Hill." *Script* (March 1949): 24–35.
———. *Southern California Country: An Island on the Land*. Freeport, NY: Books for Libraries, 1970.
Meyer, Stephen Grant. *As Long as They Don't Move Next Door: Segregation and Racial Conflict in American Neighborhoods*. Lanham, MD: Rowan & Littlefield, 2000.
Milgram, Morris. *Good Neighborhood: The Challenge of Open Housing*. New York: W. W. Norton, 1977.
Miller, Loren. "The Protest Against Housing Segregation." *The Annals of the Academy of Political and Social Science* 357 (January 1965): 73–79.
———. *The Petitioners: The Story of the Supreme Court of the United States and the Negro*. New York: Pantheon Books, 1966.
Milliken, Stephen F. *Chester Himes: A Critical Appraisal*. Columbia: Univ. of Missouri Press, 1976.
Modell, John. *The Economics and Politics of Racial Accommodation: The Japanese of Los Angeles, 1900–1942*. Urbana: Univ. of Illinois Press, 1977.
Monroy, Douglas. *Rebirth: Mexican Los Angeles from the Great Migration to the Great Depression*. Berkeley: Univ. of California Press, 1999.
Moore, Christopher Paul. *Fighting for America: Black Soldiers—The Unsung Heroes of World War II*. New York: One World, 2005.
Moore, Joan W. *Going Down to the Barrio: Homeboys and Homegirls in Change*. Philadelphia: Temple Univ. Press, 1991.
Moore, Natalie Y., and Lance Williams. *The Almighty Black P Stone Nation: The Rise, Fall, and Resurgence of an American Gang*. Chicago: Lawrence Hill Books, 2011.
Moore, Shirley Ann Wilson. *To Place Our Deeds: The African American Community in Richmond, California, 1910–1963*. Berkeley: Univ. of California Press, 2000.
Morehouse, Henry Lyman. "The Talented Tenth." *American Missionary* 50, no. 6 (June 1896): 182–83.
Morris, Richard T., and Vincent Jeffries. *The White Reaction Study*. Los Angeles: Univ. of California, Los Angeles, Institute of Government and Public Affairs, 1967.
Moynihan, Daniel Patrick. *The Negro Family: The Case for National Action*. Washington, DC: Government Printing Office, 1965.
Muchnic, Suzanne. LACMA *So Far: Portrait of a Museum in the Making*. San Marino: Huntington Library, 2015.
Muller, Gilbert H. *Chester Himes*. Boston: Twayne Publishers, 1989.
Myers, William A., and Ira L. Swett. *Trolleys to the Surf: The Story of the Los Angeles Pacific Railway*. Glendale, CA: Interurbans, 1976.

Nicholson, Stuart. *Ella Fitzgerald: The Complete Biography.* New York: Routledge, 2004.
Nickerson, Michelle M. *Mothers of Conservatism: Women and the Postwar Right.* Princeton, NJ: Princeton Univ. Press, 2012.
Nicolaides, Becky M. *My Blue Heaven: Life and Politics in the Working-Class Suburbs of Los Angeles, 1920–1965.* Chicago: Univ. of Chicago Press, 2002.
———. "The Quest for Independence: Workers in the Suburbs." In *Metropolis in the Making: Los Angeles in the 1920s,* edited by Tom Sitton and William Deverell, 77–95. Berkeley: Univ. of California Press, 2001.
Niiya, Brian, ed. *Japanese American History: An A-to-Z Reference from 1868 to Present.* New York: Facts on File, 1993.
Nishi, Midori. "Japanese Settlement in the Los Angeles Area." *Yearbook of the Association of Pacific Coast Geographers* 20 (1958): 35–48.
Nishi, Midori, and Young Il Kim. "Recent Japanese Settlement Changes in the Los Angeles Area." *Yearbook of the Association of Pacific Coast Geographers* 26 (1964): 23–36.
Norrell, Robert J. *Reaping the Whirlwind: The Civil Rights Movement in Tuskegee.* Chapel Hill: Univ. of North Carolina Press, 1998.
Orser, W. Edward. *Blockbusting in Baltimore: The Edmondson Village Story.* Lexington: Univ. Press of Kentucky, 1994.
Ottensmann, John R. "Requiem for the Tipping-Point Hypothesis." *Journal of Planning Literature* 10, no. 2 (November 1995): 131–41.
Pagán, Eduardo Obregón. *Murder at the Sleepy Lagoon: Zoot Suits, Race, & Riot in Wartime L.A.* Chapel Hill: Univ. of North Carolina Press, 2003.
Parson, Don. "Breeding Grounds of Communism: The Gwinn Amendment in Los Angeles' Public Housing." In Keil and Branfman, *Public Los Angeles,* 122–44.
———. "'Houses for the Rich Were also for the Birds': Designing a Better World." In Keil and Branfman, *Public Los Angeles,* 54–95.
———. *Making a Better World: Public Housing, the Red Scare, and the Direction of Modern Los Angeles.* Minneapolis: Univ. of Minnesota Press, 2005.
Pattillo-McCoy, Mary. *Black Picket Fences: Privilege and Peril Among the Black Middle Class.* Chicago: Univ. of Chicago Press, 2000.
Payne, J. Gregory, and Scott C. Ratzan. *Tom Bradley: The Impossible Dream.* Santa Monica, CA: Roundtable Publishing, 1986.
Perine, Robert. *Chouinard: An Art Vision Betrayed: The Story of the Chouinard Art Institute, 1921–1972.* Encinitas, CA: Artra Publishing, 1985.
Peter, Carolyn, and Damon Willick. "Gallery 32 and Los Angeles's African American Arts Community." *Nka: Journal of Contemporary African Art,* no. 30 (Spring 2012): 16–26.
Peterson, Jon A. *The Birth of City Planning in the United States, 1840–1917.* Baltimore: Johns Hopkins Univ. Press, 2003.
Pfeffer, Paula F. *A. Philip Randolph, Pioneer of the Civil Rights Movement.* Baton Rouge: Louisiana State Univ. Press, 1990.
Pitt, Leonard. *The Decline of the Californios: A Social History of the Spanish-Speaking Californians, 1846–1890.* Berkeley: Univ. of California Press, 1966.
Plotkin, Wendy. "'Hemmed In': The Struggle against Racial Restrictive Covenants and Deed Restrictions in Post–WWII Chicago." *Journal of the Illinois State Historical Society* 94, no. 1 (Spring 2001): 39–69.
Prigoff, James, and Robin J. Dunitz. *Walls of Heritage, Walls of Pride: African American Murals.* San Francisco: Pomegranate, 2000.

Pulido, Laura. *Black, Brown, Yellow, and Left: Radical Activism in Los Angeles*. Berkeley: Univ. of California Press, 2006.
Rampersad, Arnold. *Jackie Robinson: A Biography*. New York: Alfred A. Knopf, 1997.
———. *The Life of Langston Hughes, vol. 1: 1902–1941, I, Too, Sing America*. New York: Oxford Univ. Press, 2002.
Rasmussen, Cecilia. *L.A. Unconventional: The Men and Women Who Did L.A. Their Way*. Los Angeles: Los Angeles Times, 1998.
"Real Property, Restrictive Covenants, Prohibition against Use or Occupation by Racial Groups." *Virginia Law Review* 33, no. 5 (September 1947): 658–60.
Regan, Michael. *Mansions of Los Angeles*. Los Angeles: Regan Publishing, 1965.
Rice, Christina, and Emma Roberts, eds. *Bunker Hill in the Rearview Mirror: The Rise, Fall, and Rise Again of an Urban Neighborhood*. Los Angeles: Photo Friends of the Los Angeles Public Library, 2015.
Robinson, Greg, and Tony Robinson. "*Korematsu* and Beyond: Japanese Americans and the Origins of Strict Scrutiny." *Law and Contemporary Problems* 68, no. 2 (Spring 2005): 29–55.
Robinson, Jackie. *Baseball Has Done It*. Philadelphia: J. B. Lippincott, 1964.
Robinson, Ray Charles, Jr. *You Don't Know Me: Reflections of My Father, Ray Charles*. New York: Harmony Books, 2010.
Romo, Ricardo. *East Los Angeles: History of a Barrio*. 7th paperback ed. Austin: Univ. of Texas Press, 1988.
Rosenzweig, Roy, and Elizabeth Blackmar. *The Park and the People: A History of Central Park*. Ithaca: Cornell Univ. Press, 1992.
Rothstein, Richard. *The Color of Law: A Forgotten History of How Our Government Segregated America*. New York: Liveright Publishing, 2017.
Sallis, James. *Chester Himes: A Life*. New York: Walker, 2001.
Salomon, Carlos Manuel. *Pío Pico: The Last Governor of Mexican California*. Norman: Univ. of Oklahoma Press, 2010.
Saltman, Juliet. *A Fragile Movement: The Struggle for Neighborhood Stabilization*. New York: Greenwood, 1990.
Sánchez, George J. *Becoming Mexican American: Ethnicity, Culture and Identity in Chicano Los Angeles, 1900–1945*. New York: Oxford Univ. Press, 1993.
Satter, Beryl. *Family Properties: How the Struggle over Race and Real Estate Transformed Chicago and Urban America*. New York: Henry Holt, 2009.
Schneider, Mark Robert. *"We Return Fighting": The Civil Rights Movement in the Jazz Age*. Boston: Northeastern Univ. Press, 2002.
Schrank, Sarah. *Art and the City: Civic Imagination and Cultural Authority in Los Angeles*. Philadelphia: Univ. of Pennsylvania Press, 2009.
Schulberg, Budd, ed. *From the Ashes: Voices of Watts*. New York: New American Library, 1967.
Schuparra, Kurt. *Triumph of the Right: The Rise of the California Conservative Movement, 1945–1966*. Armonk, NY: M. E. Sharpe, 1998.
Schwartz, Bernard. *Swann's Way: The School Busing Case and the Supreme Court*. New York: Oxford Univ. Press, 1986.
Scott, Allen J., and Edward W. Soja, eds. *The City: Los Angeles and Urban Theory at the End of the Twentieth Century*. Berkeley: Univ. of California Press, 1998.
Seiber, Roy, and Arnold Rubin. *Sculpture of Black Africa: The Paul Tishman Collection*. Los Angeles: LACMA, 1969.

Self, Robert O. *American Babylon: Race and the Struggle for Postwar Oakland.* Princeton, NJ: Princeton Univ. Press, 2003.
Seligman, Amanda I. *Block by Block: Neighborhoods and Public Policy on Chicago's West Side.* Chicago: Univ. of Chicago Press, 2005.
Selz, Peter. *Art of Engagement: Visual Politics in California and Beyond.* Berkeley: Univ. of California Press, 2005.
Serrano, Basilio. *Juan Tizol: His Caravan through American Life and Culture.* San Bernardino, CA: Xlibris, 2012.
Shevky, Eshref, and Molly Lewin. *Your Neighborhood: A Social Profile of Los Angeles.* Los Angeles: The Haynes Foundation, 1949.
Sides, Josh. "A Simple Quest for Dignity: African American Los Angeles Since World War II." In *City of Promise: Race & Historical Change in Los Angeles,* edited by Martin Schiesl and Mark M. Dodge, 109–36. Claremont, CA: Regina Books, 2006.
———. "Battle on the Home Front: African American Shipyard Workers in World War II Los Angeles." *California History* (Fall 1996): 251–63.
———. *L.A. City Limits: African American Los Angeles from the Great Depression to the Present.* Berkeley: Univ. of California Press, 2003.
———. "Straight into Compton: American Dreams, Urban Nightmares, and the Metamorphosis of a Black Suburb." *American Quarterly* 56, no. 3 (September 2004): 583–603.
Sitkoff, Harvard. *A New Deal for Blacks: The Emergence of Civil Rights as a National Issue.* New York: Oxford Univ. Press, 1978.
———. *The Struggle for Black Equality, 1954–1992.* New York: Hill and Wang, 1993.
Sitton, Tom. *Los Angeles Transformed: Fletcher Bowron's Urban Reform Revival, 1938–1953.* Albuquerque: Univ. of New Mexico Press, 2005.
Sloper, Don. *Images of America: Los Angeles's Chester Place.* Charleston, SC: Arcadia Publishing, 2006.
Smethurst, James Edward. *The Black Arts Movement: Literary Nationalism in the 1960s and 1970s.* Chapel Hill: Univ. of North Carolina Press, 2005.
Smith, J. Clay, Jr. *Emancipation: The Making of the Black Lawyer, 1844–1944.* Philadelphia: Univ. of Pennsylvania Press, 1993.
Smith, R. J. *The Great Black Way: L.A. in the 1940s and the Los African-American Renaissance.* New York: PublicAffairs, 2006.
Snider, Sandra Lee. *Elias Jackson "Lucky" Baldwin: California Visionary.* Los Angeles: Stairwell Group, 1987.
Soares, André. *Beyond Paradise: The Life of Ramon Novarro.* Jackson: Univ. of Mississippi Press, 2010.
Somerville, J. Alexander. *Man of Color: An Autobiography of Dr. J. Alexander Somerville.* Los Angeles: Lorrin L. Morrison, 1949.
Sonenshein, Raphael J. *Politics in Black and White: Race and Power in Los Angeles.* Princeton, NJ: Princeton Univ. Press, 1993.
Spaulding, Charles B. "Housing Problems of Minority Groups in Los Angeles County." *Annals of the American Academy of Political and Social Science* 248 (November 1946): 220–25.
Squires, Gregory D., ed. *The Fight for Fair Housing: Causes, Consequences, and Future Implications of the 1968 Federal Fair Housing Act.* New York: Routledge, 2018.
Starr, Kevin. *California: A History.* New York: Random House, 2007.
———. *The Dream Endures: California Enters the 1940s.* New York: Oxford Univ. Press, 1997.

———. *Inventing the Dream: California through the Progressive Era.* New York: Oxford Univ. Press, 1985.
Stein, Clarence S. *Toward New Towns for America.* New York: Reinhold Publishing, 1957.
Stevenson, Janet. *The Undiminished Man: A Political Biography of Robert Walker Kenny.* Novato, CA: Chandler & Sharp Publishers, 1980.
Stuart, Merah Steven. *An Economic Detour: A History of Insurance in the Lives of American Negroes.* College Park, MD: McGrath Publishing, 1969.
Sugrue, Thomas. "Crabgrass-Roots Politics: Race, Rights, and the Reaction against Liberalism in the Urban North, 1940–1964." *Journal of American History* 82, no. 2 (September 1995): 551–78.
———. *The Origins of the Urban Crisis: Race and Inequality in Postwar Detroit.* 3rd ed. Princeton, NJ: Princeton Univ. Press, 2014.
Summers, Martin. *Manliness and Its Discontents: The Black Middle Class and the Transformation of Masculinity, 1900–1930.* Chapel Hill: Univ. of North Carolina Press, 2004.
Sweeting, Charles Anthony. "The Dunbar Hotel and Central Avenue Renaissance, 1781–1950." PhD diss., Univ. of California, Los Angeles, 1992.
Tapscott, Horace. *Songs of the Unsung: The Musical and Social Journey of Horace Tapscott.* Edited by Steven Isoardi. Durham, NC: Duke Univ. Press, 2001.
Taylor, Keeanga-Yamahtta. *Race for Profit: How Banks and the Real Estate Industry Undermined Black Homeownership.* Chapel Hill: Univ. of North Carolina Press, 2019.
Taylor, Quintard. *In Search of the Racial Frontier: African Americans in the American West, 1528–1990.* New York: W. W. Norton, 1998.
Torres-Rouff, David Samuel. *Before L.A.: Race, Space, and Municipal Power in Los Angeles, 1781–1894.* New Haven, CT: Yale Univ. Press, 2013.
Turner, Ike, with Nigel Cawthorne. *Takin' Back My Name: The Confessions of Ike Turner.* London: Virgin Books, 1999.
Turner, Tina, with Kurt Loder. *I, Tina.* New York: William Morrow, 1986.
Tushnet, Mark V. *Making Civil Rights Law: Thurgood Marshall and the Supreme Court, 1936–1961.* New York: Oxford Univ. Press, 1994.
Tyler, Bruce Michael. "Black Radicalism in Southern California, 1950–1982." PhD diss., Univ. of California, Los Angeles, 1983.
———. "The Rise and Decline of the Watts Summer Festival, 1965 to 1986." *American Studies* 31, no. 2 (Fall 1990): 61–81.
United States Commission on Civil Rights. *A Generation Deprived: Los Angeles School Desegregation.* Washington, DC: Government Printing Office, 1977.
———. *Hearings Held in Los Angeles, California, January 25, 1960, January 26, 1960; San Francisco, California, January 27, 1960, January 28, 1960.* Washington, DC: Government Printing Office, 1960.
Valle, Victor M., and Rodolfo D. Torres. *Latino Metropolis.* Minneapolis: Univ. of Minnesota Press, 2000.
Veblen, Thorstein. *The Theory of the Leisure Class.* New York: Penguin Books, 1994.
Viesca, Victor Hugo. "The Battle of Los Angeles: The Cultural Politics of Chicana/o Music in the Greater Eastside." *American Quarterly* 56, no. 3 (September 2004): 719–39.
Vivian, Octavia B. *The Story of the Negro in Los Angeles County.* Federal Writers' Project of the Works Progress Administration, 1936. Reprint, San Francisco: R and E Research Associates, 1970.

Vorspan, Max, and Lloyd P. Gartner. *History of the Jews of Los Angeles.* San Marino, CA: Huntington Library, 1970.
Vose, Clement E. *Caucasians Only: The Supreme Court, the NAACP and the Restrictive Covenant Cases.* Berkeley: Univ. of California Press, 1959.
Wagner, Walter. *Beverly Hills: Inside the Golden Ghetto.* New York: Grosset & Dunlap, 1976.
Walker, Victor Leo. "The Politics of Art: A History of the Inner City Cultural Center, 1965–1986." PhD diss., Univ. of California, Santa Barbara, 1989.
Washington, Booker T. *Up From Slavery: Authoritative Text, Contexts, and Composition History, Criticism.* Edited by William L. Andrews. New York: Norton, 2006.
Waters, Ethel, with Charles Samuels. *His Eye Is on the Sparrow.* Garden City, NY: Doubleday, 1951.
Watson, Peter. *From Manet to Manhattan: The Rise of the Modern Art Market.* New York: Random House, 1992.
Watts, Jill. *Hattie McDaniel: Black Ambition, White Hollywood.* New York: Amistad, 2005.
Weddle, David. *Among the Mansions of Eden: Tales of Love, Lust, and Land in Beverly Hills.* New York: William Morrow, 2003.
Wei, William. *The Asian American Movement.* Philadelphia: Temple Univ. Press, 1993.
Weinberg, Meyer. *Race and Place: A Legal History of the Neighborhood School.* Washington, DC: Government Printing Office, 1967.
Weir, Margaret. "Urban Poverty and Defensive Localism." *Dissent* 41, no. 3 (Summer 1994): 337–42.
Weiss, Marc A. *The Rise of the Community Builders: The American Real Estate Industry and Urban Land Planning.* New York: Columbia Univ. Press, 1987.
West, Michael Rudolph. *The Education of Booker T. Washington: American Democracy and the Idea of Race Relations.* New York: Columbia Univ. Press, 2006.
White, Richard, and John M. Findlay, eds. *Power and Place in the North American West.* Seattle: Univ. of Washington Press, 1999.
Widener, Daniel. *Black Arts West: Culture and Struggle in Postwar Los Angeles.* Durham, NC: Duke Univ. Press, 2010.
———. "'Perhaps the Japanese Are to Be Thanked?' Asia, Asian America, and the Construction of Black California." *Positions* 11, no. 1 (Spring 2003): 135–81.
———. "'Way Out West': Expressive Art, Music, and Culture in Black LA." *Emergences* 9, no. 2 (1999): 271–89.
———. "Writing Watts: Budd Schulberg, Black Poetry, and the Cultural War on Poverty." *Journal of Urban History* 34, no. 4 (May 2008): 665–87.
Wiese, Andrew. *Places of Their Own: African American Suburbanization in the Twentieth Century.* Chicago: Univ. of Chicago Press, 2004.
Wild, Mark. *Street Meeting: Multiethnic Neighborhoods in Early Twentieth-Century Los Angeles.* Berkeley: Univ. of California Press, 2005.
Wilson, William Julius. *The Truly Disadvantaged: The Inner City, the Underclass, and Public Policy.* 2nd ed. Chicago: Univ. of Chicago Press, 2012.
Wolfinger, Raymond E., and Fred I. Greenstein. "The Repeal of Fair Housing in California: An Analysis of Referendum Voting." *The American Political Science Review* 62, no. 3 (September 1968): 753–69.
Wollenberg, Charles M. *All Deliberate Speed: Segregation and Exclusion in California Schools, 1855–1975.* Berkeley: Univ. of California Press, 1976.

Wu, Chin-tao. *Privatising Culture: Corporate Art Intervention since the 1980s.* New York: Verso, 2002.

Young, Joseph E. *Three Graphic Artists: Charles White, David Hammons, Timothy Washington.* Los Angeles: Los Angeles County Museum of Art, 1971.

Young, Louise M. *In the Public Interest: The League of Women Voters, 1920–1970.* New York: Greenwood, 1989.

Zesch, Scott. *The Chinatown War: Chinese Los Angeles and the Massacre of 1871.* New York: Oxford Univ. Press, 2012.

Zuckerman, Bruce, Zev Garber, Jeremy Schoenberg, Lisa Ansell, eds. *The Impact of the Holocaust in America: The Jewish Role in American Life, An Annual Review,* vol. 6. West Lafayette, IN: Purdue Univ. Press, 2008.

Index

Abbott, Mercedes, 35
African American Art and Artists (Lewis), 227
African American Cultural Center, 213
Ahmanson, Howard, 126–27
Alameda corridor: racial borders and, 55–56; residents' Proposition 14 views, 185; White homeownership and, 18–19
Alexander, Robert, 95, 152
Ali, Muhammad, 132
Allen, Aulette D., 86, 101, 102
Allen, Debbie, 4
Allen, W. Clyde, 86
Alonso, Alex, 159–60
Alston, Charles H., 118, 214
Altoon, John, 217
Amde, Father, 220
American Apartheid (Massey and Denton), 14
Anderson, Eddie, 64
Anderson, Eva Simon, 64
Anderson, Glenn, 191
Anderson, Mamie Nelson Wiggins, 64
Anderson v. Auseth. See Sugar Hill case
Angels Flight Railway, 38
Ankrum Gallery, 217
Anti-African Housing Association, 60
Antoine, Le Roi, 65
Apartment Owners' Association, 195
apartments, 194–95
Arbuckle, Roscoe Conkling, 76
Arcadia Block, 34
Architectural Forum, 135
Arguello, José, 31
Art West Associated, Incorporated (AWA), 218, 233
Arvey, Verna, 65
Ashburn, Allen W., 109
Asian American movement, 199, 205, 228–30
Asian Americans: Asian American movement, 199, 205, 228–30; Baldwin Hills Estates demographics, 151–52, 154; Baldwin Village demographics, 151–52, 155; Baldwin Vista demographics, 153, 154; Leimert Park demographics, 144; as part of White flight, 12–13, 144, 150, 160; View Park, View Heights, and Windsor Hills demographics, 150; Village Green demographics, 153, 154–55. See also Chinese Americans; Japanese Americans
Asian American Studies Center at UCLA, 229
automobiles, 43
the Avenues section, 137, 199, 228
Avila, Eric, 156–57
AWA. See Art West Associated, Incorporated

Babe's and Ricky's Inn, 245
BAC. See Black Arts Council
Bailey, Edith B., 86, 97, 101
Bailey, William E., 86, 97, 102–3
Baker, Robert Symington, 35
Baker Block, 35
Baldwin, Burt R. and Dianne, 200
Baldwin, Elias Jackson "Lucky," 127
Baldwin Hills: Black migration into, 150–55; post-Watts survey of White residents, 194
Baldwin Hills Cultural Enrichment Center, 195
Baldwin Hills Elementary School, 166, 167, 202, 242
Baldwin Hills Estates: Black migration into, 125–26, 151–52, 153–54; property values, 154, 243
Baldwin Village: Black migration into, 151–52, 155; gangs and, 159–60
Baldwin Vista: Black migration into, 151, 152–53; property values, 154, 243
banks: Black-owned, 62–63, 120–21
Baraka, Amiri, 207

333

Barlow, Fred, 152
Barrows, Olive, 116
Barrows v. Jackson, 12, 116
Baruch, Dorothy, 94–95
Baskett, James and Margaret Elizabeth Bonvill, 65
Bass, Charlotta, 60, 71, 109, 141
Bass, Joseph Blackburn, 71
Bay Street Beach, 43
beach resorts, 42, 43–44
Bearden, Romare, 214
Beaudry, Prudent, 37
Beavers, George A., Jr.: appointed to HACLA board, 96; on Black migration, 3–4, 13; civil rights activism of, 157; cofounding of Golden State, 58; on Golden State's relocation, 117, 118; on *Shelley* ruling, 114
Beavers, Lola Lillian Cunningham, 4
Beavers, Louise, 65, 84, 85, 97, 101
Belafonte, Harry, 134
Belcher, Greg, 84
Benny, Jack, 64
Berkeley Square, 76–77
Beverly Hills, 73, 77
Beverly Hills High School, 197
BGP. *See* Brockman Gallery Productions
Biggers, John Thomas, 213
Bingham Ordinance, 45
Black Art: An International Quarterly, 226
Black art/artists: Black arts movement defined, 205; Black Beverly Hills and, 240; Brockman Gallery and (*see* Brockman Gallery); development of Black art scene in Los Angeles, 215–21; Leimert Park Village as hub for, 237; in Leimert Park Village during 1990s, 244–46; major groups and galleries, 224–28, 233; opening of White-led art market to, 237–38; Whites buyers and, 206–7, 230
Black Artists, The (film), 226
Black Artists Association, 227
Black Artists on Art (Waddy and Lewis), 226
Black Arts Council (BAC), 225, 233
Black arts movement, 205
"Black belt": Eastside as, 8, 10; Watts as part of, 189

Black Beverly Hills: continued affluence of, 240–47; as moniker for Crenshaw area, 4–5
Black Bourgeoisie (Frazier), 20, 84
Black cultural nationalism: activism following Watts rebellion, 212–13; criticism of Davis brothers, 207–8; versus revolutionary nationalism, 207
Black elite: criticisms of, 4, 66–68; intra-racial tensions and, 66–68; as leading challenge to housing discrimination, 5–6, 65–66; vacation homes and, 71–72; West Adams Heights/Sugar Hill and, 82–88, 157–58; Westside migration as viewed by, 68–69. *See also* Black entertainers; Black middle class
Black Enterprise, 244
Black entertainers: highlighted in Sugar Hill case, 106–7; in Leimert Park, 142–43; in Sugar Hill, 82–84; in West Jefferson, 64–65; Westside migration as viewed by, 68–69
Black homeowners' rights movement, 10–11, 56–57
Black Manual Arts High School, 196
Black middle class: criticisms of, 4, 20–21, 66–68; history, markers, and growth of, 17–21; intra-racial tensions and, 19–20, 66–68, 189–90; new Black middle class, 17, 126; settlement in West Jefferson, 60–69
Black migration/settlement: Baldwin Hills and, 150–55; Black Beverly Hills and, 4–5, 240–47; Central Avenue corridor and, 54–56, 57 (*see also* Central Avenue corridor); Crenshaw area and (*see* Crenshaw area); early history of Los Angeles and, 5–13; Eastside and, 54–56, 134–35 (*see also* Eastside); during golden era of Black Los Angeles, 28–29, 39–44; Hancock Park and, 129–32; Ladera Heights and, 241–43; Lafayette Square and, 129–30, 132–35; Leimert Park and, 135–44; overview of Westside migration, 3–5, 10–13, 58–69, 125–29; post-*Shelley* obstacles and White resistance, 116–22, 125–35, 137–41, 147, 175; racial restrictive covenants and (*see* racial restrictive covenants); real estate blockbusting and,

162, 172–76; suburban expansion of Los Angeles and, 13–23; View Park/View Heights/Windsor Hills and, 144–50; Watts and, 94, 97, 135, 189; West Adams Heights/Sugar Hill and, 82–88; West Jefferson and, 60–69; White flight and, 12–13, 144, 150, 154, 160, 246–47

Black nationalism: civil rights movement and, 213–14; cultural versus revolutionary, 207; Watts rebellion and rise of, 190, 212–13

Black-owned businesses: banks, 62–63, 120–21; Golden State Mutual Insurance Company, 3–4, 58–59, 62–63, 116–18, 157; Leimert Park Village in the 1990s, 244–46; Westside entrepreneurs, 118–19

Black Panther Party, 213

Black Peace Stone Nation, 159

Black Power movement, 207

Black real estate agents: in Crenshaw area, 173–76; discriminated against, 111, 121; Sidney Dones, 71–72

Black revolutionary nationalism: activism following Watts rebellion, 212, 213; versus cultural nationalism, 207

Blacks: Baldwin Hills Estates demographics, 154; Baldwin Village demographics, 155; Baldwin Vista demographics, 153, 154; defense industry and, 67, 91, 93; Double V campaign, 12, 91, 96, 105; early Los Angeles County demographics, 35, 36–37; early Los Angeles demographics, 6, 35, 39–40; gangs involving, 128–29, 158–60; homeownership rates, 18; Leimert Park demographics, 144; Los Angeles politics and, 54–55, 141–42, 183; multicultural coalitions, 15–16; Proposition 14 views, 186; school completion and, 19; View Park, View Heights, and Windsor Hills demographics, 150; Village Green demographics, 153, 154–55; white-collar employment and, 19

Blackstone Club, 61

Black tax, 162, 175

Black women: role in Sugar Hill case, 101; role in westward migration, 10; survey of Black female artists, 225–26

Black working class: Brockman Gallery and, 230–31; intra-racial tensions and, 20–21, 66–68, 189–90; as marker distinguishing Black middle class, 19–21; Proposition 14 views, 186

Blair, Janet, 84

blockbusting. *See* real estate blockbusting

Blodgett, Louis Matthew (L. M.), 62–63

Bloods (gang), 159–60

Blum, Irving, 216

Boger, Othelia "Fifi," 169–70, 195–96

Boger, Tom, 170

Bogle, Donald, 68, 84

Bond, J. Max, 16, 60–61

Bon Odori (festival), 144

Booker, Claude, 224–25, 233

Bound for Freedom (Flamming), 16–17

Bourgeois Utopias (Fishman), 14

Bowdoin, Lorenzo, 102

Bowen, William Miller, 217–18

Bowman, Laura, 65

Bowron, Fletcher, 92–93, 95–96, 97, 120

Boyle, Andrew, 53

Boyle Heights, 41, 53

Bradley, Ethel Mae Arnold, 139, 141

Bradley, Tom, 139–42, 183, 192, 200

Brandeis, Louis, 112

Branton, Geraldine Pate Nicholas, 65, 134

Branton, Leo, Jr., 134

La Brea Avenue, 153

Breye, Brian, 244

Brick Block, 40

Brilliant, Mark, 90

Broadway Federal Savings and Loan Association, 120

Brockman Gallery: Black artists represented by, 231–32; Black buyers and, 230–31; business approach of, 208, 227–28; as center of Black art in Leimert Park, 222–31; in context of Los Angeles's Black arts scene, 215–21; Crenshaw Neighbors collaborations, 223–24; founders of, 208–14; legacy of, 241; overview of, 204–8; public art and outreach, 231–39; White buyers and, 206–7, 230

Brockman Gallery Film Festival, 235

Brockman Gallery Productions (BGP), 208, 231, 235, 236

Bronzeville, 94–95, 96

Brooklyn Avenue, 53

Brooklyn Heights, 41

Brown, Edmund "Pat," 141, 142, 183, 186, 191
Brown, Elaine, 219
Brown, Willie, Jr., 183
Brown v. Board of Education, 164
Bruce, Willa and Charles, 42, 43–44
Bruce's Beach, 42, 43–44
Bryant, Clora, 119
Buchanan, Robert, 47
Buchanan v. Warley, 47, 50
Buckley, John, 50
Bullock, Anna Mae. *See* Turner, Tina
Bunker Hill, 37, 75–76
Burke, Yvonne Brathwaite, 174, 200
Burns, Fritz B., 119, 145–46
Burton, Phillip, 142

cable railways, 38
Caldwell, Ben, 244
Caldwell, John, 141
California: civil rights bills of 1959, 142; defense industry and, 93; early lawsuits challenging racial land restrictions, 45; early legislation related to race and gender, 50–51; Fair Housing Act of 1963, 183–84; founding and early history of, 27–28, 30–33; Proposition 10 (1950), 120; Proposition 14 (1948), 119; Proposition 14 (1964), 121, 182–88, 191
California Apartment Owners' Association, 184
California Art Club, 215
California Democratic Council, 141
California Eagle: Sidney Dones and, 71; on Olympic freeway construction, 156; on post-*Shelley* housing discrimination, 147; on racial restrictive covenants, 30, 61, 109; on school desegregation, 167; on White homeowners' protective associations, 60
California Fair Housing Act of 1963, 183–84
California Federal Savings and Loan, 175
California Governor's Commission on the Los Angeles Riots, 193
Californians Against Proposition 14 (CAP 14), 186, 187
California Real Estate Association (CREA), 46, 115, 184
California Supreme Court cases: *Fairchild v. Raines*, 100–101; *Jackson v. Pasadena City School District*, 165; *Janss Investment Co. v. Walden*, 49; *Los Angeles Investment Company v. Gary*, 48–49; *Mulkey v. Reitman*, 191; *Perez v. Sharp*, 121; Sugar Hill case, 108–11; *Wayt v. Patee*, 13, 61–62
Californios, 31, 34–35
Calle de los Negros, 33–34
Calloway, Cab, 84
Cannon, J. Alfred, 220
CAP 14. *See* Californians Against Proposition 14
Carillo, José Antonio, 32
Carlisle, David K., 147
Carmichael, Stokely, 213–14
Carter, Alprentice "Bunchy," 229
Carter, Ben, 65, 85, 97
Carter, Betty J., 65
Carter, Edward, 218
Castle Rindge, 78
Cayton, Horace R., 91
Central Avenue corridor: as Black hub, 41, 54–56, 63, 135; housing shortage and, 75, 93; multiethnic character of, 7, 41; name revisions and, 8; racial borders and, 55–56; redlining map and, 73. *See also* Eastside
Ceruti, Edward Burton, 29–30
Chandler, Dorothy Buffum, 126
Chandler, Harry, 69
Charity Street, 39
Charles, Ray, 143, 149–50, 157–58, 174
Charles Victor Hall tract cases, 109
Cheney, A. L., 77
Chester Place, 76
Chicago Defender, 106
Chicago housing movement, 178
Chicano movement, 191–92
China City, 51–52
Chinatown (Los Angeles): development and relocation of, 15, 33–34, 51–52; massacre of 1871, 34
Chinatown (San Francisco): Bingham Ordinance and, 45
Chinese Americans: development and relocation of Chinatown, 15, 33–34, 51–52; early Los Angeles County demographics, 35, 36, 51; massacre

of 1871, 34; targeted by early racial land restrictions, 45. *See also* Asian Americans
Chouinard, Nelbert, 217
CHP. *See* Committee for Home Protection
Christian Science Monitor, 4
Cienega Elementary School, 166
Citizens Against Socialist Housing, 120, 146
City Beautiful movement, 45
civil rights activism: Black nationalism and, 213–14; California's civil rights laws of 1959, 142; Civil Rights Act of 1968, Title VIII, 175, 200; Double V campaign, 12, 91, 96, 105; Golden State founders and, 157; Proposition 14 and, 186; racial liberalism and, 90, 92–93, 183; racial restrictive covenants as focus of (*see* racial restrictive covenants); school desegregation as focus of (*see* school desegregation); shifting political climate and demographics as supporting, 92–97
Civil Rights Act of 1968, Title VIII, 175, 200
Clark, Eli, 38–39
Clark, Horace and Vera, 85
Clark, Tom C., 12, 113–14
Clarke, Thurmond, 12, 92, 104, 107–8
Clark Hotel, 85
Clement, Rufus, 107, 108
CN. *See* Crenshaw Neighbors, Incorporated
Cobb, James A., 50
Cochran, George Ira, 77, 78
COIN. *See* Council of Integrated Neighborhoods
Cole, Maria Ellington, 130–32
Cole, Nat King, 130–32
Collins, Sharon, 19
Committee for Home Protection (CHP), 119, 120, 146, 184–85
Committee on Civil Rights, 113
Community Redevelopment Act of 1945, 119
Comprehensive Employment and Training Act, Title VI, 236
Compton, 94
Concordia Club, 53

Congress of Racial Equality (CORE), 213–14
Constituents (gang), 158
Copp, Andrew J., 131
CORE. *See* Congress of Racial Equality
Corrigan, Irene, 49–50
Corrigan v. Buckley, 30, 49–50, 56–57, 61–62, 70
Cortez, Jayne, 218, 220
Council of Integrated Neighborhoods (COIN), 192–93
Covington, Floyd, 96, 156
Crabgrass Frontier (Jackson), 14
Crank, James, 38
Crawford, James Lloyd, 82
CREA. *See* California Real Estate Association
Crenshaw, George L., 132
Crenshaw area: Baldwin Hills, 150–55; as Black arts and culture hub, 205–6; as Black Beverly Hills, 4–5, 240–47; Brockman Gallery in (*see* Brockman Gallery); formation of Crenshaw Neighbors, 176–82 (*see also* Crenshaw Neighbors, Incorporated); formation of United Neighbors, 161–63 (*see also* United Neighbors); Leimert Park, 135–44; overview of Black migration into, 22, 125–29; as part of curfew zone after Watts rebellion, 191, 212; property values, 243; racial composition of, 180–81, 200, 242, 243; real estate blockbusting and, 162, 172–76; resegregation and, 202–3; school desegregation and, 163–72, 176–77; South Central designation and, 246; View Park, View Heights, and Windsor Hills, 144–50; White flight and, 144, 150, 154, 160, 202–3
Crenshaw Coordinating Council, 170–71, 195
Crenshaw Democratic Club, 141
Crenshaw High School, 196, 202
Crenshaw Neighbors, Incorporated (CN): Brockman Gallery and, 223–24; formation of, 176–82; legacy of, 202–3, 241; members' mixed views of, 200–201; post-Watts initiatives, 192–201; Proposition 14 views and, 187–88; real estate agency, 179–80, 193–94
Crenshaw Notes, 178, 180, 198, 223

Crenshaw Square shopping center, 144
Crenshaw Walls, 235–36
Crestmore Improvement Association, 61
Crestmore tract, 61–62
Crips (gang), 159–60
The Crisis, 30, 110–11
Crossroads Arts Academy and Theater, 245
Crouch, Stanley, 220
Crowther, Jack, 167
Cryer, George, 102
Cryer, Isabel, 85, 102
cultural nationalism. *See* Black cultural nationalism
"culture of poverty" thesis, 14
Curtis, Helen, 50

Daáood, Kamau, 244
Daley, Richard, 178
Dance Collective, 245
Dandridge, Dorothy, 65
Daniels, John, 205
Davies, John, 168
Davis, Agnes Moses, 209, 210
Davis, Alonzo Joseph, Jr.: as artist and activist, 225, 235, 237; background of, 208–14; business approach of, 208, 227–28; founding of Brockman Gallery, 204–8, 222–23 (*see also* Brockman Gallery)
Davis, Alonzo Joseph, Sr., 209
Davis, Clifford L., Jr., 197
Davis, Dale Brockman: background of, 208–14; business approach of, 208, 227–28; founding of Brockman Gallery, 204–8, 222–23 (*see also* Brockman Gallery)
Davis, Joan, 84
Davis, Mike, 43, 127
Davis, Miles, 21–22
De Bruin, Joan, 236
Dedeaux, Richard, 220
defense industry, 67, 91, 93
De Graaf, Lawrence, 16
Delgado, Robert, 236
Democratic Minority Conference, 141
De Neve, Felipe, 31
Denton, Nancy, 14
Department of Housing and Urban Development (HUD), 115

Deutz, Max F., 242, 243
Deverell, William, 35
Dickinson and Gillespie, 145–46
Doheny, Edward L., 76
Donahue, Kenneth, 238
Dones, Sidney P., 71–72, 89, 98
Dorsey High School. *See* Susan M. Dorsey High School
Double V campaign, 12, 91, 96, 105
Doumakes House, 240
downtown Los Angeles: competition between Westside and, 126–27; early history of Plaza, 31–32 (*see also* Plaza)
Driskell, David, 238
Du Bois, W. E. B., 17, 30, 209
Durant, Thomas, Jr., 19
Dymally, Mervyn M., 183

East Los Angeles, 41, 54, 158
Eastside: as "Black belt," 8, 10; Black migration out of, 134–35; Black settlement in, 54–56; demarcation from Westside, 7–10, 27–30; name revisions, 8; neighborhood disrepair, 94–95; neighborhoods and enclaves of, 50–56; public housing projects and, 95, 190; racial borders and, 7–8, 55–56, 94, 246; rise of gangs in, 159; use-based zoning and, 9, 46–47
Eastside-Westside (artwork), 234
Ebony, 5, 132
Edmondson, Fred, 152
Edwards, Deloy, 173–76
Edwards, Elizabeth, 106–7
electric railways, 38
Eleven Associated (gallery), 216
Ellington, Duke, 84
Ellis, Pauline, 57
Elmore, Jessie, 105
Entwistle, James and Ellen, 27
Entwistle tract property owners, 27, 30, 57
Equal Rights Protective Association, 60, 61
Estrada Courts, 152
Euclid v. Ambler, 47, 56, 70
Eureka Villa. *See* Val Verde
Executive Order 8802, 93

Fairbanks, Douglas, 76
Fairchild, Hazel, 100

Fairchild v. Raines, 100–101
Fair Employment Practices Act of 1959, 142
Fair Employment Practices Commission, 183
Fairfax High School, 196
Fair Housing Act. *See* Civil Rights Act of 1968, Title VIII
fair housing movement: California legislation of 1959, 142; federal legislation of 1968, 200; nationwide campaigns, 177–78; Proposition 14 as undoing, 182–88, 191
Family Savings and Loan Association, 121, 194–95, 199
federal government: colonization of California and Los Angeles, 27–28; defense industry expansion, 91, 93; fair housing legislation of 1968, 200; Federal Housing Administration, 10, 73–74, 115, 200; New Deal and housing discrimination, 9–10, 70, 72–74; postwar support for racial equality, 113–14; support for public housing, 119–20
Federal Housing Administration (FHA), 10, 73–74, 115, 200
Felker-Kantor, Max, 186
Fergerson, Cecil, 224–25, 227–28, 233
Ferrell, F. Douglas, 183
Ferus Gallery, 216–17
Festival of the Arts (1967), 223
FHA. *See* Federal Housing Administration
5th Street Dick's Coffee Company, 244
film festivals, 235
First African Methodist Episcopal Church, 40
Fisher, Lloyd H., 65–66
Fishman, Robert, 14, 77, 127
Fitzgerald, Ella, 142–43
Flamming, Douglas, 16–17, 18, 40–41
Flicker, Milton, 223–24
Ford, John Anson, 92, 139
Fort, Jeff, 159
Fortier, Wilhelmina, 236
Fourteenth Amendment, 114
fragile movement, 178
Frazier, E. Franklin, 20, 84
Frazier, Marie Brown, 20
Freeney, Naomi, 81

freeway construction: racism and, 156–57
Frye, Marquette, 188
Frye, Ronald, 188
Fulton, Richard, 244
Furlong Tract, 63

Gable, Clark, 84
Gafford, Alice Taylor, 216
Gallery 32, 225–26, 233
Gallery Plus, 244
Gallery Row, 216–17
The Gallery, 227
Gandolfo v. Hartman, 45
gangs: disbanding and activism of, 229; rise and impact of, 128–29, 158–60; Watts rebellion and, 190
Gantz, Harry, 131
garden cities, 152
Garr, Todd and Randall, 166
Garrott, Homer L. and Pearl, 47–48
Gary, Alfred, 48–49
Gebhard, David, 134
Gibbs, Marla, 245
G.I. Bill, 74–75
Gidra (newspaper), 229, 233
Gladiators (gang), 159
Goff, Etta, 83
Golden State Mutual Life Insurance Company: as community staple, 157; formation and impact of, 3–4, 58–59, 62–63; relocation to Westside, 116–18
Goldmark, Josephine Clara, 112
Gonda, Jeffrey, 11, 131
Gone with the Wind (film), 84
Good Earth, The (film), 52
Gordon, Wilbur C., 62, 70–71
Gordon Manor subdivision, 70–71
Granger, Lester, 108
Grant, Earl (musician), 150
Grant, M. Earl, 120, 121
Greater Crenshaw Town Council, 171
Great Migration, 11
Green, Alfred and Senola Maxwell, 86
Gregg, Jean: Council of Integrated Neighborhoods and, 192; on Crenshaw Neighbors' real estate plan, 181; National Neighbors and, 201–2; presentation to McCone Commission, 193; Proposition 14 views, 187; resignation from Crenshaw Neighbors, 194; United

Neighbors/Crenshaw Neighbors and, 161, 169, 176, 177, 179, 180, 182
Griffin, Booker, 213
Griffin, Noah, 107
Griffith, Thomas Jr., 120
Grigsby, Eugene, 213
Gross, Laura Mae, 245

HACLA. *See* Housing Authority of the City of Los Angeles
Hahn, Kenneth, 200
Hairston, Eugene "Bull," 159
Hairston, Joseph, 201
Hall, Charles Victor, 77
Hall, Mary E., 77
Hamilton High School, 196
Hammons, David, 238
Hancock, Henry, 130
Hancock Park: Black migration into, 129–32; redlining map and, 73
Hancock Park Property Owners Association, 131
Hansberry, Carl, 111
Hansberry v. Lee, 111–12
"Harlem of the West," 55
Hastie, William, 107, 108
Hawkins, Augustus, 92, 141, 183
Hawkins Fair Housing Act of 1959, 142
Hearn, Lawrence, 206
Hendrix, Laura, 244
Heritage Gallery, 217
Higgins, Billy, 244
Hill, Linda, 219
Hillcrest Country Club, 79
Himes, Chester, 20, 66–68, 72, 189
Hinton, John W., 27
Hinton, Lulu Nevada Entwistle, 27
Hiroshima (band), 234
Hirsch, Arnold, 10, 171
His Eye Is on the Sparrow (Waters), 85
Hispanics. *See* Latinos; Mexican Americans
HOLC. *See* Home Owners' Loan Corporation
Holiday Bowl, 143–44
Homage to John Outterbridge (mural), 237
homeowners' associations: West Adams Heights Improvement Association, 80–82; West Adams Heights Protective Association, 97–103, 106–7 (*see also*

Sugar Hill case); White associations' role in opposing Black migration, 60, 80–82, 137–38
homeownership: Black homeowners' rights movement, 10–11, 56–57; Black rates of, 18; historical importance of, 18–19
Home Owners' Loan Corporation (HOLC), 10, 72–73, *74*
Home Protective Association, 109
Hopps, Walter, 216–17
Horne, Gerald, 118, 189, 190
HoSang, Daniel Martinez, 90, 183–84, 185
Hotel Somerville, 86
Hotel Watkins, 119
Housing and Urban Development Act of 1968, 200
Housing Authority of the City of Los Angeles (HACLA), 95, 119
housing discrimination: after *Euclid* and *Corrigan,* 69–75; Black elite as leading challenges to, 5–6, 65–66; early California lawsuits challenging racial land restrictions, 45; fair housing movement and, 177–78 (*see also* fair housing movement); formation of WAHPA to combat, 97–103; limitations of *Shelley* and, 115–16; New Deal and, 9–10, 70, 72–74; overview of history in Los Angeles, 8–12; overview of Sugar Hill case, 89–92 (*see also* Sugar Hill case); post-*Shelley* obstacles and White resistance, 116–22, 125–35, 137–41, 147, 175; Proposition 14 and, 182–88, 191; racial violence and, 134, 140–41, 165; redlining and, 73, *74,* 200; sanctioned by state, 9–10, 44–50. *See also* racial restrictive covenants; residential segregation; use-based zoning
housing shortage, 91, 93–97
Houston, Charles Hamilton, 113
Houston, Doris Talbot Young, 63–64
Houston, Edythe Pryce, 4, 59, 78–82
Houston, Ivan, 64, 118
Houston, Lillian Jackson, 58
Houston, Norman O.: appointed to HACLA board, 96; Central Avenue residence of, 63; civil rights activism of, 157; cofounding of Golden State, 3–4, 58–59; early life, 58–59; on intra-racial

tensions, 190; move into West Adams Heights, 4, 59, 78–82; move into West Jefferson, 62, 64; other business ventures, 62, 63, 120; WAHPA and, 97, 102, 107
Howard, Ebenezer, 152
Howard, H. J., 120
Howland, Charles H., 38
El Hoyo Maravilla, 158
HUD (Department of Housing and Urban Development), 115
Hudson, H. Claude, 120–21
Hughes, Howard, 136
Hughes, Langston, 99
Huntington, Henry E., 43
Hyde Park-Kenwood Community Conference, 178

If He Hollers Let Him Go (Himes), 20, 66–68, 189
Immigration Act of 1924, 52
Industrial District Ordinance, 46
Inglewood Board of Education, 242–43
Inglewood Neighbors, 242
Inglewood Public Library exhibit, 232
Inner City Cultural Center, 220
Inouye, Kazuo K., 172–73
In re Lee Sing (court case), 45
The Integrator, 198–99, 200
interurban transportation, 43
intra-racial tensions: Black westward migration and, 66–69; as contributing to Watts rebellion, 189–90; Golden State's relocation and, 118; Proposition 14 and, 186; rise of gangs and, 128–29
Isoardi, Steven, 245

Jackson, C. Bernard, 220
Jackson, Jay, 165
Jackson, Kenneth, 14
Jackson, Leola, 116
Jackson, Suzanne, 225–26, 228, 233, 236
Jackson v. Pasadena City School District, 165
Jacobs, Riley and Edythe, 182
Jacobson, Joyce, 181
Jacquette, Tommy, 213, 220
Janel Johnson v. Inglewood Unified School District, 242–43
Janes, Laura C., 71

Janss Investment Co. v. Walden, 49
Japanese American Citizens League, 111
Japanese Americans: Asian American movement, 199, 205, 228–30; Fletcher Bowron's disregard for, 97; in Crenshaw area, 137, 143–44, 205; Crenshaw Neighbors participation, 197–98; early settlement patterns, 52–53; gangs involving, 128–29, 158, 159; immigration to US, 15; intersections of Blacks and, 16; population in early Los Angeles County, 35, 36, 52; Proposition 14 views, 187; wartime incarceration and resettlement, 93–94, 96–97; working as real estate agents, 172–73. *See also* Asian Americans
Jefferson, Alison Rose, 42
Jefferson, Bernard, 156
Jefferson, Edwin L., 96
Jefferson Boulevard, 205
Jeffries, Vincent, 194
Jewish Americans: Boyle Heights and, 53; migration into West Adams/Westside, 79; population in early Los Angeles County, 36
J-Flats community, 53
John H. Francis Polytechnic High School, 64
Johnson, Evangeline Woods, 147
Johnson, Evelyn Allen, 125–26
Johnson, Pat, 236
Johnson, Raymond, 126
Johnson, Reginald, 152
Jones, Clarence A., 89, 99
Jungle Stones (gang), 159, 160

Kahen, Harold, 105
KAOS Network, 244
Karenga, Maulana, 207, 212–13, 220
Kashu Realty, 173
Kaub, Karen, 197
Kenny, Robert Walker, 12, 109–10
Kienholz, Ed, 216–17
Kimbrough, Theopolis D., 179
Kinchlow, Adolphus D. and Mattie, 61
King, Leslie U., 84–85, 97, 98, 102
King, Mamie, 84–85
King, Martin Luther, Jr., 213, 234
King, Rodney, 244
King Cole Trio, 130

Knight, Rhoda May, 78
Knowland, William, 142
Kojima, Masamori, 197–98
Kraemer, Louis and Fern, 112
Ku Klux Klan, 44, 70
Kurashige, Lon, 52
Kurashige, Scott, 16, 80, 144, 163

L.A. City Limits (Sides), 17
LACMA. *See* Los Angeles County Museum of Art
Ladera Heights, 241–43
Lafayette Square: Black migration into, 129–30, 132–35; demographic shifts, 134
Laing, John, 179, 181
Lake Elsinore Valley, 71
Landry, Bart, 17, 19, 126
LARB. *See* Los Angeles Realty Board
Latinos: Baldwin Village and Baldwin Hills Estates demographics, 151–52. *See also* Mexican Americans
L.A. Weekly, 5
Laws, Henry and Anna, 109
League of Women Voters, 169
Leimart Park Democratic Club, 141–42
Leimert, Walter, 135
Leimert Park: Black migration into, 135–44; Brockman Gallery and Black art scene in, 222–31; demographics/population shifts, 137, 144, 204–5; post-Watts survey of White residents, 194
Leimert Park Plaza, 223
Leimert Park: The Story of a Village (film), 246
Leimert Park Village: Black art and activism during 1990s, 244–46; as Black art hub, 237; Brockman Gallery and (*see* Brockman Gallery); history of, 136–37; reactions to demographic shifts, 223–24
Leimert Theater, 136–37
Letteau, George H., 27
Letteau heirs, 29, 30, 57
Lewis, Norman, 214
Lewis, Oscar, 14
Lewis, Samella S., 217, 218, 226–27
Life, 135
Lindsay, Gilbert, 142, 183
Lindsay, Jeannette, 246

Little Tokyo: as Bronzeville, 94–95, 96; establishment of, 15, 53
Lomax, Almena, 211
Long, Tatiana, 236
Long, William H. and Eunice, 27, 30
Lopéz, César, 33
Los Angeles: Black homeownership rate, 18; Black migration and suburban expansion of, 13–23; Black political representation, 54–55, 141–42, 183; characterizations of, 30, 66–68, 72, 91; competition between downtown and Westside, 126–27; defense industry and, 67, 91, 93; development of Black art scene in, 215–21 (*see also* Black art/artists); Eastside-Westside demarcation, 7–10, 27–30; envisioned as "white spot," 69; founding and early history of, 27–28, 30–33; freeway construction and racism in, 156–57; Great Migration and, 11; history of segregation in, 5–13, 33–37, 43–44; housing shortage in, 91, 93–97; implementation of use-based zoning, 45–47; mixed reaction to Sugar Hill ruling, 107; as multicultural center, 15; public housing in, 95–96, 119–20; rise and impact of gangs in, 128–29, 158–60; shifting political climate and demographics, 92–97; uprising of 1992, 244; Watts rebellion, 188–92 (*see also* Watts rebellion)
Los Angeles, 1972: A Panorama of Black Artists (exhibit), 238
Los Angeles Board of Education: racial census of schools, 202–3; school desegregation and, 164, 165–68, 171, 176–77
Los Angeles Cable Railway Company, 38
Los Angeles Consolidated Electric Railway Company, 38
Los Angeles County: early demographics, 35, 36–37, 51, 52; Proposition 14 vote, 188
Los Angeles County Committee on Human Relations, 139
Los Angeles County Conference on Community Relations, 152
Los Angeles County Museum of Art (LACMA), 218, 224–25, 238
Los Angeles County Museum of History, Science, and Art, 217–18

Los Angeles County Regional Planning Commission, 47
Los Angeles Cultural Arts Center for Youth, 195
Los Angeles Electric Railway, 38
Los Angeles Investment Company, 145
Los Angeles Investment Company v. Gary, 48–49
Los Angeles Negro Artist Association, 216
Los Angeles Negro Victory Committee, 96
Los Angeles Pacific Railway Company, 39
Los Angeles Railway Company, 43
Los Angeles Realty Board (LARB), 45–46, 115–16, 121
Los Angeles Security Map, 73, *74*
Los Angeles Sentinel: on Double V campaign, 105; founding of, 99; on racial restrictive covenant cases, 107, 109, 111, 114; on school desegregation, 168
Los Angeles Street Graphics Committee, 237
Los Angeles Superior Court cases: *Janel Johnson v. Inglewood Unified School District*, 242–43; other racial restrictive covenants cases, 109, 182; Sugar Hill case, 90, 104–8; *Title Guarantee & Trust Company v. Garrott*, 47–48
Los Angeles Times: on Baldwin Vista, 153; on Berkeley Square, 77; Black Beverly Hills moniker and, 4–5; on dual housing market, 175; interview with Deloy Edwards, 174; on Proposition 14, 182–83; on racial restrictive covenants, 48, 106; racist vision of, 69; on Windsor Hills Elementary, 203
Los Angeles Tribune, 211
Louden, Joyce, 19
Lummis, Charles, 36
Lynwood, 94

Macbeth, Hugh Ellsworth, 48, 61
Mack, Kenneth, 11, 103
Mafundi Institute, 220, 233
Magnin, Edgar Fogel, 79
Manhattan Beach, 42, 43–44
"Mapping L.A." project, 246
March Against Fear, 214
Marla's Memory Lane, 245
Marlow, Fred H., 145, 146
Marlow-Burns and Company, 145–46

Marshall, Louis, 50
Marshall, Thurgood, 103, 108, 112
Marvin Avenue Elementary School, 166
Mason, Bridget "Biddy," 40–41
Massey, Douglas, 14
Matthews, Miriam, 215–16
Maverick's Flat, 205–6
McAdoo, William G., 77
McCone Commission. *See* California Governor's Commission on the Los Angeles Riots
McDaniel, Hattie, 65, 82–84, 98, 105, 106
McDaniel, Sam and Lulu, 65
McGovney, Dudley Odell, 105
McKissick, Floyd, 213–14
McQueen, Butterfly, 84
McWilliams, Carey, 77, 78–79, 81
Memory Lane Supper Club, 206, 245
Meredith, James, 213
Merrill, Edwin, 152
Mesa Vernon Market, 136
Metz, Elizabeth, 166–67
Mexican Americans: Fletcher Bowron's disregard for, 97; Chicano movement, 191–92; gangs involving, 158; Proposition 14 views, 187; settlement in East Los Angeles, 54; settlement in Sonoratown, 34; settlement in West Adams Heights, 79–80; Village Green and Baldwin Vista demographics, 153
Mexican American War, 31
Mexico: California settlement, 27, 31; Los Angeles settlement, 32
middle class, Black. *See* Black middle class
Miles, Mitchell B. and Mabel C., 87
Milgram, Jean Gregg. *See* Gregg, Jean
Milgram, Morris, 201, 300n96
Miller, Juanita Ellsworth, 100
Miller, Loren: as attorney for WAHPA, 98–103; background of, 99–100; on ongoing nature of housing discrimination fight, 121–22; other racial restrictive covenant cases, 103, 109, 111; on residential segregation, 163; school desegregation and, 163, 164, 167; *Shelley* litigation and, 112–13; Sugar Hill litigation and, 11–12, 89, 104–6, 107, 108–9, 110–11
Millier, Arthur, 215
Mills, Billy G., 142, 183

INDEX

Minikus, Lee, 188
Ministers (gang), 159
Mirror-News, 134–35
Misumi, Donald, 198
Mitchell, Courtland G. and Rosa Lee, 86
mixed-use districts, 46
Miyashiro, Sam S., 173
Mizukami, R. M., 173
Moore, William, 77
Moorehead, Agnes, 84
Morehouse, Henry Lyman, 17
Moreland, Mantan and Hazel, 65
Morris, Richard T., 194
Mott, Stephen H., 37
Moynihan, Daniel Patrick, 14
Mulkey v. Reitman, 191
Multi-Cul gallery, 227
Multimedia Public Arts Services Program, 236
Mumford, Lewis, 152
murals, 235–36, 237
Murray, Henry "Juggy," 149
Museum in Black, 244
Museum of African American Art, 227
The Music Center, 126
My Neighbor's Island (Johnson), 125

NAACP. *See* National Association for the Advancement of Colored People
Nakada, Suma, 224
Nakada, Yoshinao, 197, 198
The Nation, 94–95
National Association for the Advancement of Colored People (NAACP): critique of Hattie McDaniel, 84; legal challenges to racial restrictive covenants, 29–30, 50, 57, 103, 108, 111, 112–13; legal challenge to race-based zoning, 47; school desegregation and, 164–67, 165–67; *Shelley* litigation, 112–13; Somervilles and, 55, 86; Sugar Hill case and, 108, 111
National Association of Real Estate Boards, 121, 184
National Association of Real Estate Brokers, 111
National Neighbors, 163, 201–2
Native Americans: population in early Los Angeles County, 35, 36; settlement of California region, 31

Navarro, Charles, 156
Negro Digest, 91
Negro in American Art, The (exhibit), 238
Negro in California from 1780–1910, The (Matthews), 216
neighborhood school concept, 164
neighborhood stabilization movement, 163, 178, 201–2
Neighborly Endeavors, Incorporated, 137–38
Nelson, Anne, 195
Nelson, Oliver, 150
Nengudi, Senga, 226
Neutra, Richard, 95
New Black Middle Class, The (Landry), 17
New Deal: housing discrimination and, 9–10, 70, 72–74
Newsweek, 203
Newton, Huey P., 213
New York City, 18
New York Times, 114
Nicholas, Fayard, 65
Nicholas, Geraldine Pate. *See* Branton, Geraldine Pate Nicholas
Nicholas, Harold, 65
Nickerson, Michelle, 170
Nickerson, William, Jr., 3, 58, 117
Nicolaides, Becky, 18, 55, 185
Niggers Ain't Gonna Never Ever Be Nothin' (exhibit), 230–31
Nishi, Midori, 143
Novarro, Ramon, 79–80

Oakland, 18
Obatala, J. K., 4
occupancy clauses: Erstwhile tract homes and, 27, 30; residential segregation and, 13; upheld by courts, 49. *See also* racial restrictive covenants
Olmsted, Frederick Law, Jr., 70–71
Olmsted Brothers (firm), 135
Olsen, Kenneth, 194, 201, 224
Olson, Culbert, 97
Olvera, Agustín, 32
Olvera Street, 51
Olympic freeway, 155–57
O'Melveny, Henry, 70–71
open housing movement. *See* fair housing movement
O'Reilly, Deborah, 102

Origins of the Urban Crisis, The (Sugrue), 14
Oshiro, Harry, 143
O'Solomon, Otis, 220
Otis, Harrison Gray, 36
Outterbridge, John: Black Arts Council and, 225; Brockman Gallery and, 227, 228, 230, 232, 237; as Watts Tower Arts Center director, 221, 234
Owens, Robert and Minnie, 40–41
Oyama v. California, 121
Ozawa, Joseph, Jr., 197

pachucos, 158
Pacific Electric Railway, 43
Pajaud, William, 118, 217
Pan Afrikan Peoples Arkestra, 219, 245–46
Parker, William H., 158, 188, 191
Parks, Bernard C., 174
Pasadena: *Fairchild v. Raines*, 100–101; public transit and early growth of, 38; Jackie Robinson on racism in, 44; school desegregation and, 164–65
Pasadena Board of Education, 164–65
Patton, K. D., 153
Paxton, Gertrude, 153–54, 160
Paxton, Lawrence, 153, 154
Peck, George H., Jr., 42, 43
Perez v. Sharp, 121
Phillips, Lee Allen, 77
Pickford, Mary, 76
Pico, Pío, 32, 35
Pittsburgh Courier, 70, 91
Plaza: development beyond, 33–35; early history of, 31–32; as hub of Mexican community, 54
Plessy v. Ferguson, 44
pobladores, 31–33
Pollard, W.L., 46
Post, Ann: Proposition 14 views, 187–88; United Neighbors/Crenshaw Neighbors and, 169, 179, 194, 195, 200–201
Post, David, 169
Poulson, Norris, 120
Powell, Judson, 221
Price, Linda, 236
Price, Rena, 188
Professional Artist Employment Program, 236

Progressive Federation of Improvement Associations of California, 61
property values: Baldwin Hills Estates and Baldwin Vista, 154, 243; Crenshaw area, 243; Sugar Hill, 87, 156; View Park, View Heights, and Windsor Hills, 150, 243
Proposition 10 (1950), 120
Proposition 14 (1948), 119
Proposition 14 (1964), 182–88, 191
public housing: campaigns against, 119–20; construction of, 95–96, 190
public housing war projects, 95
public murals, 235–36, 237
public schools: desegregation and, 163–72, 176–77; formation of United Neighbors and race relations in, 161, 168; racial census of, 202–3
public transit: early development of Westside and, 37–39; White control of land and, 43
El Pueblo de Nuestra Señora La Reina de Los Ángeles de Porciúncula, 31
Purifoy, Noah, 221, 230–31

Race Life of the Aryan Peoples (Widney), 38
racial discrimination: Double V campaign challenging, 12, 91, 96, 105; early California laws curbing, 50–51; G.I. Bill and, 74–75; racial liberalism and, 90, 92–93, 183; shifting political climate and demographics as challenging, 92–97; Sugar Hill defendants' prior fight against, 106. *See also* civil rights activism; housing discrimination; racial restrictive covenants; residential segregation
racial equality: debate over method to achieve, 209; federal government's postwar support for, 113–14; United Nations charter and, 110
racial integration: Crenshaw Neighbors' formation and first year, 176–82; Crenshaw Neighbors' post-Watts initiatives, 192–201; school desegregation efforts, 163–72, 176–77; United Neighbors' formation and, 161–63
racial liberalism, 90, 92–93, 183
racial restrictive clauses. *See* occupancy clauses

racial restrictive covenants: anti-covenanters' strategies to oppose, 65–66; *Barrows v. Jackson,* 12, 116; *Corrigan v. Buckley,* 30, 49–50, 56–57, 61–62, 70; early legal challenges and rulings, 29–30, 45, 47–50; establishment of, 9, 13, 29, 59; *Fairchild v. Raines,* 100–101; formation of WAHPA, 97–103; *Hansberry v. Lee,* 111–12; housing discrimination after legal demise of, 116–22; intra-racial tensions and, 118; Japanese resettlement and, 96–97; lawsuits nationwide against, 103; Leimert Park and, 137; other cases in the Los Angeles Superior Court, 109; *Shelley v. Kraemer,* 3, 12, 92, 112–16; struck down by US Supreme Court, 111–16; Sugar Hill case in California Supreme Court, 108–11; Sugar Hill case in Los Angeles Superior Court, 104–8; Sugar Hill case overview/context, 11–12, 89–92; West Jefferson and, 60–62; Windsor Hills and, 146. *See also* housing discrimination; residential segregation
racial violence, 134, 140–41, 165
racism: freeway construction and, 156–57; Jackie Robinson on, 44; use-based zoning and, 46; Paul Williams and, 133
Raffles restaurant, 224
railroads, 36
railways: early development of Westside and, 37–39; White elite control of land and, 43
Raines, Ross and Helen, 100–101
Ramsess, 244
Randolph, A. Philip, 93
Reagan, Ronald, 191
real estate agents: blockbusting in Crenshaw area, 162, 172–76; Crenshaw Neighbors' real estate agency, 179–80, 193–94; discrimination against Black realtors, 111, 121; Sidney Dones, 71–72; National Neighbors and, 202; opposition to Crenshaw Neighbors, 181
real estate blockbusting: addressed by 1968 federal legislation, 200; in Crenshaw area, 162, 172–76
real estate boards: discriminatory practices of, 111, 121; Proposition 14 and, 184–86; response to *Shelley* ruling, 115–16; use-based zoning and, 45–46
redlining, 73, 74, 200
Redmond, Elly Woods, 147
Reichow, Oscar and Mabel, 138
Reid, Clifford E., 145
Residence District Ordinance, 46
residential segregation: challenged by Black homeowners' rights movement, 10–11, 56–57; as context for Watts rebellion, 188–92; formation of Crenshaw Neighbors to combat, 176–82 (*see also* Crenshaw Neighbors, Incorporated); history of Los Angeles and, 5–13, 33–37, 43–44; real estate blockbusting and, 162, 172–76; redlining and, 73, 74, 200; resegregation, 12–13, 202–3, 246–47; ripple effect of, 163; role of White homeownership associations, 60, 80–82, 137–38. *See also* housing discrimination; racial restrictive covenants; use-based zoning
respectability politics, 71–72
revolutionary nationalism. *See* Black revolutionary nationalism
Riddle, Carmen Garrott, 228, 230
Riddle, John, 221, 225
Rindge, Frederick Hastings, 78
Roberts, Frederick Madison, 54–55, 92
Robinson, Bill and Fannie Clay, 64
Robinson, Della Beatrice Howard, 143, 149–50, 174
Robinson, Jackie, 44
Robinson, Jennie V., 89
Robinson, Matthew ("Mack"), 44
Robinson, Nadine, 130
Robinson, Ray Charles. *See* Charles, Ray
Robinson, Ray Charles, Jr., 149, 150
Rodia, Sabato, 220
Rosas, Abigail, 121
Rosecrans Avenue, 94
Roybal, Edward, 141
RPM International, 157–58
Rumford, William Byron, 141, 183, 184
Rumford Act, 183–84
Ruscha, Ed, 217

Saar, Betye, 217, 226
Safety Savings and Loan Association, 121
Saito, John, 156, 199

INDEX

Saito, Takeshi, 96–97
Saito, Ty, 173
Saltman, Juliet, 178, 202
Sanders, Stan, 213, 225
San Francisco: Bingham Ordinance, 45
Sansei gangs, 159
Santa Fe Railroad, 36
Santa Monica, 38, 42, 43
Santa Monica freeway. *See* Olympic freeway
Sapphire: You've Come a Long Way, Baby (exhibit), 225–26
Satter, Beryl, 10
Schomburg, Arturo (Arthur), 216
school blowouts of 1968, 191
school desegregation: Ladera Heights and, 242–43; Los Angeles and, 163–72, 176–77; Pasadena and, 164–65
school zoning, 165
Schrank, Sarah, 216
Schulberg, Budd, 219–20
Sculpture of Black Africa: The Paul Tishman Collection (exhibit), 238
Seale, Bobby, 213
Seattle, 18
Second Great Migration, 67, 91
Seidenbaum, Art, 176
Seinan Japanese district, 137
Senn, Milton, 116
Servicemen's Readjustment Act of 1944, 74–75
Shaw, Frank, 92–93
Shelley, J. D. and Ethel Lee, 112
Shelley v. Kraemer, 3, 12, 92, 112–16
Sherman, Moses H., 38–39
Shoppers' Sunday project, 202
Sides, Josh, 16, 17
Sidney, Jack, 222
Siegel, Barry, 195, 202
Silent, Charles, 76
Simon Rodia Watts Tower Jazz Festival, 234
Sissle, Noble and Ethel, 86
Sitton, Tom, 93
66 Signs of Neon (exhibit), 221
Sixty-Third Assembly District Community Council, 139
Slauson Freeway, 195
Sleepy Lagoon murder, 158
"slum clearance," 119

Smith, Francis L. and Mildred Taylor, 89
Smith, Robert and Rebecca, 40
Smith, Sydnetta Dones, 89, 98
SNCC. *See* Student Nonviolent Coordinating Committee
Soleri, Paolo, 213
Somerville, J. A., 55, 63, 86, 102
Somerville, Vada Jetmore Watson, 86
Somerville Hotel, 55, 63
Sonenshein, Raphael, 142
Sonoratown, 34
SooHoo, Peter, Sr., 52
South Central area, 8. *See also* Eastside
South Los Angeles, 8. *See also* Eastside
Spain: California settlement, 27, 31; Los Angeles settlement, 31–33
Spaulding, Theodore, 107
Spook Hunters, 128
Sprague, Frank J., 38
Spring and Sixth Street Railroad Company, 37
Stearns, Abel, 34
Stearns, Arcadia Bandini de, 34, 35
Stein, Clarence, 152
Sterling, Christine, 51–52
Stewart, Fred R. and Nellie, 61
Stewart, Horace Winfred and Edna, 64–65
Still, William Grant, 65
Stimson, Thomas, 76
Stocker, Clara Baldwin, 135
Storefront (collective), 229, 233
Storey, Moorfield, 50
straw-party sales, 131
streetcars, 38
street clubs. *See* gangs
Student Nonviolent Coordinating Committee (SNCC), 213–14
Studio Watts Workshop, 218–19, 220
Stutsman, Carl A., 57
suburban development, 13–14
Sugar Hill: Black elite and, 82–88, 157–58; Olympic freeway construction and, 155–57; property values, 87, 156; relocation of Golden State to, 116–18; revived by Black migration into, 87–88. *See also* West Adams Heights
Sugar Hill case: in California Supreme Court, 108–11, 115; formation of WAHPA, 97–103; Robert Kenny and,

109–10; in Los Angeles Superior Court, 104–8; Loren Miller and litigation for, 11–12, 89, 104–6, 107, 108–9, 110–11; overview and significance of, 11–12, 89–92
Sugrue, Thomas, 10, 14, 121, 171
Summers, Martin, 19
Susan M. Dorsey High School: Alonzo Davis and, 211; Project APEX and, 196–97; race relations and, 161, 168, 176; racial composition of, 202, 242
Suter, Joan, 161, 170–71, 195
Suter, Lyle, 171, 195, 199
Swann v. Charlotte Mecklenburg Board of Education, 242

Taft-Ellender-Wagner Housing Act of 1949, 120
Takai, Roy, 173
Talented Tenth, 17–18
Tann, Curtis, 216
Taper, Mark, 126–27
Tapscott, Horace, 219, 245
Taylor, Henry, 105
Taylor, J. Phyromn, 86
Taylor, Keeanga-Yamahtta, 115
Taylor, Pat, 245
Taylor, Pearl S., 86, 101
Teen Post, 195–96
Temple, Jonathan, 34
Temple Block, 35
Temple B'nai B'rith, 79
Temple Street section, 41
Tenan, Barbara, 195
Third Street Tunnel, 38
Three Graphic Artists (exhibit), 238
Thurburn, Malcolm, 82, 87
Time, 106
Tishman, Paul, 238
Title Guarantee & Trust Company v. Garrott, 47–48
Tizol, Juan and Rosebud (Rose) Browne, 85–86
Toberman, James, 34
Trible, Dwight, 245
Truly Disadvantaged, The (Wilson), 14
Truman, Harry, 113
Turner, Ike, 148, 149, 174
Turner, Tina, 148–49, 174
Tuskegee Institute, 209–10

Twitchell, Kent, 236
Two Centuries of Black American Art (exhibit), 238
Tyler, Willis O.: legal challenges to racial restrictive covenants, 48, 61, 70, 100–101, 103; Loren Miller and, 100–101, 103; on Sugar Hill ruling, 108

UN. *See* United Neighbors
Underground Musicians Association, 219
Union of God's Musicians and Artists Ascension, 219
United Civil Rights Council, 177
United Nations, charter of, 110
United Neighbors (UN): formation and overview of, 161–63; formation of Crenshaw Neighbors, 176–82 (*see also* Crenshaw Neighbors, Incorporated); growth of, 168–72; real estate blockbusting and, 176
Unity Finance Company, 63
Unruh, Jesse, 142
Unruh Civil Rights Act of 1959, 142
"urban crisis" narrative, 14
use-based zoning: establishment and impact of, 9, 29, 45–47; *Euclid v. Ambler*, 47, 56, 70; redlining map and, 73
U.S. News & World Report, 114
Us Organization, 212–13
US Supreme Court cases: affirmation of *Mulkey* ruling, 191; *Barrows v. Jackson*, 12, 116; *Brown v. Board of Education*, 164; *Corrigan v. Buckley*, 30, 49–50, 56–57, 61–62, 70; *Euclid v. Ambler*, 47, 56, 70; *Hansberry v. Lee*, 111–12; *Oyama v. California*, 121; *Plessy v. Ferguson*, 44; rulings against racial restrictive covenants, 111–16; *Shelley v. Kraemer*, 3, 12, 92, 112–16; *Swann v. Charlotte Mecklenburg Board of Education*, 242

vacation homes, 71–72
La Vada Apartments, 86
Val Verde, 71–72
vandalism, 134
Vaughn, George, 11, 112
Veblen, Thorstein, 206–7
vecinos, 34
Ventura County, 45

Vereen, Lady Helena Walquer, 245
Video 3333, 244
View Heights: Black migration into, 144–50; property values, 150, 243
View Park: Black migration into, 144–50; historic recognition of, 240; property values, 150, 243
Village Green, 151, 152, 154–55
Vinson, Fred M., 114
Visual Communications (organization), 229

Waddy, Ruth G., 217, 218, 226, 233
Wagner-Steagall Housing Act of 1937, 95, 119
WAHIA. *See* West Adams Heights Improvement Association
WAHPA. *See* West Adams Heights Protective Association
Walden, James J. Henry, 49
Walker, Edward W., 61
Walker, Olive, 198, 223
Walling, Betty, 49
Walter H. Leimert Company, 135
Ward, Warren, 224
Warley, William, 47
War Relocation Authority, 96
Warren, Earl, 97
Warwick, Dionne, 174
Washington, Booker T., 67, 209
Washington, Kenny, 65
Washington, Leon, Jr., 99
Washington, Timothy, 238
Waters, Ethel, 84, 85, 105
Watkins, William B., 119
Watts: art and activism in, 218–21; history and racial composition of, 94, 97, 135, 189; Watts rebellion, 188–92 (*see also* Watts rebellion)
Watts, Jill, 84
Watts Happening Coffee House, 219–20, 233
Watts Prophets, 220
Watts rebellion: events and impact, 188–92; rise of Black nationalism and, 190, 212–13; survey of White attitudes following, 194
Watts Repertory Theater Company, 220
Watts Savings and Loan Association. *See* Family Savings and Loan Association

Watts Summer Festival, 213
Watts Towers, 220–21
Watts Towers Arts Center, 221, 234
Watts Writers Workshop, 220, 233
Wayt v. Patee, 13, 61–62
Weaver, Robert, 108
Weeks, Maurice, 108
Weeks, Paul, 134–35
Weil, Raymond, 192
Wells, Thomas and Eleanor, 165
Wesley N. Taylor Realty Company, 182
West Adams, 75–78
West Adams Heights: as historically White, 69, 77–78; Houstons' move into, 59, 78–82; redlining map and, 73; settlement of Black elite in, 69, 82–88; settlement of Mexican Americans in, 79–80. *See also* Sugar Hill
West Adams Heights Improvement Association (WAHIA), 80–82
West Adams Heights Protective Association (WAHPA), 97–103, 106–7
West Jefferson: Black settlement in, 60–69; designation/boundaries of, 264–65n5; Japanese resettlement and, 96–97; redlining map and, 73
West Jefferson Press, 60
West Jefferson Street News, 60
Westside: Black entrepreneurs and, 118–19; competition between downtown and, 126–27; demarcation from Eastside, 7–10, 27–30; early Black settlement in, 41–42; early public transit and development of, 37–39; Gordon Manor subdivision, 70–71; impact of Olympic freeway and gangs, 155–60; overview of Black migration into, 3–5, 10–13, 58–69, 125–29; racial borders and, 7–8, 246; racial restrictive covenants and (*see* racial restrictive covenants); relocation of Golden State to, 116–18; rise of gangs in, 159; use-based zoning and, 46–47. *See also* Crenshaw area; *individual neighborhoods*
Westside Collective, 230
White, Charles, 217, 238
White, Walter, 84
White flight: Crenshaw area and, 144, 150, 154, 160, 202–3; resegregation and, 12–13, 202–3, 246–47

White homeowners' associations: role in opposing Black migration, 60, 80–82, 137–38; West Adams Heights Improvement Association, 80–82

Whites: Baldwin Hills Estates demographics, 151–52, 154; Baldwin Village demographics, 151–52, 155; Baldwin Vista demographics, 153, 154; as buyers of Black art, 206–7, 230; Crenshaw Neighbors' housing campaign targeting, 179–81; gangs involving, 128; history of Los Angeles and, 5–13, 34–36; Leimert Park demographics, 144; opposition to Gordon Manor subdivision, 70–71; overview of response to Blacks' Westside migration, 3–5, 10–13, 58–69, 125–29; population in early Los Angeles County, 35, 36; post-*Shelley* resistance to Black migration, 116–22, 125–35, 137–41, 147, 175; post-Watts survey of, 194; racial restrictive covenants and (*see* racial restrictive covenants); racial violence by, 118, 134, 140–41, 165; View Park, View Heights, and Windsor Hills demographics, 150; Village Green demographics, 153, 154–55; Westside-Eastside demarcation and, 7–10, 27–30; White elite in West Adams, 75–78; White-led modern art scene, 216–17

White working class: homeownership and, 18–19; Proposition 14 views, 185; racial borders and, 55–56

Widener, Daniel, 16, 205

Widney, Joseph P., 36, 38

Widney, Robert M., 37

Willard, Henry, 42

Williams, Charles and Bertha, 140

Williams, Della Mae Givens, 134

Williams, Esther, 84

Williams, Frances, 85

Williams, Paul R., 64, 95, 117, 120, 133–34

Willis, Henry M., 96–97

Willowbrook, 94

Wilshire Boulevard Temple, 79

Wilshire Country Club, 130

Wilson, Diedra, 197

Wilson, Lewis, 152

Wilson, Nancy, 150

Wilson, William Julius, 14

Windsor Hills: Black migration into, 144–50; property values, 150, 243

Windsor Hills Elementary School, 202, 203

Winters, Ann, 131

Wirin, A. L., 111

women: Black women's role in westward migration, 10; role in fighting Sugar Hill case, 101; survey of Black female artists, 225–26; United Neighbors' founders, 169–70

Wong, Tyrus, 216, 217

Woodard, Beulah, 216

Woodruff, Hale, 118, 214

Woods, James M., 121, 218

working class. *See* Black working class; White working class

World Stage, 244

Wright, Theodore, 167

YB. *See* Yellow Brotherhood

Yellow Brotherhood (YB), 229, 233

Yorty, Sam, 191

youth: Crenshaw Neighbors initiatives serving, 195–97; intra-racial generational tensions, 190; Watts Towers Arts Center and, 221

zoning. *See* school zoning; use-based zoning

zoot suit attacks, 97, 158

About the Author

JENNIFER MANDEL, PhD, serves as associate director of assessment in the University of New England's Office of the Provost. In addition to her administrative role, she has taught history at the University of New England, Granite State College, Hesser College, and the University of New Hampshire.